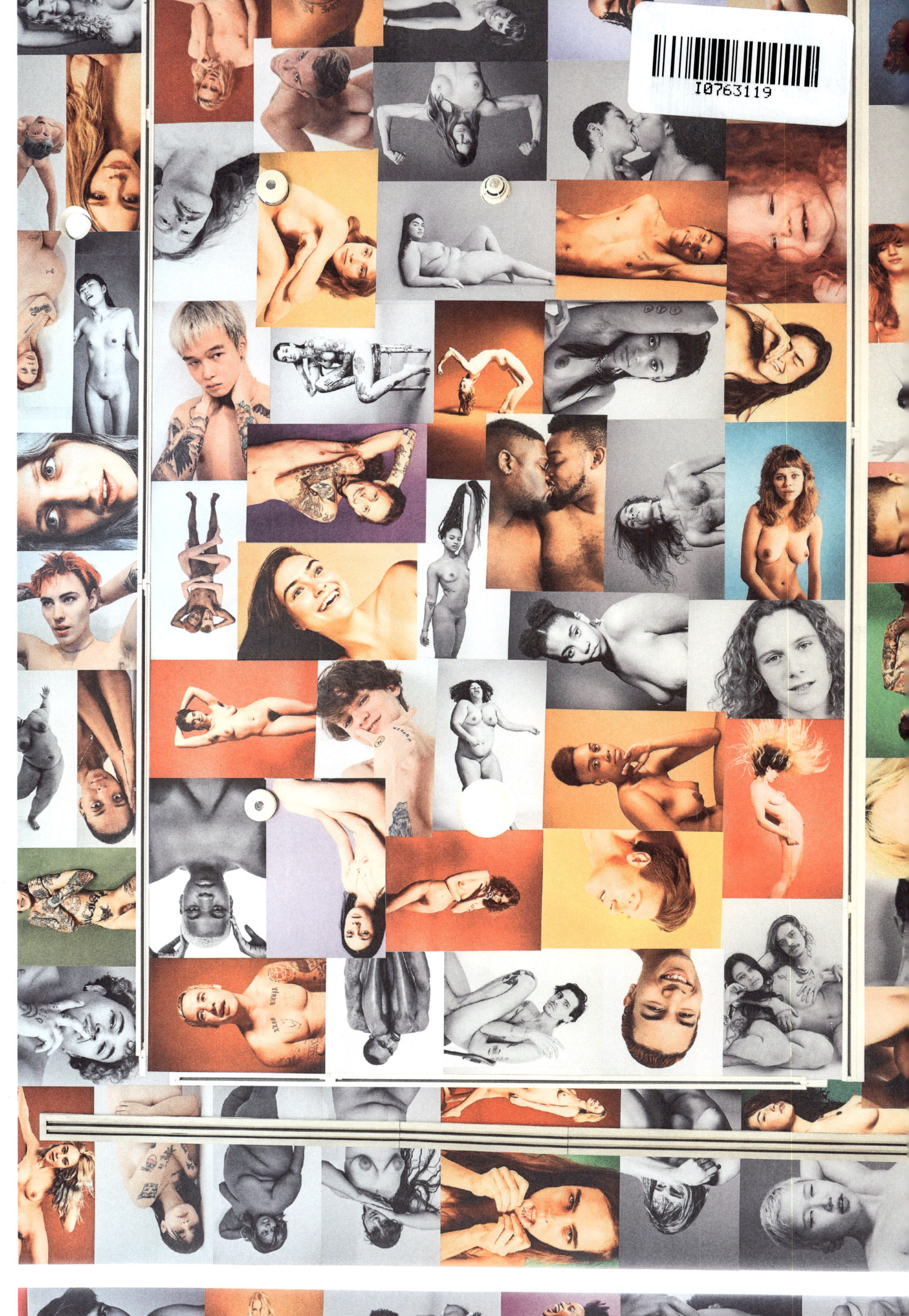

YEARBOOK

YEAR

RYAN McGINLEY

BOOK

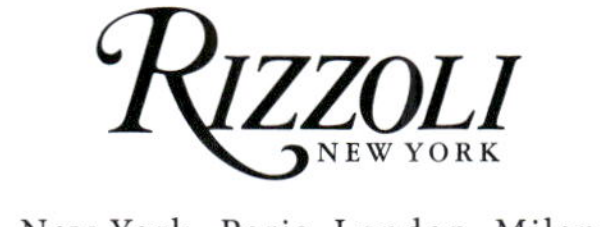

New York · Paris · London · Milan

CONTENTS

INTRODUCTION

Can a nude tell you what year it is? People say this decade was a blur: 2009-2019. If it wasn't a blur, it was fragmented. Bush to Obama to Trump. The recession and Occupy Wall Street. Black Lives Matter. Gay marriage. Grindr. MySpace ended where Facebook began while Tumblr and Instagram transformed our relationships with images, and with each other.

The photos in this book could almost be timeless. Without clothes or a city view, history blurs. You can't hear the music we were listening to or the conversations we were having. Maybe you can tell the decade from the nail art, the body hair, the jewelry, the HRT beauty, the diversity, the scars, or from the piercings and tattoos (the stick and pokes, the gay tattoos, the face tattoos . . .). Maybe the faces give it away. A lot of the people in these photos changed culture and defined a moment. The photos themselves contributed something, working to redefine beauty standards and exhibit the spirit of a new Downtown New York.

The photos kept my spirit alive. Shot over the course of ten years, from January 2009 to December 2019, the casting was my vision of Downtown New York. Not everyone lived Downtown of course. Bushwick was the new Williamsburg. People were in Bed Stuy and Ridgewood. The neighborhood around my Chinatown studio was renamed Dimes Square. Skaters who mobbed up around Dimes, the restaurant, named it that and it stuck. There are skaters in this book and artists, actors, activists, chefs, stylists, filmmakers, educators, meme collectors, comedians, multigenerational New Yorkers, and kids who were just around—every contribution you can imagine that makes up "Downtown." The casting was a web. Models would recommend their friends, then those friends recommended other artists. In the end, you get a cohort, a Yearbook.

The common age in the book is about twenty-five. A lot of the models were becoming artists when they were photographed. They came to be with art. And with the gays. I always tried to bring my queerness into the image. My queerness is my essence. Sometimes, I'd photograph people two or three times for the project, capturing them along a journey: a gender journey, a weight journey, a tattoo journey, a mother's journey, a recovery journey . . .

I set a lot of people free on their nudity journey. The way we shot, full nudity was optional. Models could do shirtless only, opt for a side view, or wear a thong. Through retouching and cropping, we could imply nudity while honoring people's boundaries. It was a lot of people's first nude shoot. Shooting nude was out of a lot of people's comfort zones and many came, they said, because of this. They wanted to try something new or open up in a new way. Some of those people went on to model nude for other photographers and in their own artwork.

Nudity itself changed over the decade. Between dick pics, thirst traps, cell phone cameras and selfies, Snapchat, Grindr, hookup apps, and later, OnlyFans, sharing nudes became more common in the 2010s. But it wasn't without censorship. "Your post has been removed for violating Community Guidelines." I lost my first Instagram account because I posted nudity. Over the years, so many people had their Yearbook photos taken down and even got kicked off the platform because of them. (Maybe this is why people used to call me "the King of Tumblr"—nudity flourished on that platform until 2018.) "Free the Nipple" tried to counter IG censorship. We later learned that the algorithm was racist, classist, ableist, and fatphobic. It boosted select bodies, while discriminating against others.

This Yearbook is sex positive, queer and trans affirming, body positive, and class conscious. The nudity is about community—witnessing one another in our diversity, lifting each other up, and finding freedom and joy in vulnerability. This is what community looks like.

People came as themselves. We had no hair stylists or makeup artists, it was just me, a choreographer, an assistant or two, and the models. Everything in the room was considered. The temperature. The music. The lighting. We always had these tools on hand: snacks, a Makita fan for blowing hair, a mini trampoline, a changing tent, disposal robes, and rolls of Colorama seamless paper. The paper was the model's space. No one else walked on it. We'd always say, at the end, "Thank you for coming and sharing the space with us." Everyone got paid and ran off and spent their checks right away.

Compulsive, repetitive. Shooting every month for a decade. Taking a thousand frames to get one picture. Each photo adding up to a total picture of our time in Downtown New York.

By the end of the project, I only knew people by their IG names: *golden Polaroid*, *Rochelle fat leopard*, *Jarlos*, *fat Albert 420* . . . Phone addiction: that's the 2010s. Yearbook weekends were a break from looking at social. We'd start shooting in the morning. Nine hours later, I'd be so satisfied and wiped out, high off the energy, tired from being on my feet. The goal was to capture someone in a flow state. The project's choreographers, Luisa and Brandee, both had such vibrant energy and could get people there. I liked to be a fly on the wall between the choreographer and the models, the camera and I becoming so small and nimble, the self-consciousness a camera can imply wouldn't apply. Then a genuine energy exchange could happen. I'd get to a point of being so present and connected, I could anticipate the model's movements almost before they happened, as if in slow-motion; that's how you get the shot.

My studio in Chinatown, where most of these photos were taken, was above a fire station and next to a Chinese wedding photography studio. We had a fake business sign on the front door that said "Life Adjustment Center." Telfar Clemens was in the building. He was winning major fashion awards and making the bag of the decade when he was our neighbor. The building was filled with artists, designers, and musicians. It was like the Chelsea Hotel of Chinatown. I remember watching the Freedom Tower go up from outside my window 2011-12-13. Hurricane Sandy fucked up the city in 2012. The power went out in the studio for a week and I had to postpone a Yearbook shoot. Otherwise, we shot every month for a decade, the intercom and siren of the fire station bleeding through the walls, remixing the music we were playing.

Music set the tone for every shoot. At the start of the project, we played a lot of Gaga's "Born This Way," Die Antwoord, Björk, and psych rock: Ty Segall, Tame Impala, Mac DeMarco, Ariel Pink... Sky's "Everything Is Embarrassing" played nonstop for what seemed like years. To get models to jump around, we'd listen to Offspring's "Self Esteem." Mid-decade, the repeat albums were Drake's "If You're Reading This . . . ," all the Lanas, and Solange's whole album. Rihanna's "Anti" carried us through 2016-17-18. By the end of the project, the models were requesting a lot of Azealia.

It was important to me to get the Yearbook models onto the walls of museums and galleries. "The Gang's All Queer" and they belong in those spaces, just as they belong in this book; to be seen, honored, and valued. When it came to installing in an art institution, I was inspired by New York's wheatpaste advertising, printing the images big and layering them up the wall. As the work traveled to San Francisco, Basel, New York, Tokyo, Seoul, Denmark, Abu Dhabi, London, La Termica in Spain, and Australia, this is what we did.

In Abu Dhabi, I wasn't allowed to show any nudity, so I mostly showed headshots. I wanted it to be subversive, so I only chose queer models for that installation. It was cool to be in the UAE and have hundreds of queers looking back at the viewers. In London, my exhibition opened on March 20, 2020, the day the world shut down. The work sat there, installed, with no one to see it. The Yearbook was in quarantine, just like everyone else.

How to end a project? The Yearbook really feels like Before the Pandemic, a decade leading up to this world changing event. It also started right after Obama had been elected president. So much happened during this bracket of time. Necessary uprisings. A queer revolution. Petra Collins and Jari Jones blew up, my sisters. People moved in and out of New York. Stores closed, parties moved locations. Inside of my studio, we could keep certain things constant. Overall, the throughline of the Yearbook is joy—finding freedom, joy, and authenticity with each other and capturing the essence of that joy in an image.

We lost some important people along the way. Adam Perkins, Chris Glockson, Sara Anne Jones, CJ Jorgensen, White Ring's Kendra Malia, Rad aka Lighter, Tommy Playboy, Brett DeGroot, and Eva Evans. Sudden deaths, young deaths, the passing of talented, beautiful individuals. When I look through this book, I hear their voices and their stories.

This is a book of memories. If this yearbook has a school, it's the school of one another. No matter what decade it is, art and community can be made and they have to be made. They're made through listening, witnessing, holding space, and giving back. Art and community are what carry me through change, through losses and successes, aging and rebirths, project to project, year after year.

—RYAN MCGINLEY

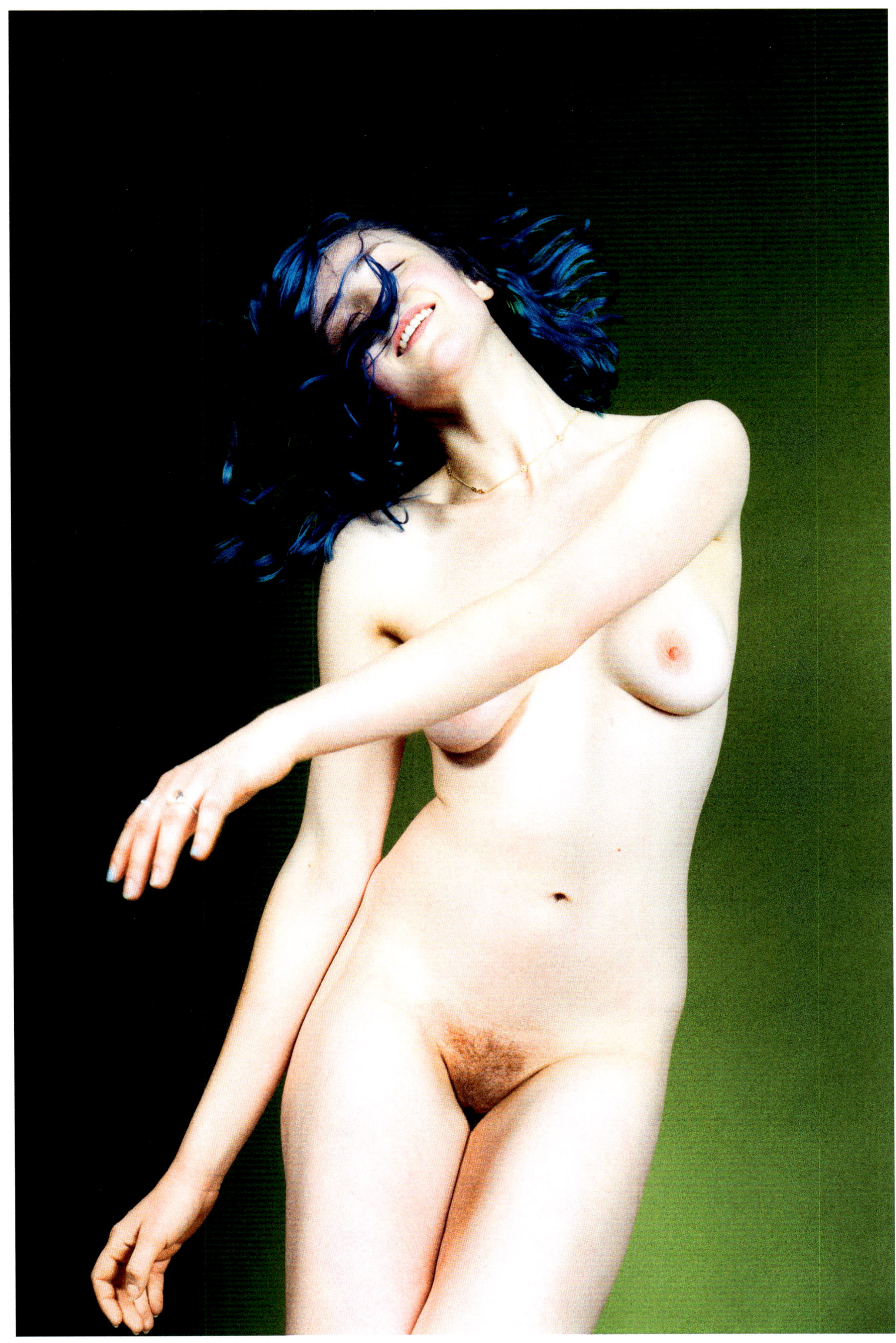

Nellie, December 2014

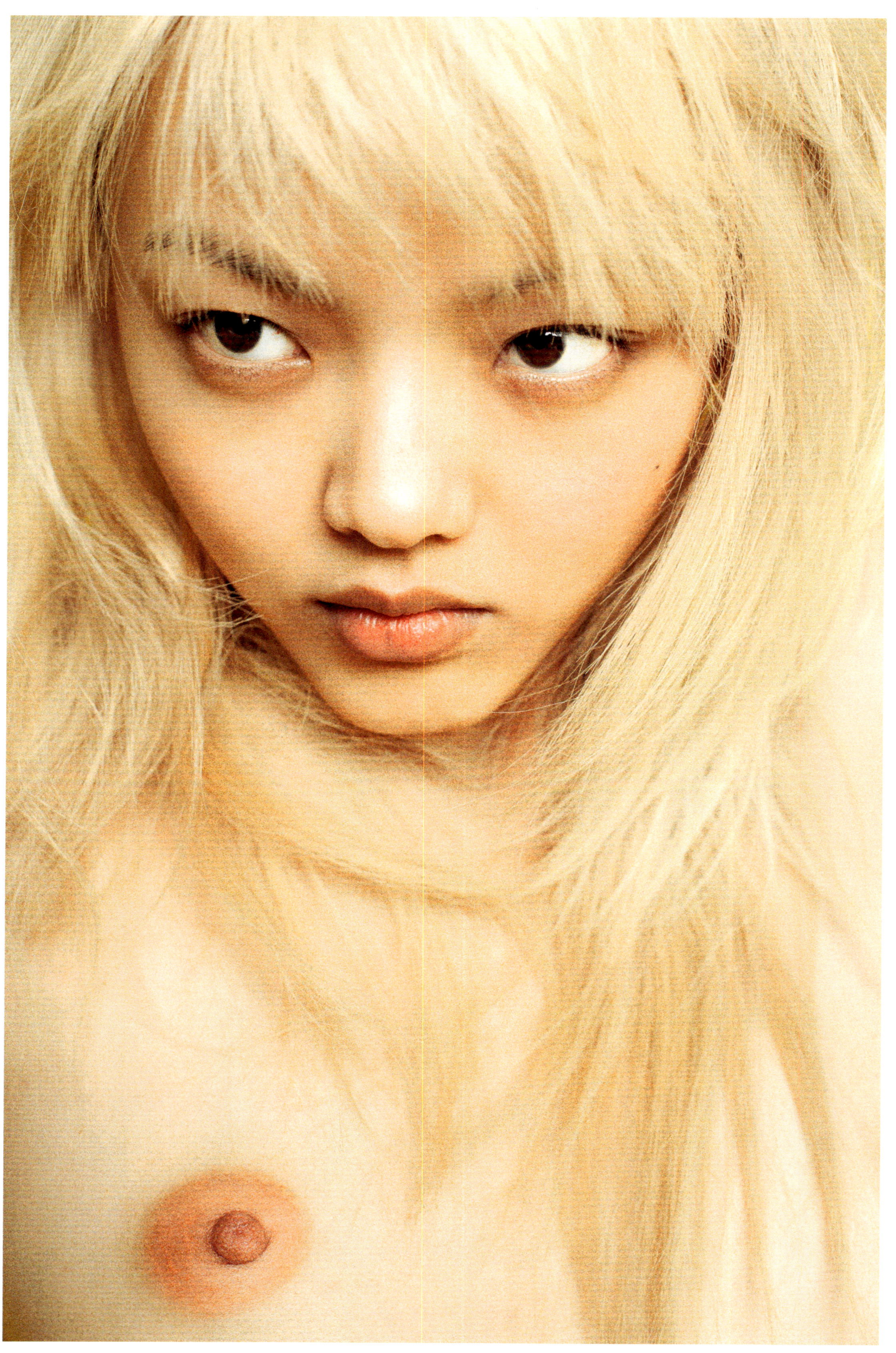

Rila, January 2010

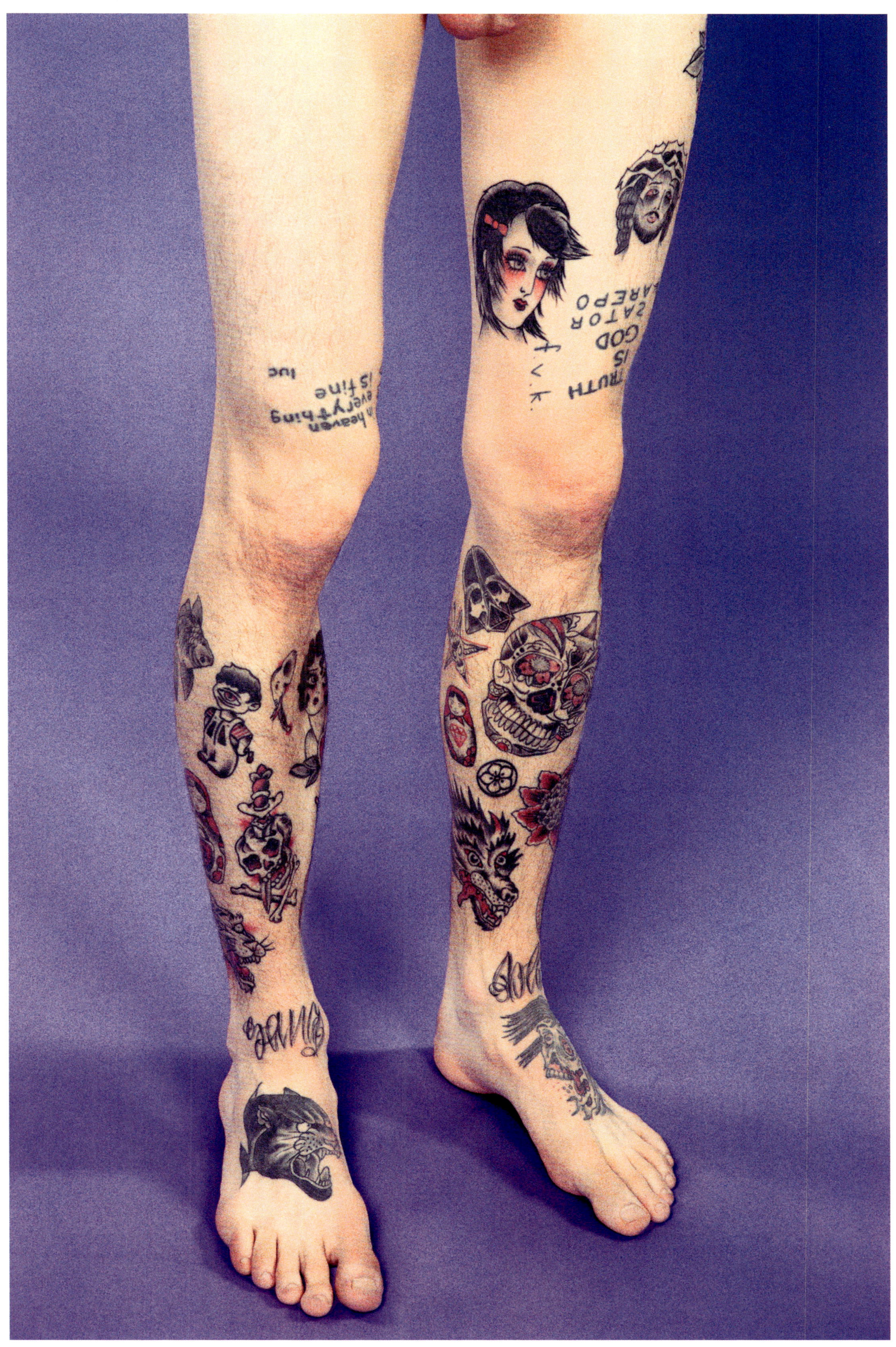

Sean, March 2011

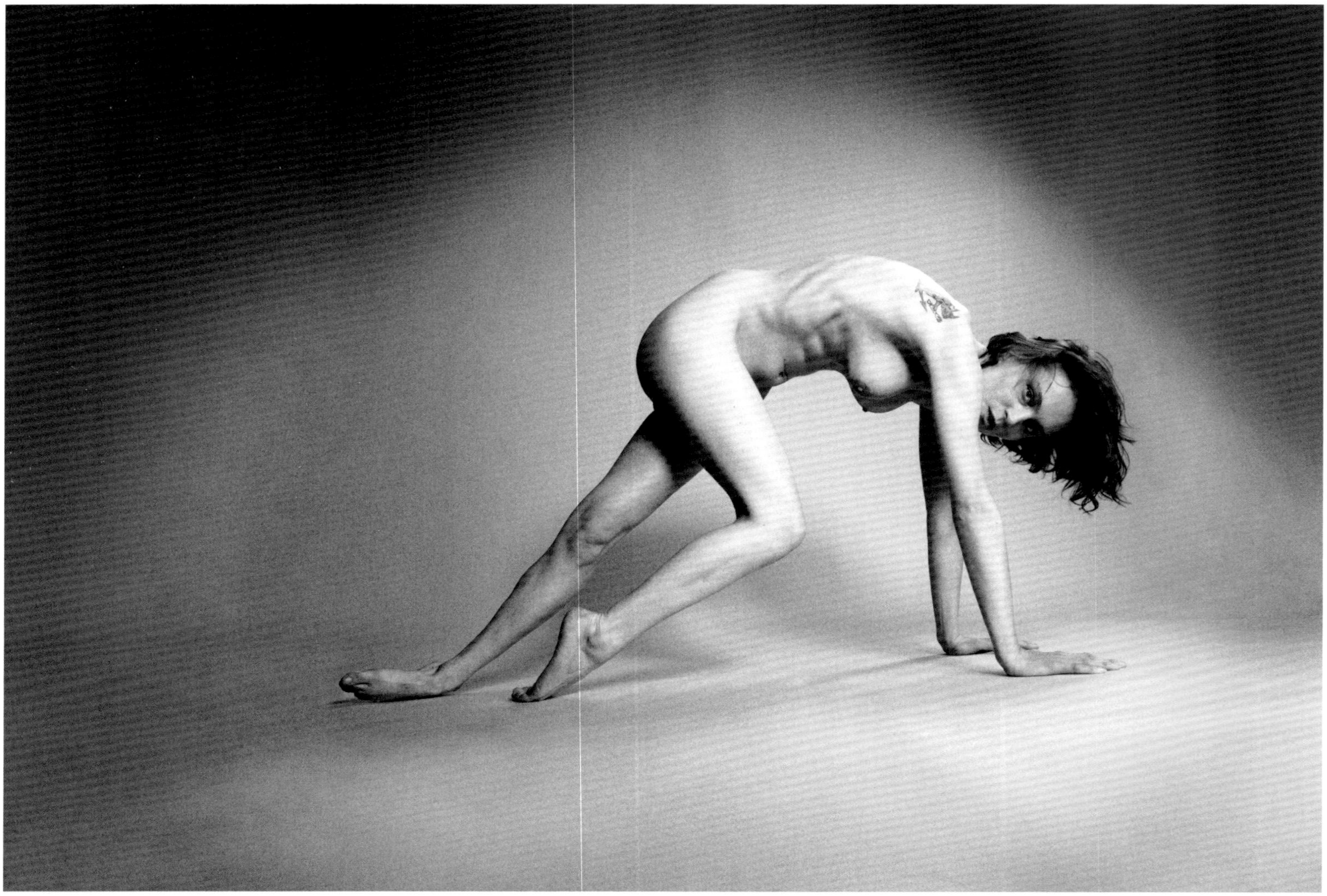

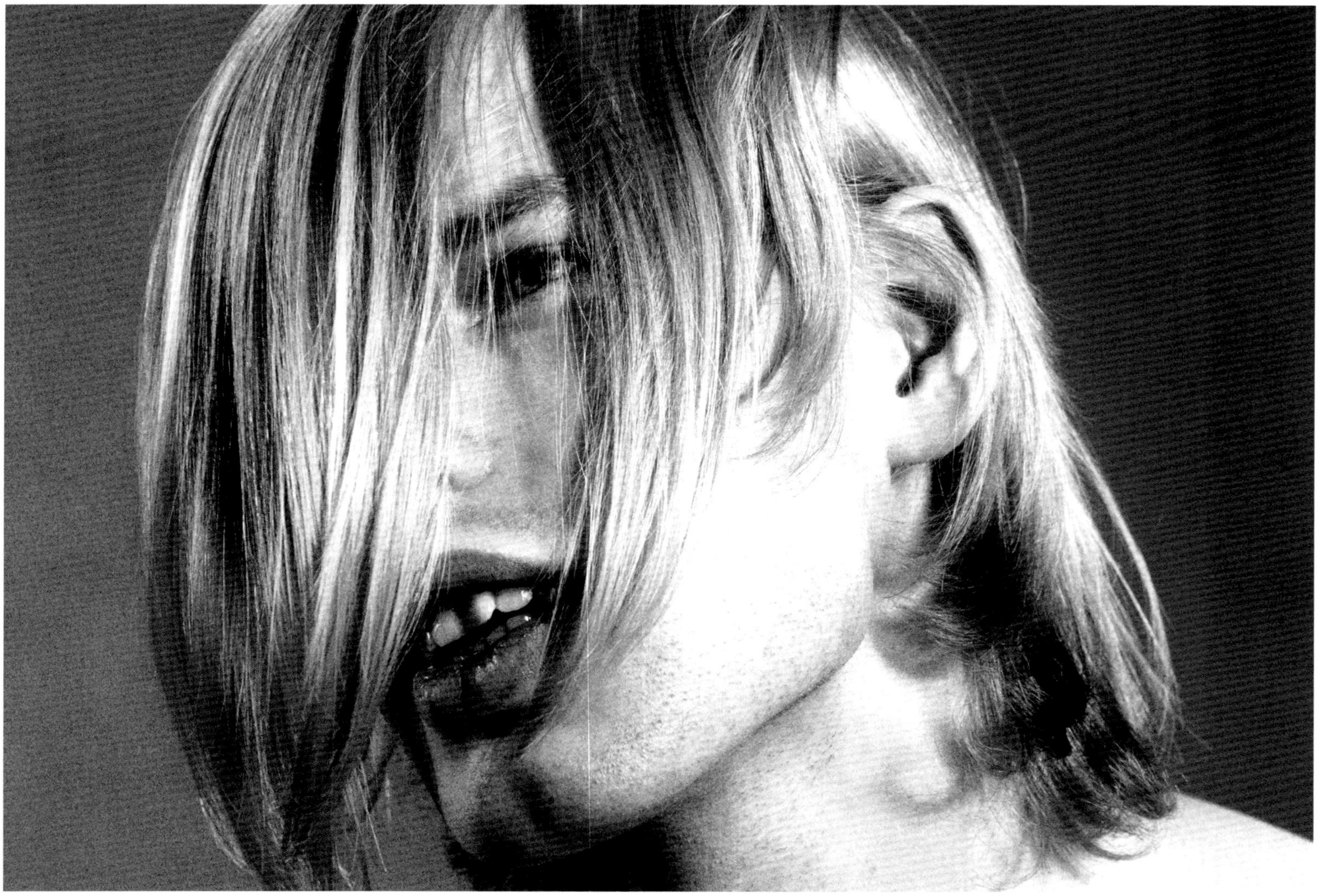

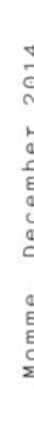

Lucia, January 2015 Momme, December 2014

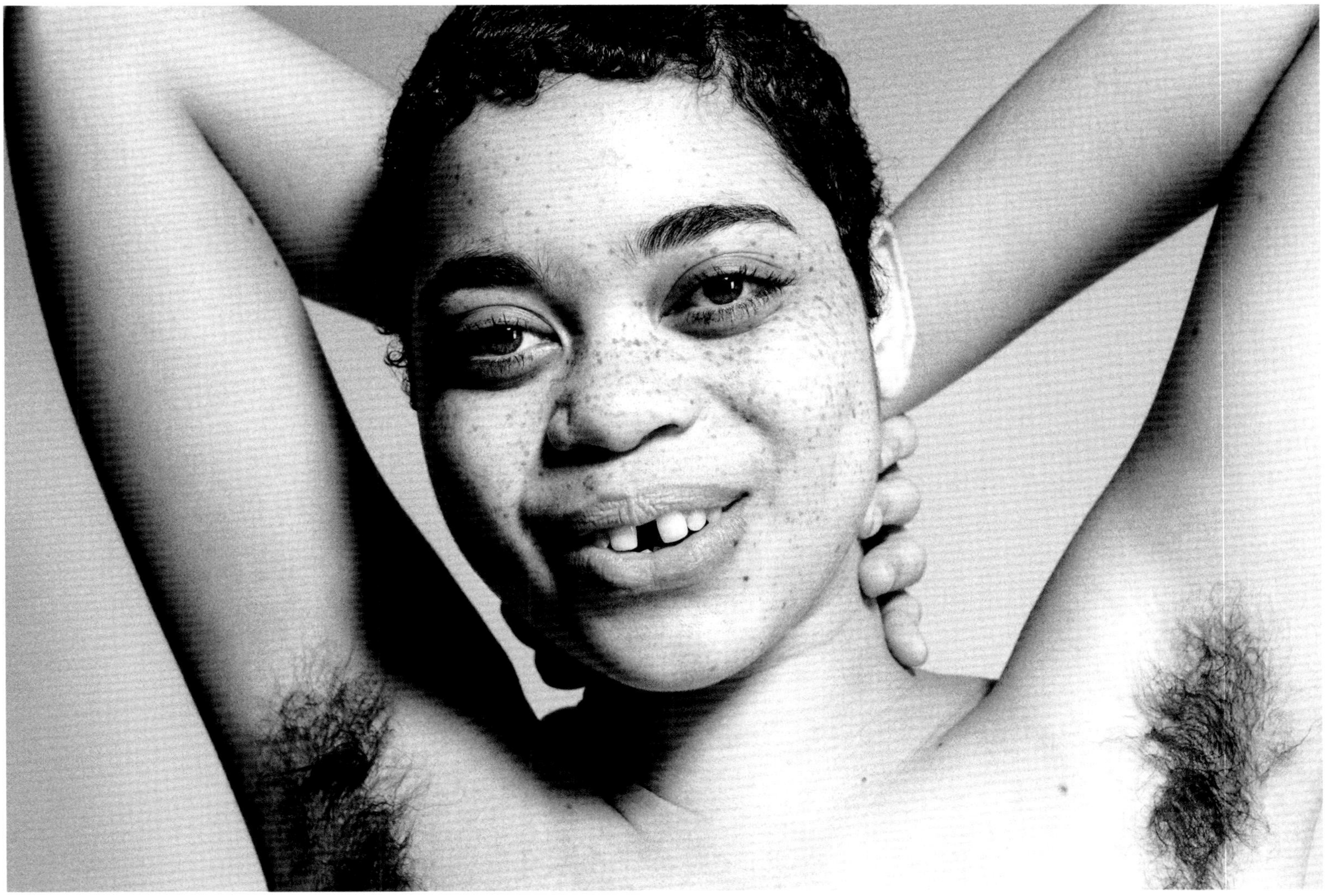

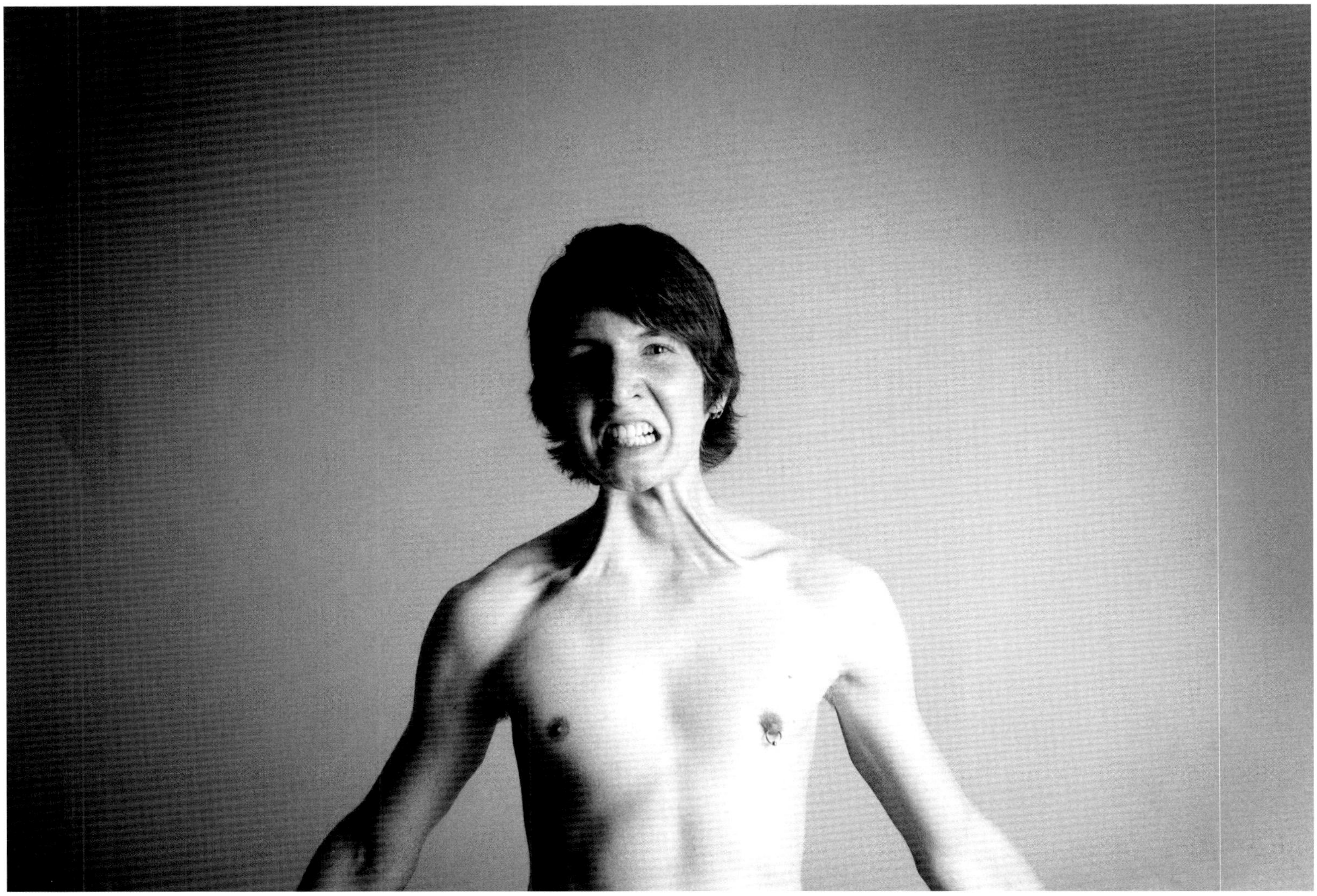

Itchel, January 2016

James, July 2015

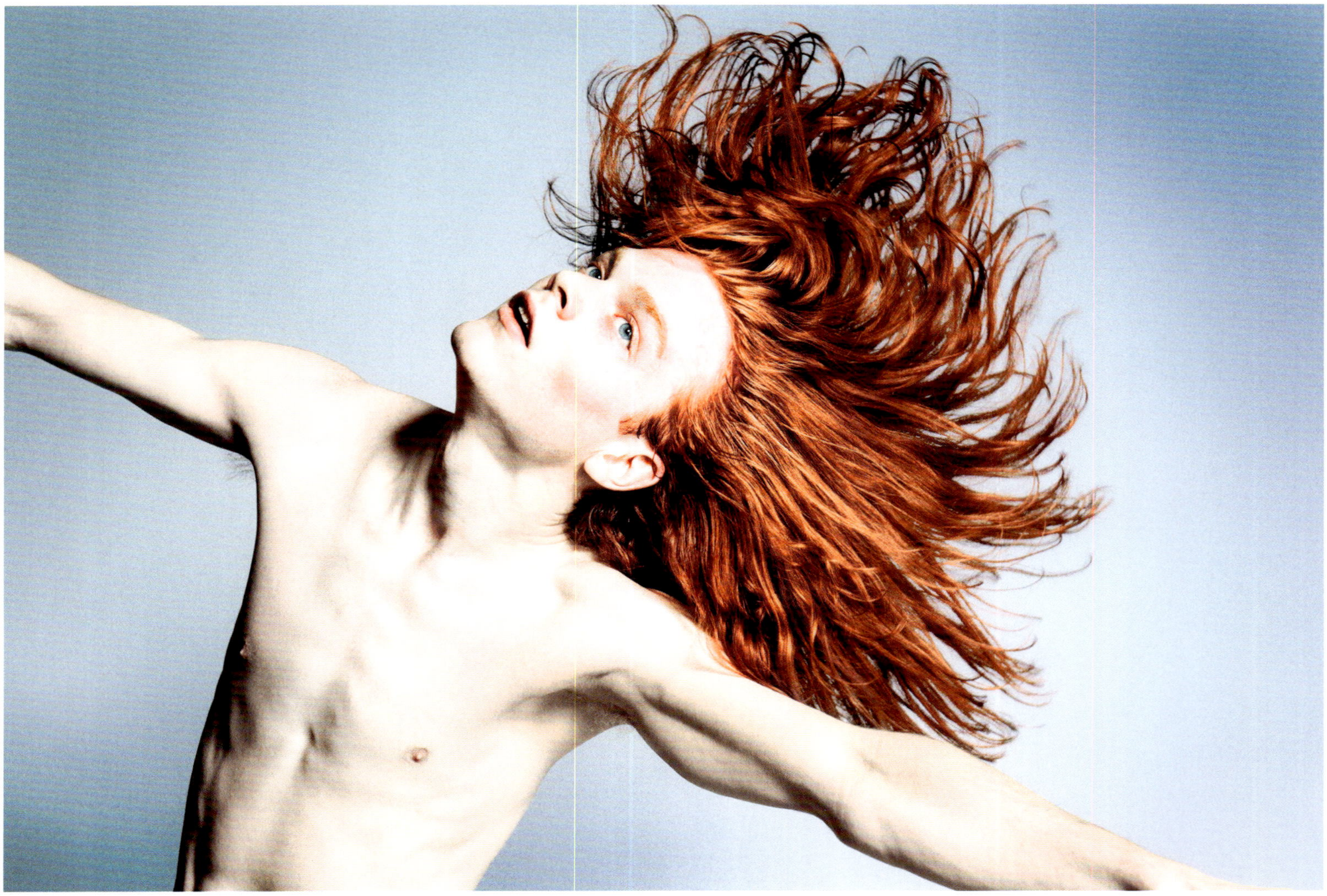

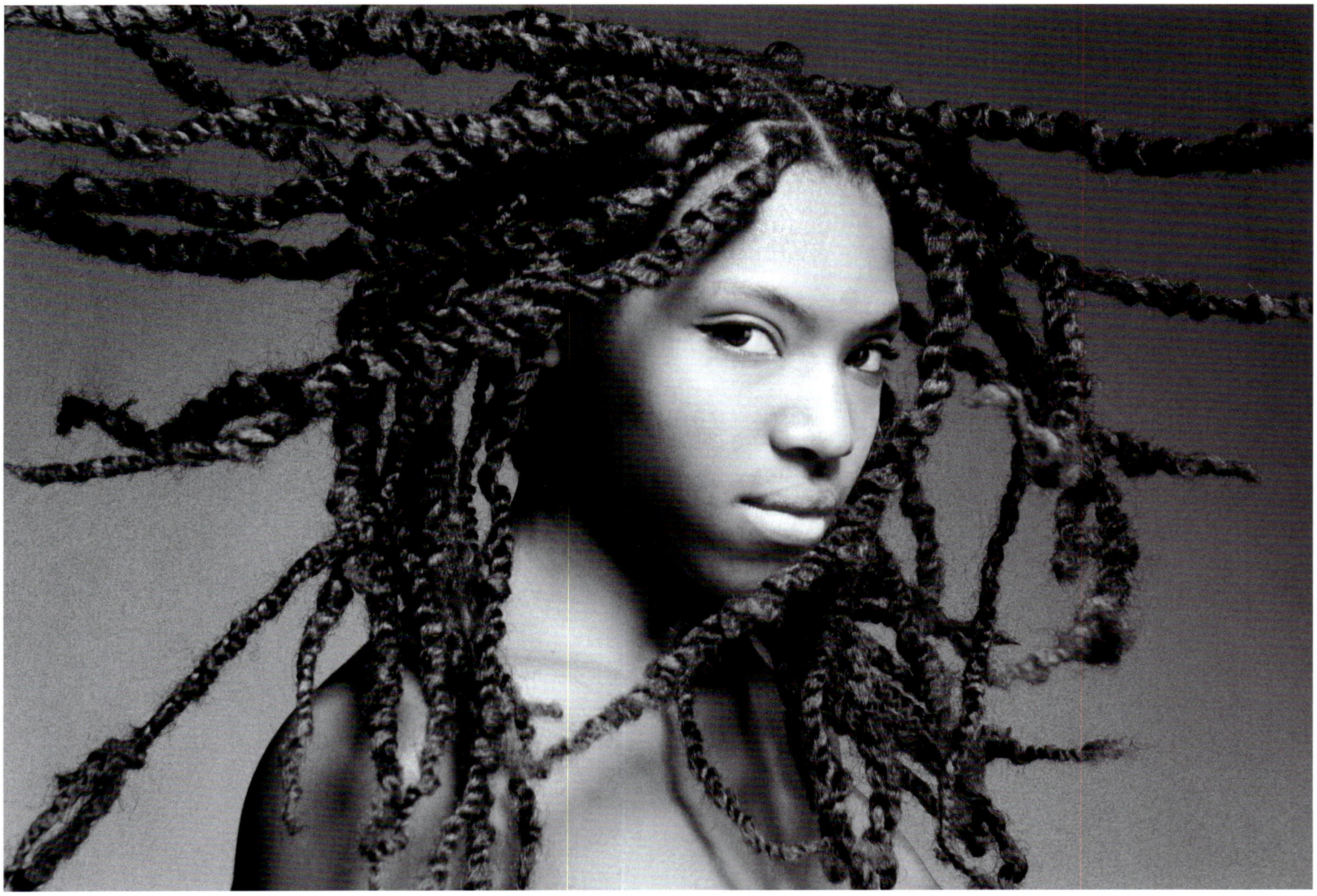

Christopher, November 2015   Lynn, February 2015

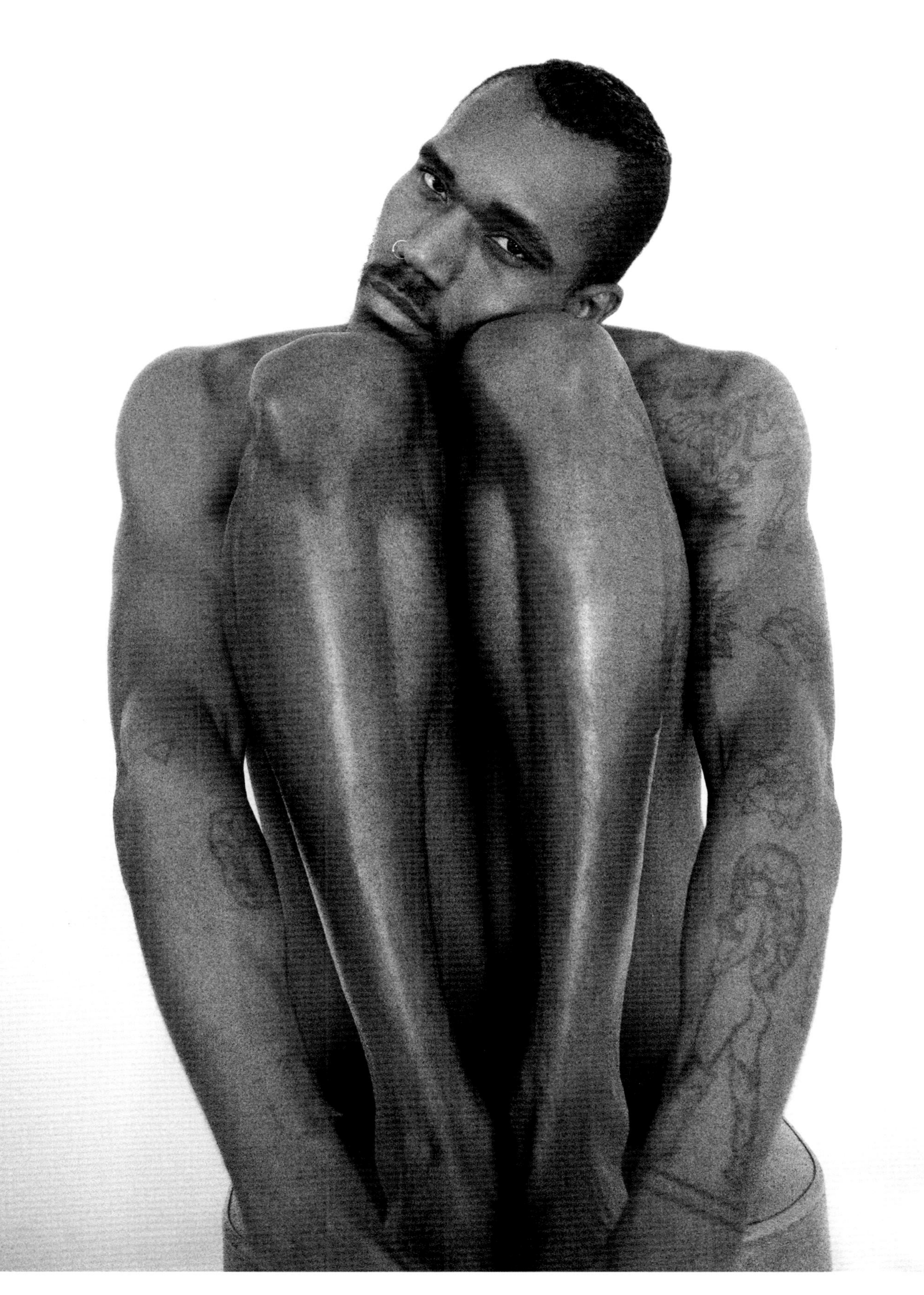

Jordan, December 2019

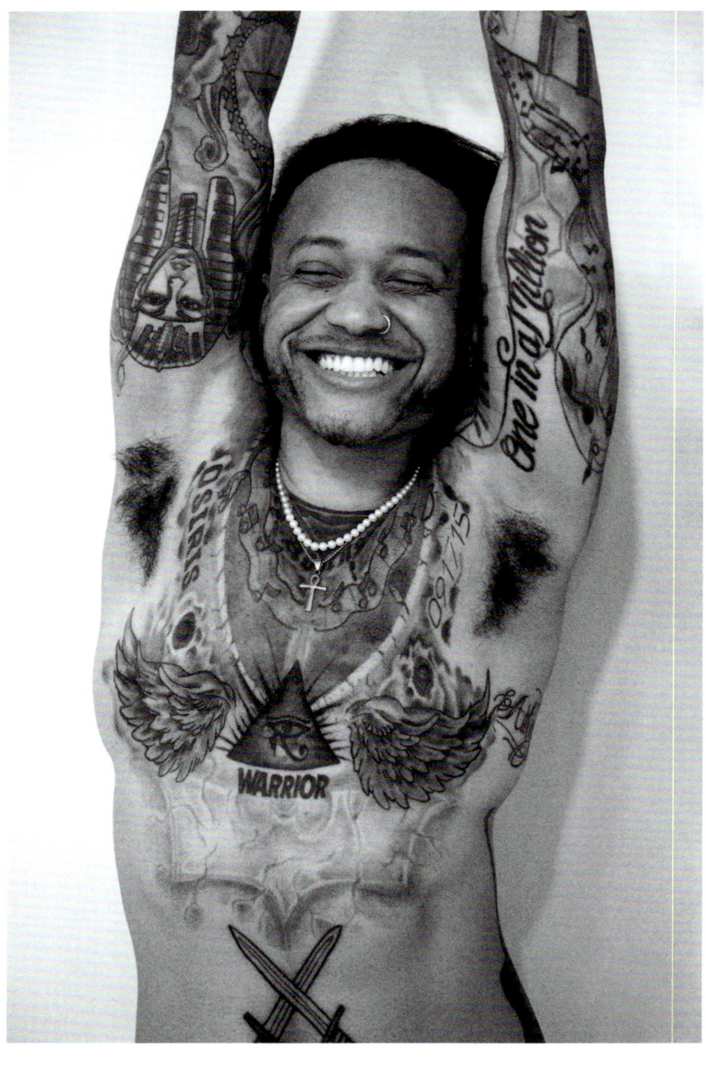

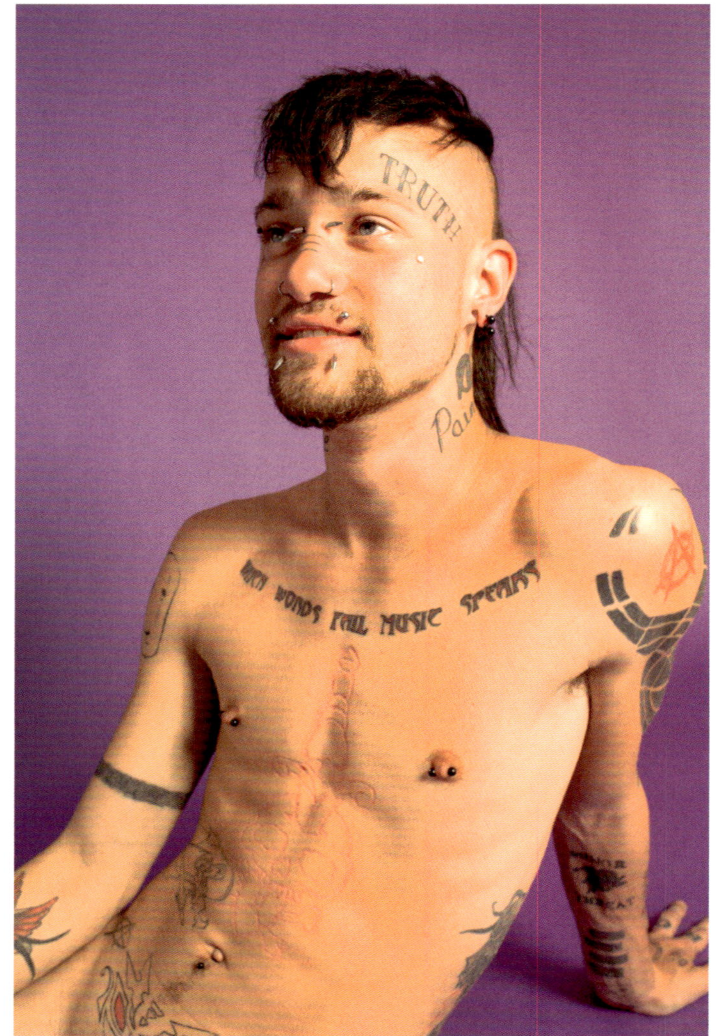

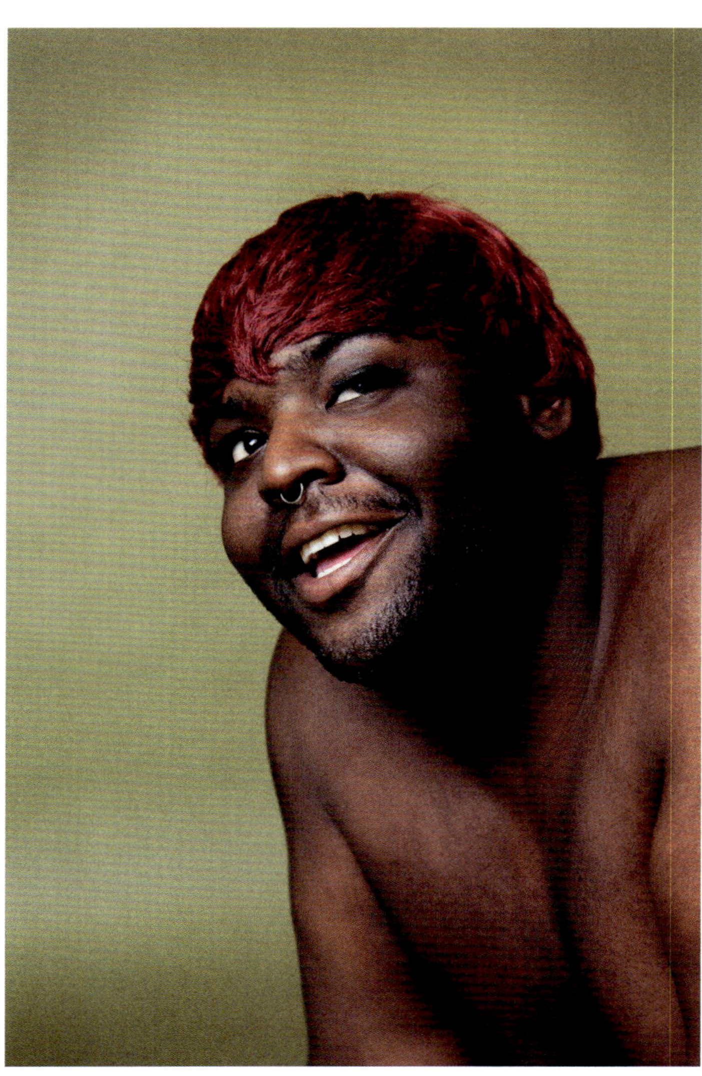

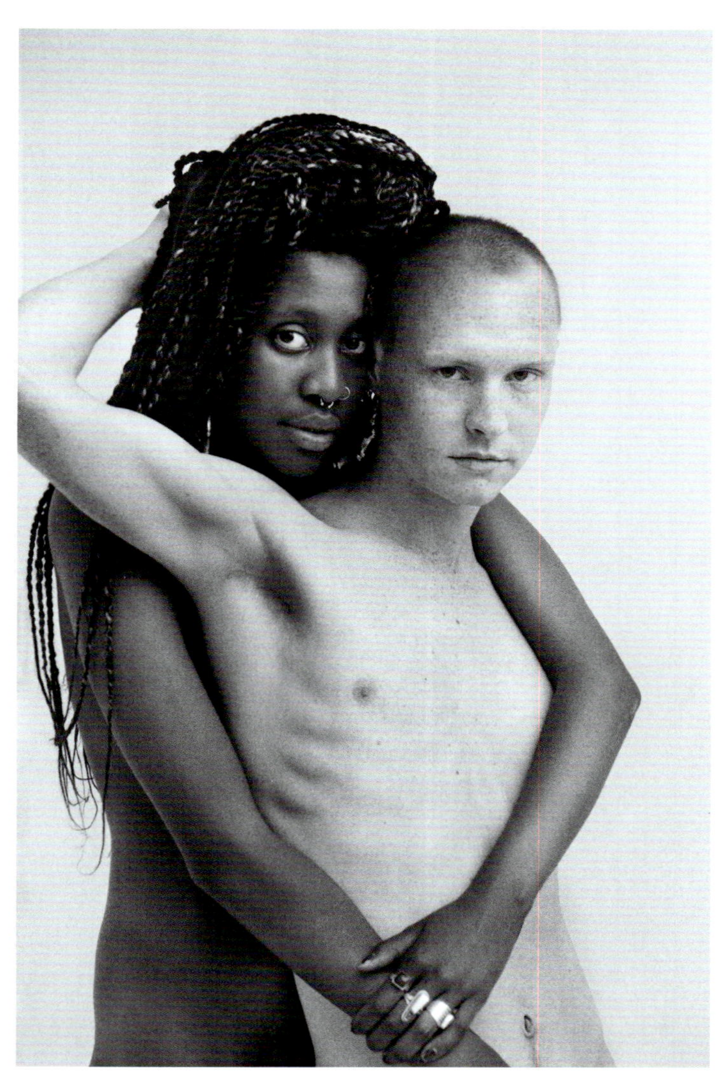

Sir K, February 2019 Taylor, April 2013 Jamal, December 2016 James & Mayan, July 2017

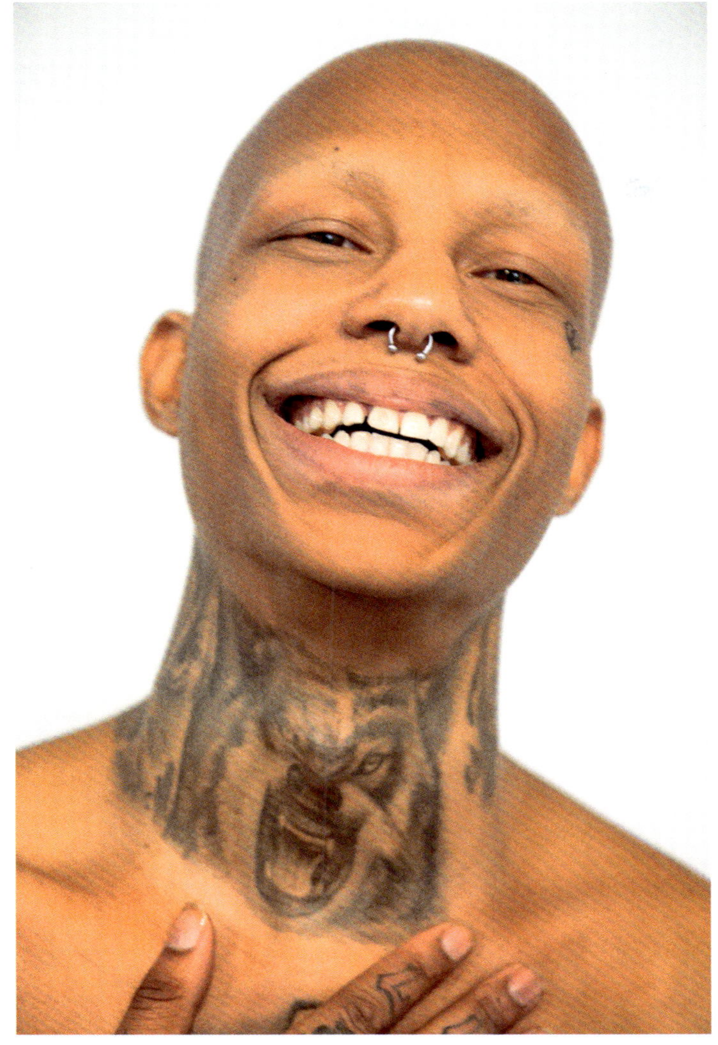

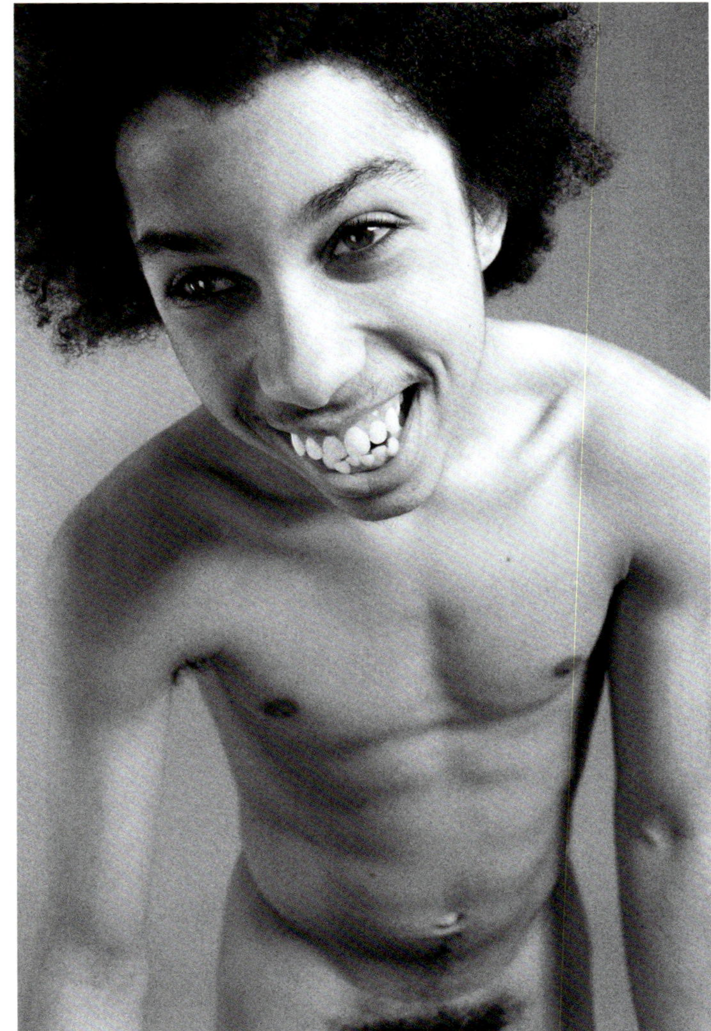

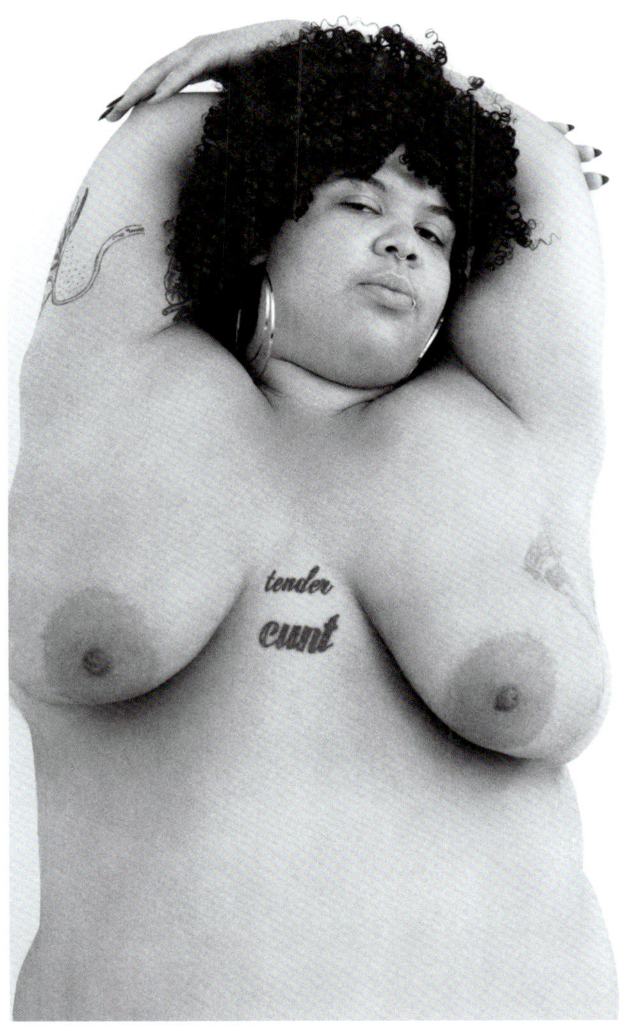

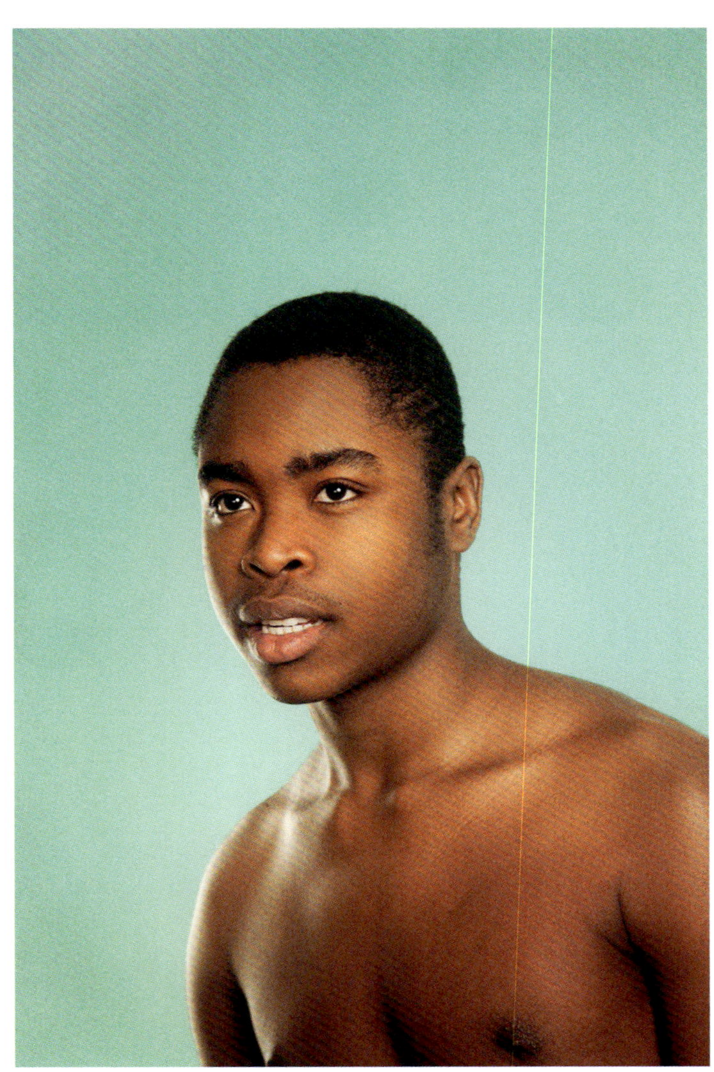

Miles, February 2019   London, December 2012   Kathleen, June 2017   Kern, January 2011

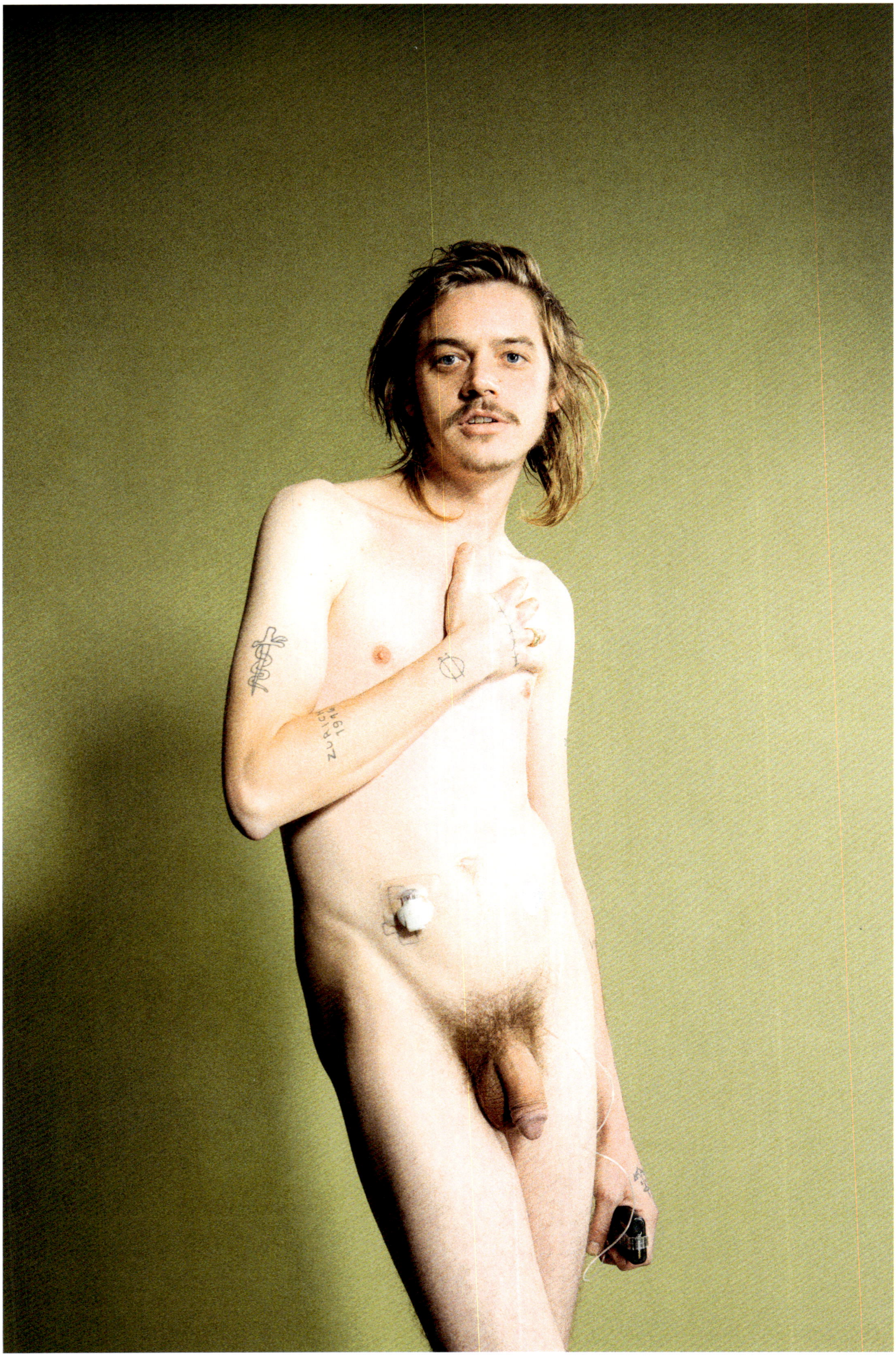

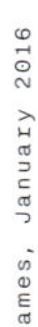
James, January 2016

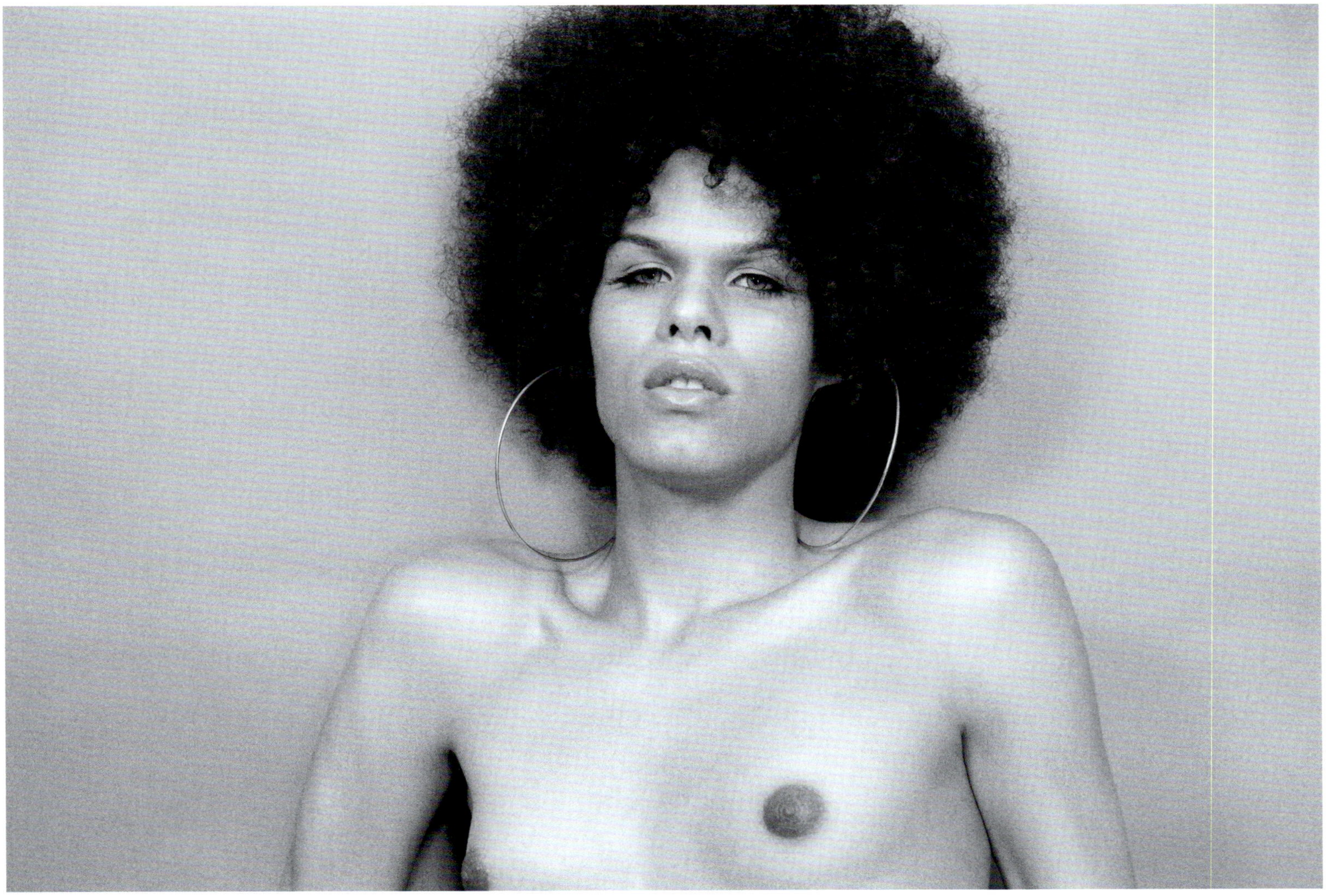

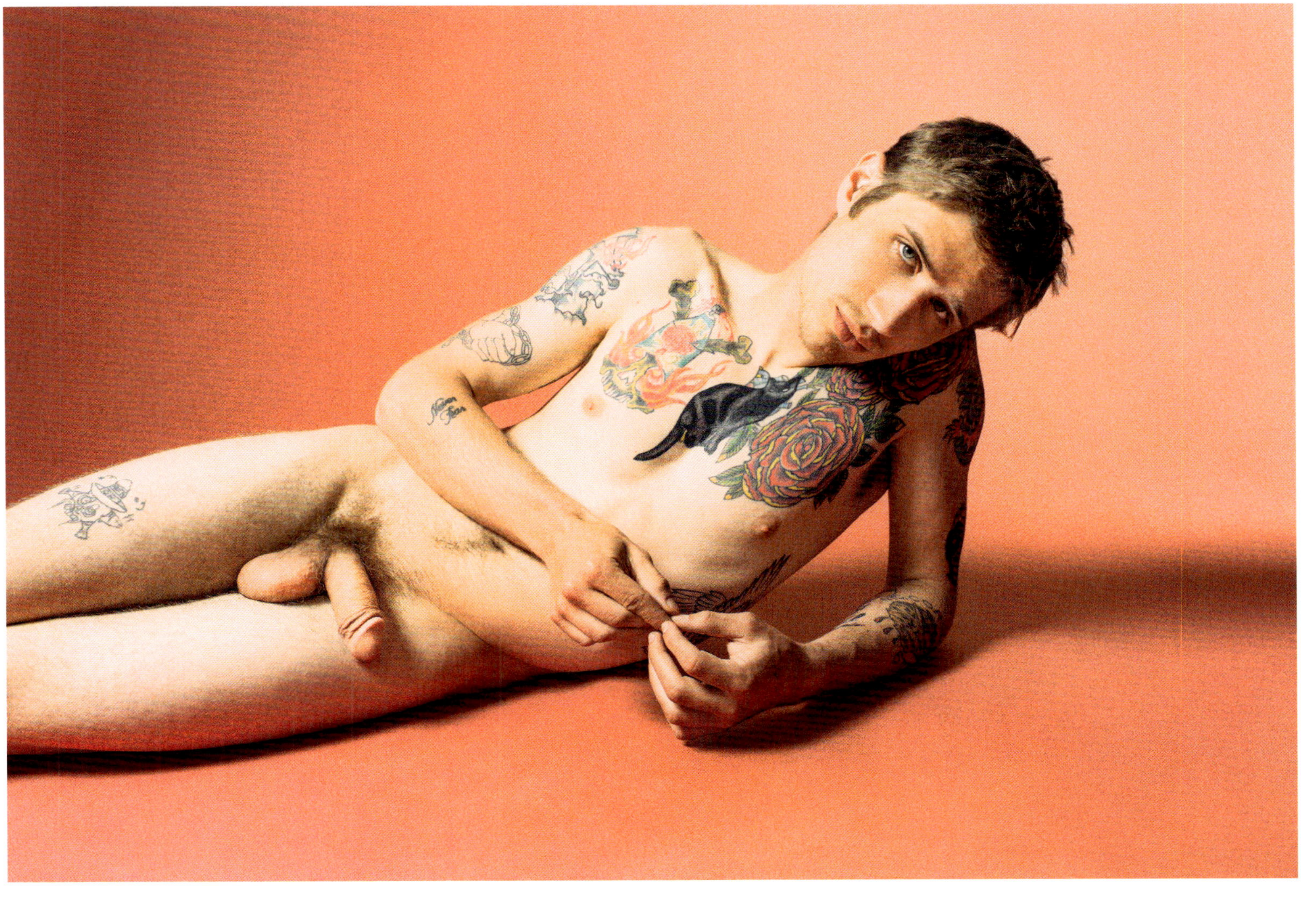

Maya, May 2016 Dylan, May 2013

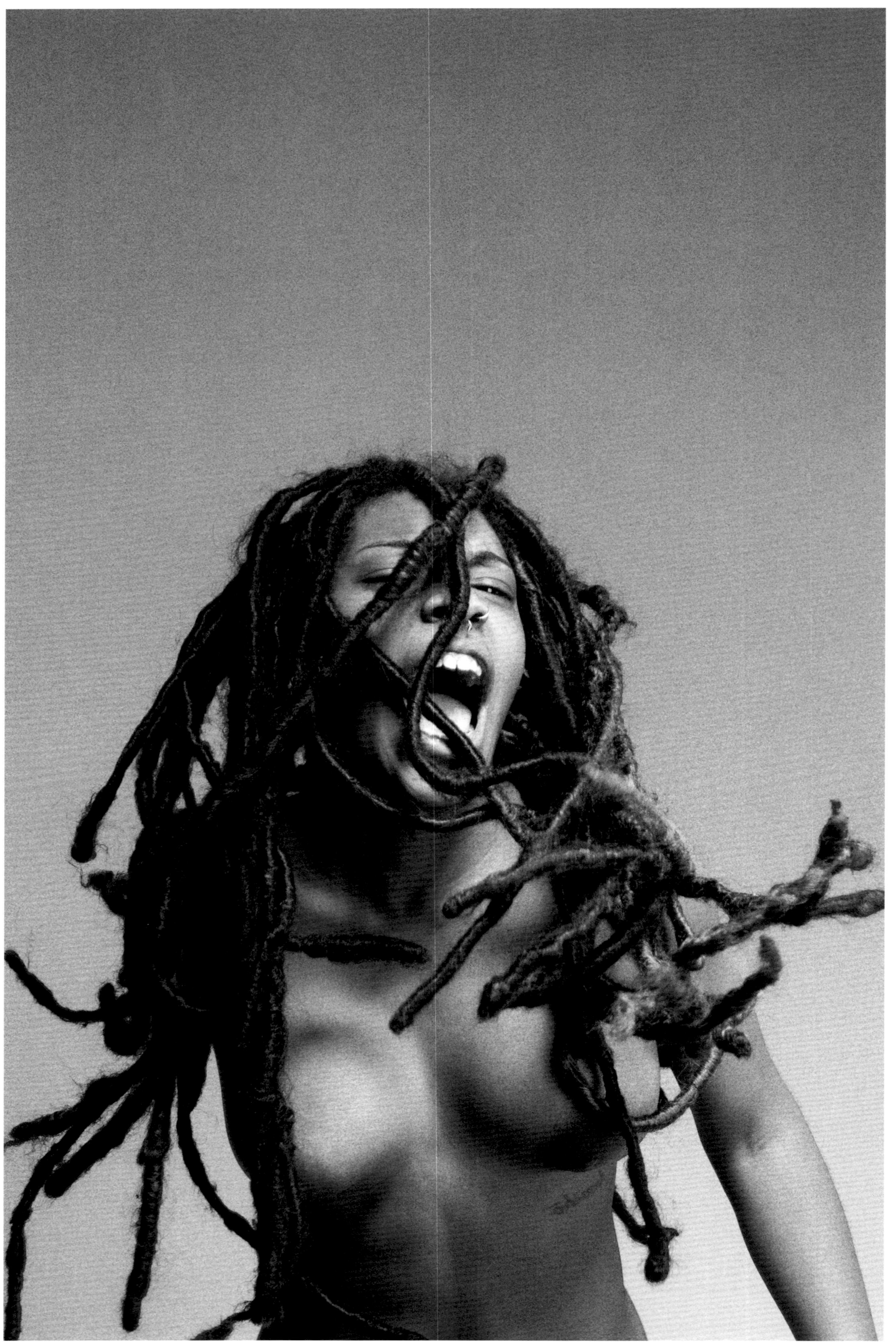

Katarah, February 2015

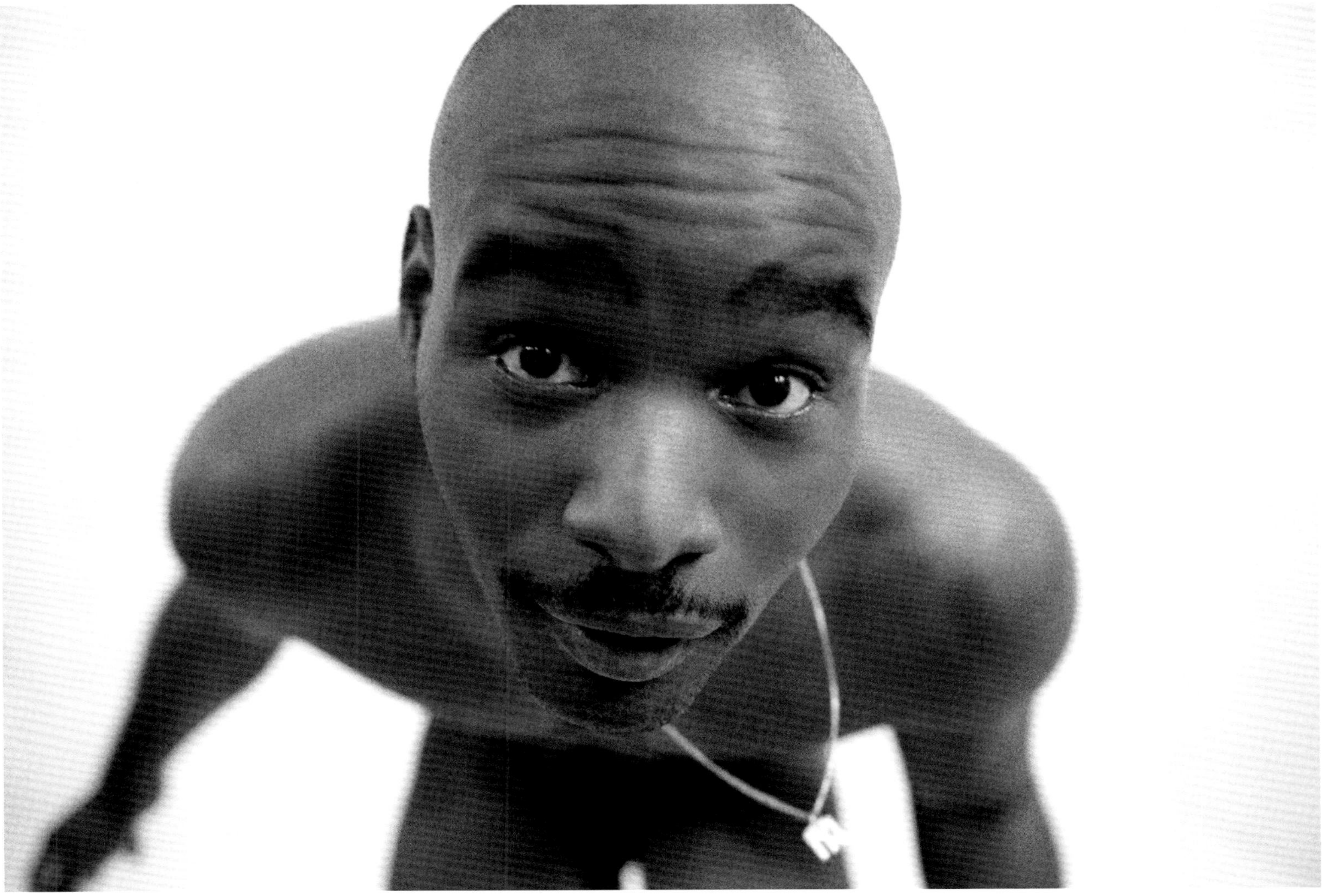

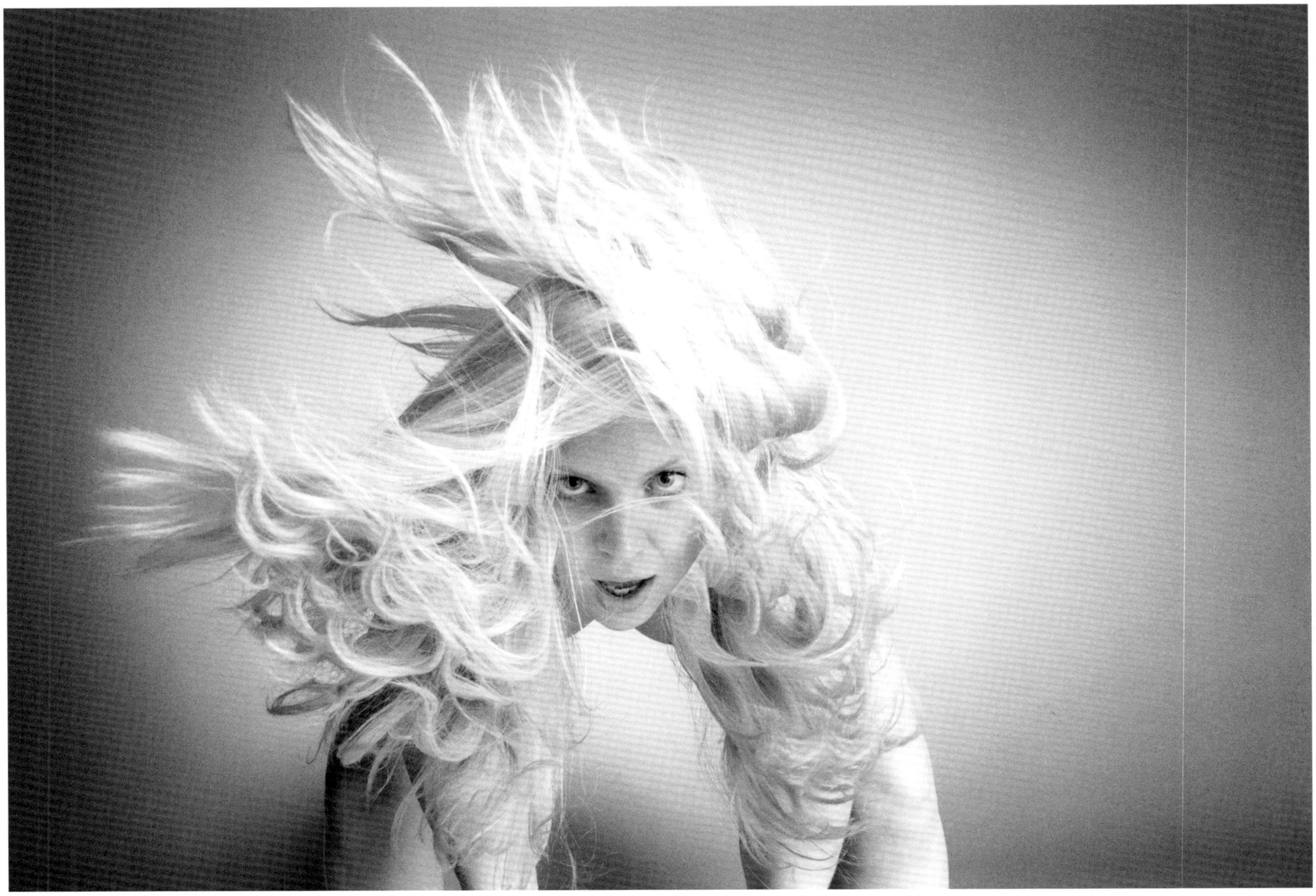

Lamar, November 2018   Maggie, September 2015

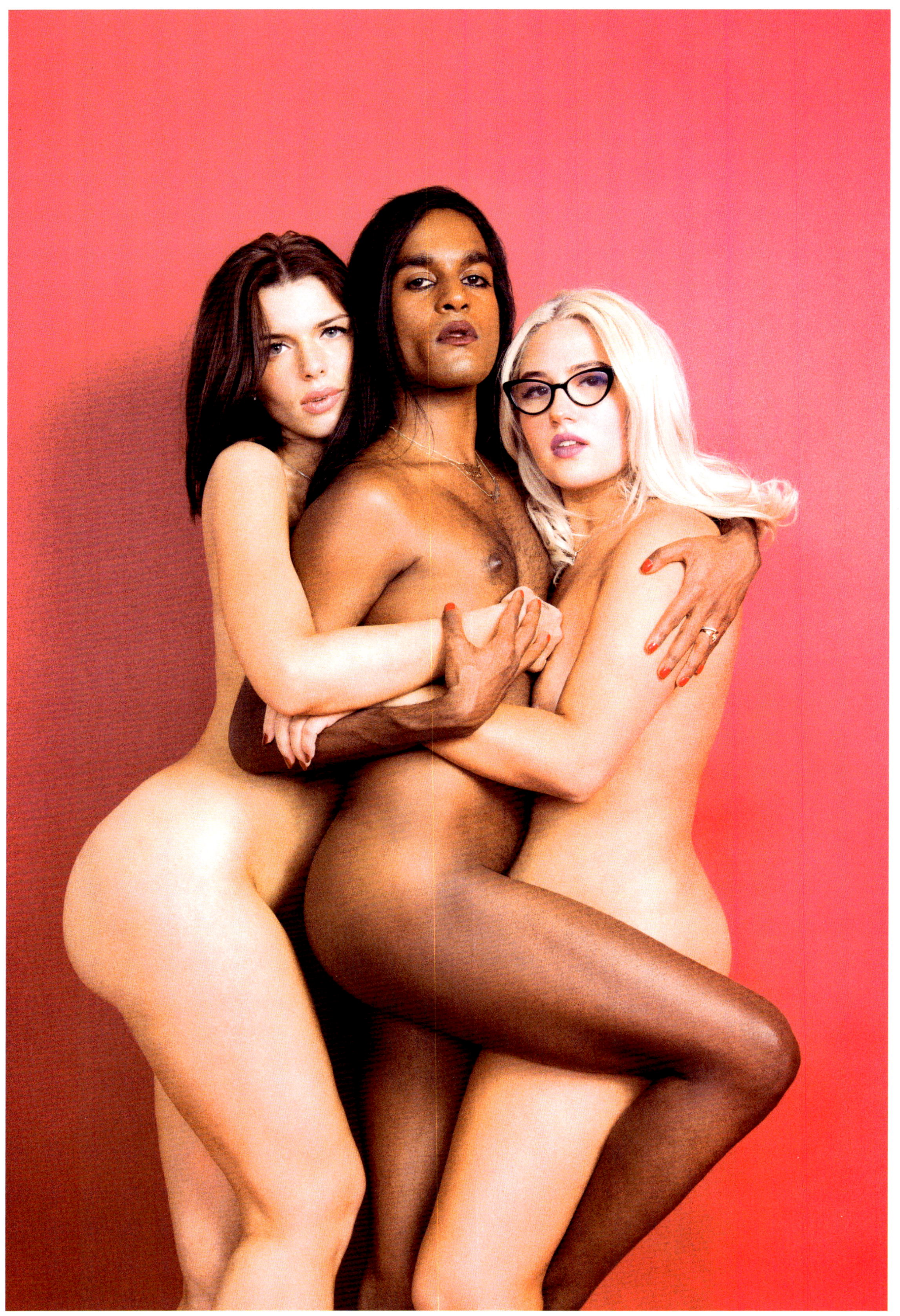

Julia & Richie & Briana, January 2017

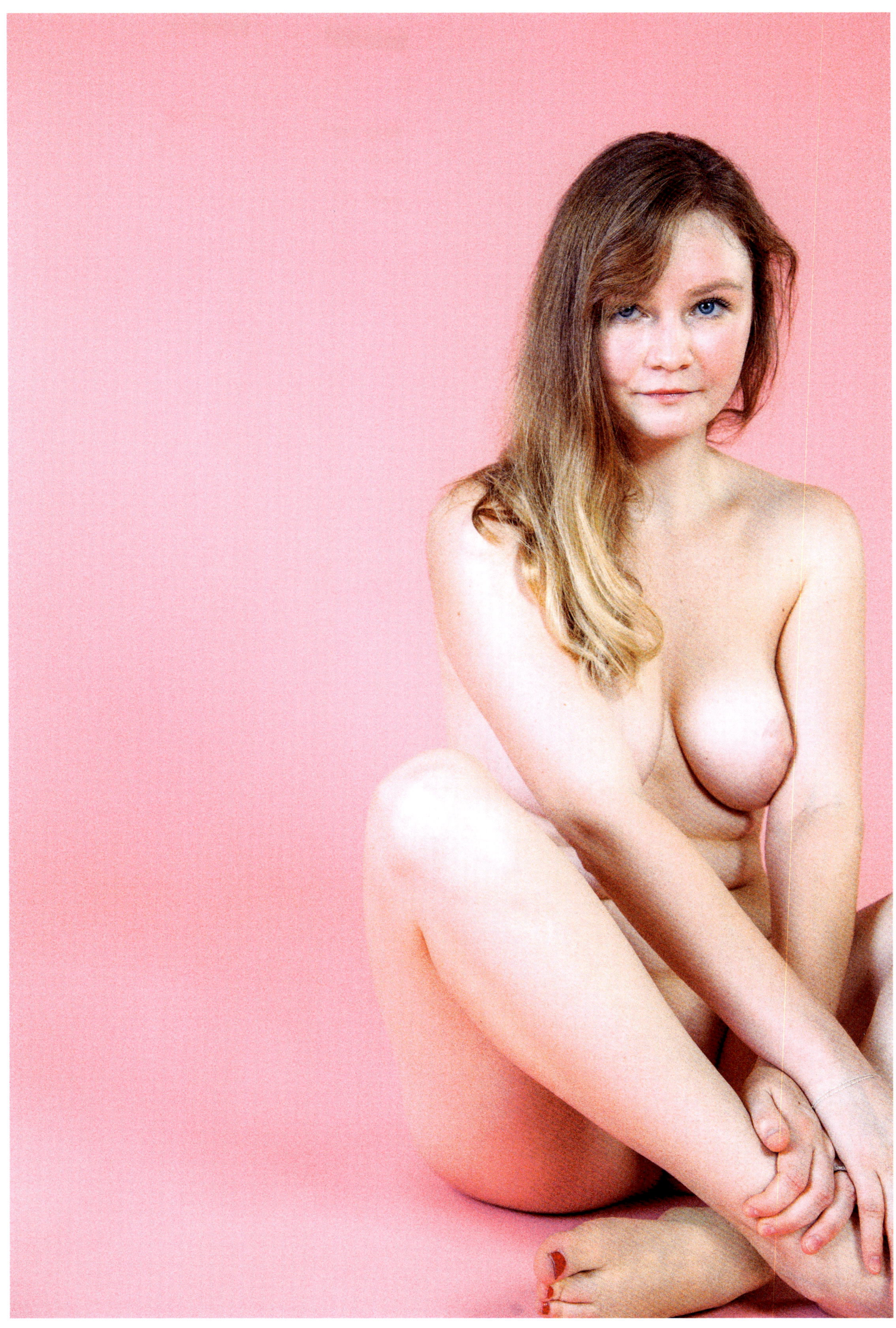

Anna, November 2013

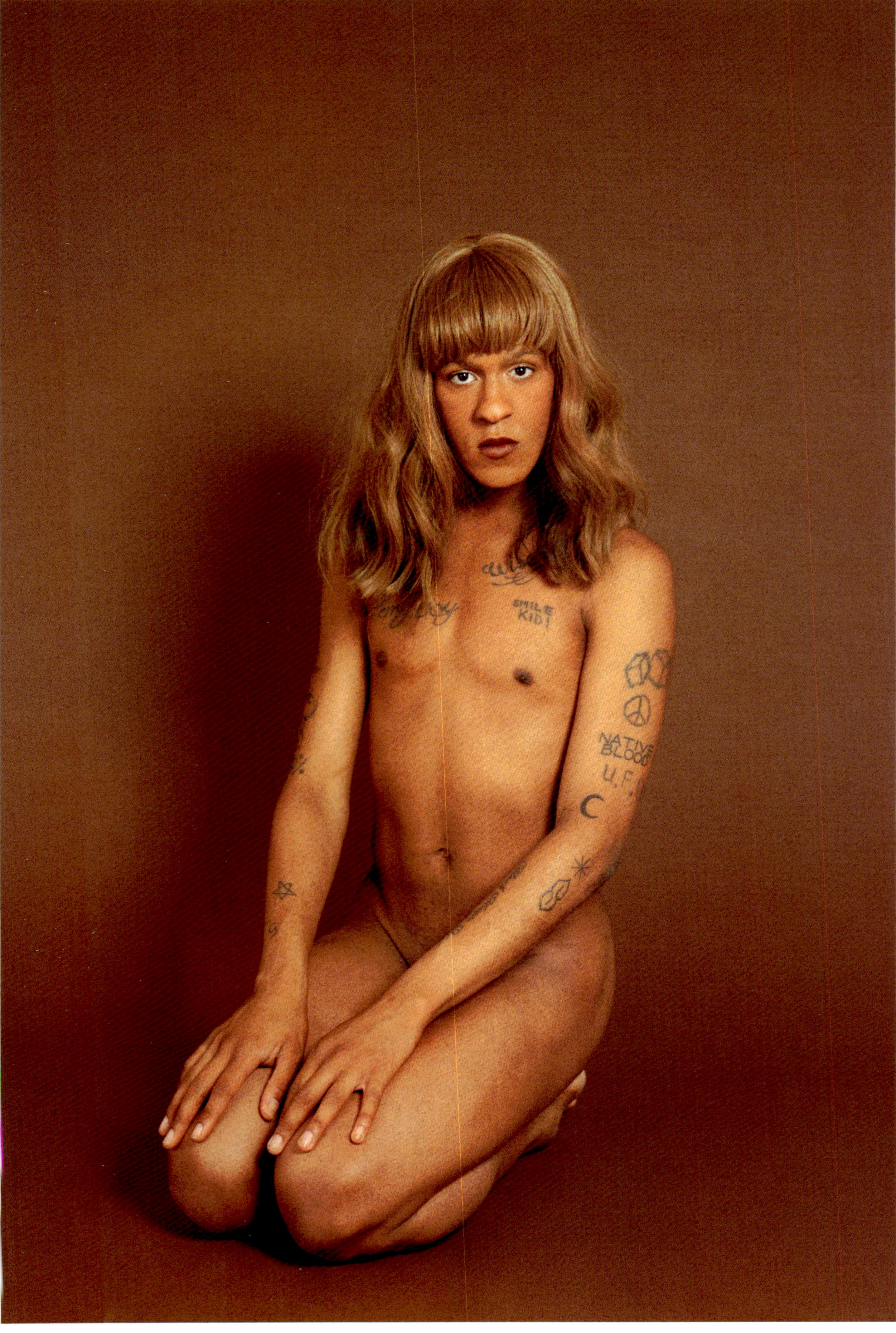

Mykki, June 2012

I was a teenager when I first ran away to New York. There was this book that was really popular at the time in anarchist punk circles called *Days of War, Nights of Love: Crimethink for Beginners*. This book literally said, "Run away from home, start your own life, fuck everything." It was very positive about how "you can do it, you can be an adult." That combined with "get free, get free, get free" from Lauryn Hill *Unplugged*—I packed a suitcase. I stole a hundred bucks out of my mom's wallet, literally only a hundred. My mom makes fun of me to this day. She's like, "I wish you had stolen more." I took a Greyhound bus from North California to New York. I was so naive, I hid my suitcase in Tompkins Square Park and obviously it was stolen within an hour.

I was heavily influenced by *Paper*, *The Face*, *i-D*, and *Index Magazine*. That's how I knew about Electroclash, Williamsburg, and Ryan's stuff. The masthead of *Index* had all these people's emails. Before coming to New York, I'd emailed Kathleen Hanna, Vincent Gallo, and Vaginal Davis. Vincent Gallo emailed me back. He was like, "Don't come to New York. You're an idiot." So I wrote to him again and I'll never forget this. He could tell I was planning on running away and said, "If you get sick, email me again."

I was sixteen at the Cock. I made fifty dollars dancing naked on the bar. I met Alexander McQueen. I had no filter and was just like, "You're Alexander McQueen." As soon as I said it, two gay guys swooped in to shield him from me. *I was sixteen at the Cock.*

My mom hired a private investigator but they couldn't find me—I was always calling from different payphones. Then I got an internship with *Elle Girl*, the teen *Elle*. I wrote a letter to the editor asking to be an intern, and she accepted. My mom fully supported me doing that. She gave me money and paid for me to stay in a hostel called Jazz on the Park while I interned. Then I came home and was grounded for four or five months.

Years later, back in New York, I started doing music, not because I was so into music, but because I wanted my peers to think what I was doing was cool. After college, I had wanted to do studio art, but I couldn't afford the supplies. Then a bunch of people encouraged my poetry. I published a book of poetry and all of a sudden I had an article in *Interview Magazine*. I realized older people were listening to my poetry but my peers didn't think it was so cool. So I started a band called No Fear. We were really, really arty. It was my training ground, laying the foundation to eventually become Mykki Blanco.

When people ask where "Mykki Blanco" came from, I can honestly say, "One day, I just had an idea." It was in the midst of a pop culture moment. Nicki Minaj's feud with Lil' Kim was just starting. I was thinking about Cindy Sherman and was super inspired by the photographer Nikki S. Lee when I had this idea about a teenage girl who wanted to be a famous rapper. I got makeup and a wig and started making these videos and putting them directly on Facebook. One day, I got all dressed up and went outside. It was that simple. I'll never forget this guy running across the street to ask me for my number. At McDonald's, a guy held the door open for me. Going through life as a gay boy and then all of a sudden to have people treat you like a hot girl, it was like opening Pandora's box.

Everything happened so quickly. Venus X from GHE20G0TH1K was like, "If Mykki wants to be a rapper, you should rap." The very first Mykki Blanco rap is still on YouTube: "Black Sailor Moon, Doom Generation, Dark Joan of Arc, Now give me my veneration . . ." The second Mykki Blanco song was produced by fucking Arca. Francesco Carrozzini directed and produced the video for my song "Wavvy" for free. I blew up on Tumblr.

I don't even own a copy of my poetry book anymore. I have a PDF of it, but God. I'm doing my master's degree now. Professor Blanco.

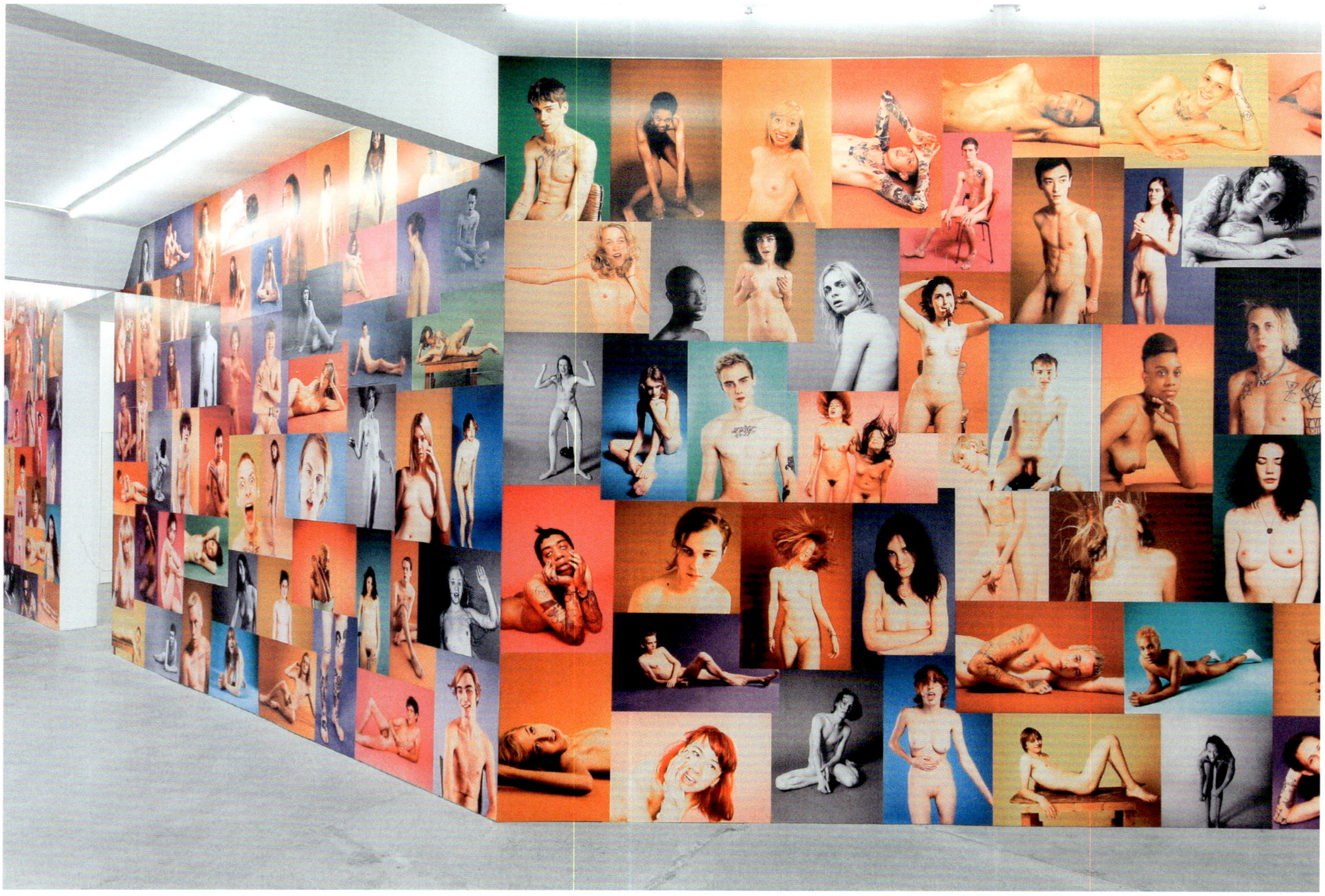

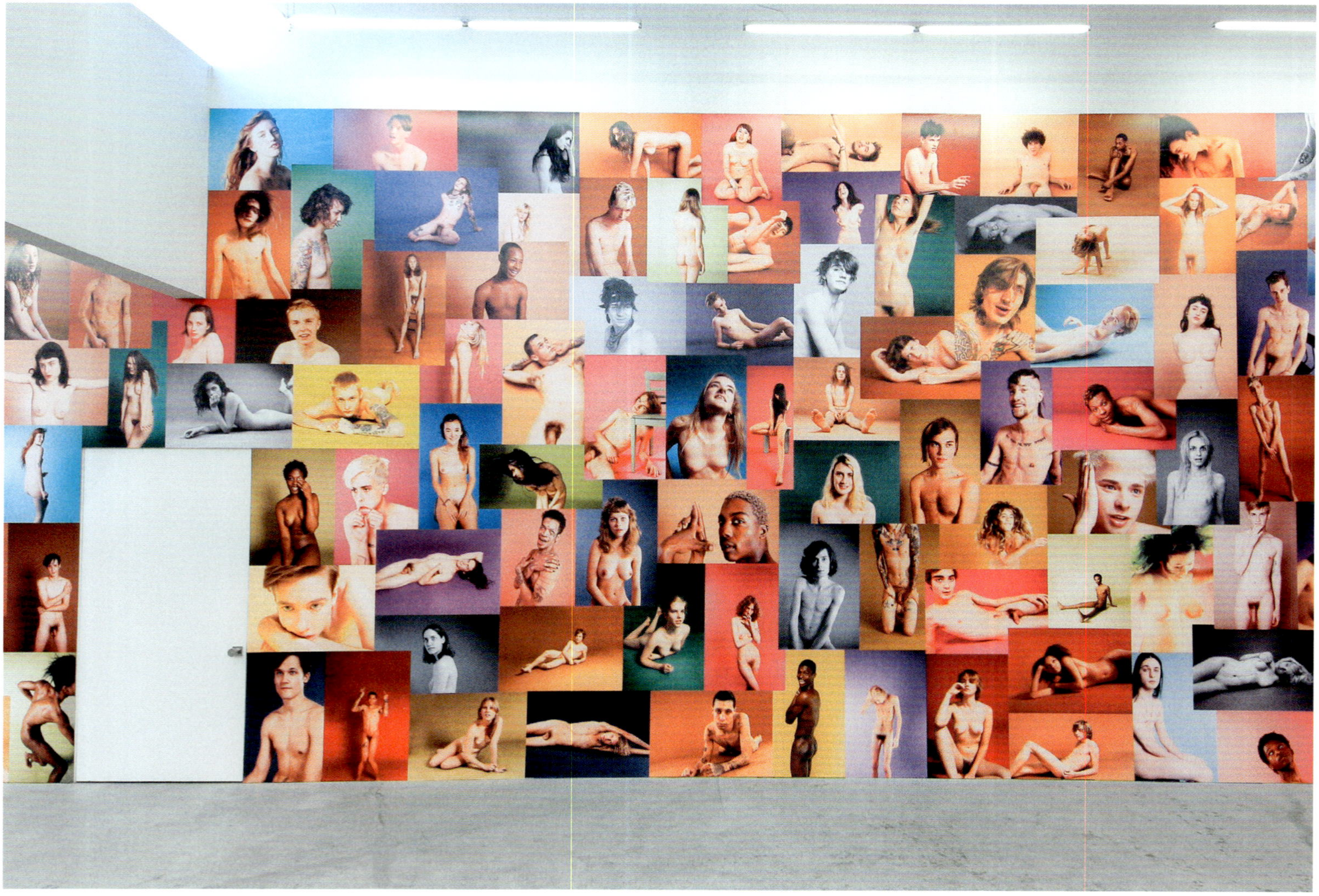

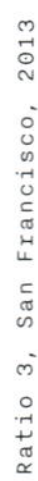
Ratio 3, San Francisco, 2013

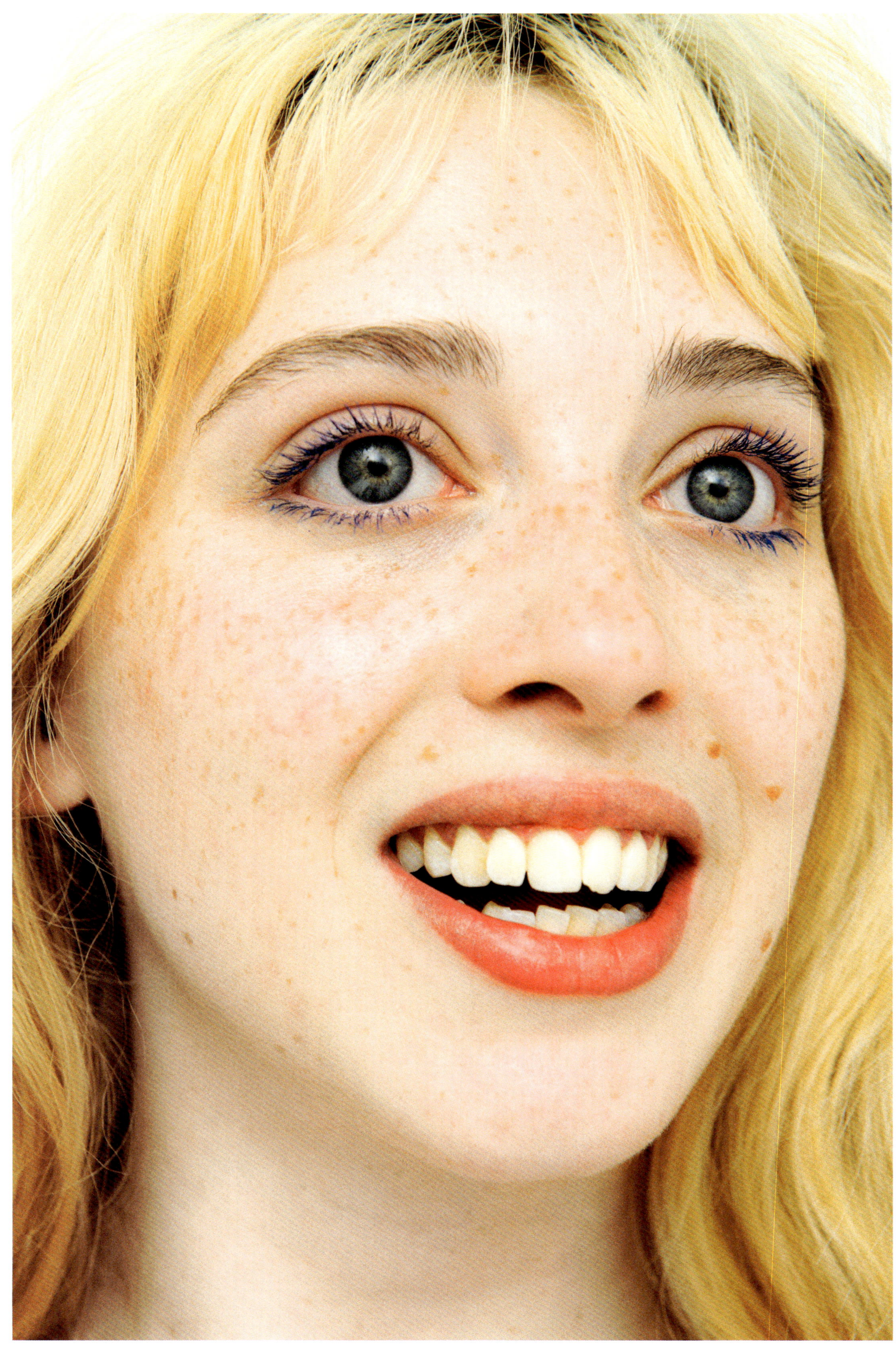

Nika, June 2017

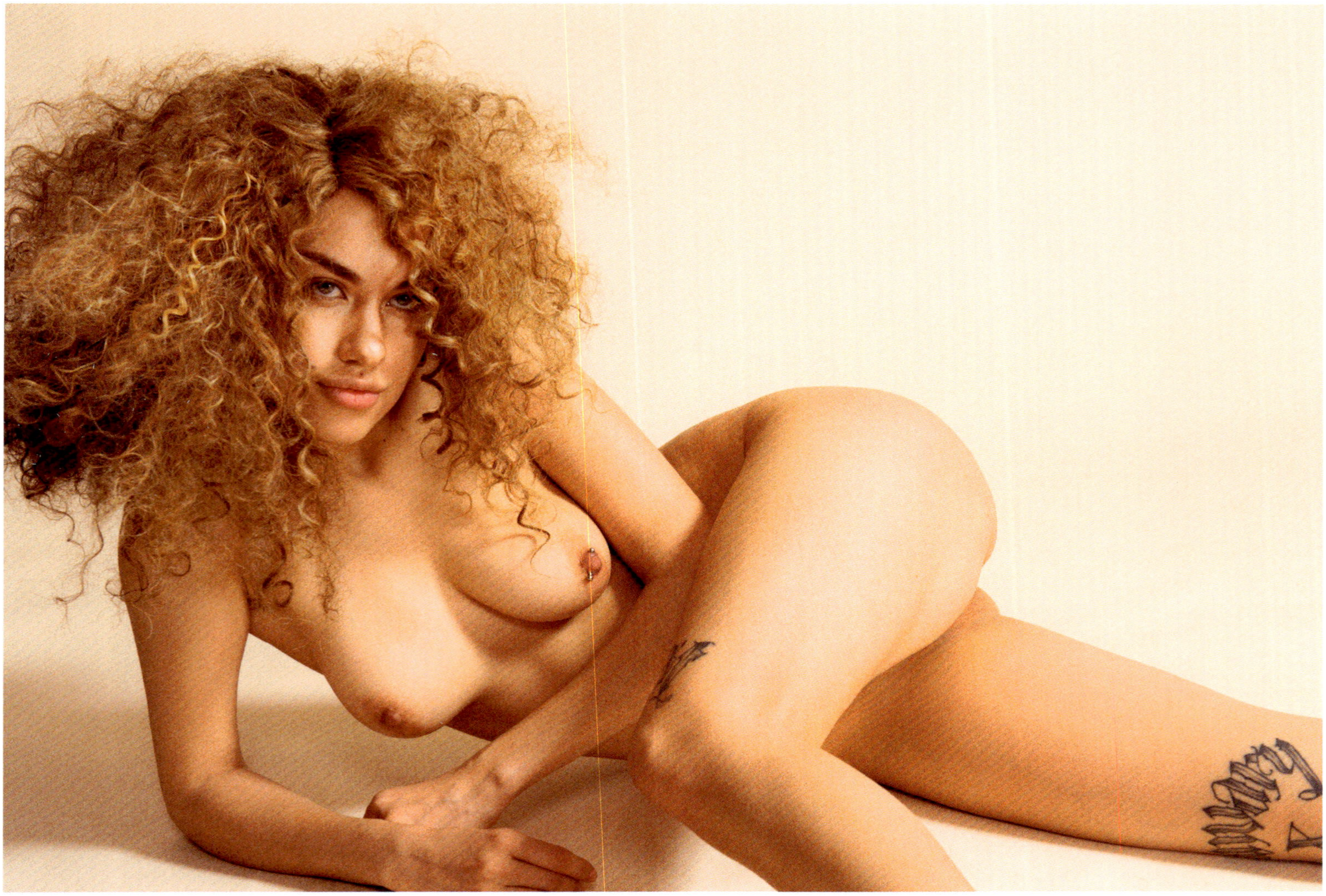

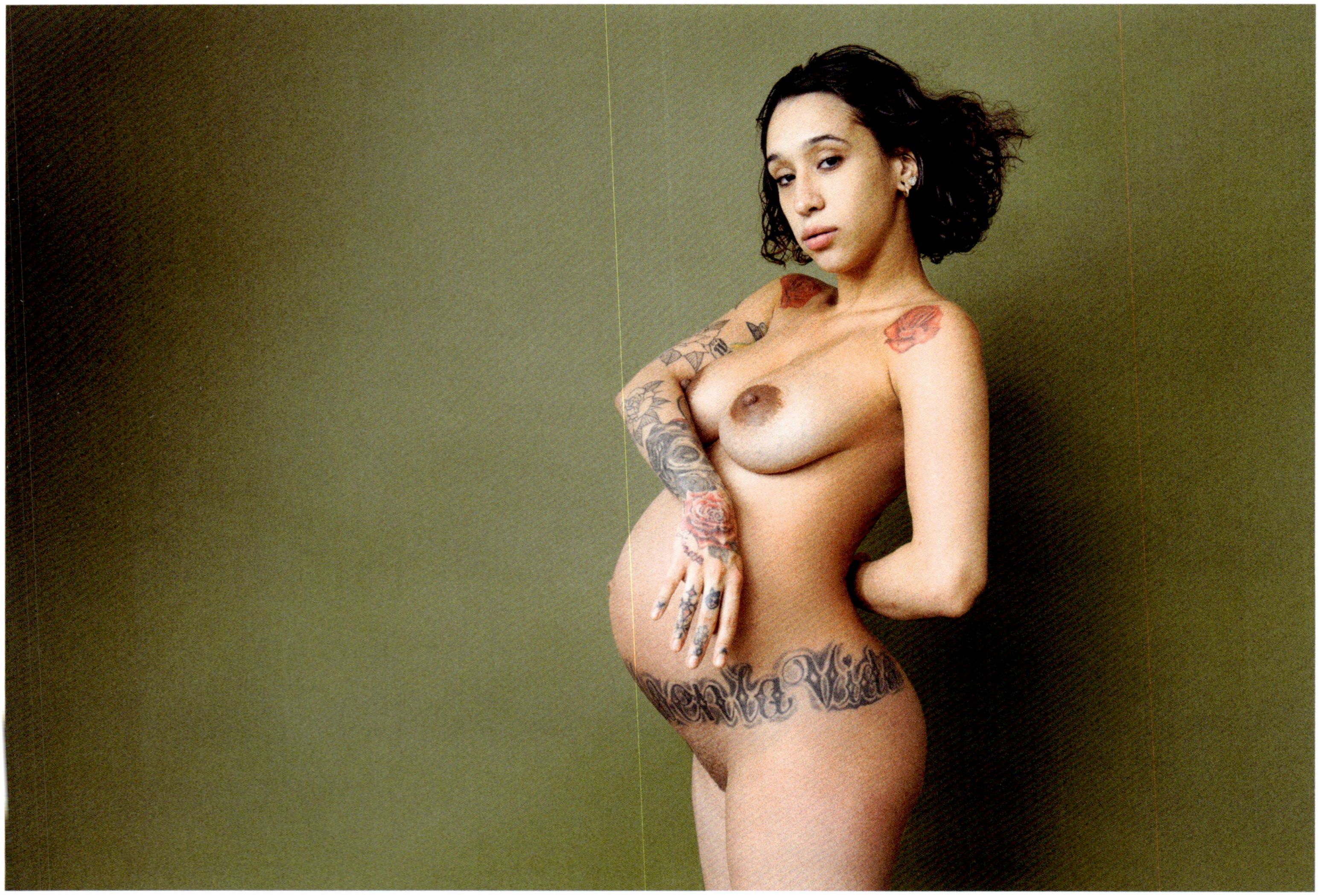

Apple, May 2016

Mela, December 2016

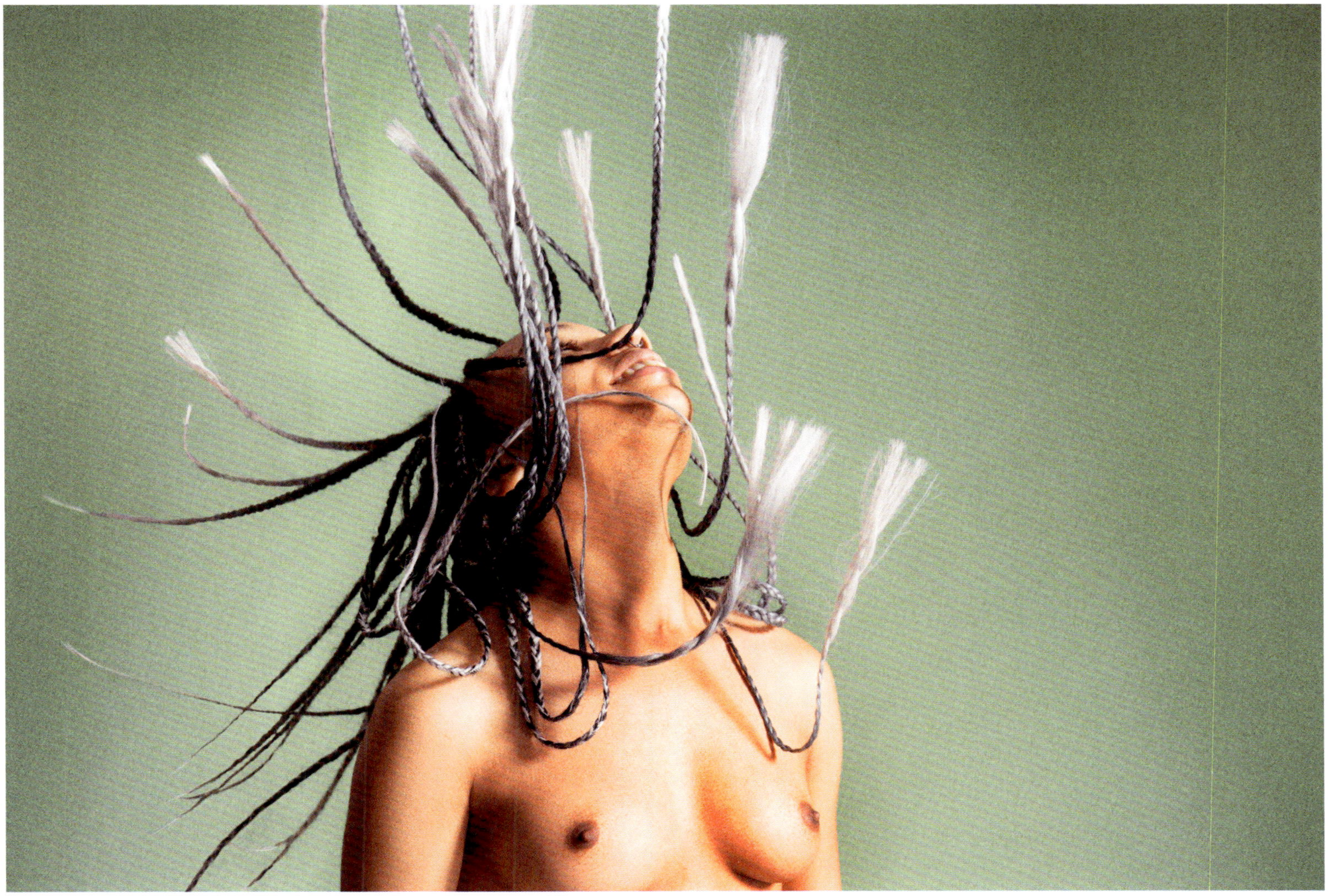

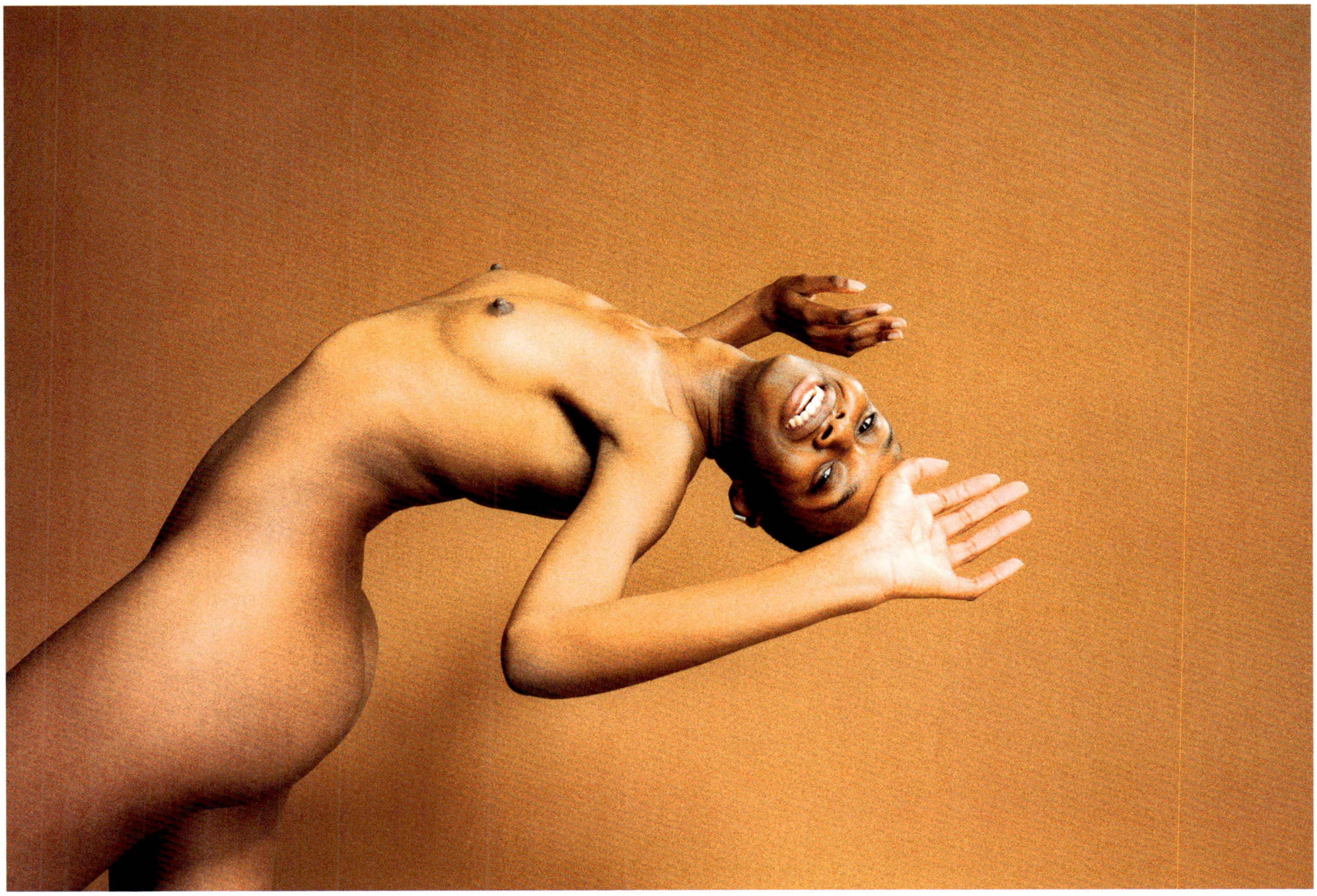

Jessica, March 2016   Ashley, January 2016

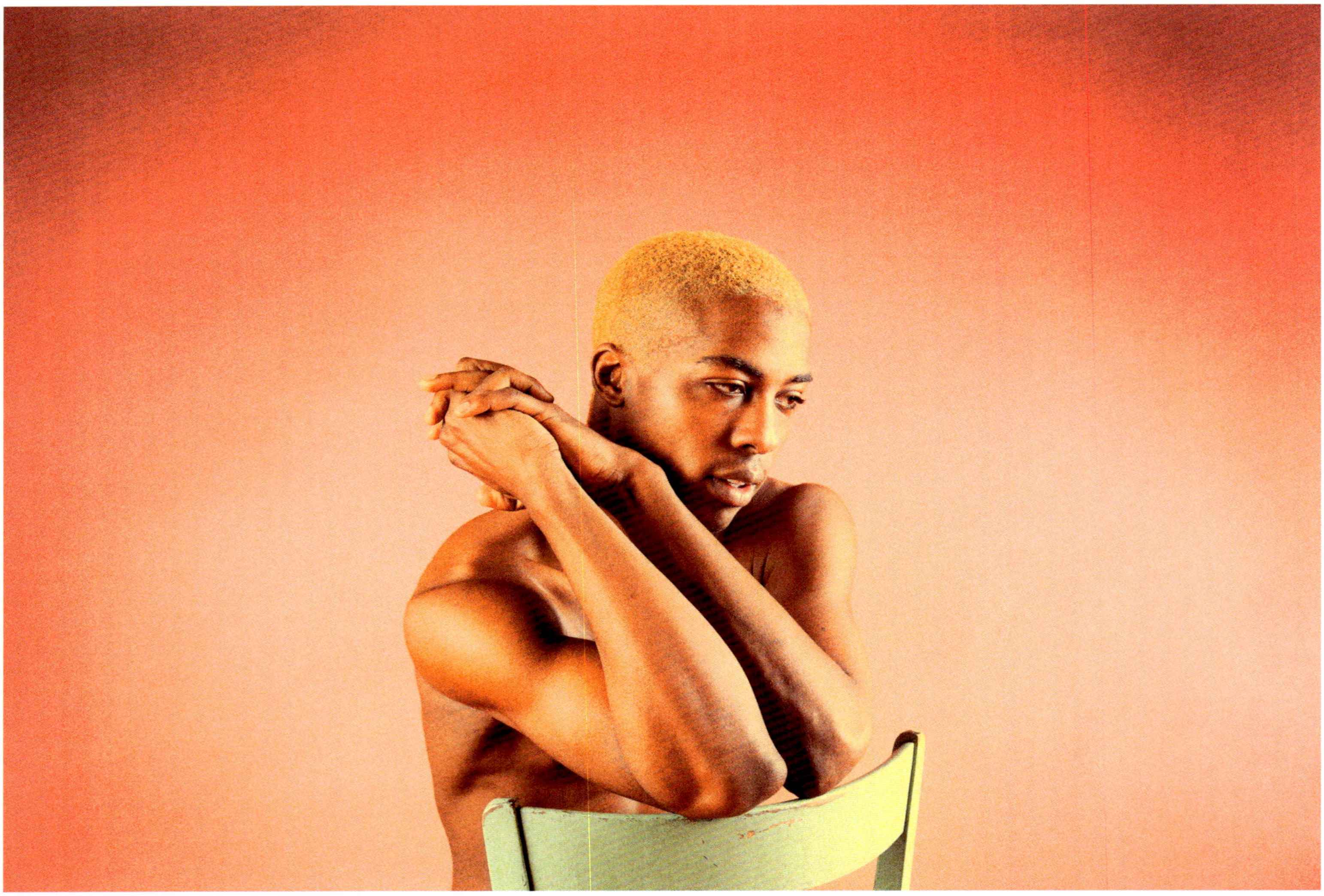

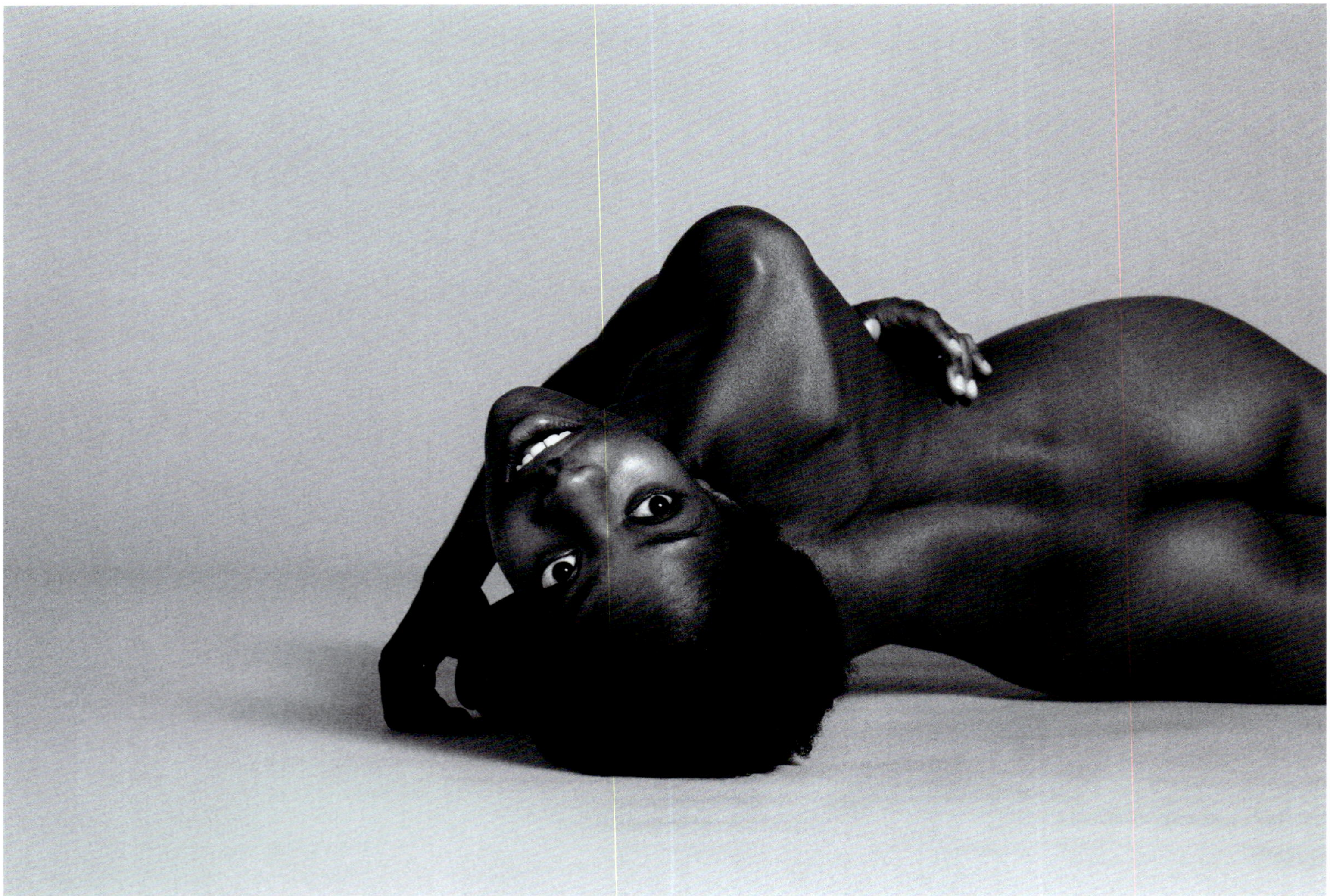

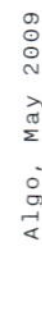

Eliot, December 2011   Algo, May 2009

Calson, September 2015

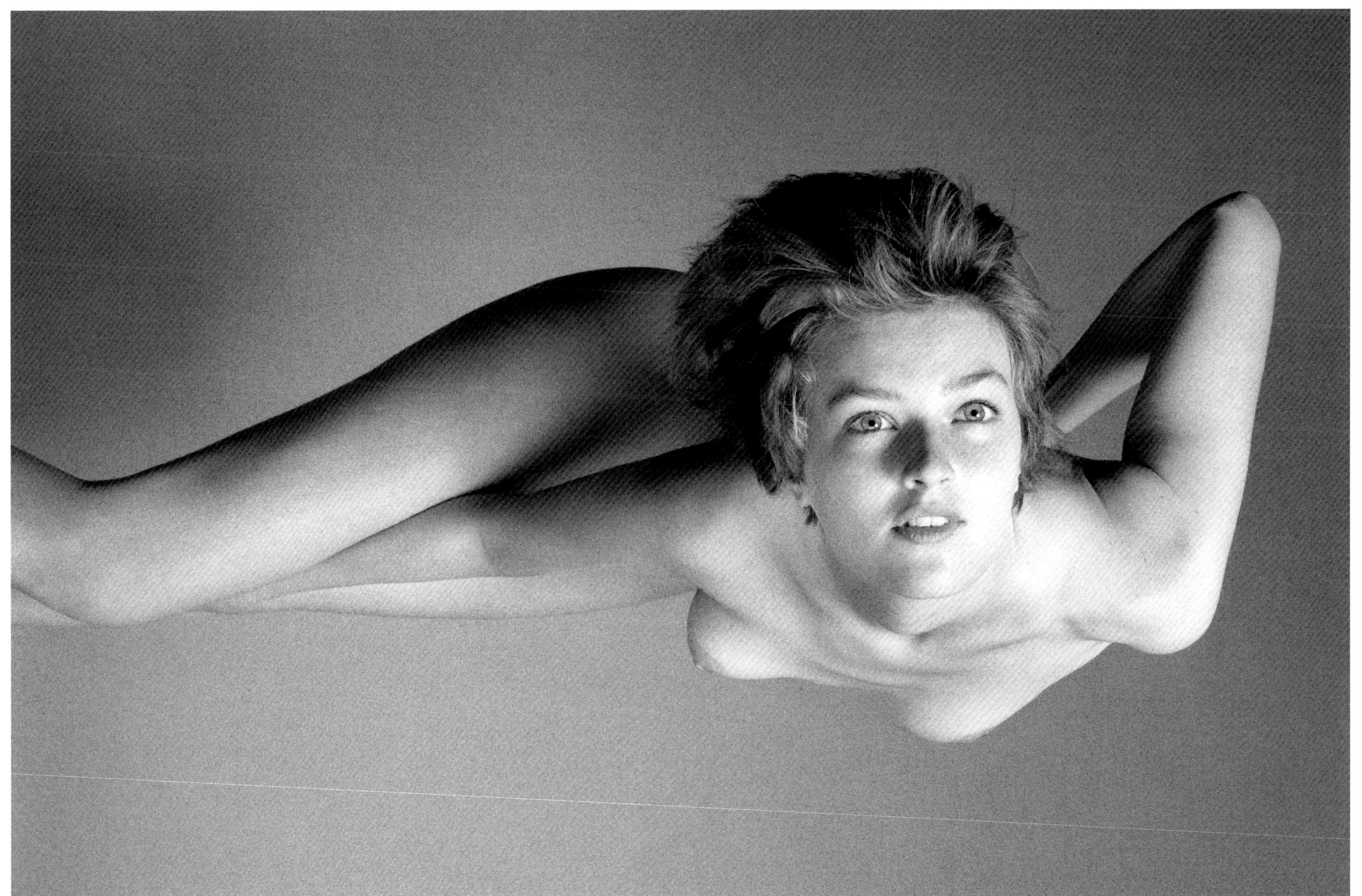

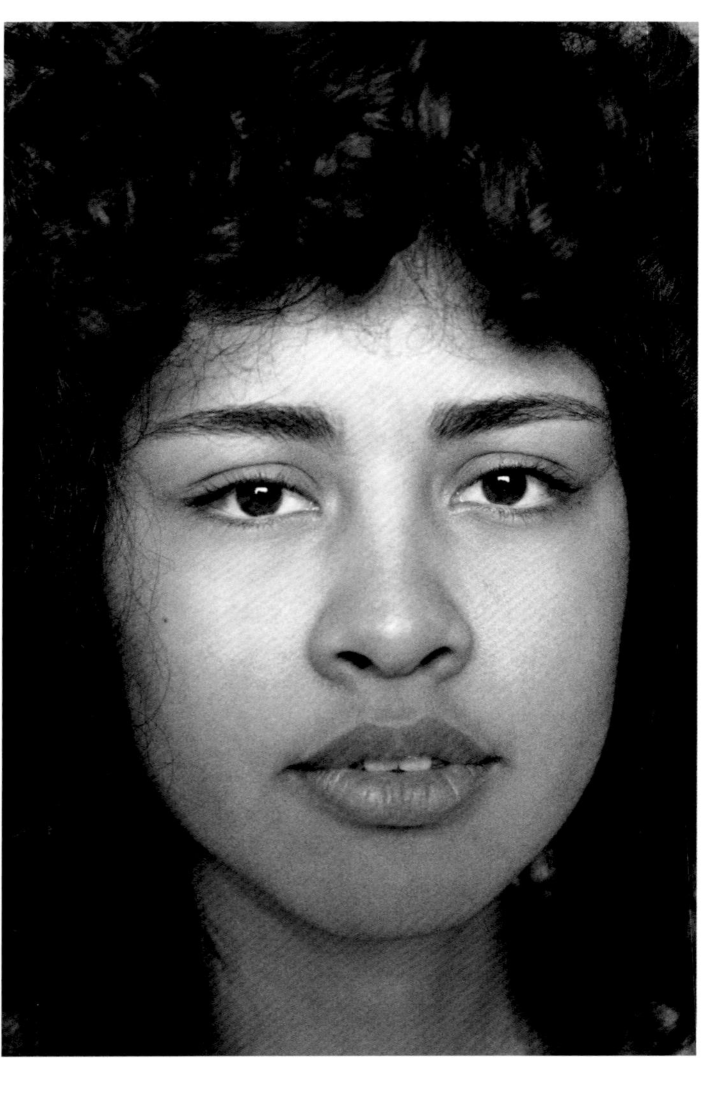

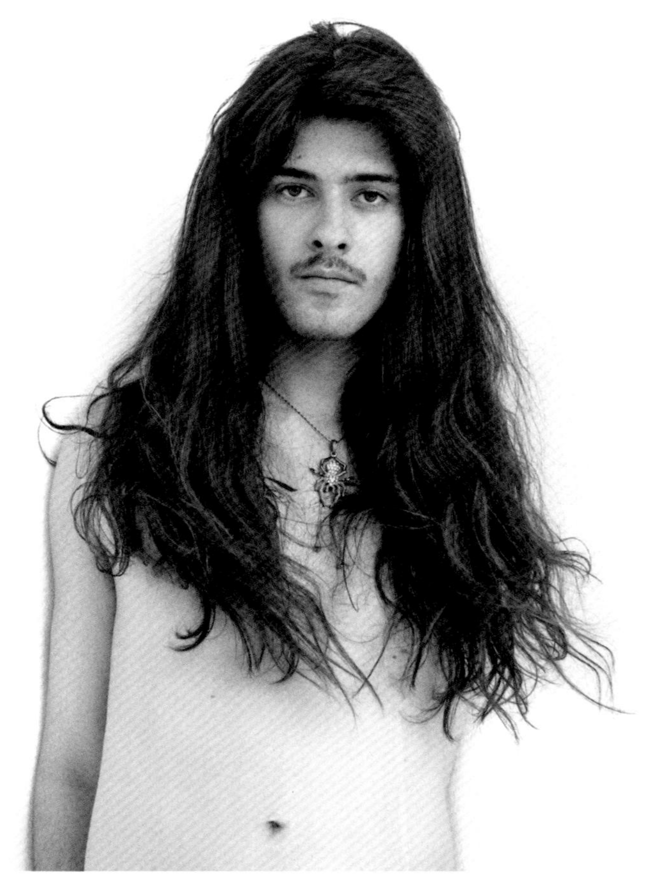

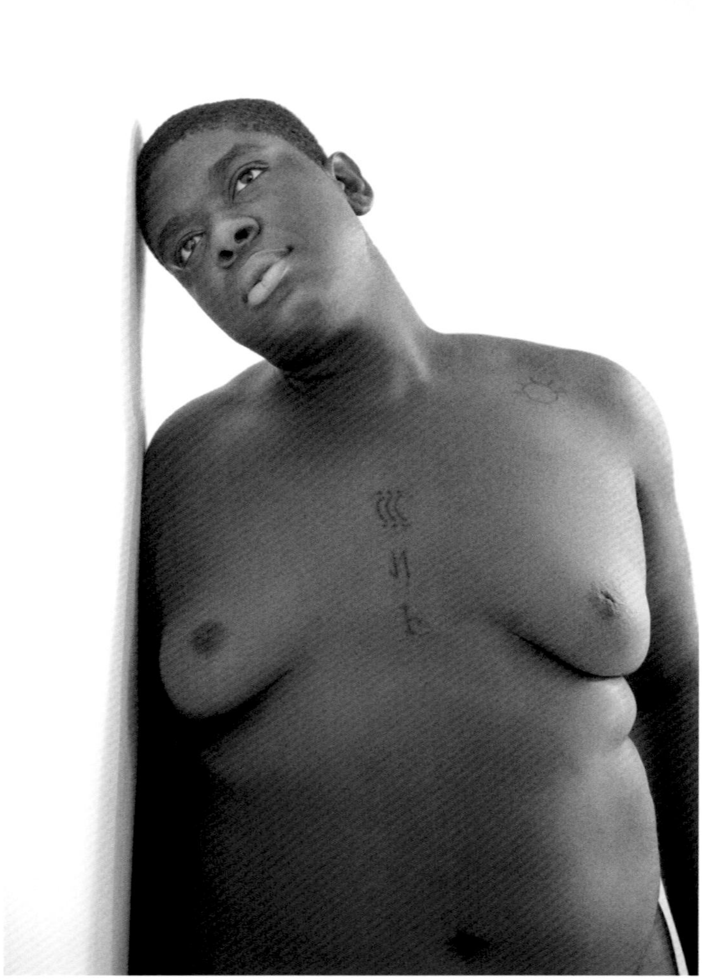

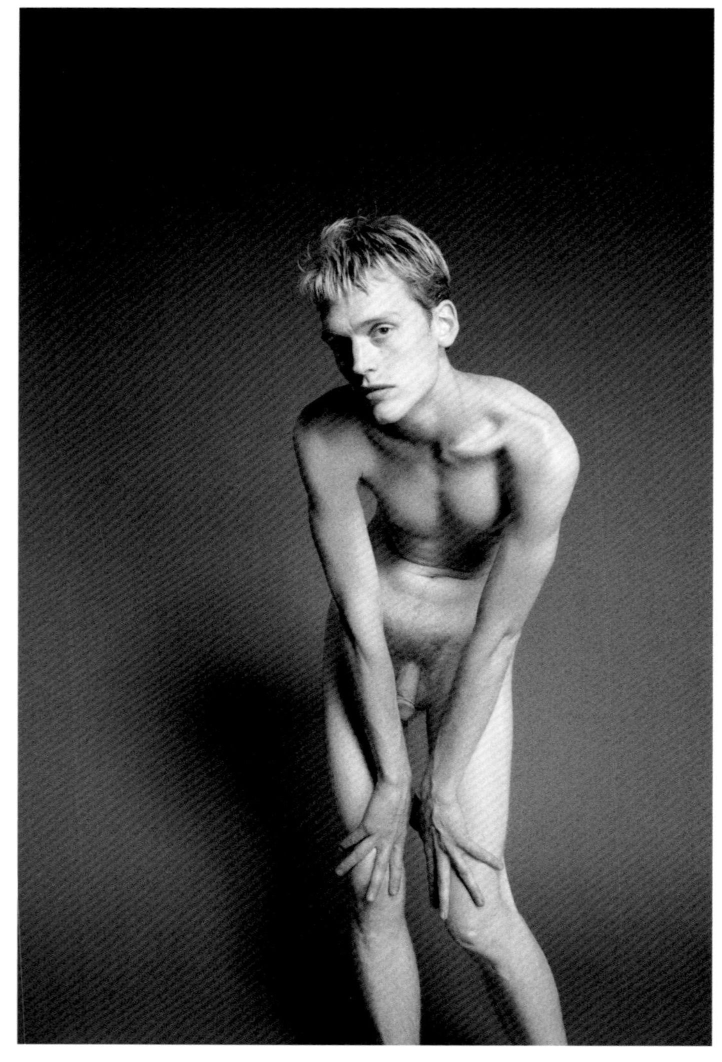

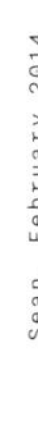

Luz, January 2010   Alex, September 2017   Cherry, December 2018   Sean, February 2014

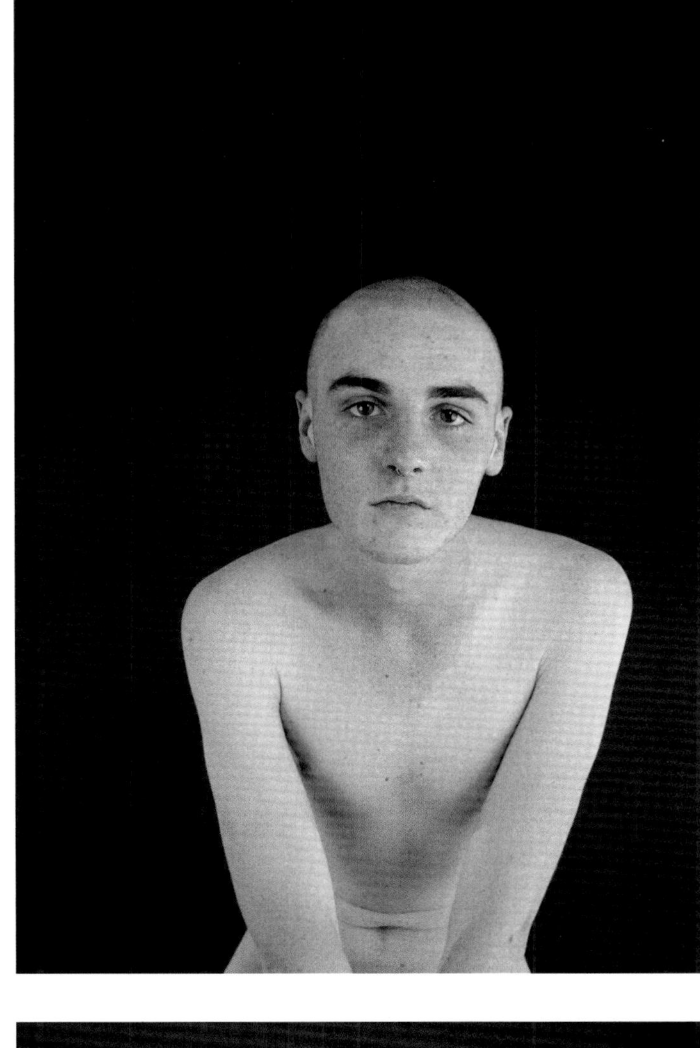

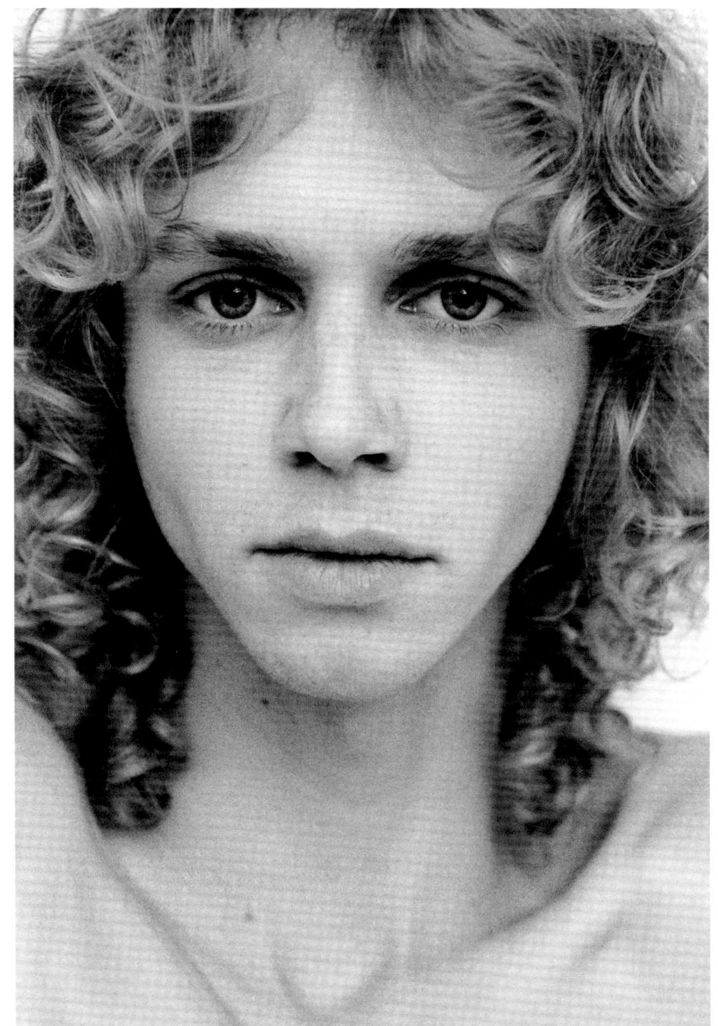

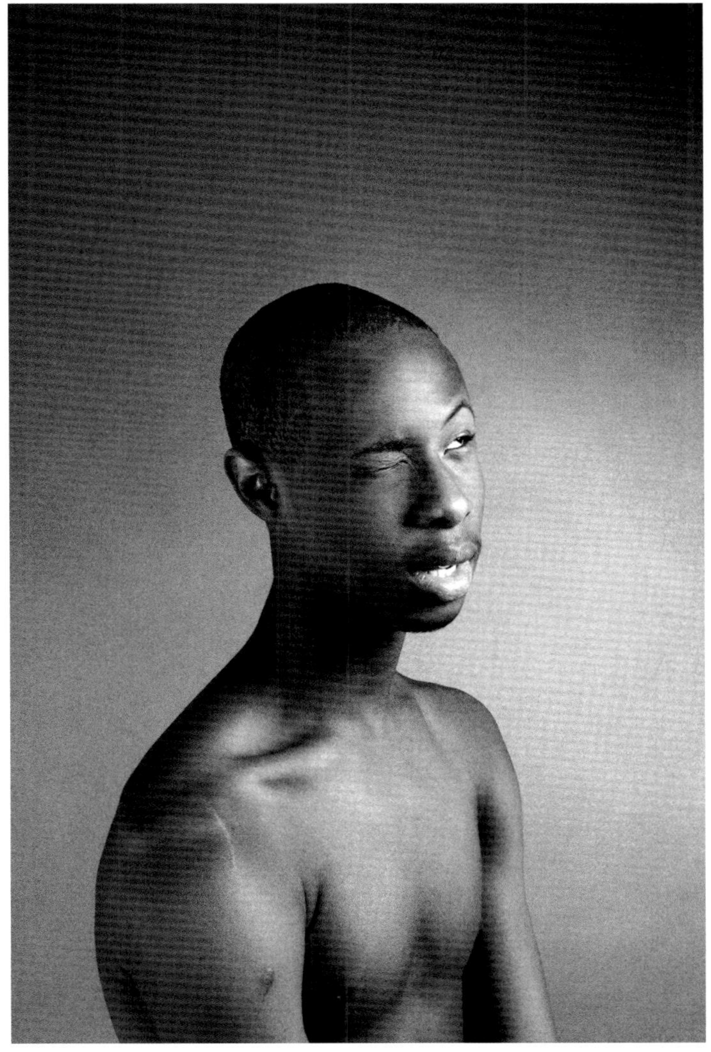

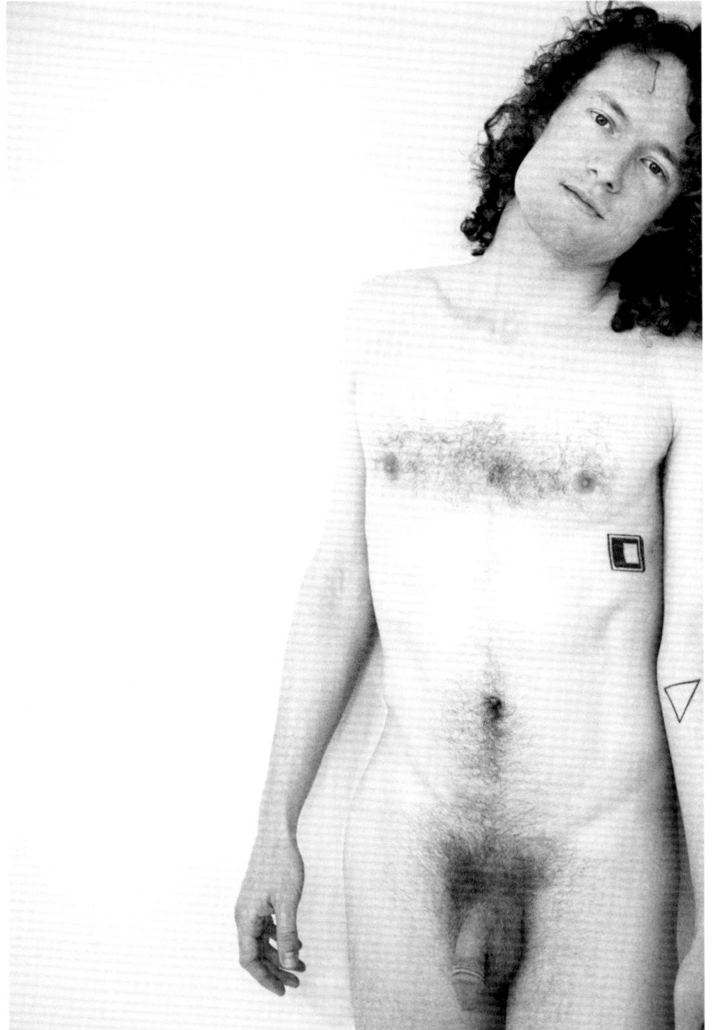

Thomas, January 2013   Brett, July 2017   Jei, October 2012   Daniel, November 2018

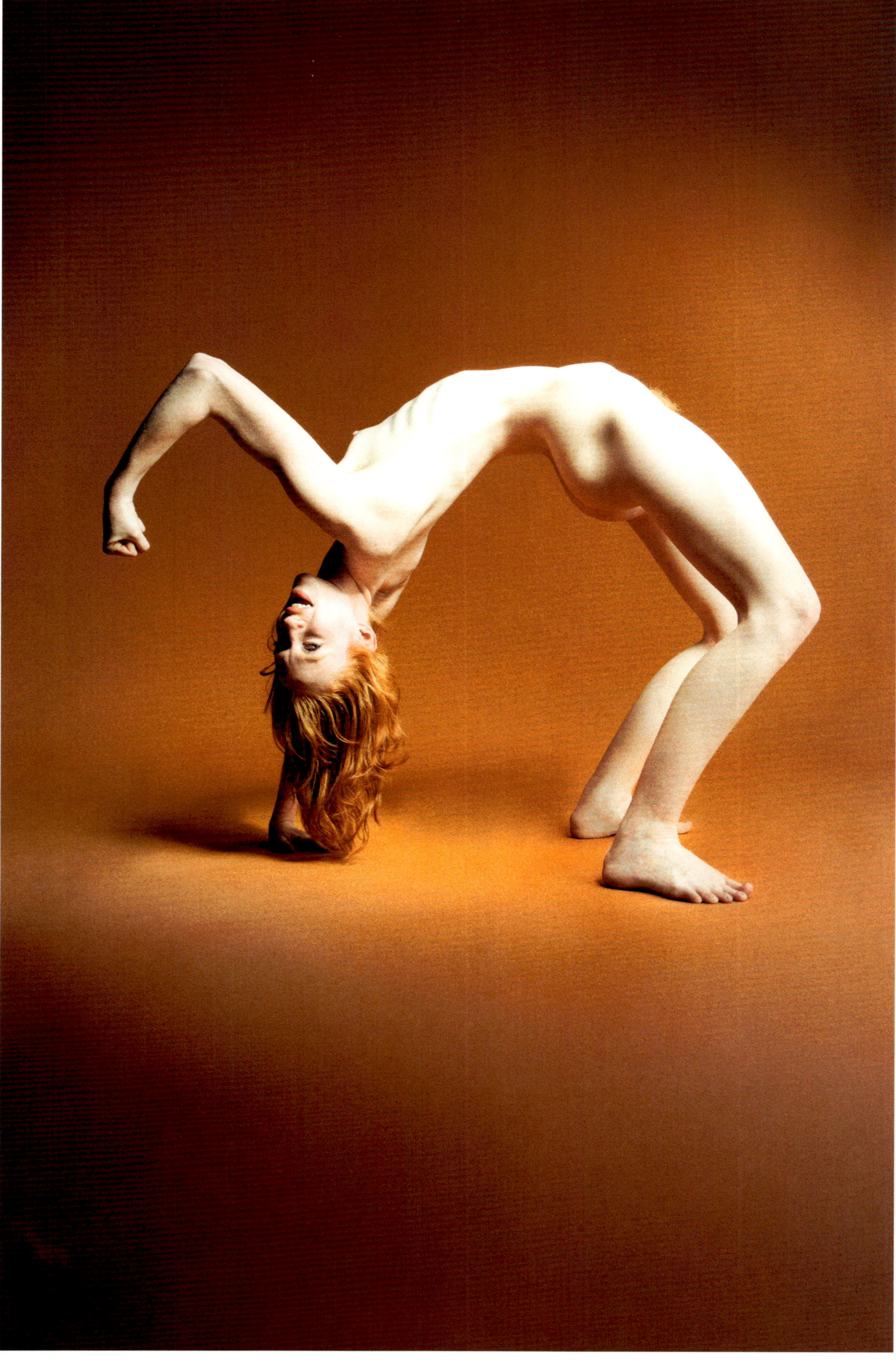

Ely, March 2015

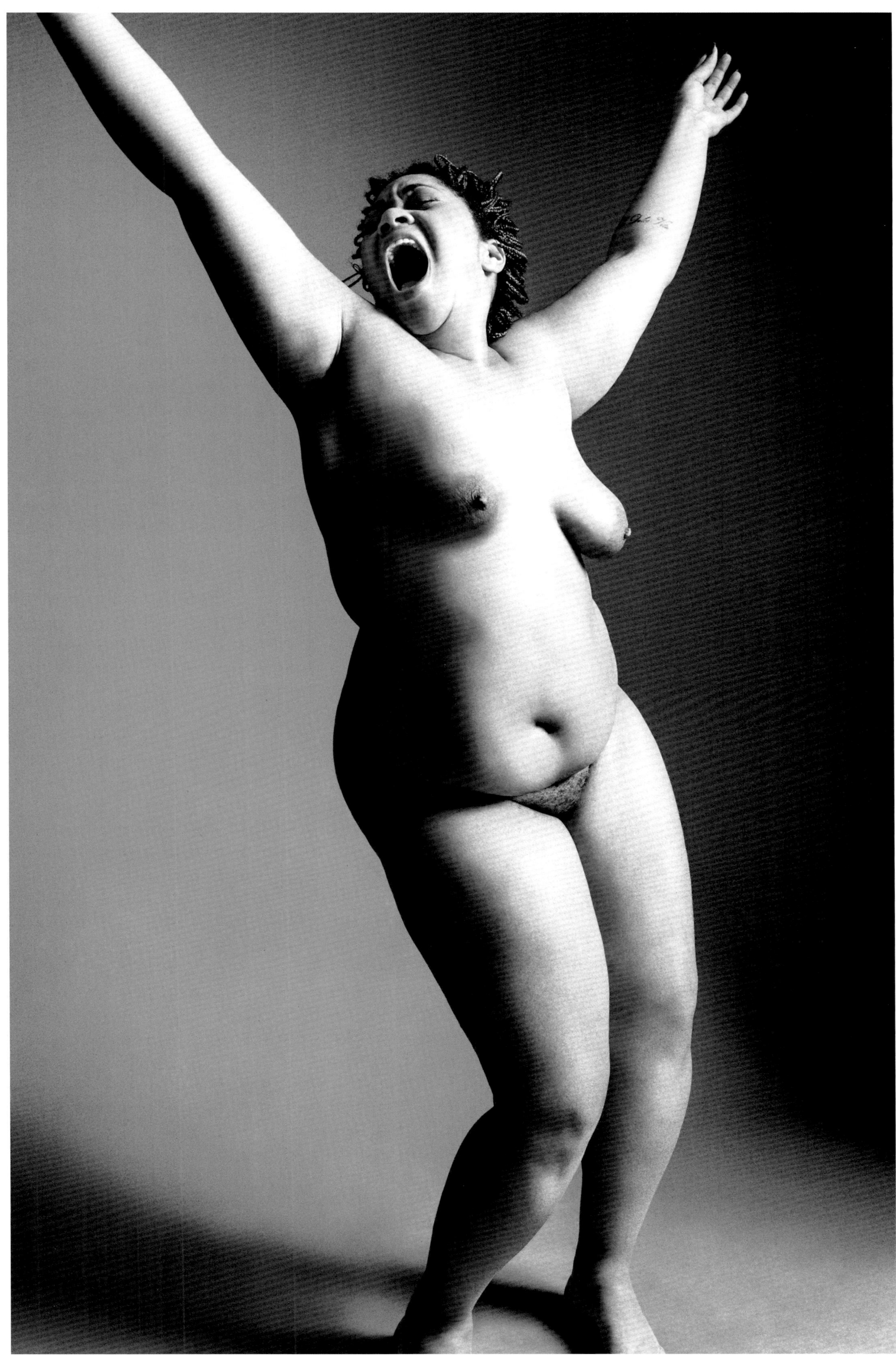

Ebere, February 2016

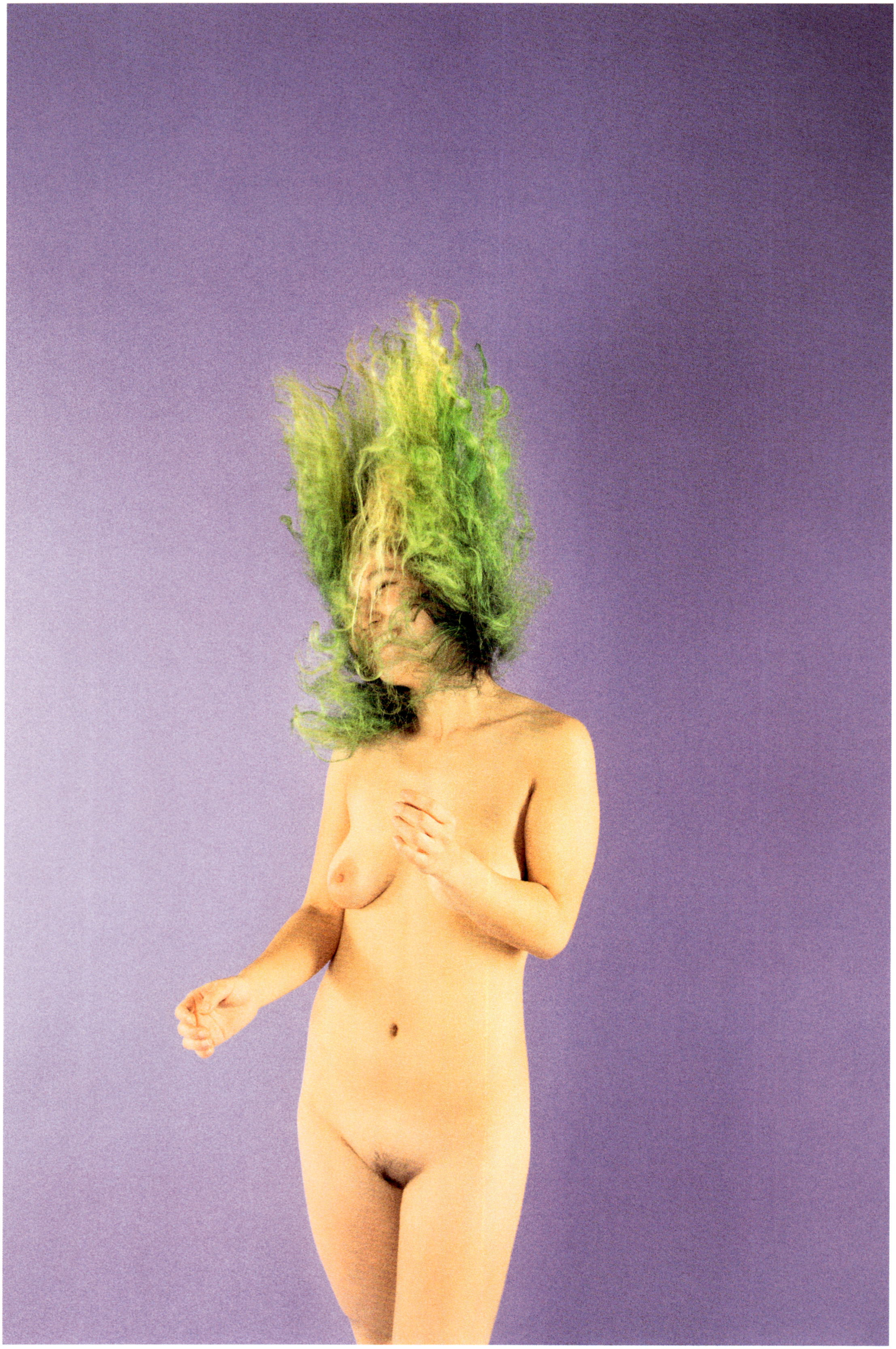

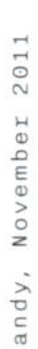

Sandy, November 2011

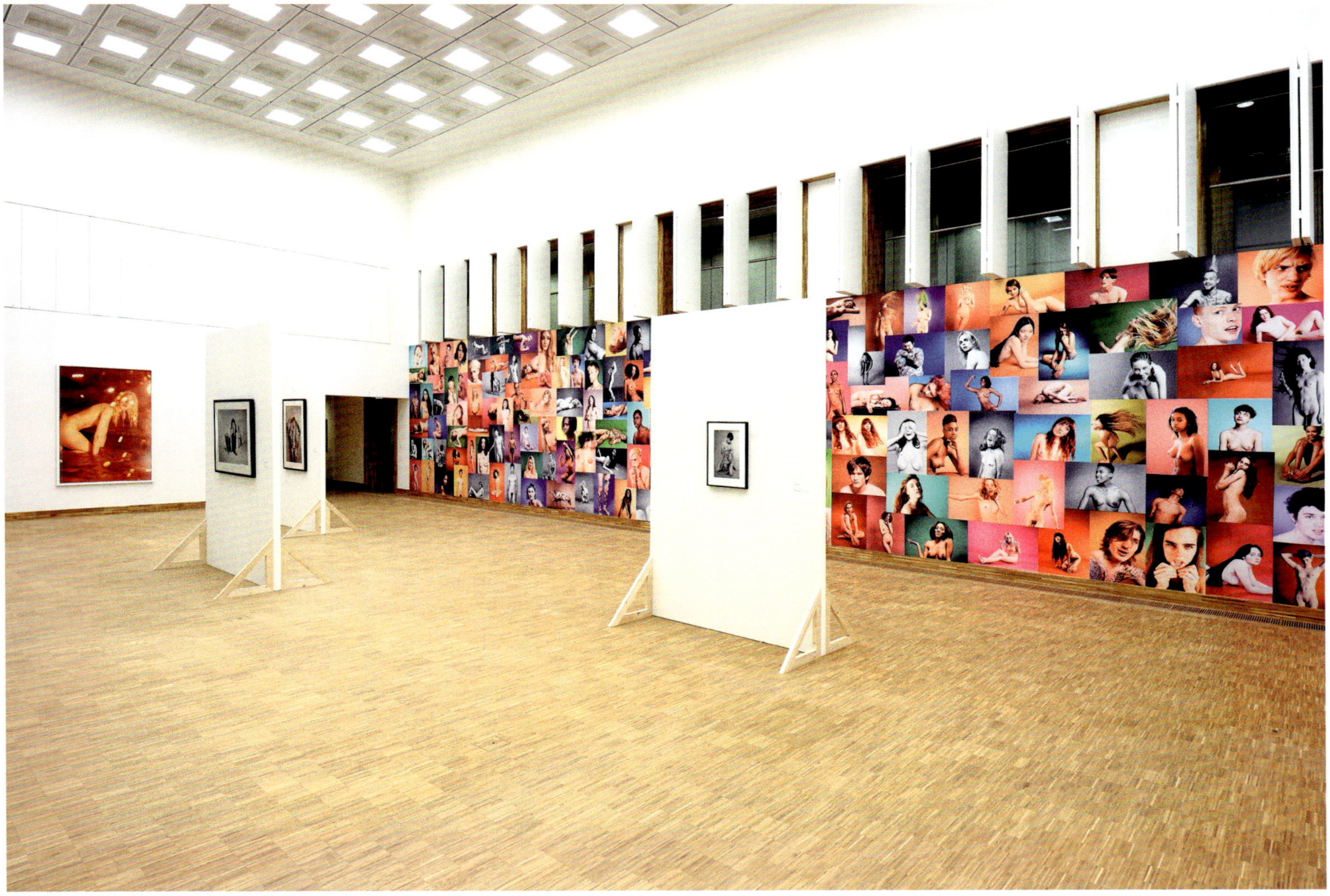

Kunsthal KAdE Museum, The Netherlands, 2015

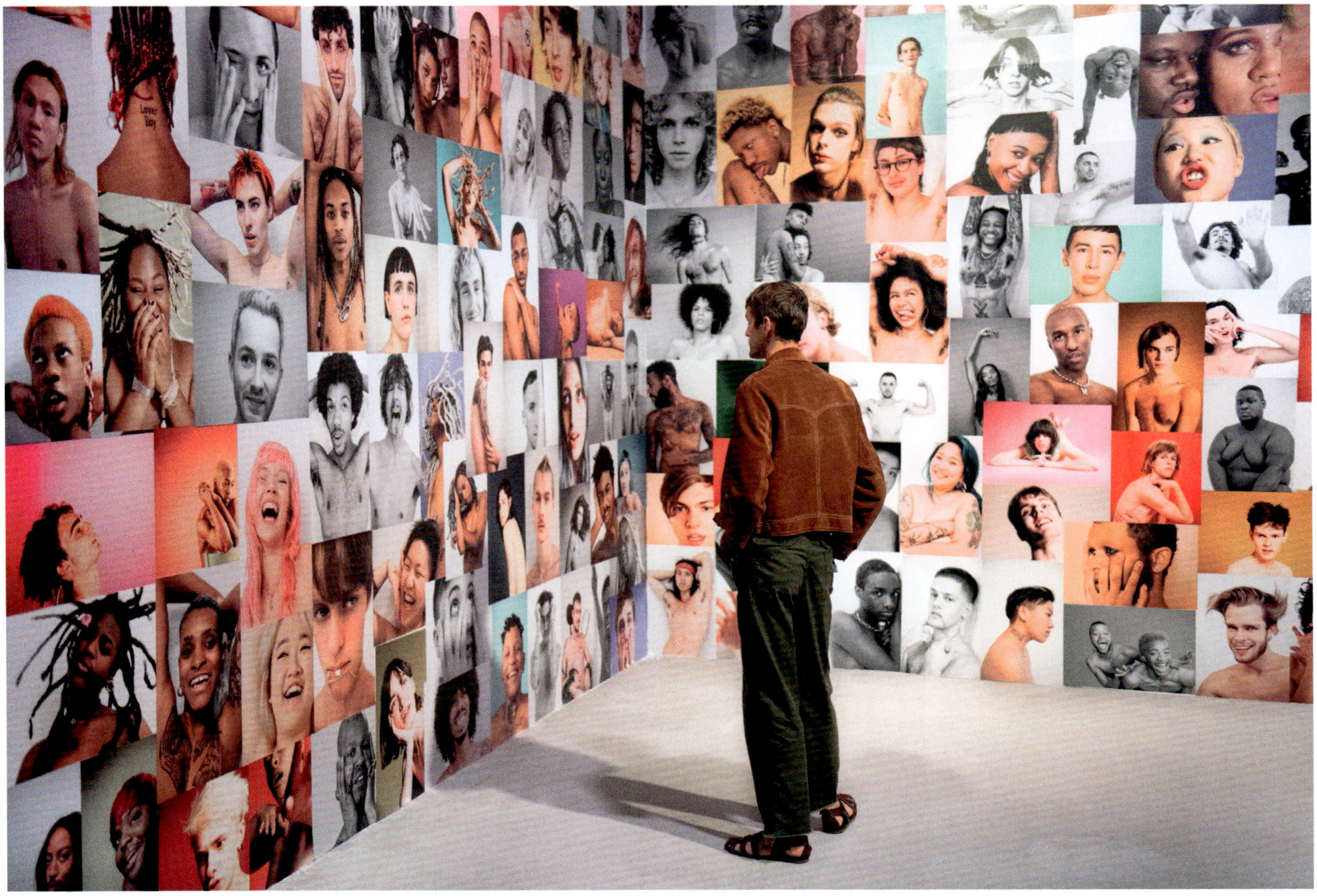

Abu Dhabi Semi Permanent, 2021

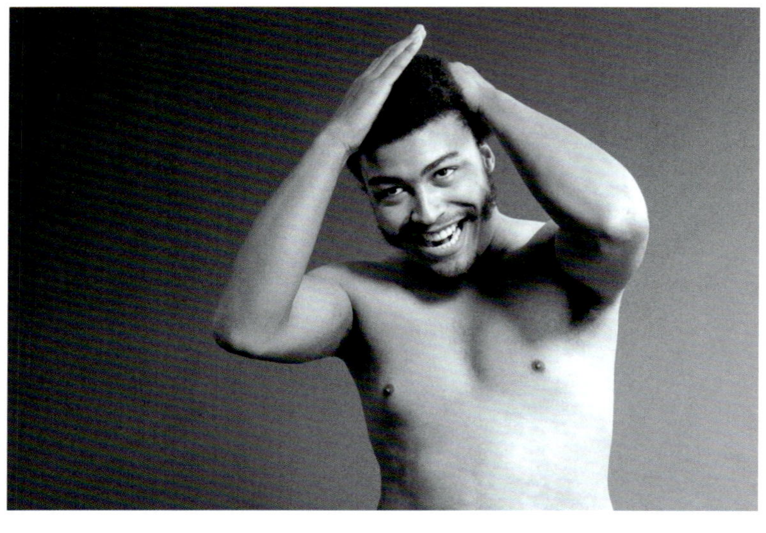

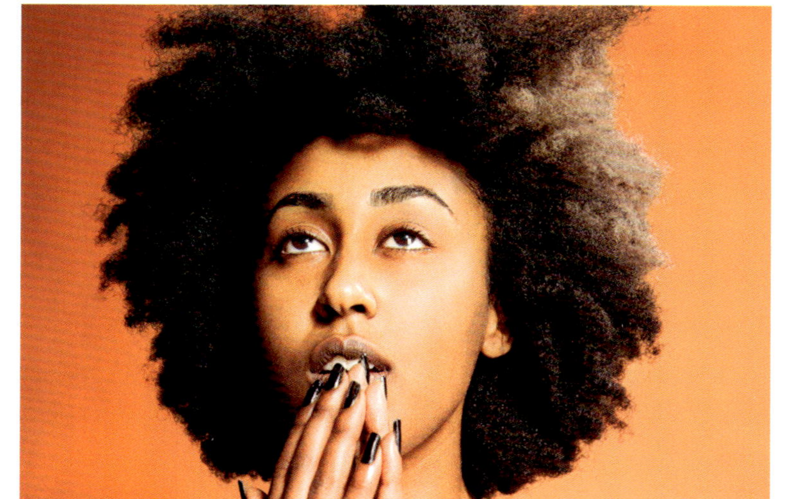

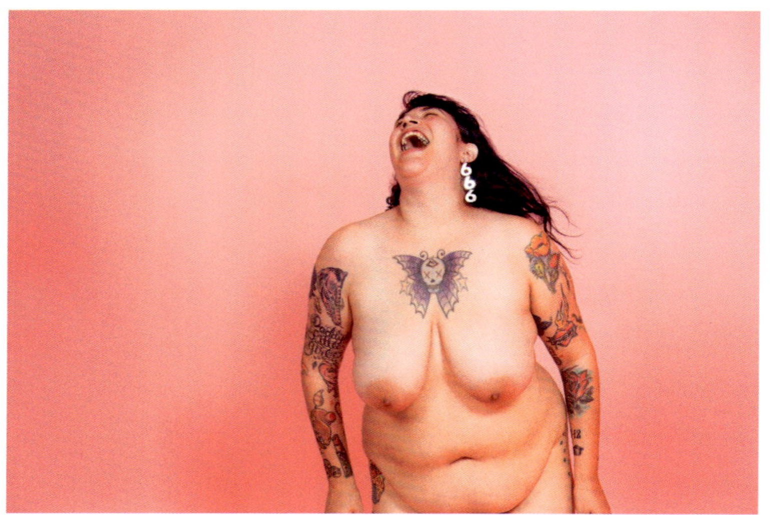

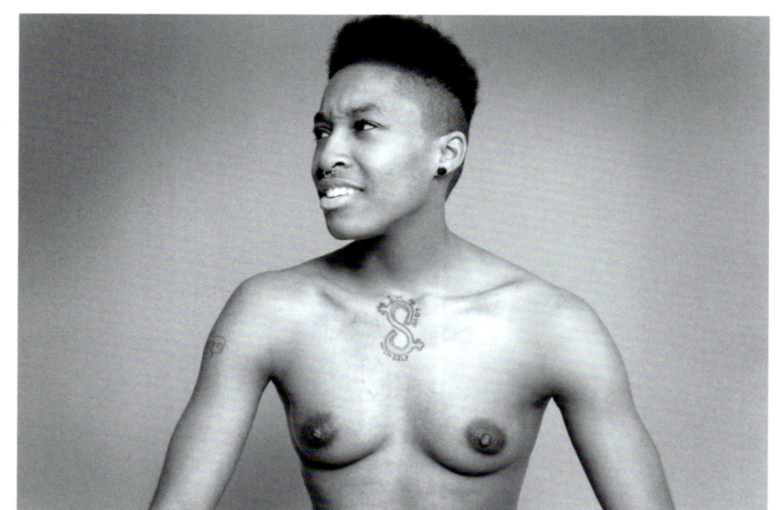

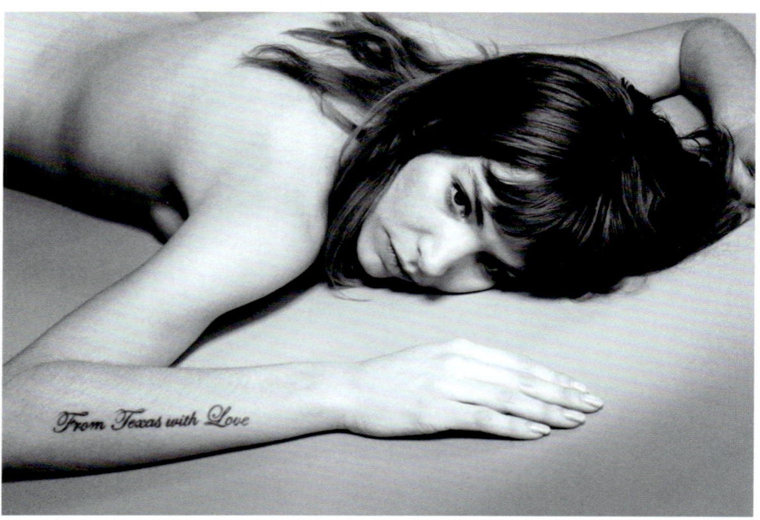

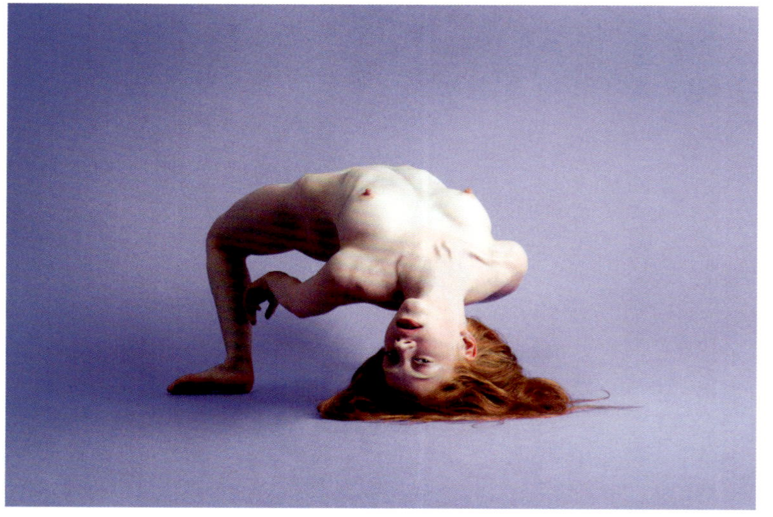

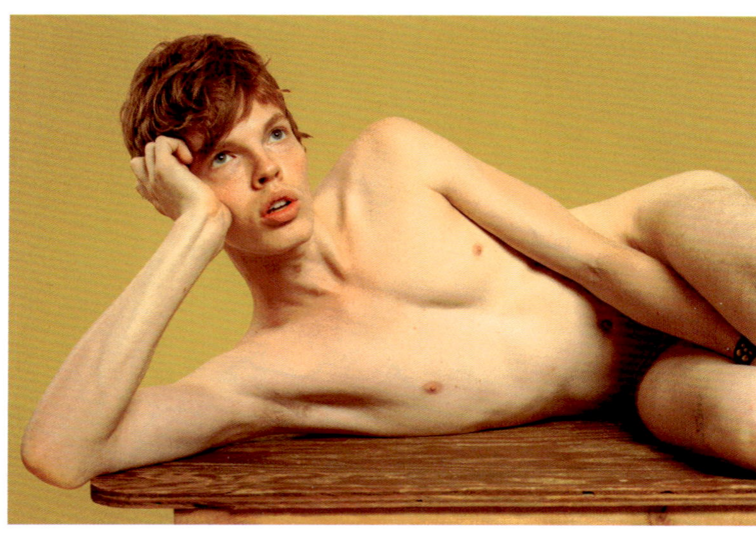

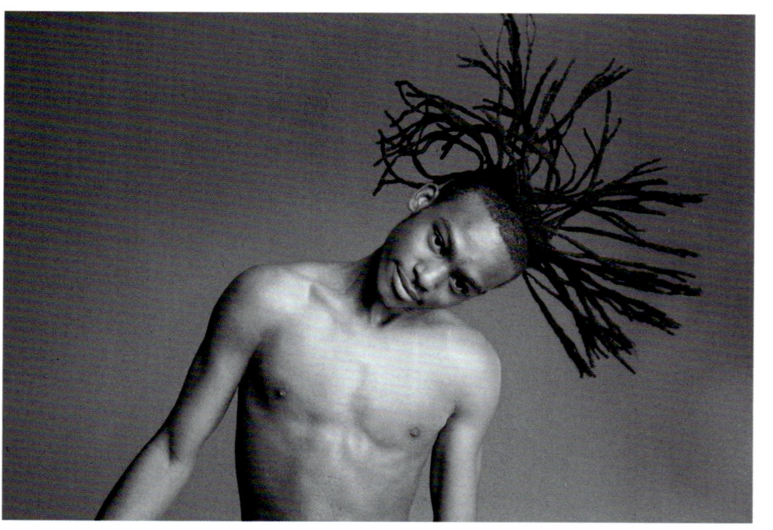

Ramon, December 2015 Masaye, January 2016 Chockie, July 2016 Shontasia, January 2014 Lauryn, November 2015 Lily, March 2015 Frey, June 2010 LeRonn, May 2014

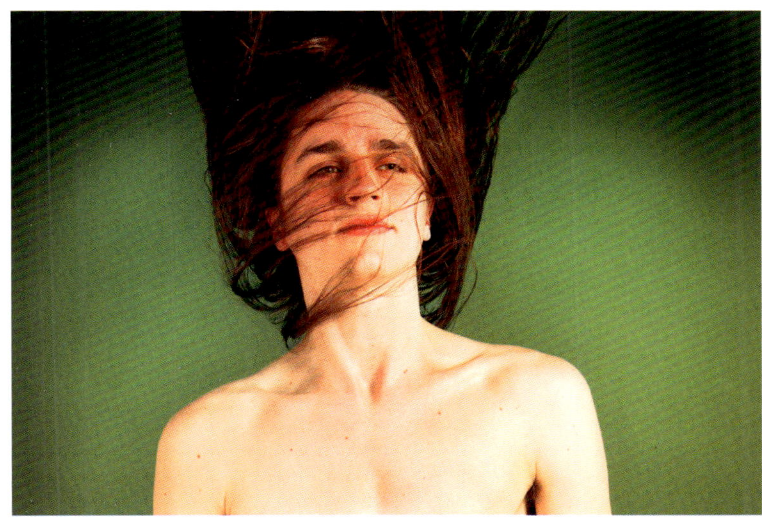

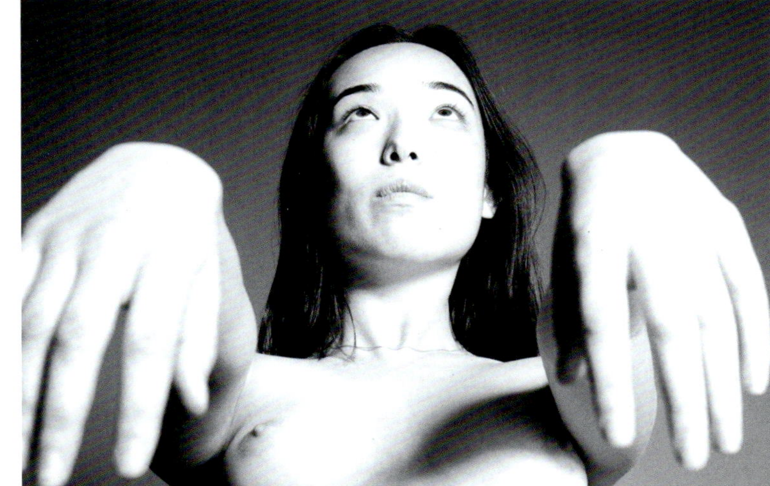

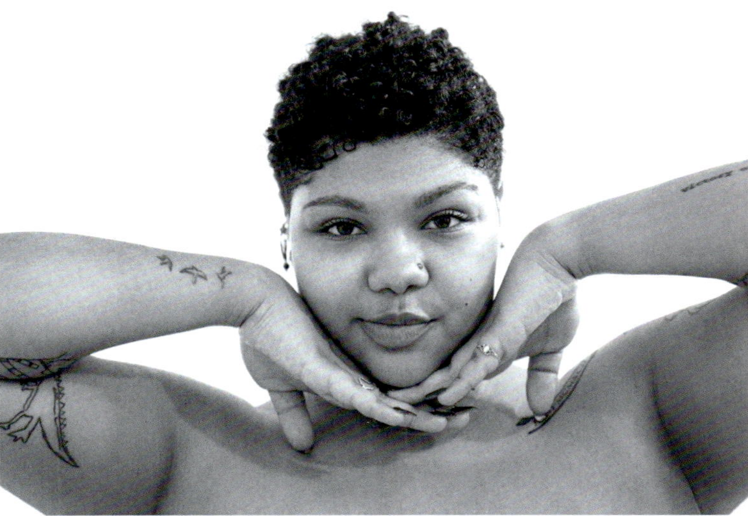

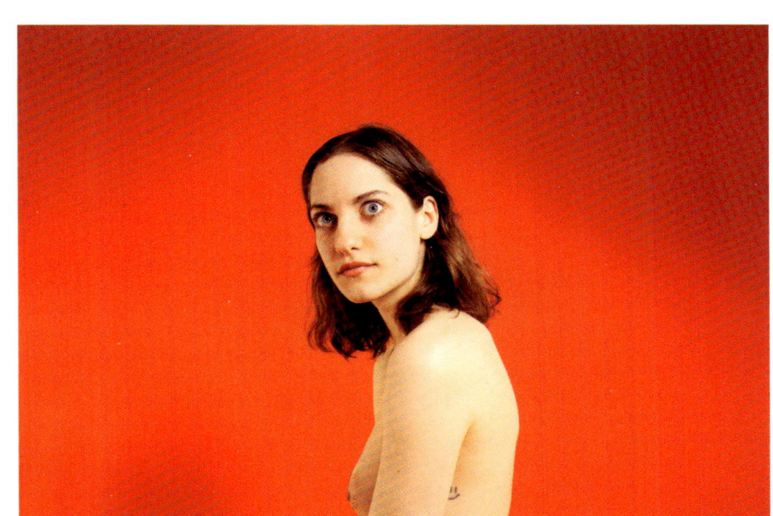

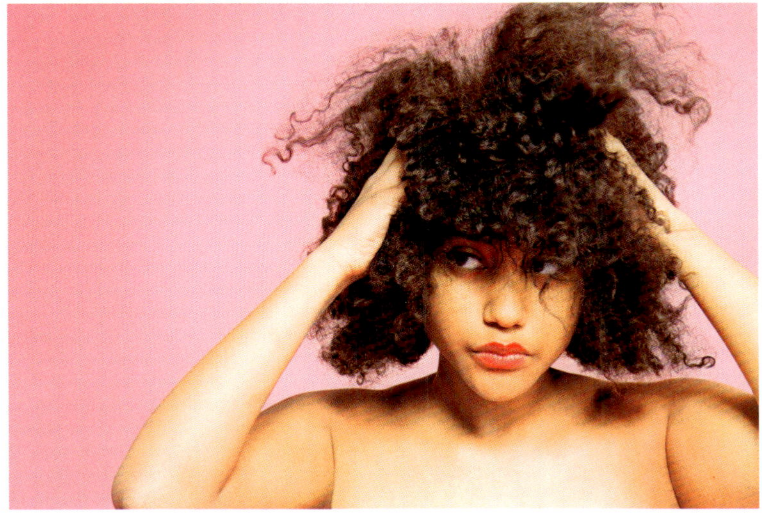

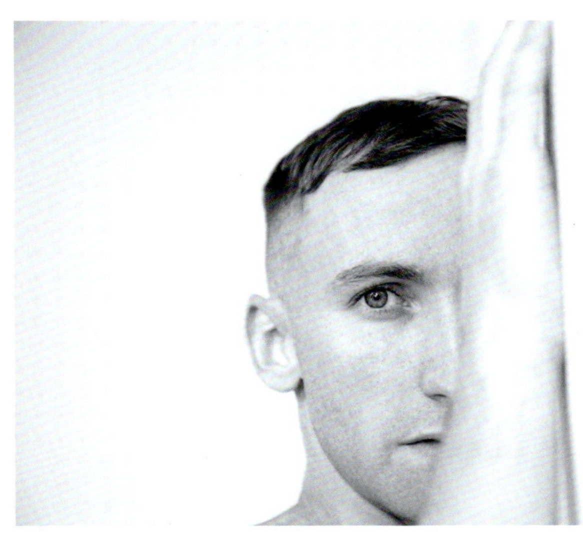

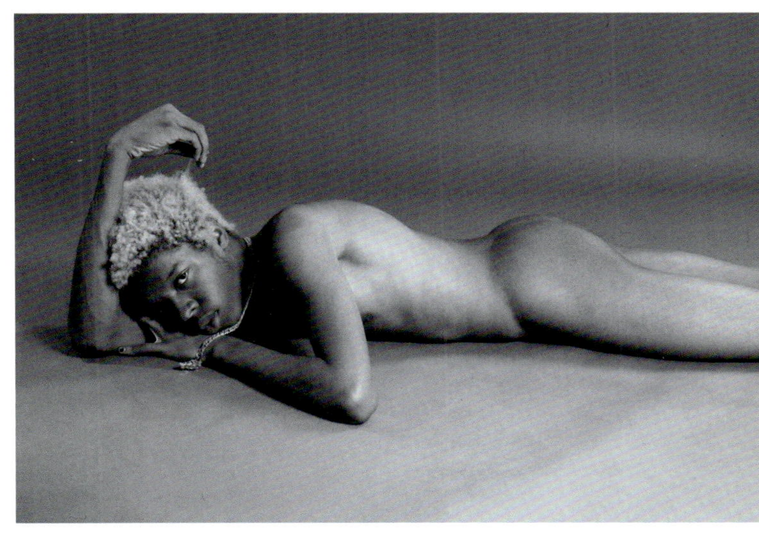

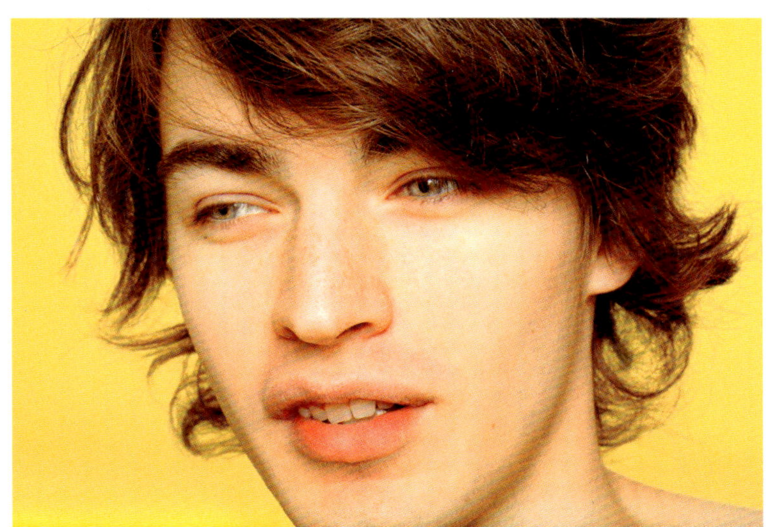

David, January 2012 Megan, November 2015 Christina, December 2018 Alice, December 2012 Randi, January 2014 Monte, November 2018 Caleb, September 2015 Mike, December 2009

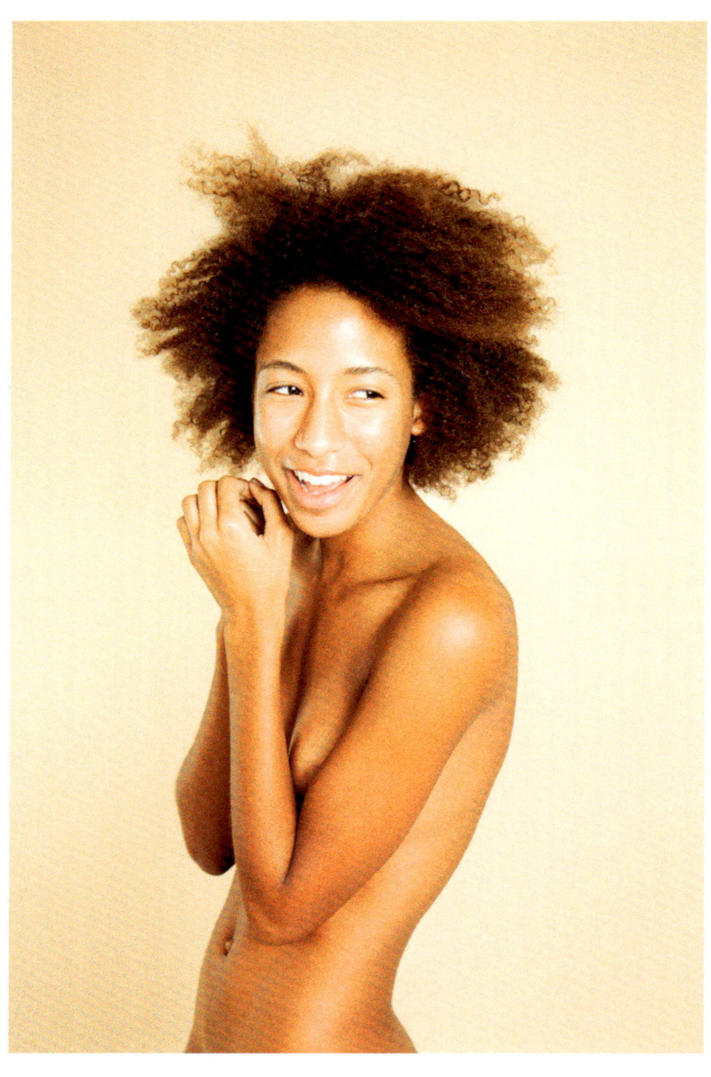

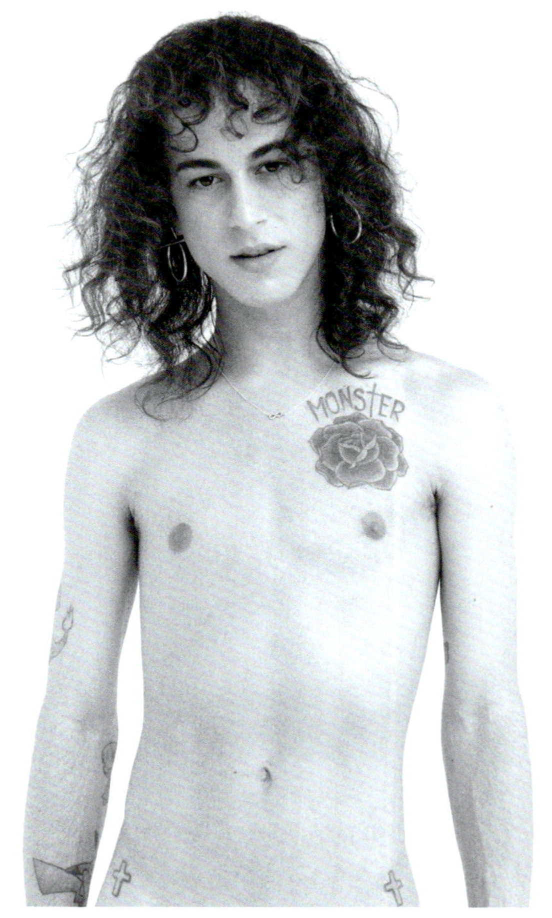

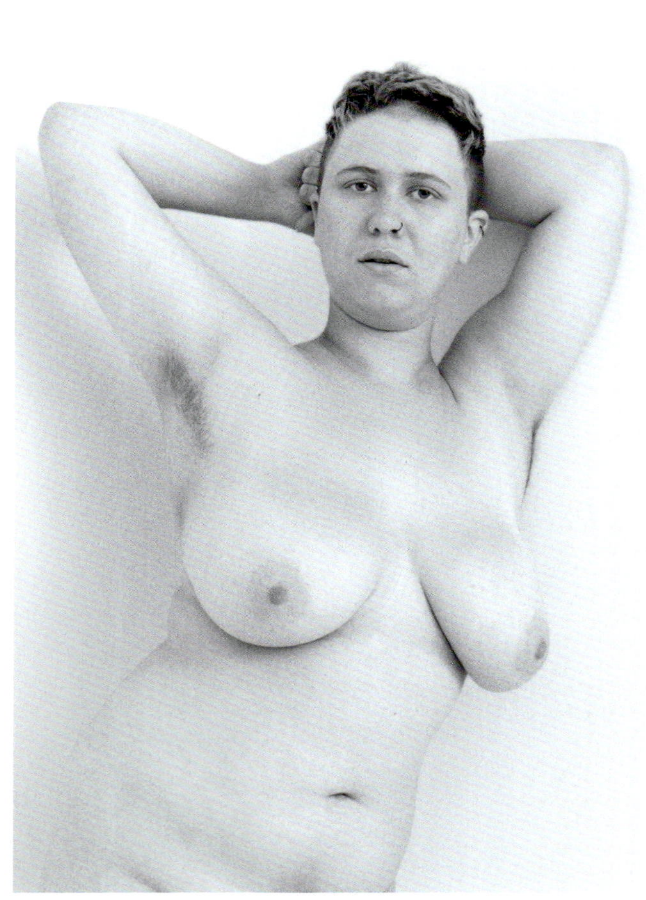

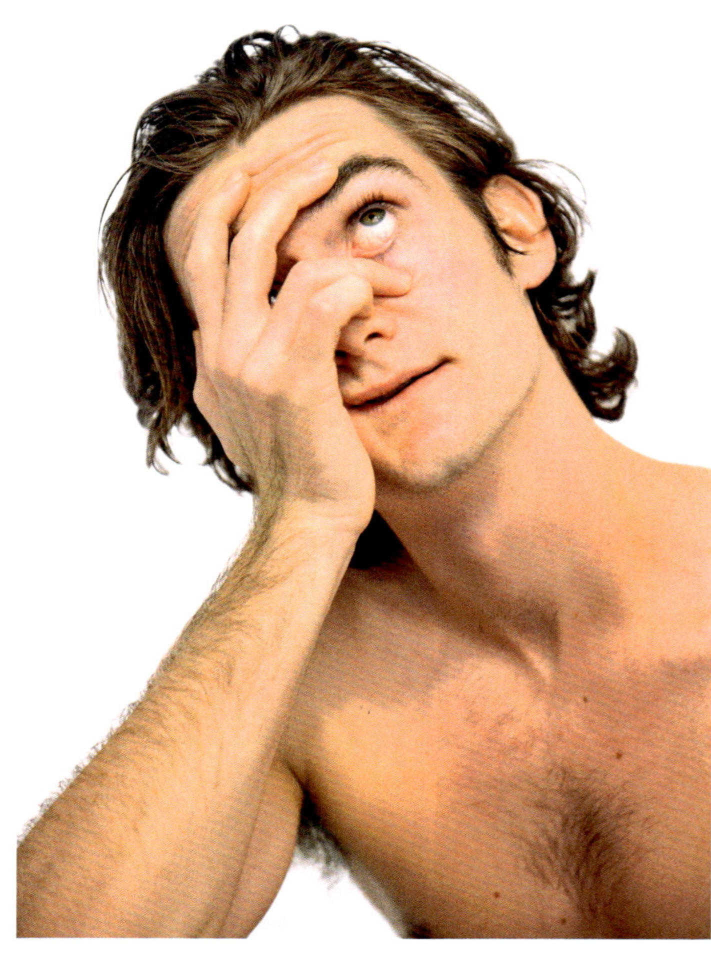

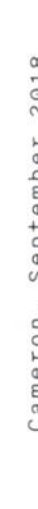
Ashley, September 2010 Richie, July 2017 Chandler, August 2017 Cameron, September 2018

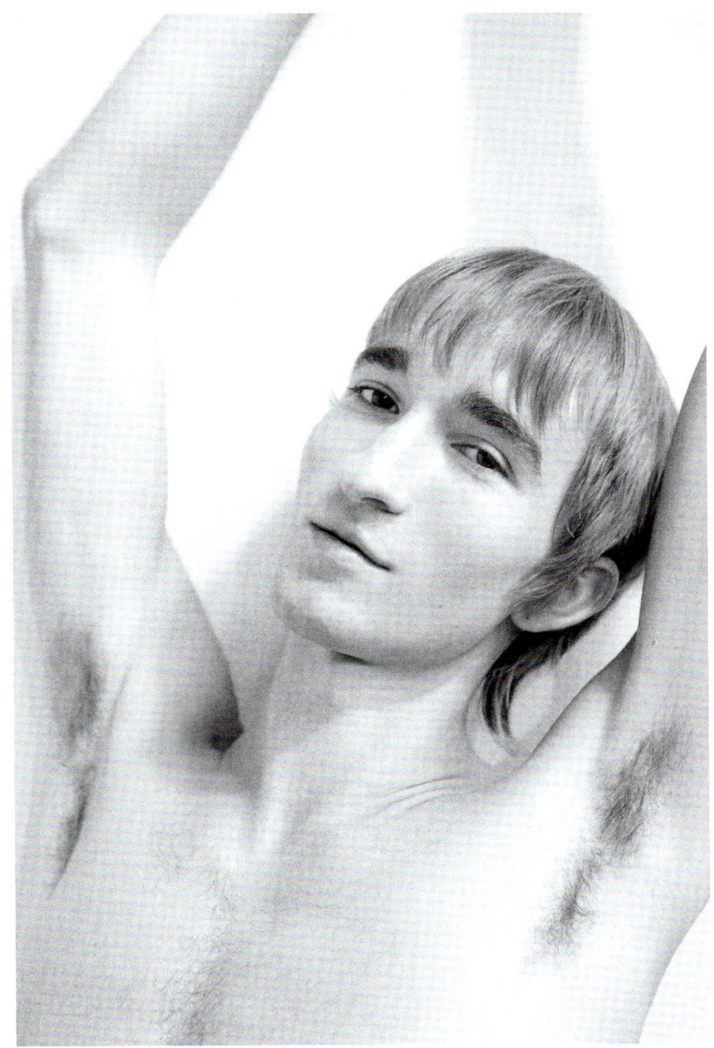

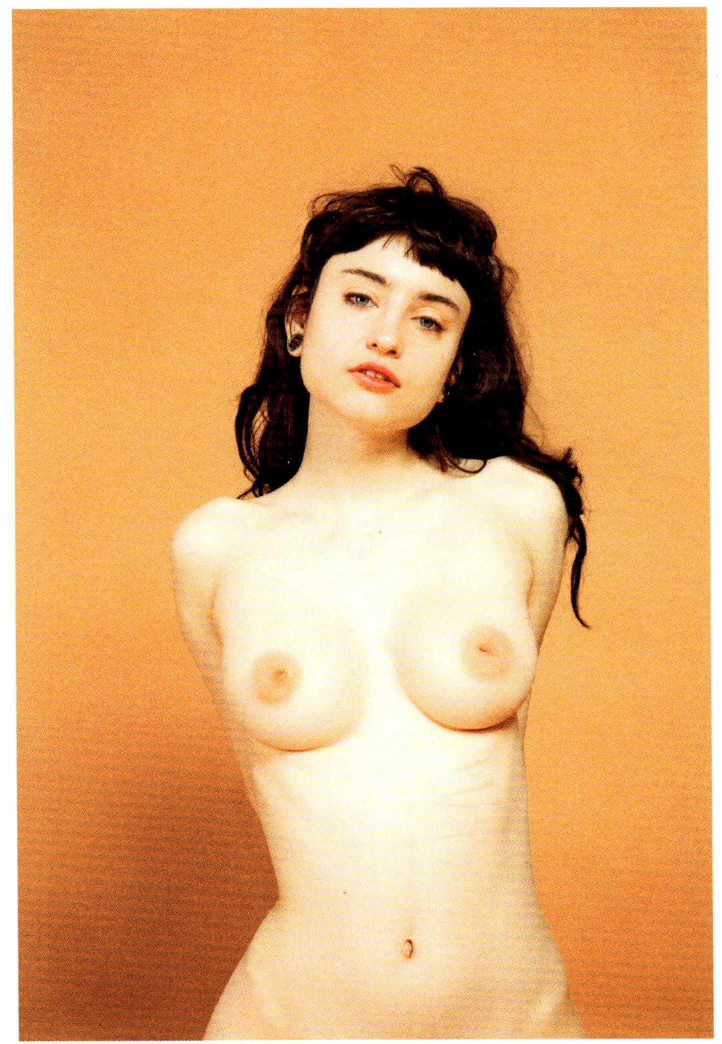

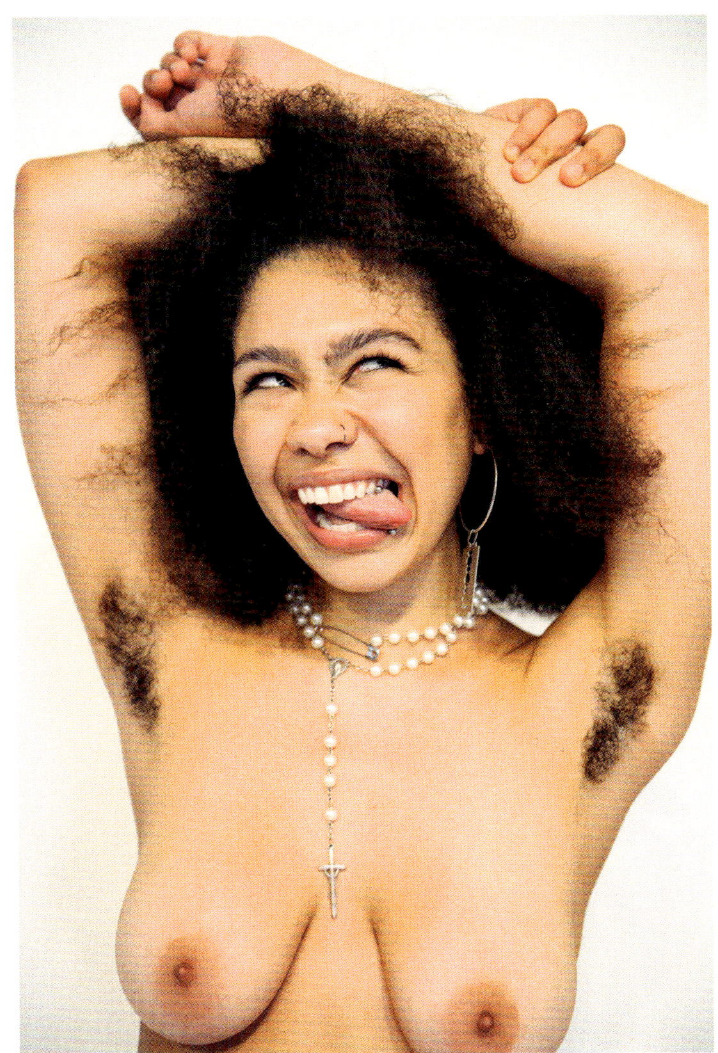

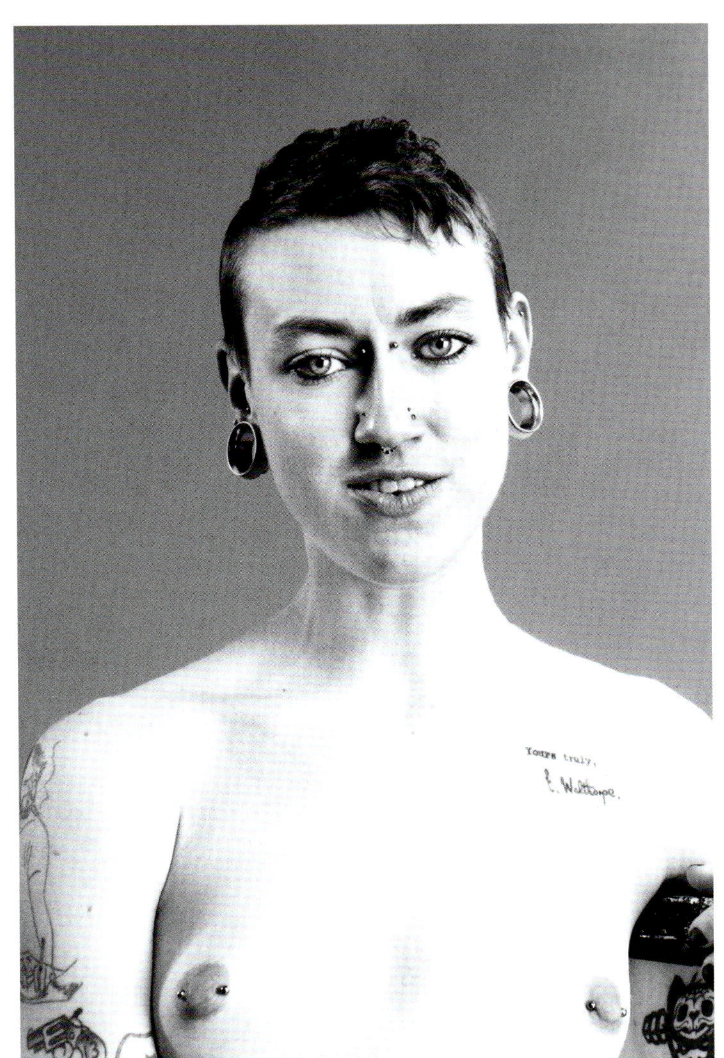

Francis, October 2019   Faina, March 2012   Devin, October 2019   Emily, January 2015

This is not a picture of a girl.

My body has changed so much since this image was taken. I have more tattoos. I no longer have breasts. I've modified my body in line with my own exploration of my gender.

There are other images from around this time, where I was often modeling in a commercial setting and would be all femmed up like "a pretty girly girl."

When I look at this image, I don't think I look like a girl. It's rather, "There's my animal body, which I know."

I knew I was queer and I would name that to people, but no one was really interested in what that meant because I also technically had a boyfriend. Most of my income was generated by being pretty and being perceived in this particular way.

In the relational space of having a body within a culture that is cis-focused, trans-exclusionary, and binary, part of what excited and motivated me to make changes was this way of connecting to my own agency through action. Being female socialized, it was a healing action, almost like a ritual action, to go through these changes. Things like tattoos: I do have some in that photo, but I have more now. I'm even thinking about getting rid of some, going in all directions, in this nonlinear way. The body is this thing marked through time. Big changes, and changes you choose to make, draw lines in the sand, waves oncoming . . .

I grew up in New York City. When I was in high school, I lived on Grand and Forsyth. I would pick my brother up from daycare across the street from Ryan's studio. We were in very literal close proximity. By eighteen, I'd started going full-time to Hunter College. I was a part of an art collective that I'd started with friends called Luck You. I'd just shot my first film, with Olivier Assayas. And I was seeing Ryan around, at openings, sneaking into parties.

Ryan was always just such a sweetie pie. I remember getting breakfast. I would tell him about crushes I had. In this big brother way, he would give me his two cents.

New York is a magnet. There are parts of the city that are totally portals. New York's magic can be used for good or evil (not that it's so simple). If people come here to find their people and to do something connective, then that's exciting to me—that makes this place feel better. On the flip side, there remains so much opportunity to come here and just be extractive.

Working with Ryan, I keep thinking about fun. As a performer, I'm interested in the limits of my body and how my body wants to move in relation to different input. What does it look like to follow an impulse in my body? And so things like going on road trips, or a naked photoshoot, I can find that really fun, like an experiment.

When I say fun, I'm thinking again of connection. Obviously as soon as someone's naked, there's a charge of vulnerability. It's like a cheat code, but it also works. We get to enter this vulnerable space together.

Something special about Ryan is that he never made me feel like my body was an inherently sexualized object, which is hard to do when you're photographing someone naked. I've only ever photographed people naked in a sexual context, personally. Plus, of course, the nude is also this loaded historical thing. I think Ryan is very much trying to find something beyond what he would or could plan for. It's not about the camera and the person behind the camera; it's about finding these in-between moments that are unscriptable and connective.

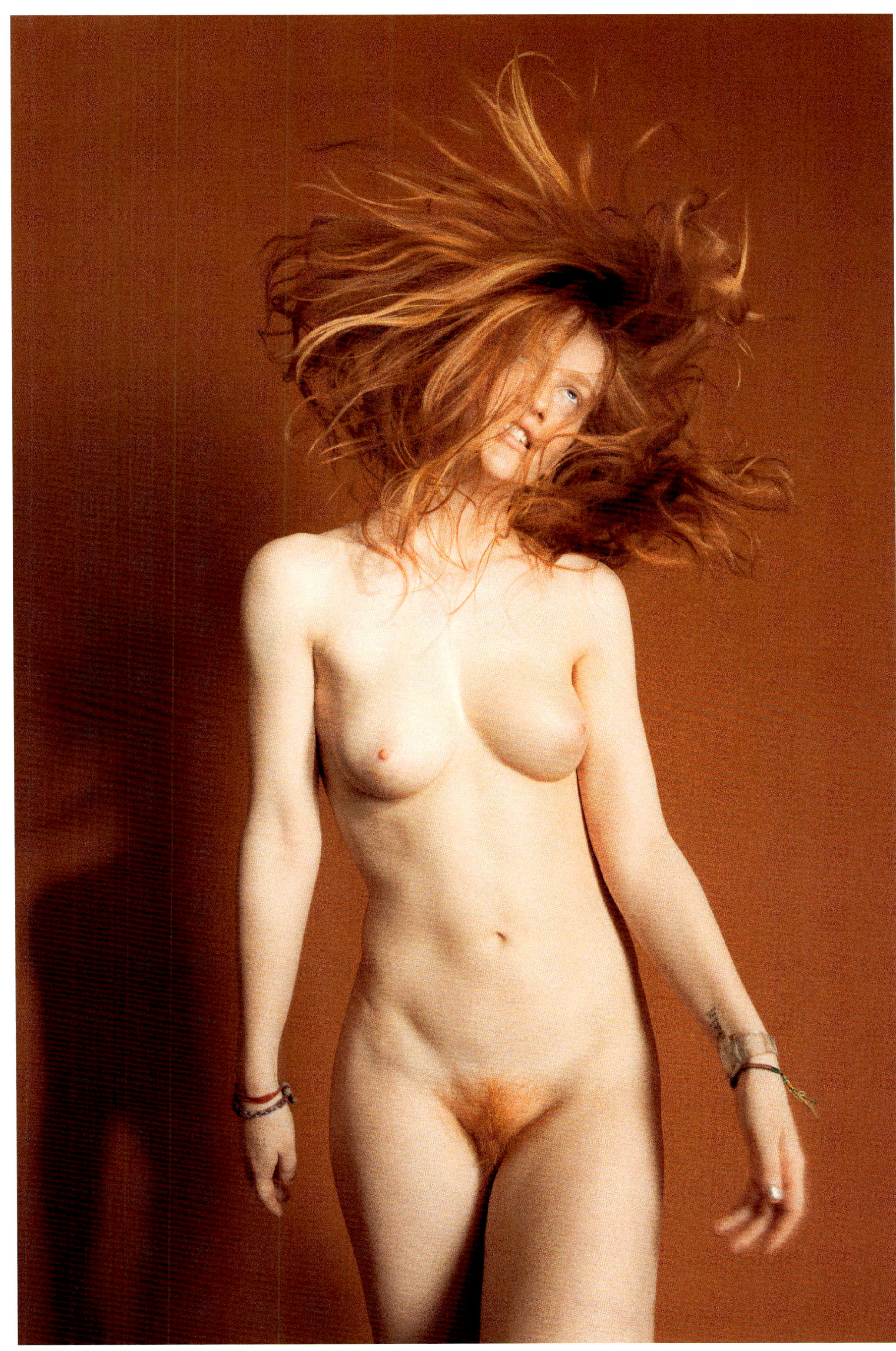

Bobbi, June 2012

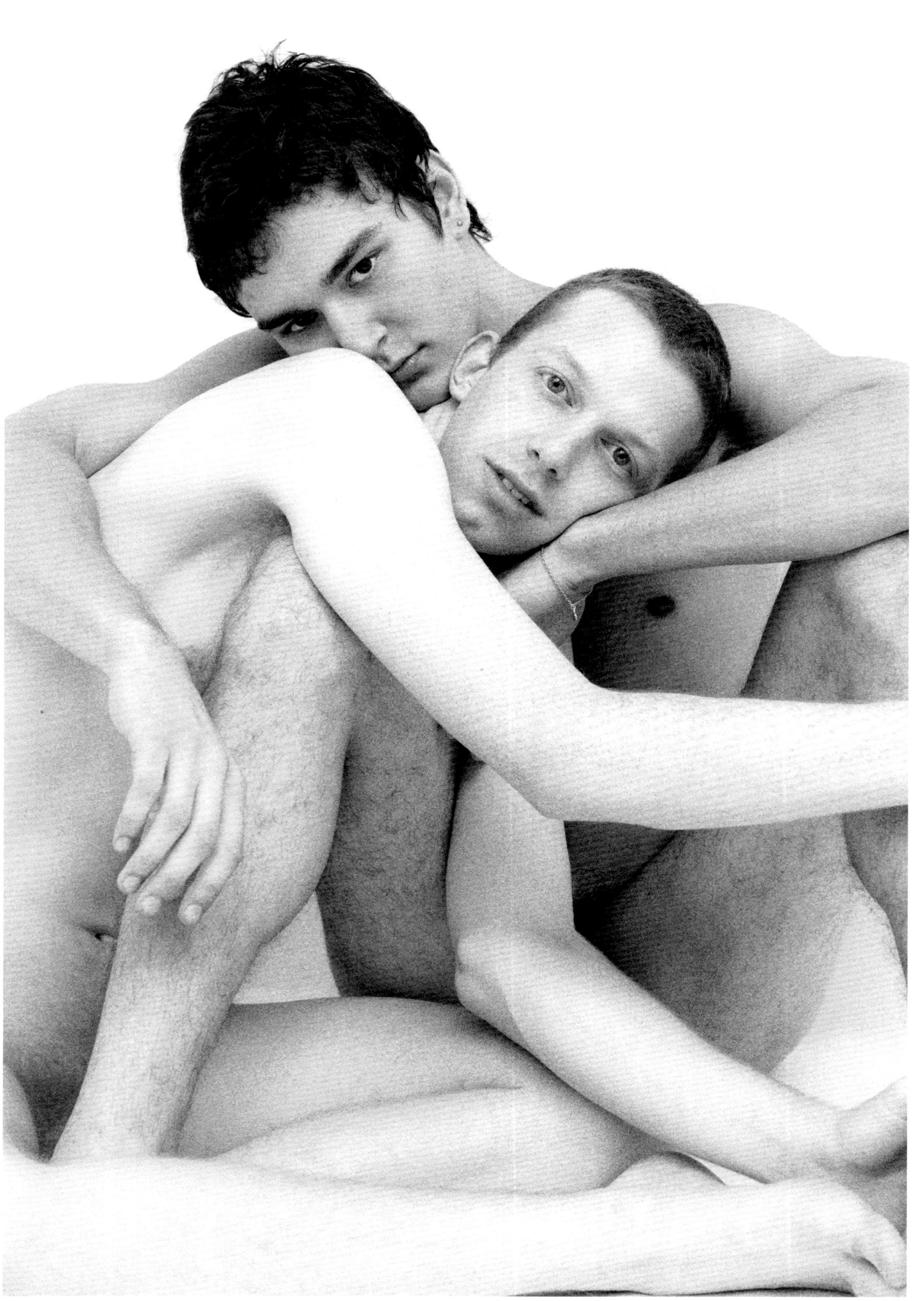

Nick & Austin, July 2017

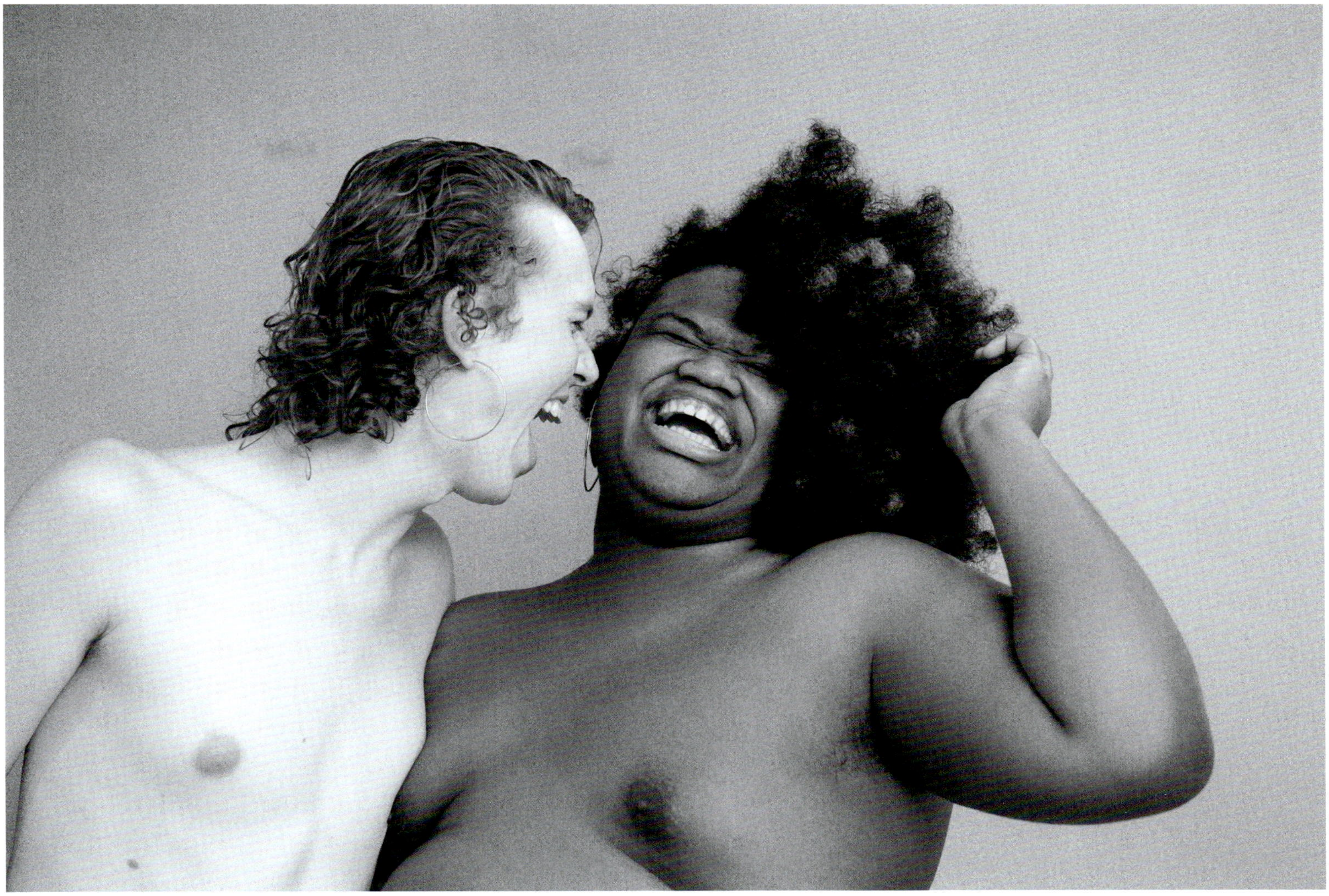

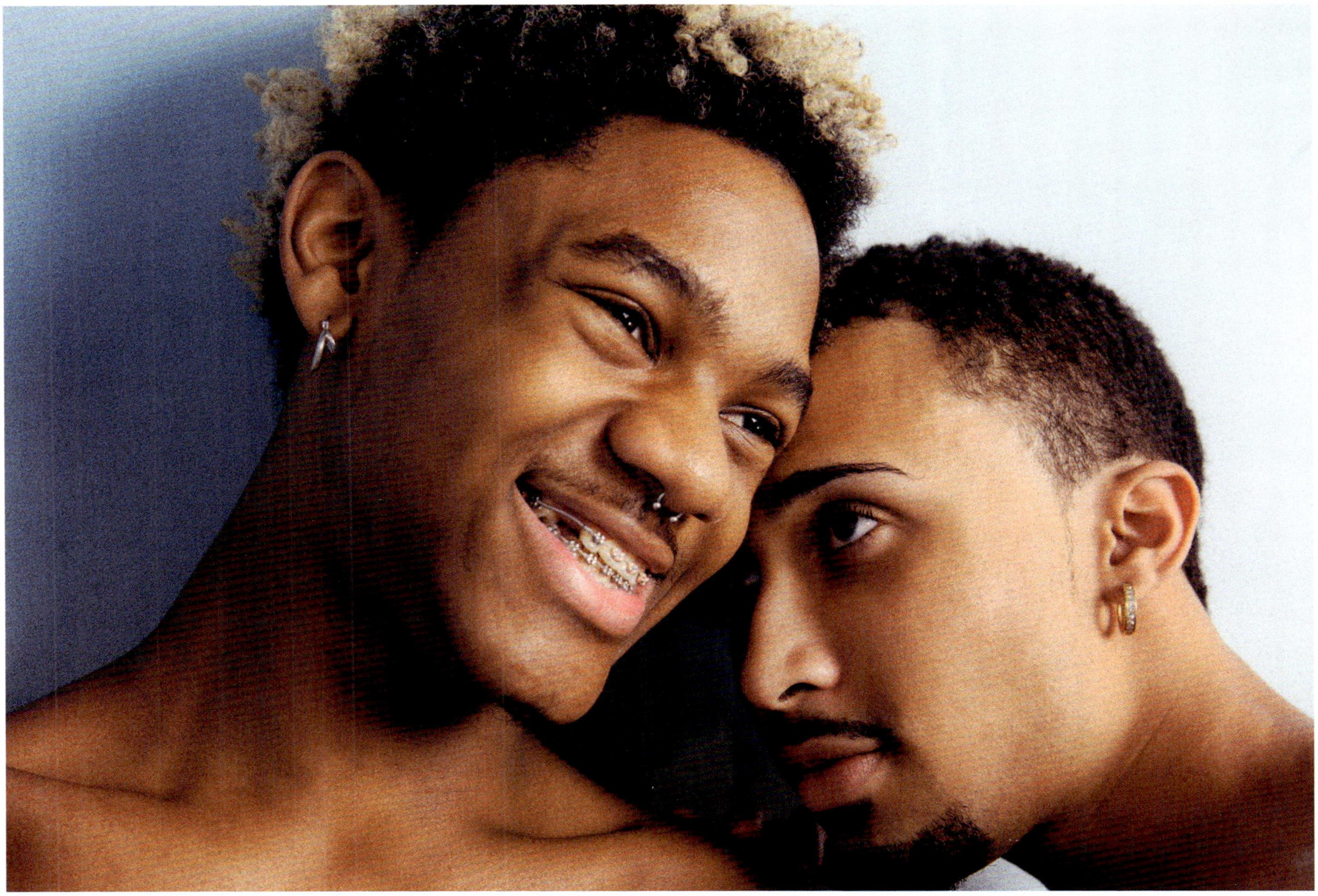

Jari & Corey, December 2016   Eddy & Darryl, December 2016

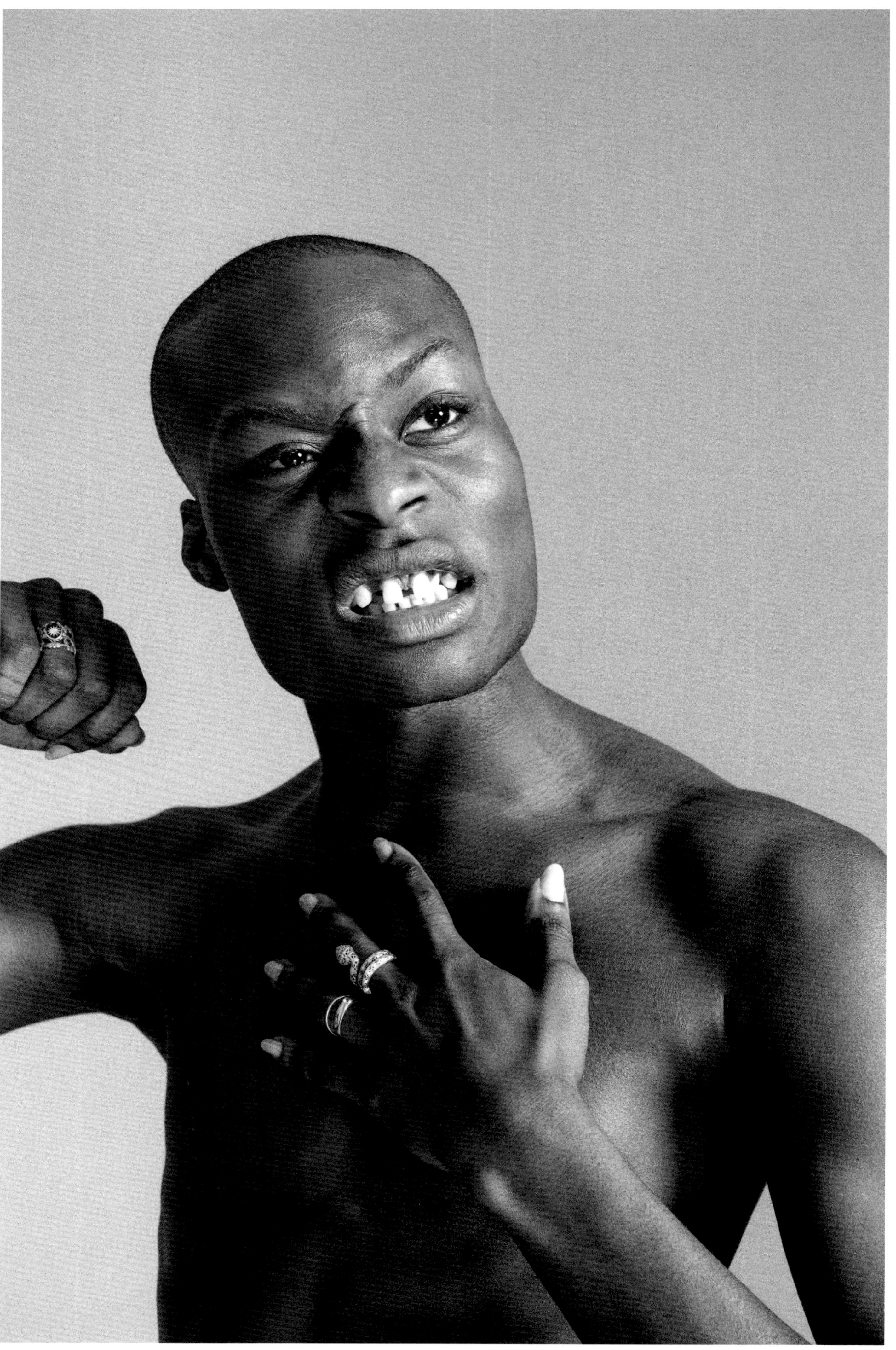

Jahmal, May 2016

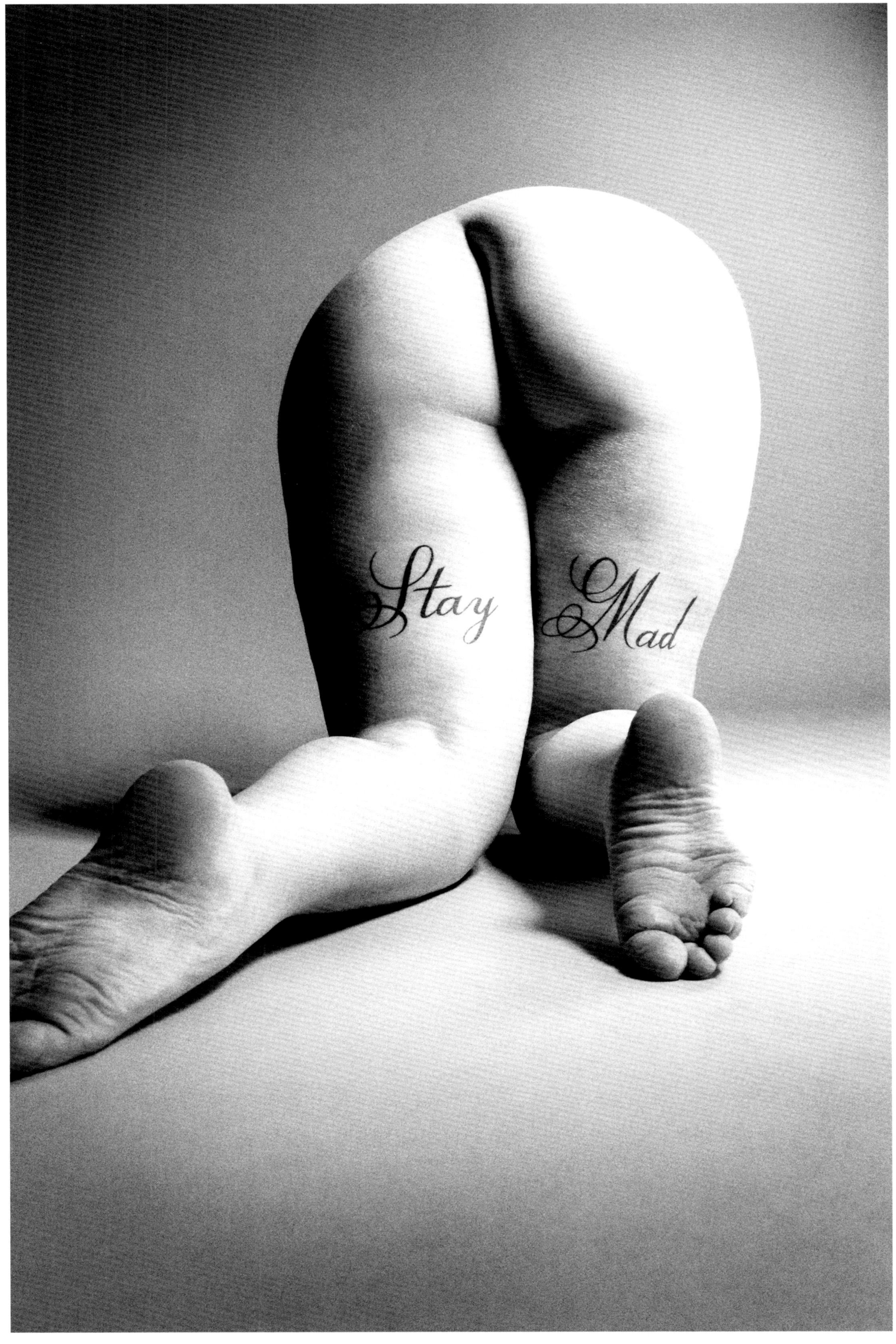

Annie, December 2015

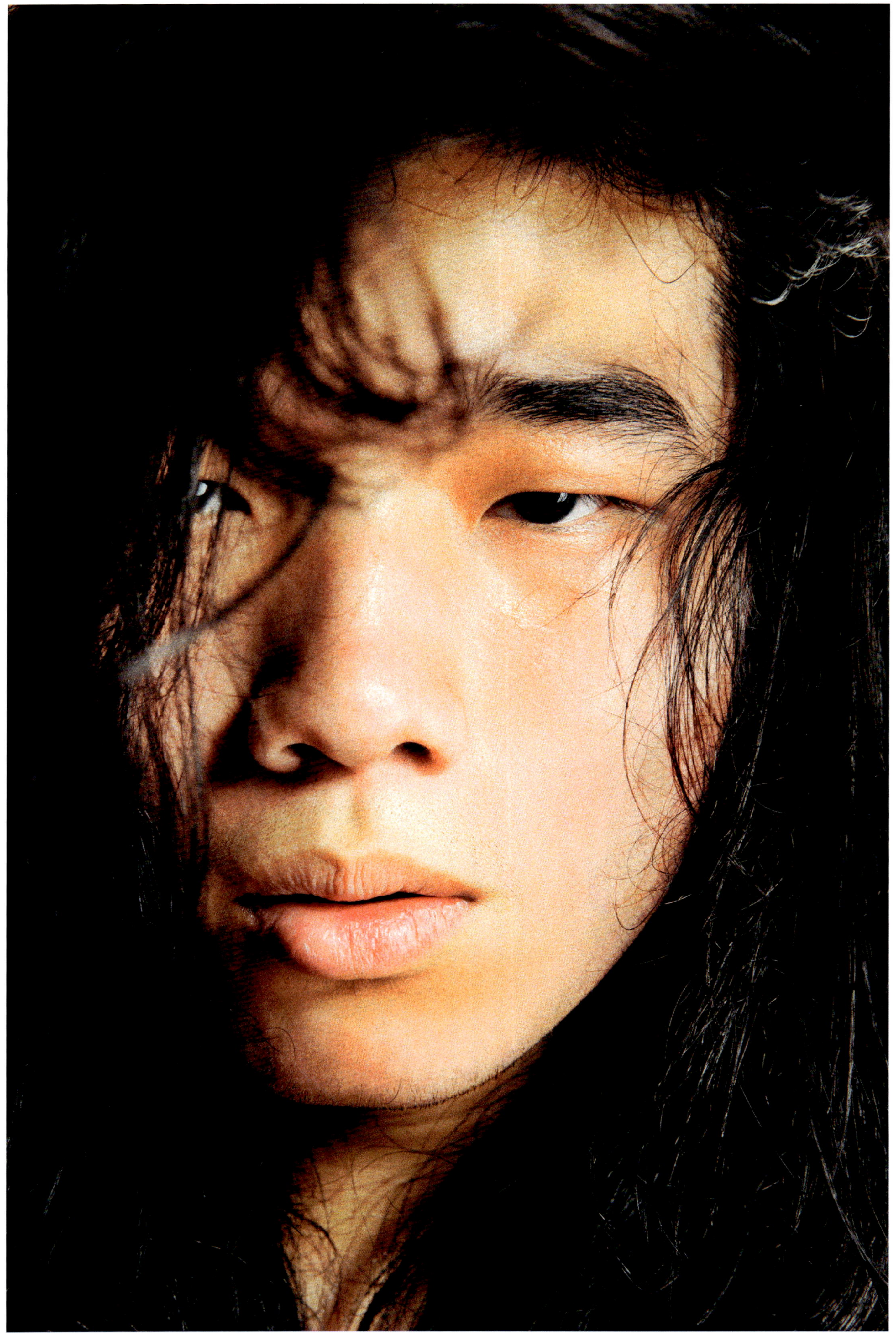

Alex, June 2015

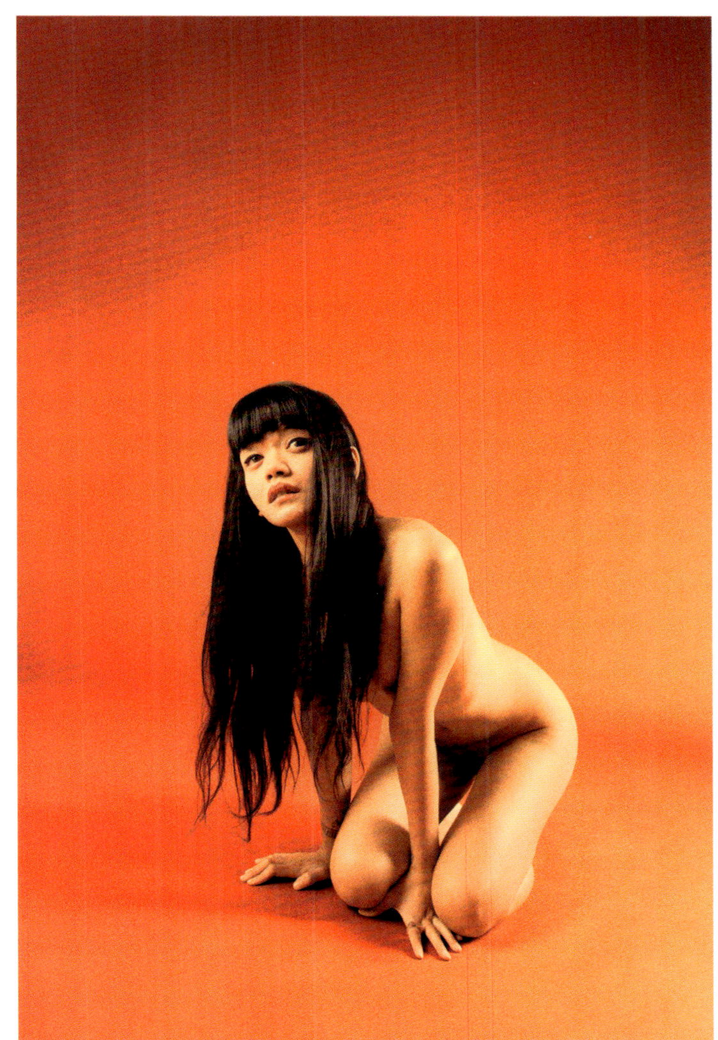

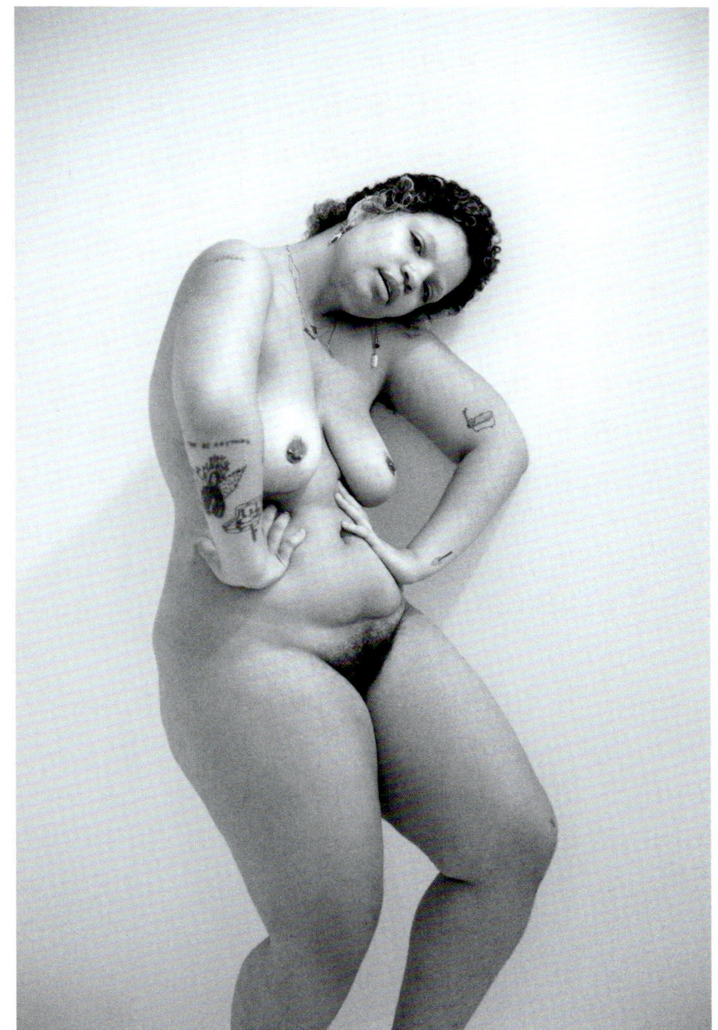

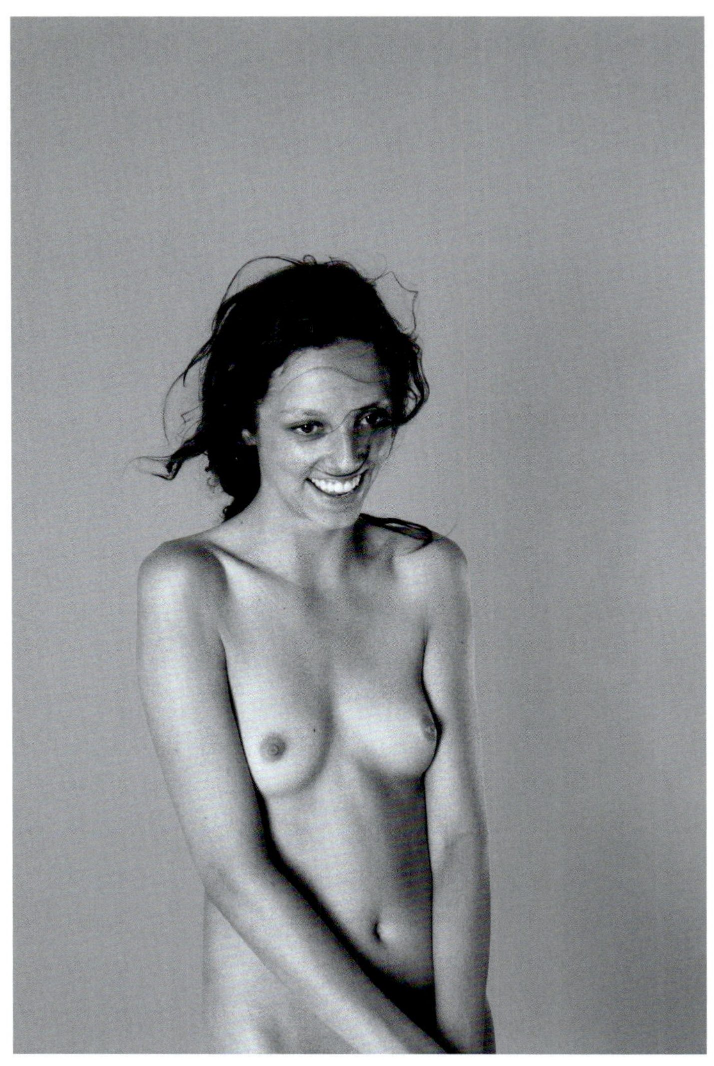

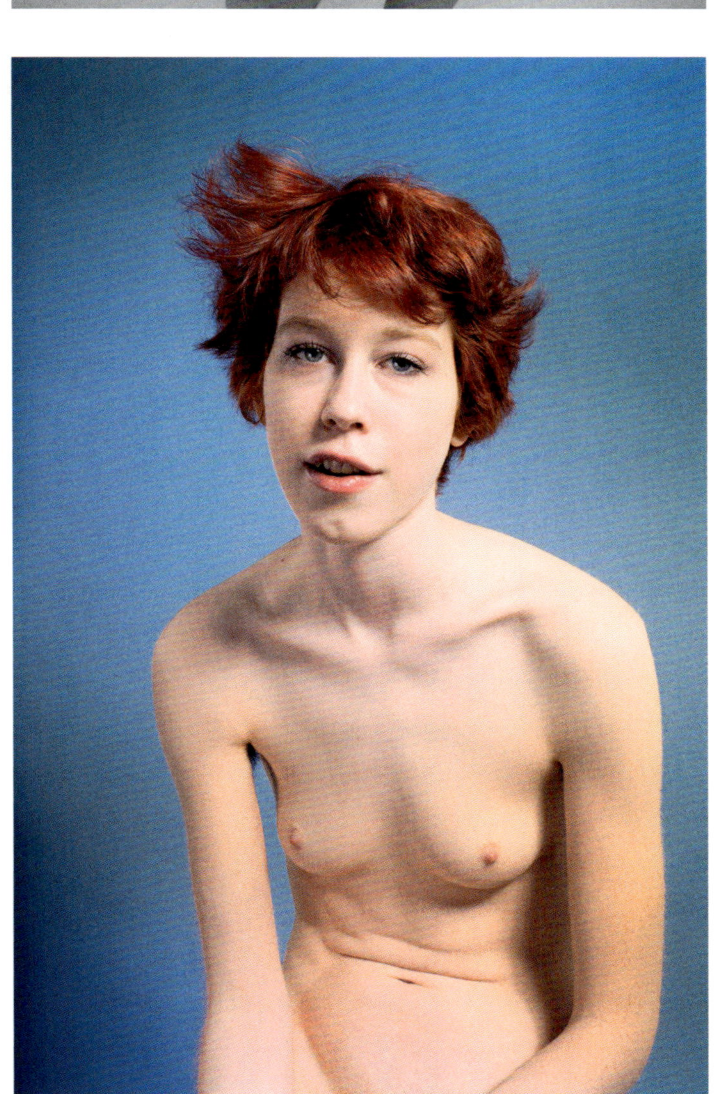

Dylan, December 2011 Maya, September 2018 Hanna, June 2009 Alannah, March 2013

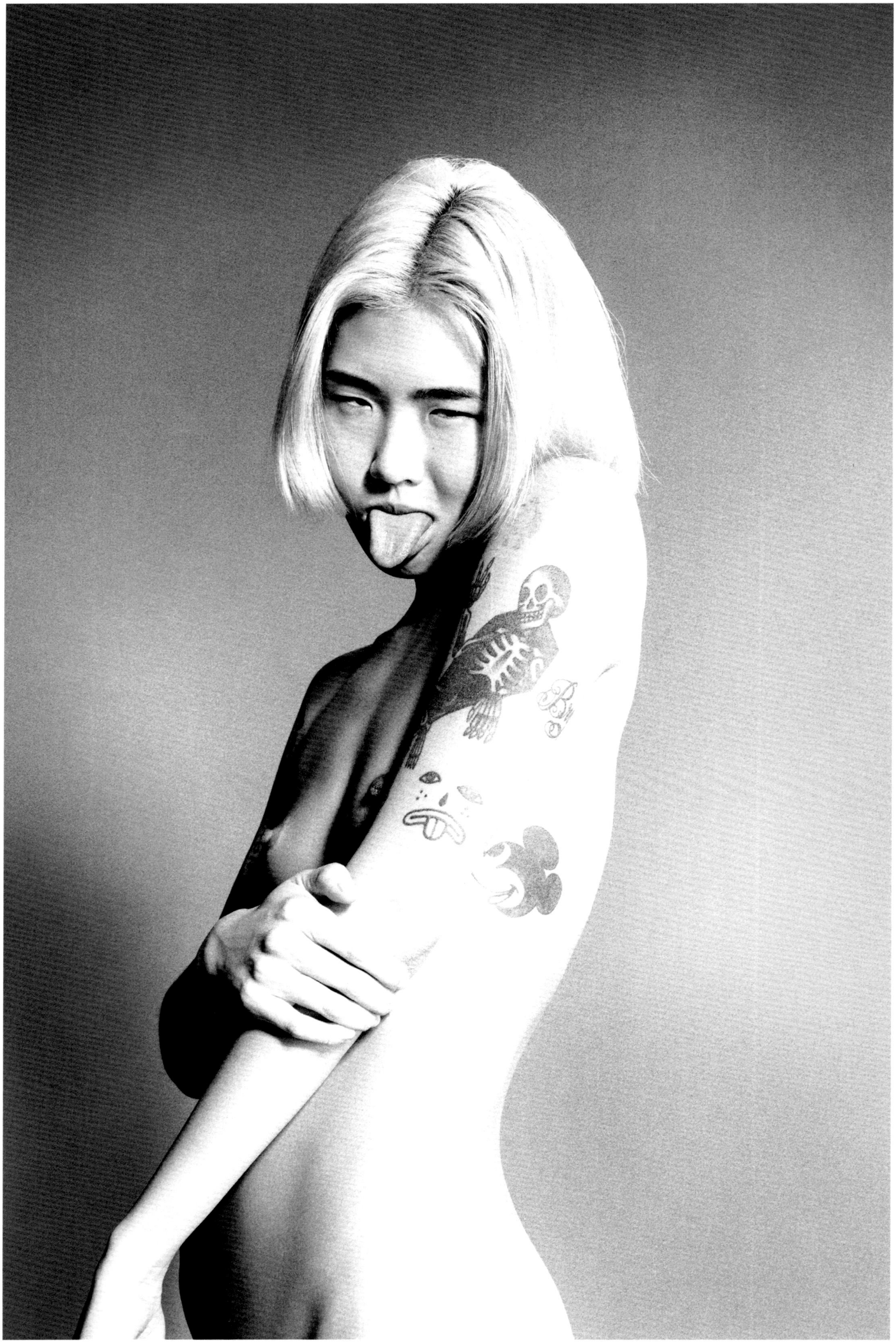

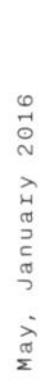
May, January 2016

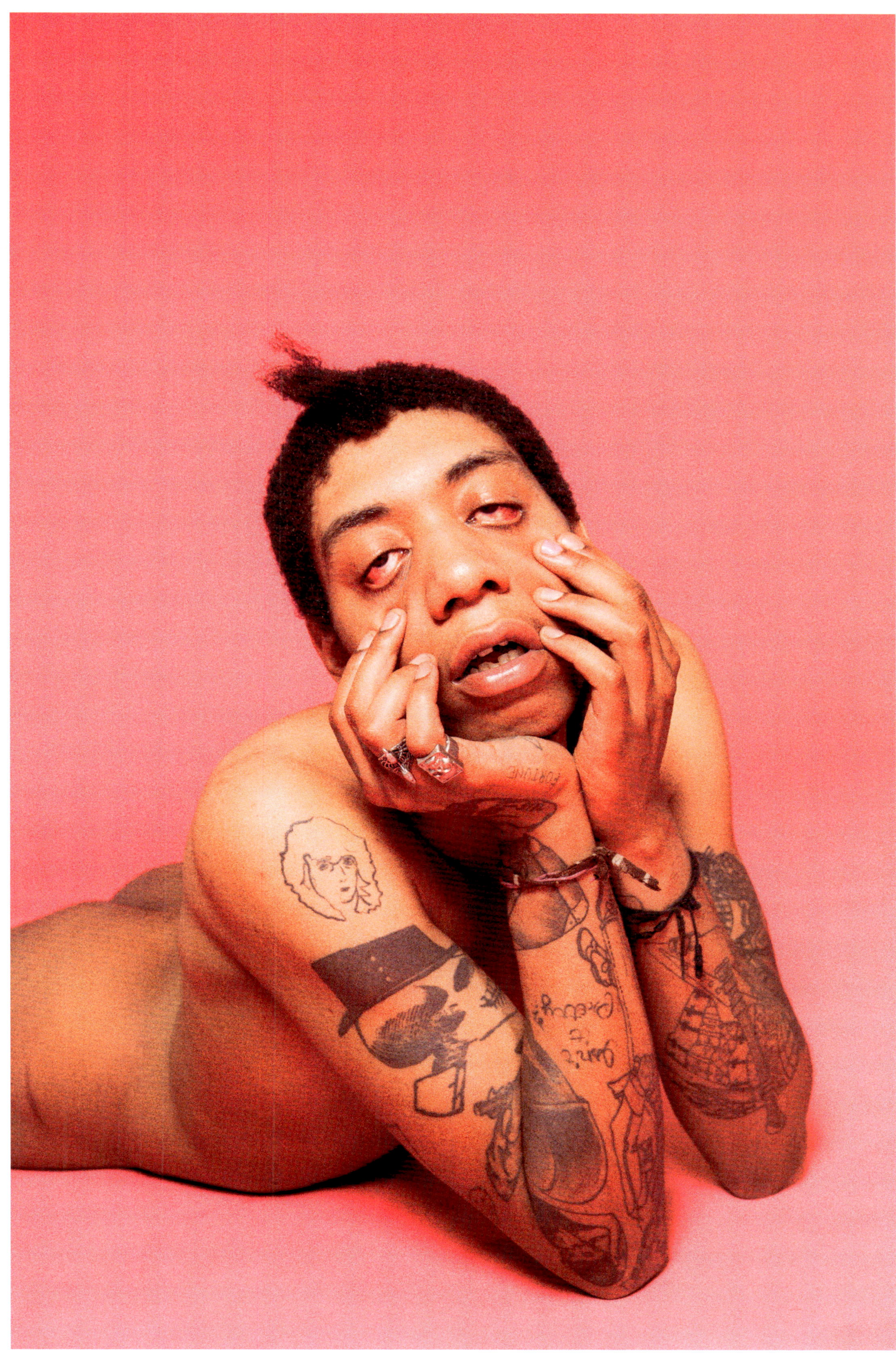

Honor, June 2012

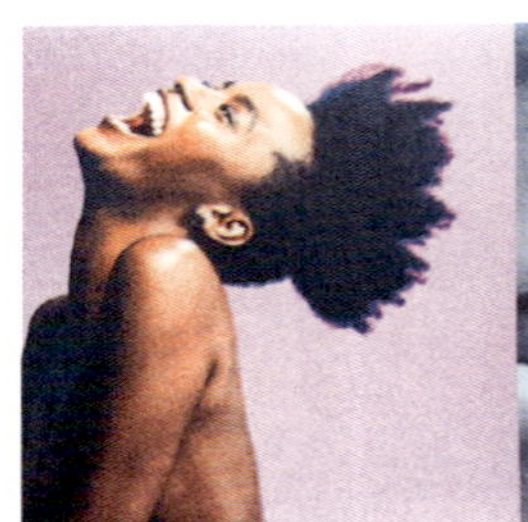

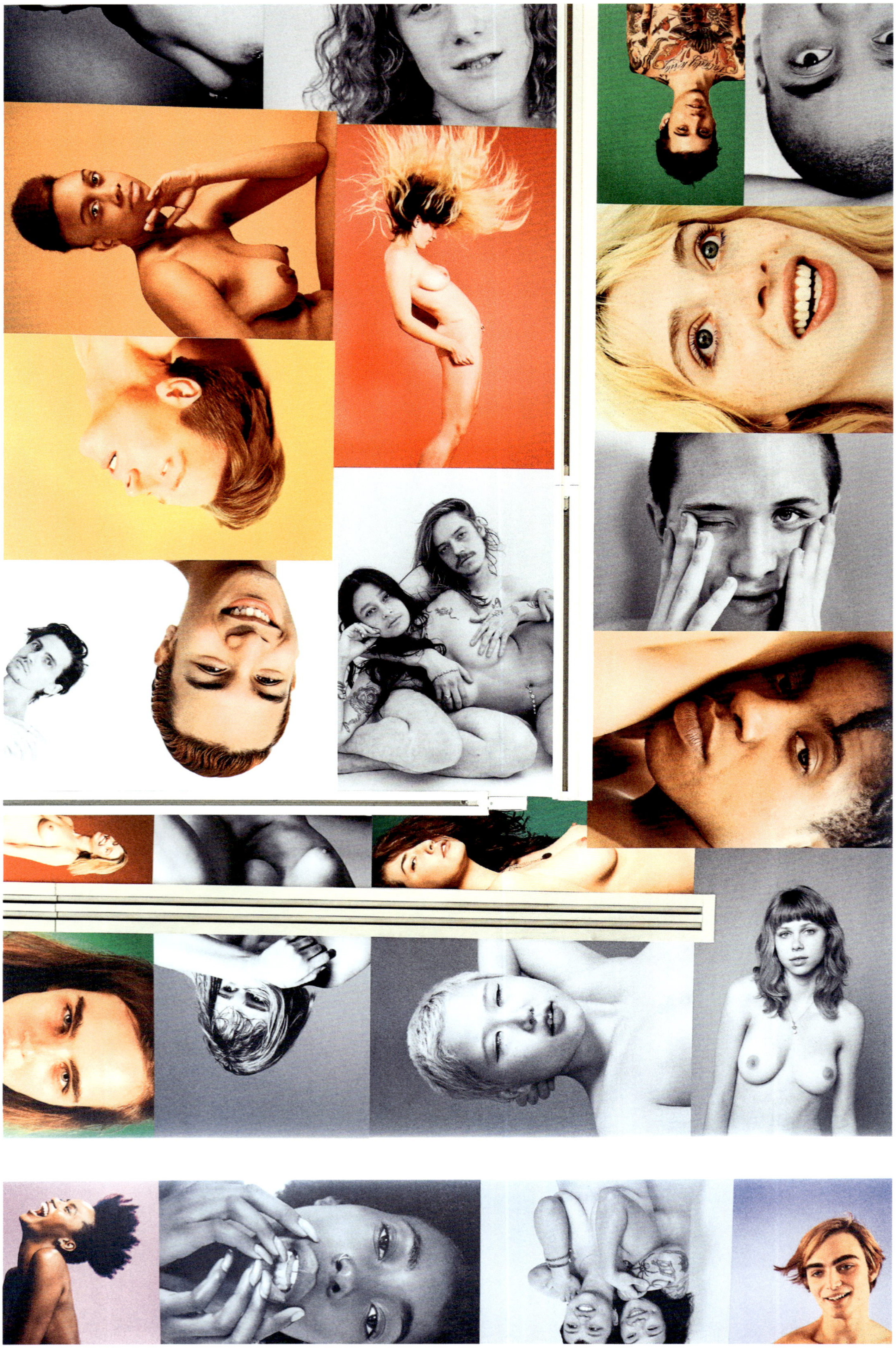

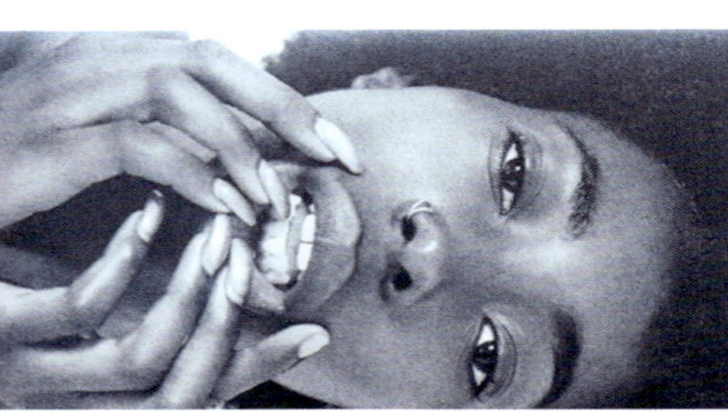

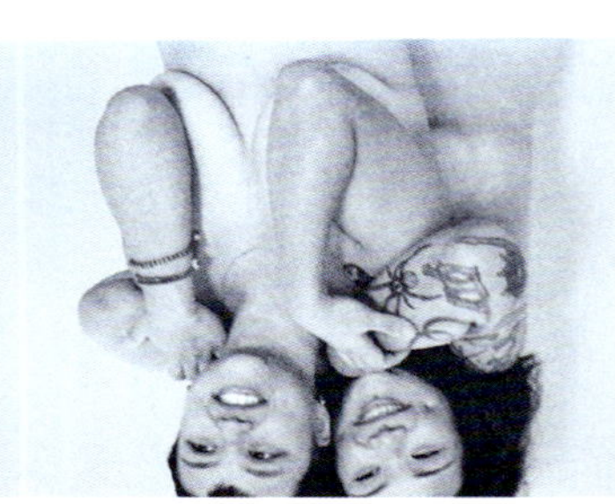

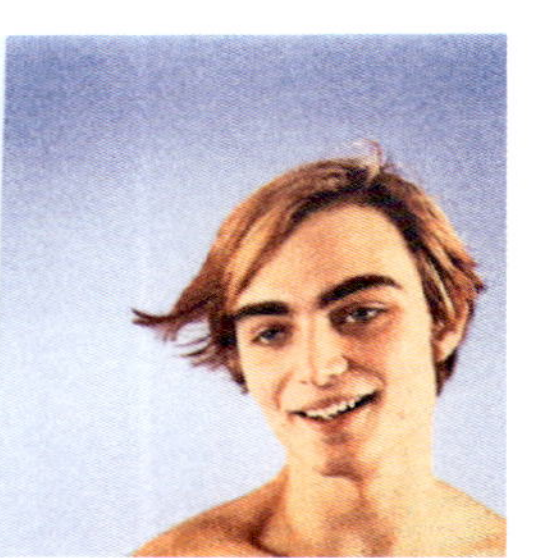

Pretty Free, Marlborough London, 2020

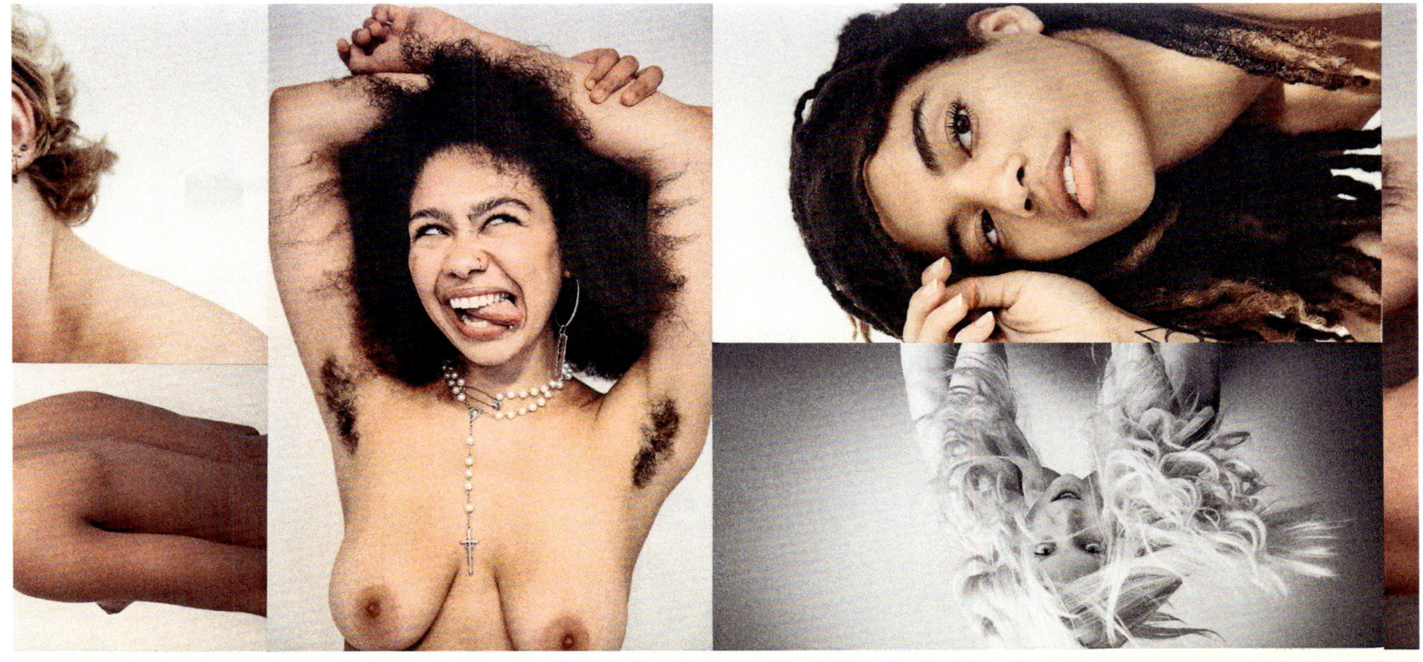

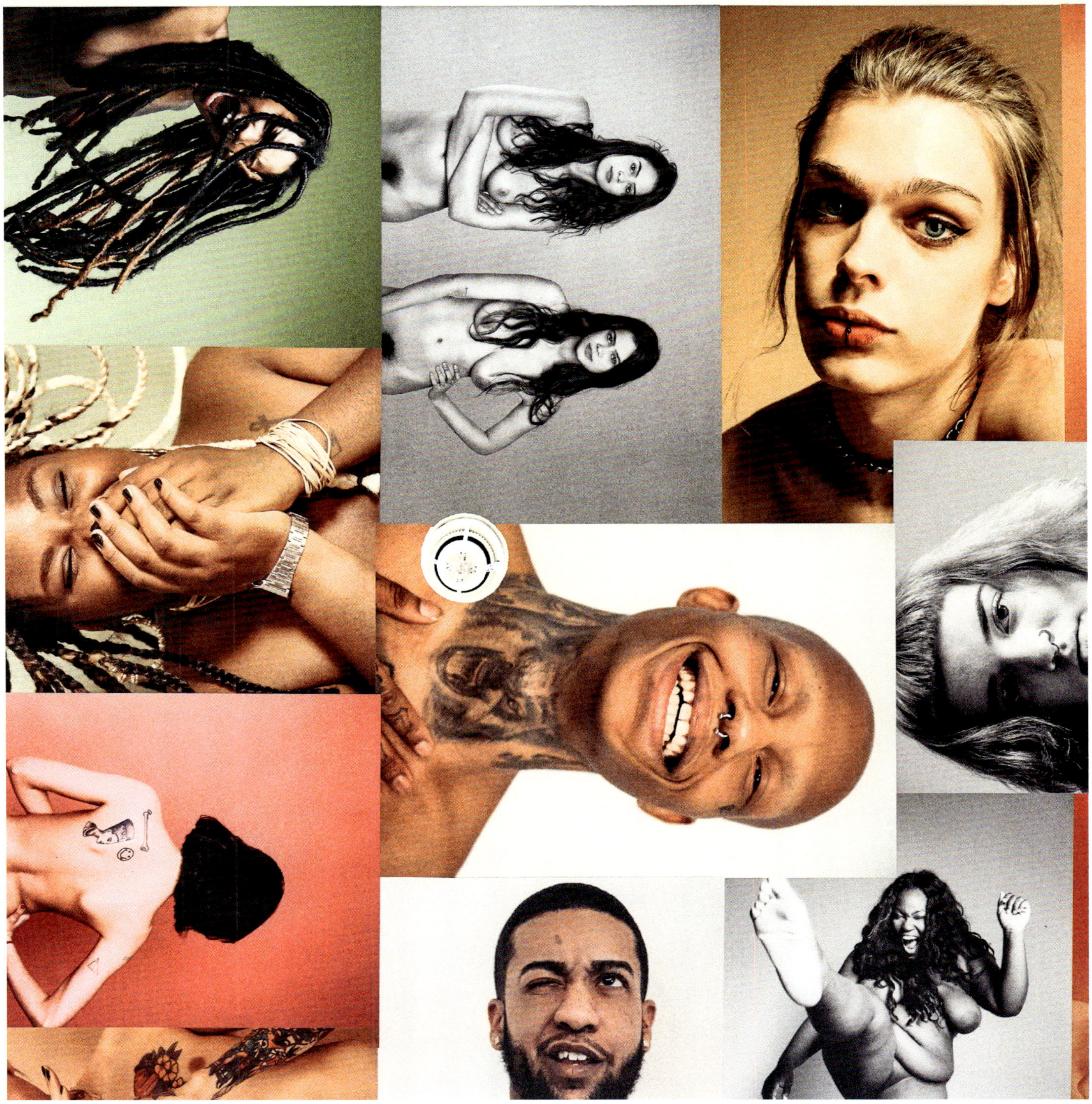

Pretty Free, Marlborough London, 2020

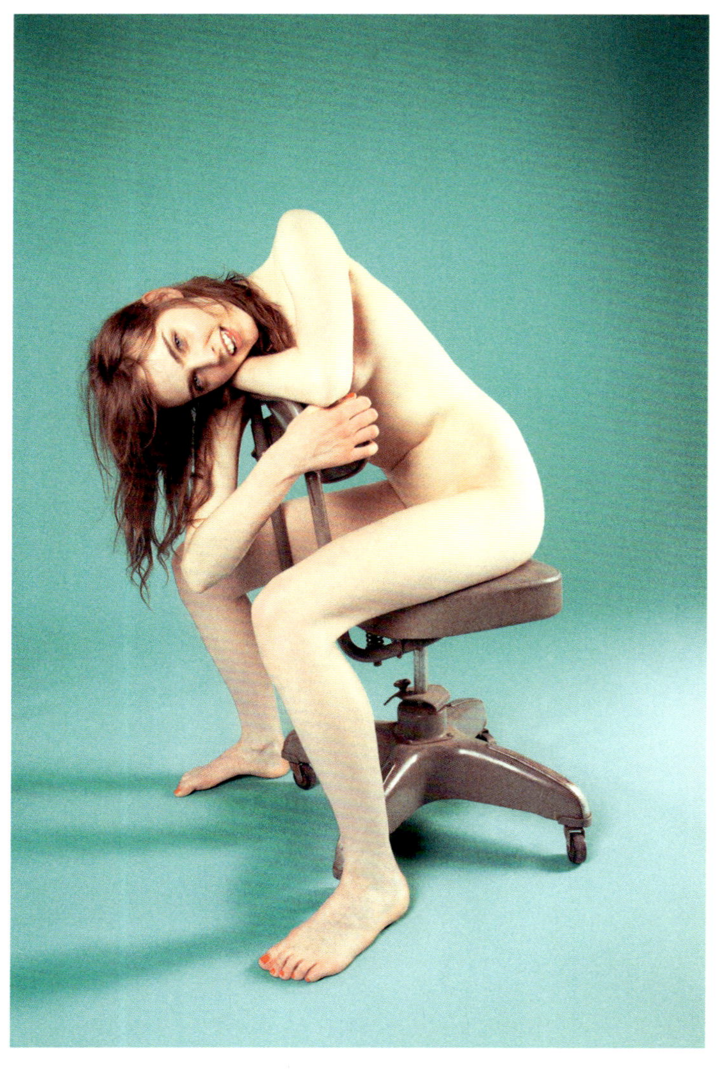

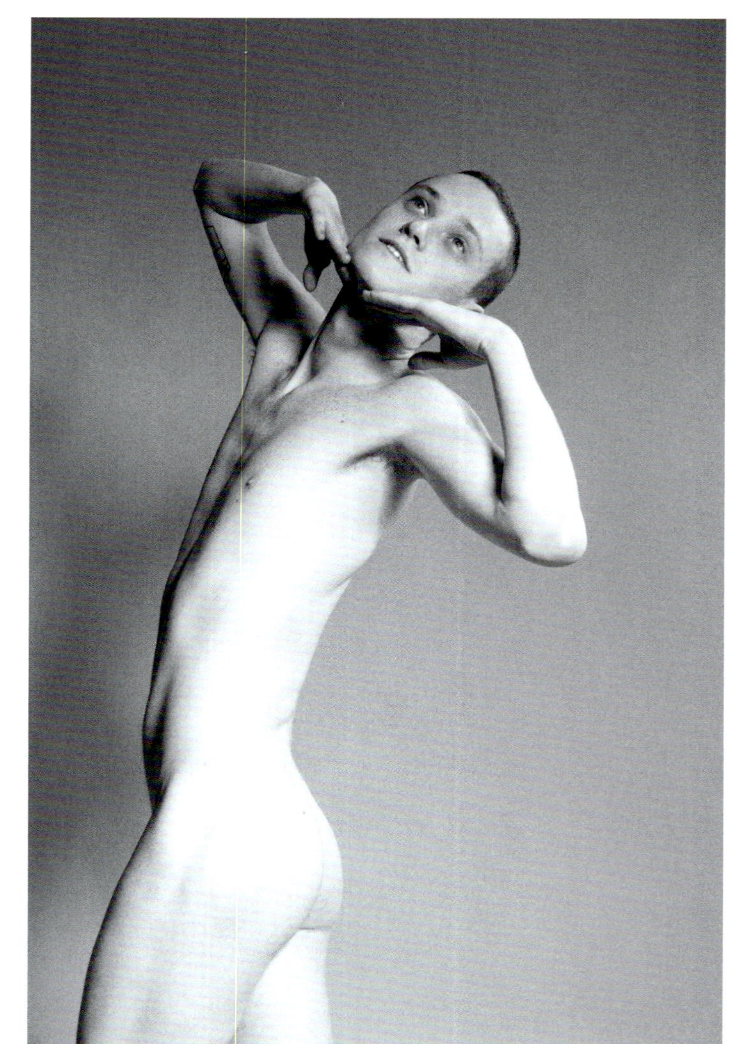

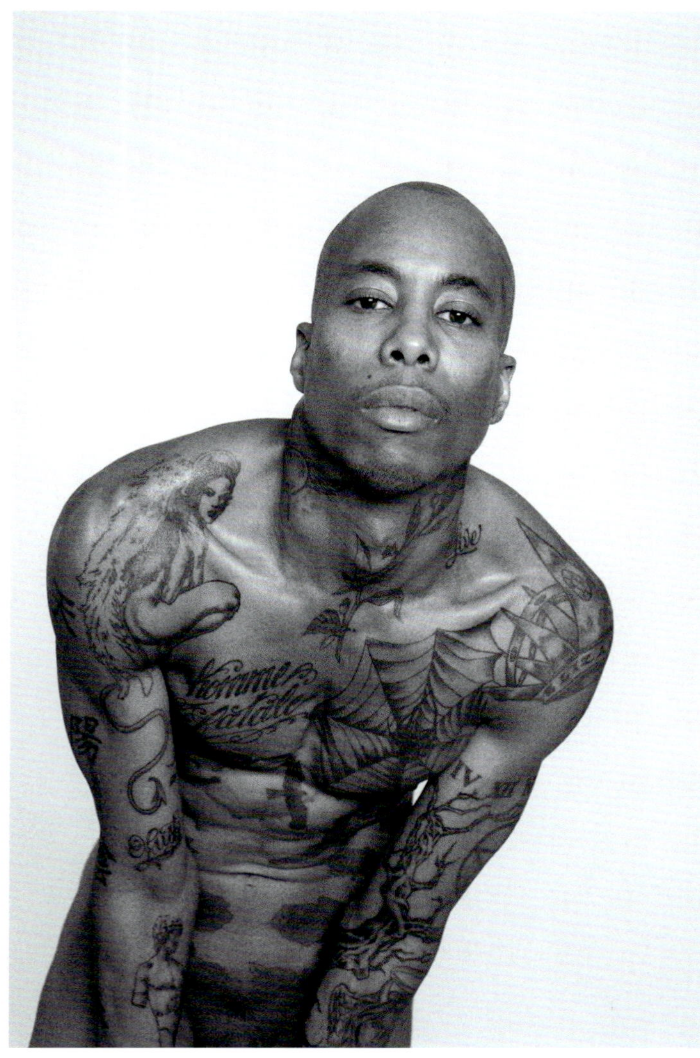

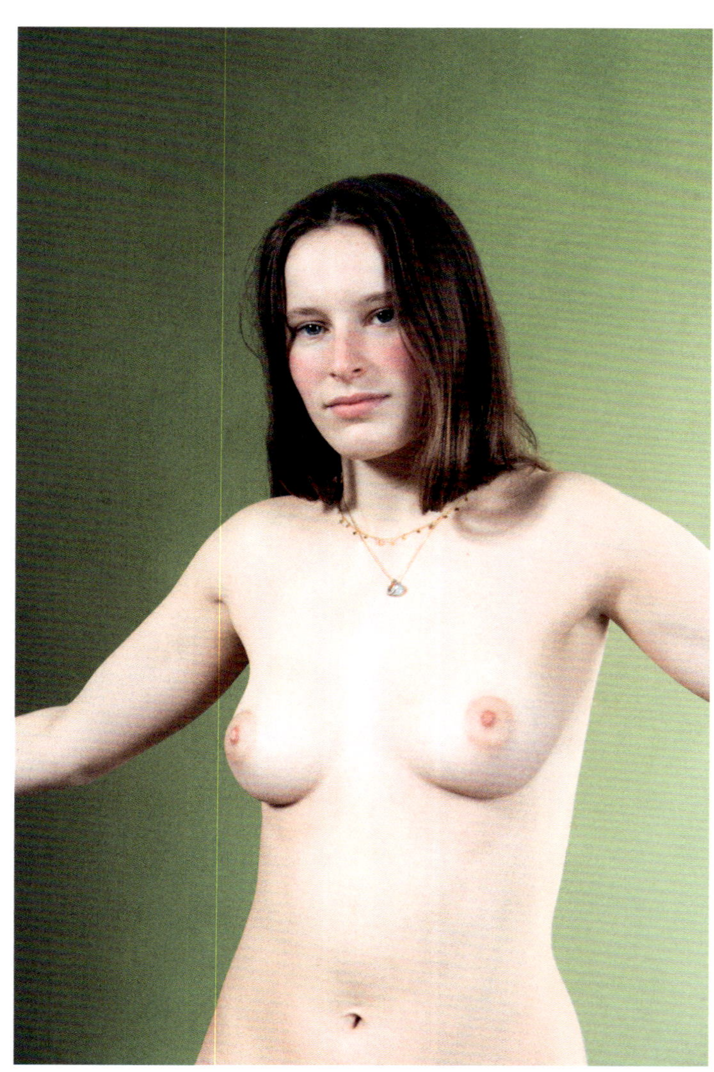

Myf, November 2011   Chad, January 2016   Angelo, June 2010   Claire, December 2014

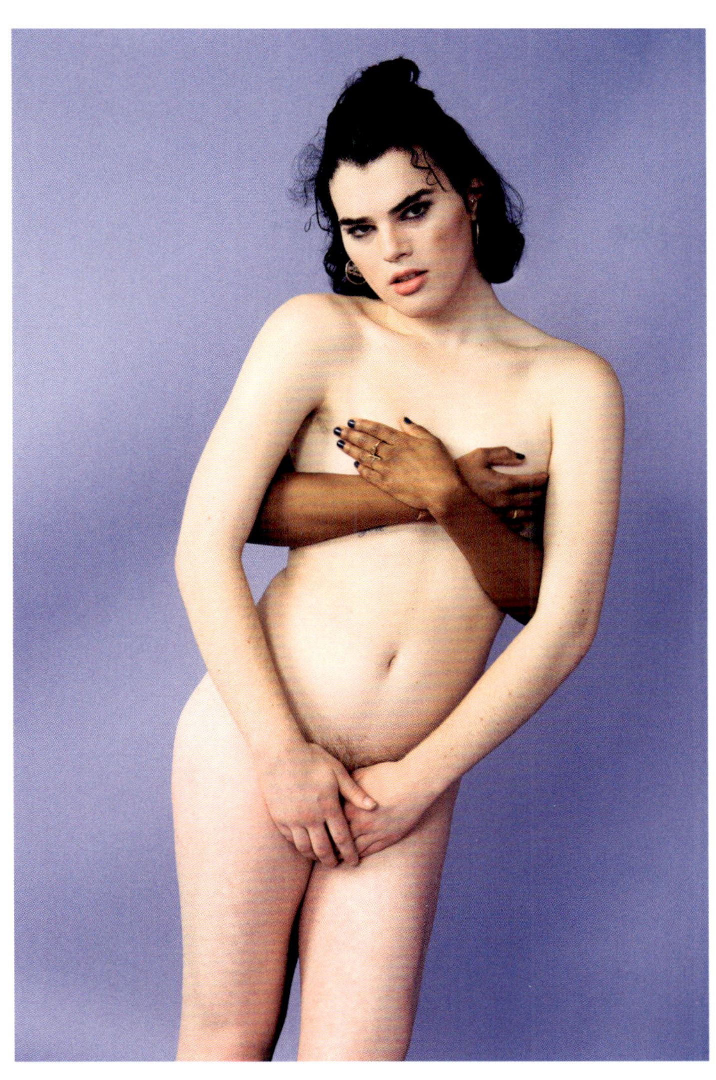

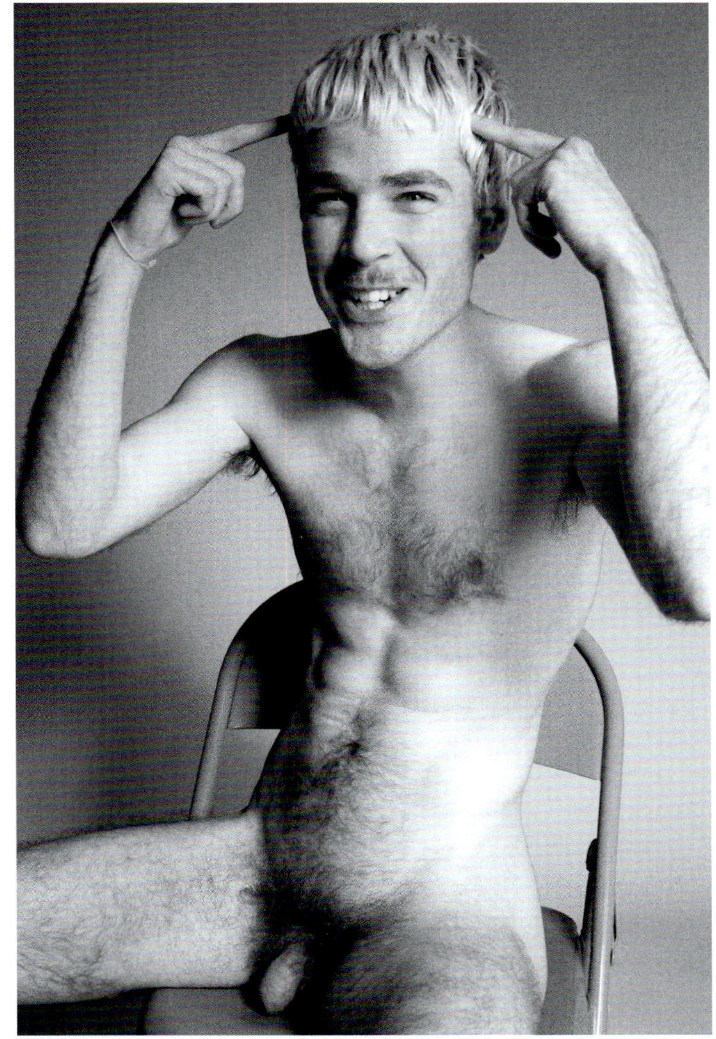

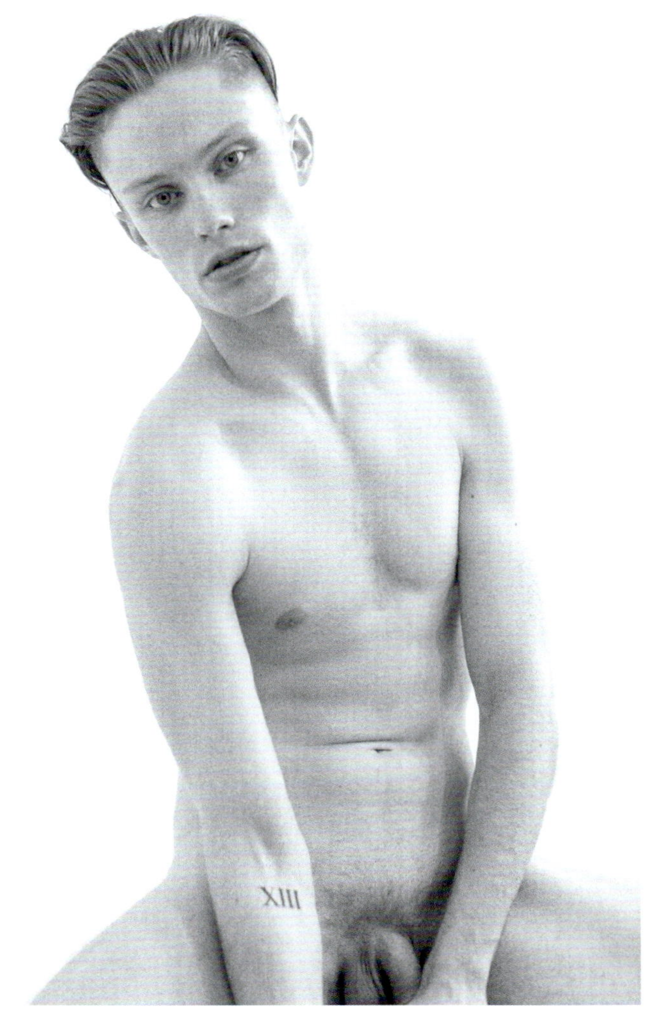

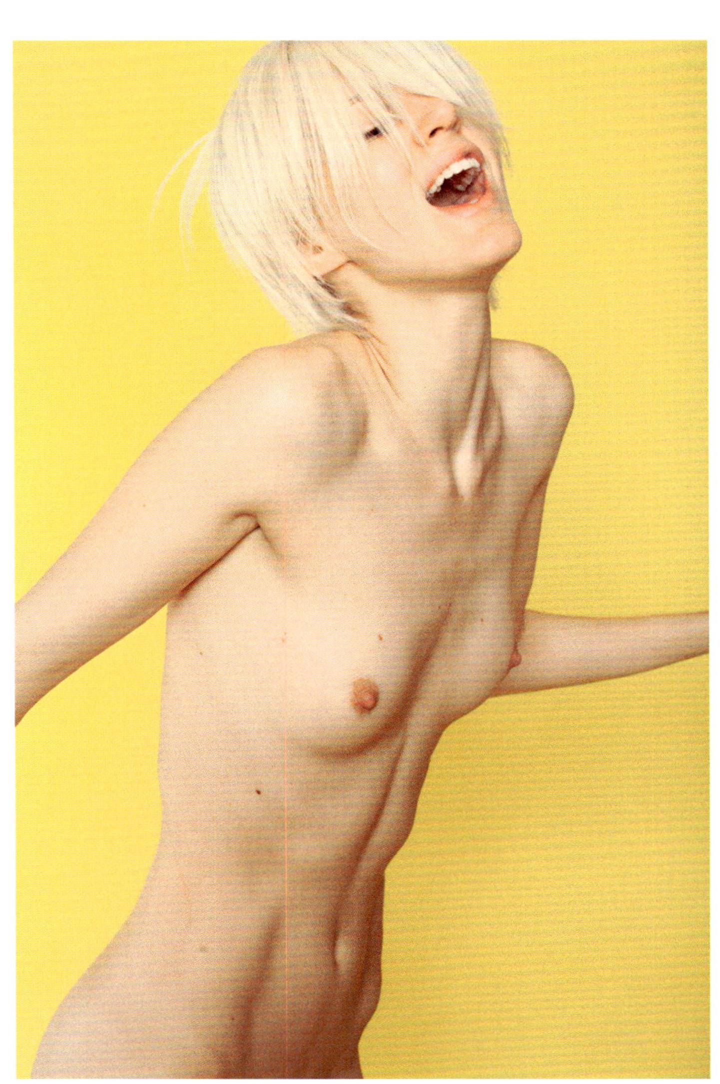

Chloe & Adrienne, January 2017   Mick, January 2014   Matthew, December 2018   Kelly, December 2009

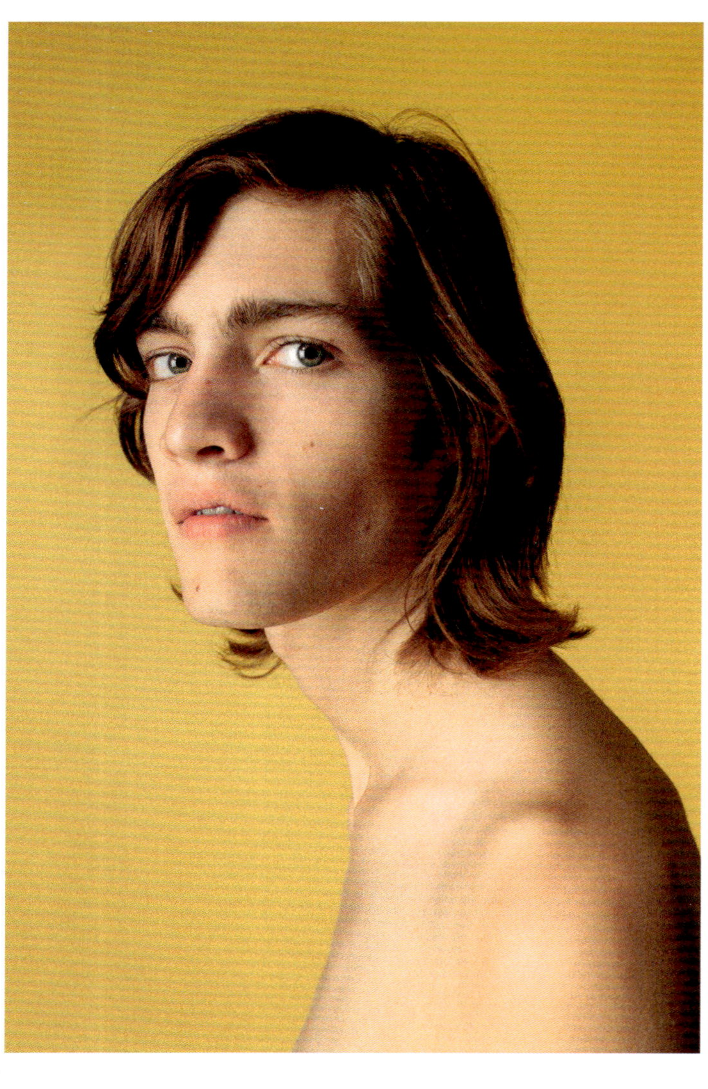

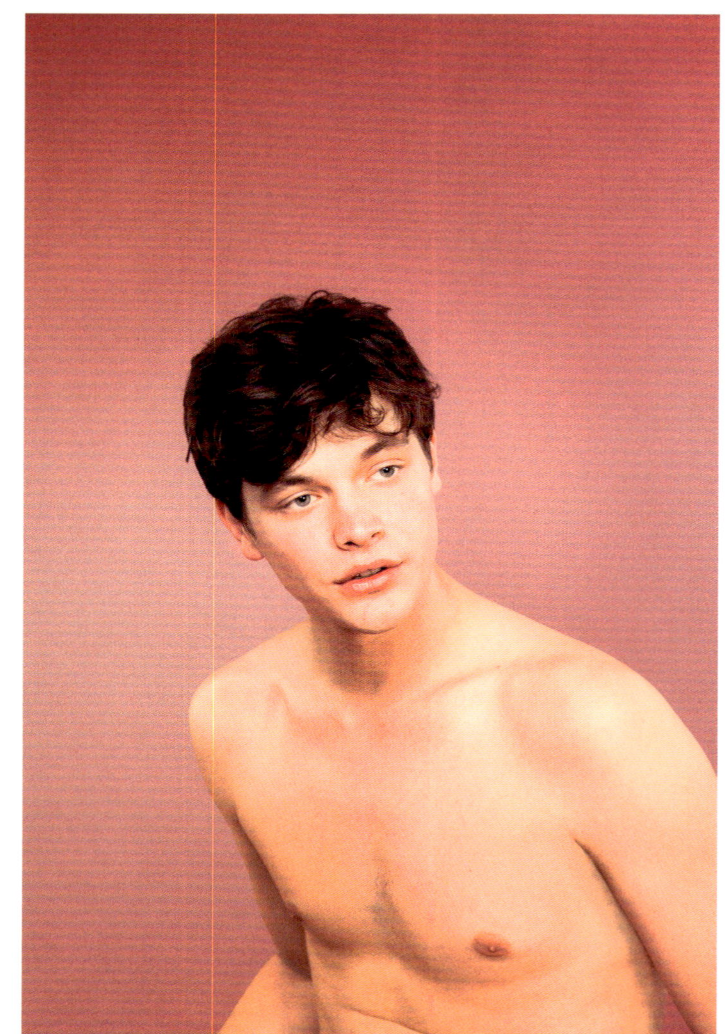

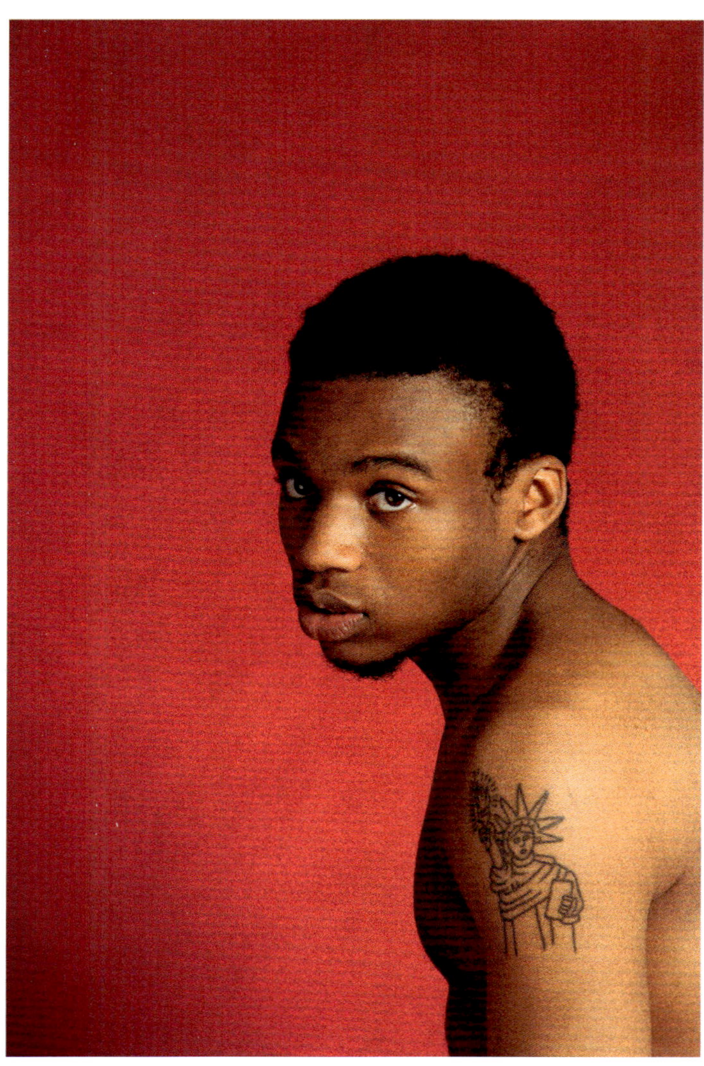

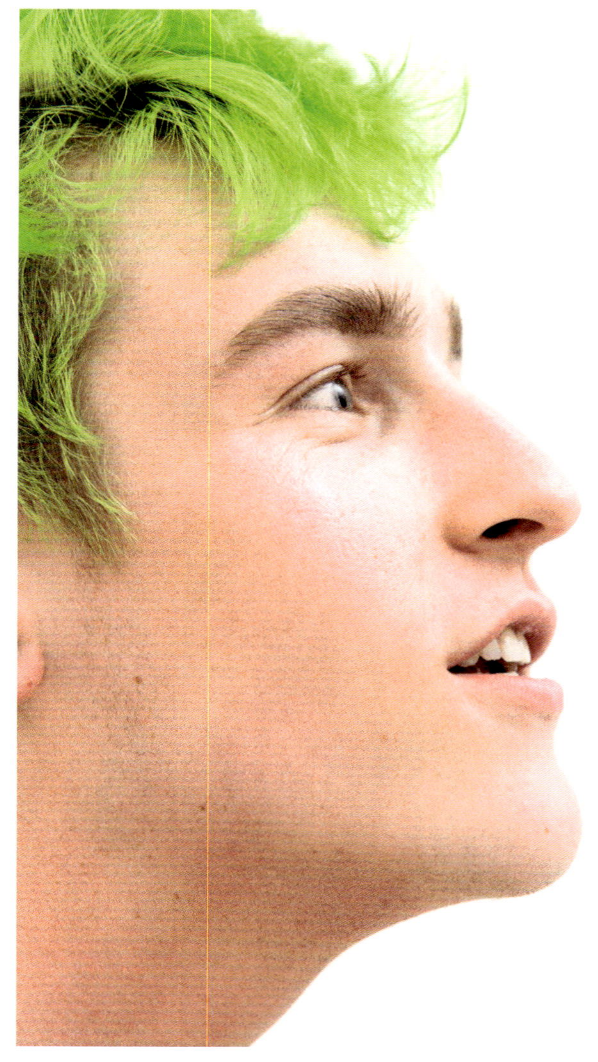

Marcel, November 2008 Jason, March 2011 Zachary, May 2012 John, August 2017

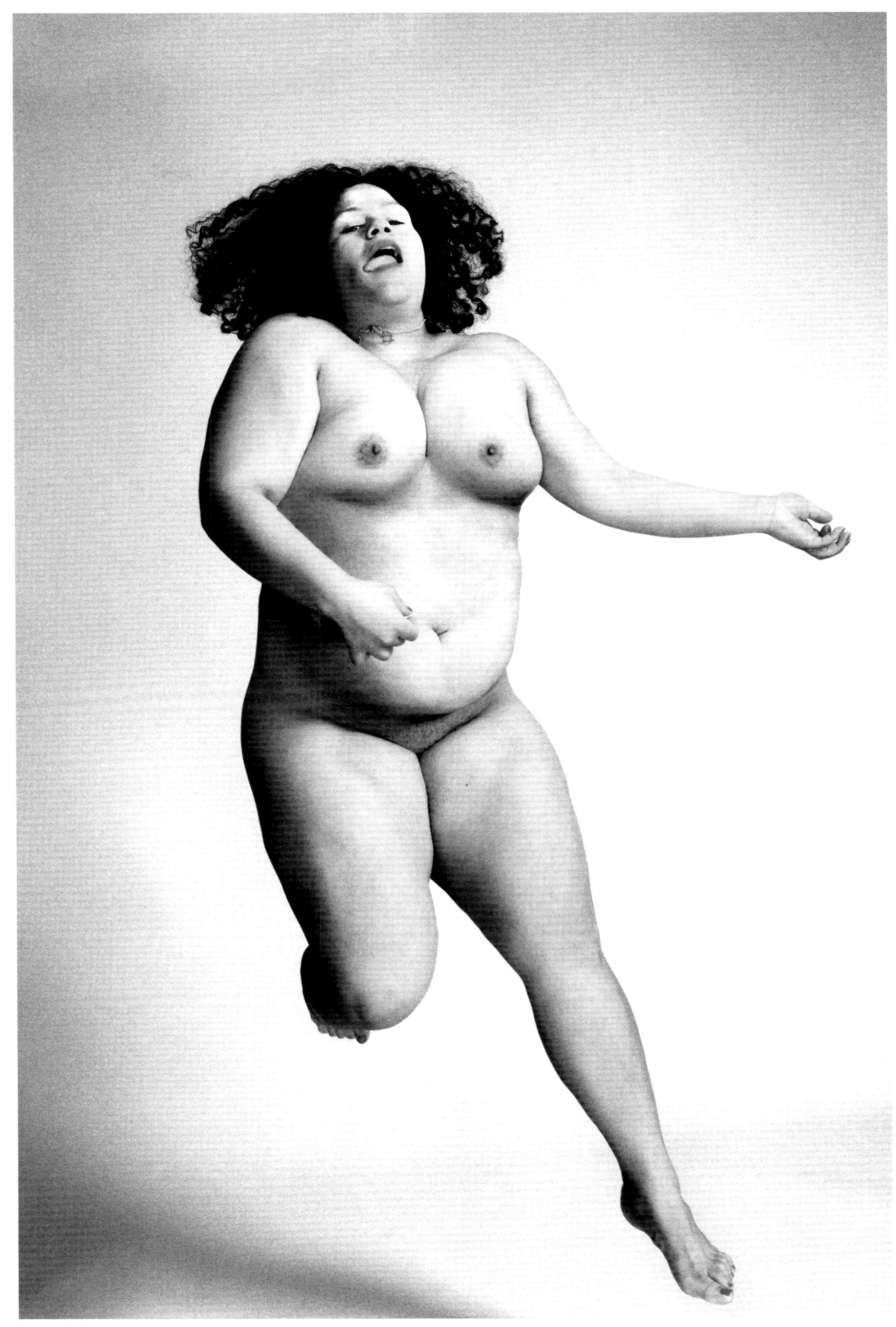

Adena, May 2016

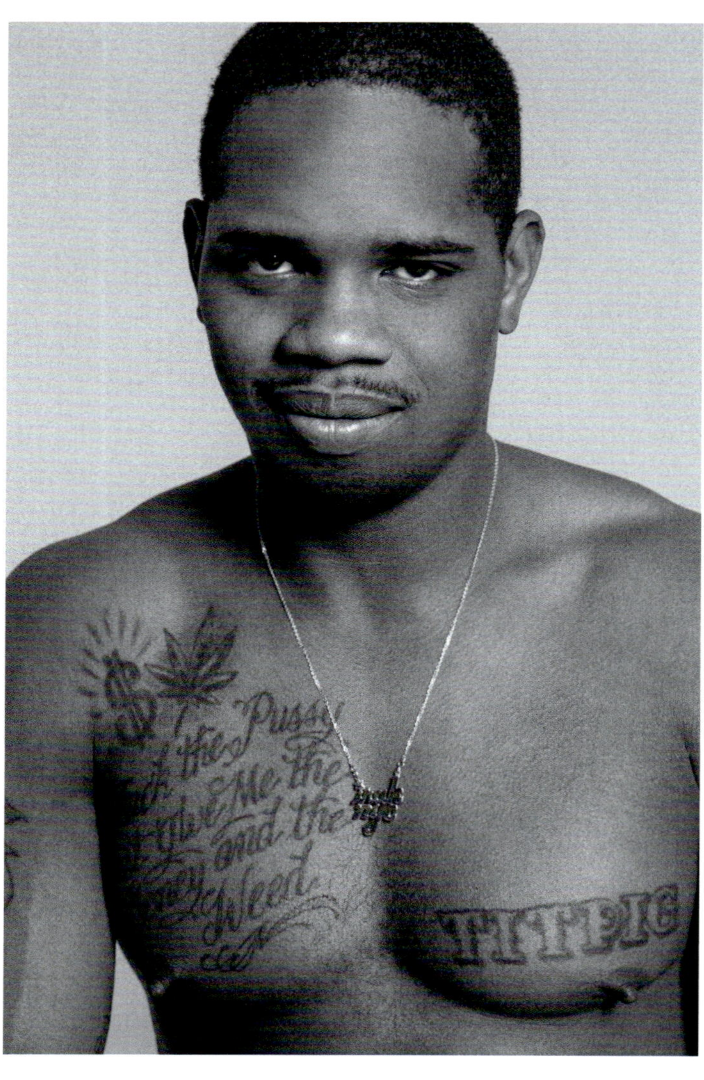

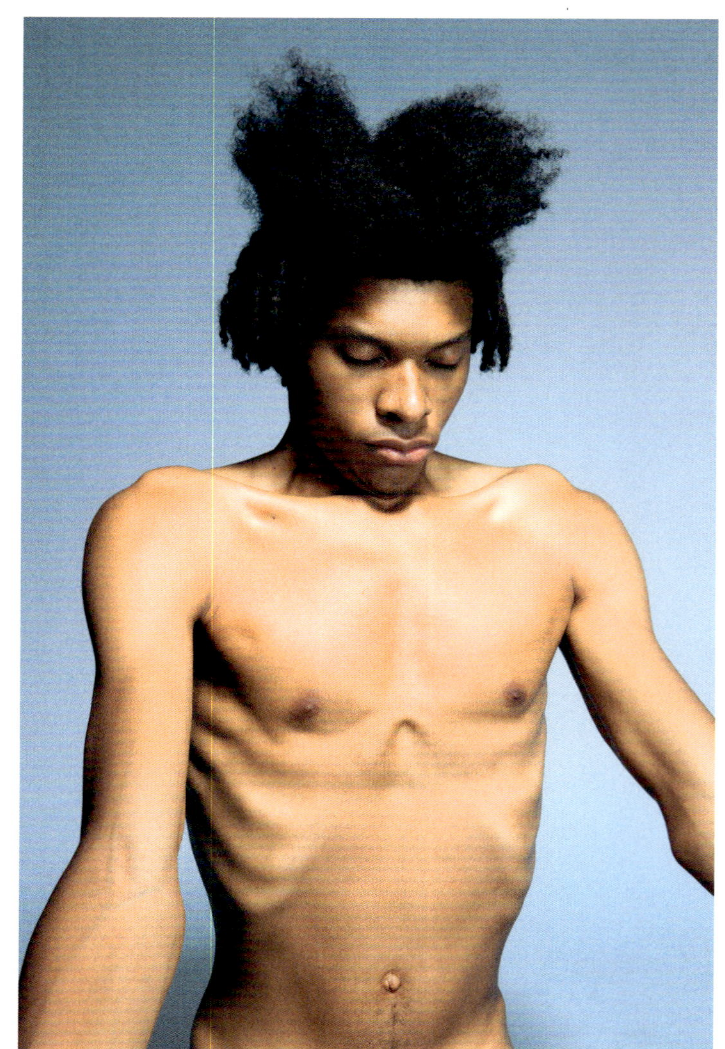

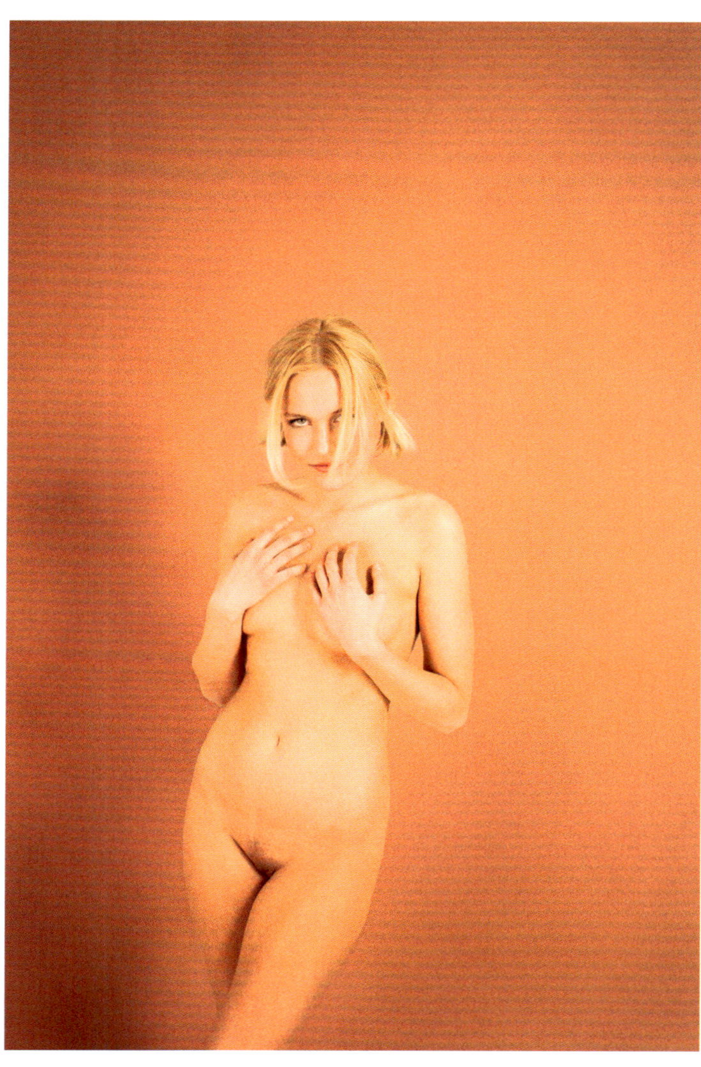

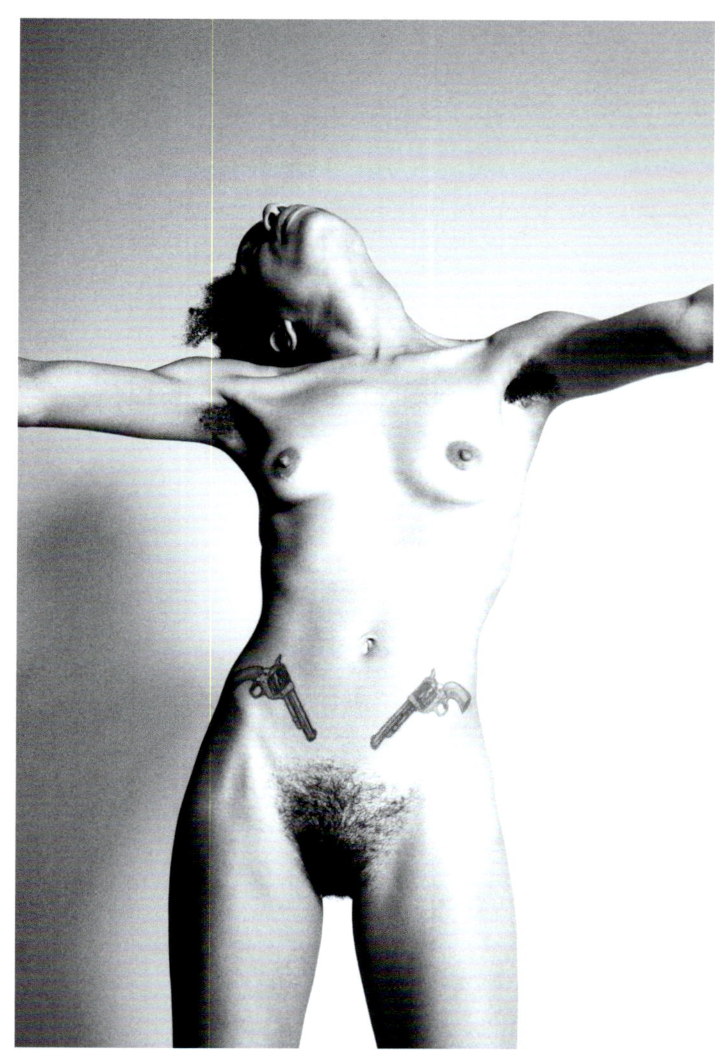

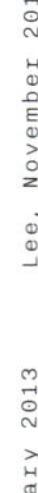

Kunle, January 2009   Lam, September 2015   Carlotta, January 2013   Lee, November 2015

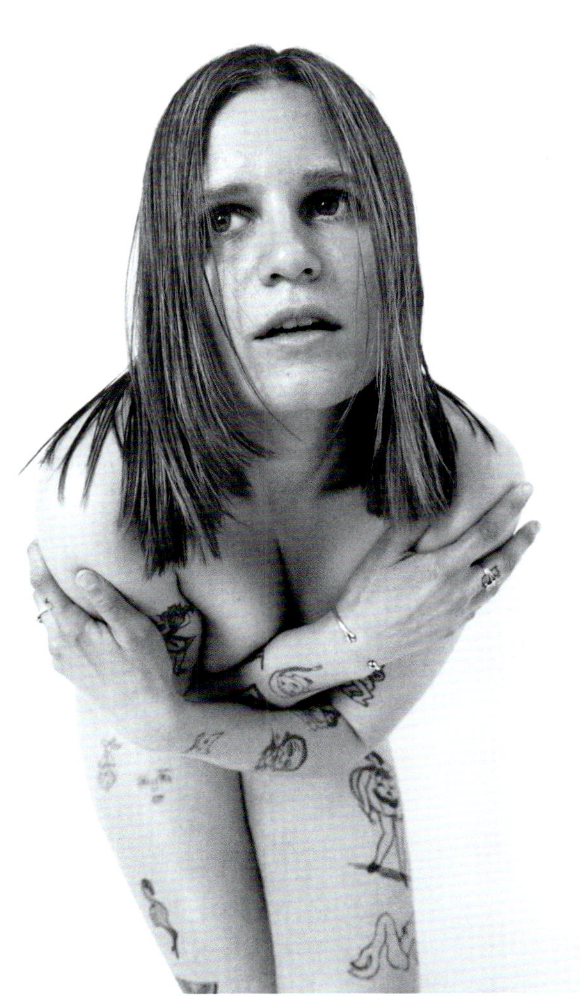

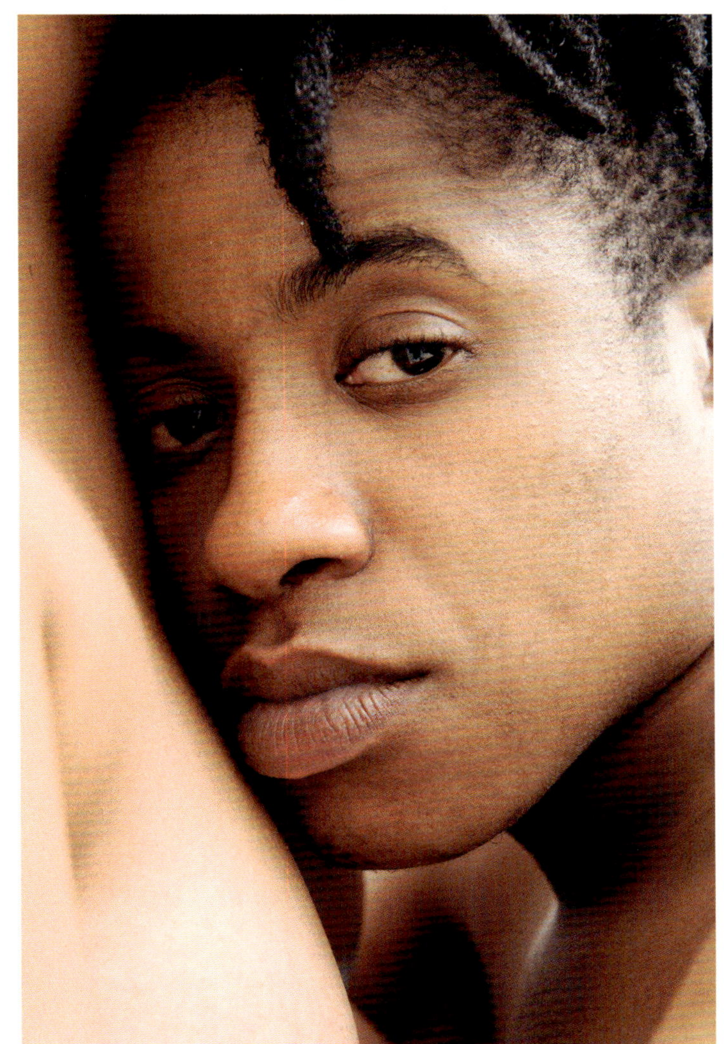

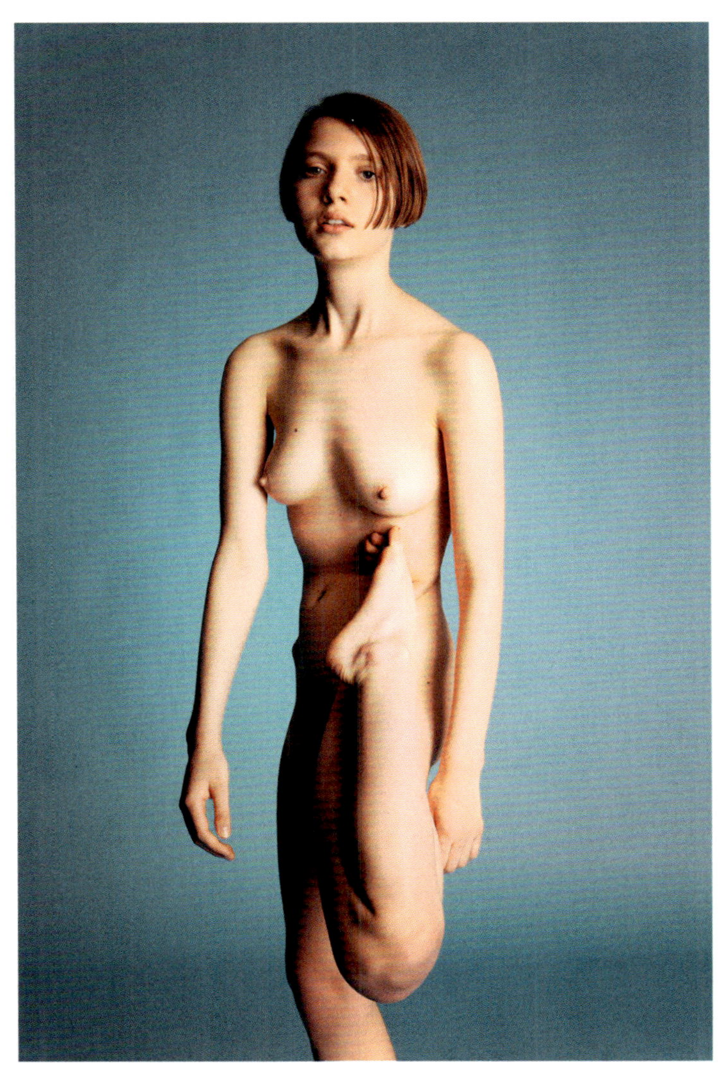

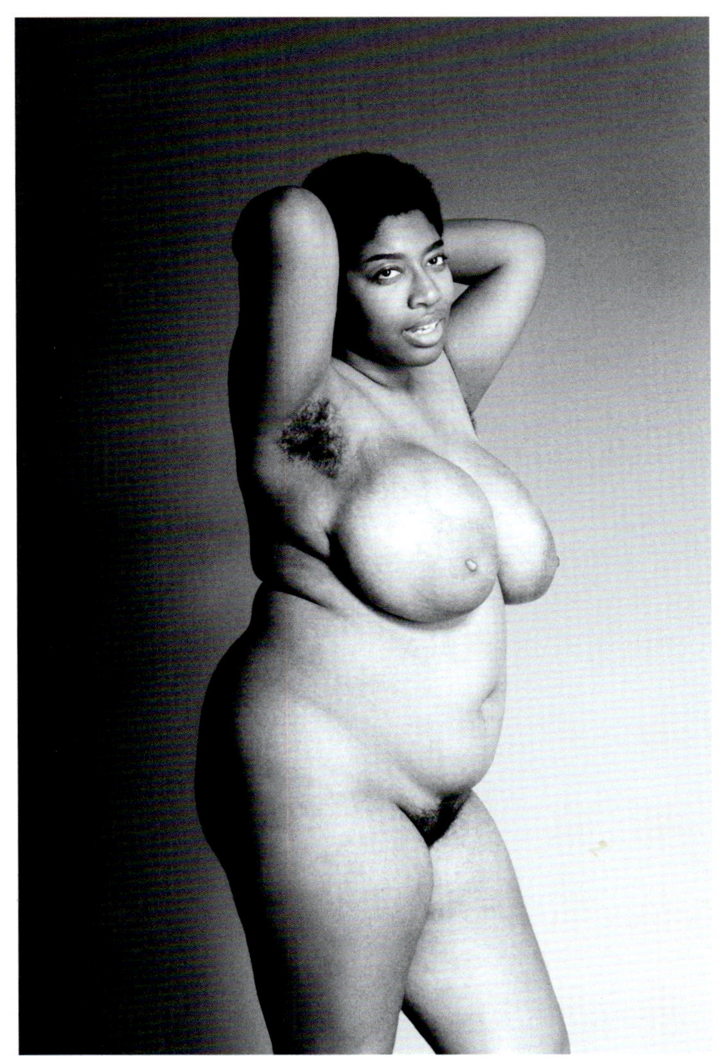

Claire, June 2017   Meliq, August 2017   Sasha, May 2015   Morgan, October 2015

I met Ryan in 2016 after I went topless at a music festival to raise awareness for breast cancer.

When my mom was diagnosed with breast cancer when I was thirteen, and even later, when I was going through my own treatment, I didn't see a lot of representation of Black people and breast cancer. And then, as a nonbinary queer person, I absolutely didn't see anybody who was queer or nonbinary in the breast cancer advocacy world. The representation was for a white, cisgender, married with three kids, drives a minivan, and lives in the suburbs kind of person.

I had been going to this festival every year and knew a lot of Black queer and trans people went as well. At music festivals, people are often topless. And it's hot in New York in August! I couldn't imagine it would be an issue. I just thought, "I'm going to go topless to raise awareness; it'll make a difference to show my scars."

From that one moment of wanting to make a difference, so many opportunities came. I didn't imagine that people would come up to me and be like, "You're an inspiration." Or, "What happened to your chest?" And, "Can you tell me more about this?"

I'm an educator. My primary focus is sex education with a more in-depth focus on racial and social justice and gender. How do systems of oppression impact pleasure and our access to it? How does the fact that our governmental systems keep us from having our material needs met impact our ability to feel good in our bodies? Things that should be as simple as access to clean water, clean air, food on the table, and free time—not working around the clock constantly—will impact sex and sexuality.

I also talk about the ways in which people relate to people's bodies. As a Black person, people have related to me and my body like it was a threat or going to cause violence, like it was angry. And then, being diagnosed with breast cancer, there was a new element of how people relate to my body. Something that I've pushed up against is not relating to me as solely as an inspiration. I know a lot of people with chronic illnesses and disability navigate the ableist perspective that we are just inspirational porn, and we're not worthy of desire and pleasure or sex.

If you think about sex scenes, I don't know any sex scenes, or even porn scenes, that feature a person with a double mastectomy. How does that shape who we see as deserving of love and pleasure?

This photo was taken at such a transitional point in my life. I had just gotten divorced and had just finished chemo treatment, maybe eight months before. I had this whole new outlook on life, but I also felt like a fish out of water. It was towards the end of my twenties. I felt like my twenties were a bit of a blur; I spent a lot of time giving myself away to people who did not celebrate me or honor me. Now I was learning who I was anew.

Looking back, I'm like, "Wow, that is a different person." I've changed so much. My body has changed. I have way more stretch marks and more discernment, wisdom, and grounding in my body and in my spirit.

I shot with Ryan again after this with my current partner. I don't remember when exactly, but it was very early in our relationship. My partner doesn't really like to be on camera but is a Gemini, so likes attention. The shoot took place on the back of a truck. We rode all over Manhattan. I think it was four in the morning, the only time, maybe, when there was not much traffic. We were held on by a bungee cord and had to be really kissy, in love, and attentive to each other while Ryan got the shot. It was terrifying and beautiful. It was on the cover of the *New York Times Magazine*. It's one of my favorite images ever, and it's still framed in our house.

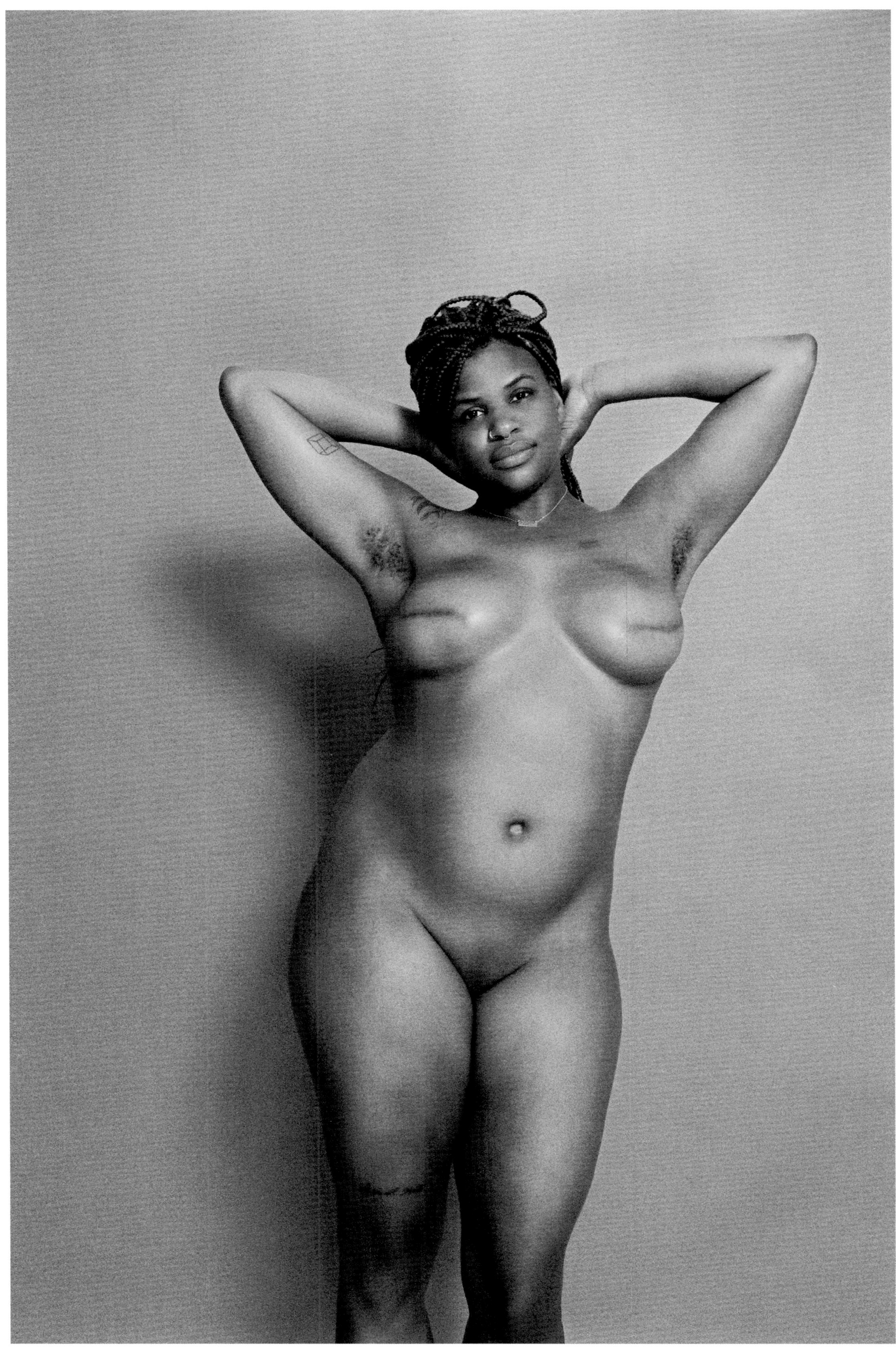

Ericka, September 2016

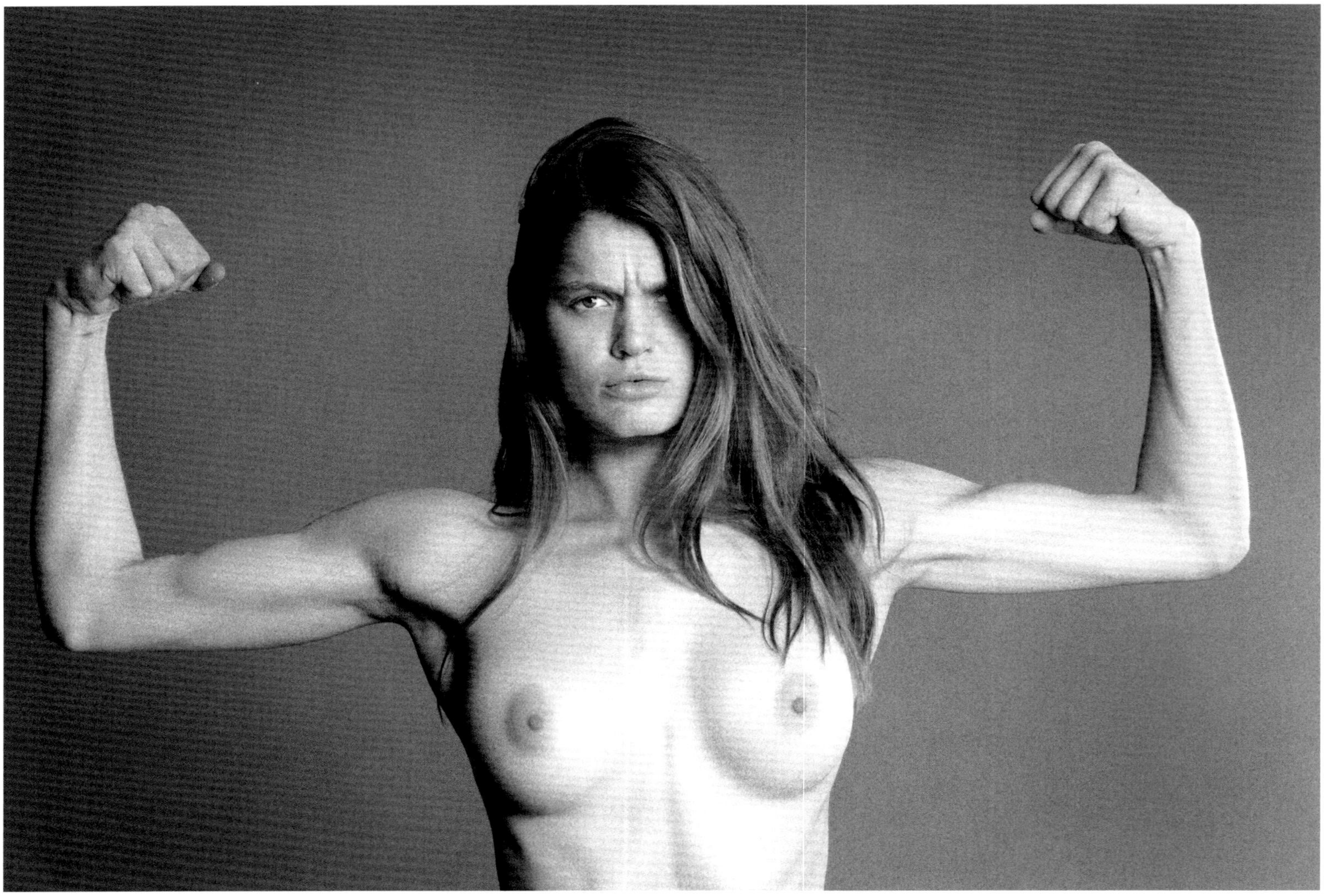

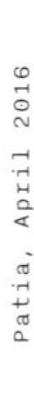

Rebekah, January 2014 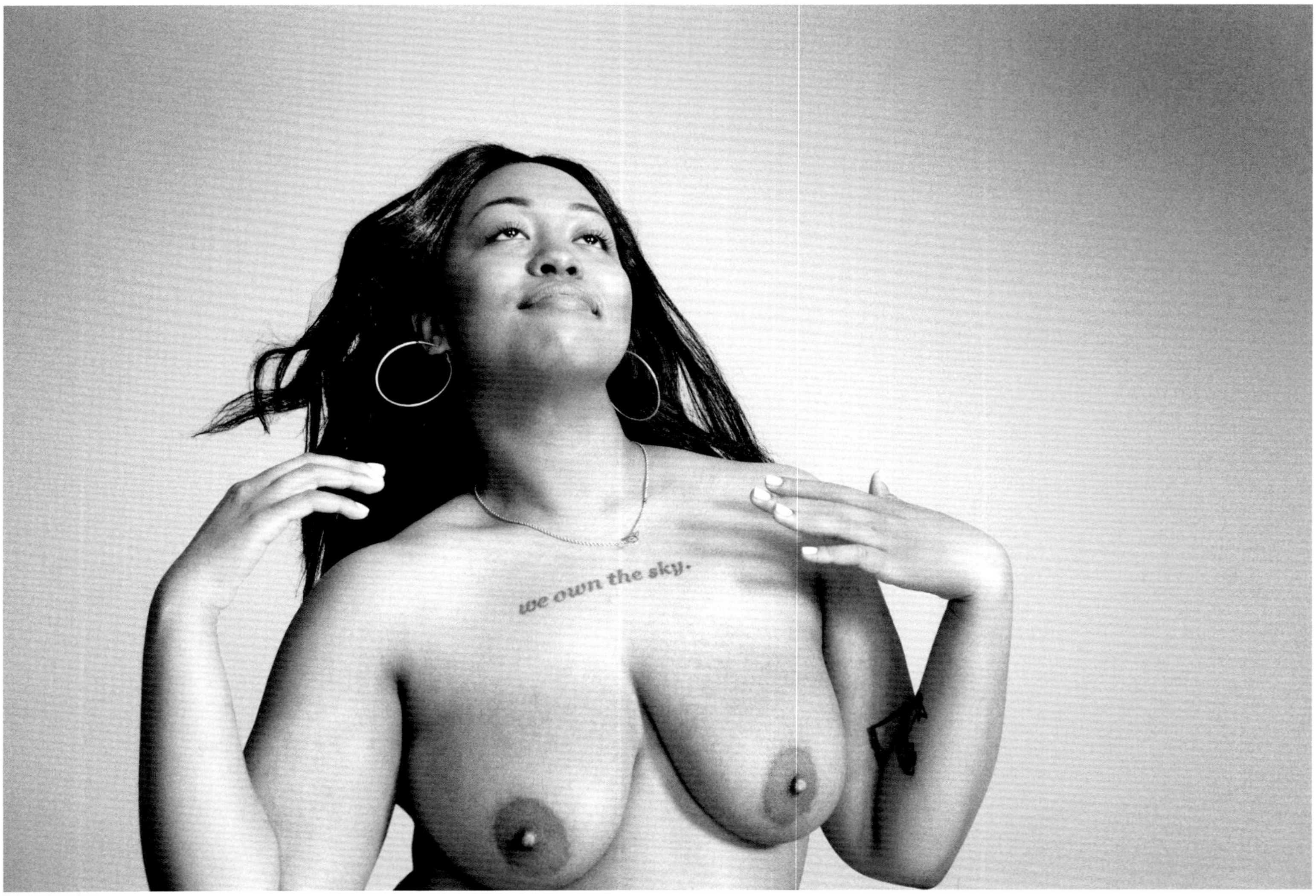   Patia, April 2016

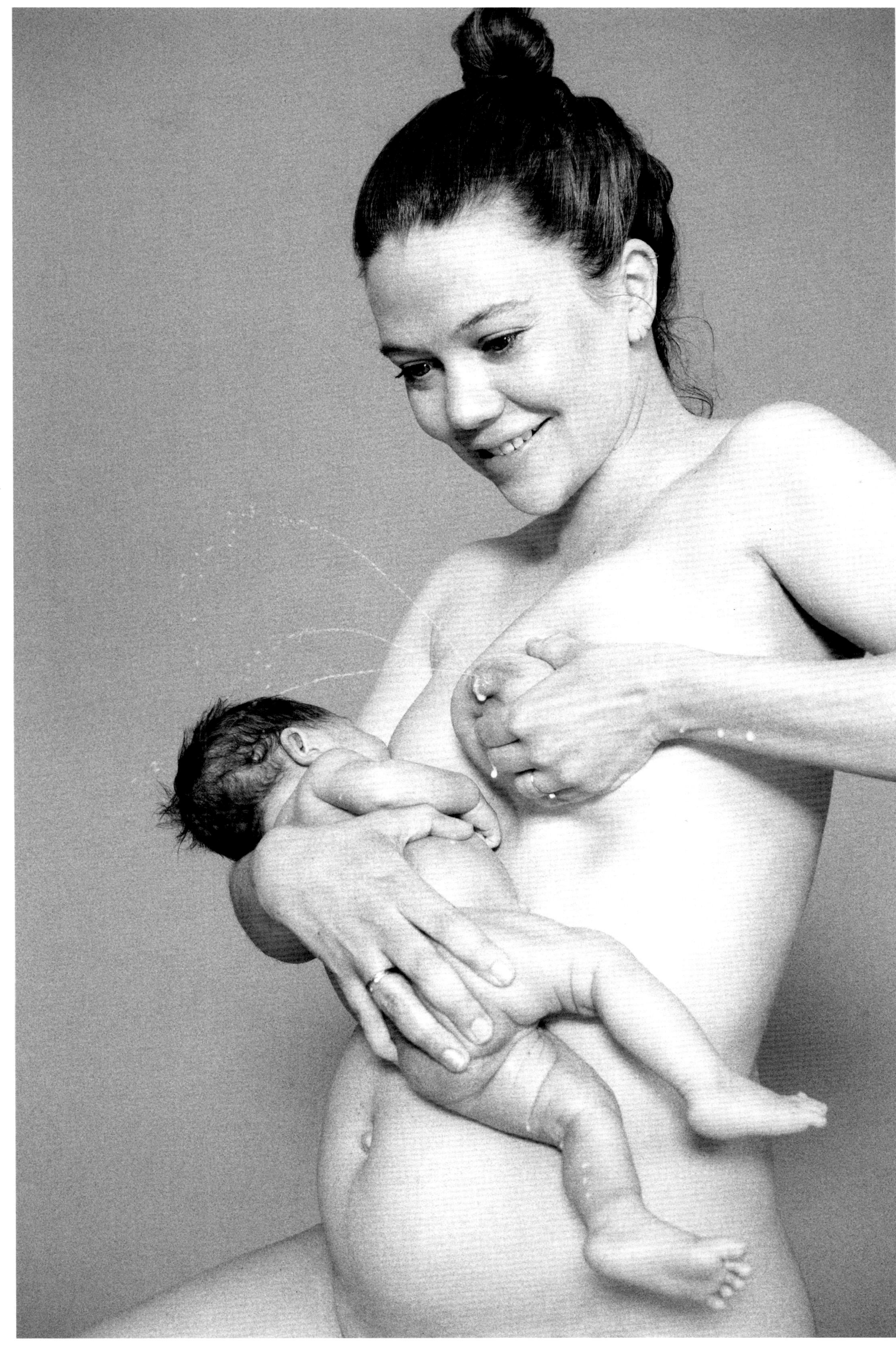

Louise & Frankie, April 2016

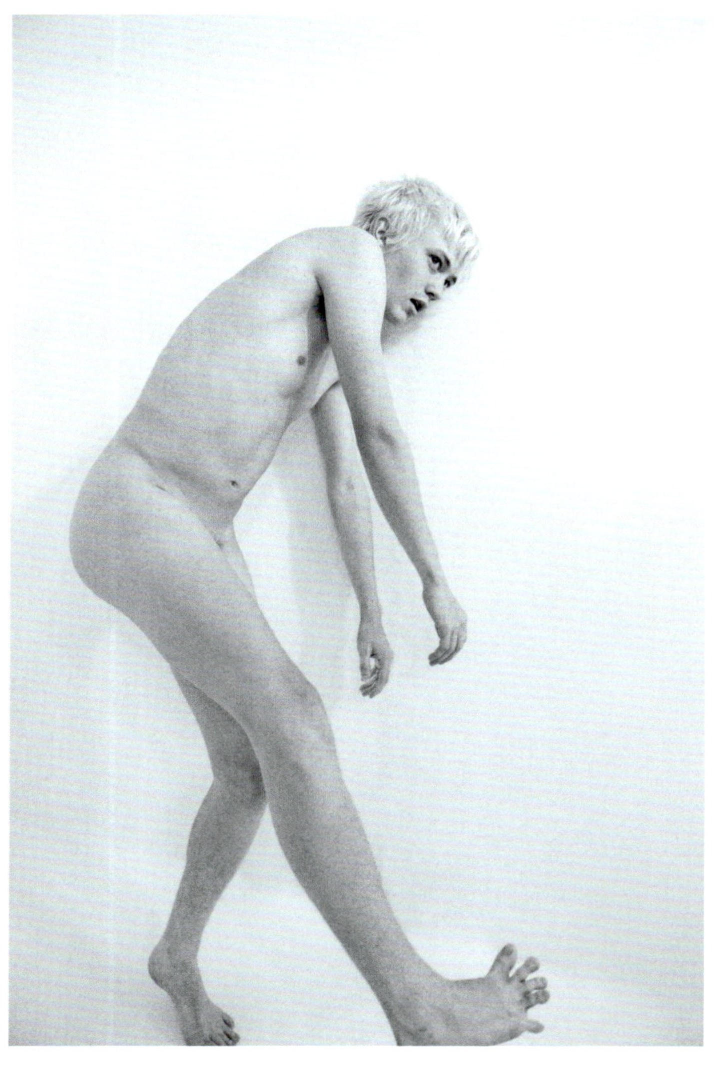

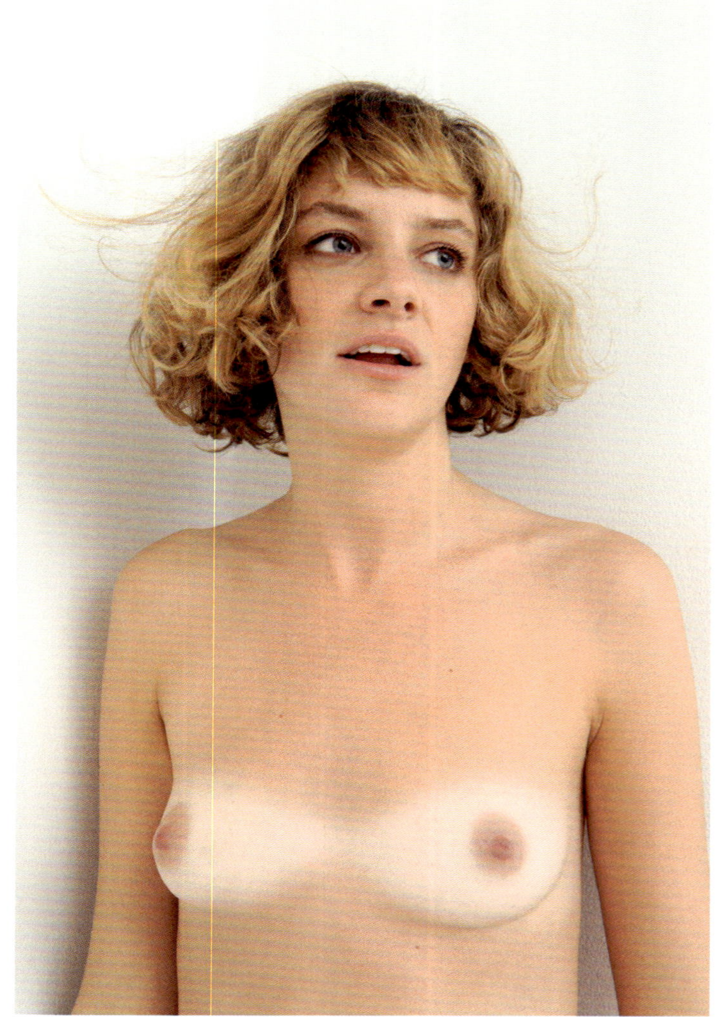

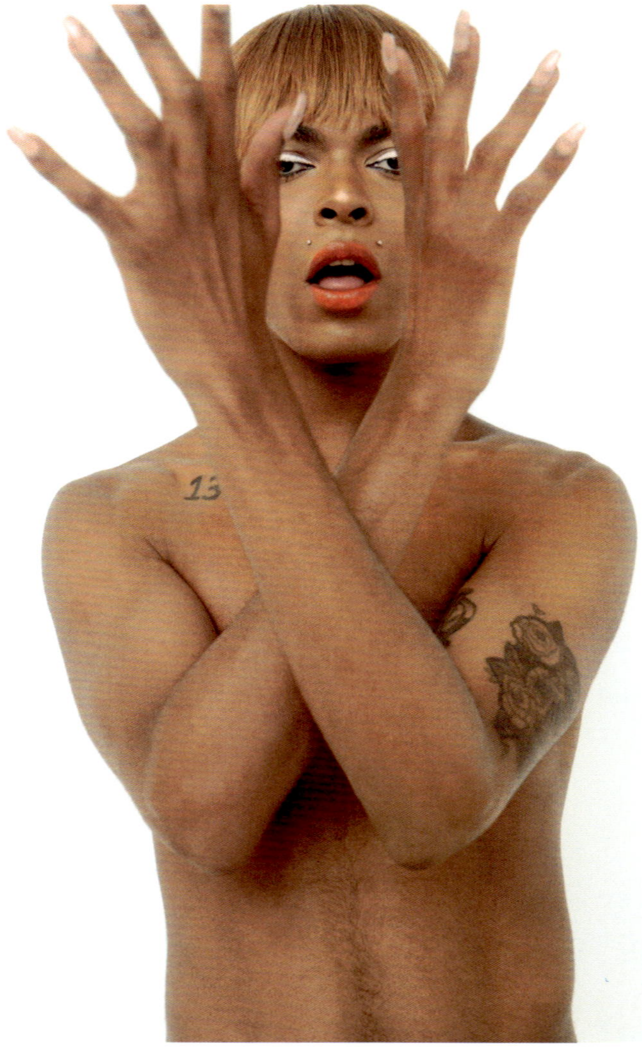

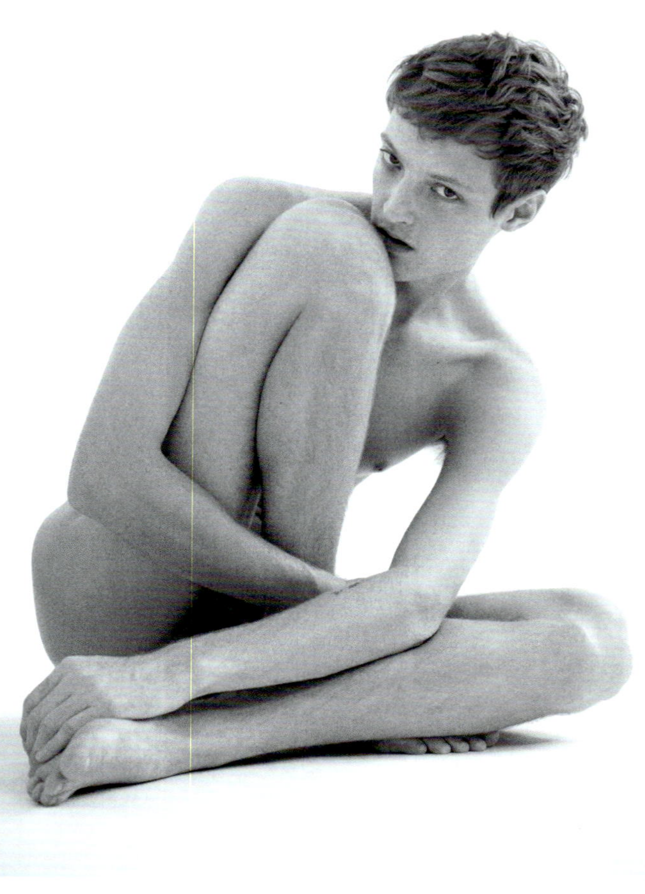

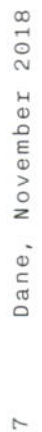

Kyle, October 2019   Alexandra, June 2017   Imaj, June 2017   Dane, November 2018

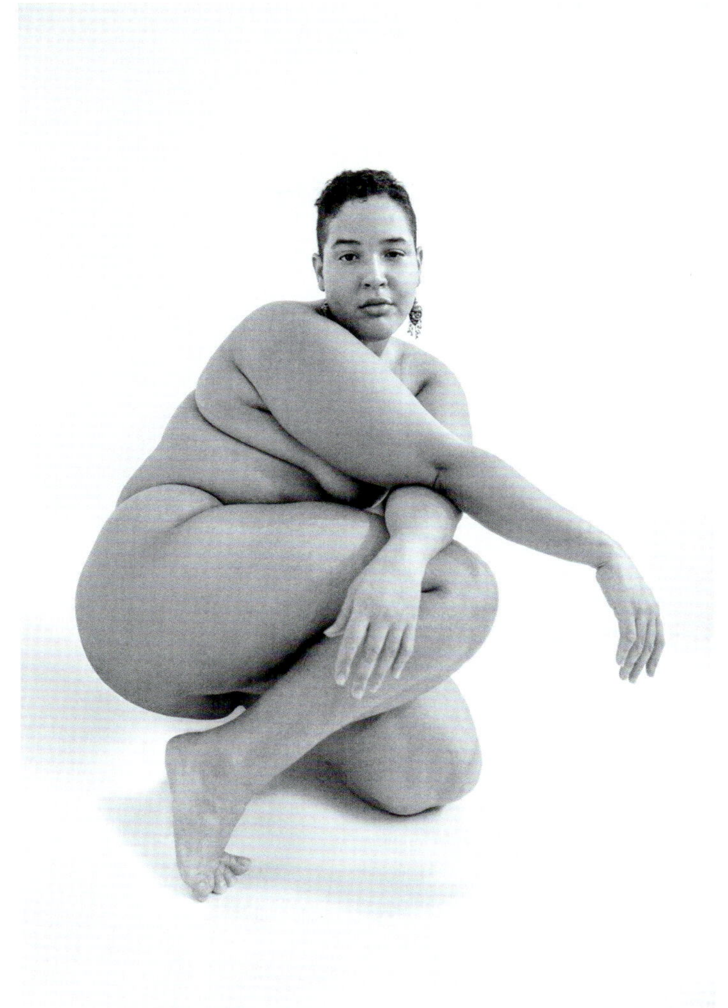

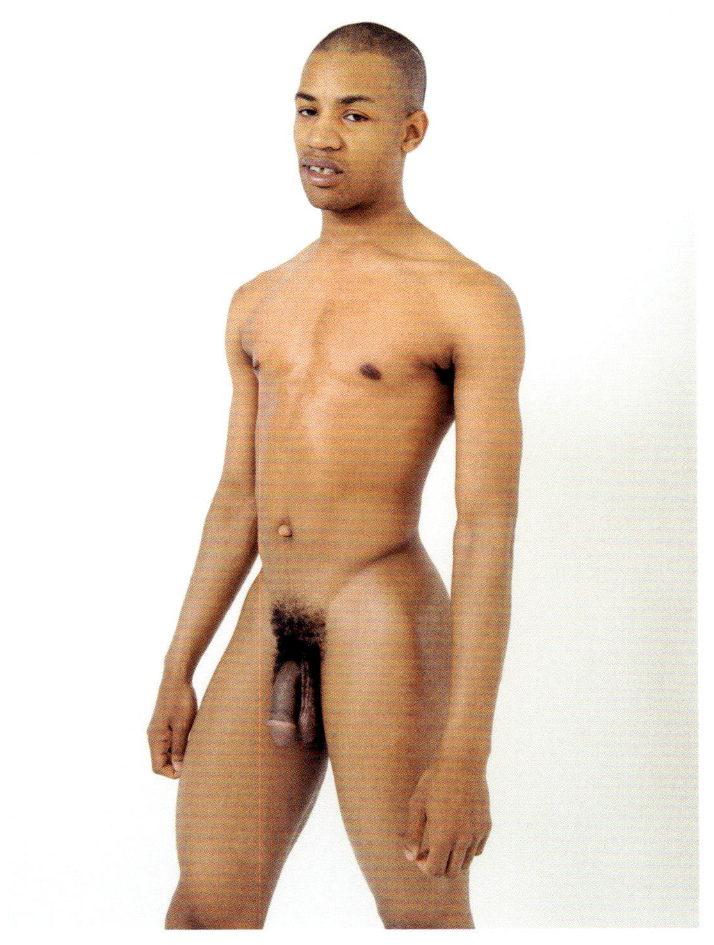

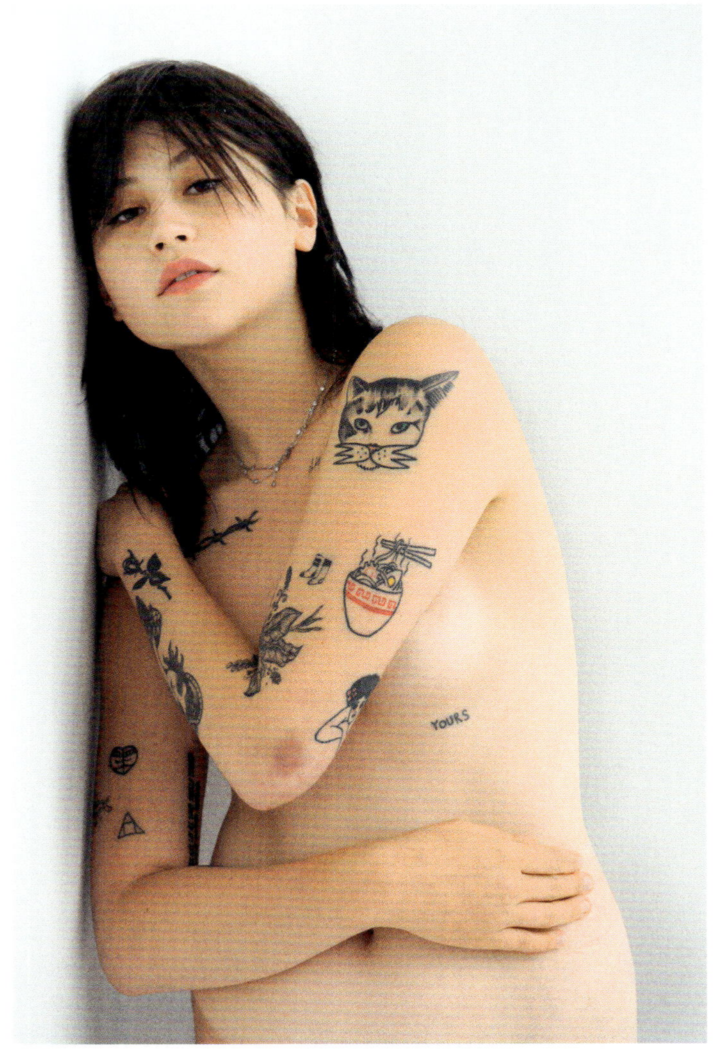

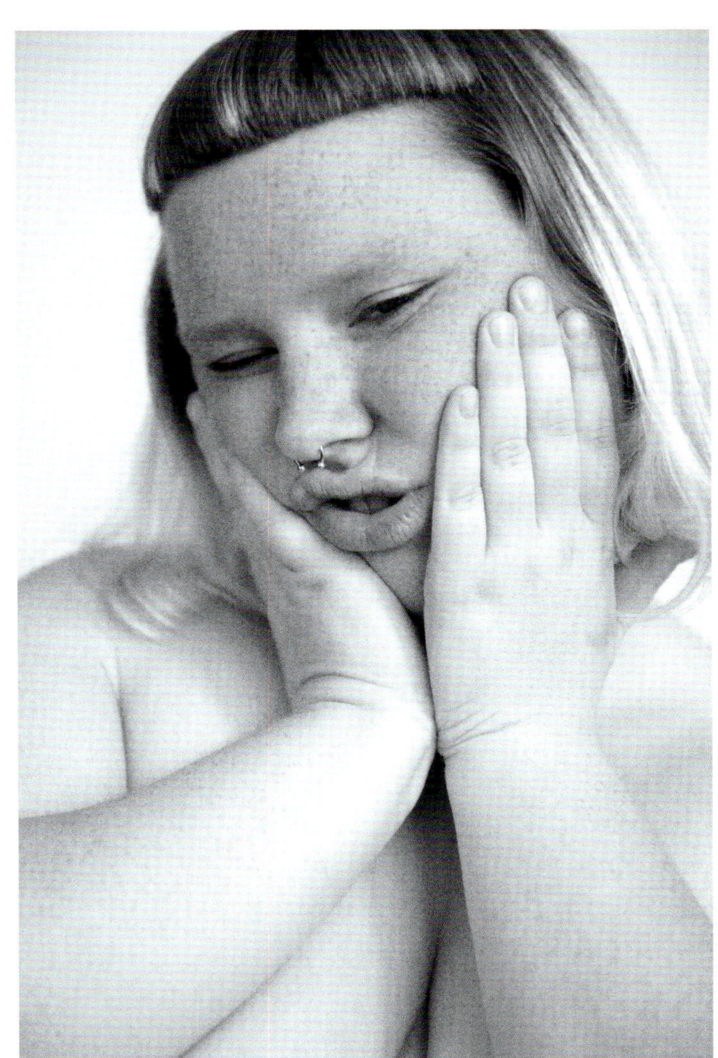

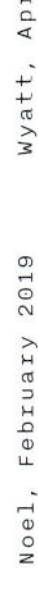

Noel, February 2019 Wyatt, April 2017 Kayla, July 2017 Claire, September 2018

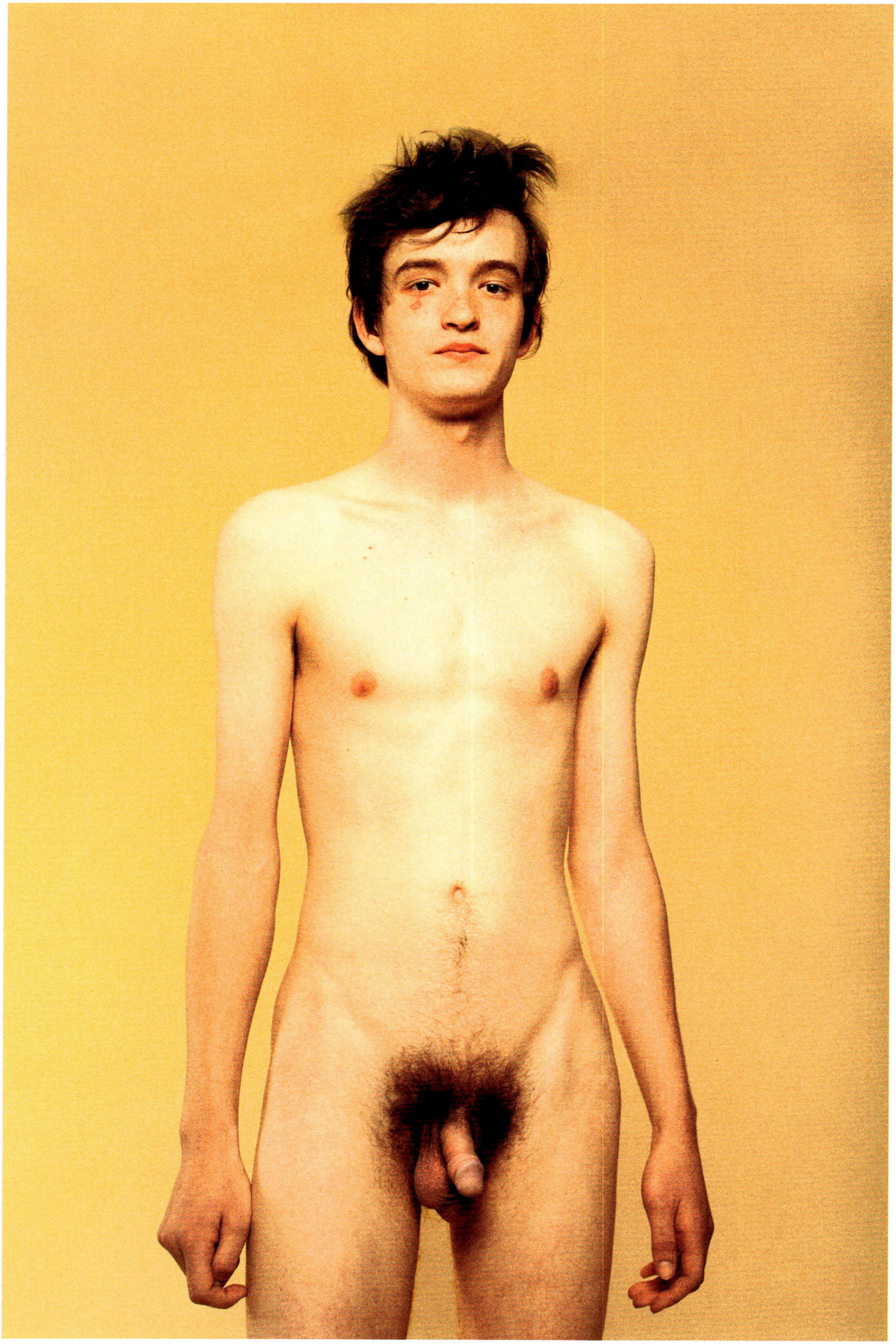

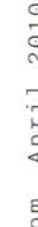

Tom, April 2010

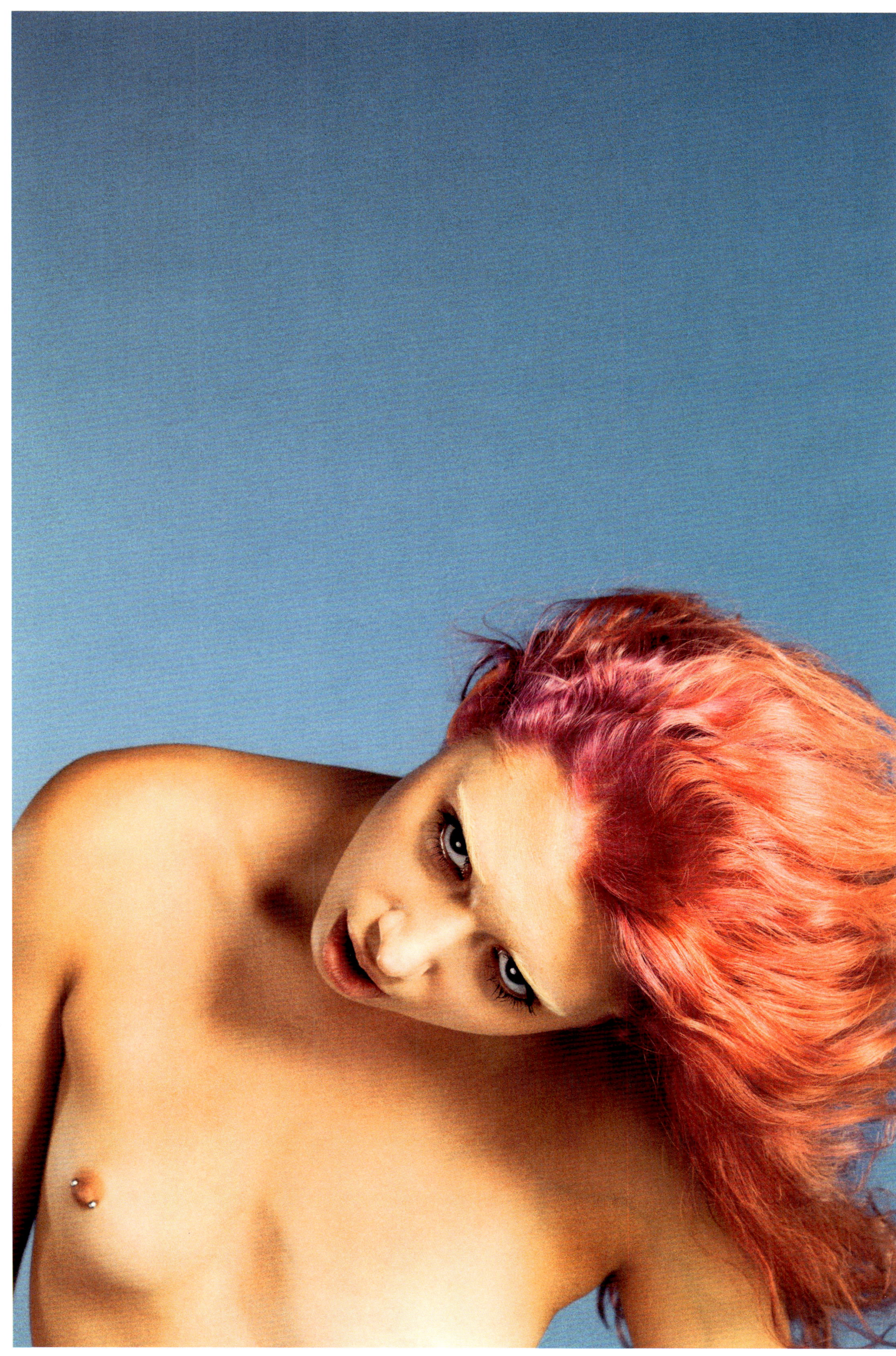

Tate, August 2012

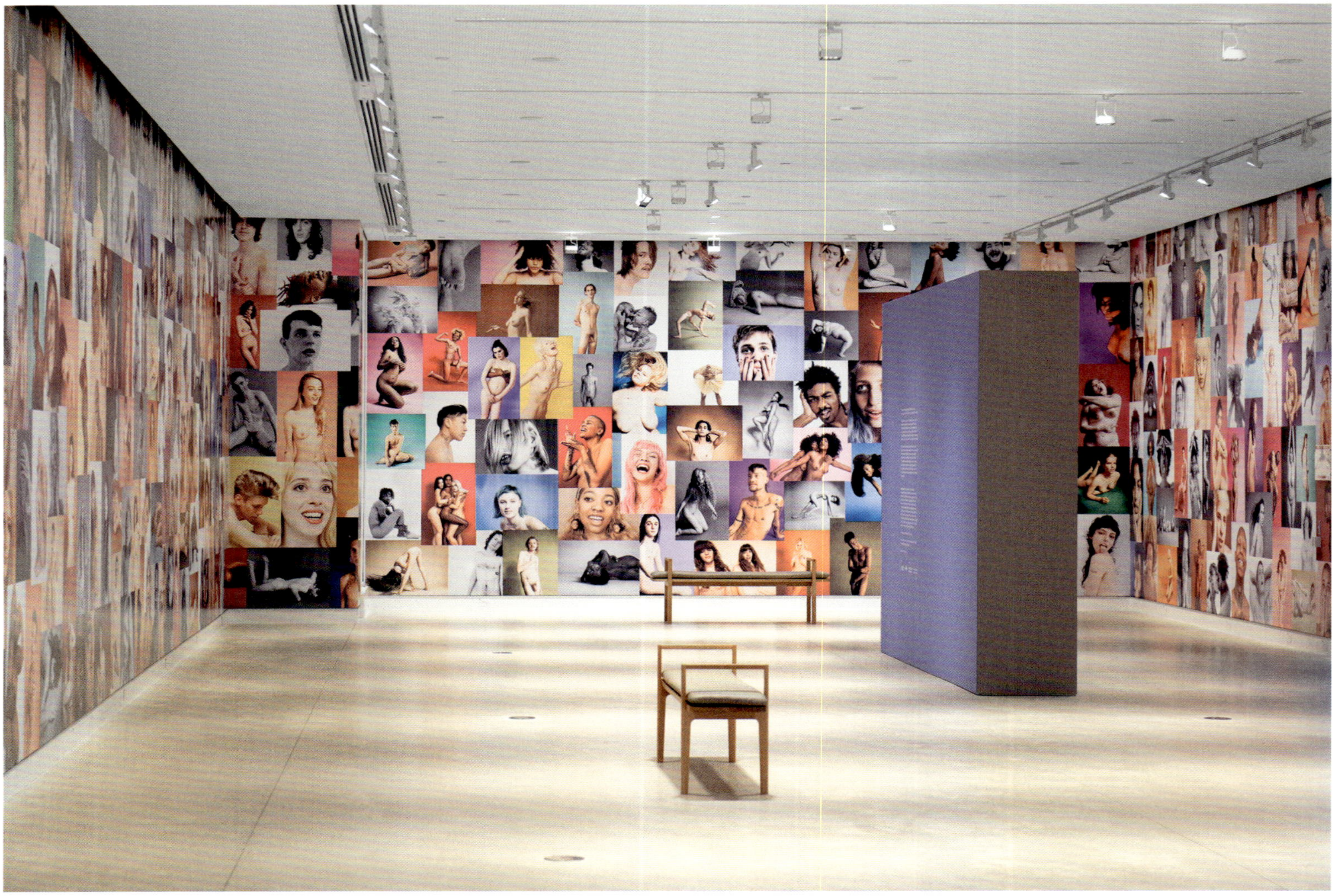

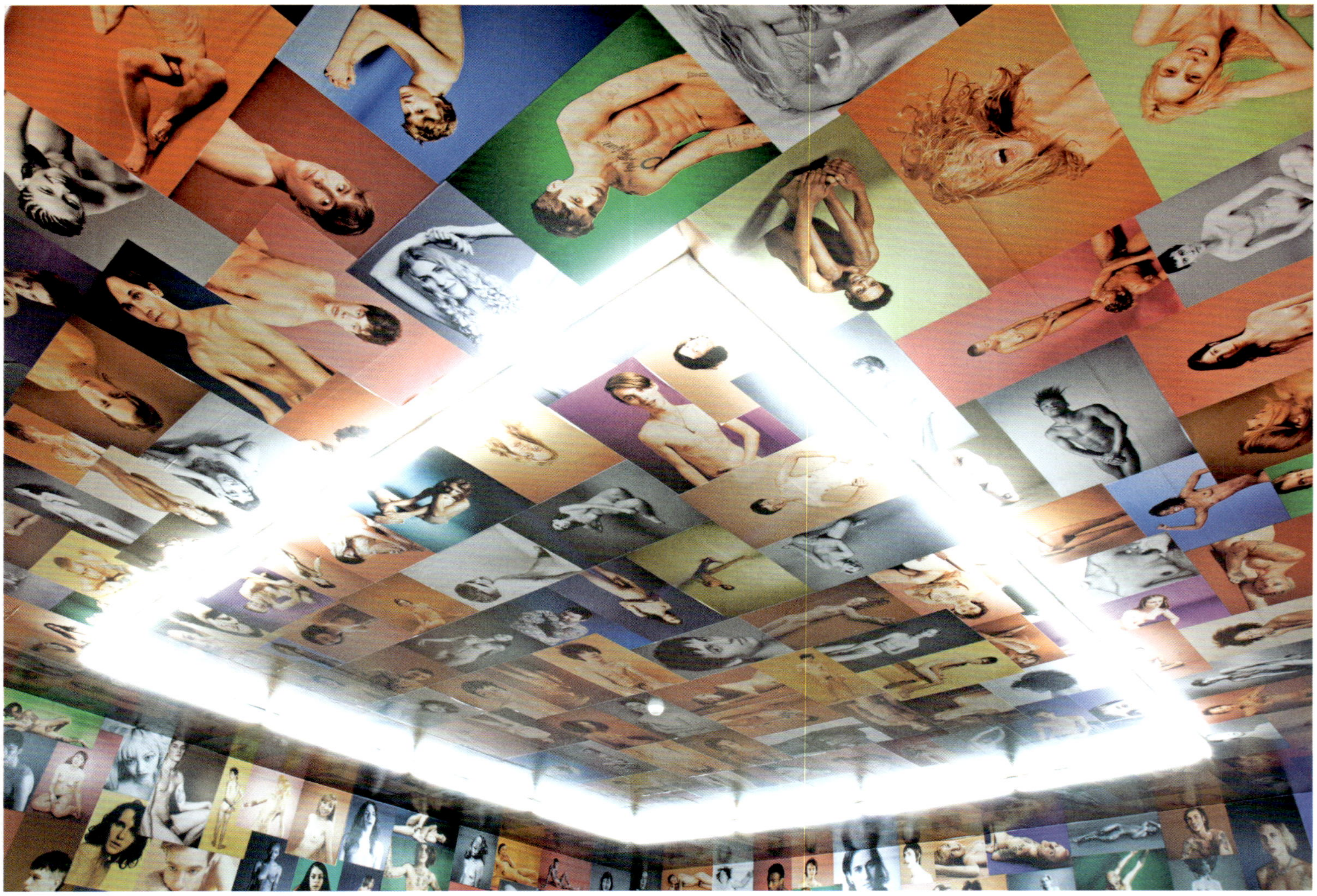

Shepparton Art Museum, Australia, 2024 Art Basel 'Unlimited,' Switzerland, 2015

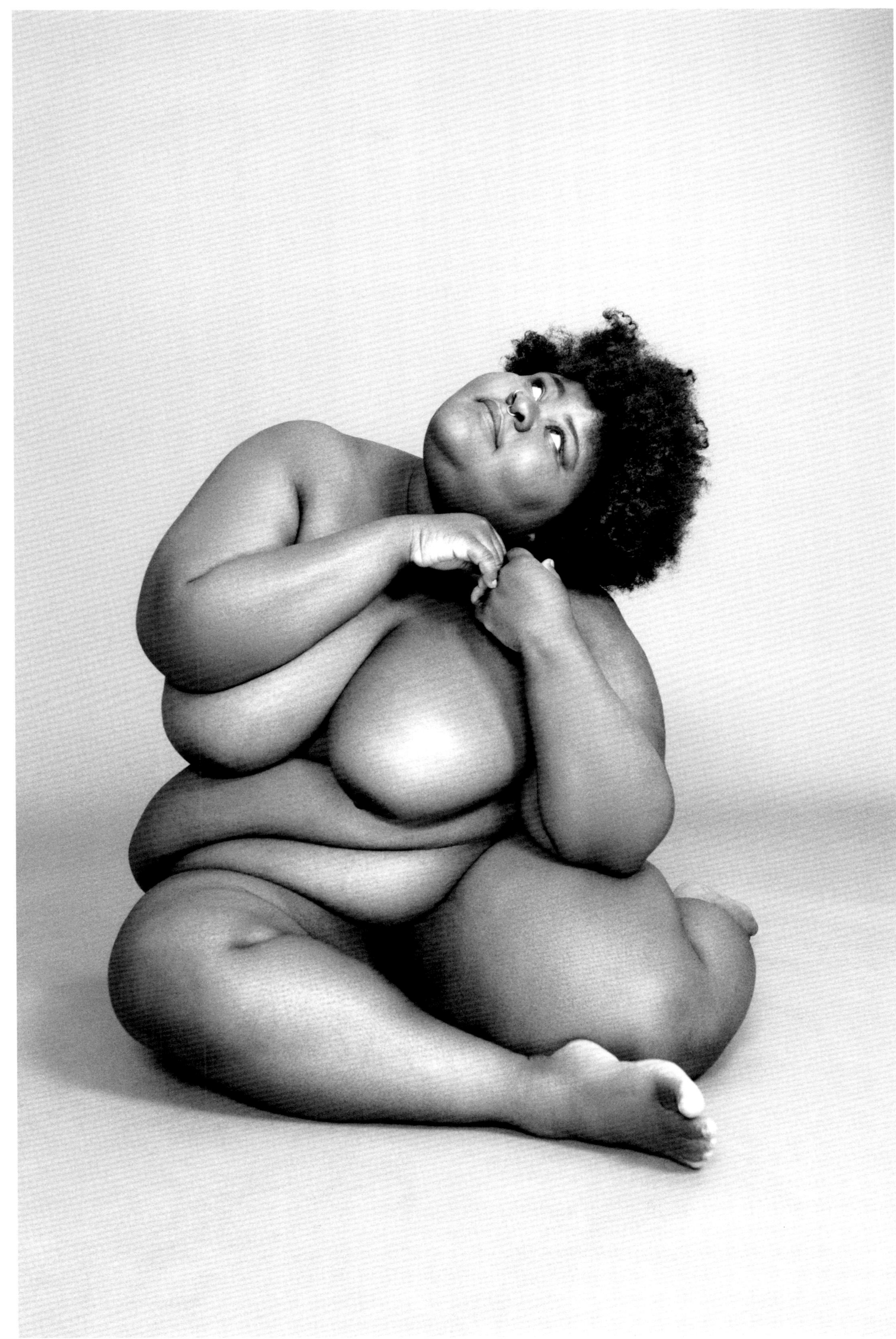

Rochelle, April 2016

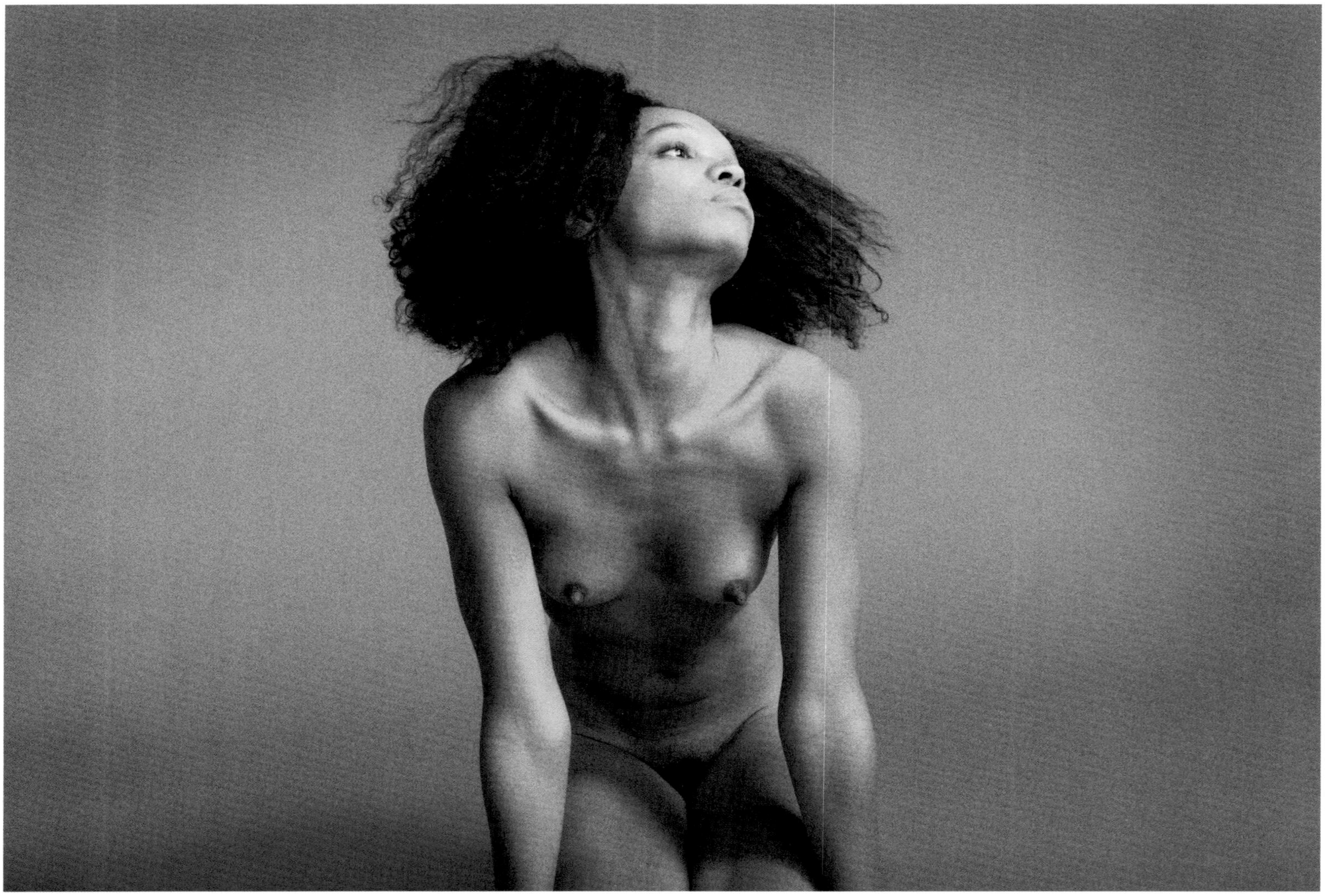

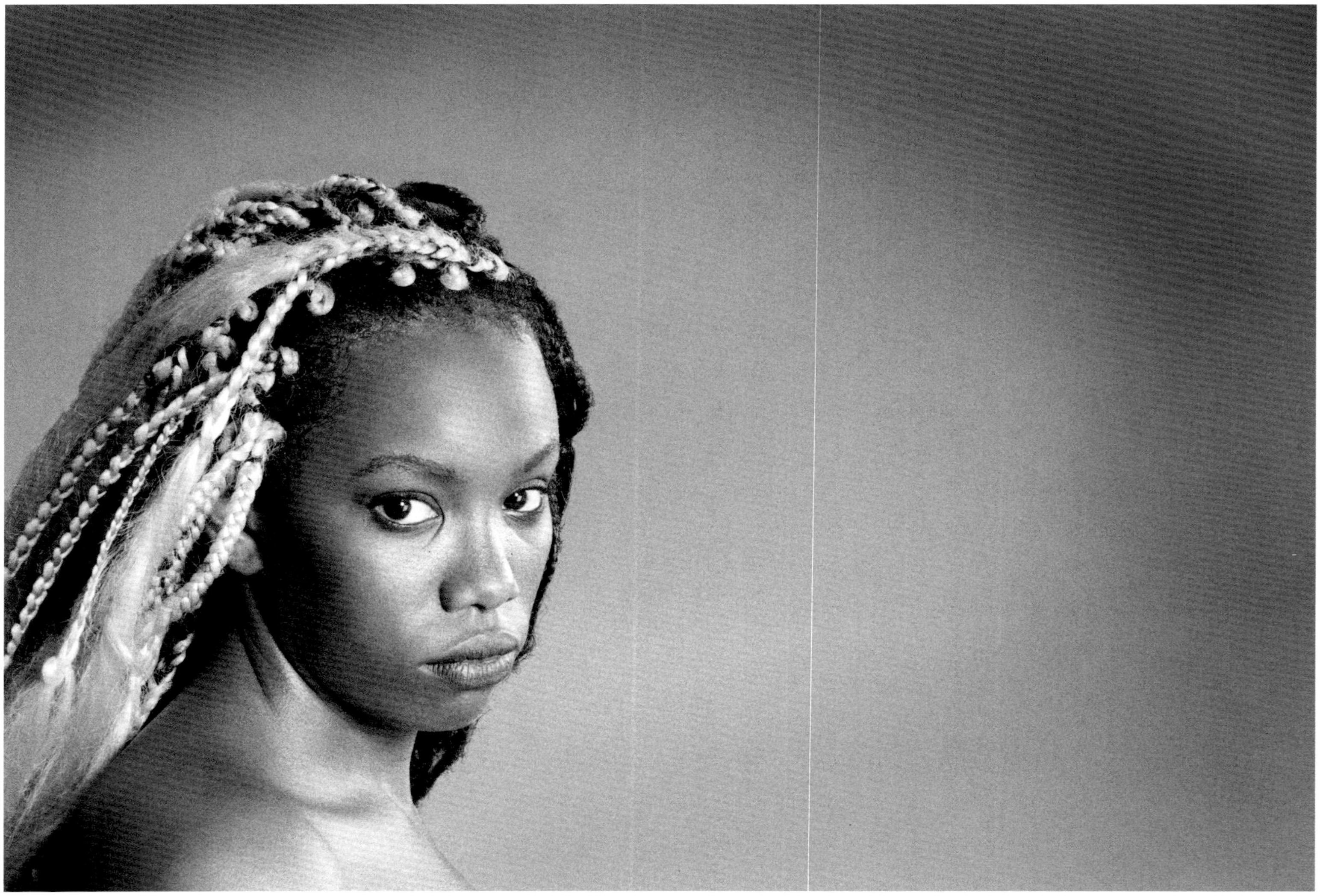

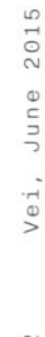

Taryn, July 2012   Vei, June 2015

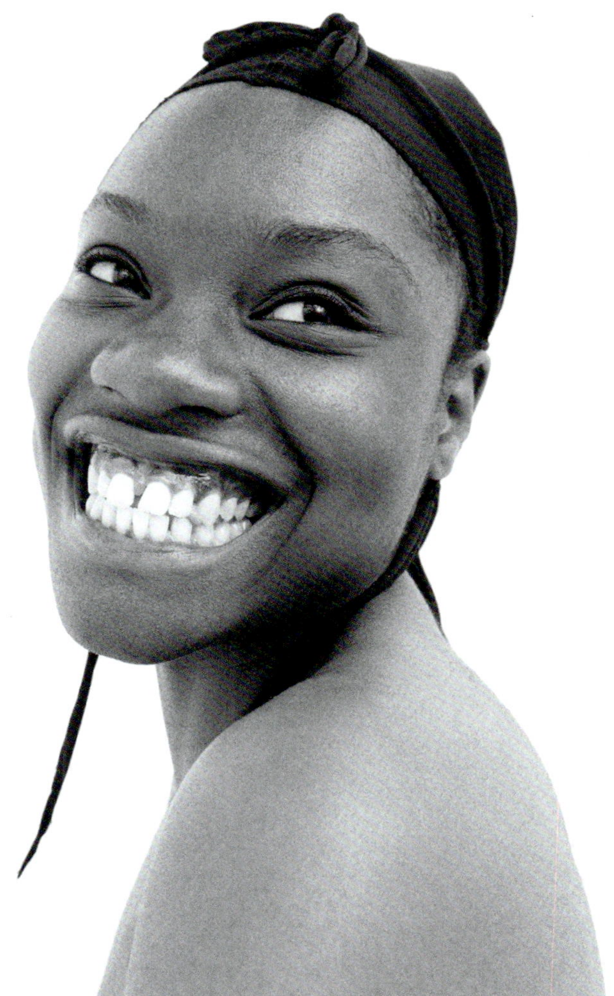

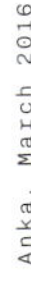

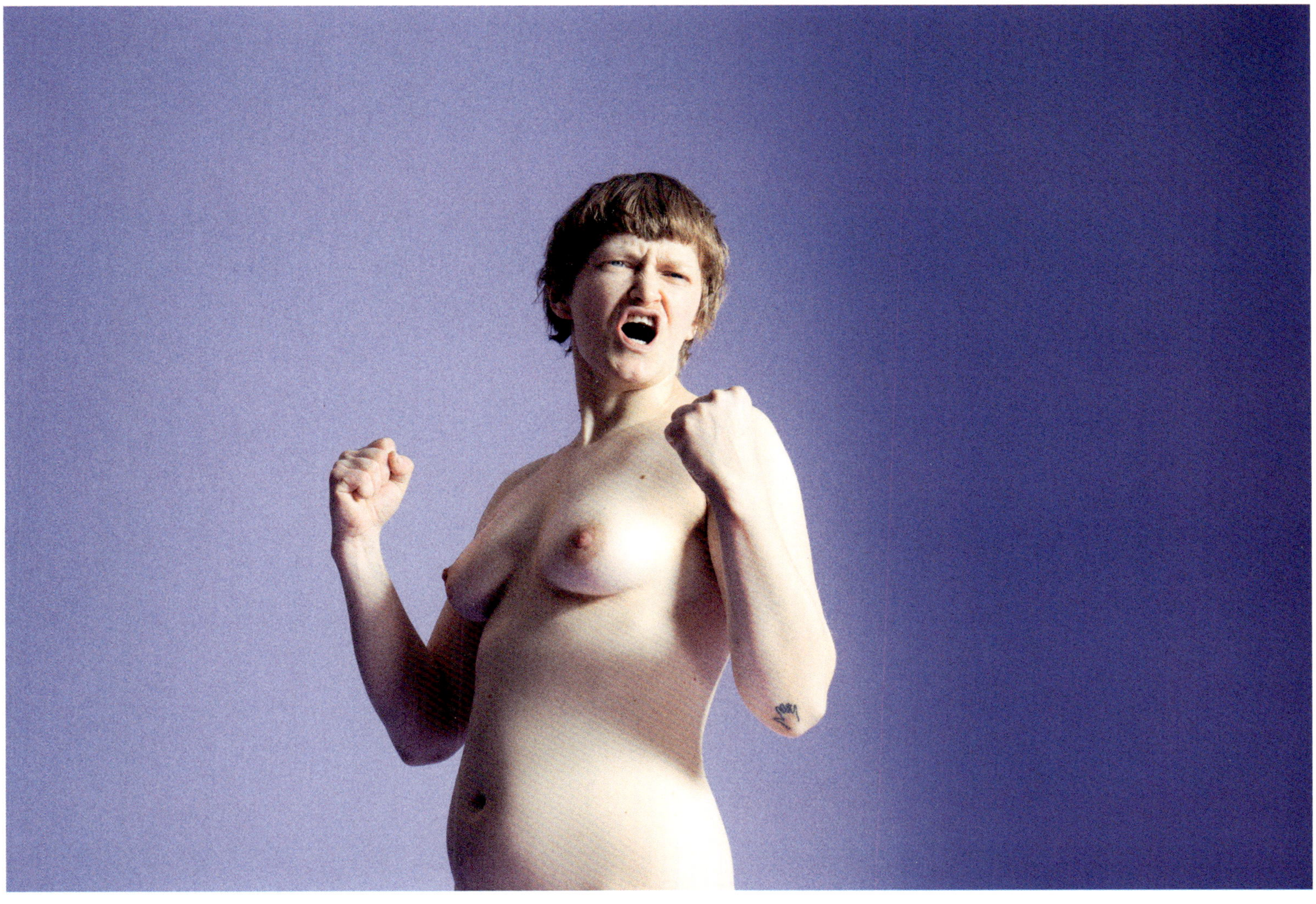

Rock, July 2017

Anka, March 2016

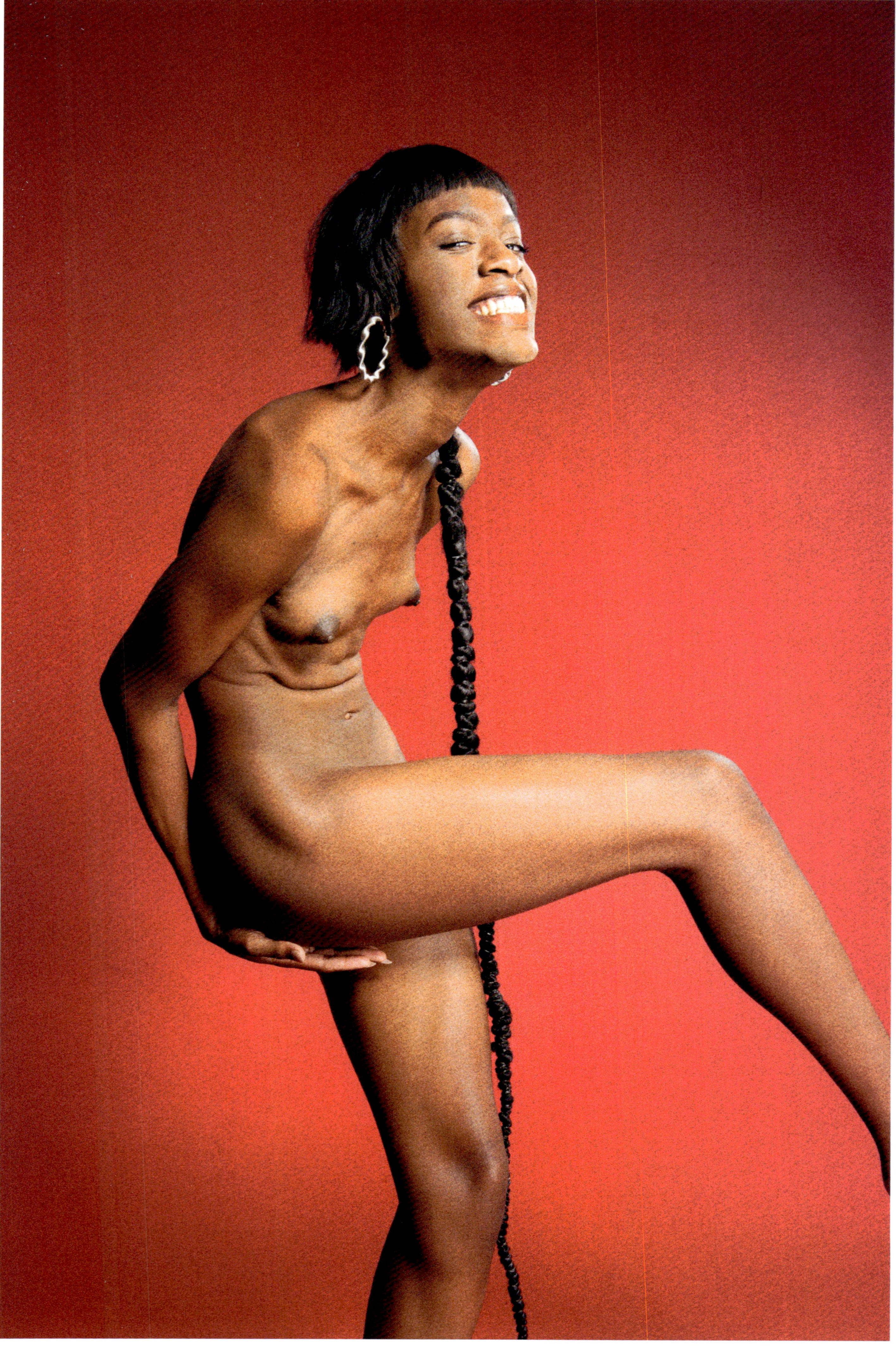

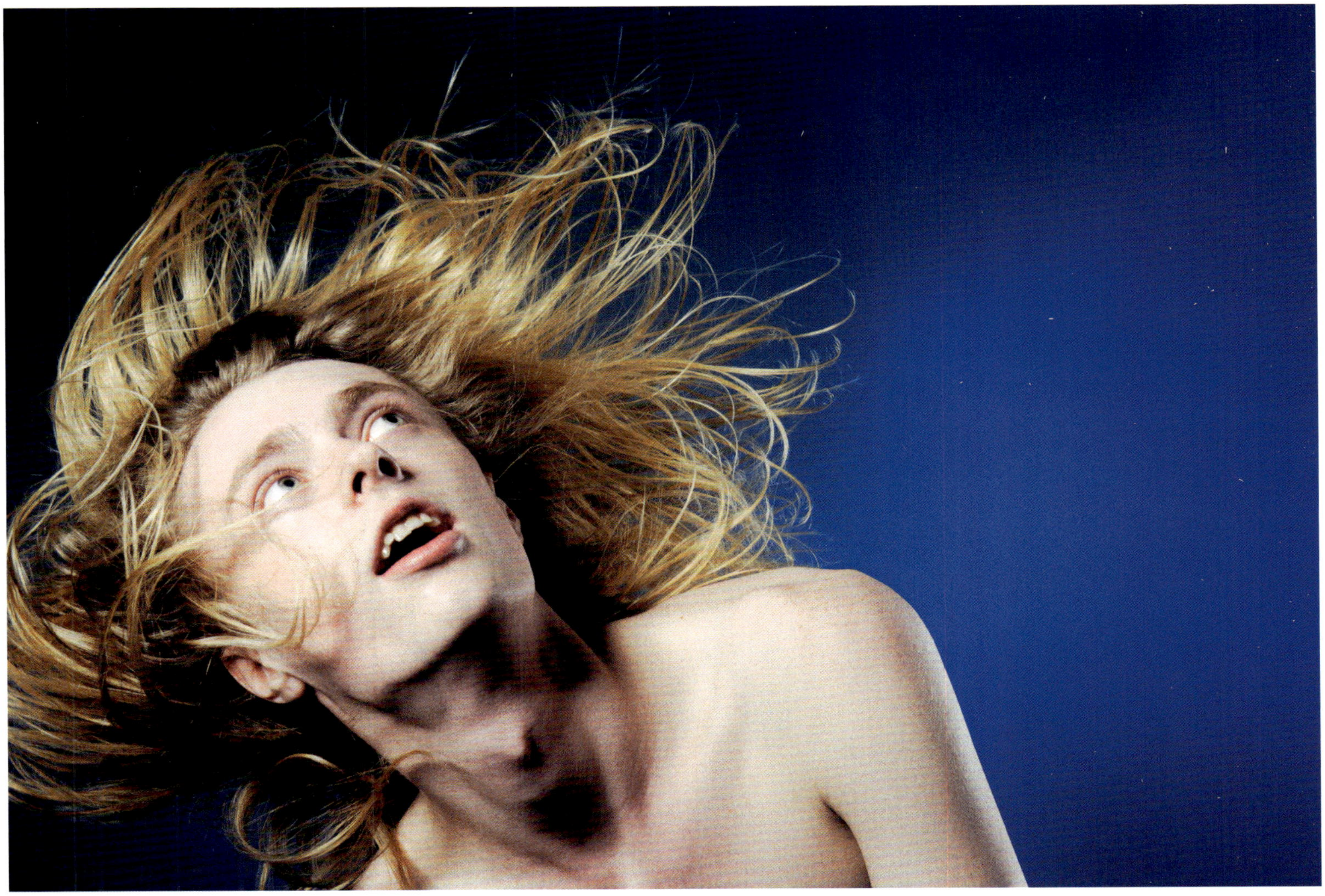

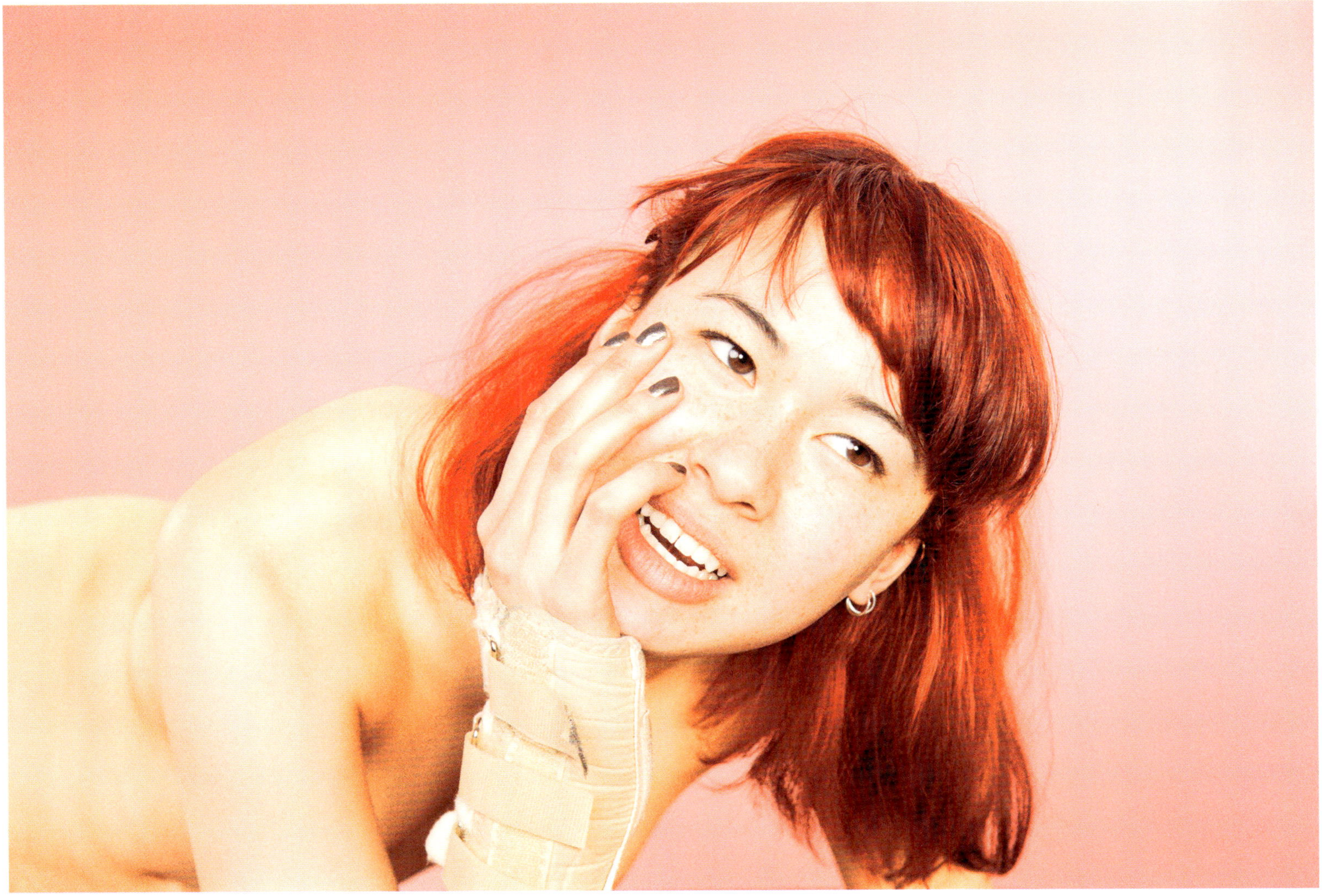

Jacob, July 2015 Erin, March 2011

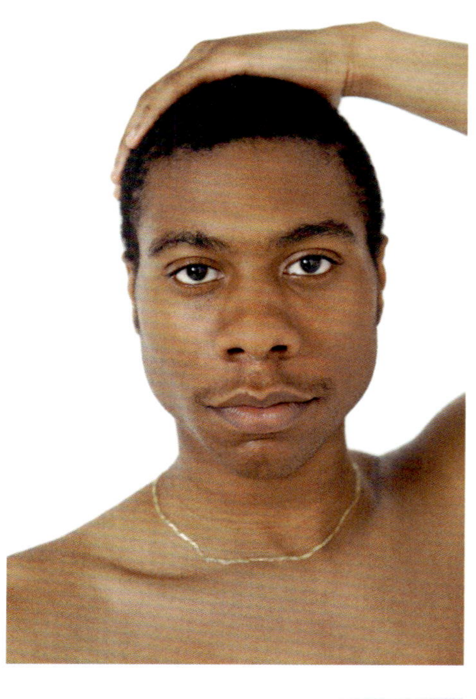

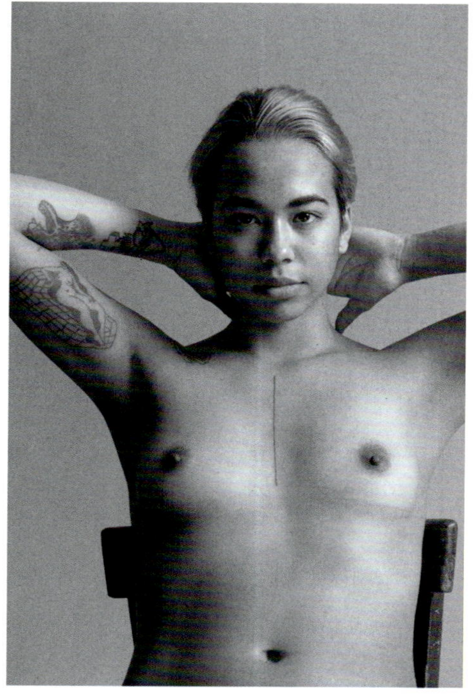

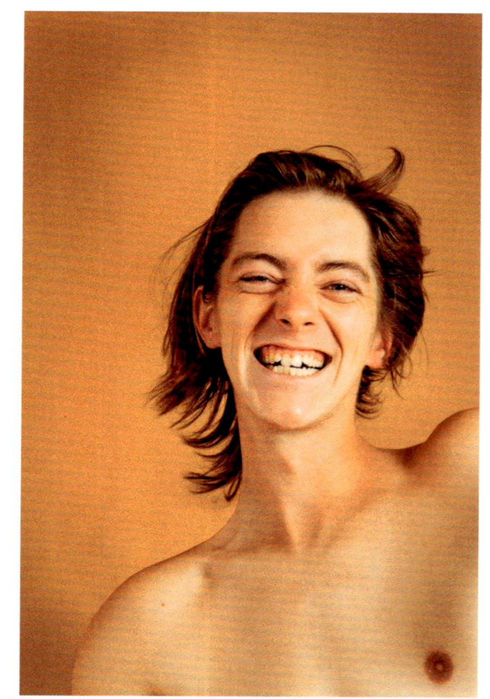

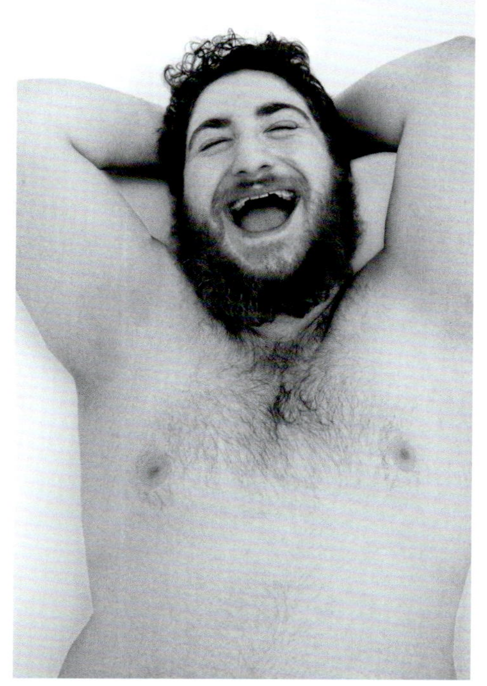

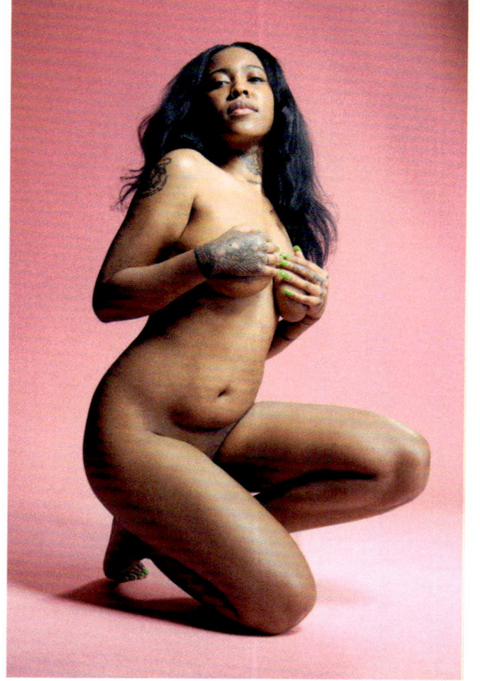

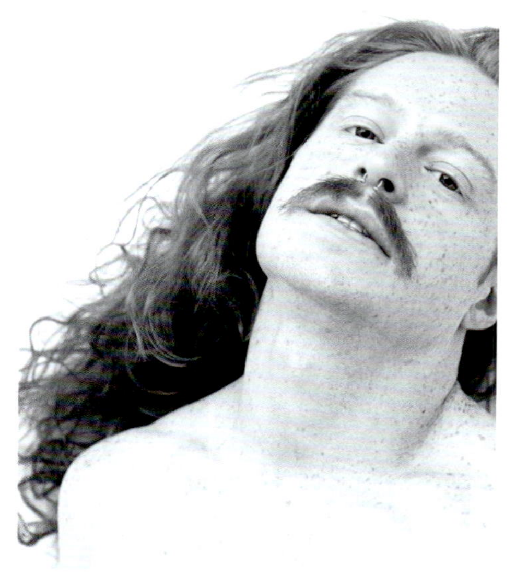

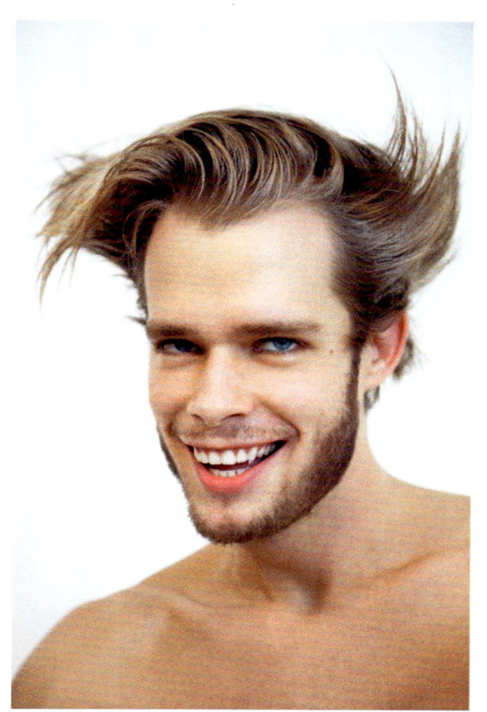

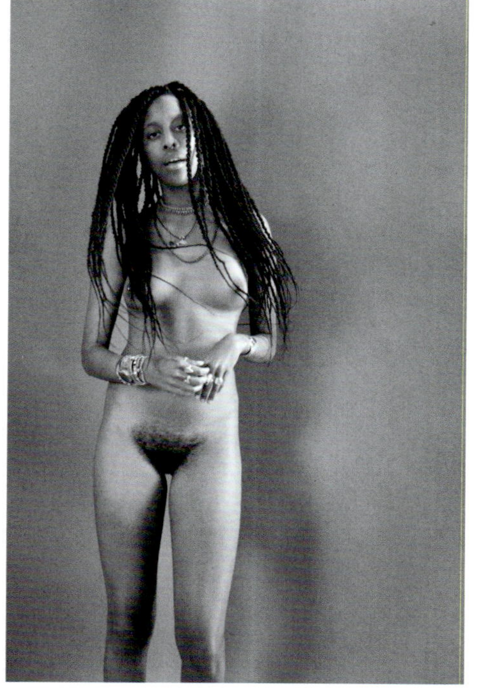

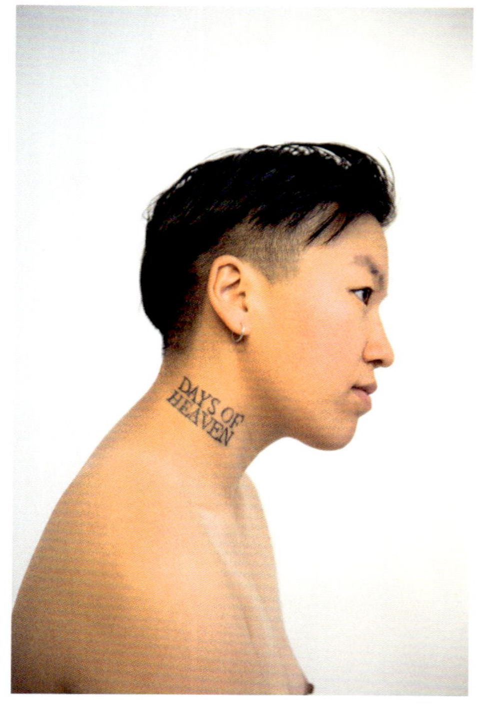

Orrin, April 2017 Chloe, February 2016 Dennis, September 2011 Hunter, June 2017 Euphoria, June 2015 Patrick, July 2017 Andrew, December 2018 Mayan, September 2016 Yoma, October 2018

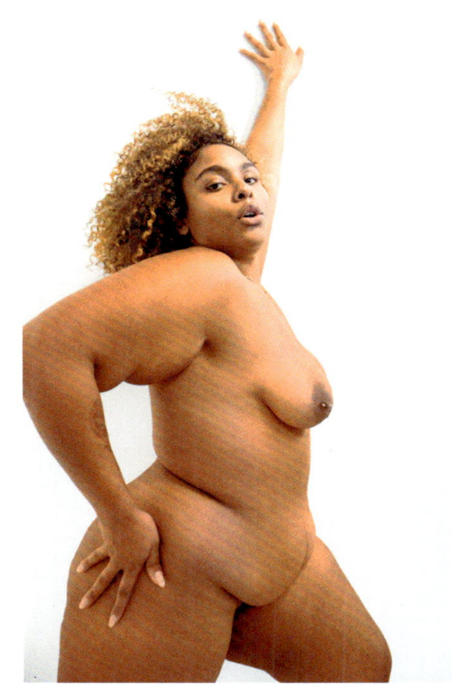

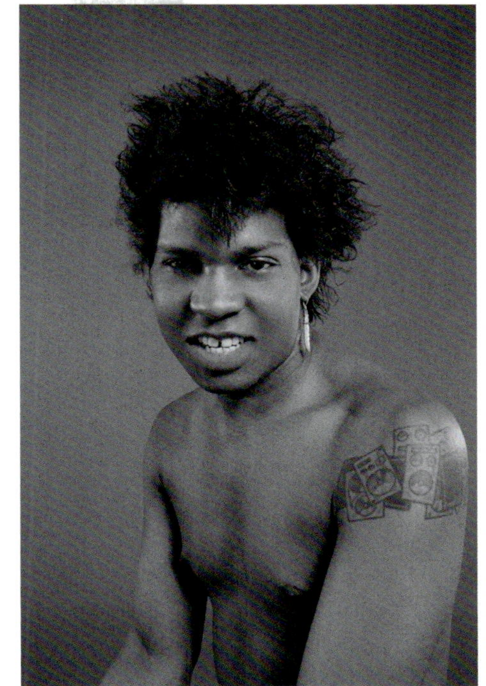

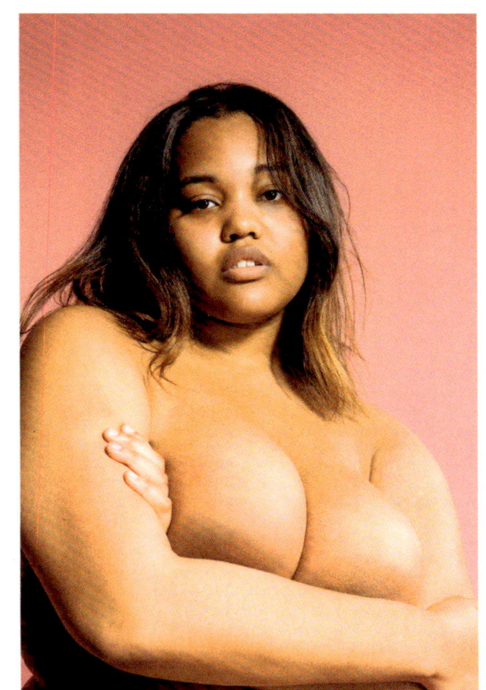

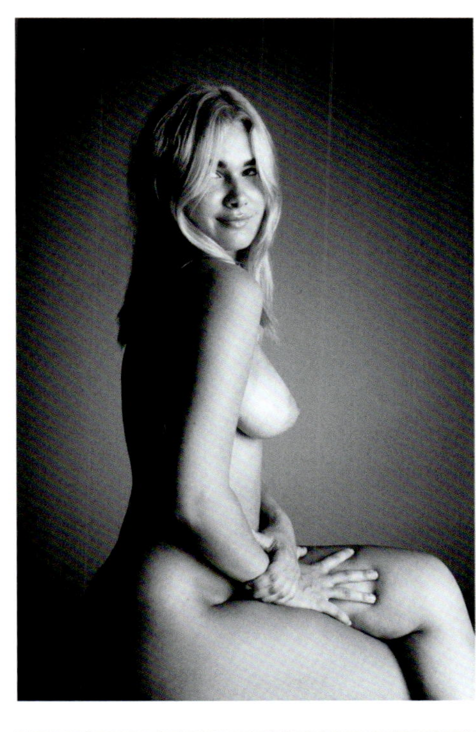

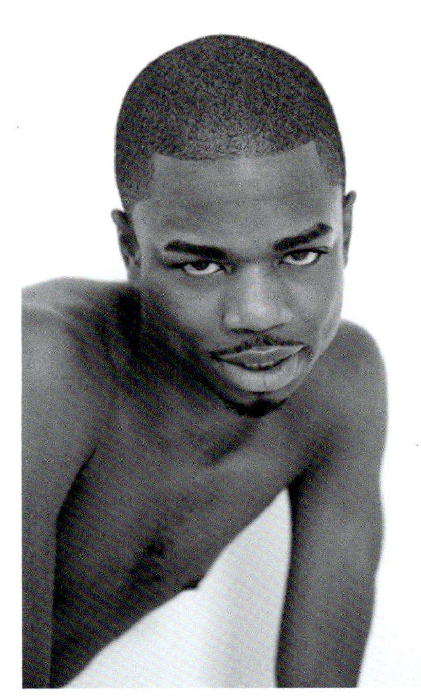

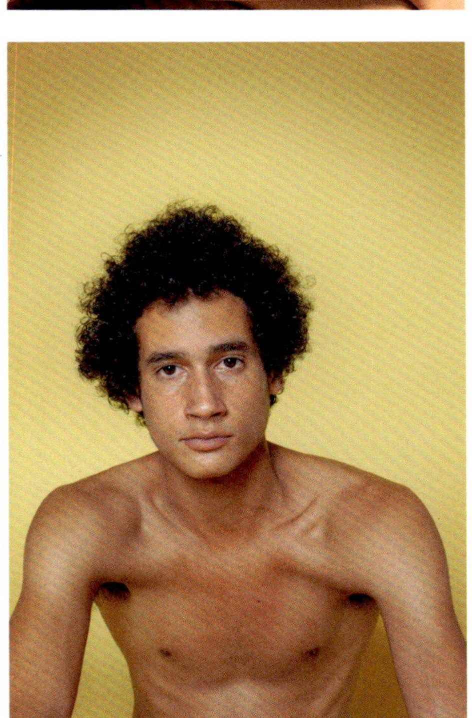

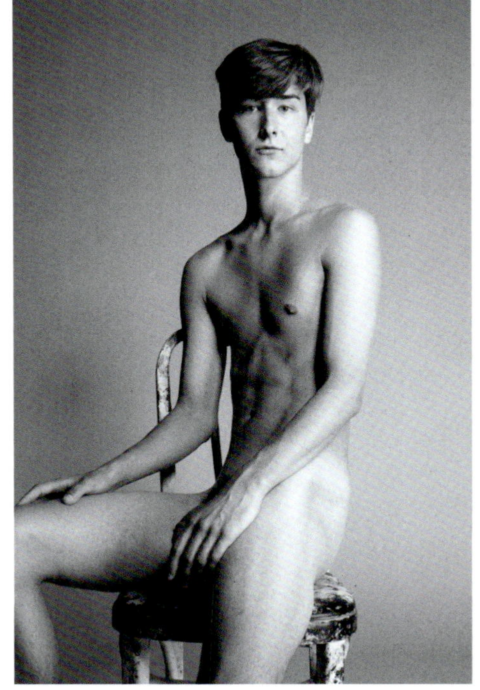

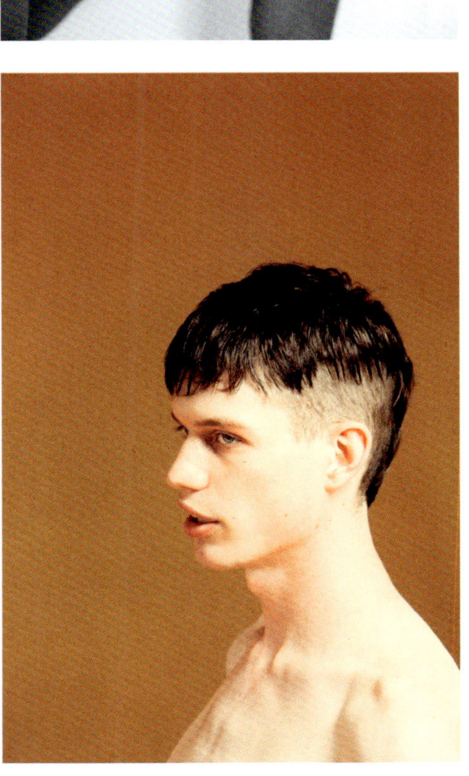

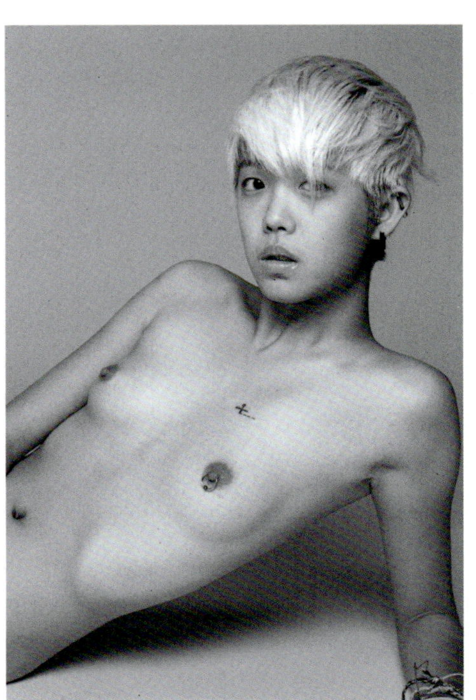

Kendra, October 2019   Terry, February 2013   Charisse, January 2016   Shawn, July 2015   Marquale, December 2018   Eric, August 2009   Ryan, April 2015   Jay, June 2012   Jen, November 2008

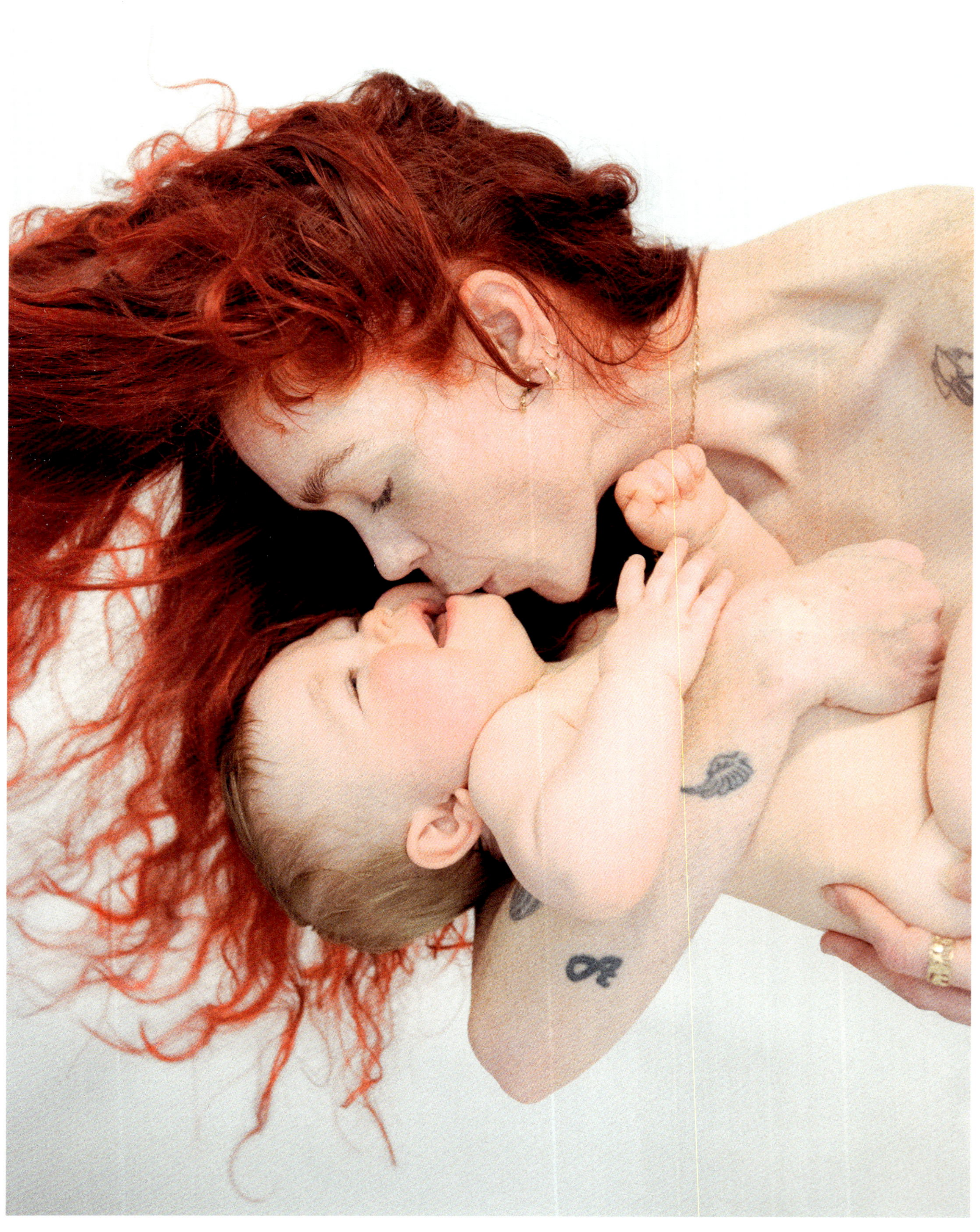

Maeve & Vashti, December 2019

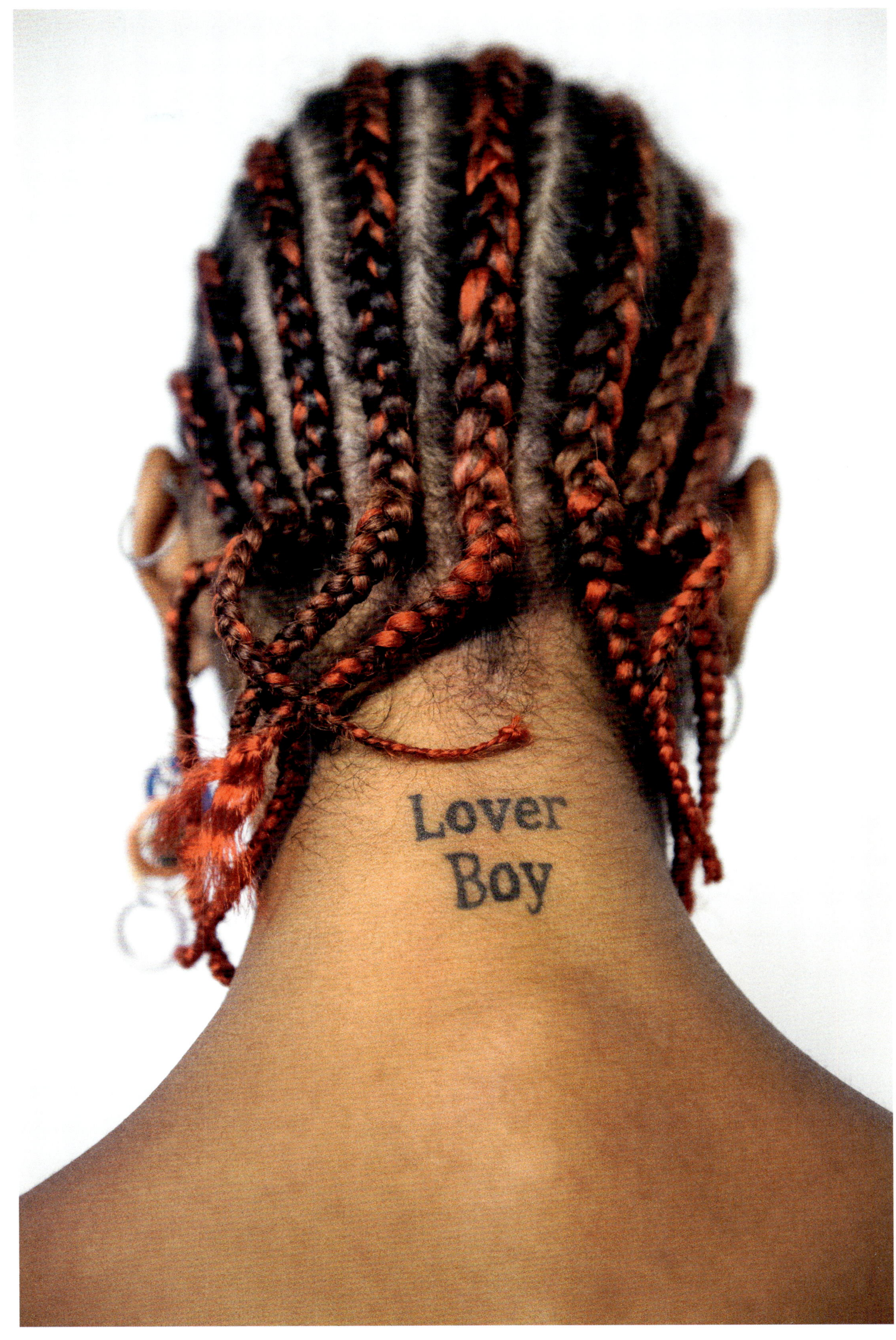

Anthony, October 2019

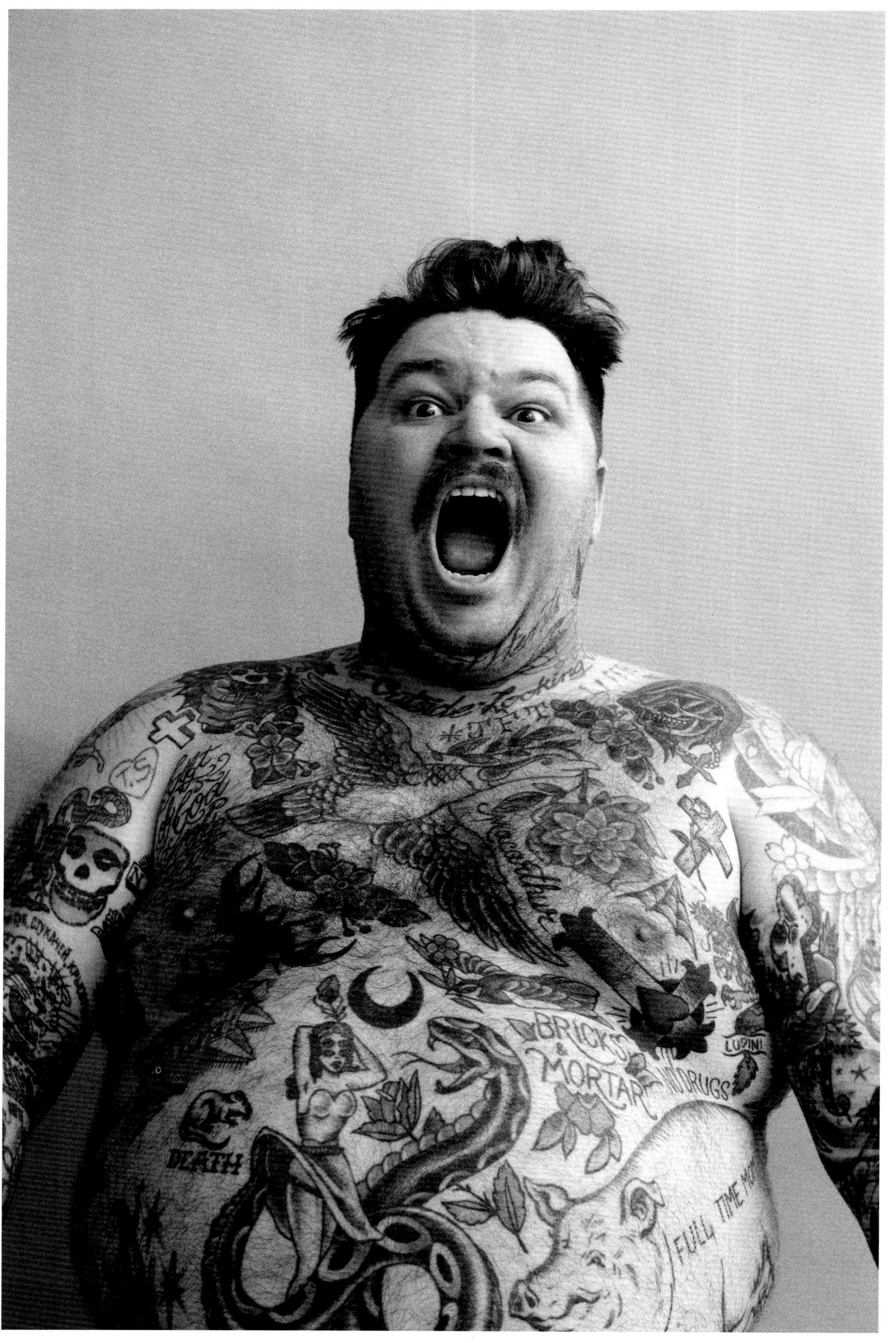

Matty, January 2018

I grew up in a small Canadian border town across from Buffalo. It was all ice fishing, running around on a Ski-Doo, and running through the woods and away from coyotes. A hardcore scene, subs from the gas station, and little family restaurants. I barely graduated from high school. I had to negotiate with my vice principal to just get out. I got accepted into culinary school. I was good at it. Every opportunity in my life has come from food.

After college, I worked at Le Sélect Bistro, which was across the street from the *Vice* store in Toronto. Le Sélect was a haven for artists, singers, painters, and poets. I'd never hung out with cultured adults like that before. I was a punk, hardcore kid. I was like, "You're a jazz singer? You paint?" I'd never been to a play. Everyone smoked French cigarettes and drank fucking tons of wine.

Vice was everything. I'd hang out at the store before work and party there afterward. I met a lot of people through *Vice*. I remember seeing Dash, Kunle, Ryan, Colen, and the hamster shit—Ryan's photos in *Vice*—and thinking, "This is it. This is what we want to do. We want to go to houses and smash stuff. We want to party. I want to get punched in the face and knocked out. I want to shove blow in my ass. That was the epitome of youth, ignorant youth. Photography like that is still the sickest thing. All people want to do is look at people. They want to judge them, lust over them. They want to love them. They want to hate them. There's nothing more original than a photo of a human.

I don't take my shirt off for anyone anymore. After I did it once, every photographer wanted me to take my shirt off and "scream" or "do something crazy." Shooting with Ryan was amazing because of the movement. He had Luisa helping him. They gave me direction and got me to move. I don't take my shirt off anymore though. There are things where I'm just like, "I'm done with that." There was an end to my *Vice* era, too.

Being a plus-size man, a big dog, is a double-edged sword. There are highs and lows. I've always been big, it's all I've known. I've two brothers who I always say are like greyhounds. They're all ribs and dick; skinny, ripped. I was the fat brother, cool. My brothers looked the same. Why would I want to look like them? I learned to use being fat early on, making fun of myself, using physical comedy, shoving shit in my face. [Chris] Farley was my God. I'm probably very confident for someone my size. I'm just a thick dude and I'm attracted to it. I think it's hot. I think skinny people are dweebs. If seeing me helps people—and I understand that it does—amazing. They should feel sexy as shit. I'm going to keep being me.

I'm very indifferent to fame, I'll tell you that much. I come from nothing. My parents worked really hard and still got nothing. I want to be able to provide for my entire family, and if I'm able to use my fame to make money, I'll continue to do that. That's it. Chef Matty is a brand: kitchen cultures, party hardy, hospitality every day. But we're spiritual boys now, I'm not trying to do too many things to my body.

I used to want everyone to be drunk, fucked up, and full all the time. I wanted this Valhalla thing every day, but it's not sustainable. Recovery and really loving yourself is so crazy. We're up against ourselves that's the thing. You think you're up against the world, but we're just up against ourselves.

I don't live in LA or New York for a reason. I live in Ridgeway, Ontario. That's how I stay cool. I do my work and I go home. I focus on my family. Being a dad's the best. They don't tell you it's easily the hardest thing. You love this thing uncontrollably, and it's going to break your brain, scare you, and make you happier than you've ever been. When I come home and my kids open that door and start screaming, "Daddy," there's nothing better.

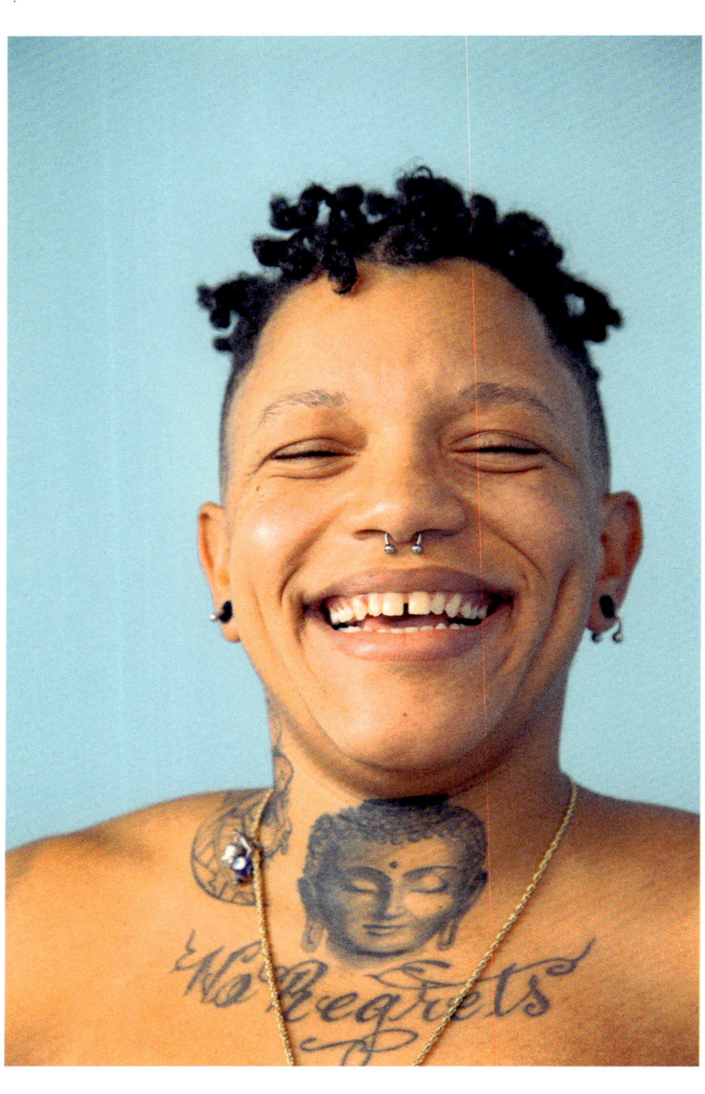

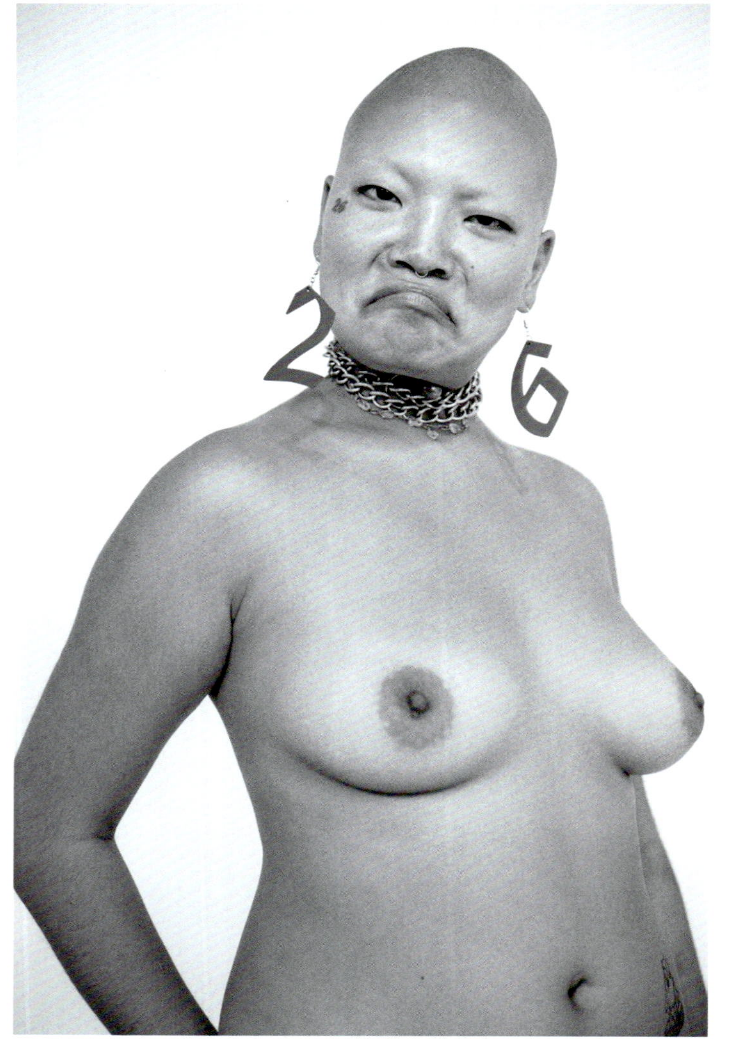

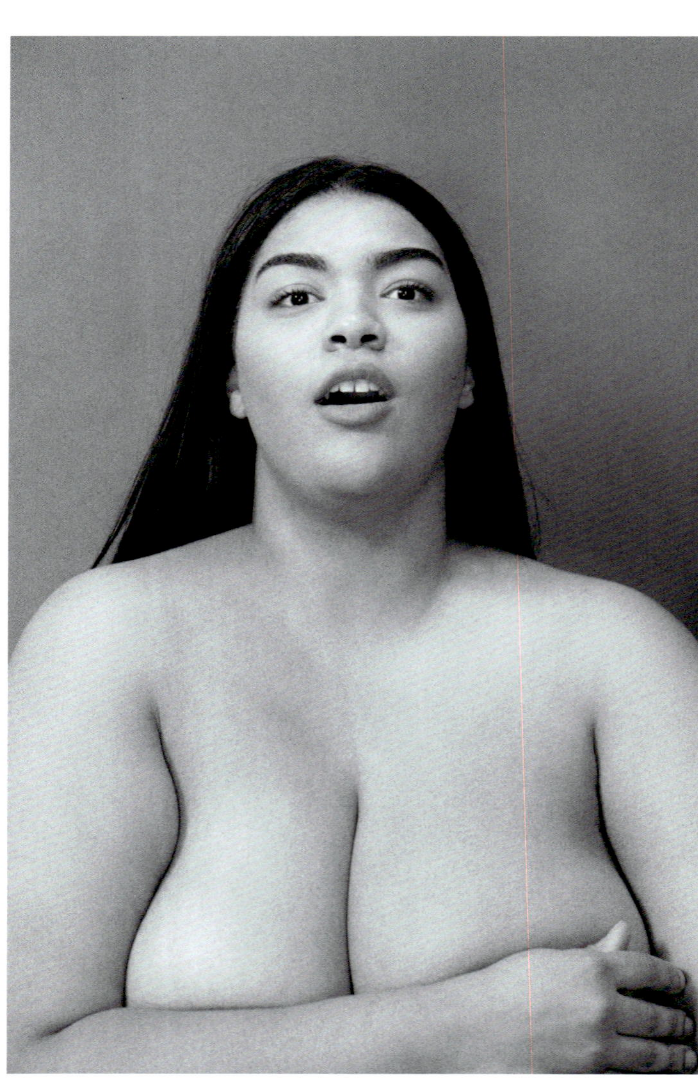

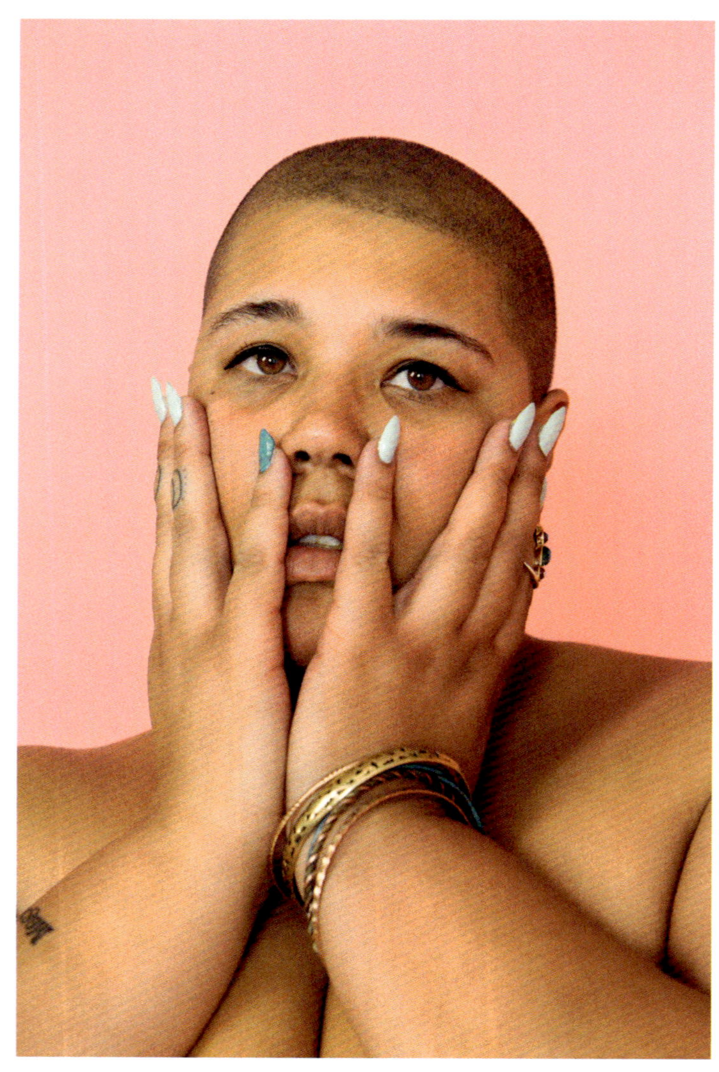

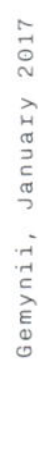
Kat, December 2016   Z, October 2019   Jovanna, November 2016   Gemynii, January 2017

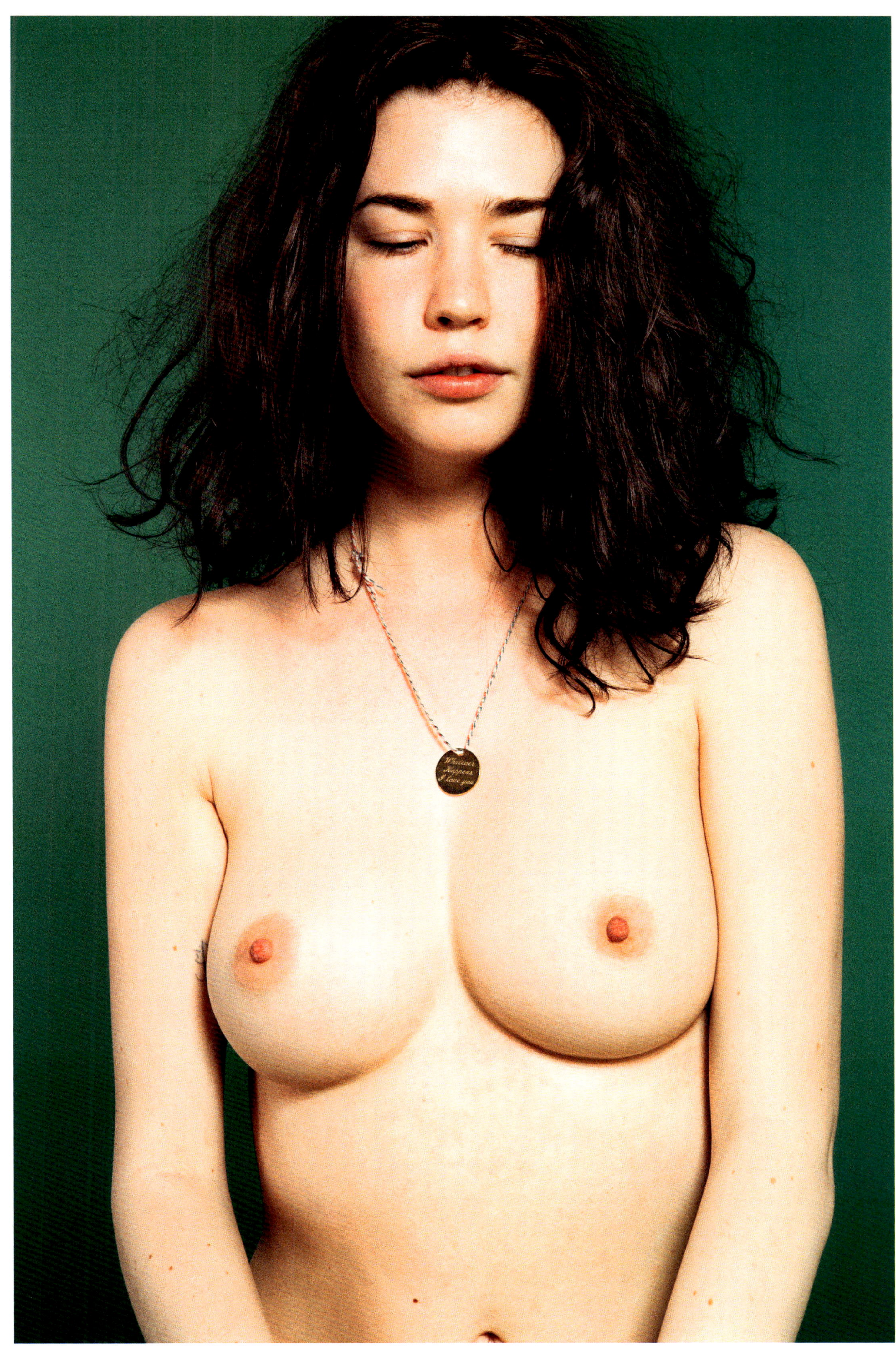

Sara, January 2012

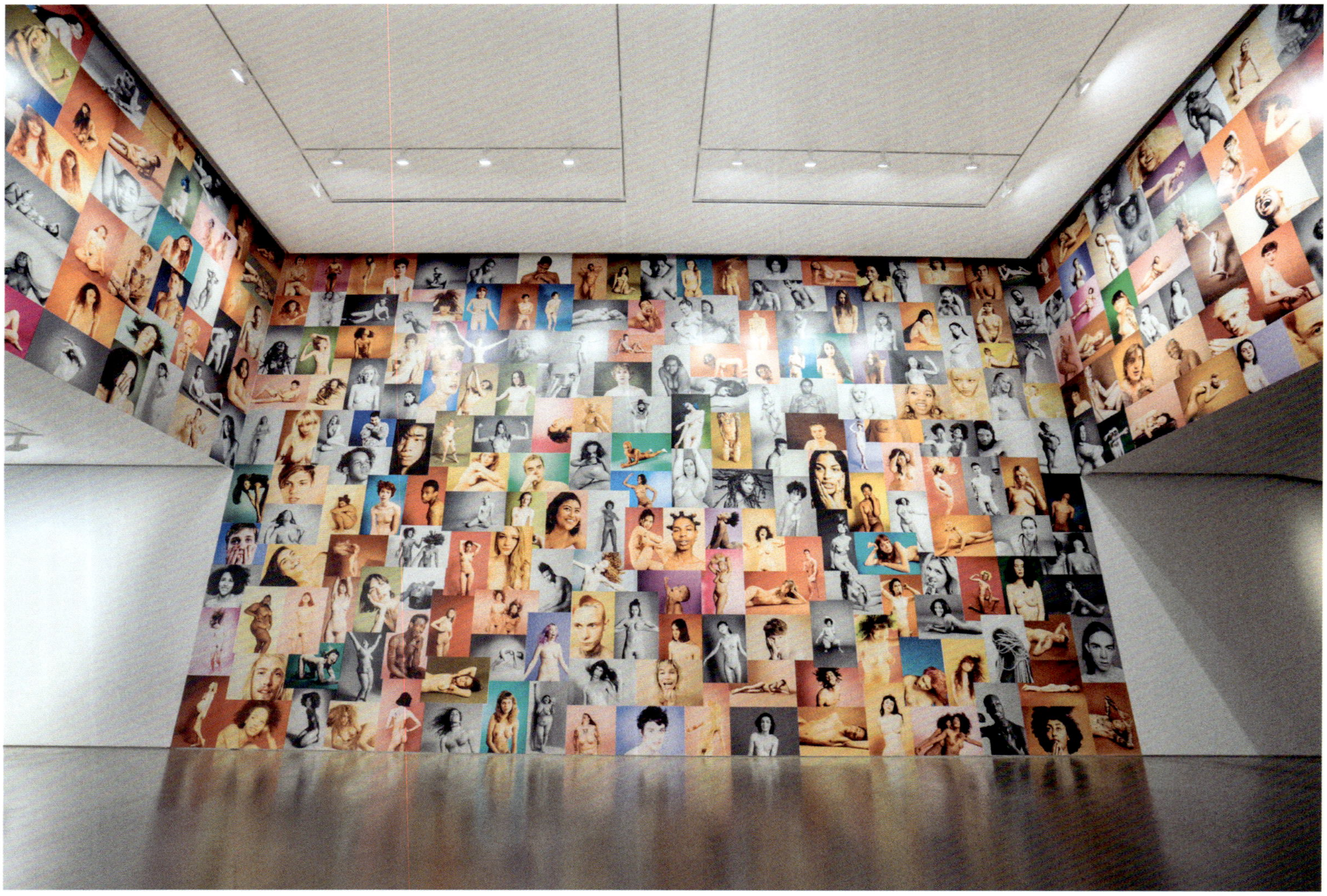

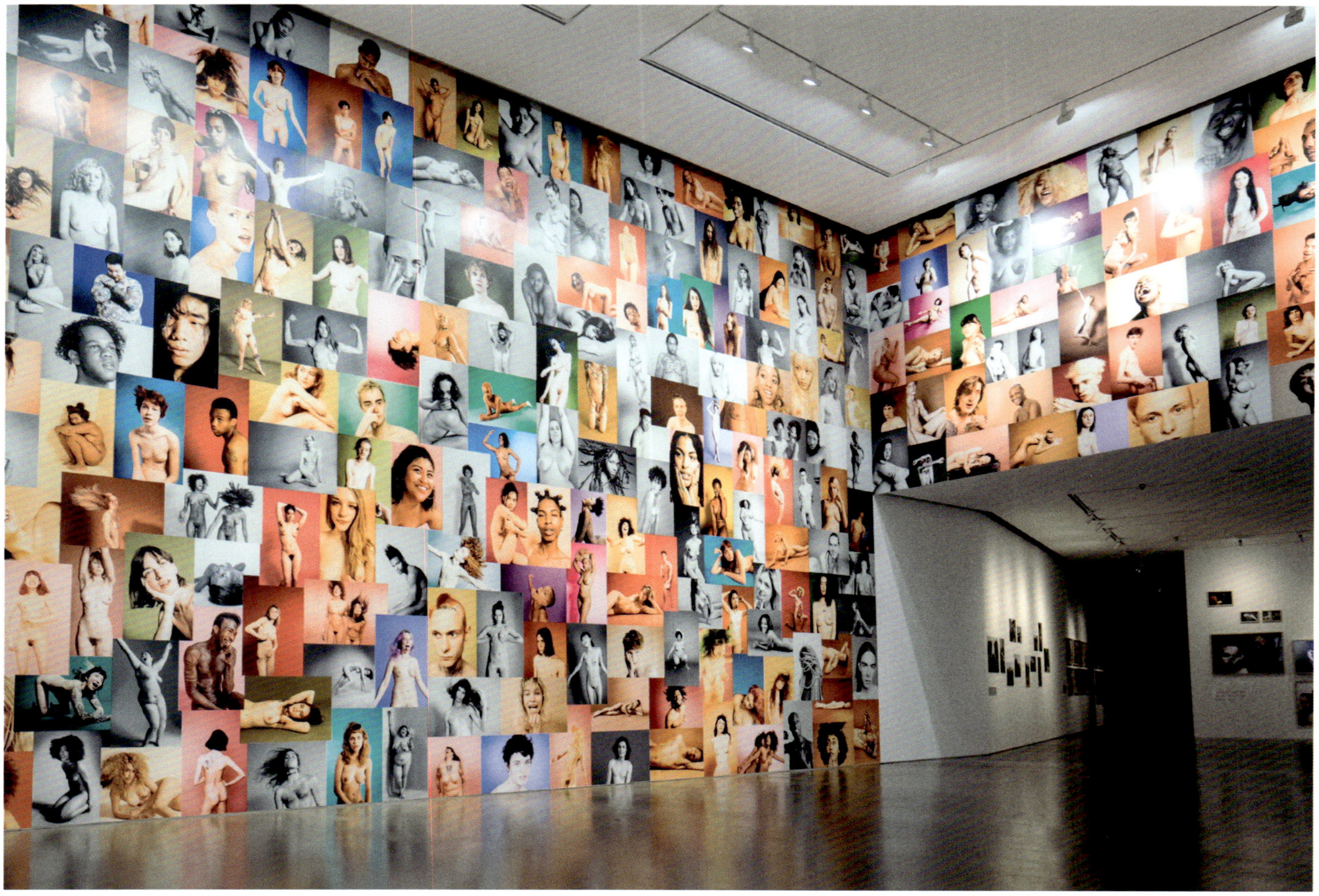

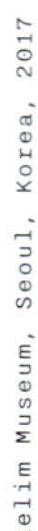
Daelim Museum, Seoul, Korea, 2017

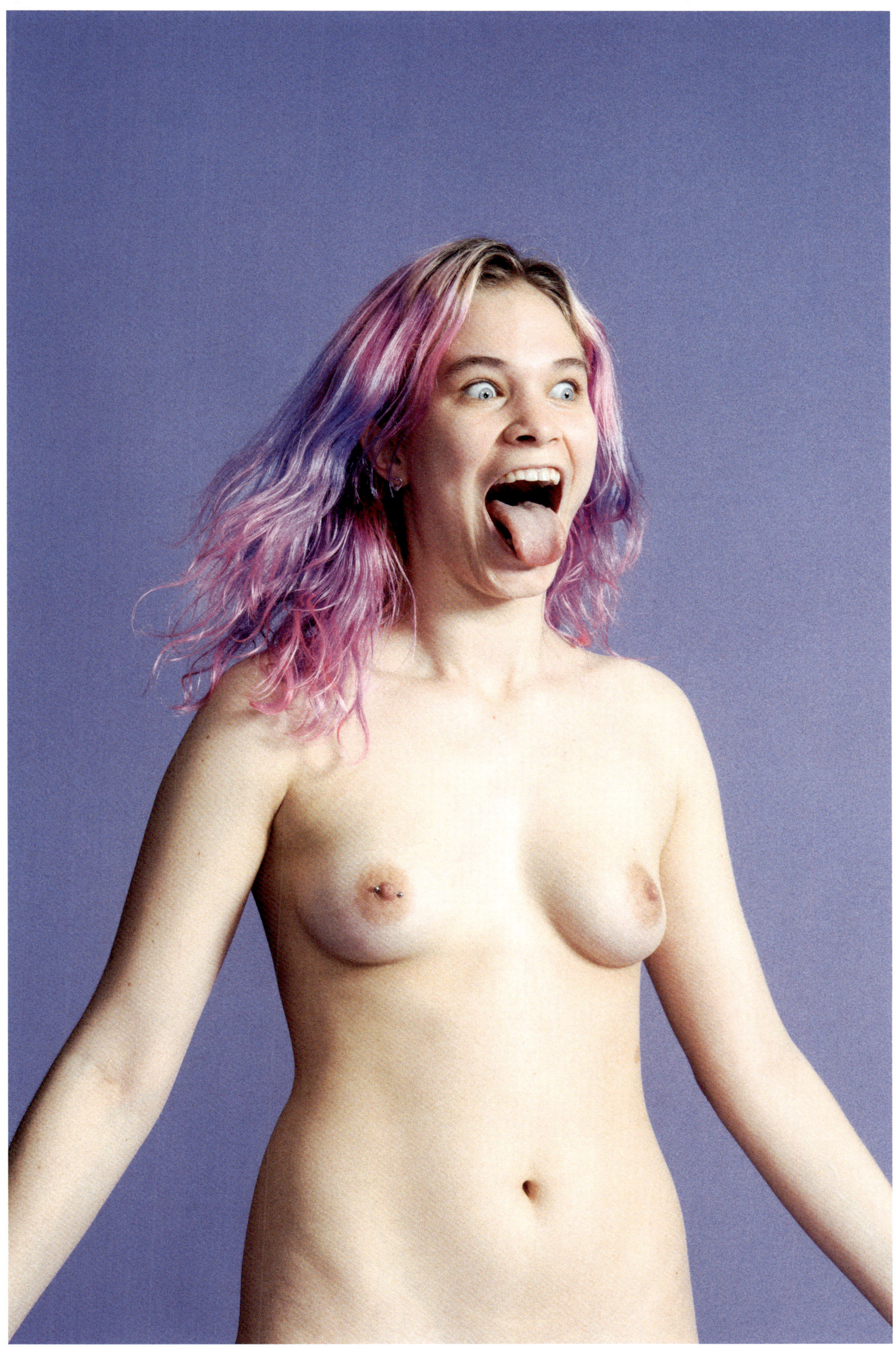

Eva, April 2016

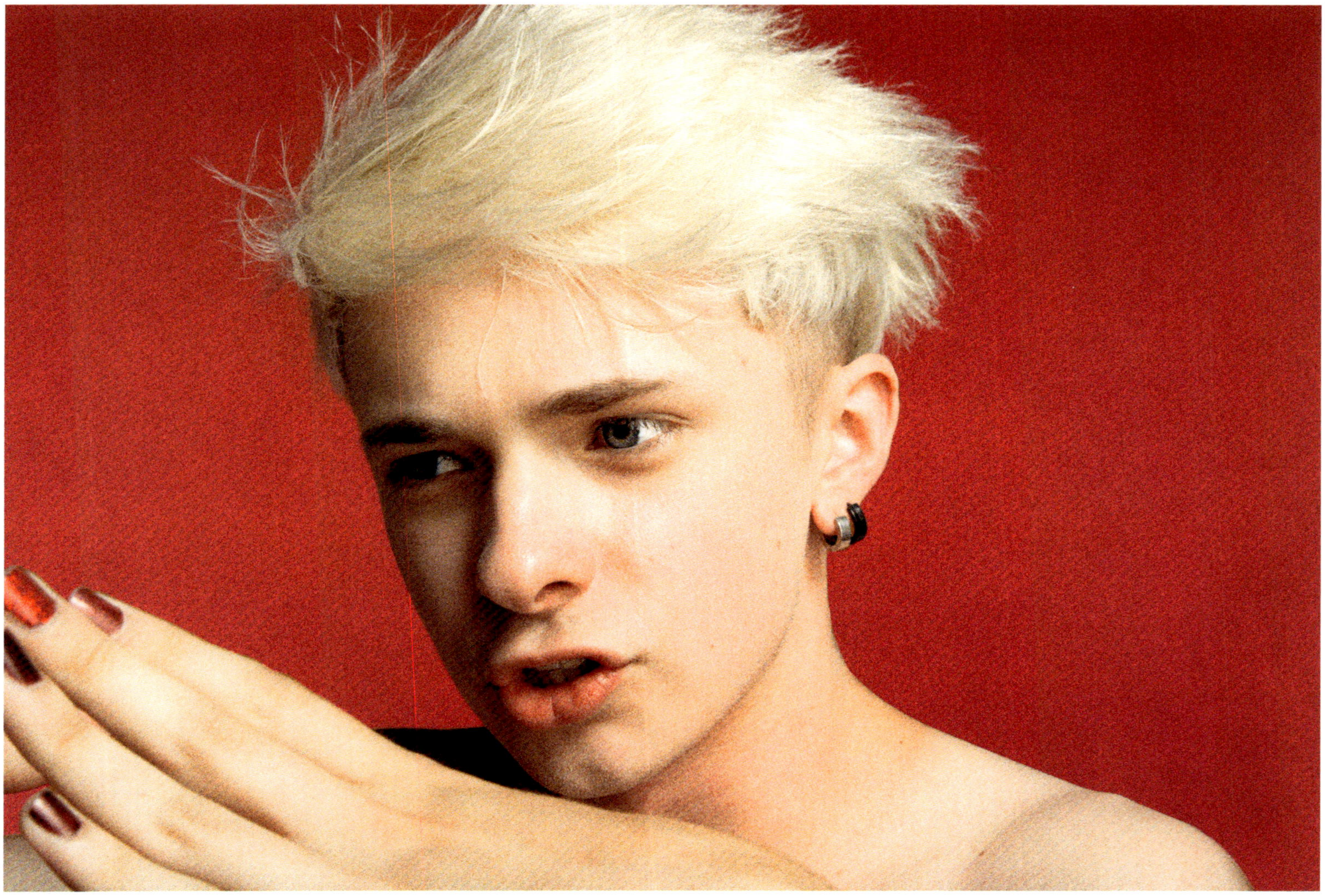

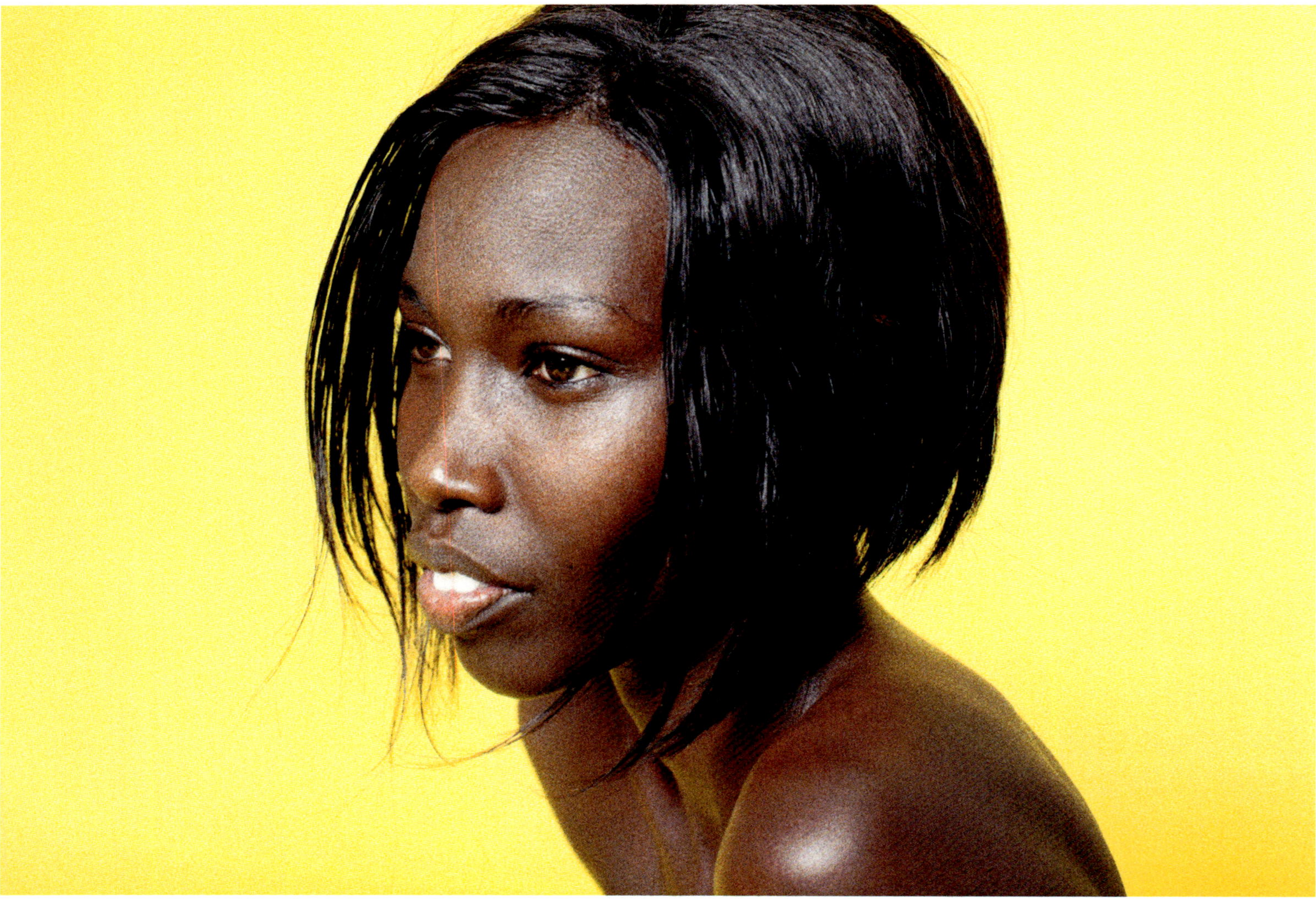

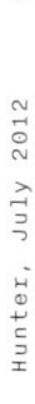
Hunter, July 2012

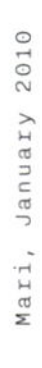
Mari, January 2010

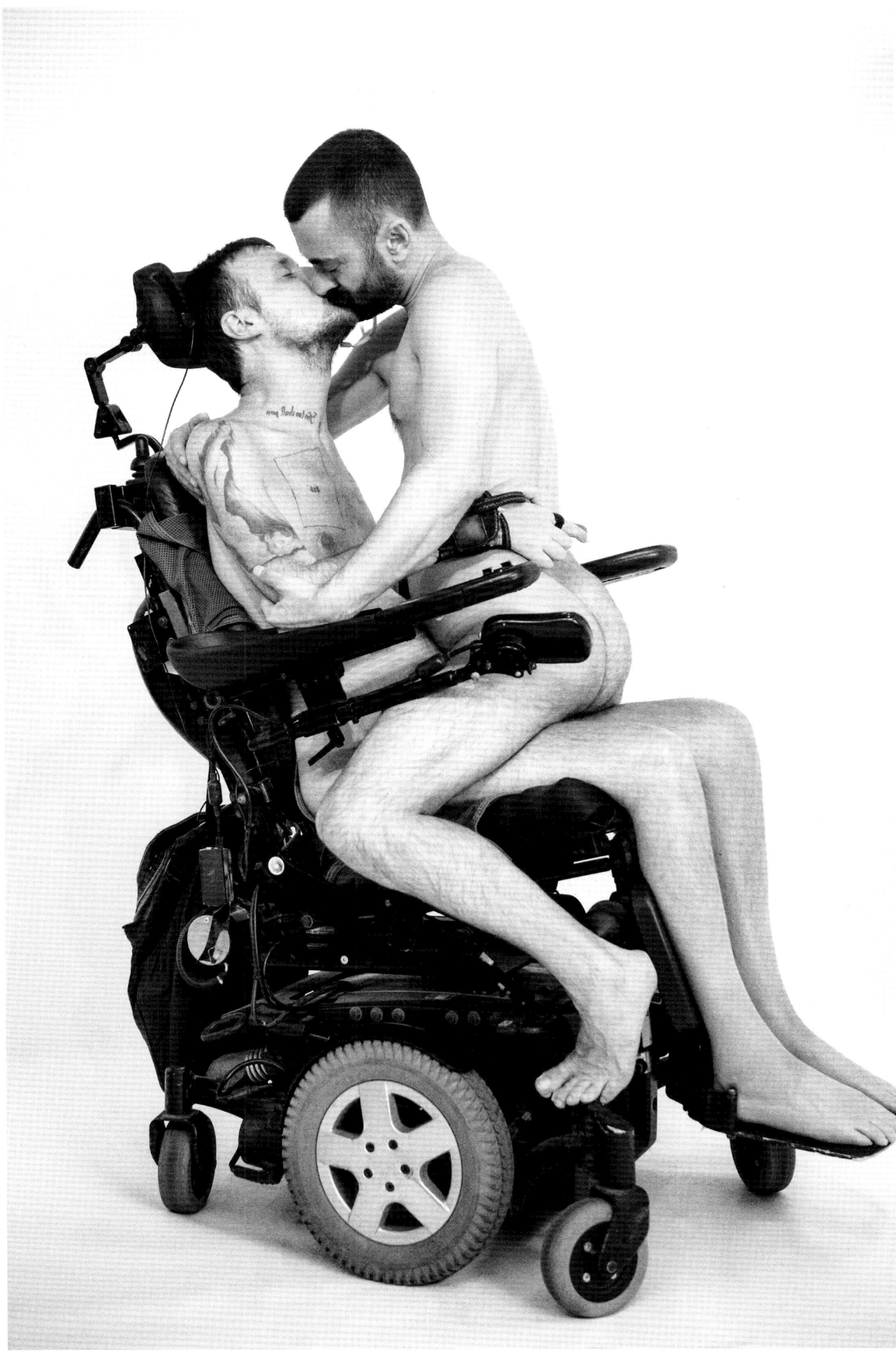

Robert & Benjamin, October 2019

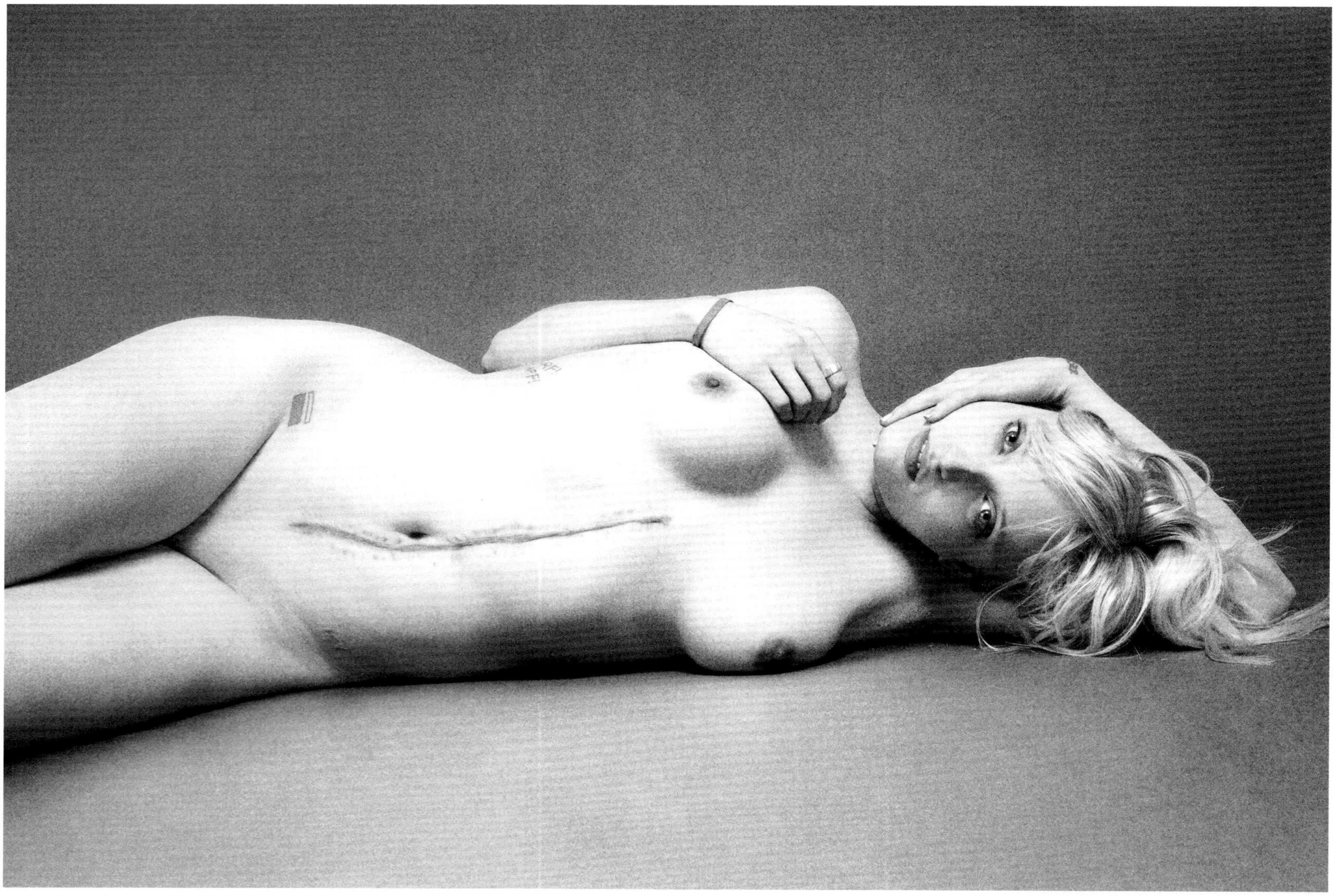

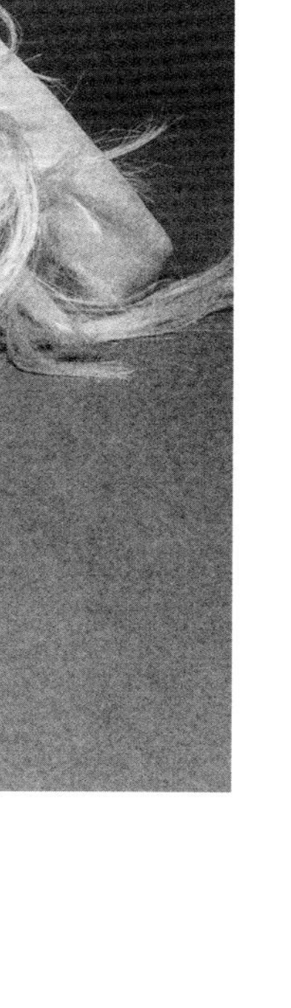

Kay, March 2012

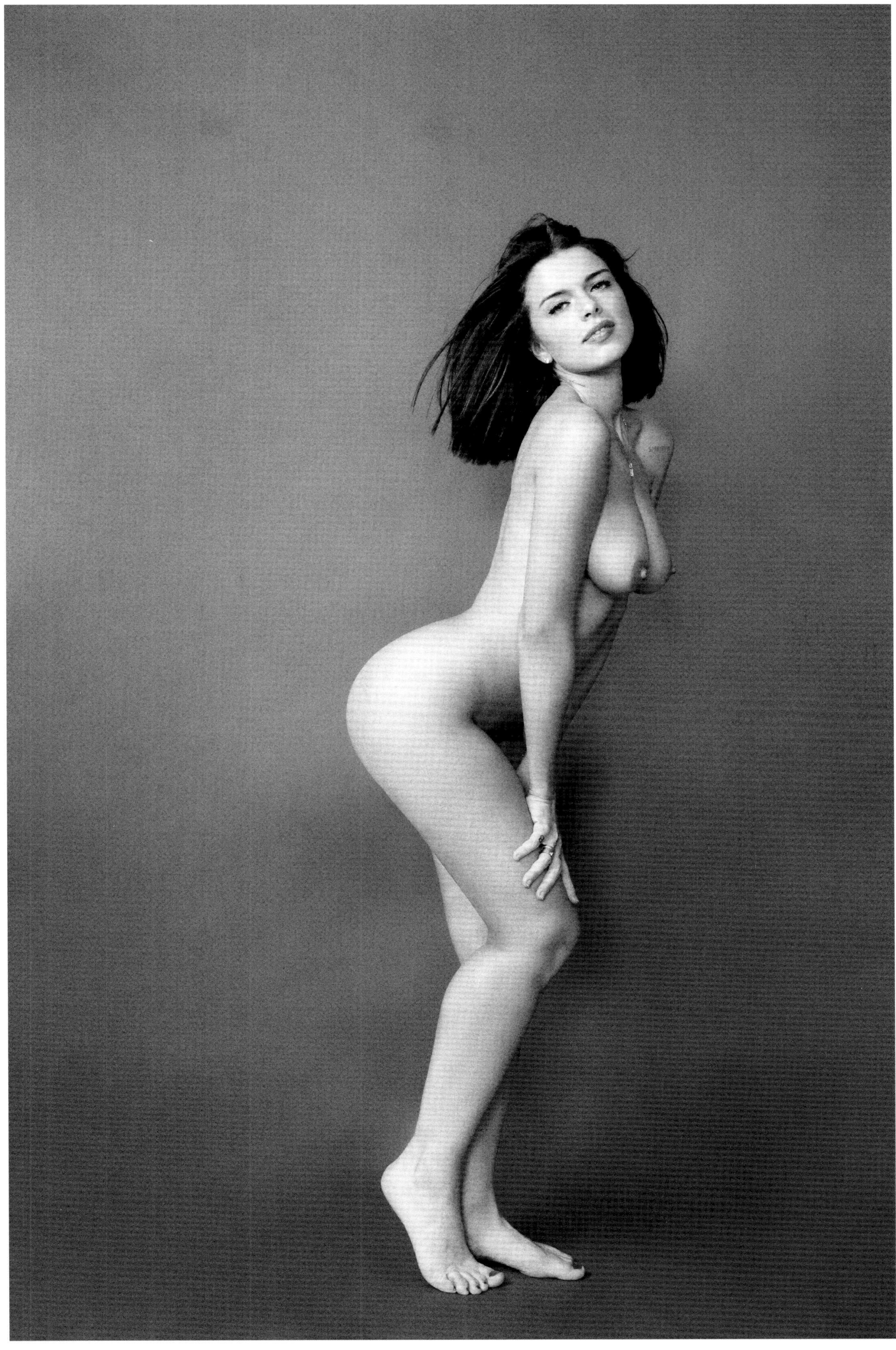

Julia, January 2017

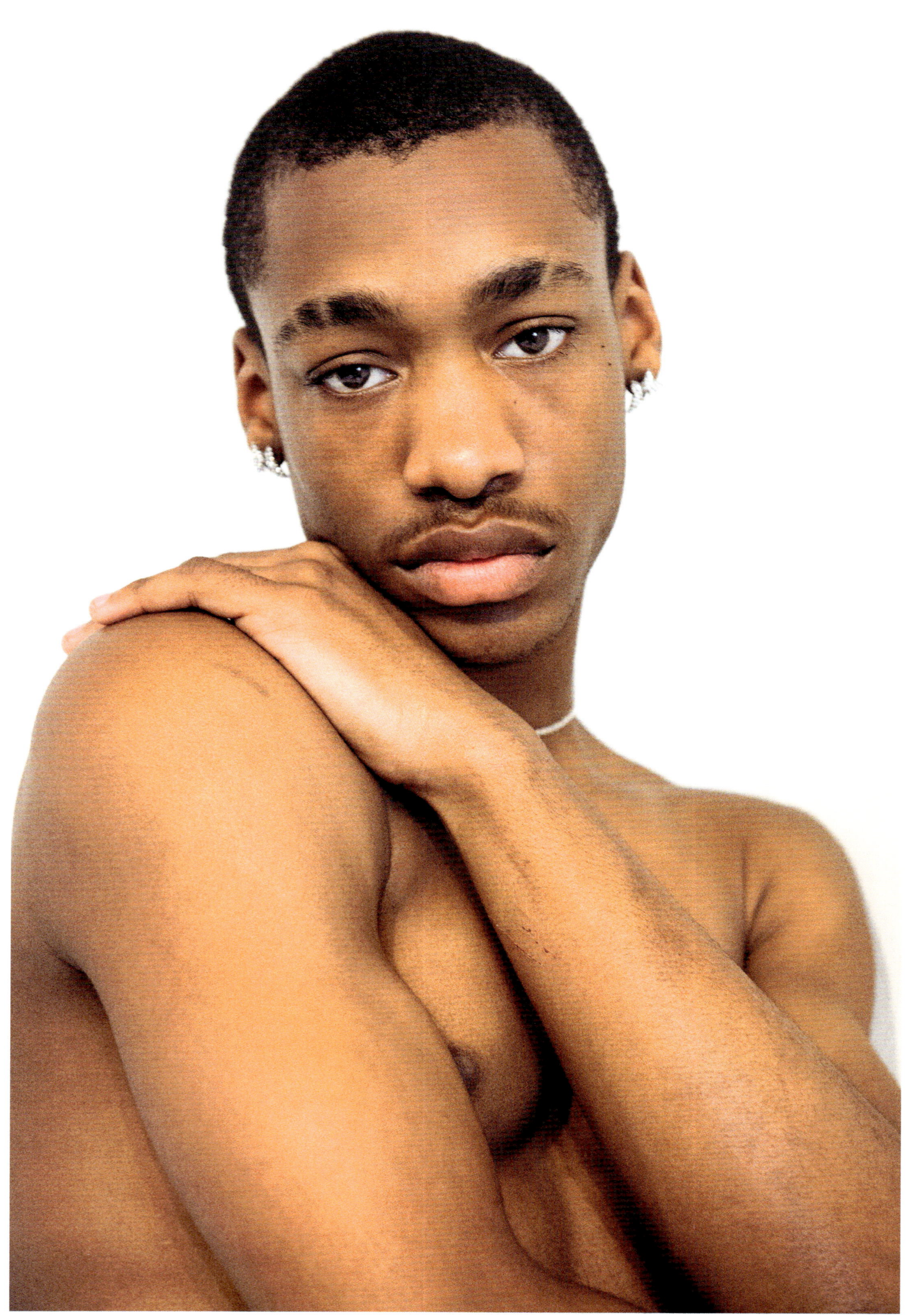

Kafiq, February 2019

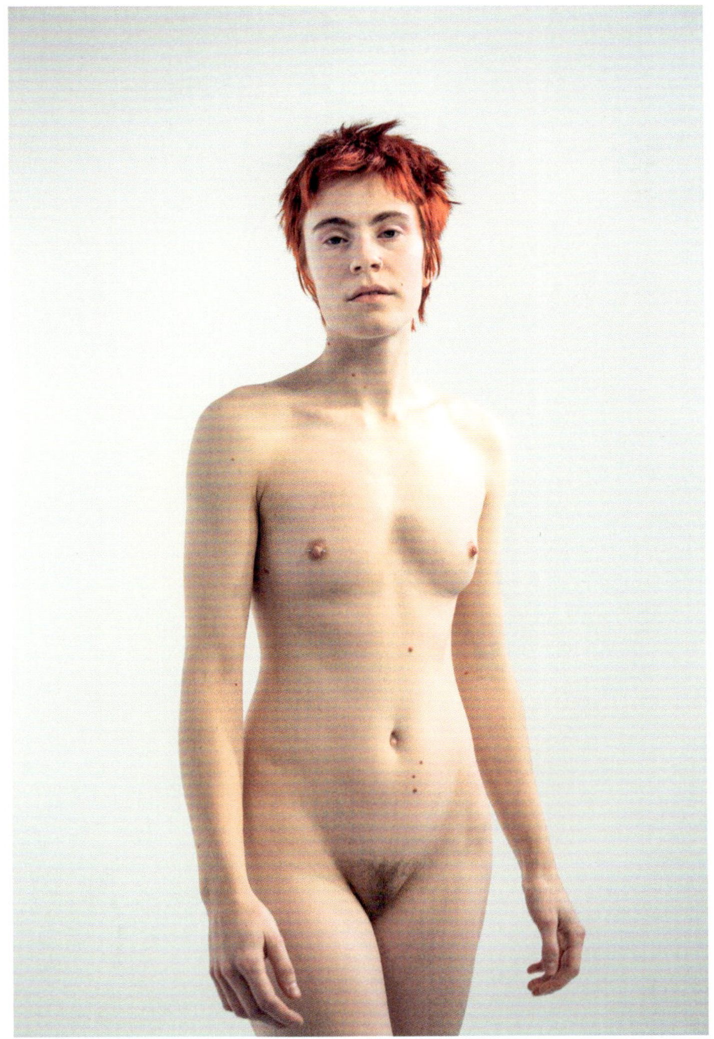

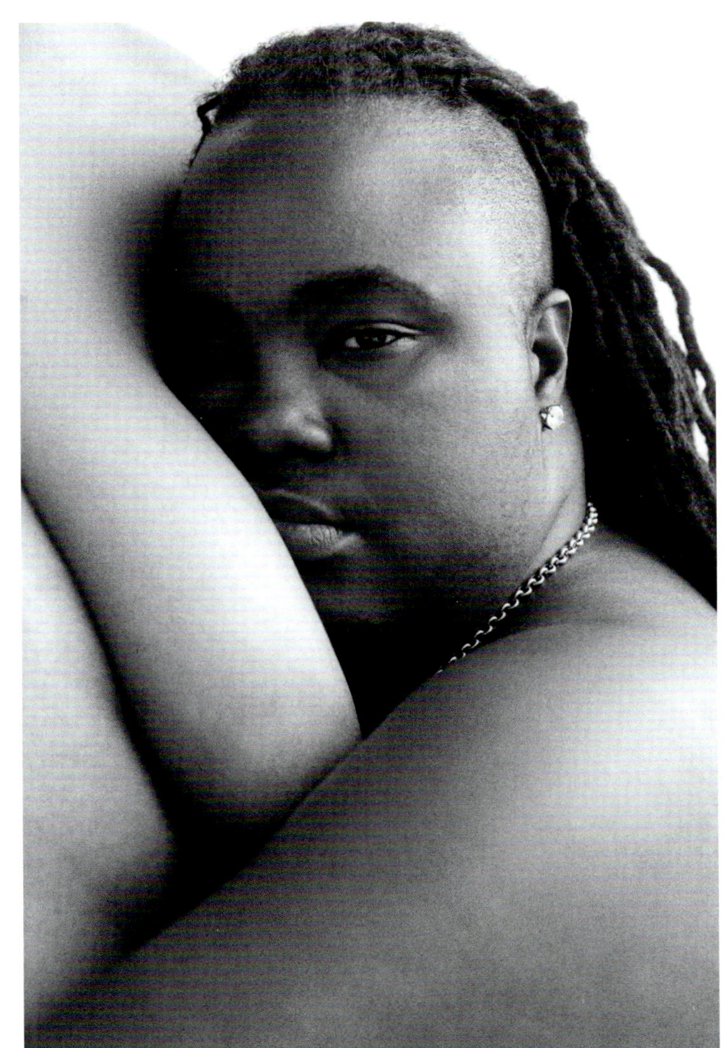

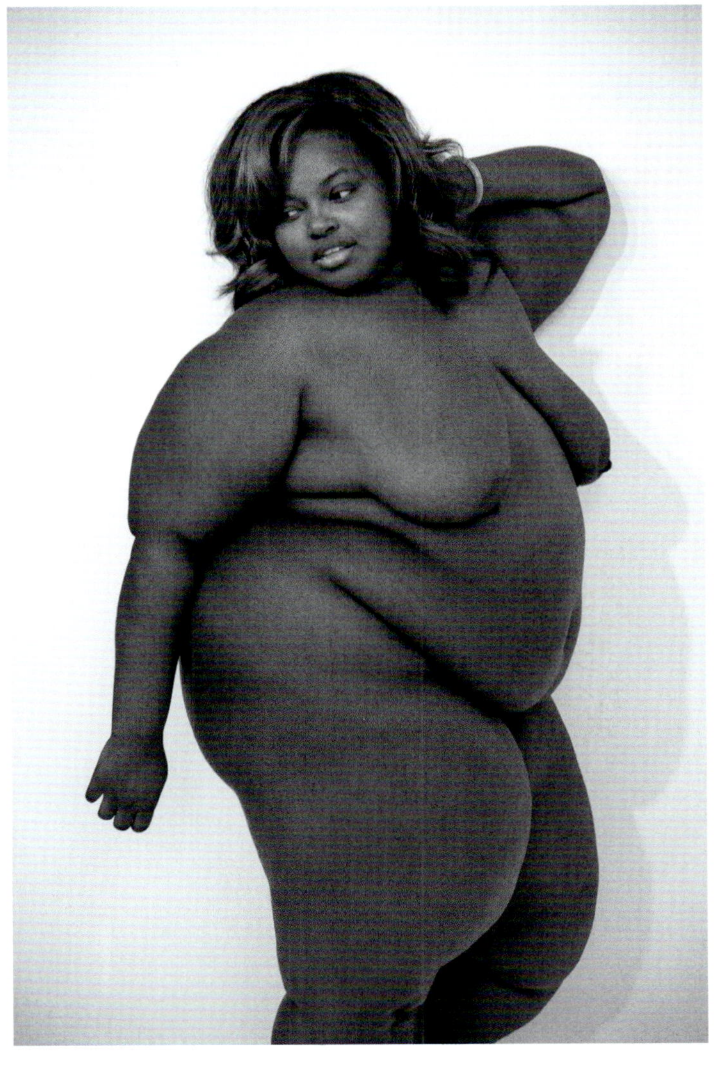

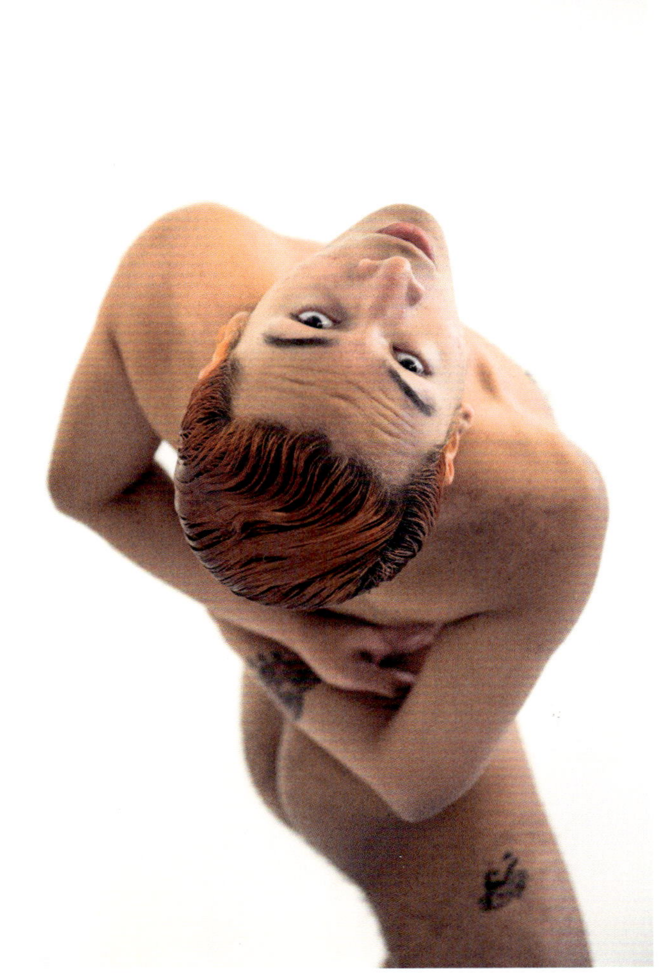

Zeke, October 2018   Apyphanie & Dani, July 2017   Candice, August 2018   Maxwell, October 2019

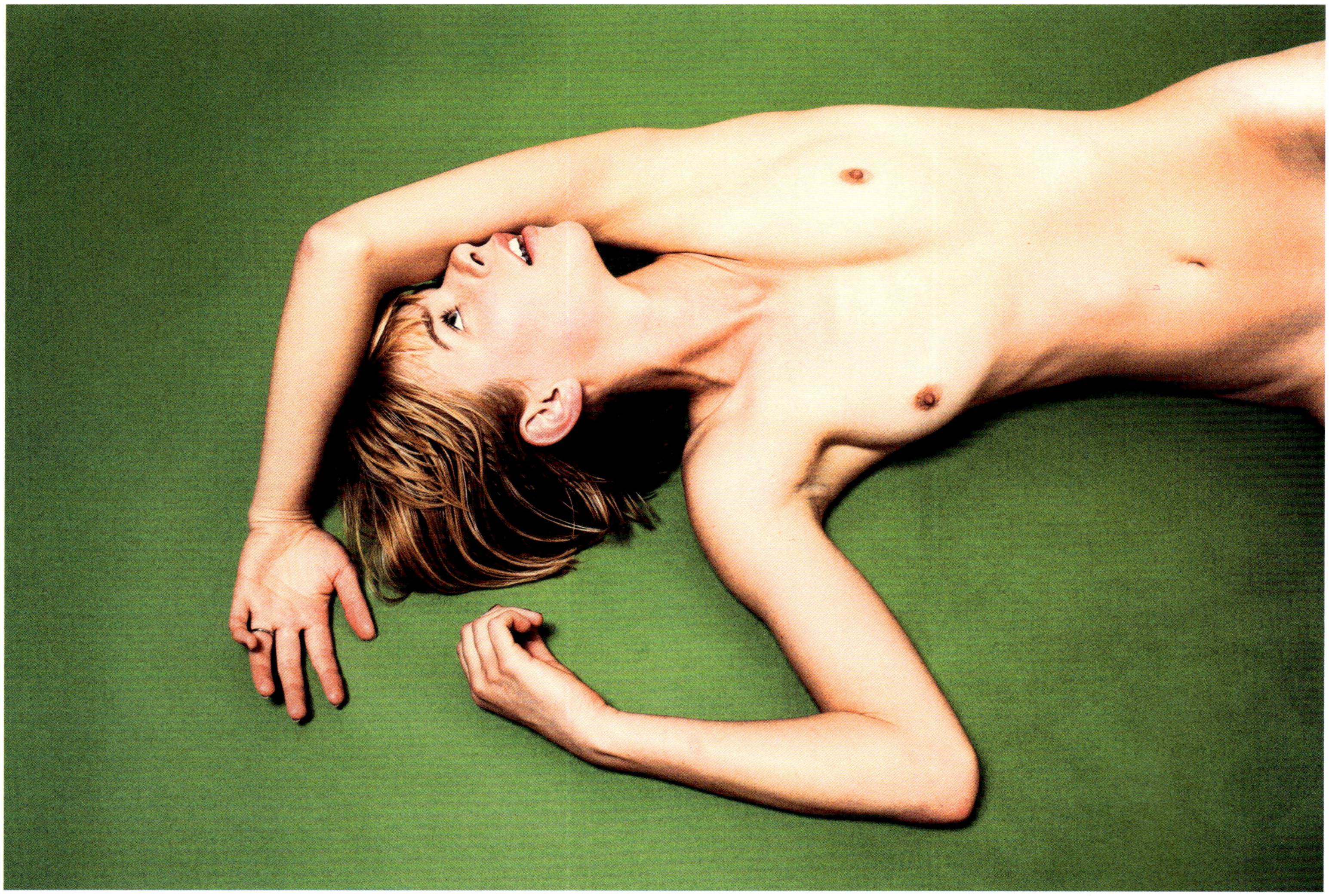

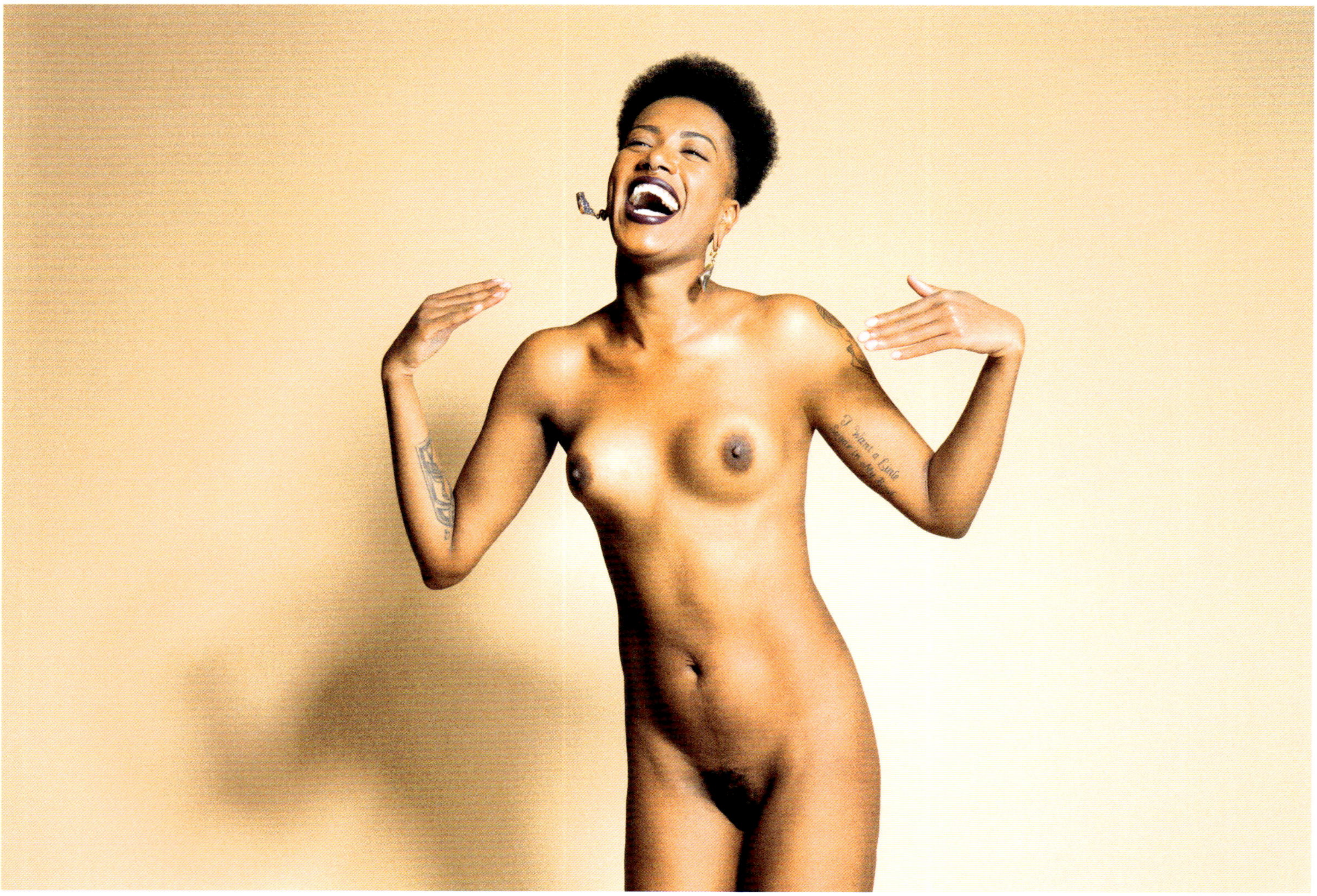

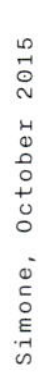

Mollie, May 2013 Simone, October 2015

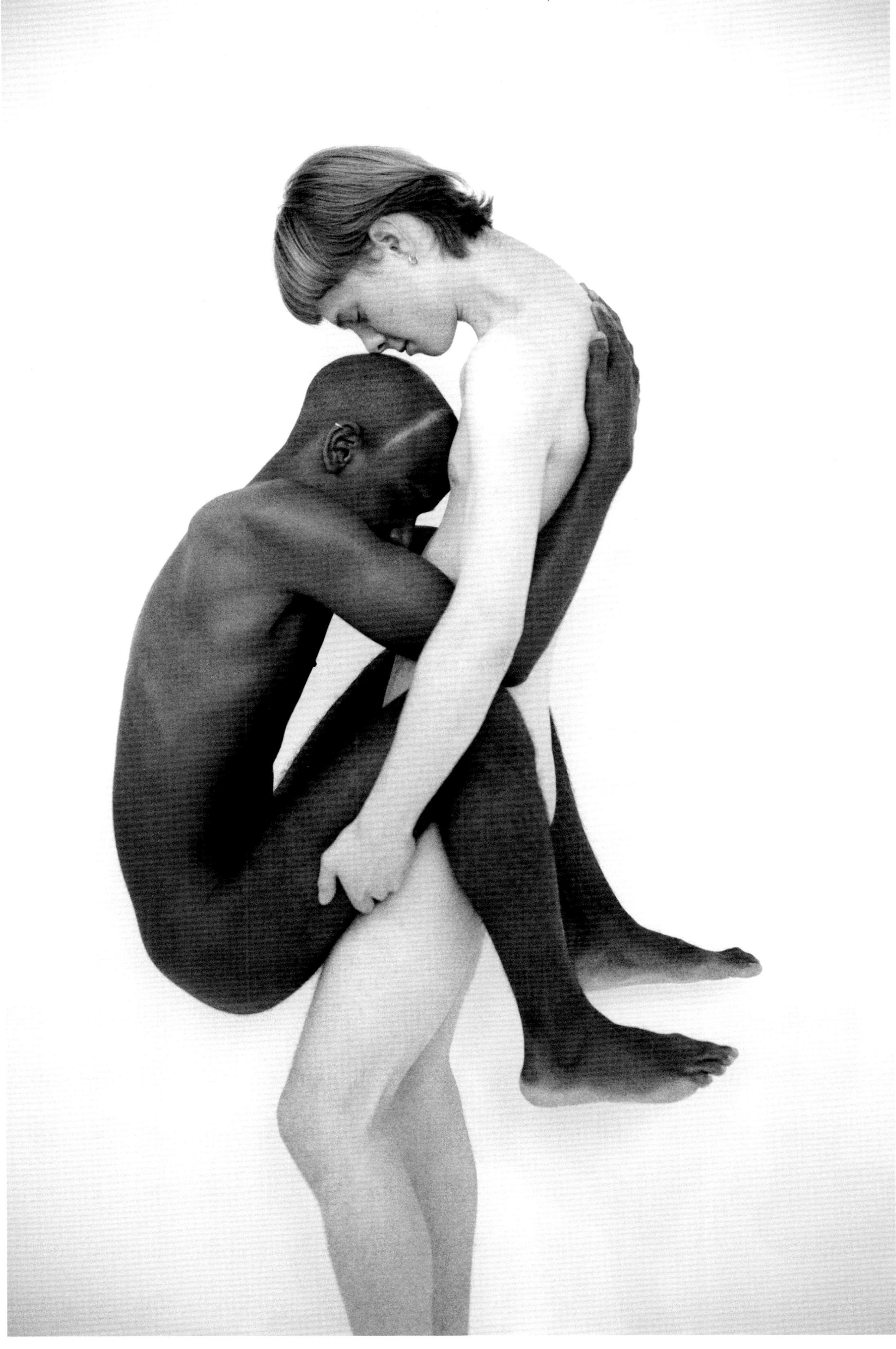

Sam & Emmanuel, November 2018

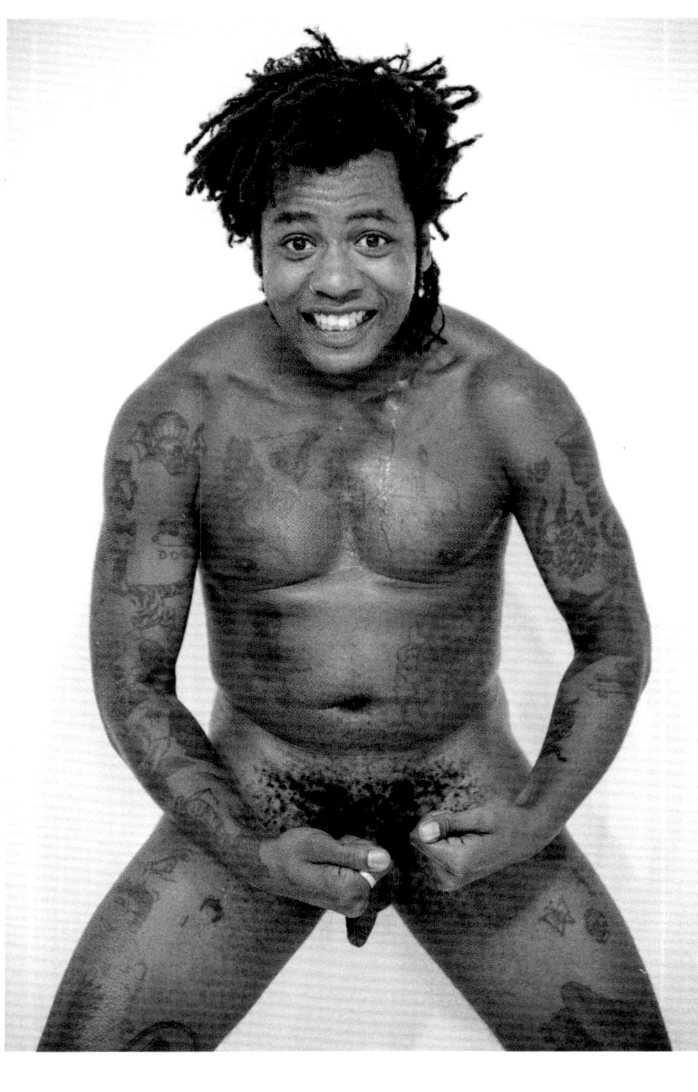

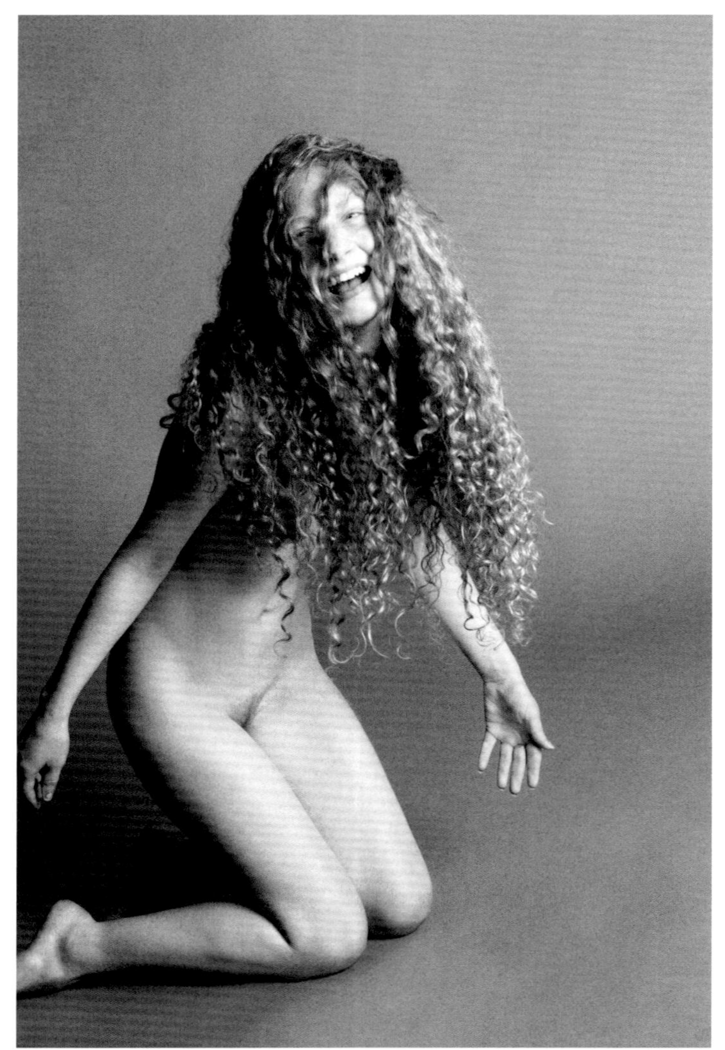

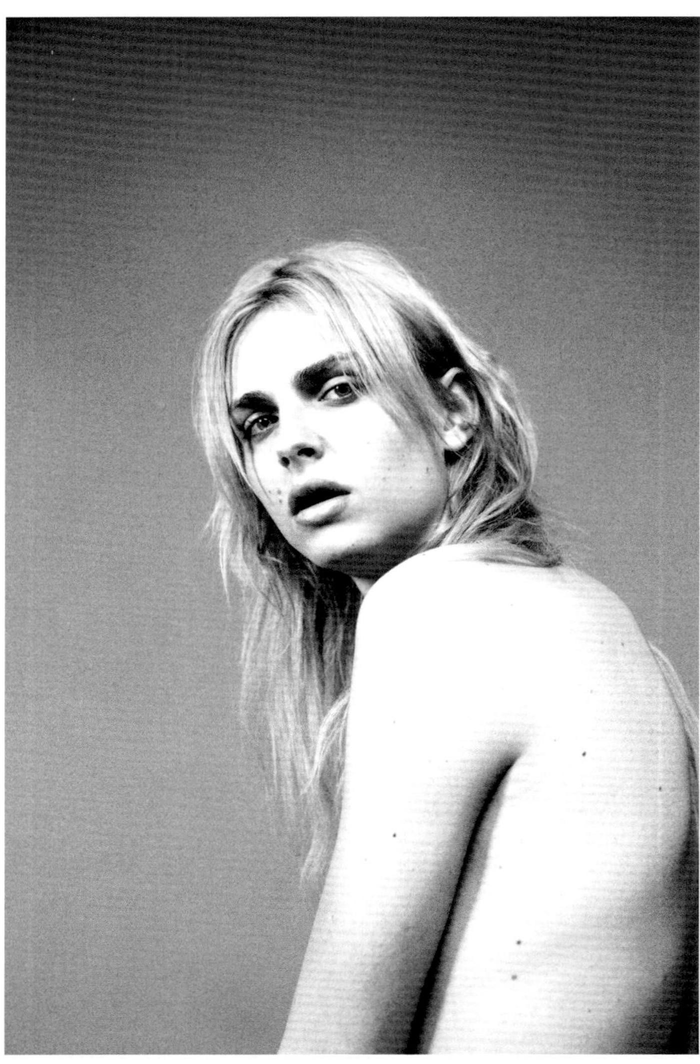

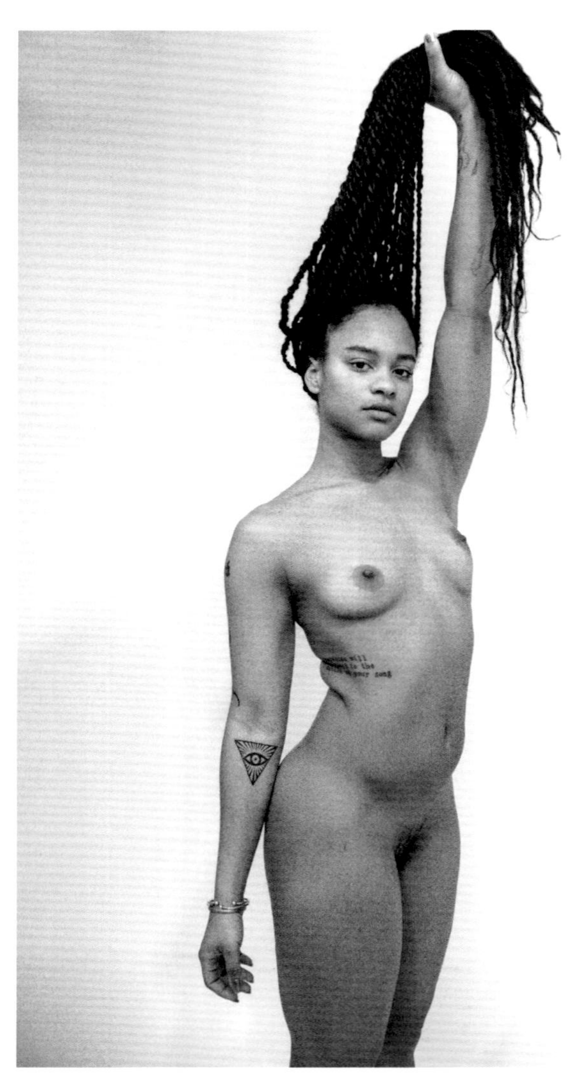

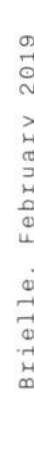

Dennis, October 2019 Abigail, March 2014 Andrej, May 2011 Brielle, February 2019

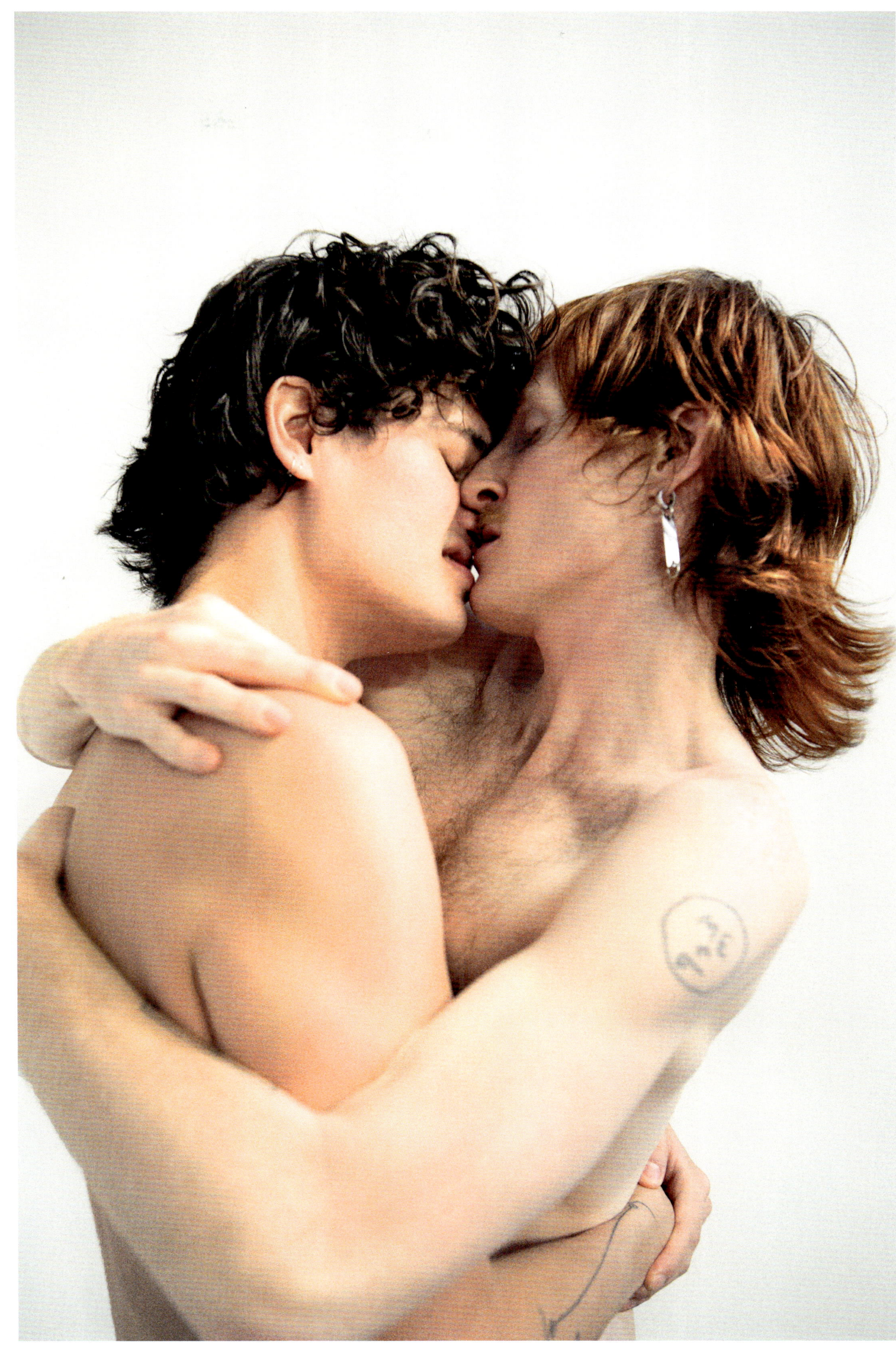

Austin & Johnny, October 2018

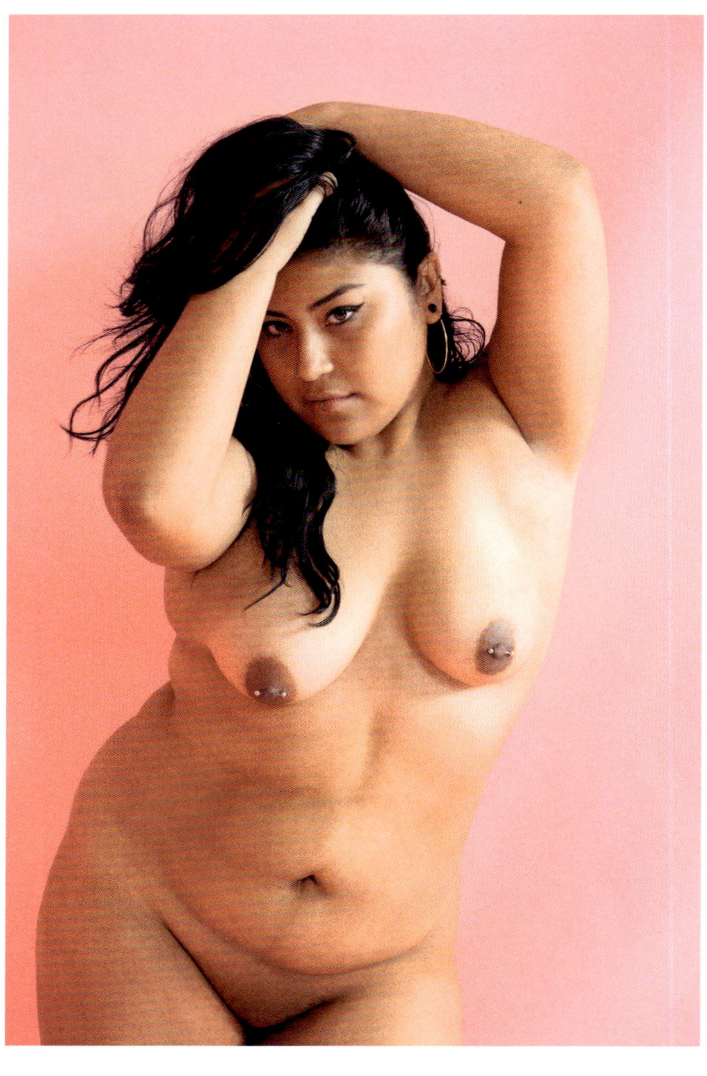

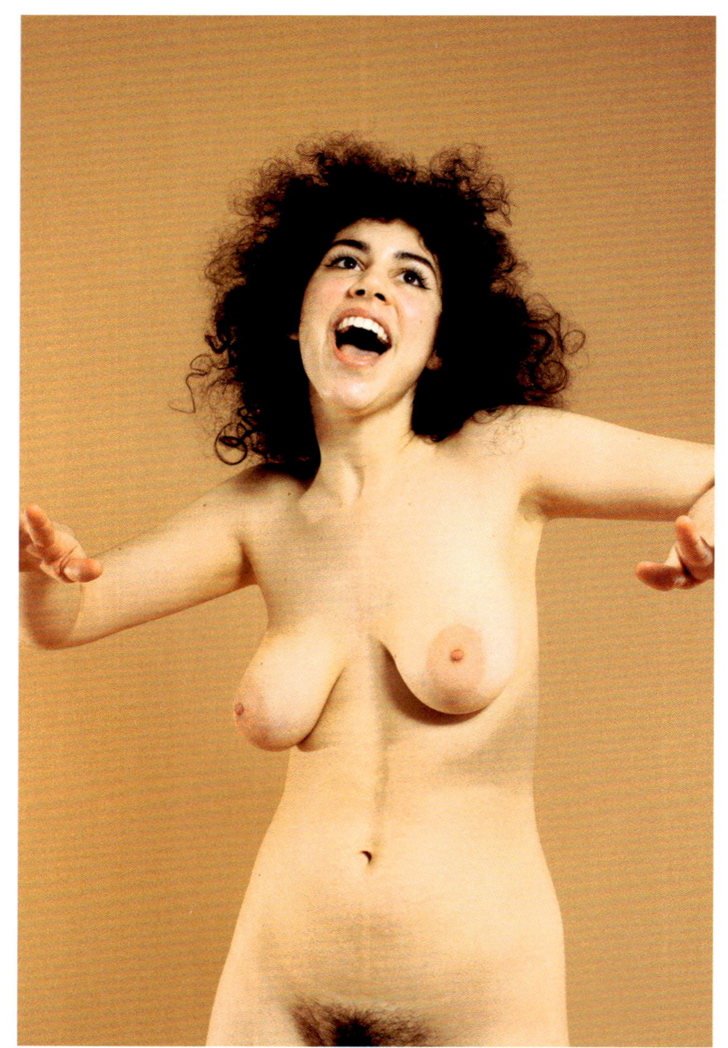

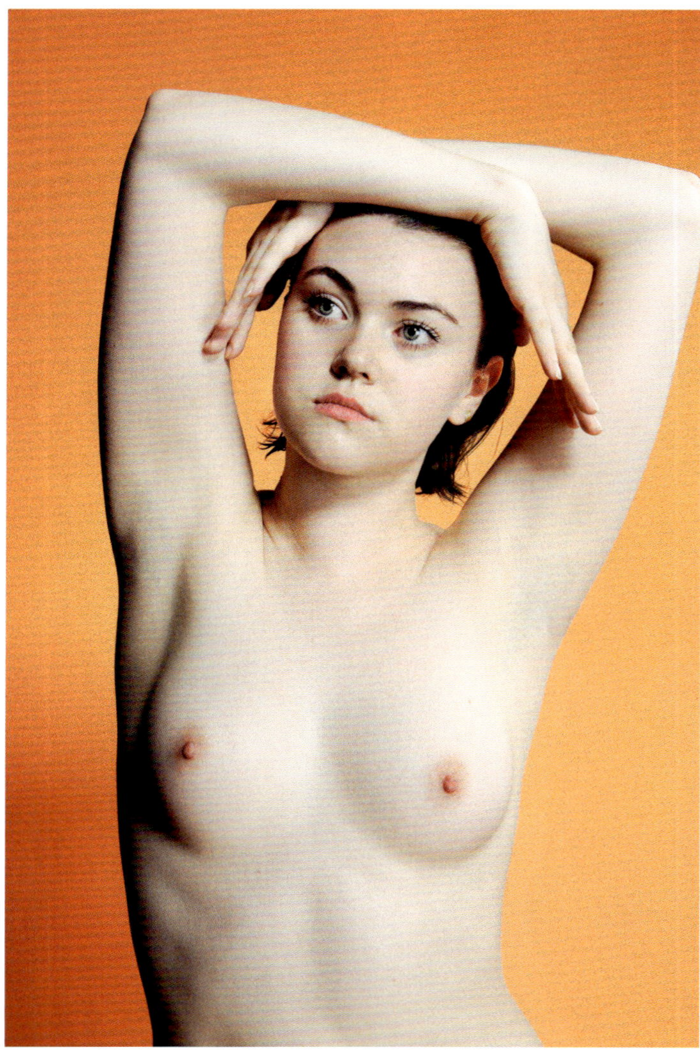

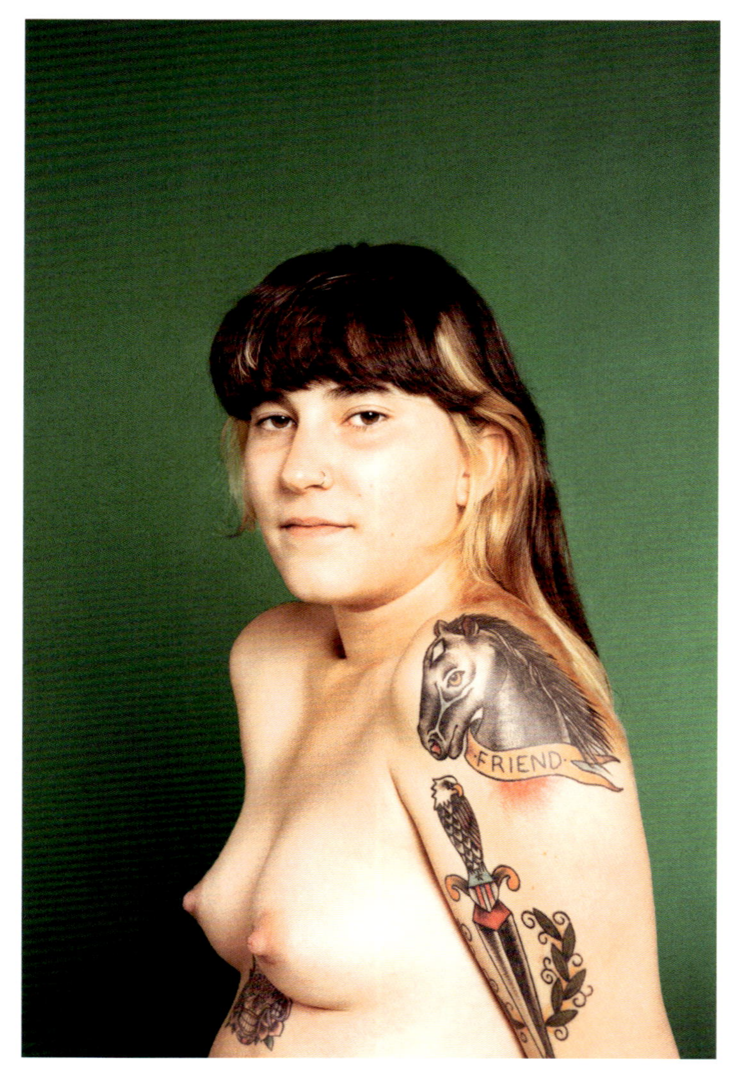

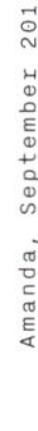

Johmaris, July 2016 Jessica, February 2013 Eva, June 2015 Amanda, September 2011

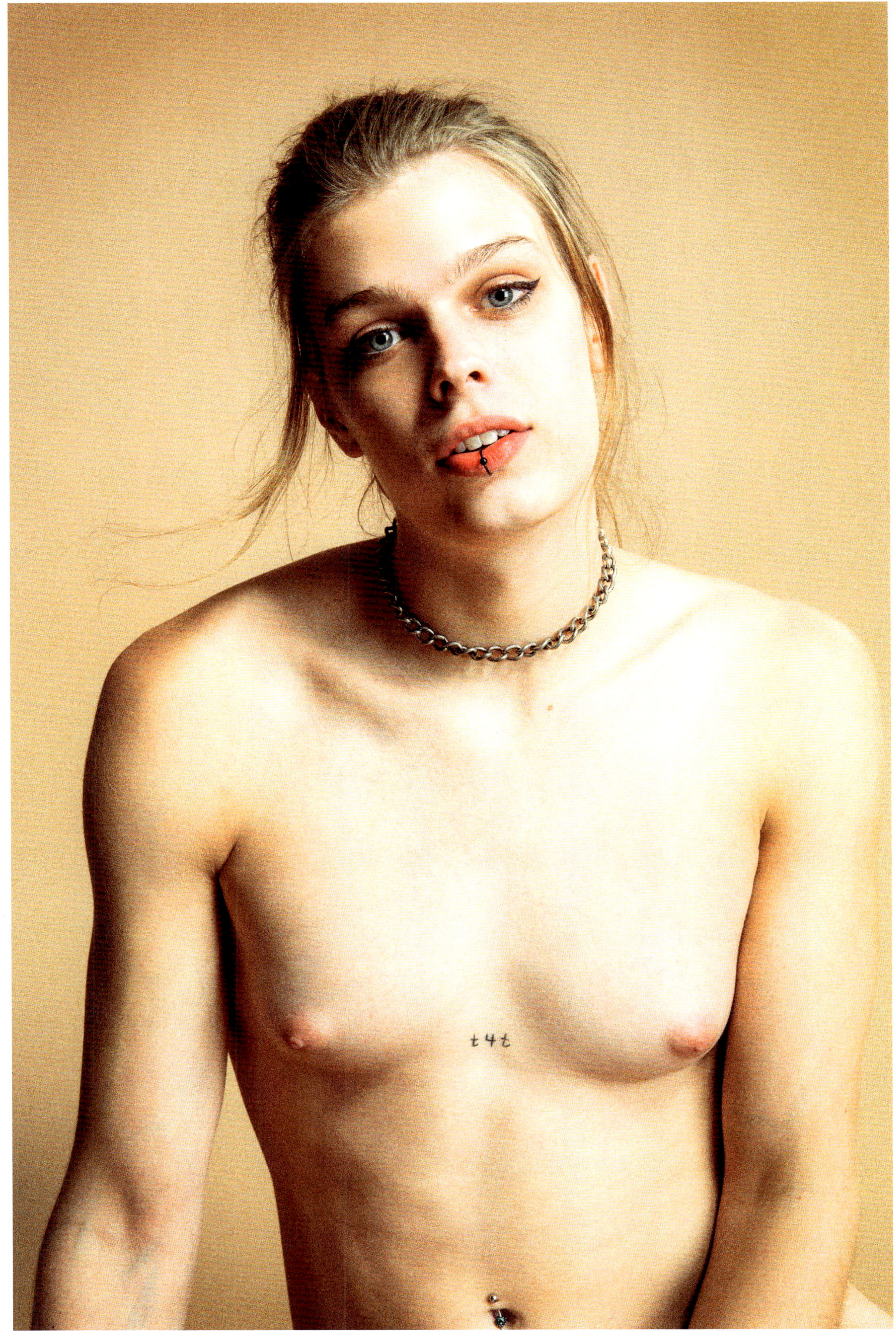

Serena, November 2015

I would've been twenty-seven at the time. I felt like such an adult. I remember thinking, "Oh my God, if I don't achieve X by thirty, then it's pointless because after thirty you're basically old and irrelevant." Looking back, I'm like, wow, I was such a kid.

I was living in Brooklyn in one of those illegal loft warehouse buildings on Kent. It was the end of an era of disgusting, junky Williamsburg. You would build these plywood shacks inside of the loft. I had a bedroom with literally no windows. It was pitch black. Mattress on the floor. I was probably just being a ho from hell, and getting drunk, and going to warehouse parties, the usual.

I was working for *Vice* at the time, like everyone was. I had just started doing this web series, *Slutever*, about sex and relationships. 2013 was funny. The book *Fifty Shades of Grey* had become really popular so like every basic bitch on the planet was going S&M crazy. We were interviewing a lot of the BDSM community in New York. I remember meeting Julia [Fox] in this era. I was working as a dominatrix, and she had worked in a dungeon, so she gave me dominatrix tips. I remember thinking, "She's better at it than me."

There were sex parties in Brooklyn that I was going to, like One Leg Up and Chemistry. They were generally in Brooklyn warehouses and generally with mattresses on the floor. You could bring your own alcohol. Kind of grungy. I remember there was one fancy sex party that emerged called Top Floor; it took over the whole top floor of the Thompson Hotel. Discussions of kink, BDSM, and non-monogamy had become a topic, and going to a swingers or sex party felt new.

It was also the era of Petra Collins and the beginning of what people would call a fourth wave of feminism. There was this real reclaiming of sluttiness for women. Particularly women online. There was the "girl blog," and I don't mean that in a pejorative way. I'm saying this as someone who wrote a blog called *Slutever*. There was a reason people cared about it.

Now you see all these articles about how Gen Z doesn't have sex or how young people haven't had sex in a year. When I was that age, all my friends in New York were fucking around a ton. We re-named the "walk of shame" the "limp of shame" because clearly you got fucked so much that you had to limp home.

Being on the periphery of it and looking in, I thought, "Oh, this is our generation's Warhol's factory." Being in Ryan's studio, it's like Warhol superstars. The idea of who the artist's eyes are on. Warhol's thing was that people wanted to be chosen by him. I don't mean this in a negative way, but there just was a reality that people wanted to be chosen by Ryan and photographed by him to be deemed cool and beautiful.

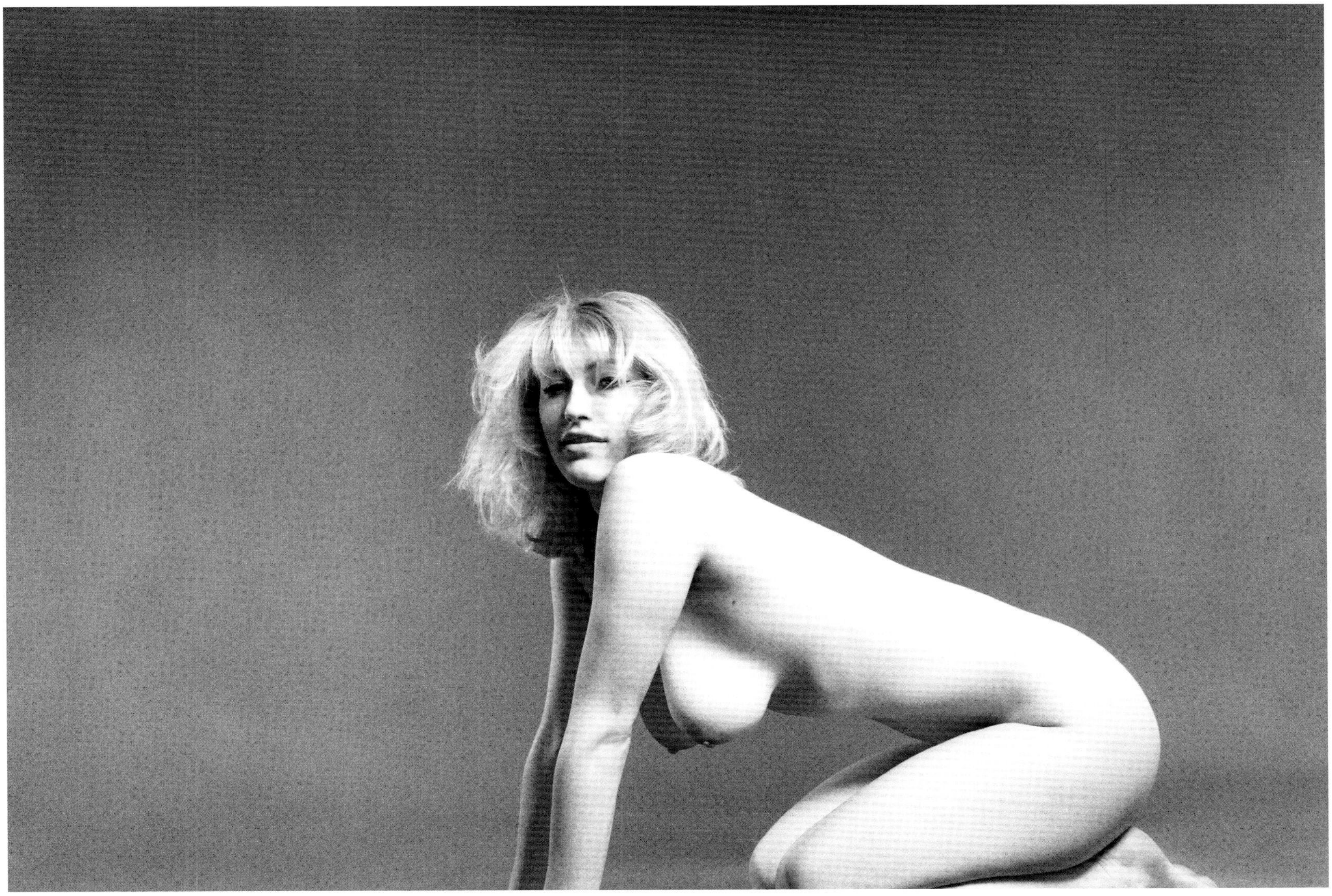

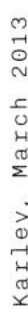

Karley, March 2013

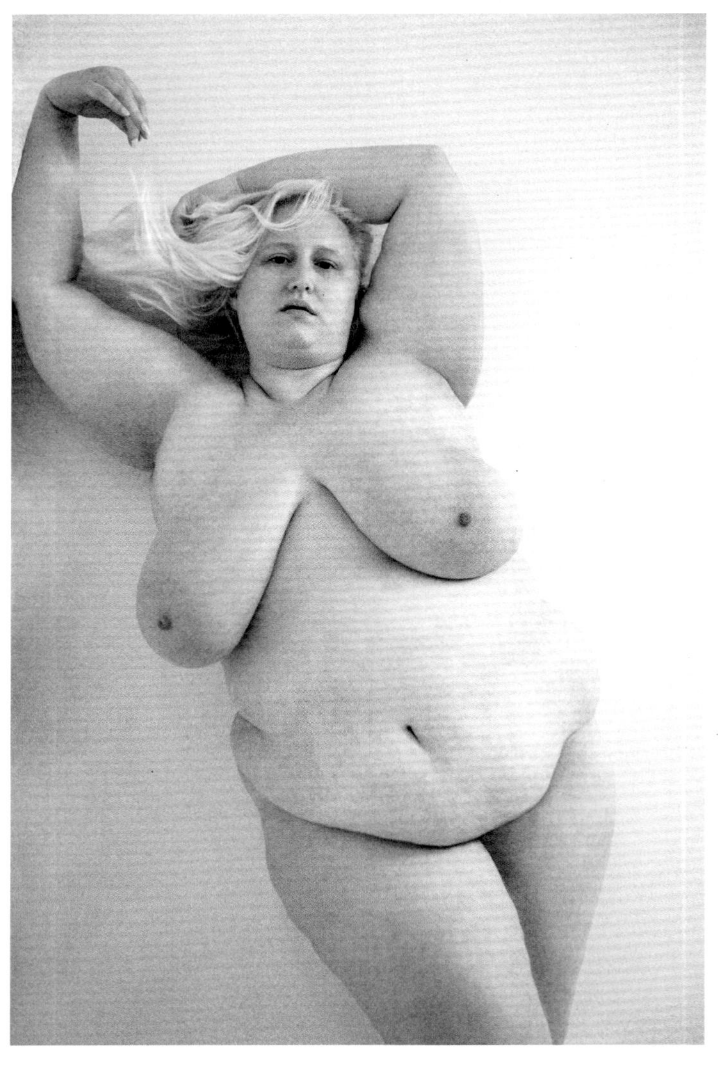

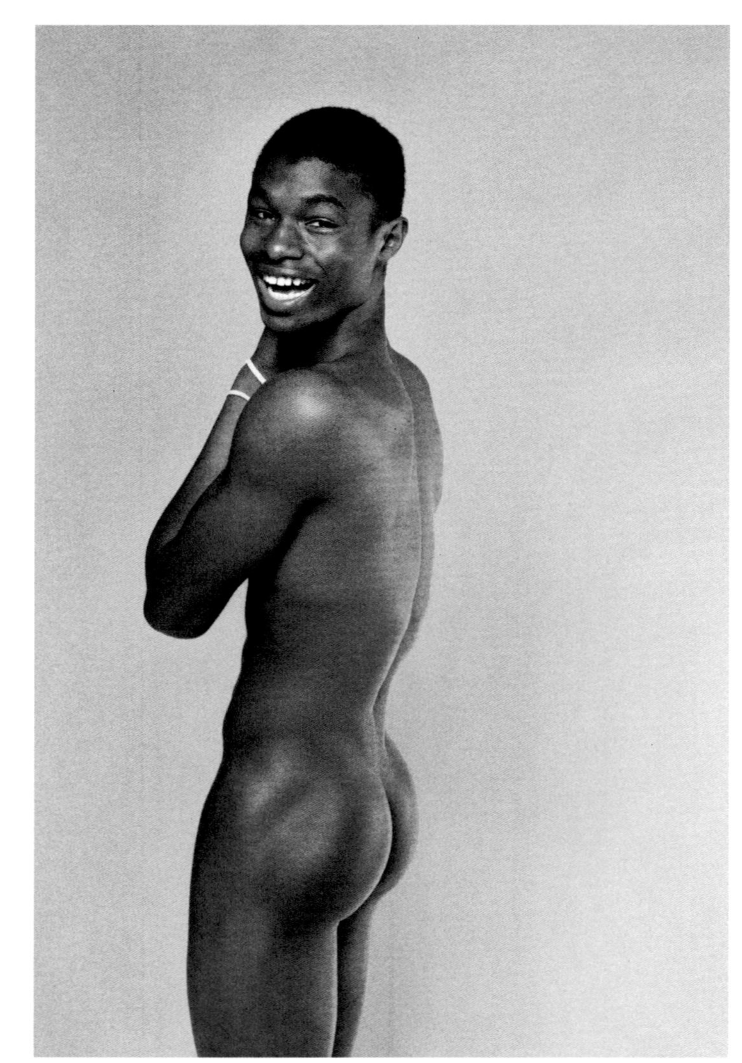

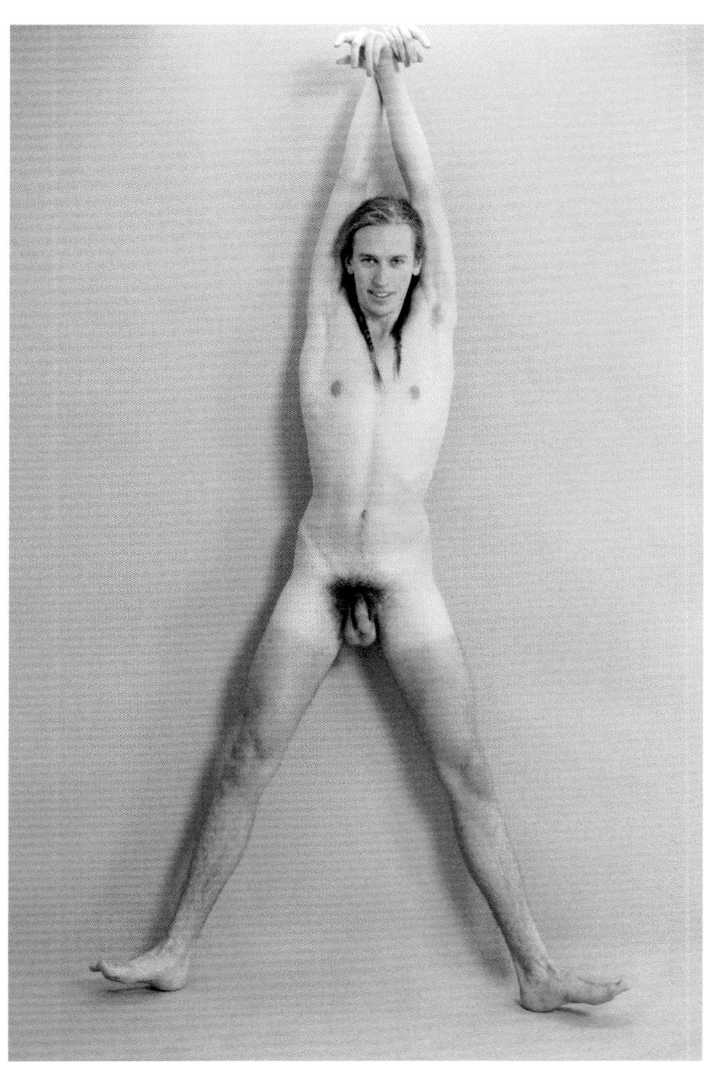

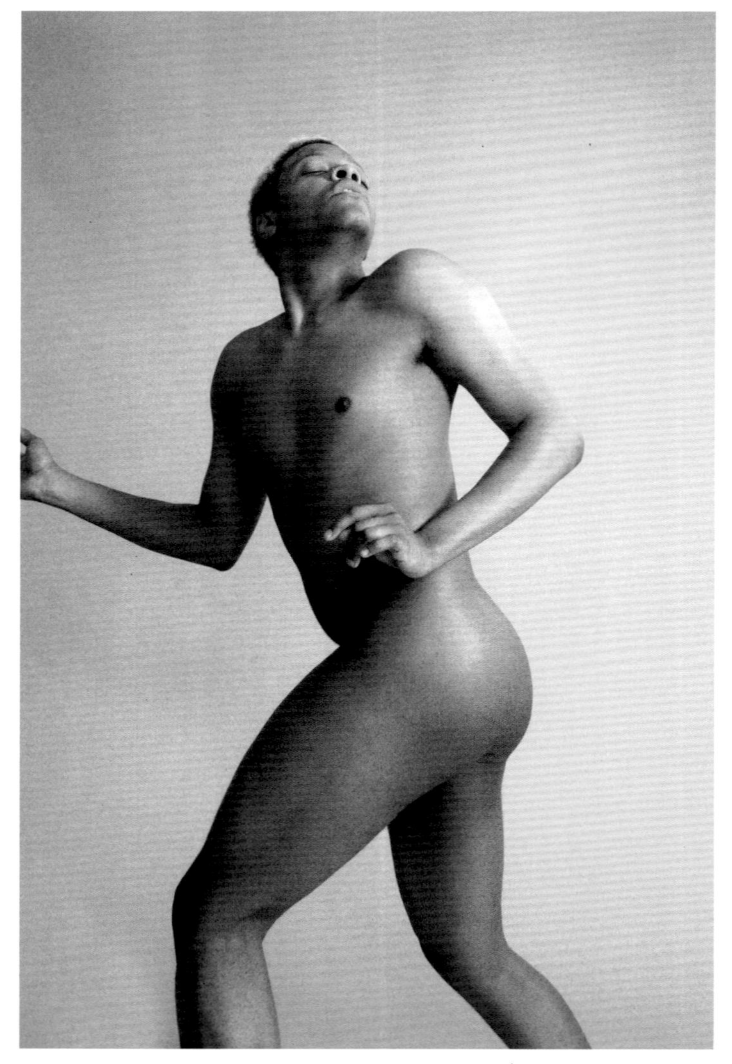

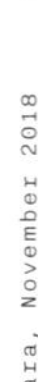

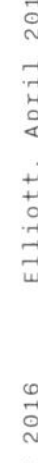

Clara, November 2018   Salieu, September 2009   CJ, November 2016   Elliott, April 2016

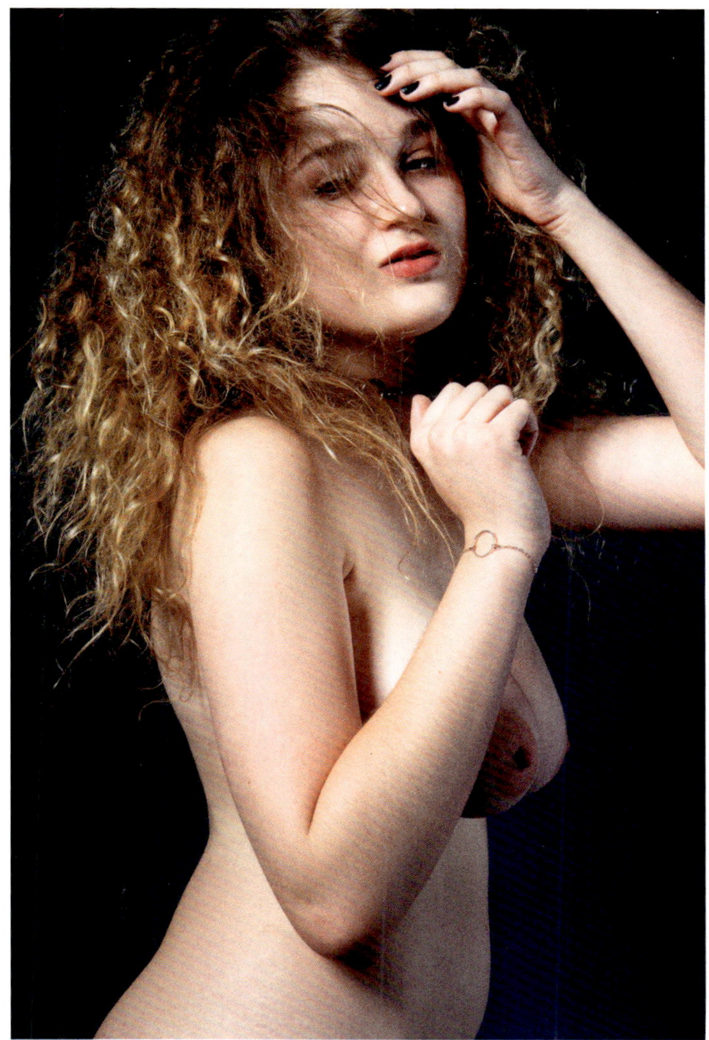

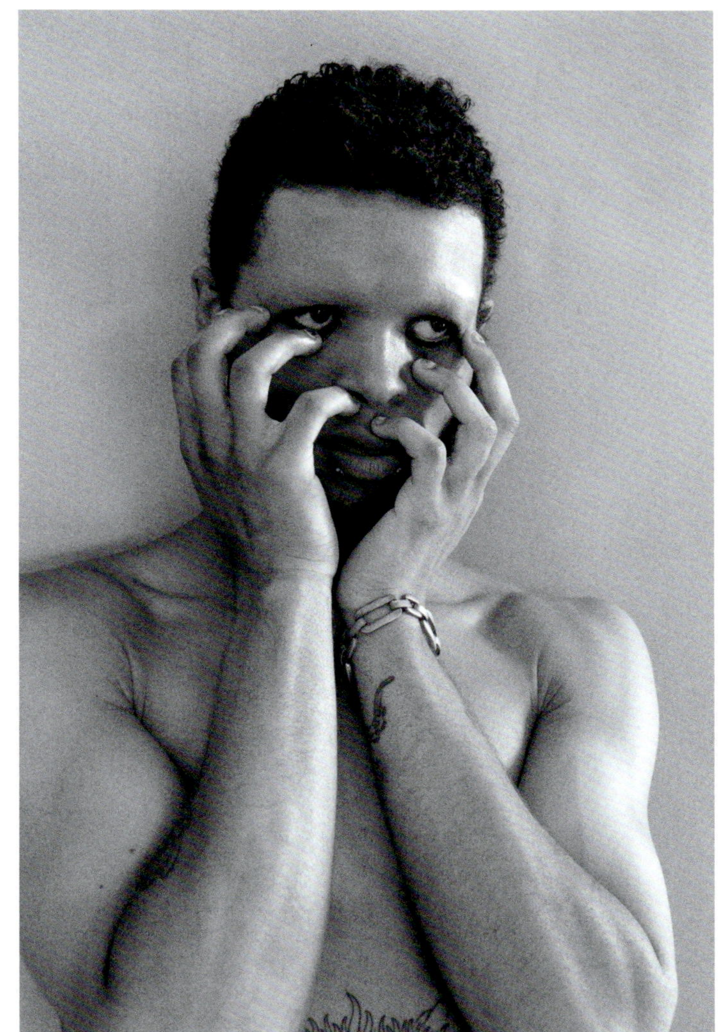

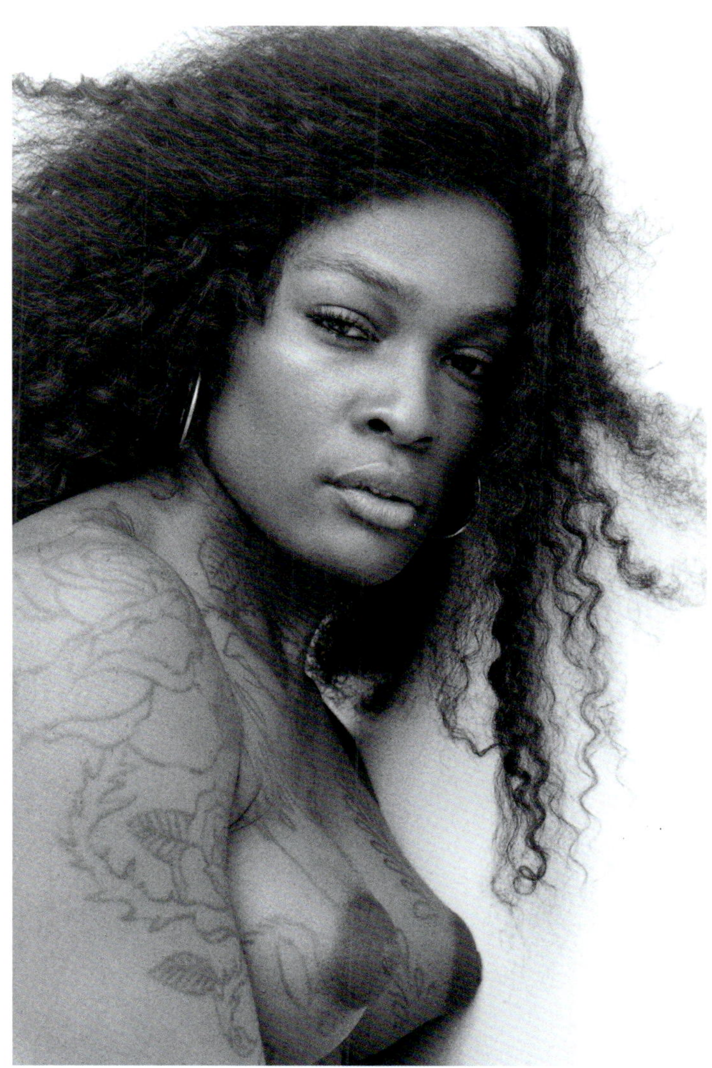

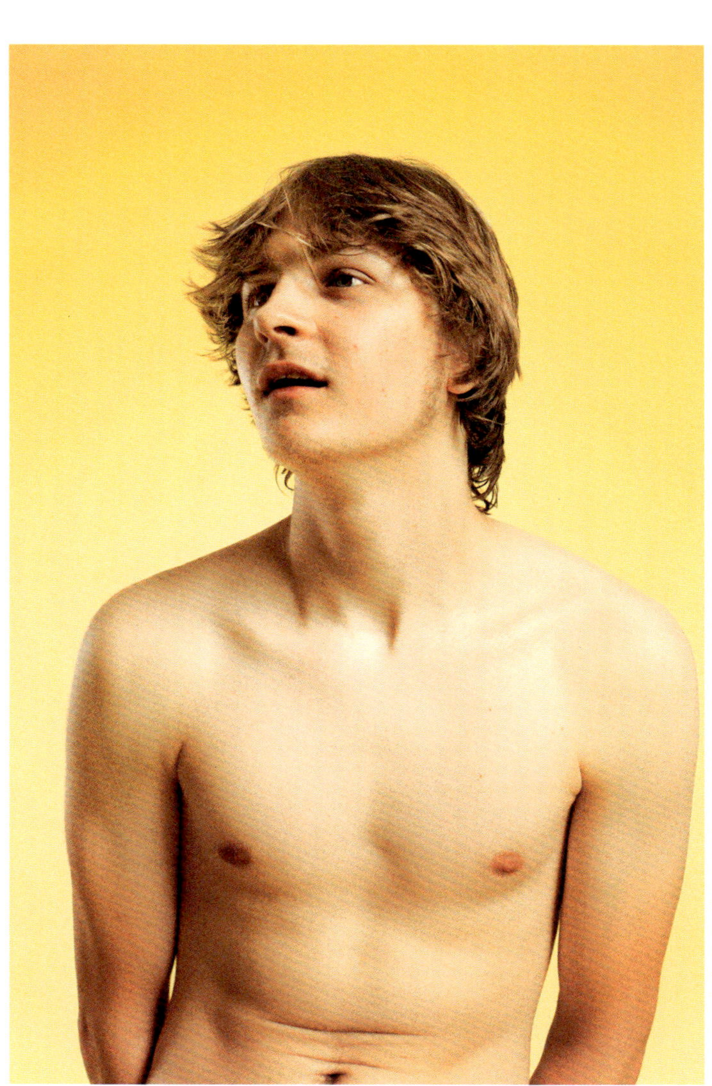

Sasha, July 2015   Vlad, September 2016   Imma, June 2017   Cheney, July 2010

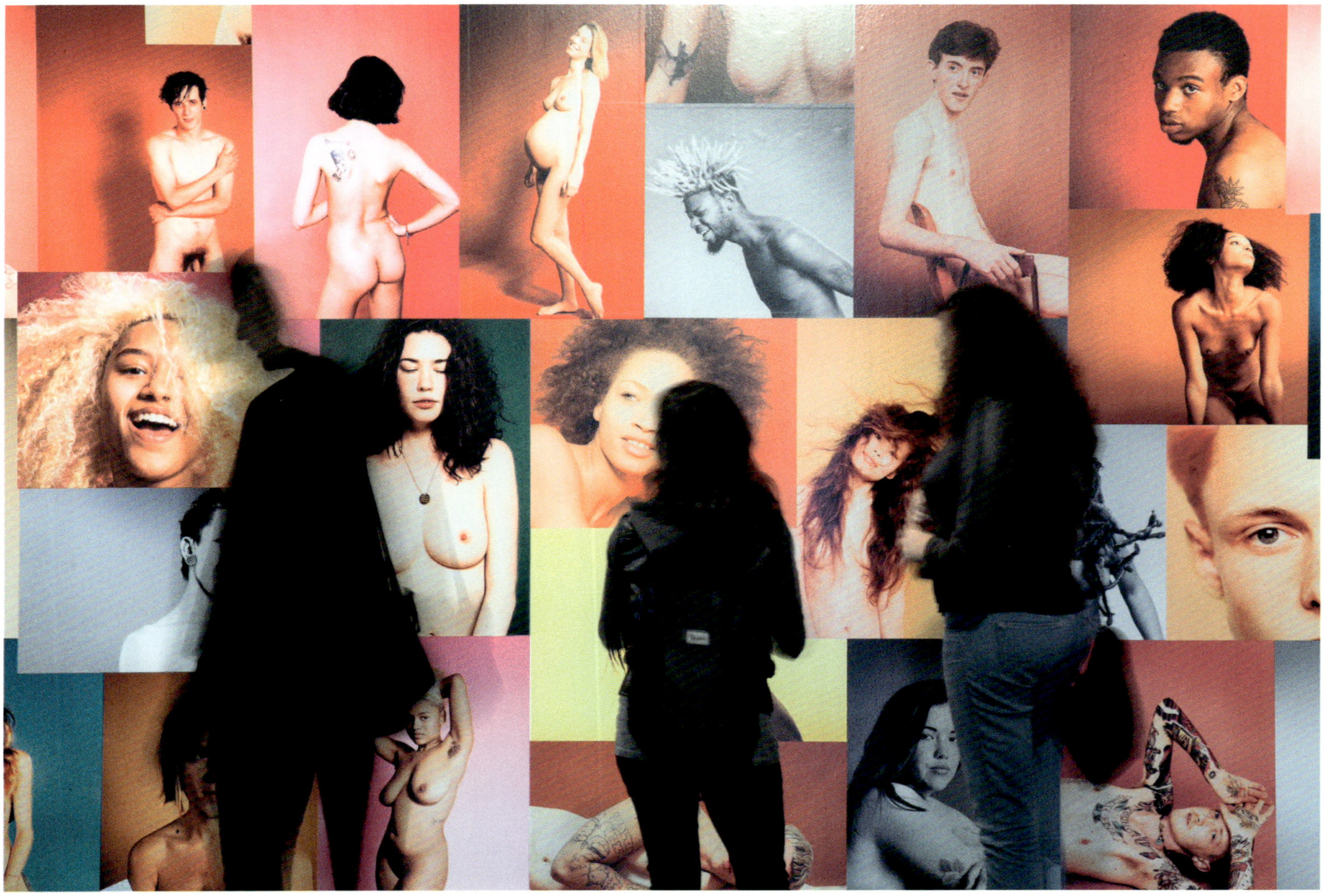

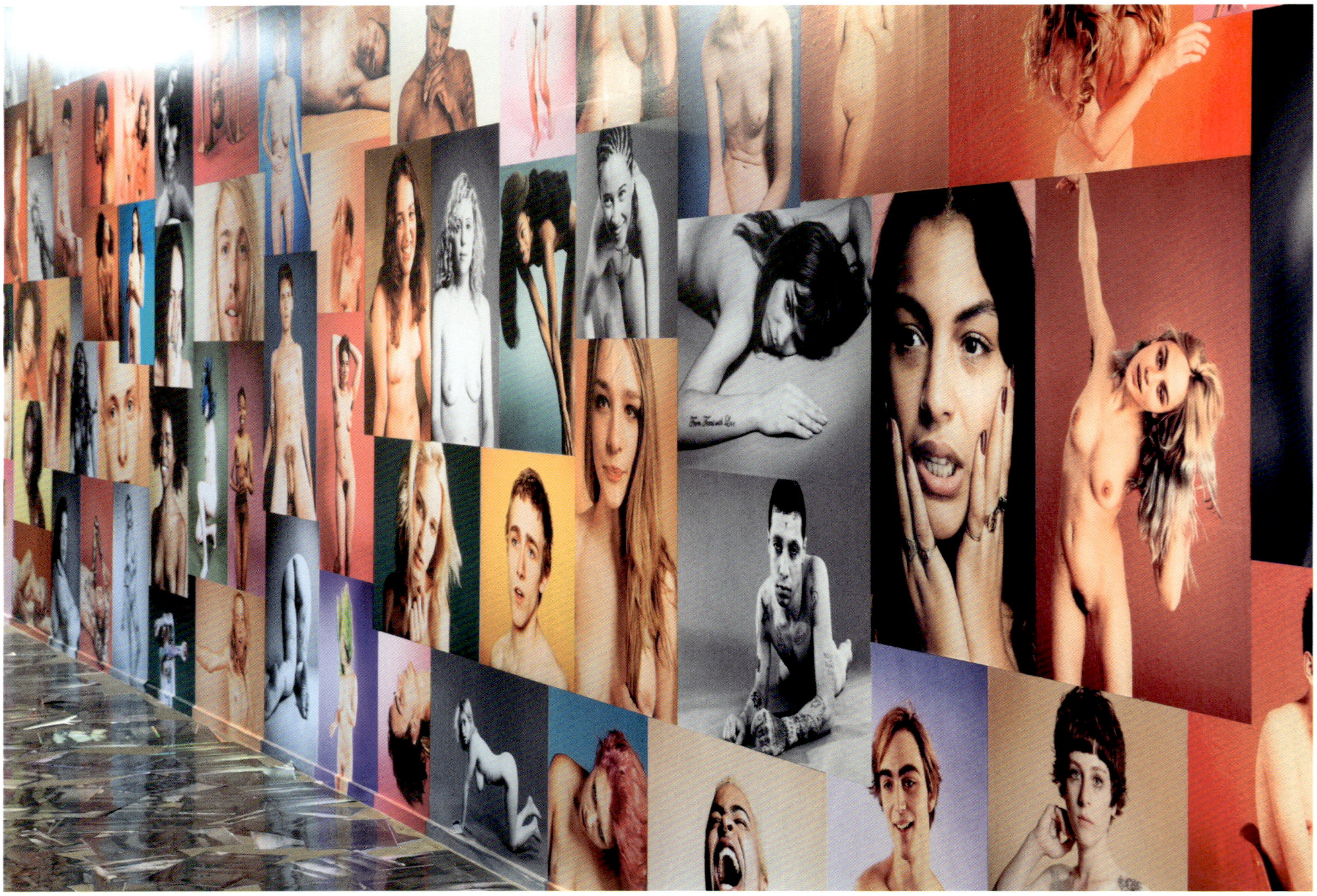

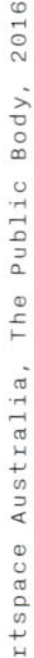

Artspace Australia, The Public Body, 2016

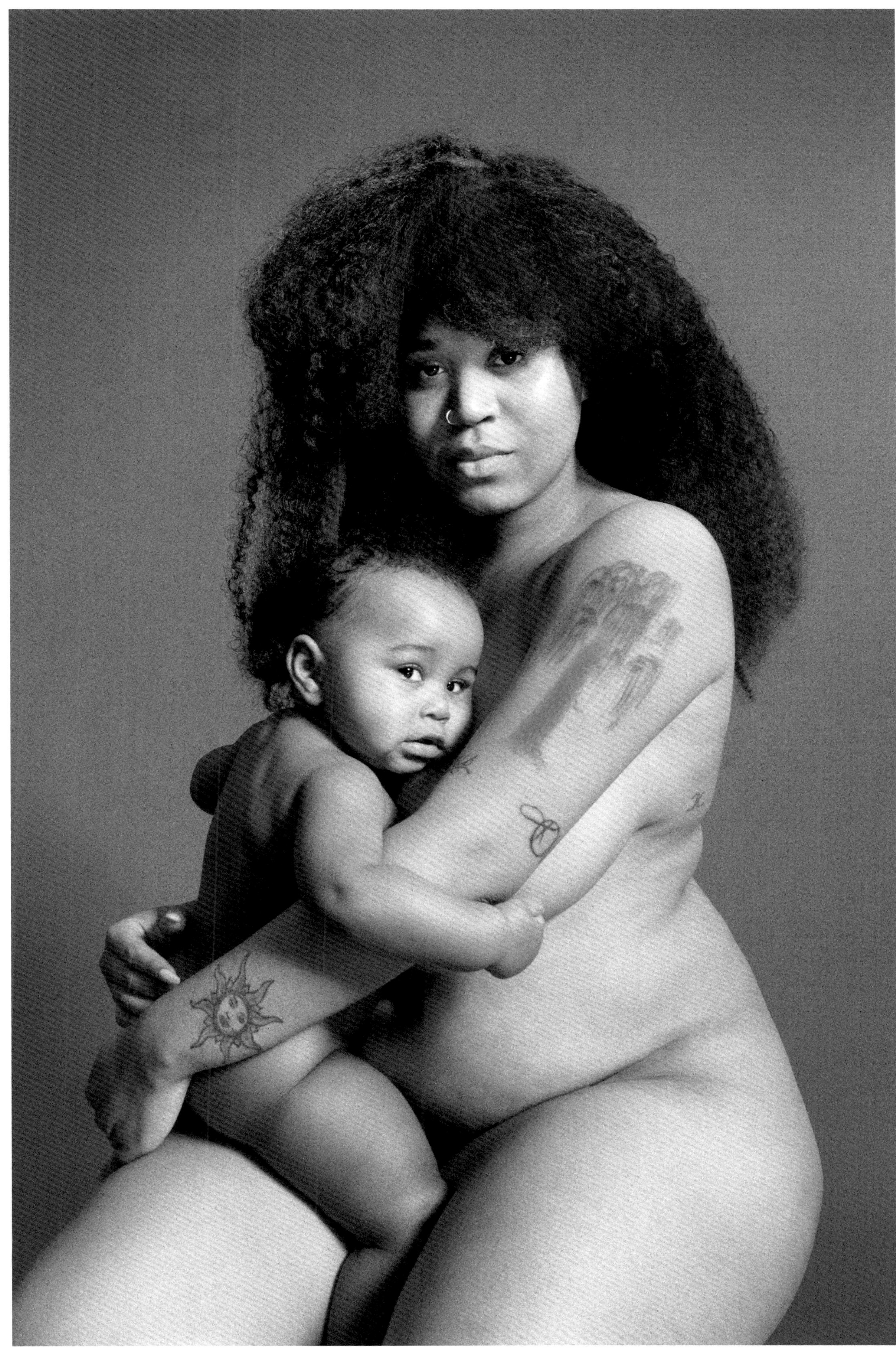

Eryn & Sirius, March 2016

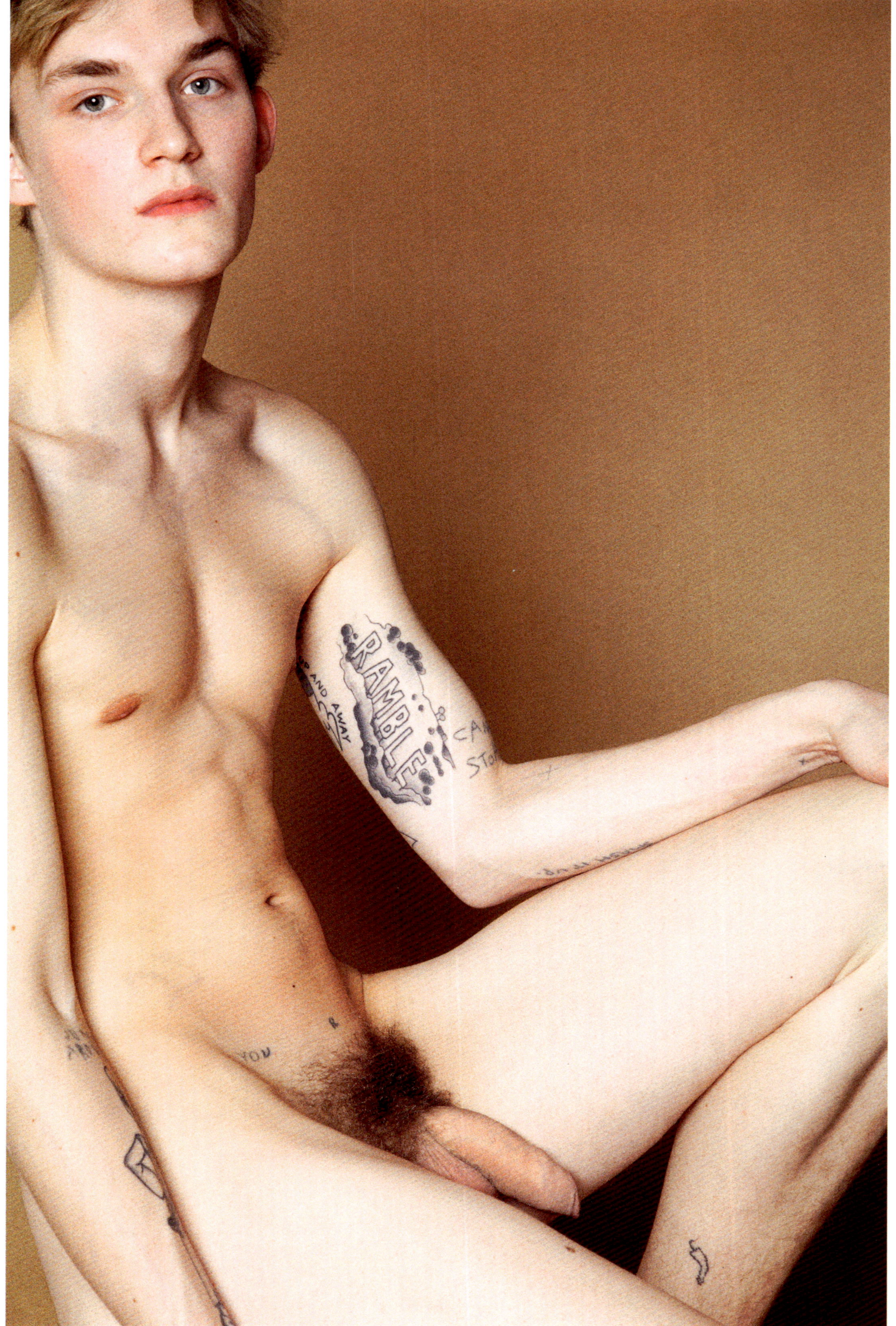

Charlie, February 2011

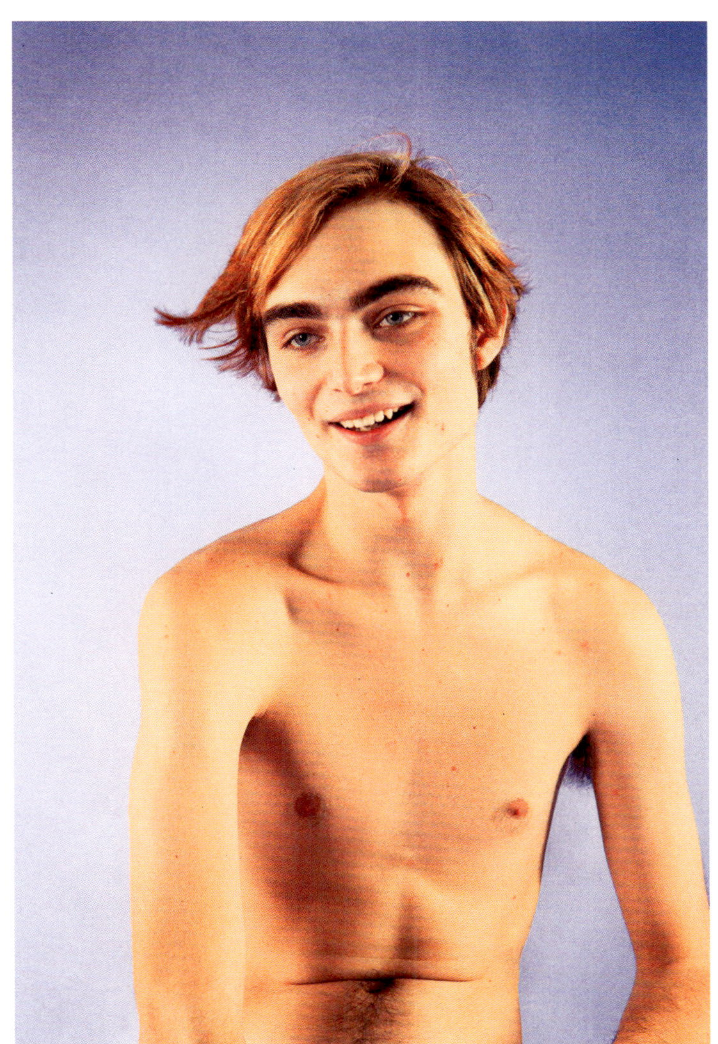

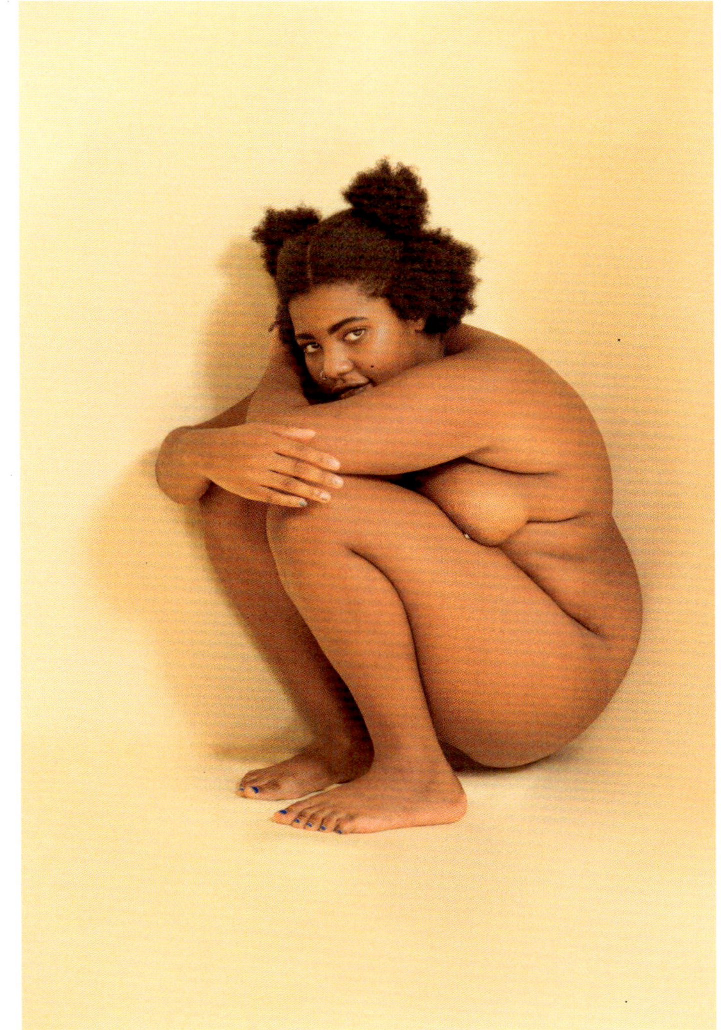

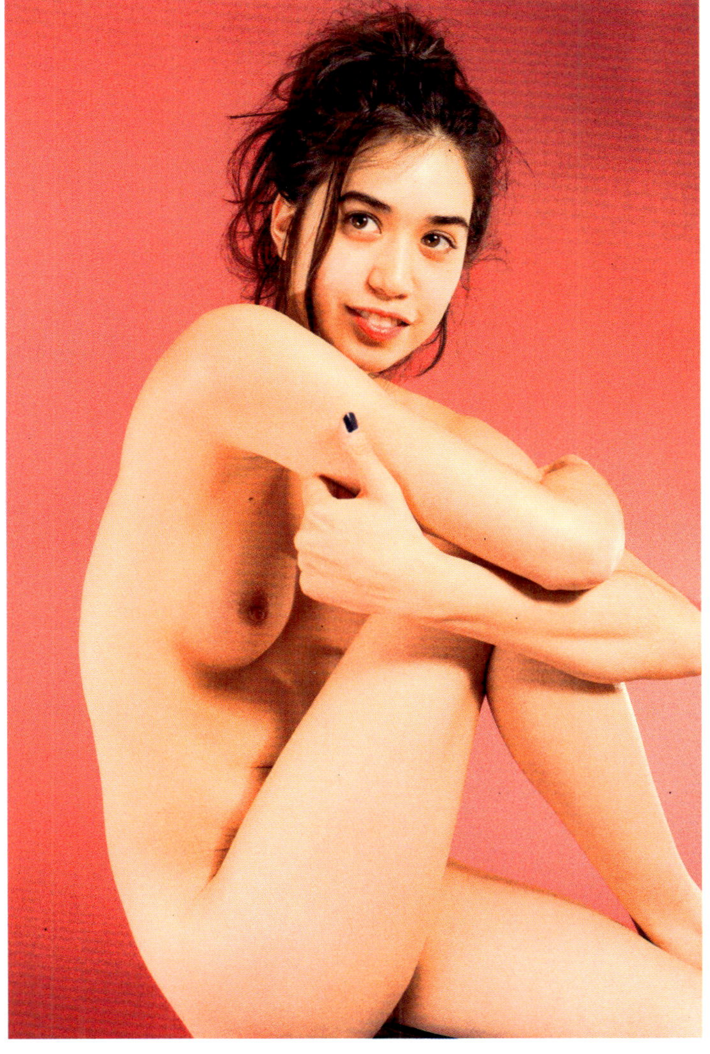

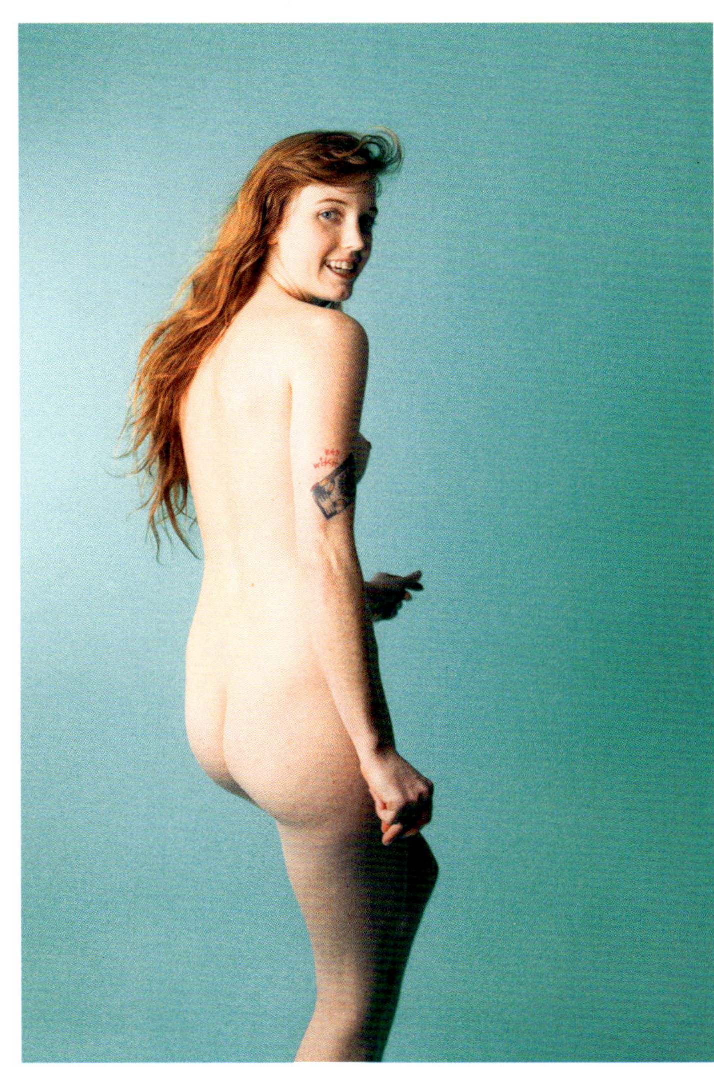

Chris, June 2012   Dajiu, July 2016   Sara, February 2013   Jessica, January 2011

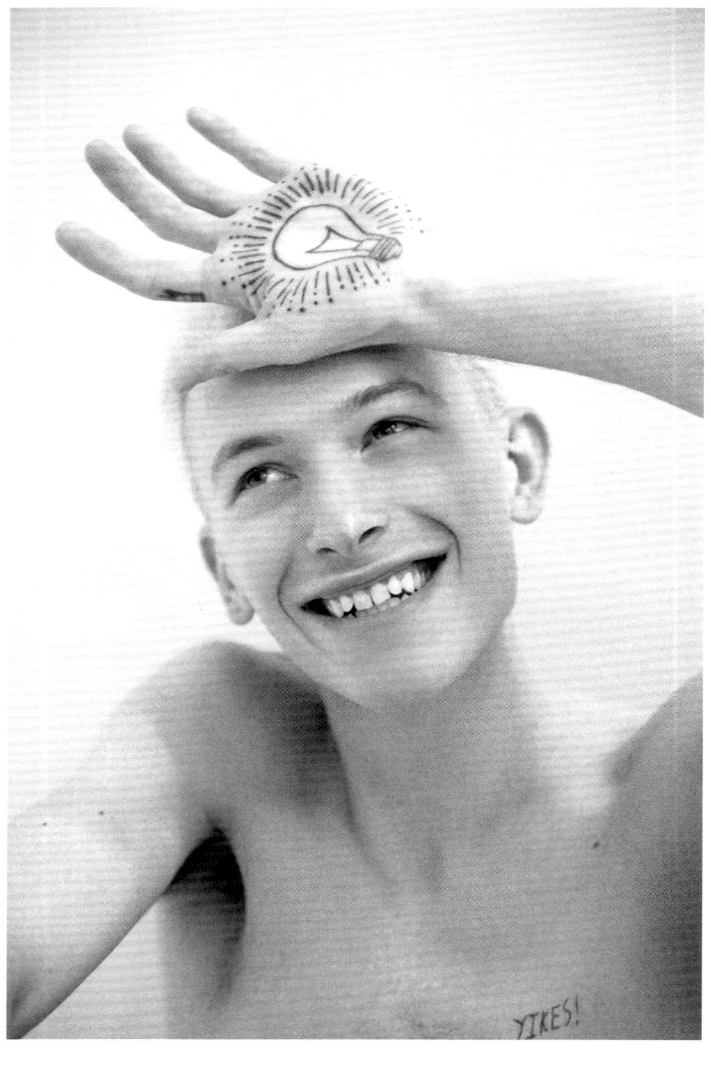

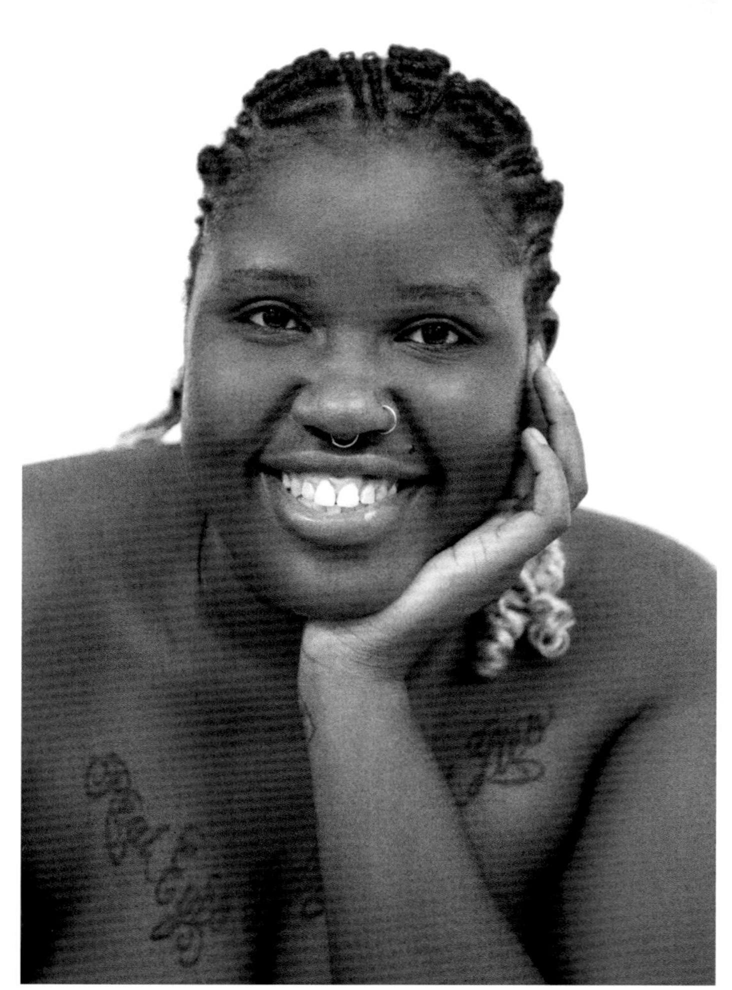

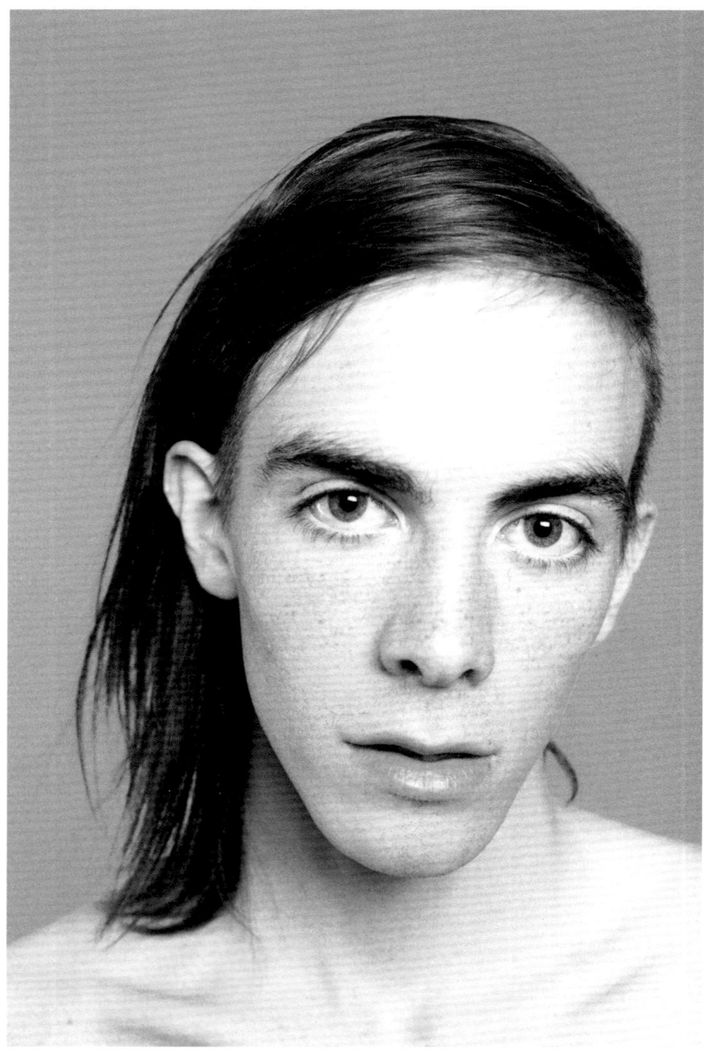

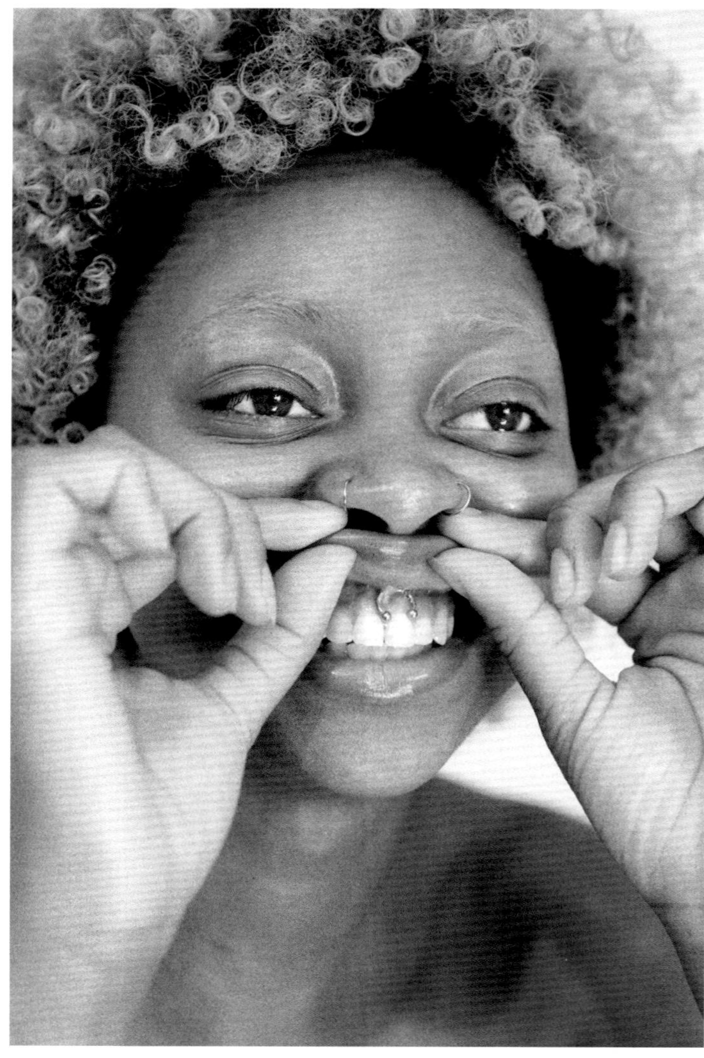

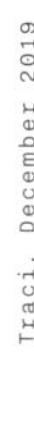
Jake, September 2018 Konyin, October 2018 Joe, April 2010 Traci, December 2019

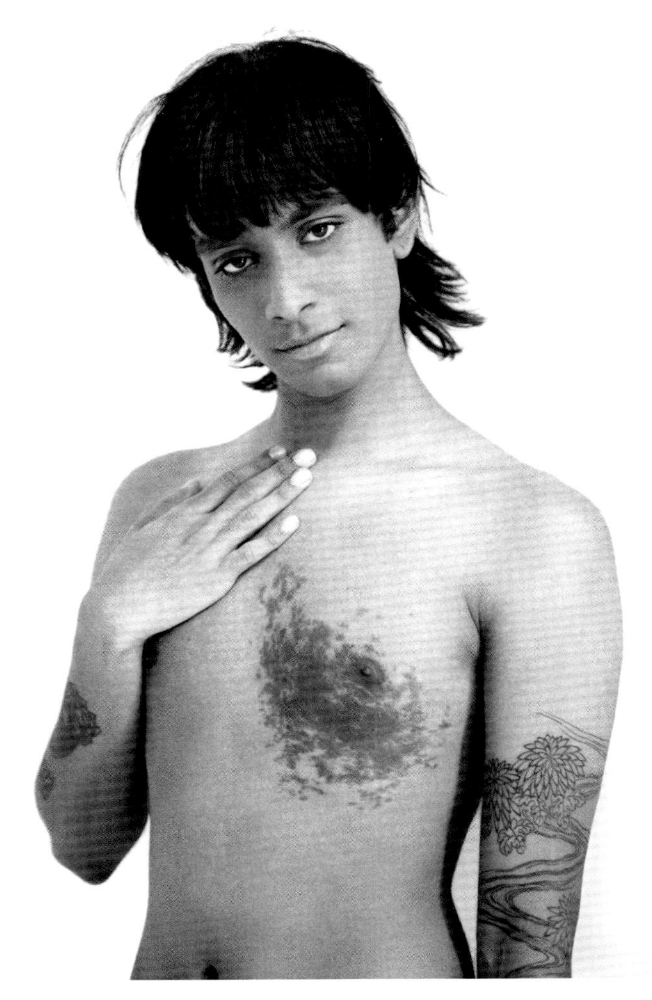

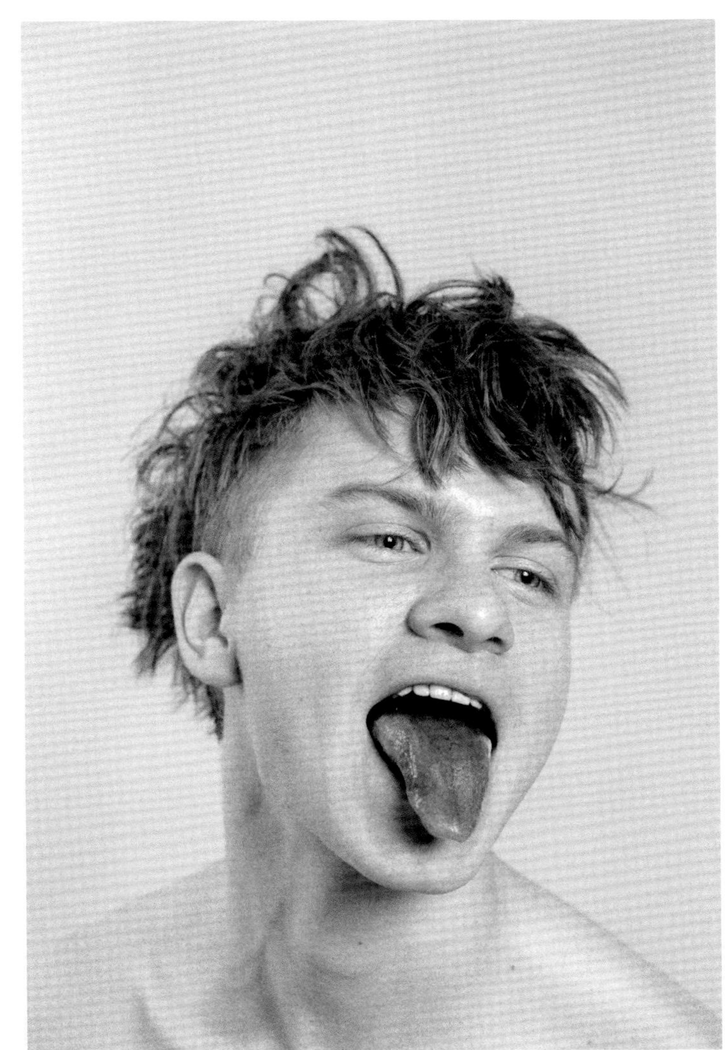

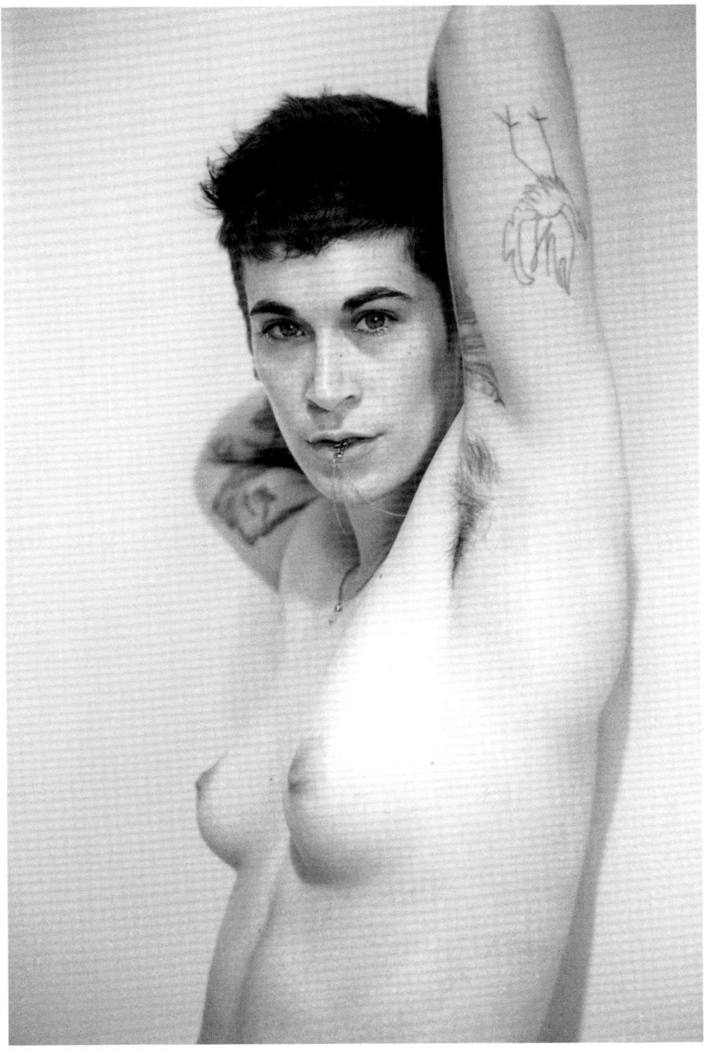

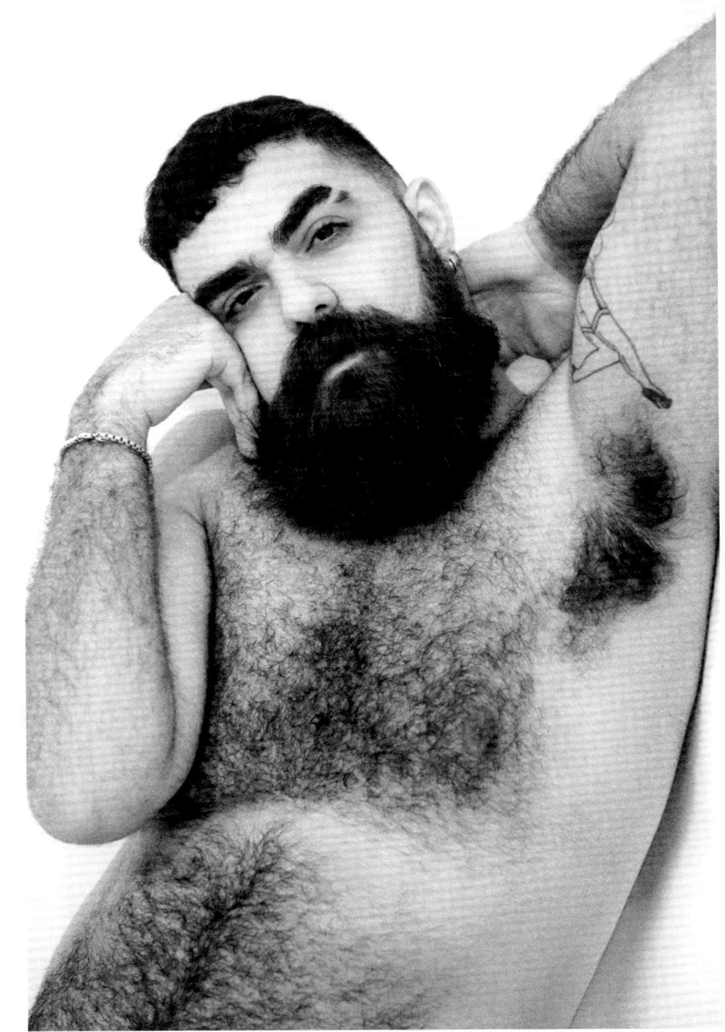

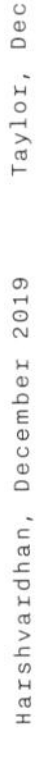

Harshvardhan, December 2019 Taylor, December 2010 Ali, October 2019 Alex, February 2019

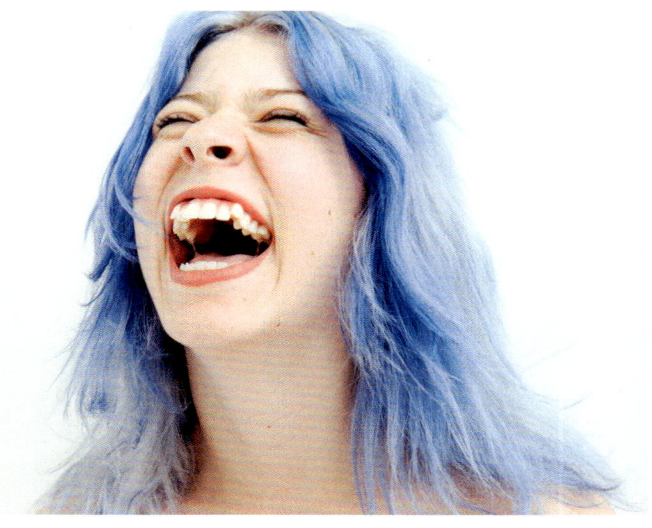

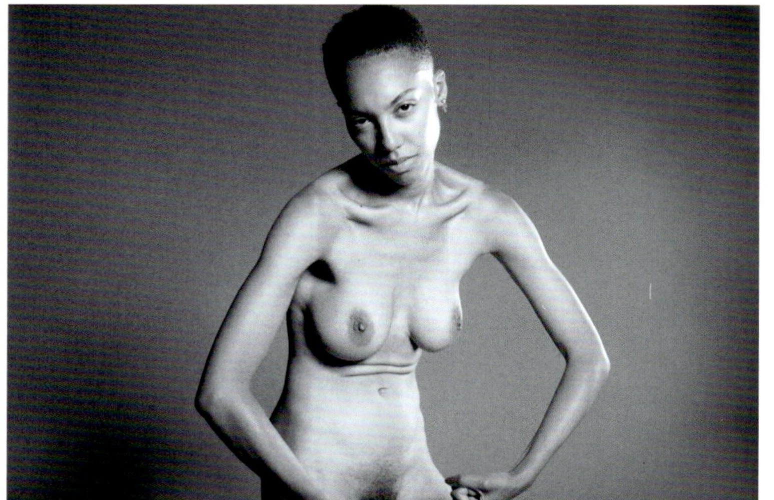

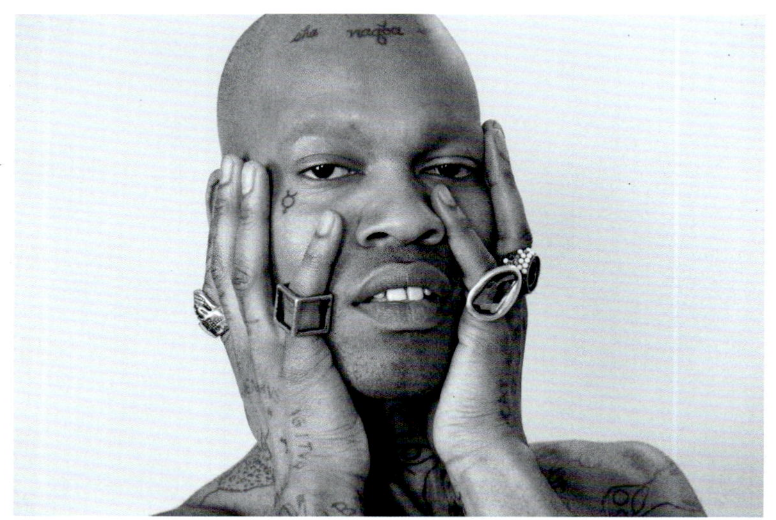

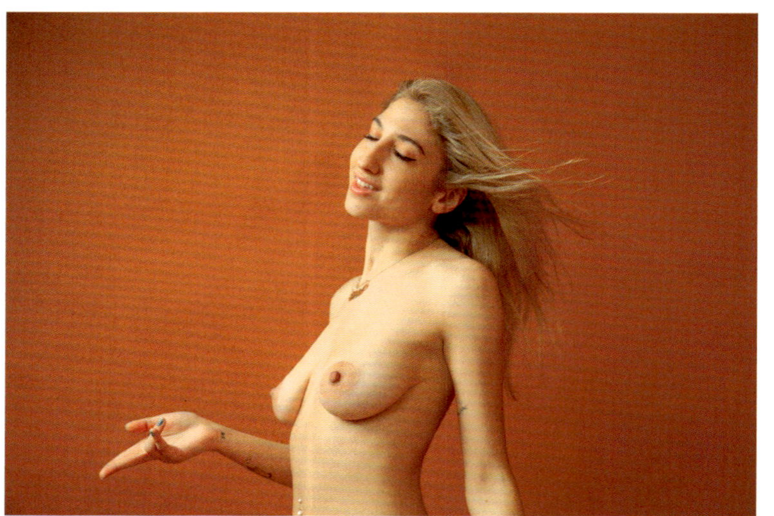

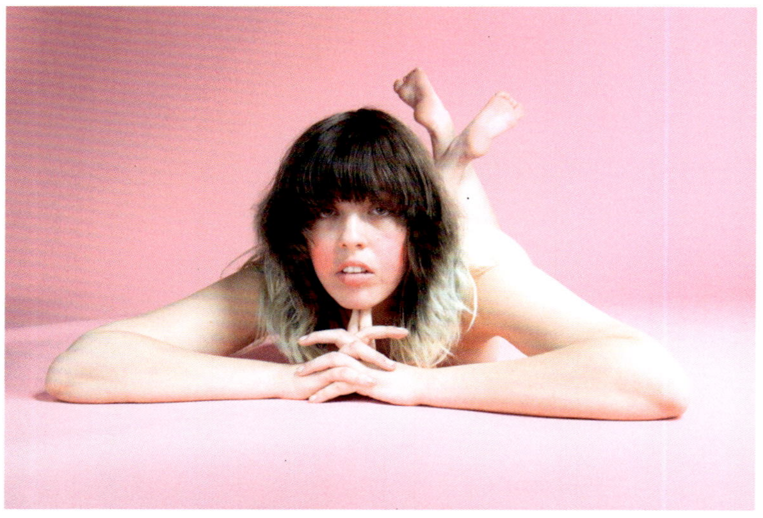

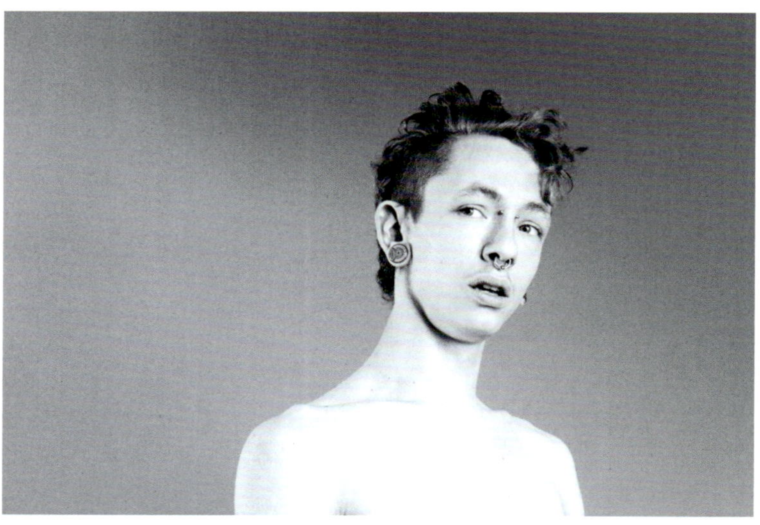

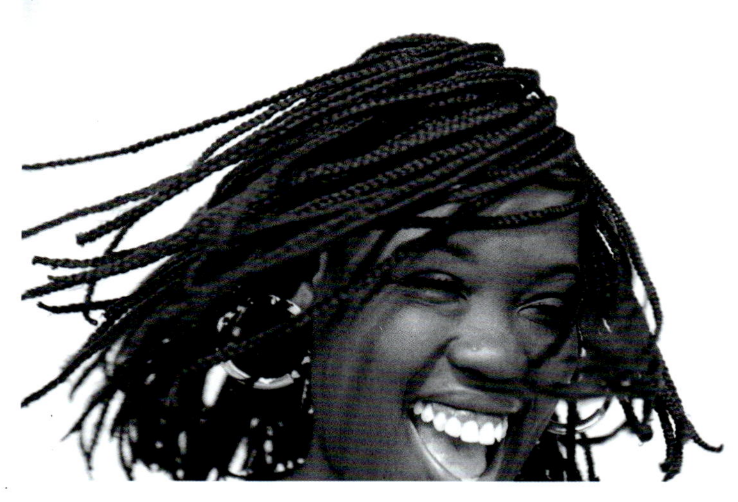

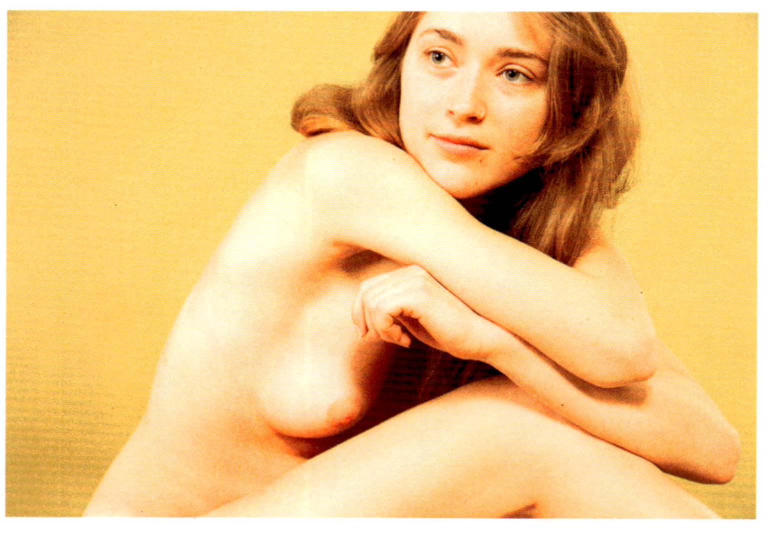

Sydney, June 2017 Chanel, July 2015 Dick, January 2017 Nikki, December 2016 Danielle, April 2015 Ethan, 2014 Mariam, December 2019 Jules, November 2013

Anthony, September 2017 Richard, April 2009 Chinatsu, May 2016 Brody, July 2017 Jinhee & Shaina, January 2017 Brittany, September 2011 Luca, June 2011 Ashley, December 2009

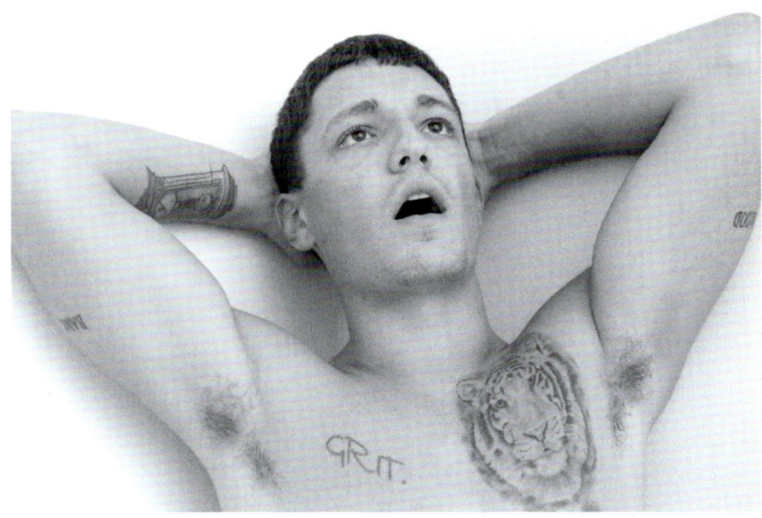

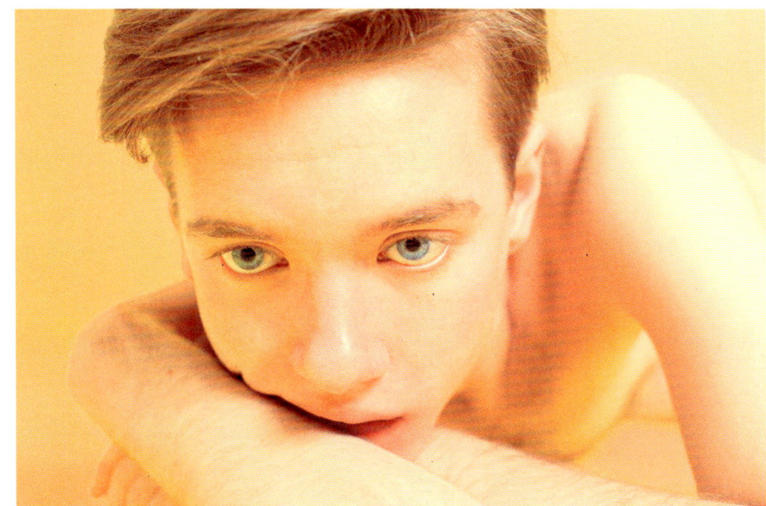

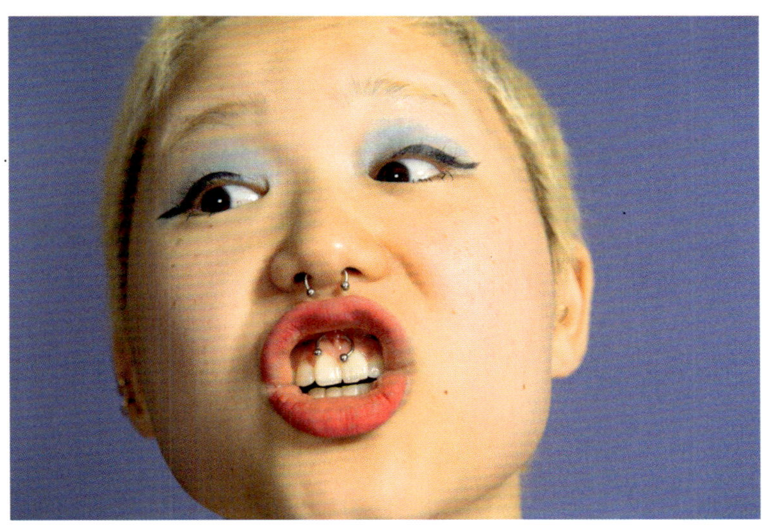

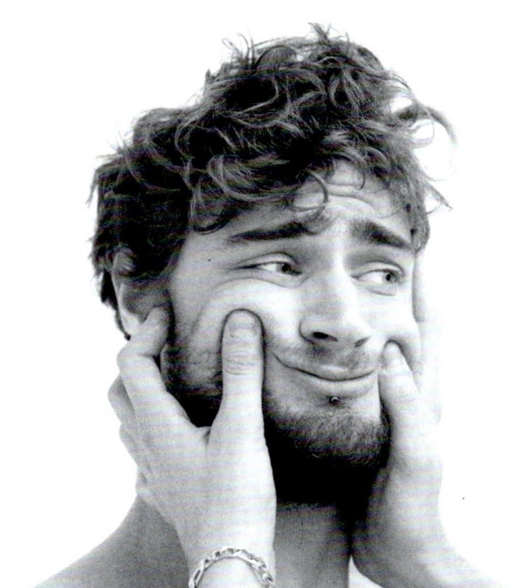

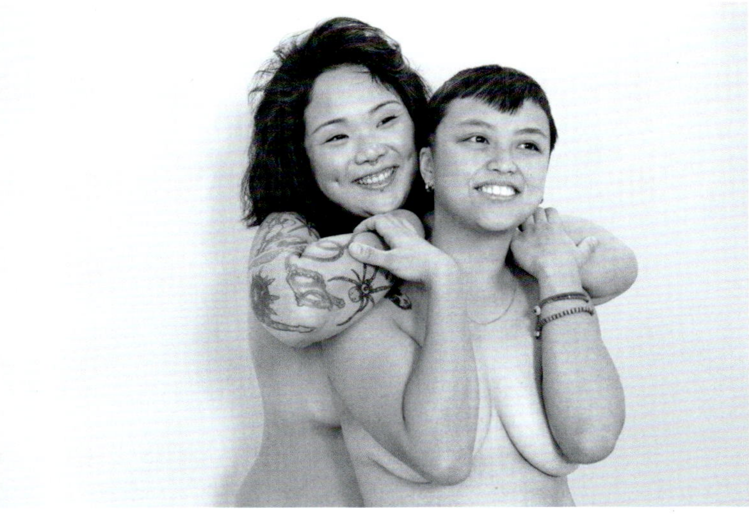

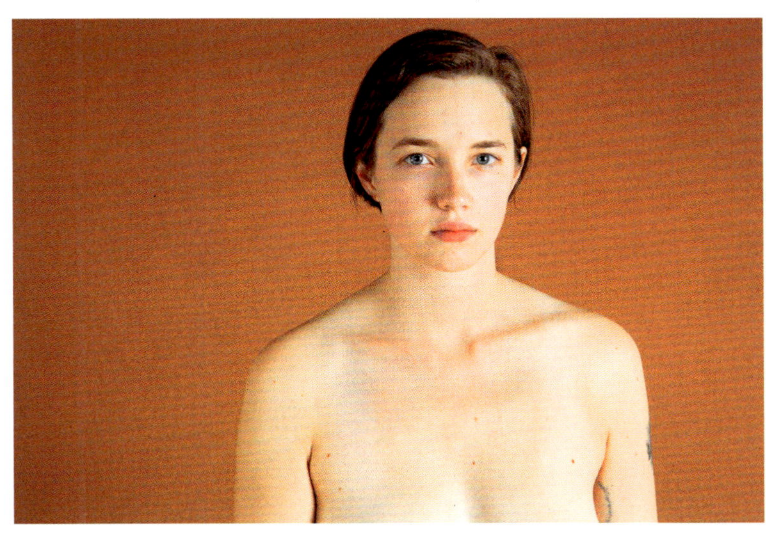

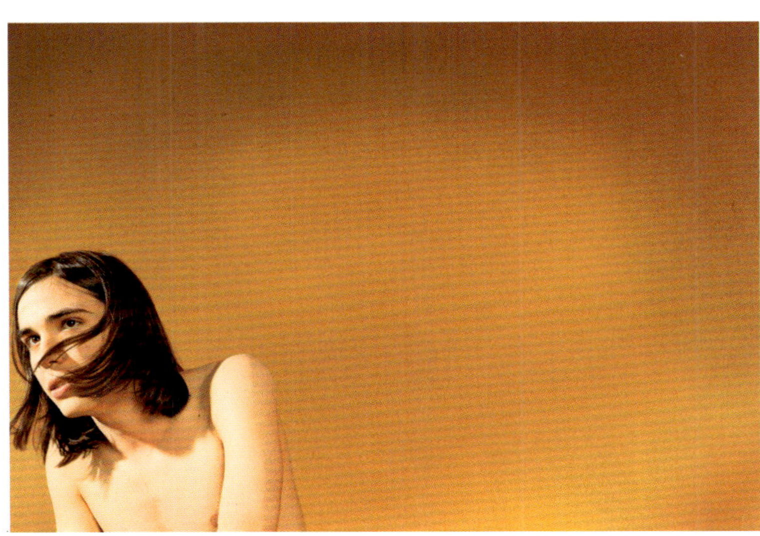

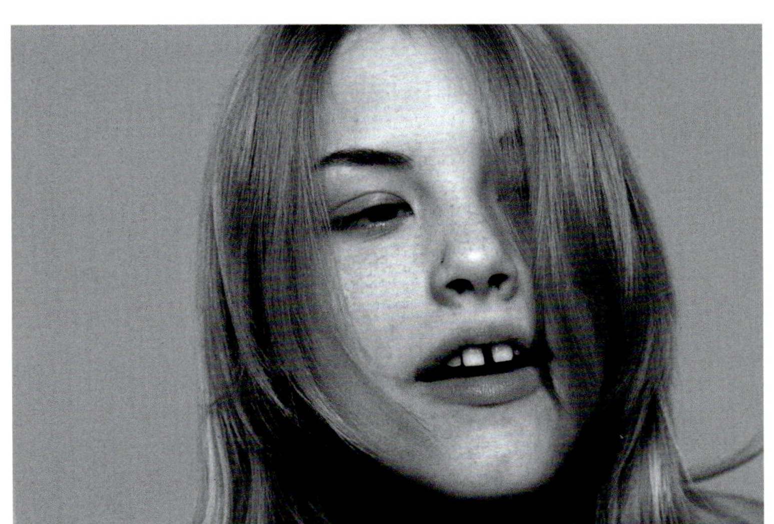

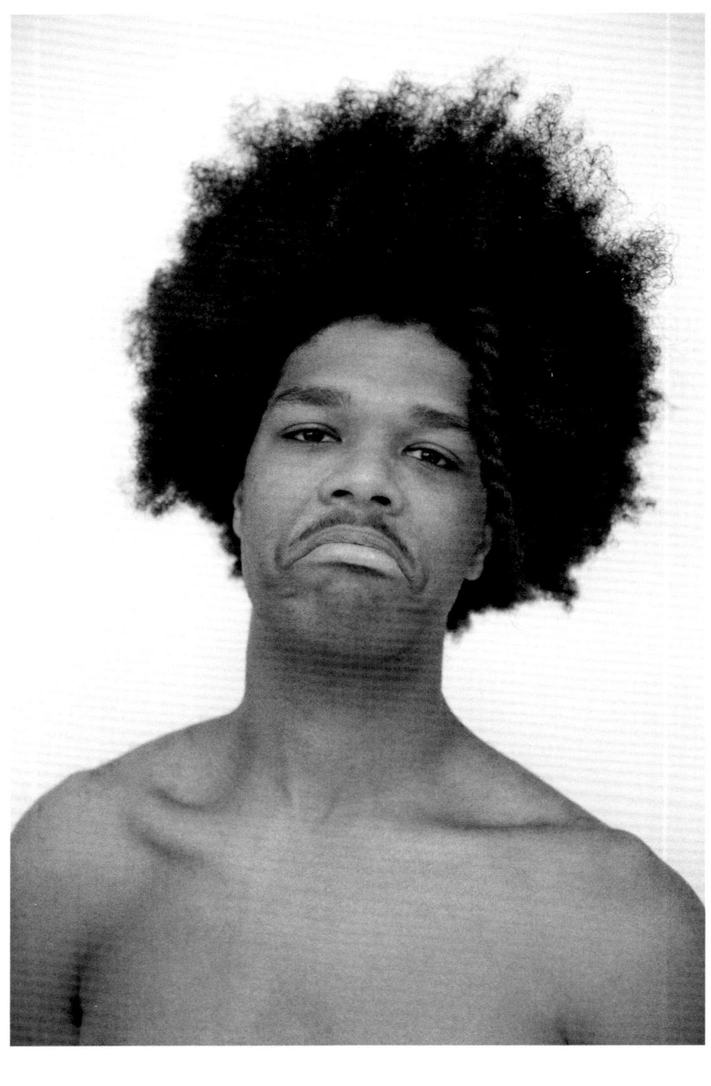

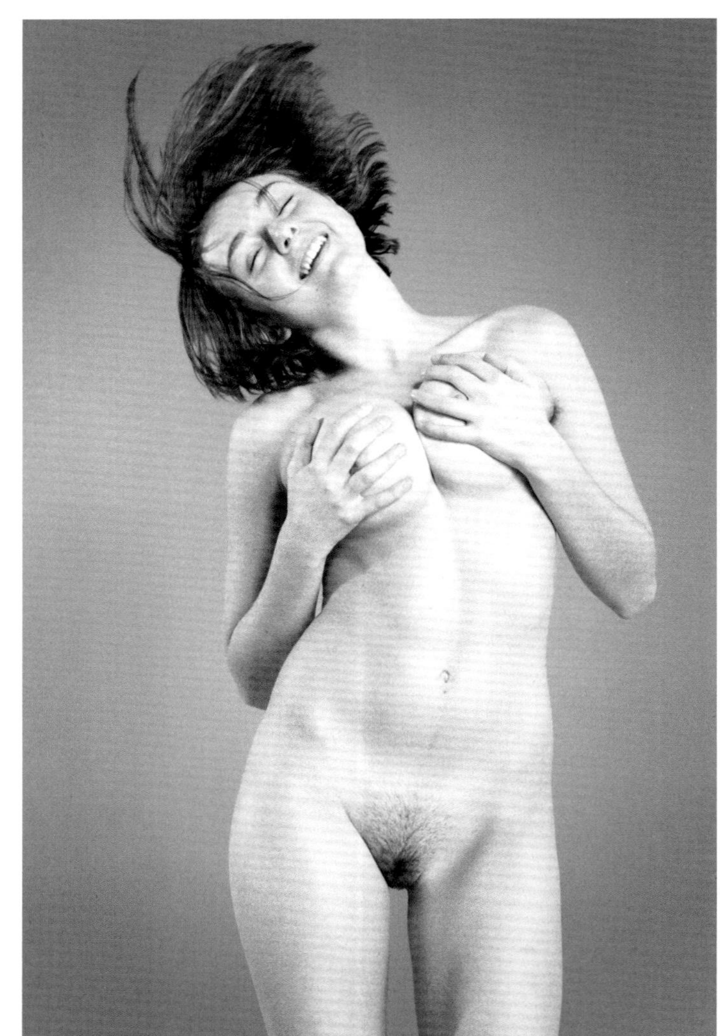

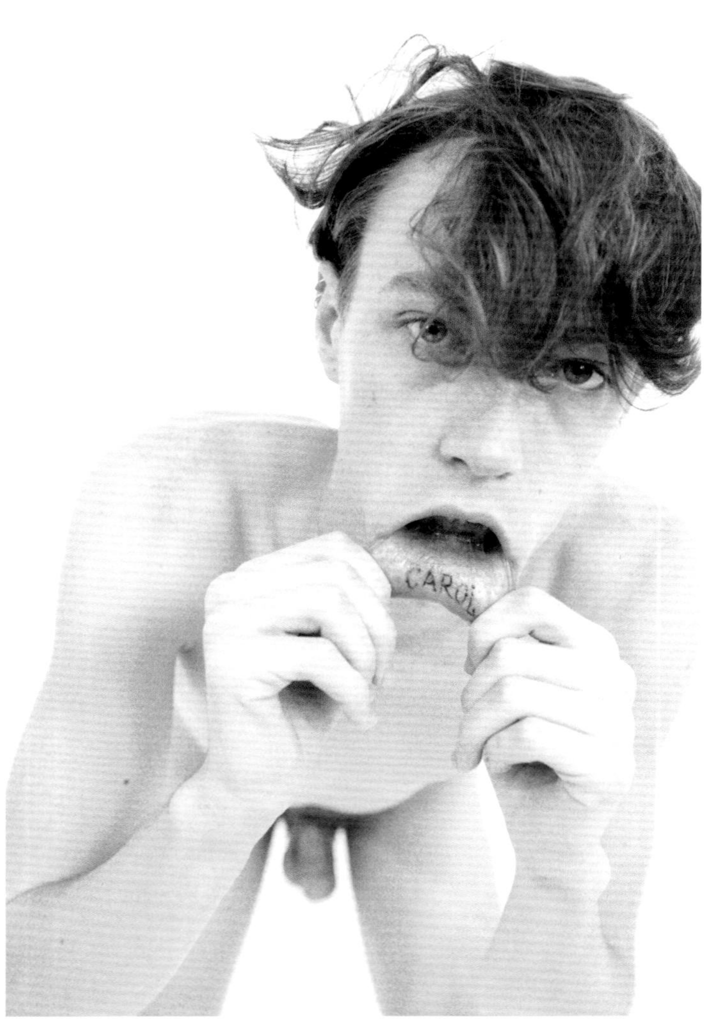

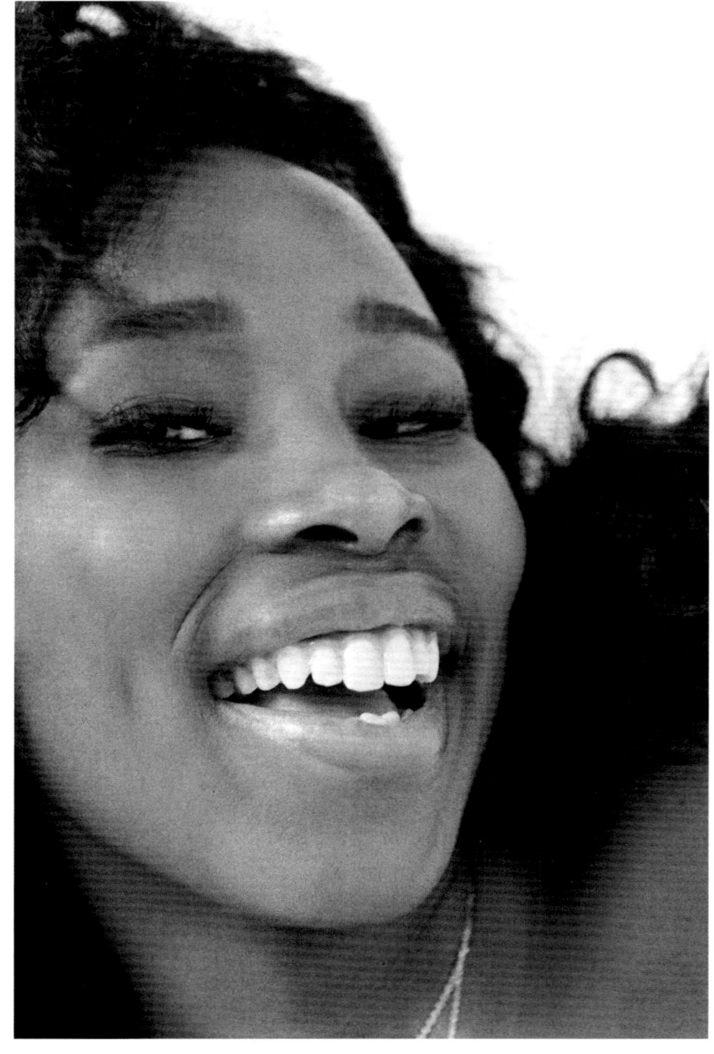

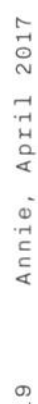

Christian, September 2018   Ivy, December 2014   Noah, October 2019   Annie, April 2017

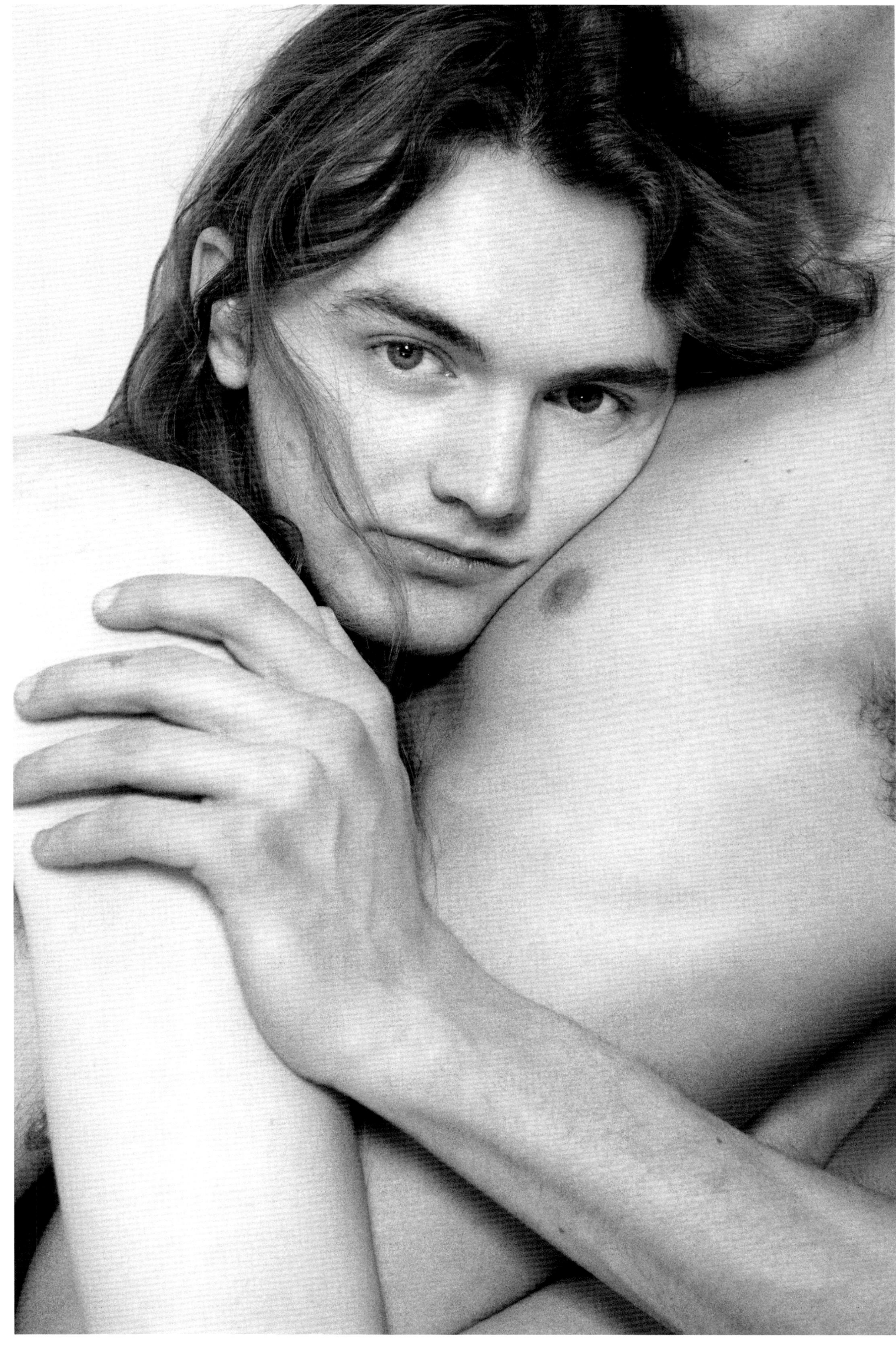

Richard & Bolt, May 2016

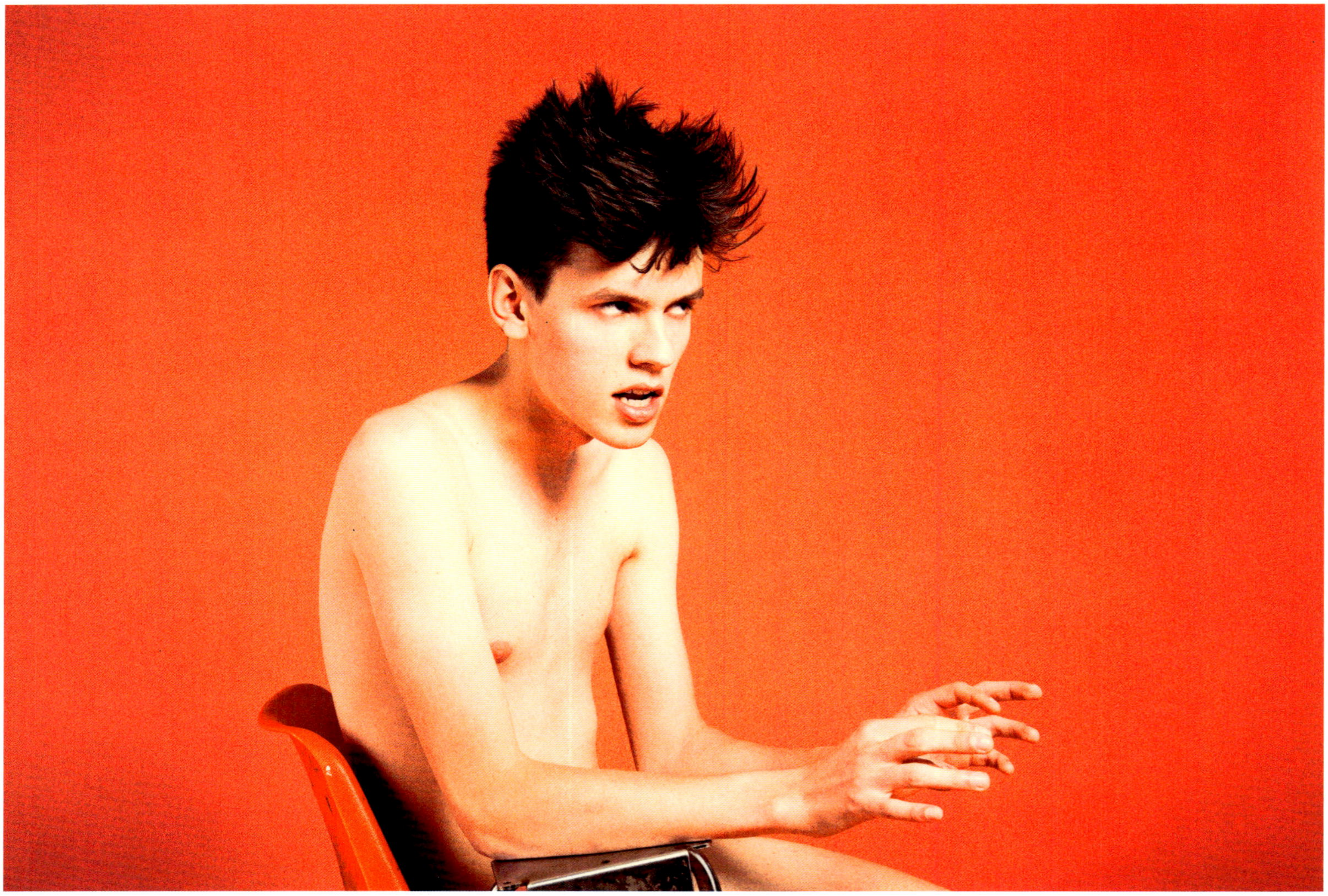

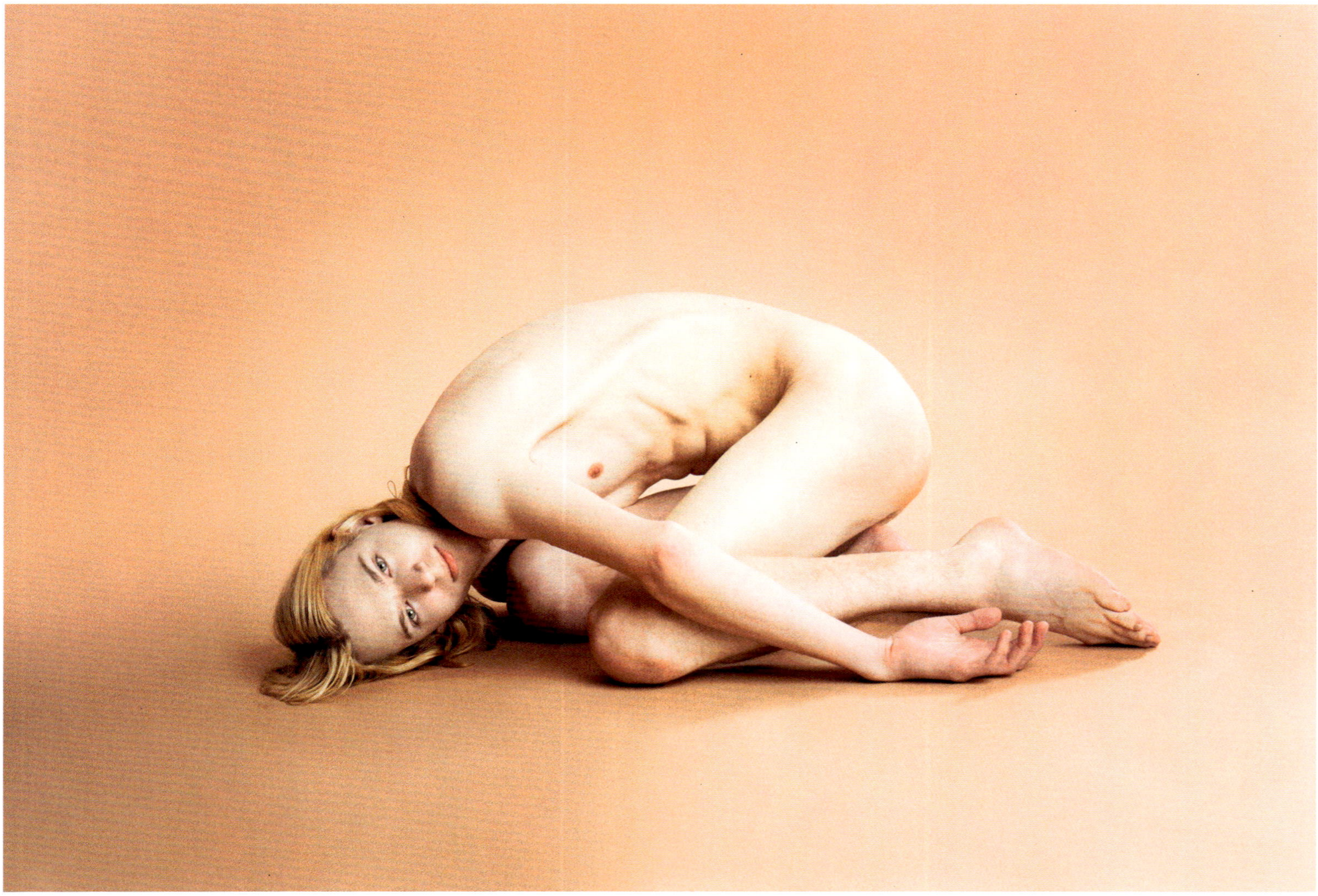

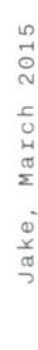

Henry, June 2012

Jake, March 2015

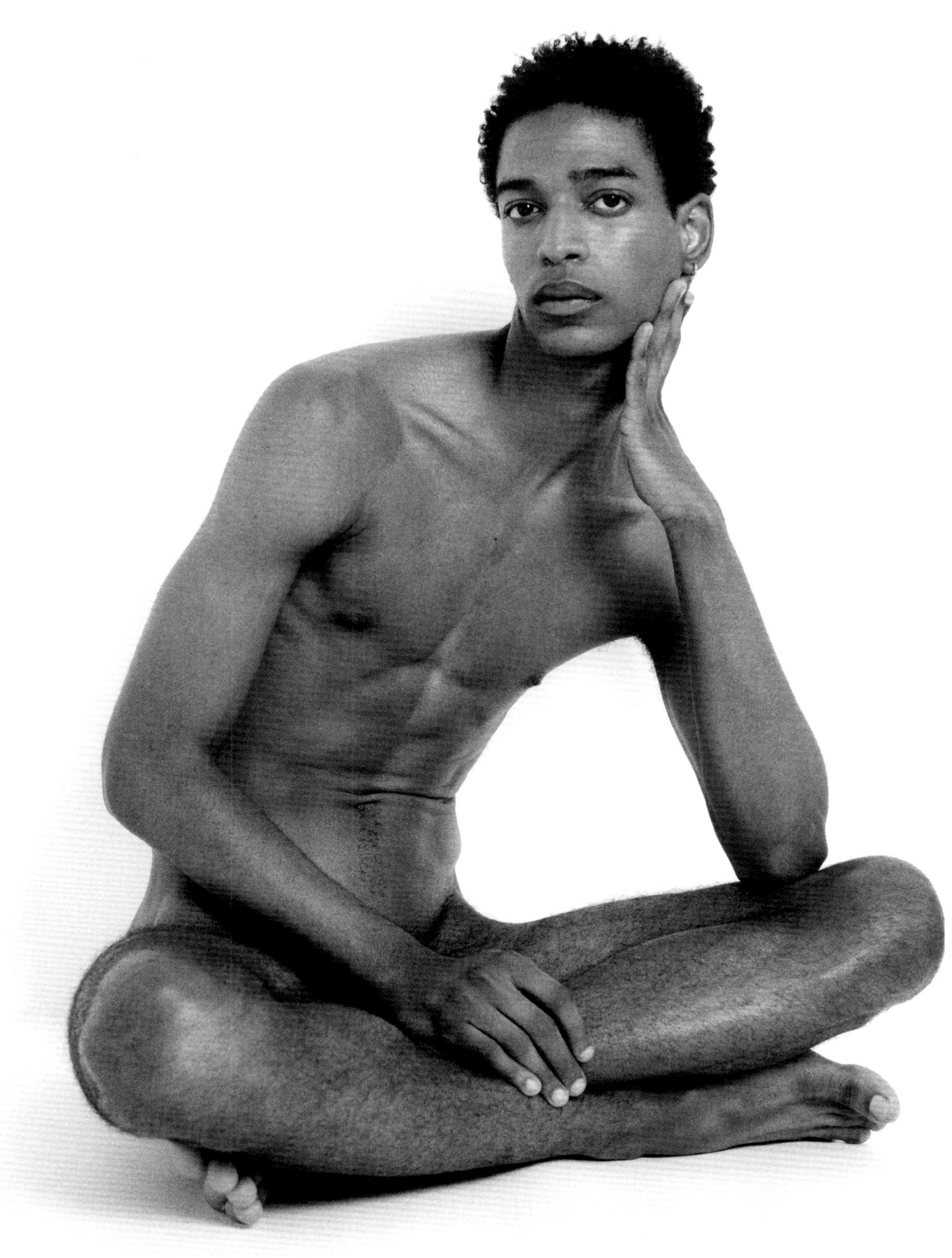

Darron, April 2017

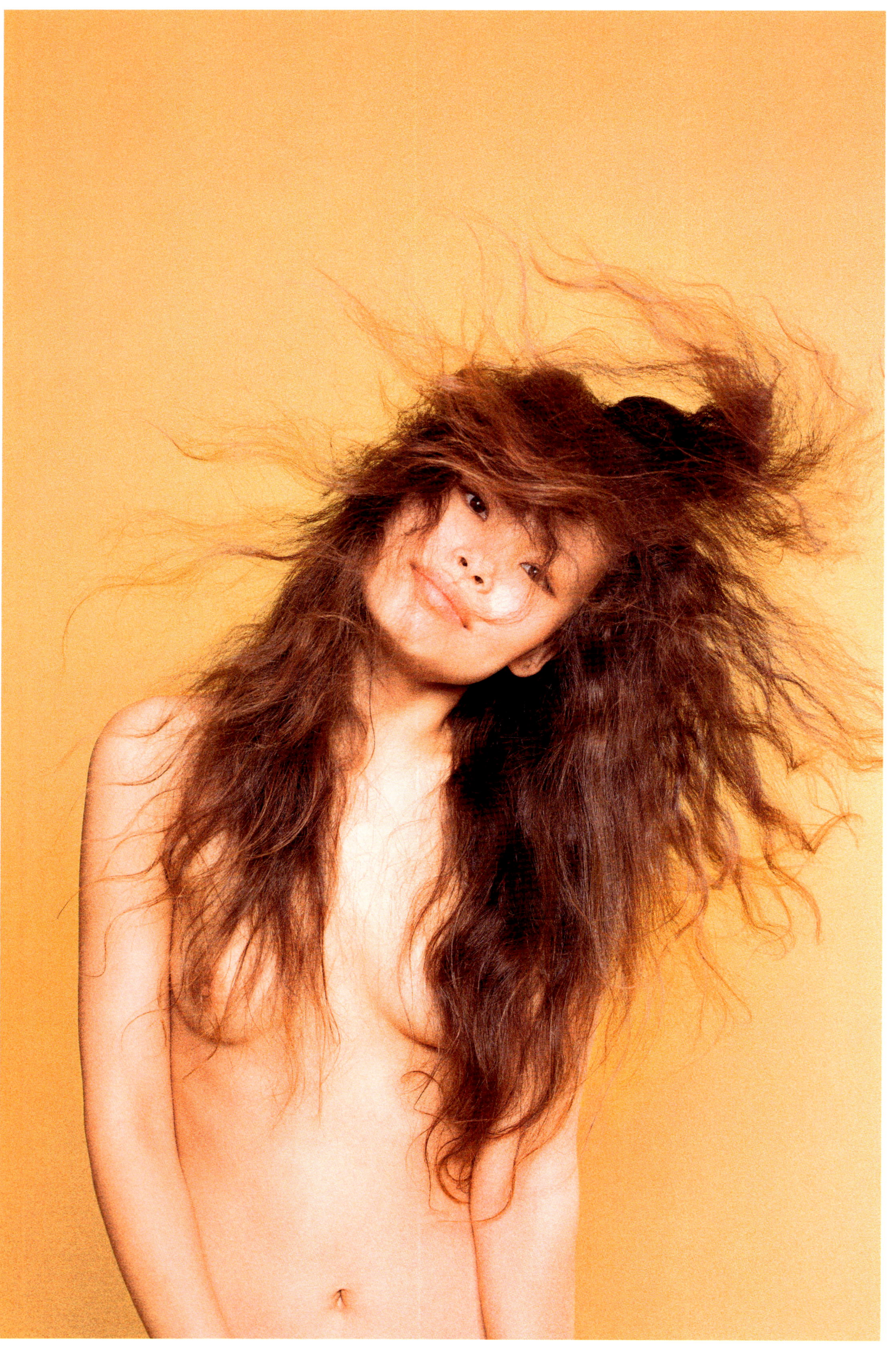

Saglara, September 2009

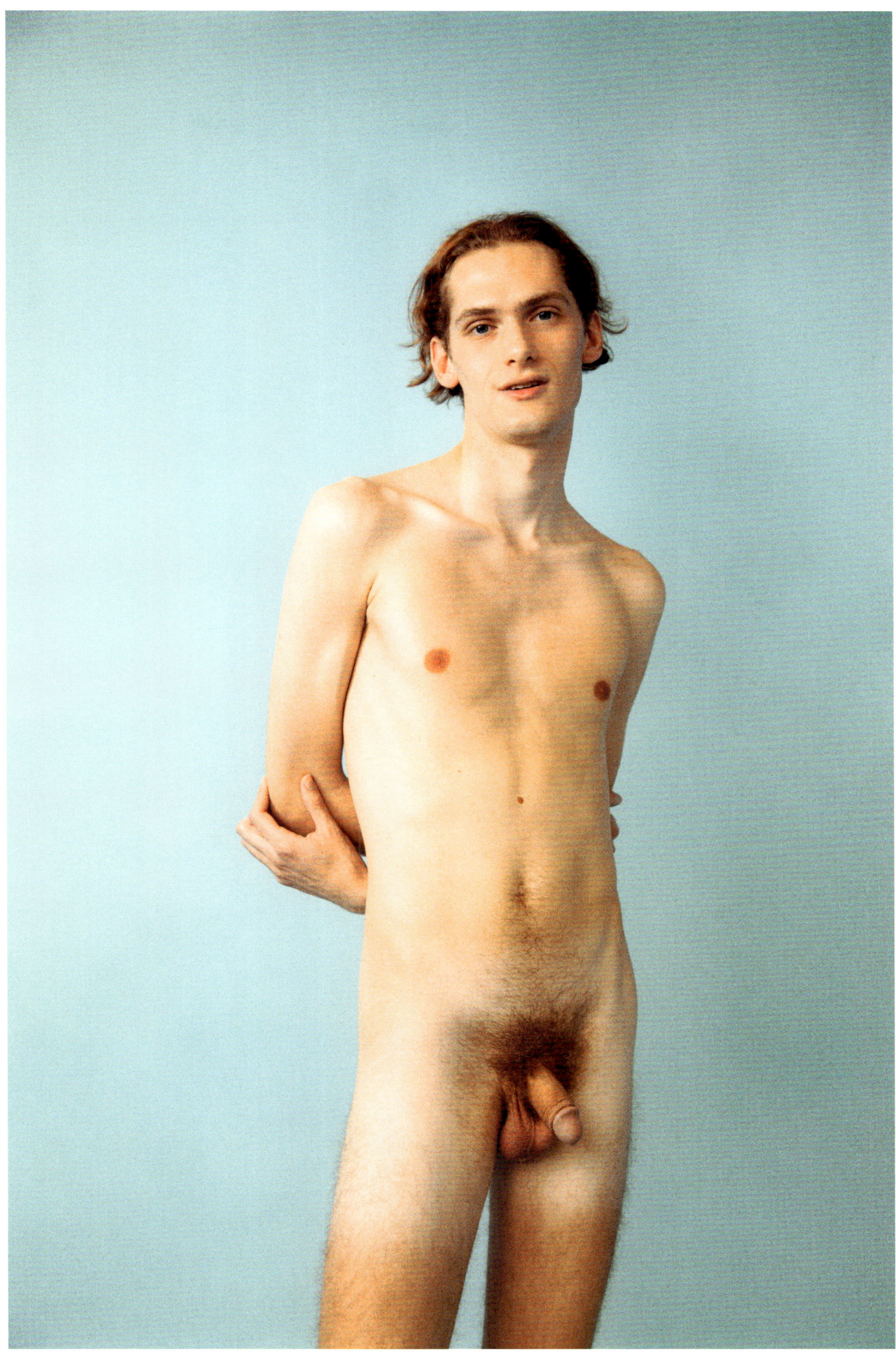

Devin, December 2016

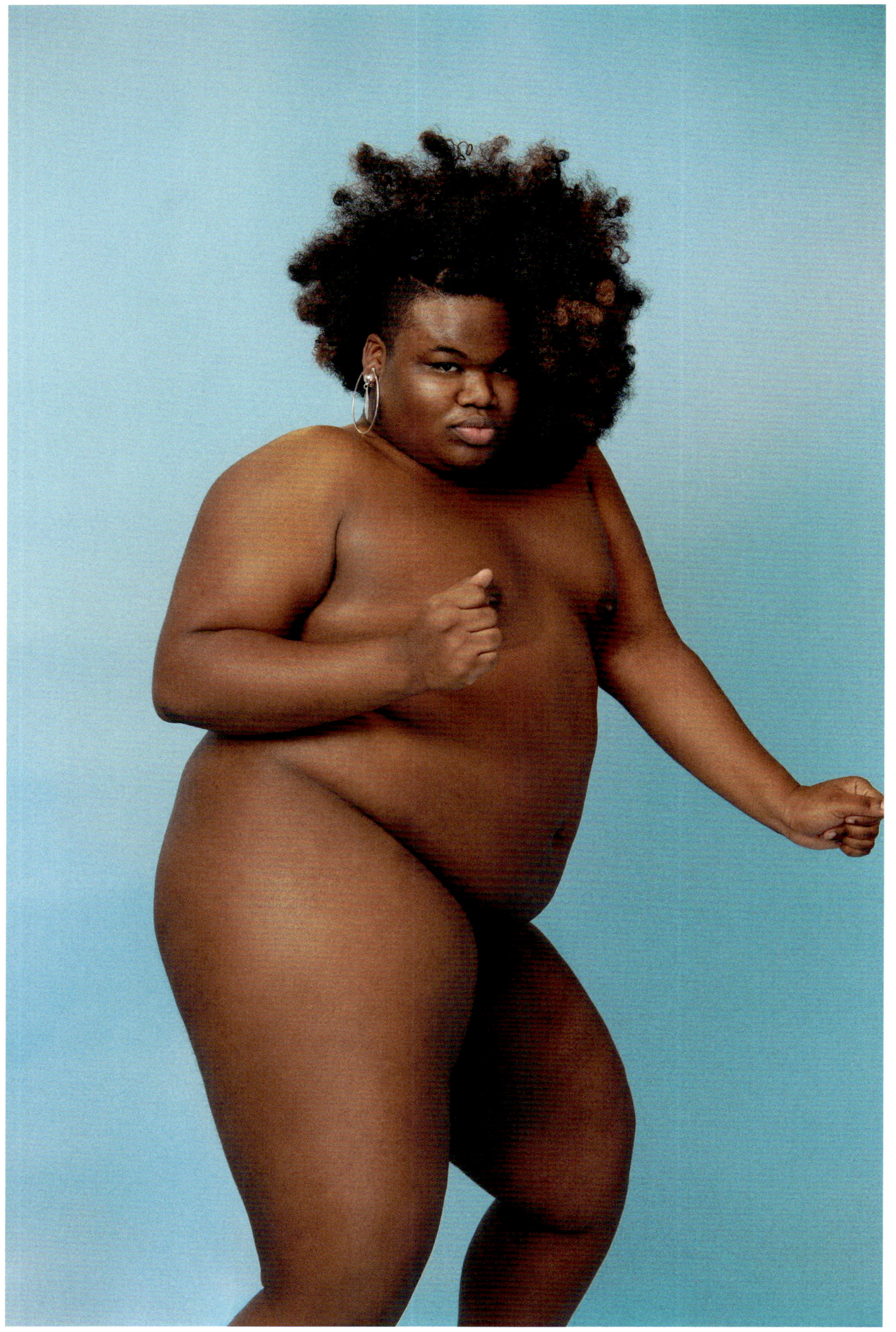

Jari, December 2016

It had to be a Gaga era. A Beyoncé era for sure. We're definitely in a Rihanna realm too. I can tell because of my hair. I don't use the term anymore, but I was doing this alt-Afrofuturism thing. Like Rihanna shaving her head, I have half of my head shaved with this big fro, infusing punk, staying close to my roots.

It was also the era of *high faggotry*—that's what I called it. I was so embedded in my queerness and so proud of it. I was detaching myself from the gay male world. I remember waking up my partner one day and being like, "I don't think gay fits me anymore." In New York, that's what gay meant to me at the time. "I feel queer," I told her. "I feel trans. And I'm embracing it. If you're going to call me faggot, why not?" I remember being called faggot on the street and saying, "Duh!"

I was also a photographer and had studied Ryan's work and the way he shot bodies. Ryan was shooting fat folks. Ryan was shooting darker-skinned folks. He was shooting trans folks. And he was doing it in a way that wasn't like, "How close can we get them to the proximity of thinness, whiteness, or the beauty standard?" He was shooting people as human beings.

Ryan pushes for inclusivity in a way that most people don't. Where most people are like, "But I included them in the shoot," Ryan's like, "I'm going to get you the cover. I'm going to make you the lead feature." And that's what happened. Ryan took care of me.

After this, Ryan shot us on a double-decker bus kissing in the middle of Times Square. I shot another, maybe three more series after that with him. For *Paradiso*, we went up to the Adirondacks. We were staying in this lake house with wraparound windows. I remember, one morning, I was doing my makeup, listening to Sade, and looking in the mirror when I heard a shutter. I turned around and it's Ryan. He's like, "I just had to get that image."

I believe the Calvin Klein billboard was next. There I was on set with a lot of bodies that weren't like mine. I was the only plus-size model and the only, at the time, trans woman. Those spaces can feel very secluded but Ryan welcomed me on set like, "Here's our celebrity. Here's our queen for the shoot." That meant a lot to me.

When you're in this weird celebrity limelight kind of thing, people assume that people are taking care of you or always looking out for you, and it's not the case. But Ryan has done that and not only for me, but for girls like me, consistently. Whether we're talking about Gia Love or Qween Jean, Ryan has been there for the girls in a way that's about more than making us the face, he really stays in community. I think people worry that their work will get stale if they photograph the same people over and over, but Ryan has this knack of finding us in different parts of our lives, and the images are completely different. Ryan has captured me in some of the most beautiful and some of the saddest moments of my life. This image compared to my Calvin Klein billboard or how I am in *Paradiso*, they look like different humans.

You're documenting somebody's journey, so the art is never stale.

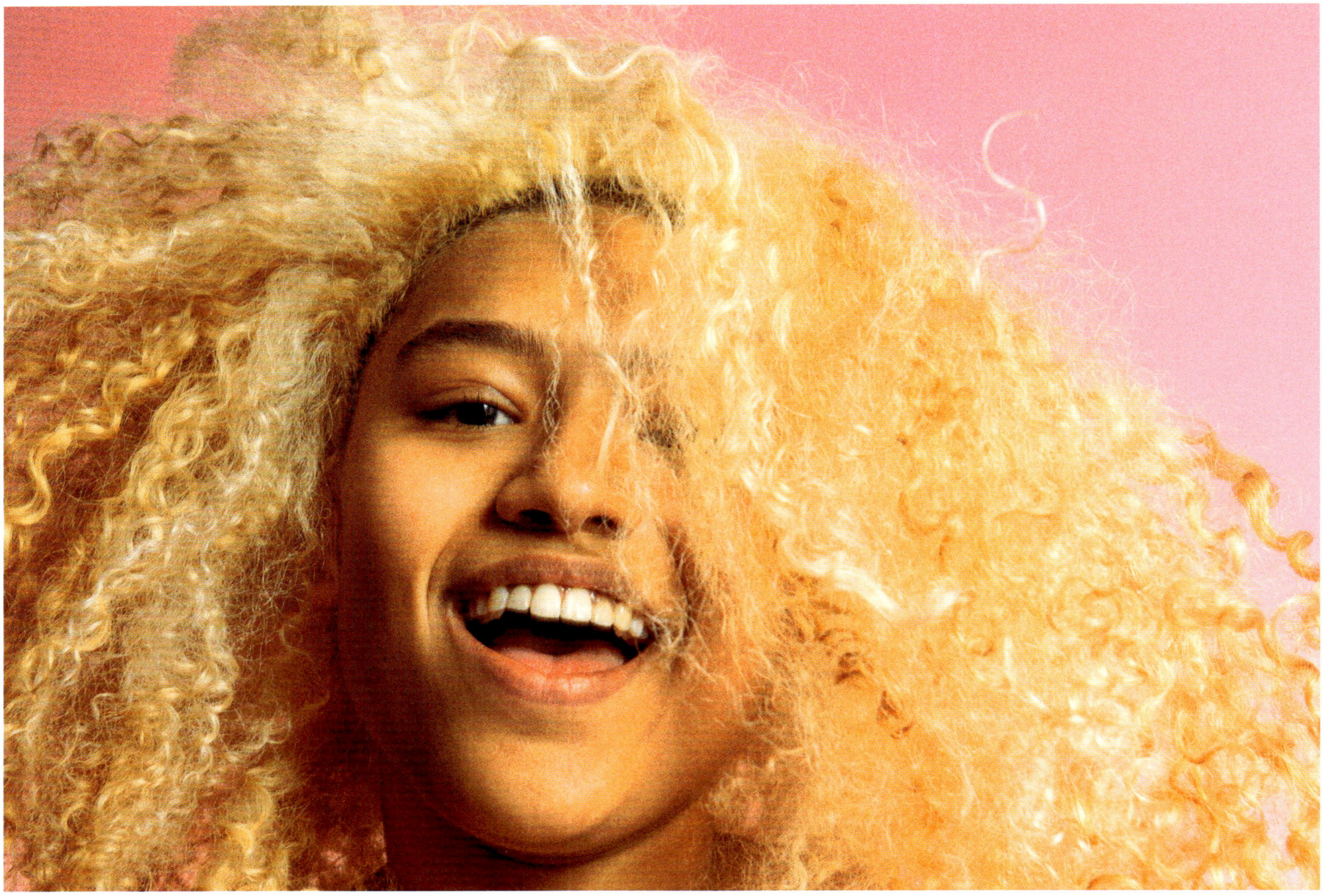

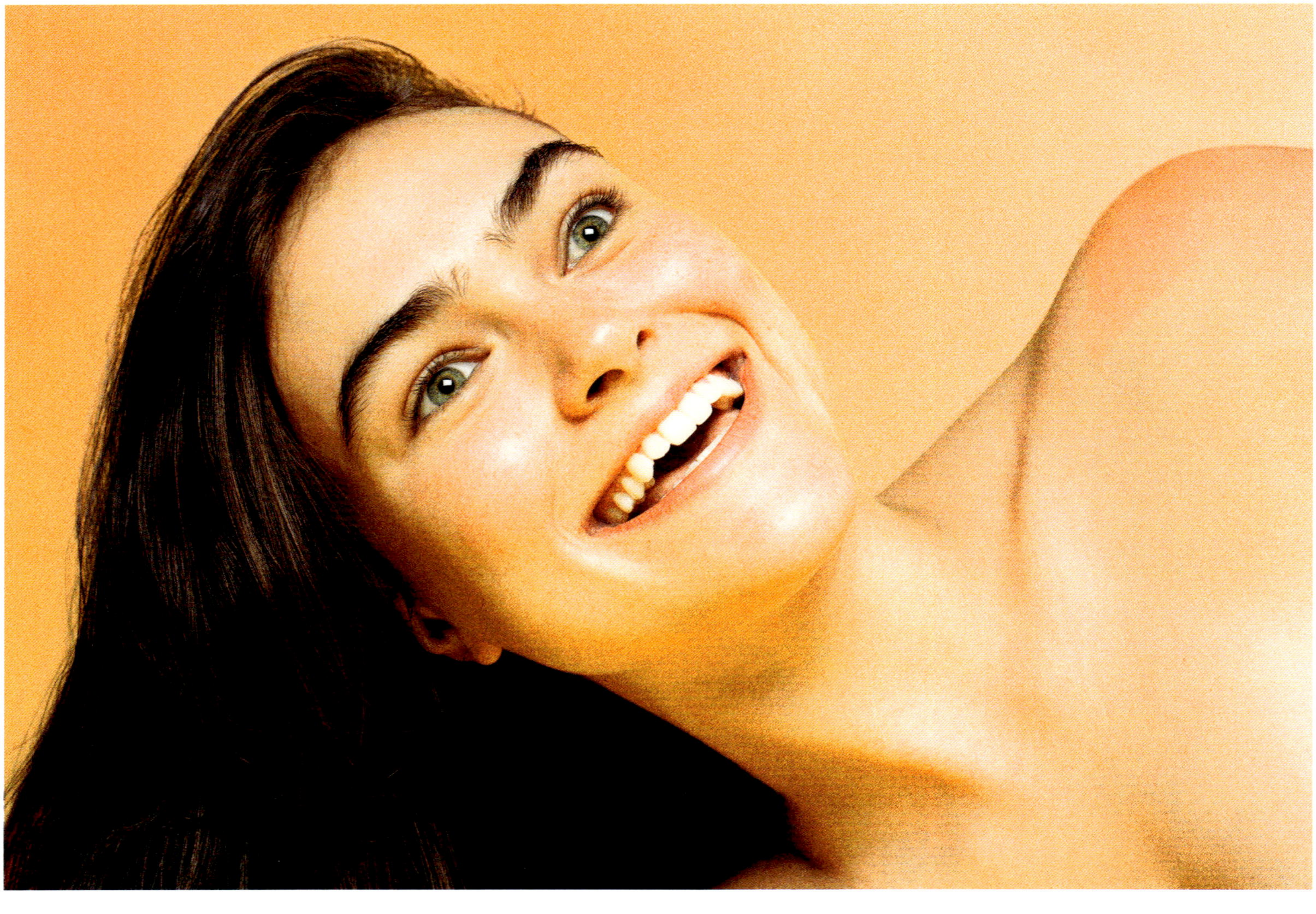

Nikki, November 2015

Myla, September 2009

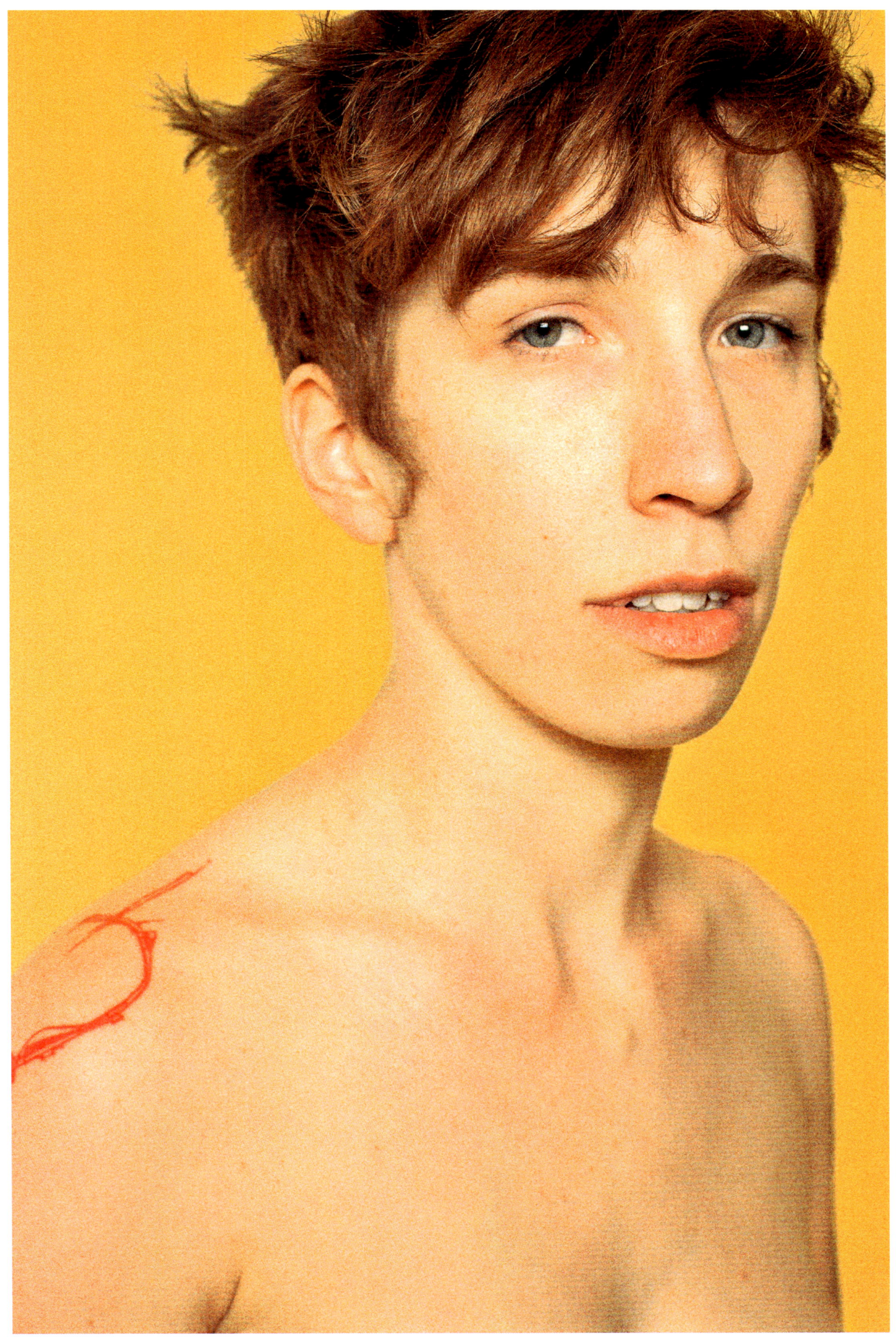

Io, January 2010

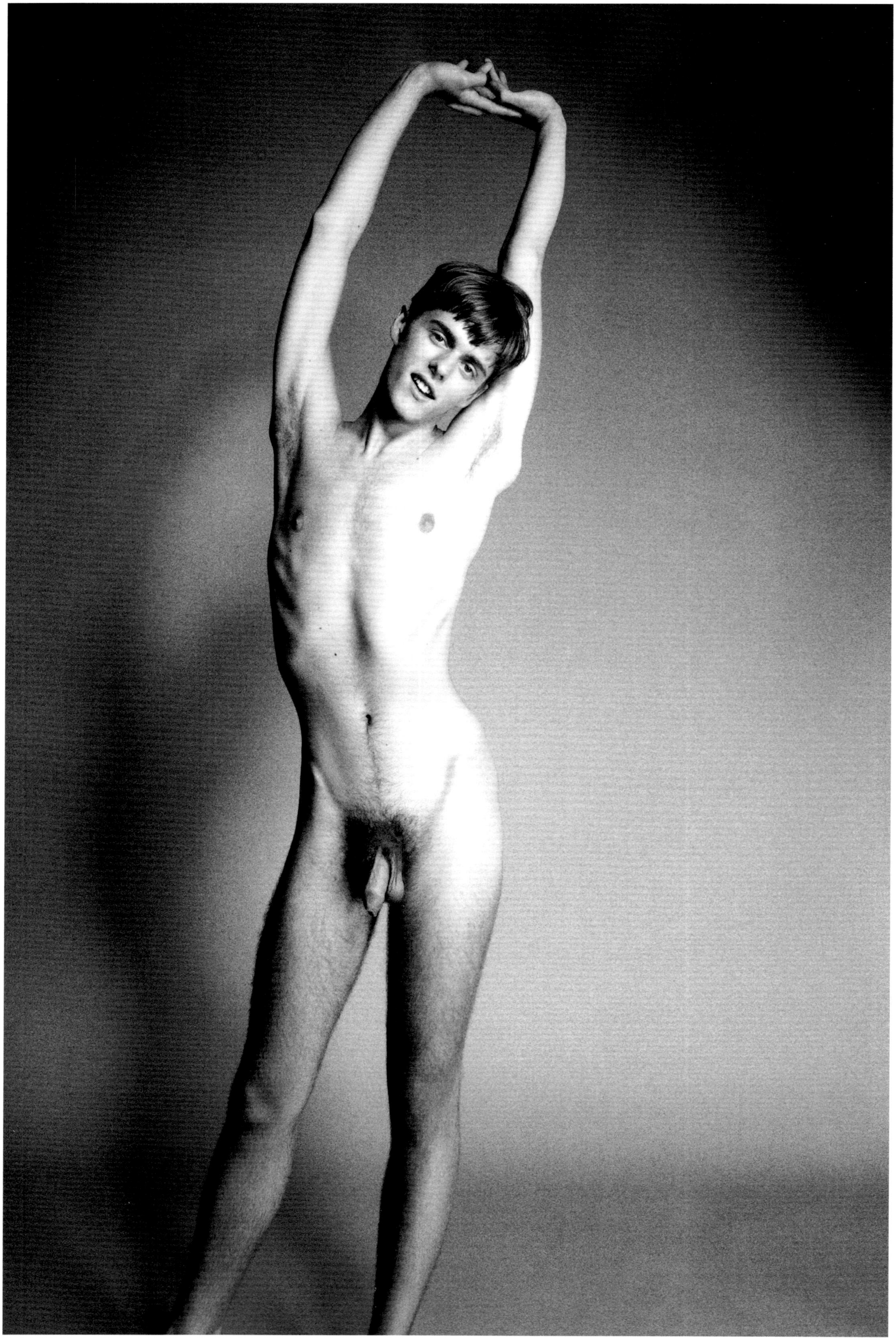

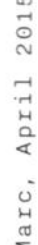

Marc, April 2015

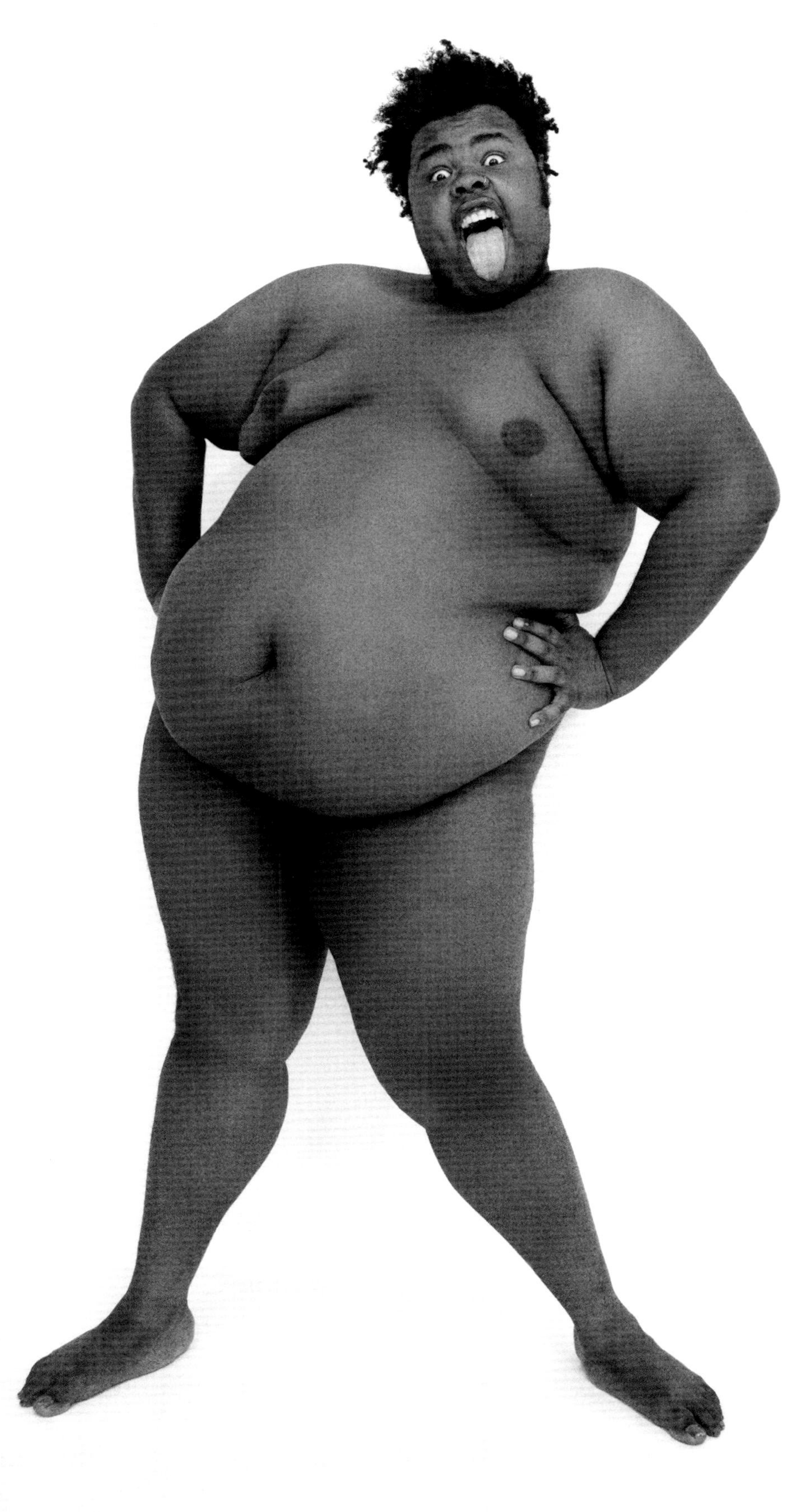

Khaaliq, September 2018

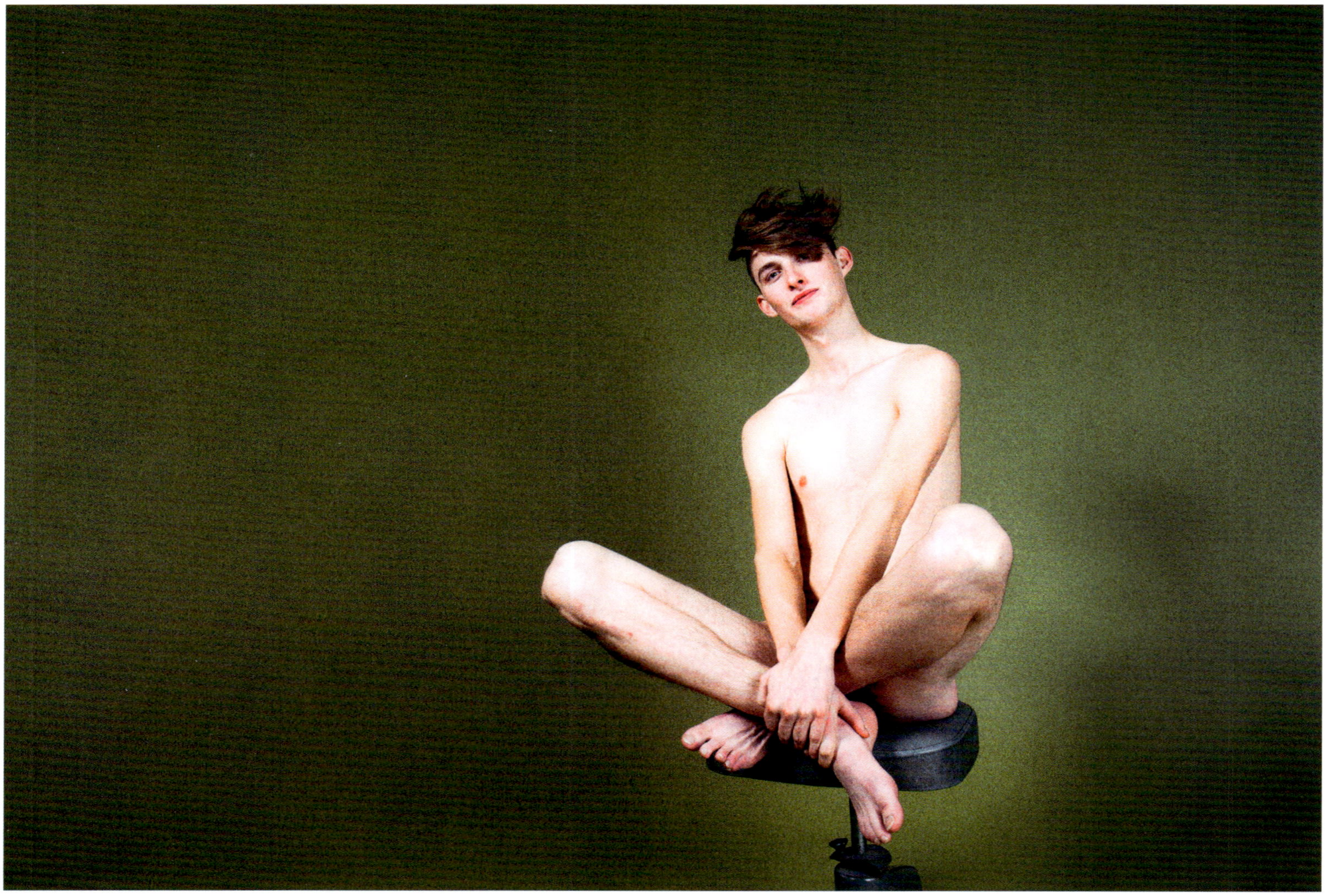

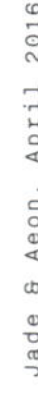

Lewis, December 2014

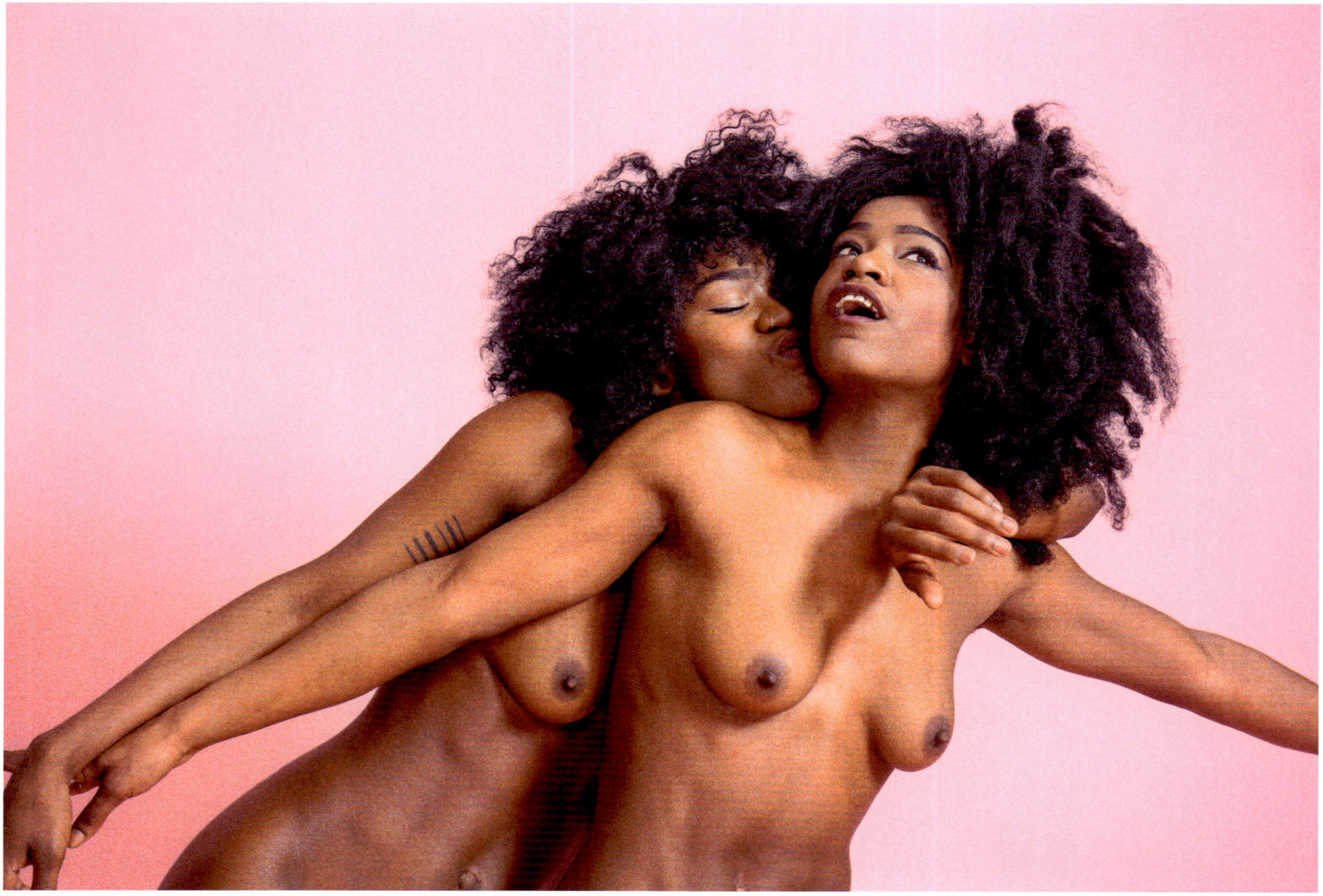

Jade & Aeon, April 2016

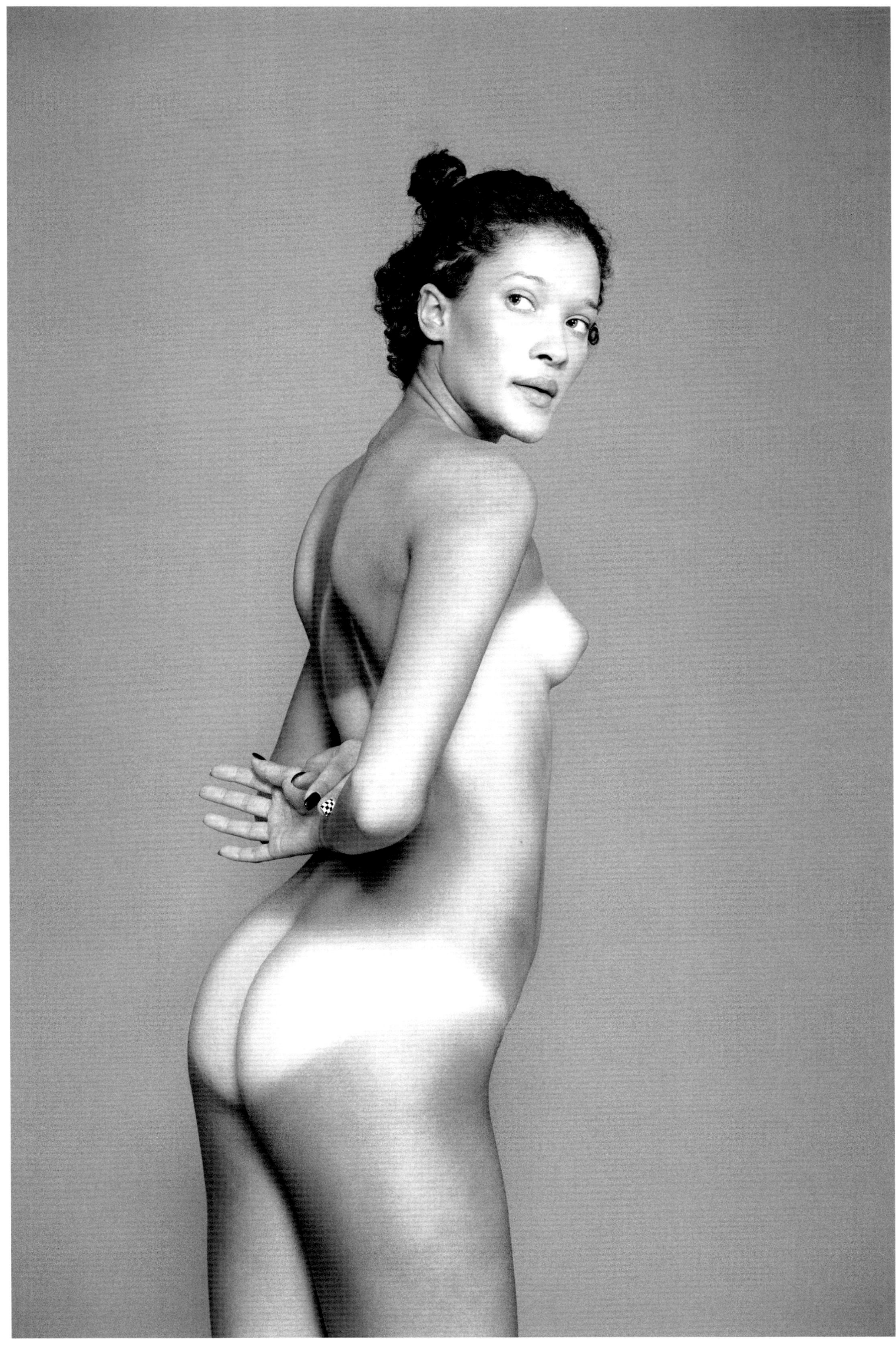

Olivia, April 2016

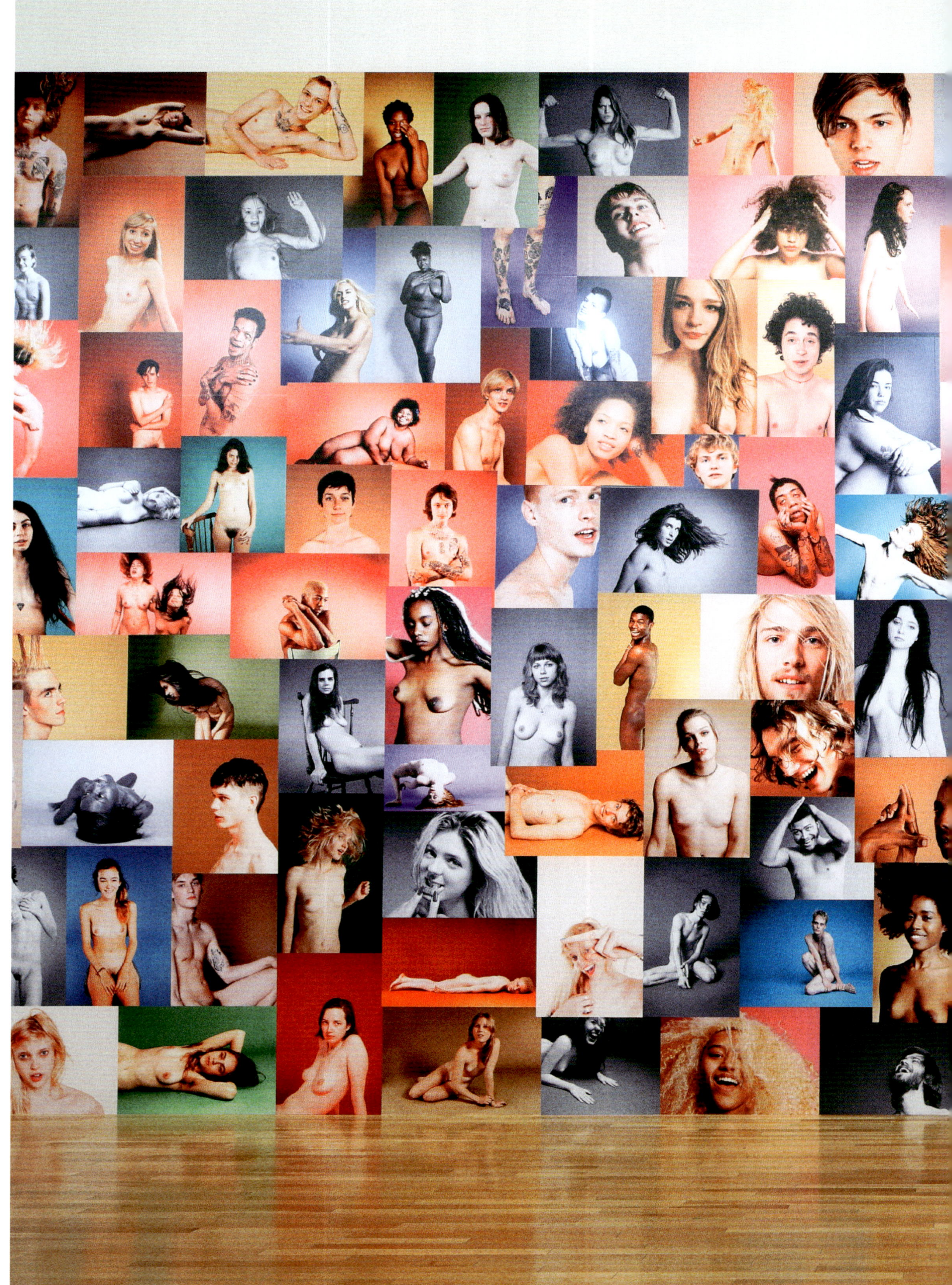

Body Loud, Tokyo Opera City Museum, Japan, 2016

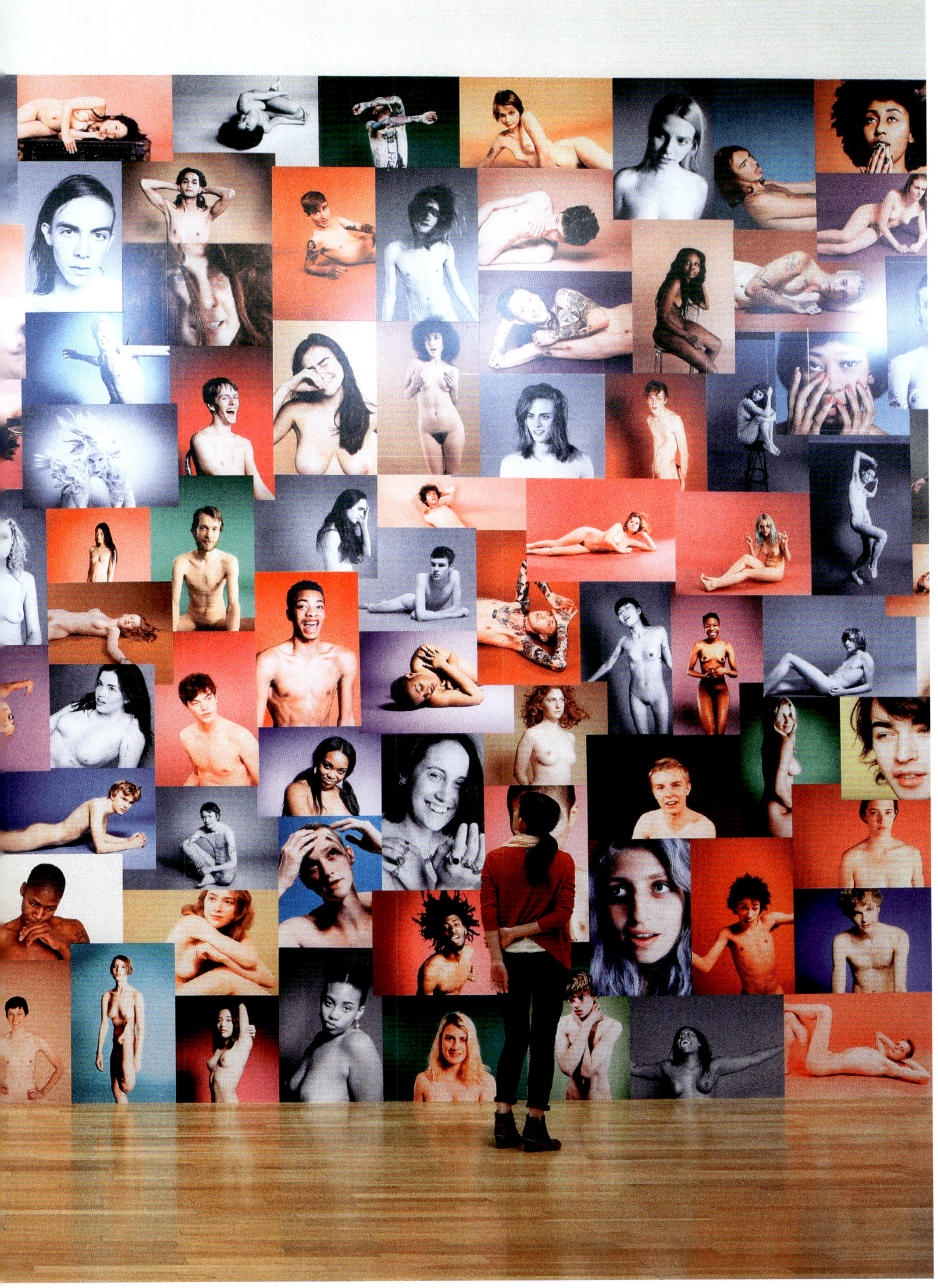

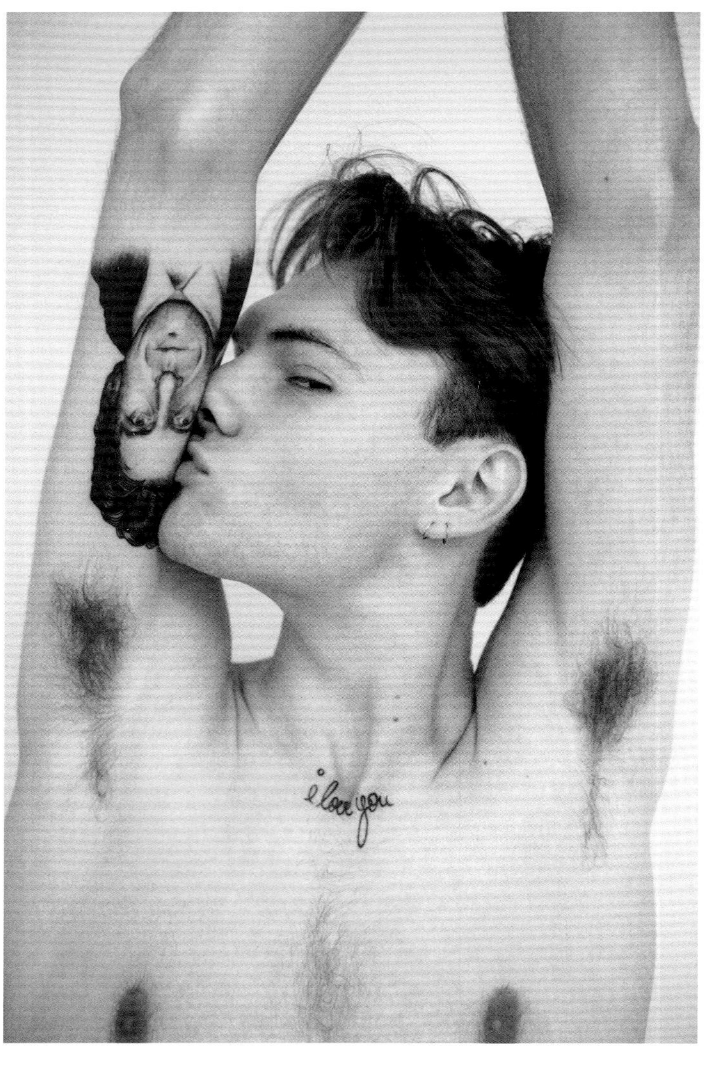

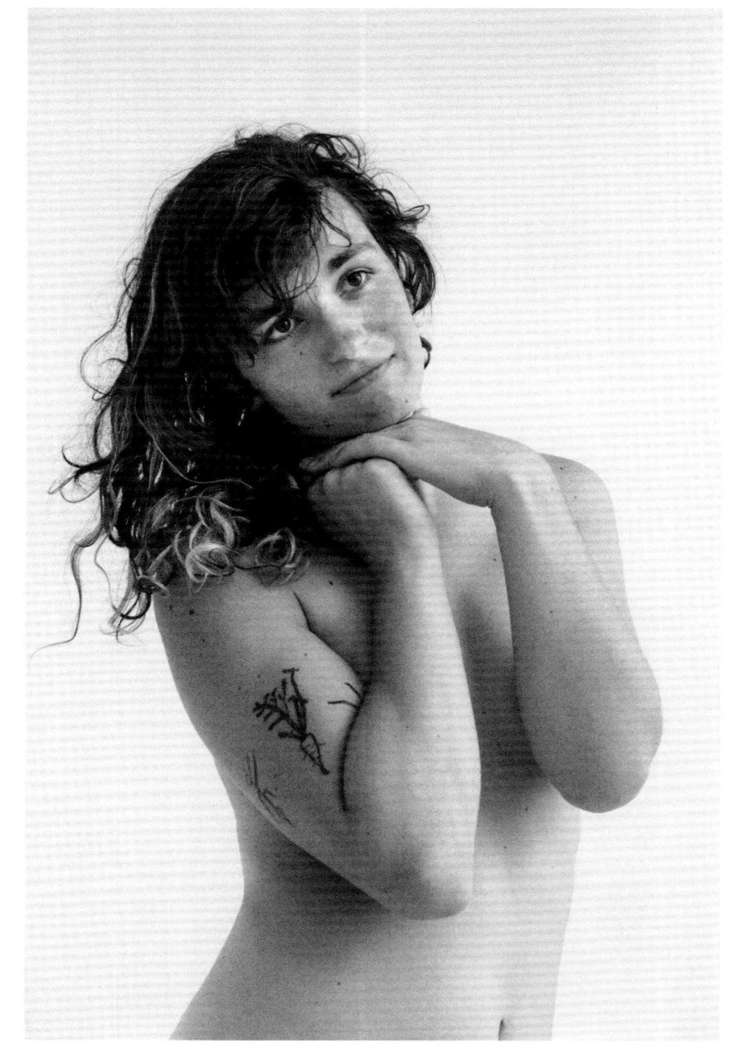

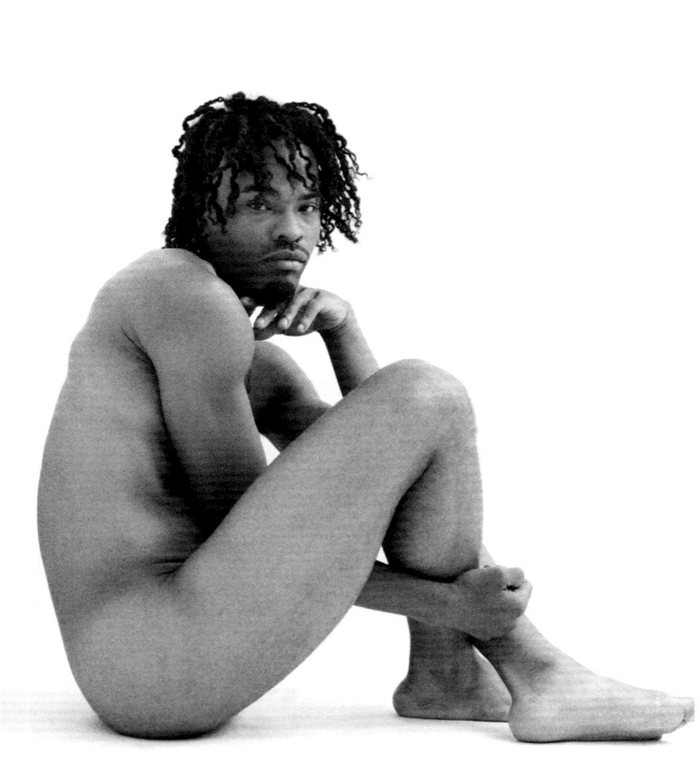

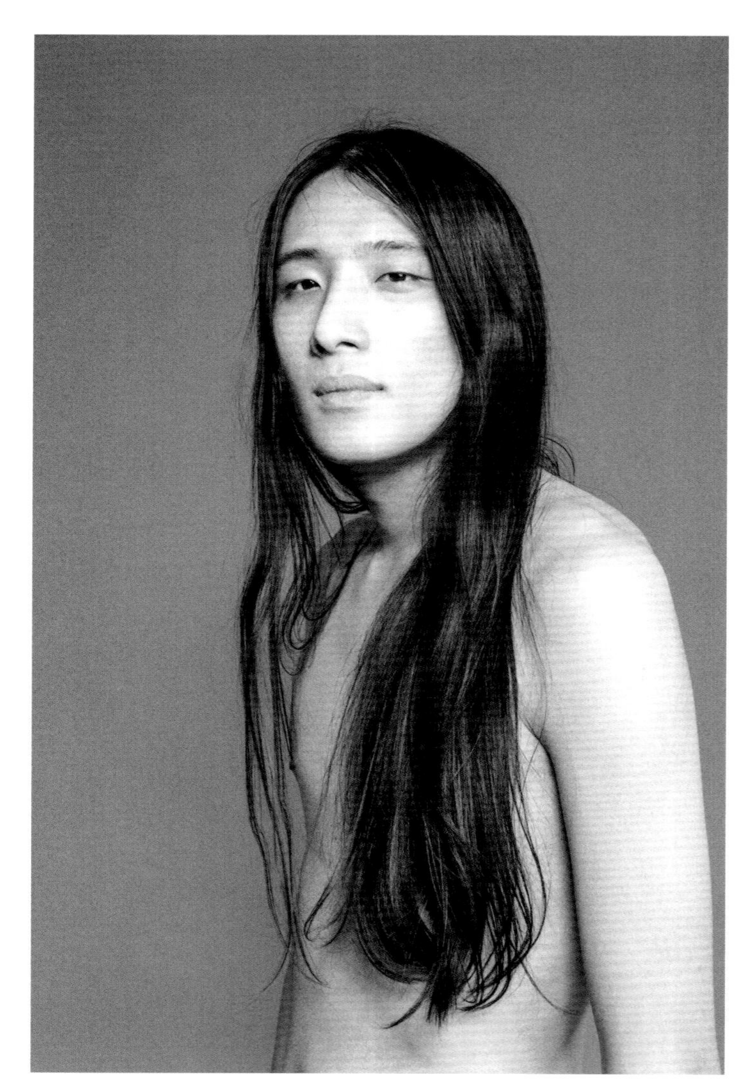

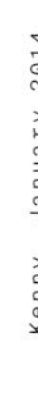
Chase, September 2018   Josslynn, July 2017   Marcus, September 2017   Kenny, January 2014

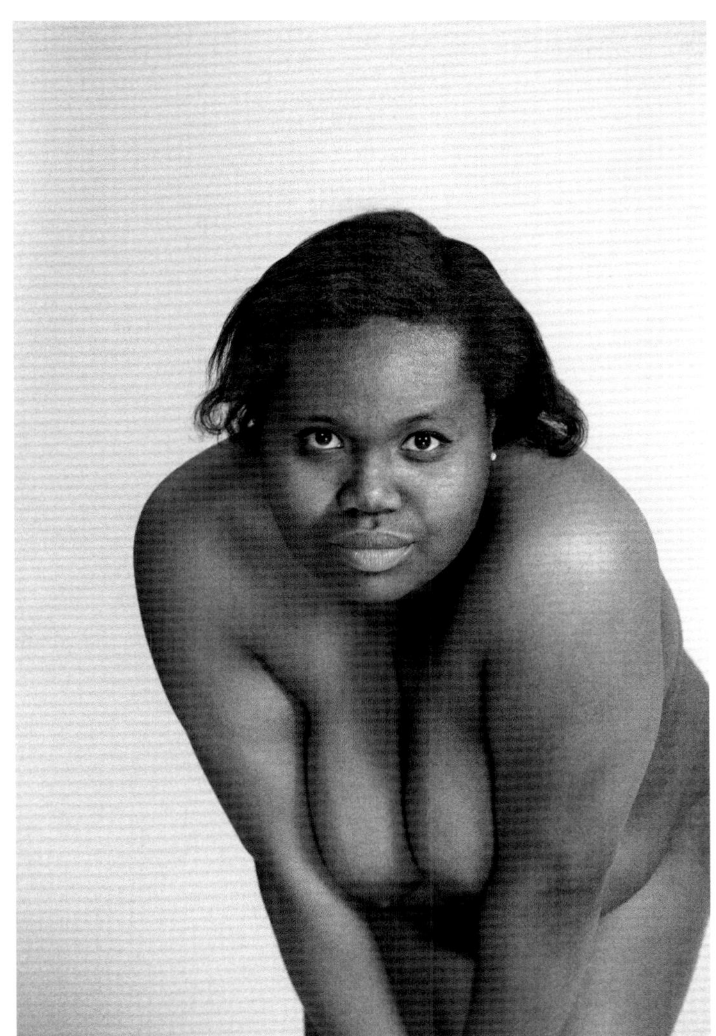

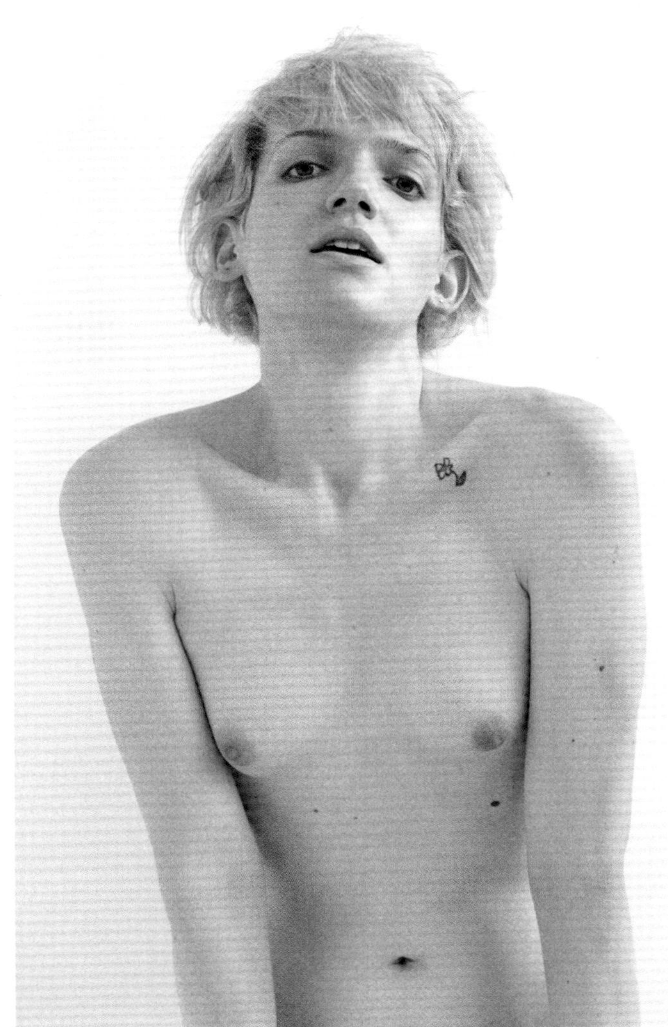

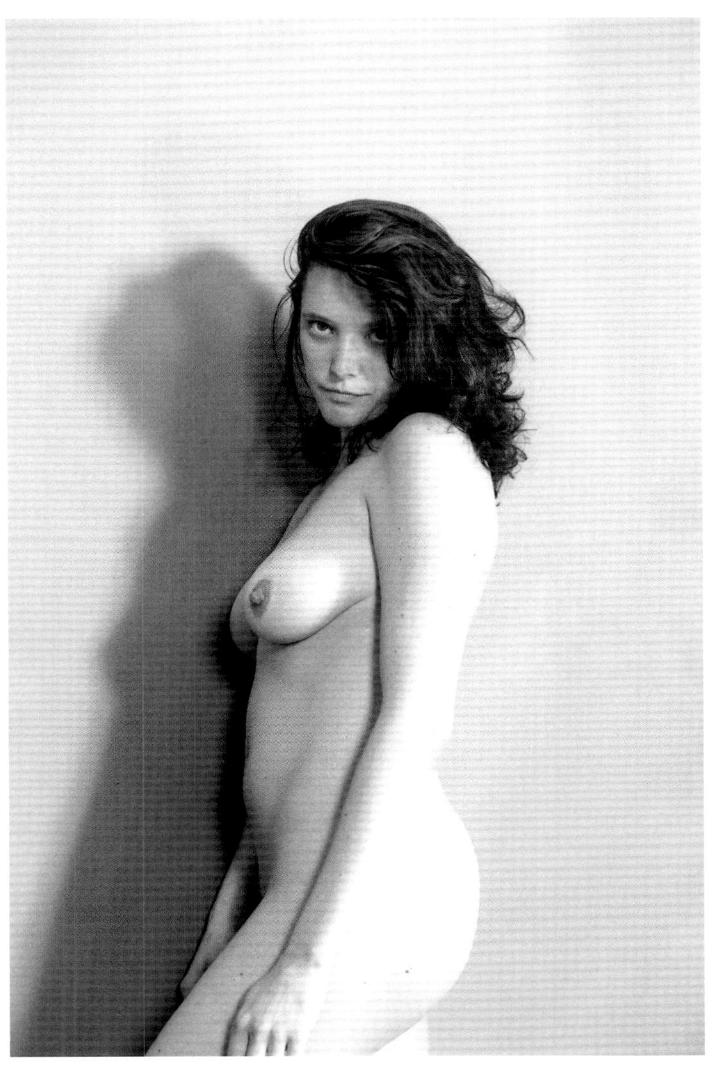

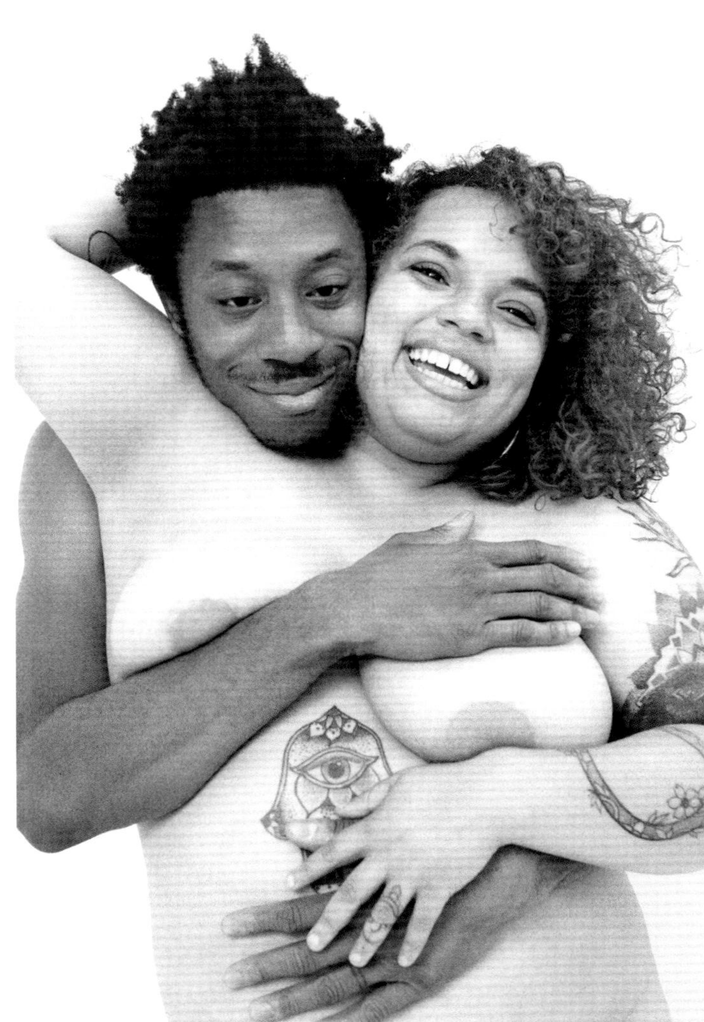

Zora, May 2016   Mattie, September 2017   Sophie, May 2016   Liv & Chris, June, 2017

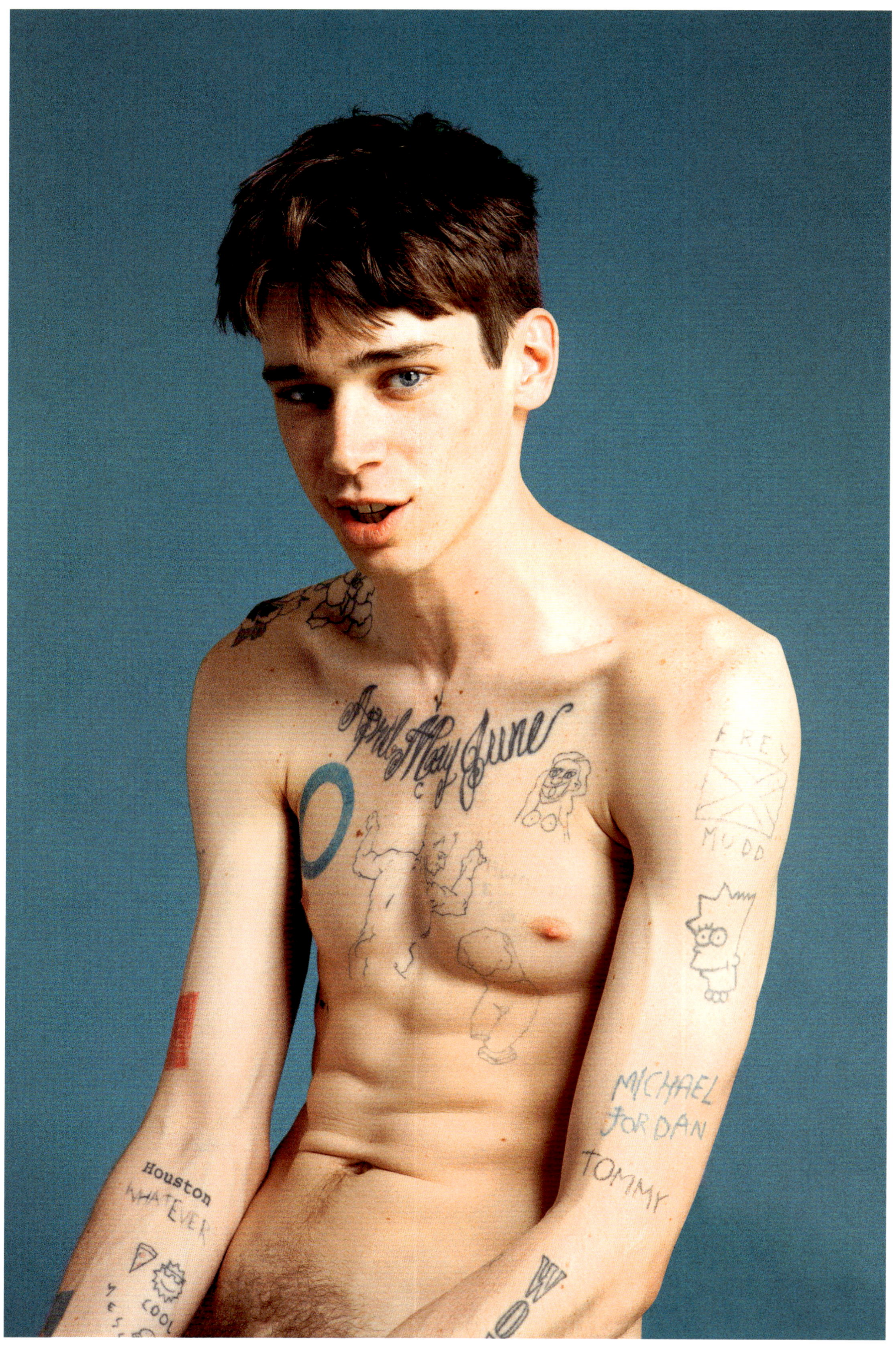

Cole, April 2012

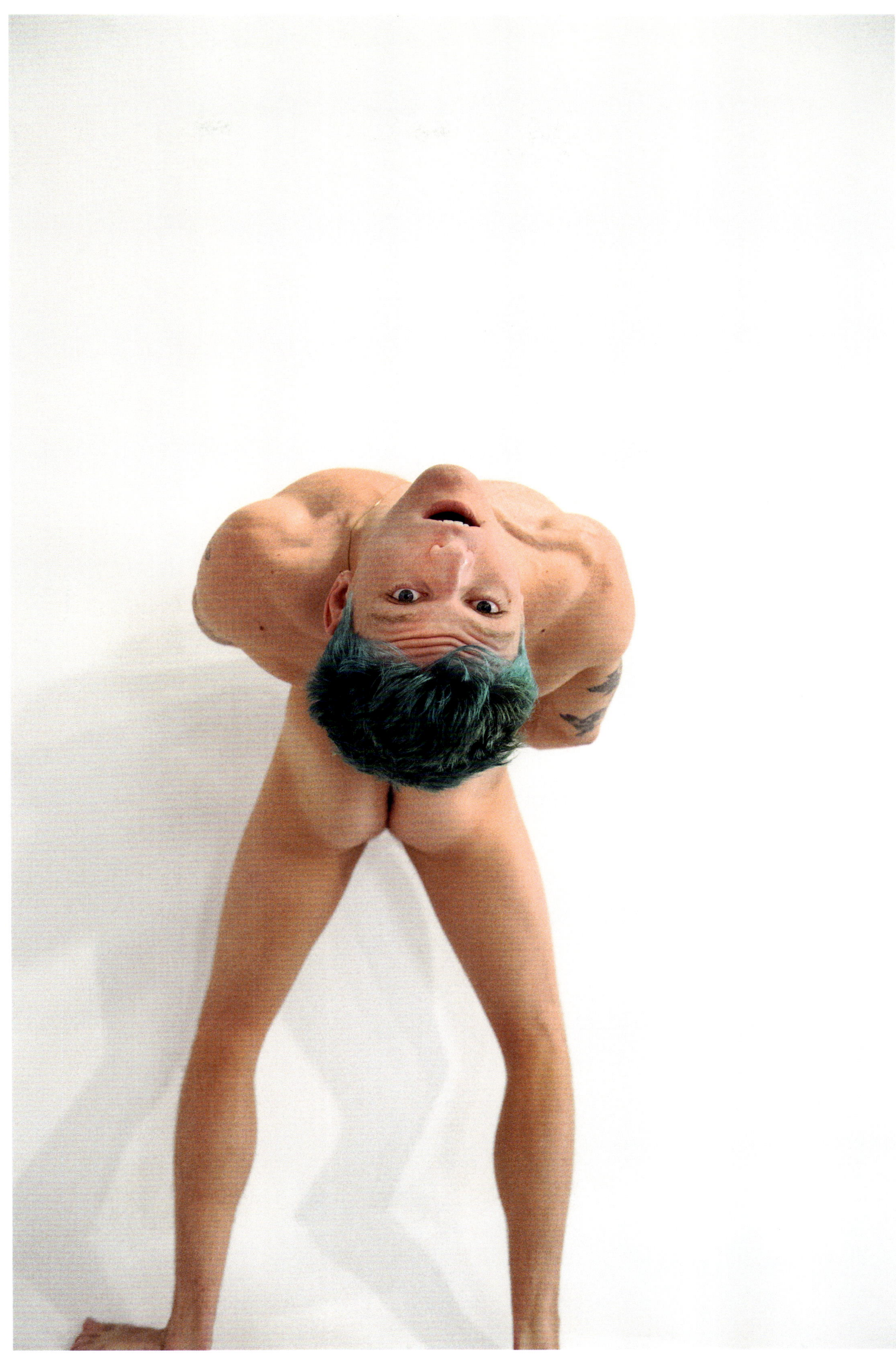

Asher, December 2019

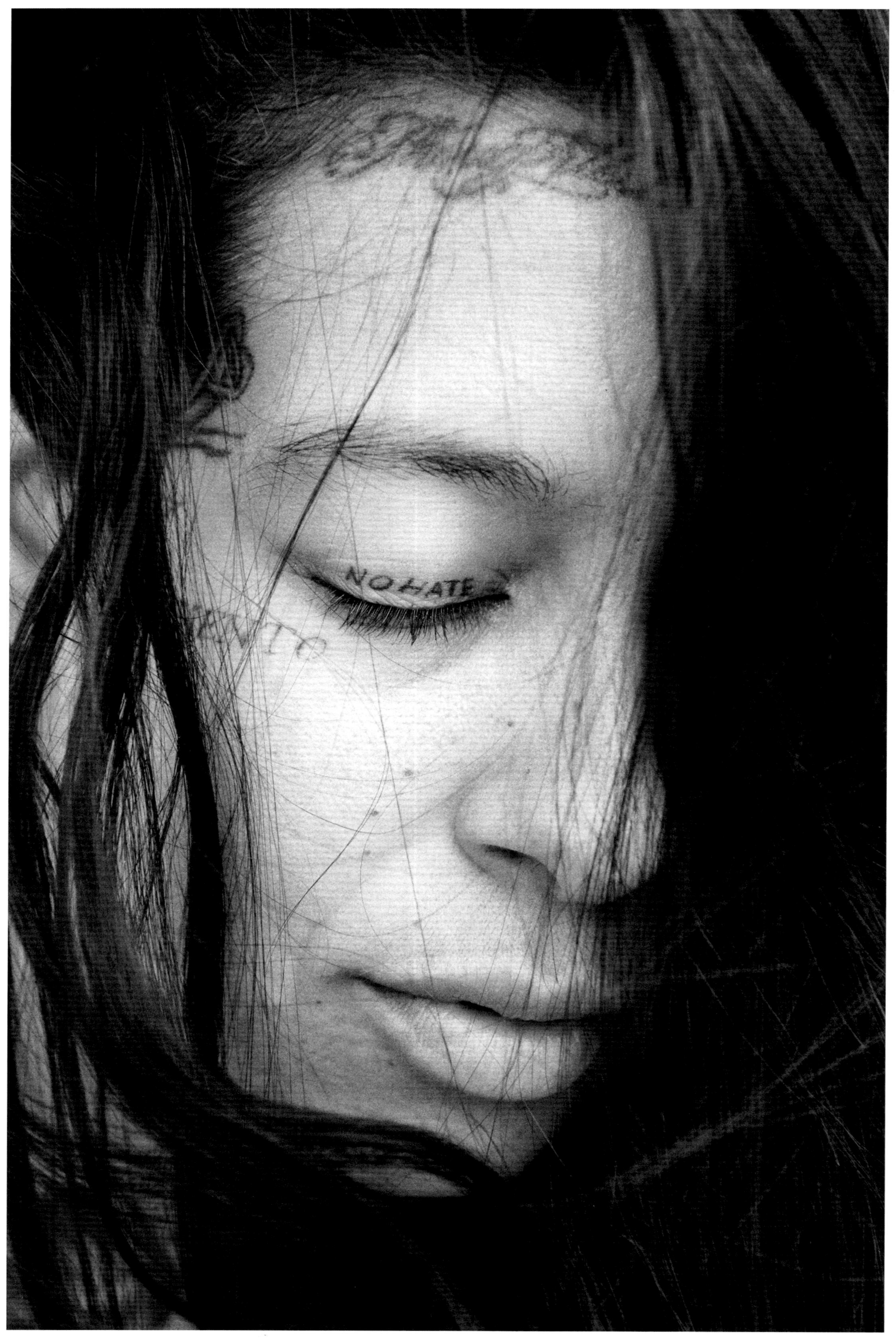

Marilyn, September 2017

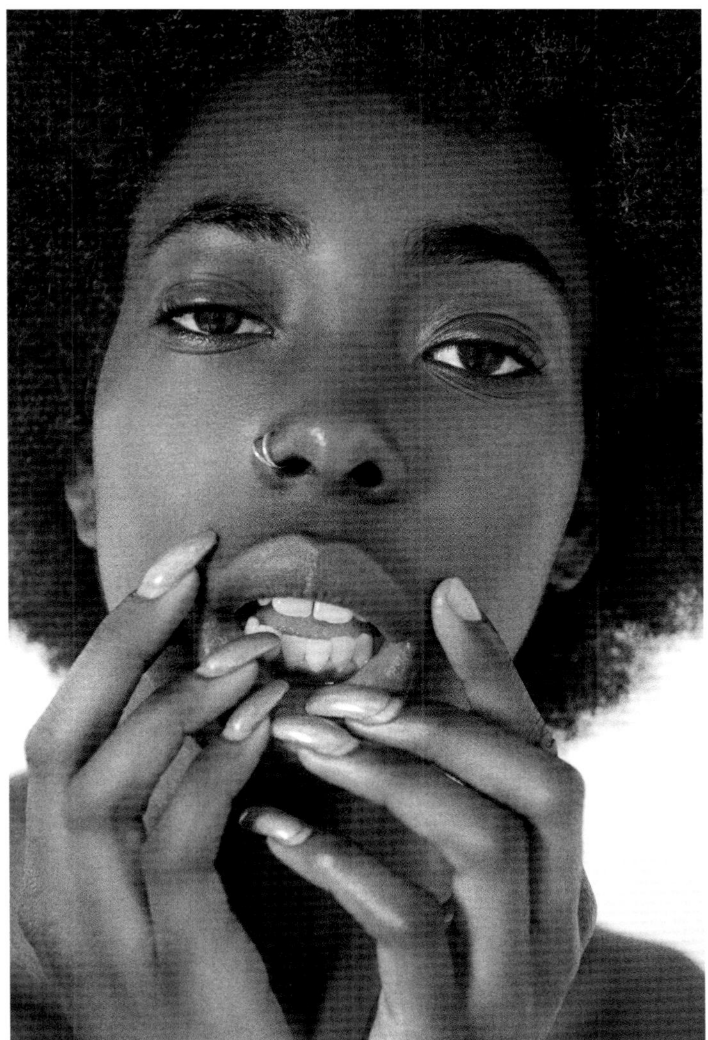

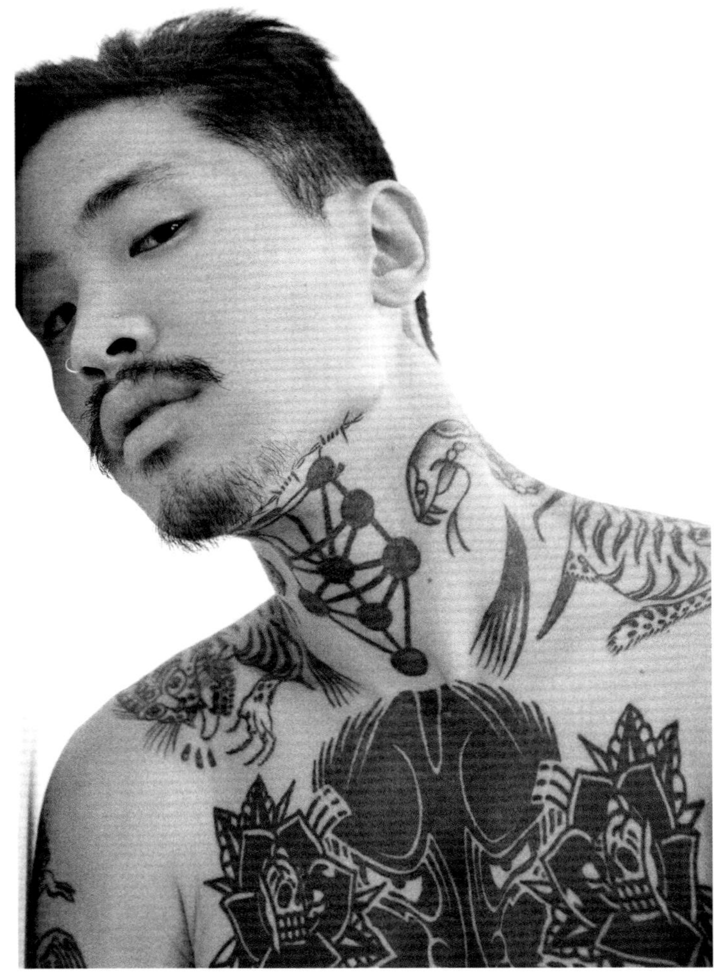

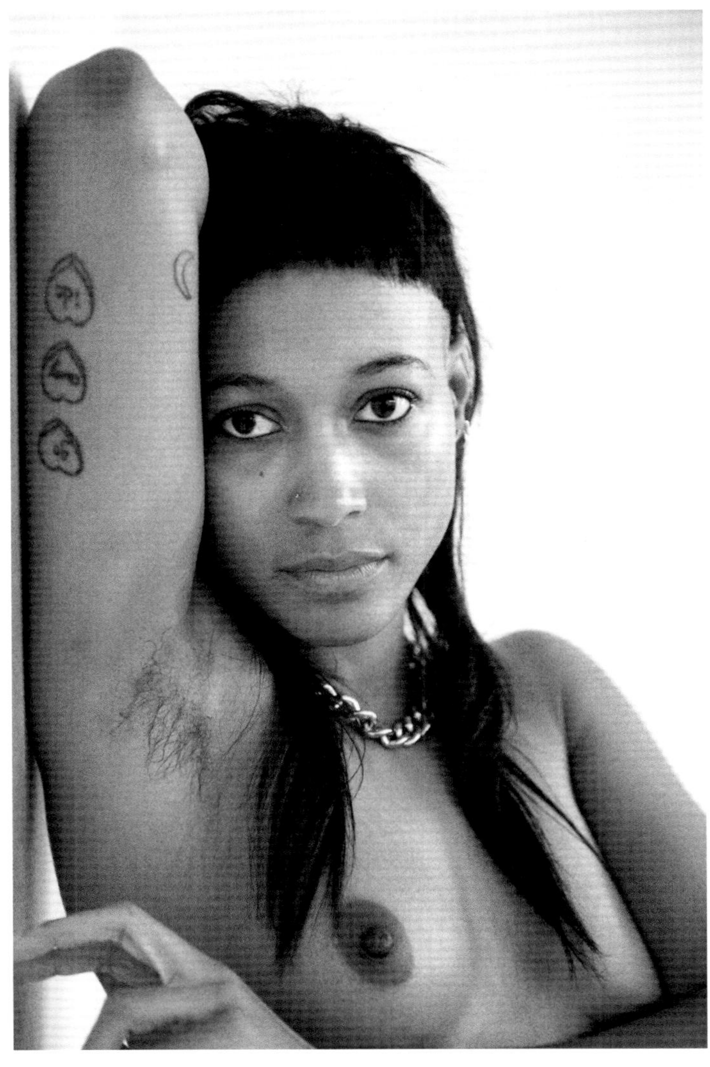

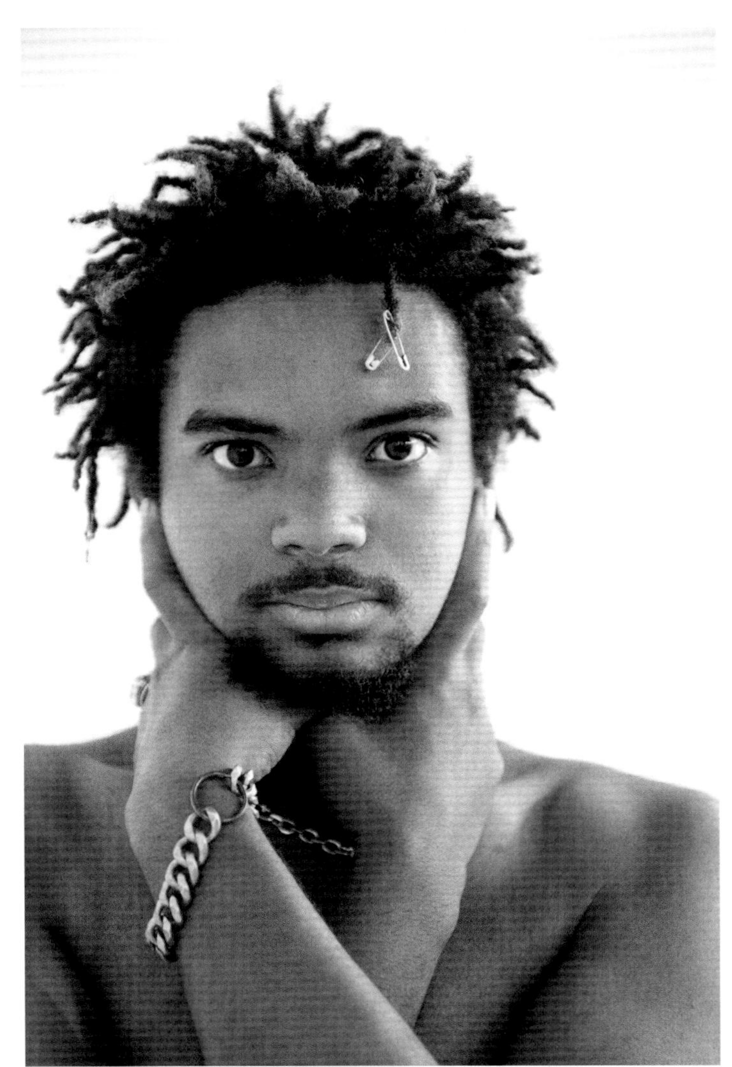

Bianca, April 2017 Jae, October 2019 Tina, October 2018 Allen, October 2019

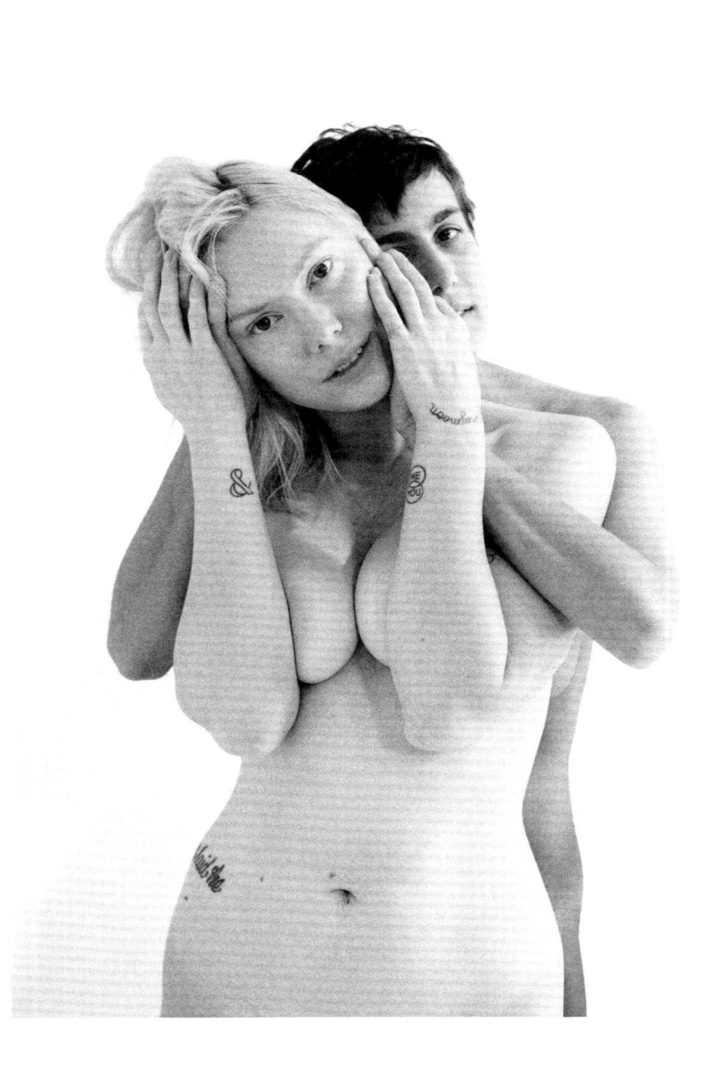

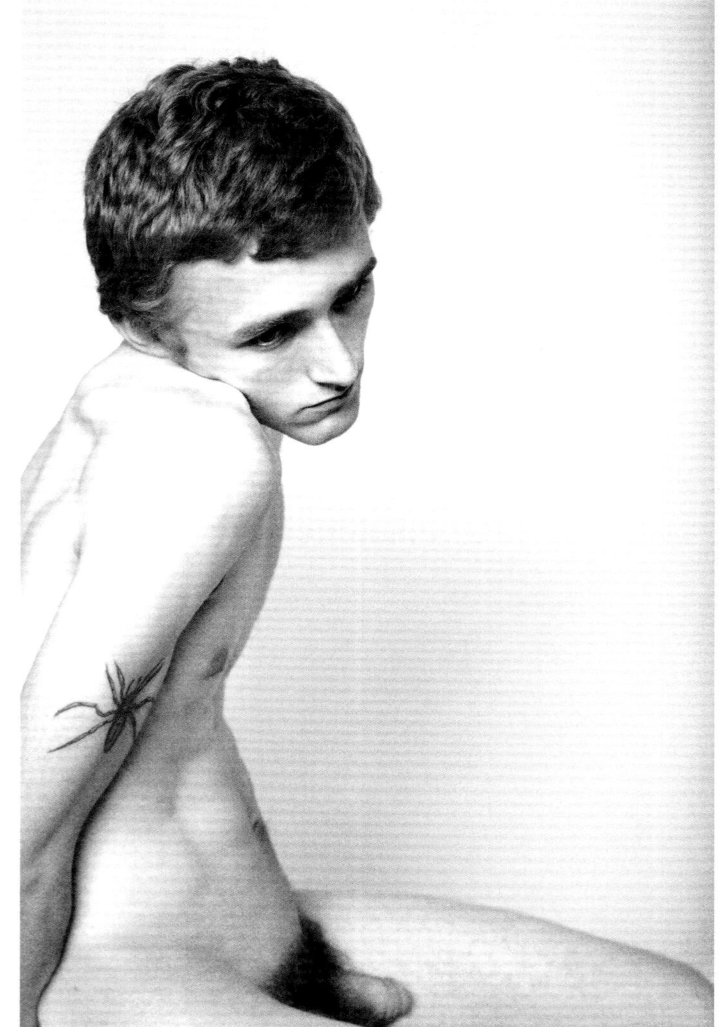

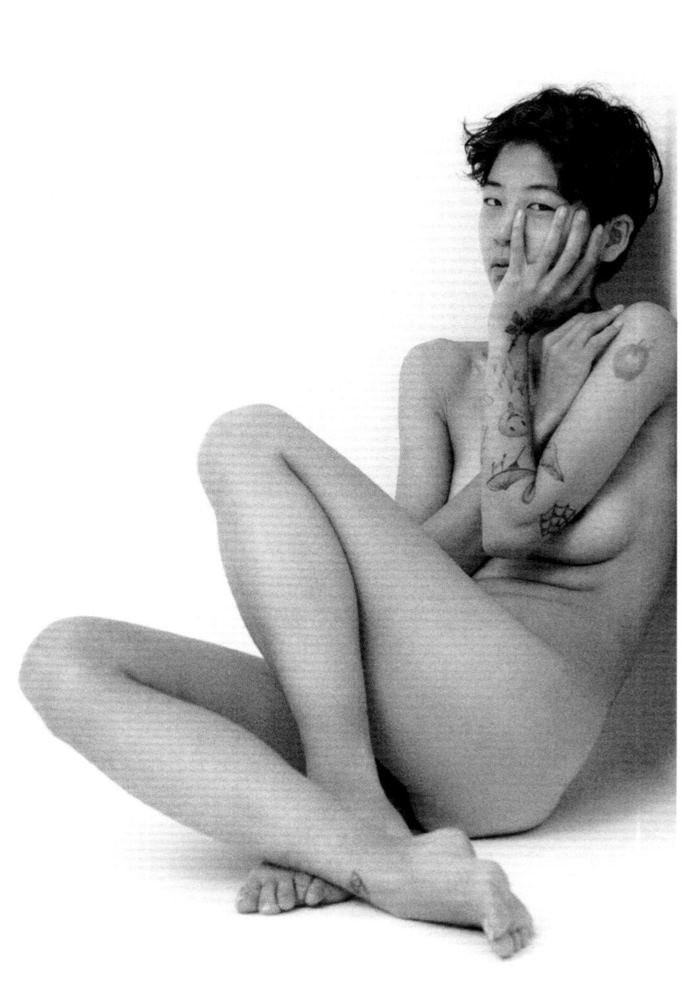

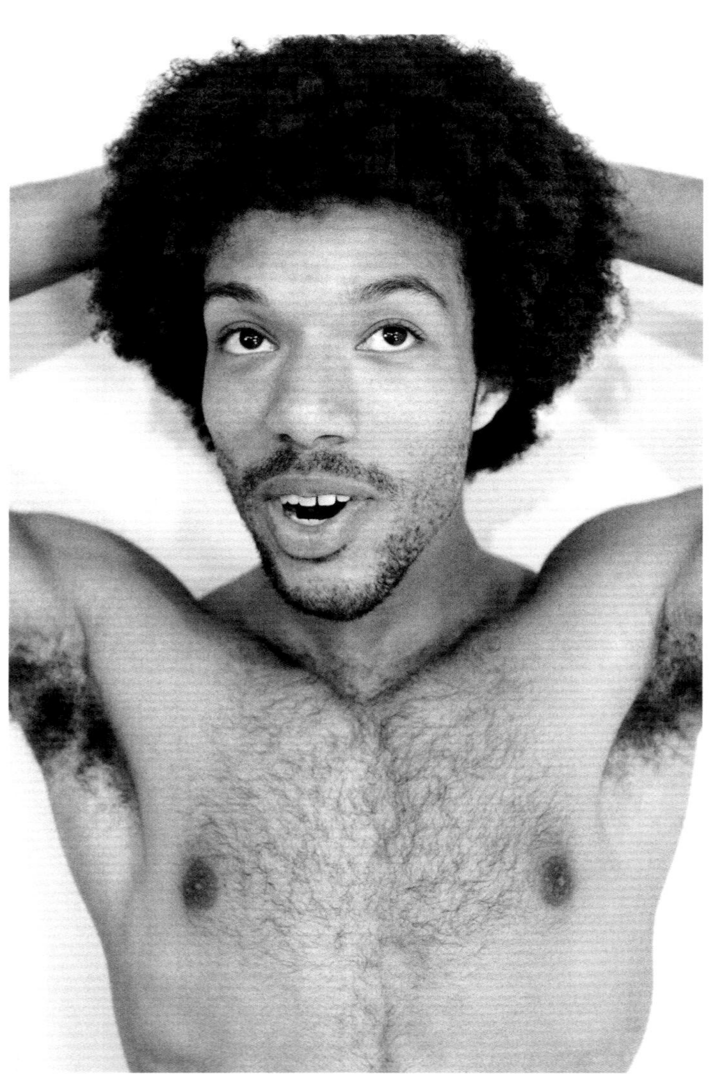

Robin & Charlotte, December 2019 Roger, January 2010 Masami, July 2017 David, December 2019

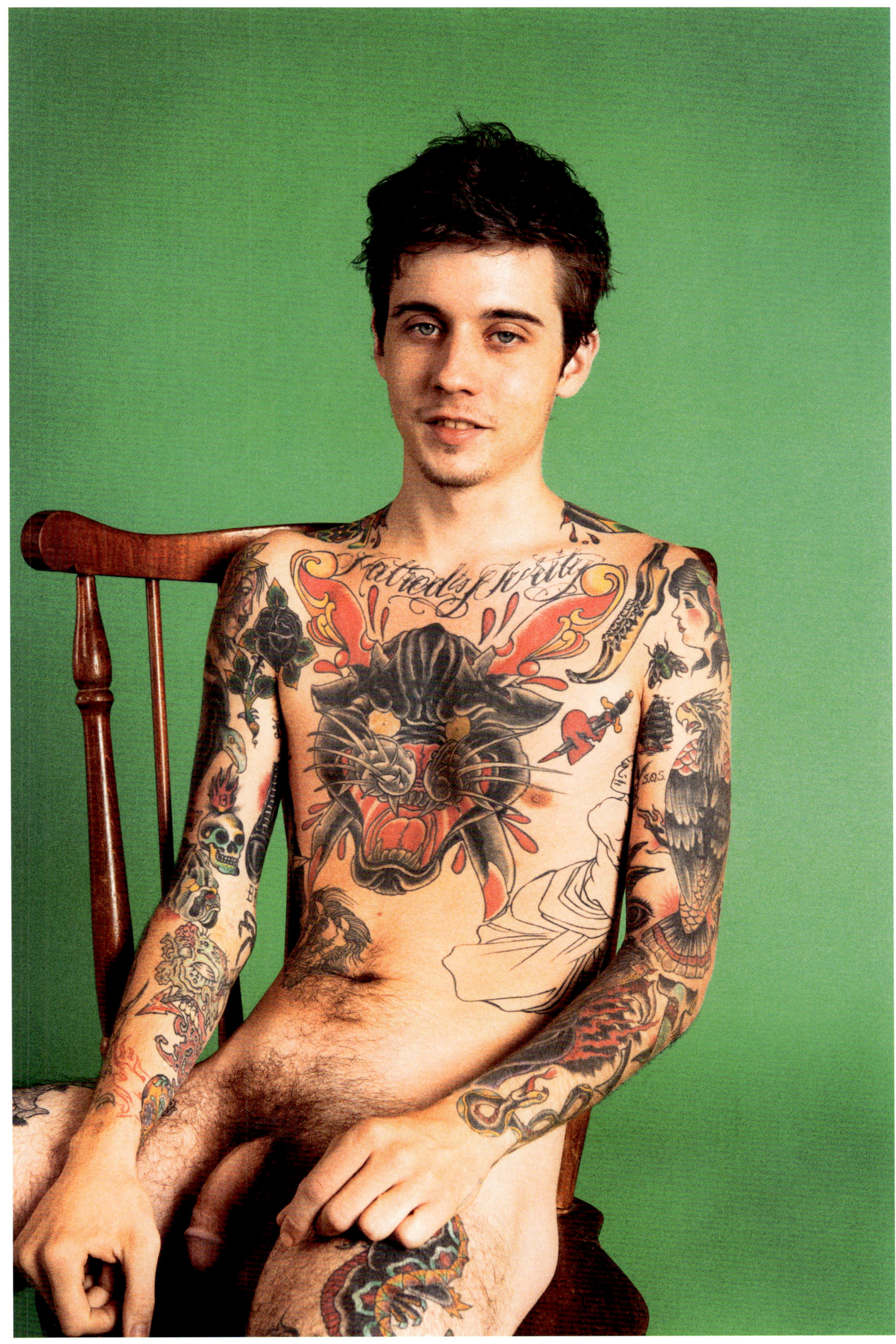

Tom, September 2011

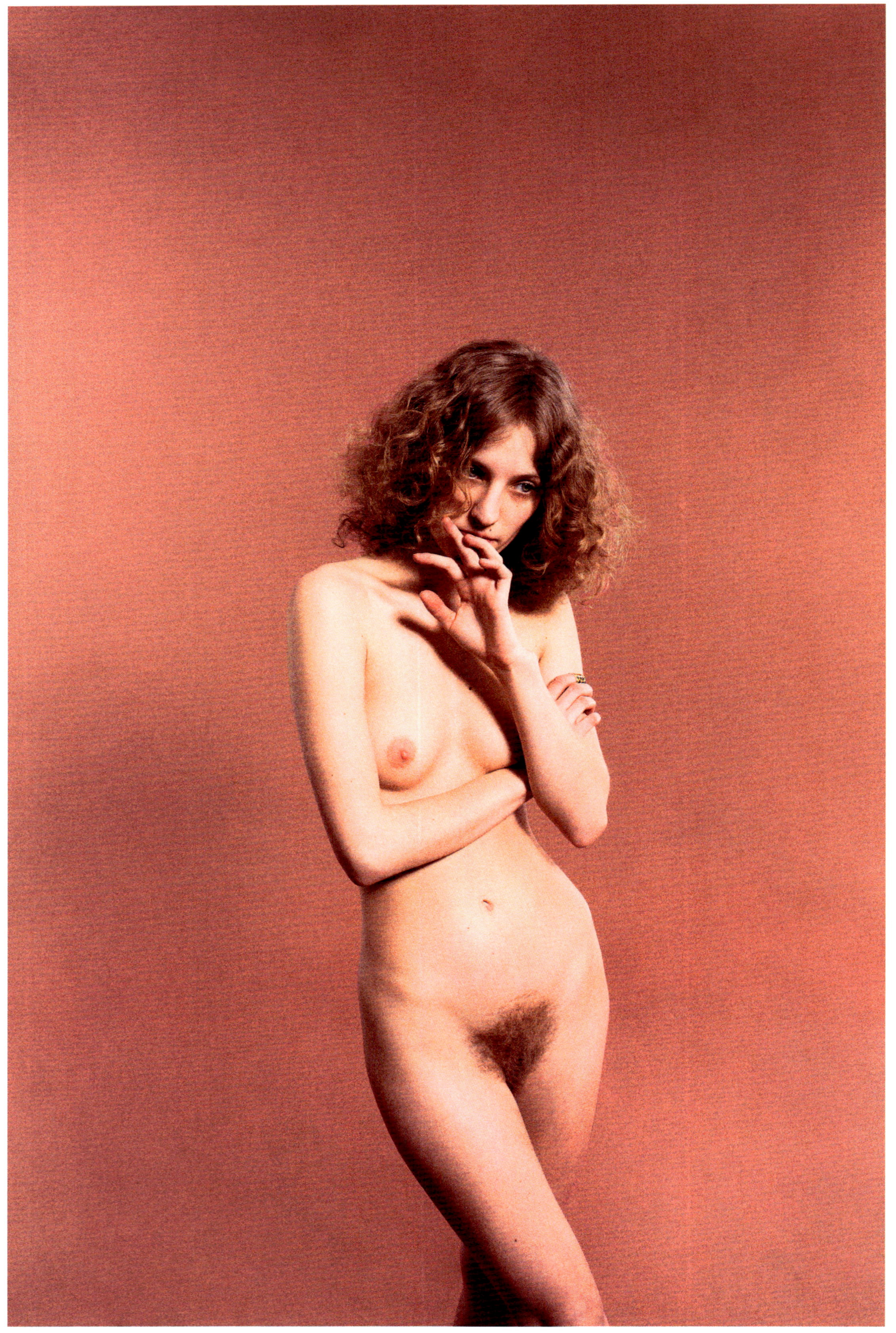

Petra, March 2013

In high school, I had a really horrible photography teacher who didn't like Ryan's work at all. I was always bringing Ryan's photos into class and having to defend them. I loved his work and wanted to see more like it. That teacher was not having it.

I didn't study photography formally after that class. Years later, the School of Ryan McGinley taught me so much, like how to use lights on any kind of set.

Ryan and I met in Toronto when I was eighteen or nineteen. He came to a show I curated while I was a student at OCAD [the Ontario College of Art and Design]. I ended up dropping out soon after because I couldn't afford it. Then I moved to New York, in large part because of this photo and what it represents.

This photo was from my test shoot with Ryan. The night before, I'd taken a Megabus, this super cheap bus, from Toronto to New York. My ticket might have been a dollar. Ryan was looking for people to come on his next road trip and was test shooting for that. I really wanted to go. During the interview, when they asked, "Are you able to run around and jump on things? Do you have allergies?" I lied. I've a connective tissue disorder that makes me dislocate my knees all the time and I've crazy allergies, to the point where I can't really be outside. For the trip, we'd be in nature, naked, running around. I lied because I knew I had to do it. I'd been afraid to move my body for too long and needed to get out.

I've never talked about this before. But I left home when I was pretty young and was in a very abusive relationship. I was still in that relationship when this photo was taken. I wanted to leave this person but I didn't have the money or anywhere to go. The road trip was a way that I could get out. It was also something that I wanted to do for myself. It was truly the best trip of my life.

It was one of Ryan's last big road trips. There were three legs; I was on the first. We went from New York to Texas. It was transformative. I felt safe in my body for the first time. I'd get welts, my eyes would be puffy, and my nose would run, but I felt beautiful and so free. We had very little cell service. We weren't on our phones. This was before social media and Instagram were such a thing. I was present. And this person couldn't reach me. By the end of the trip, my body was strong from having done such strenuous activities. When I got home, I felt invincible. I had the courage to leave. I moved to New York. Ryan was very supportive. And that was the beginning of the rest of my life.

Before then, I'd done things with *Rookie* and *Vice* magazine. I was a Tumblr girl. Tumblr was an important space for many people, the kind of space that doesn't exist online anymore. There was an innocence to it. I learned so much from finding films and images and connecting with people on Tumblr. Once I got to New York, I got more opportunities. I was around more artists. My work picked up. It was a sweet spot in history. For one second, it didn't feel like the world was ending. You could get political in a fun way.

I don't know if Ryan knows this but many of my lighting techniques come from him. Ryan's more technical as a photographer than me. My interest in the medium really comes from film and I was self-taught until I passed through the School of Ryan McGinley. I learned so much from just being around him. On the road trip, I saw how scrappy you could be. With lights you can buy at a hardware store, you can create spotlights and other set-ups that transform what you can do with an image. That trip was a catalyst for so much change in my life, and I always think about it.

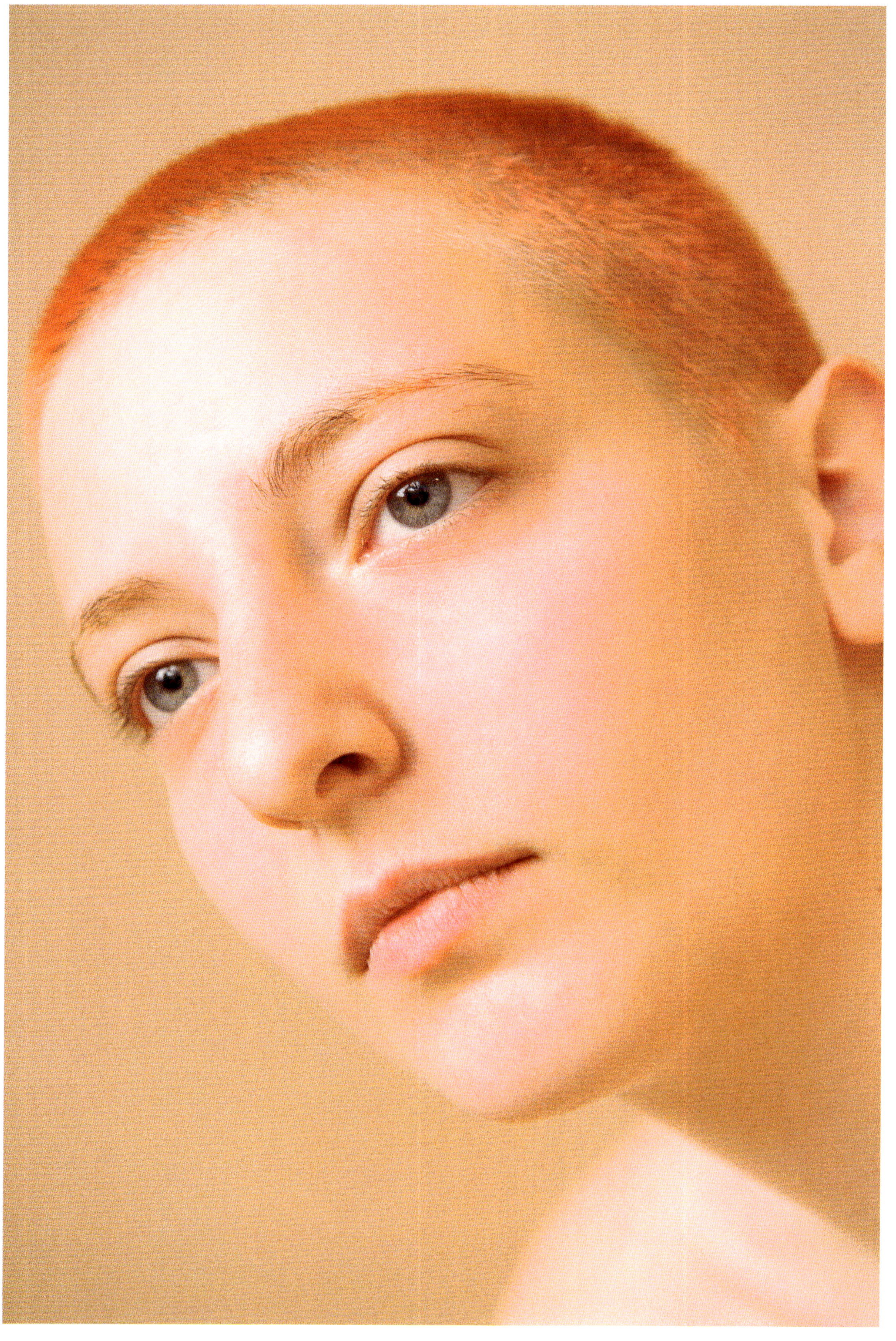

Meredith, December 2016

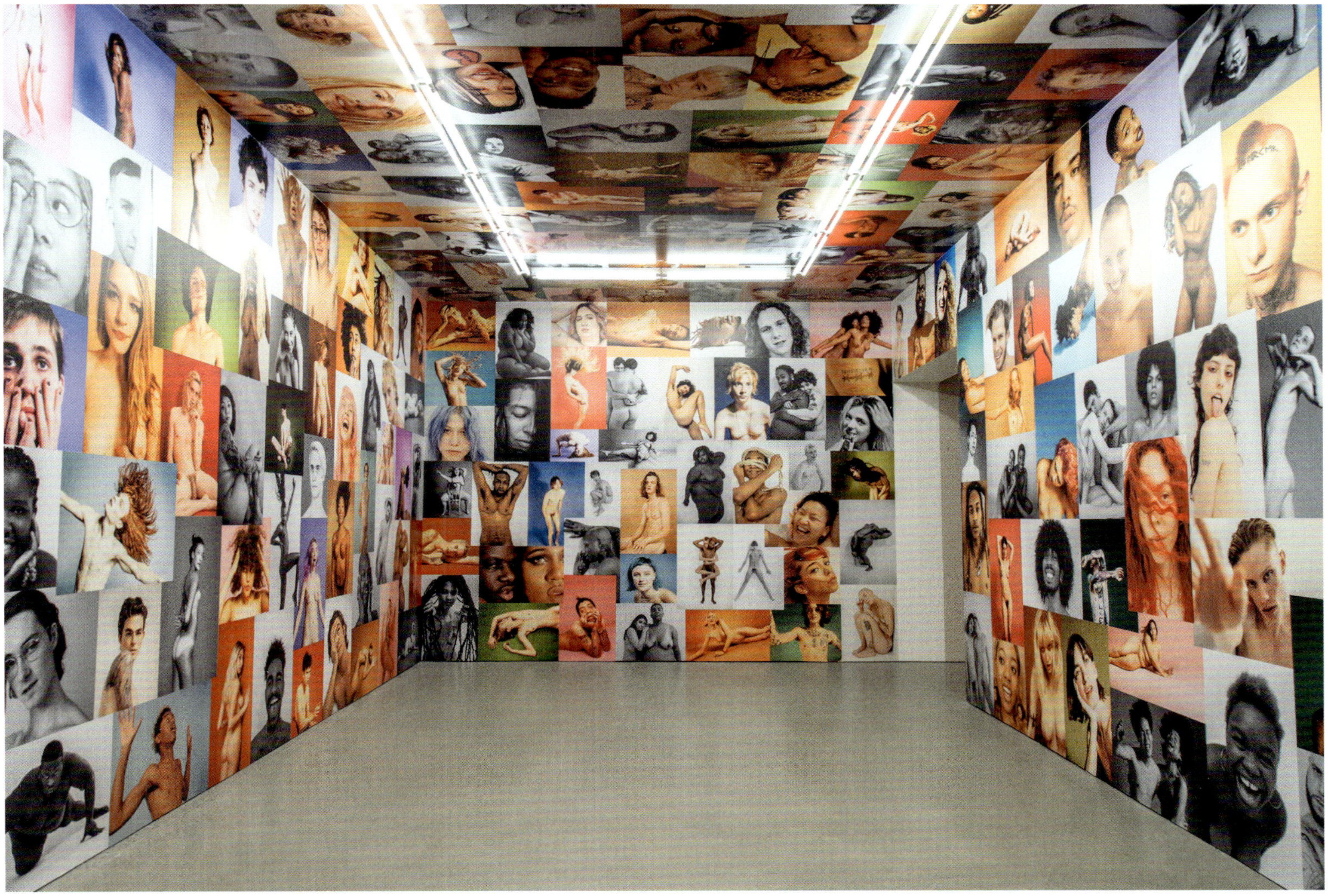

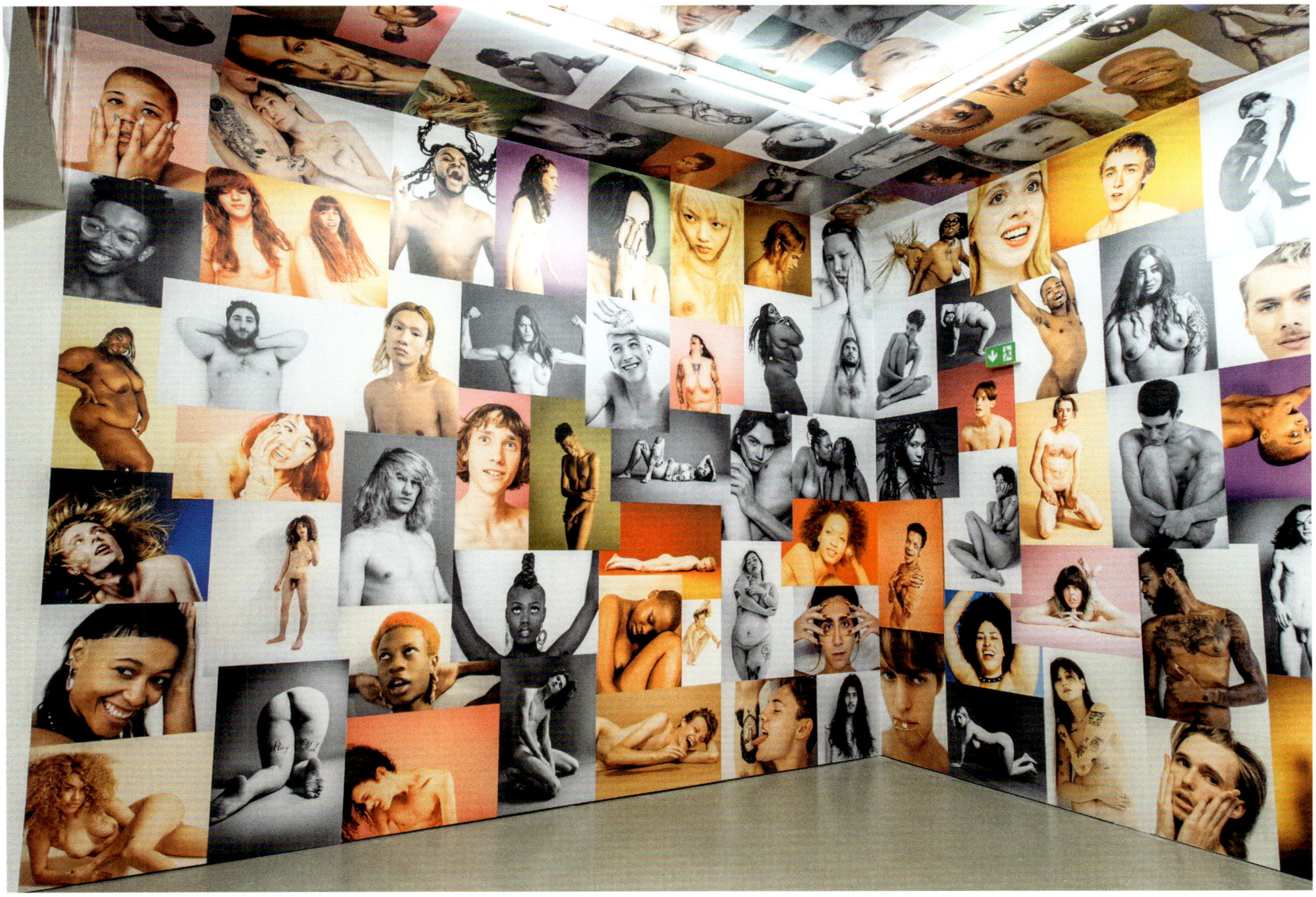

AROS Aarhus Art Museum, Denmark, 2019

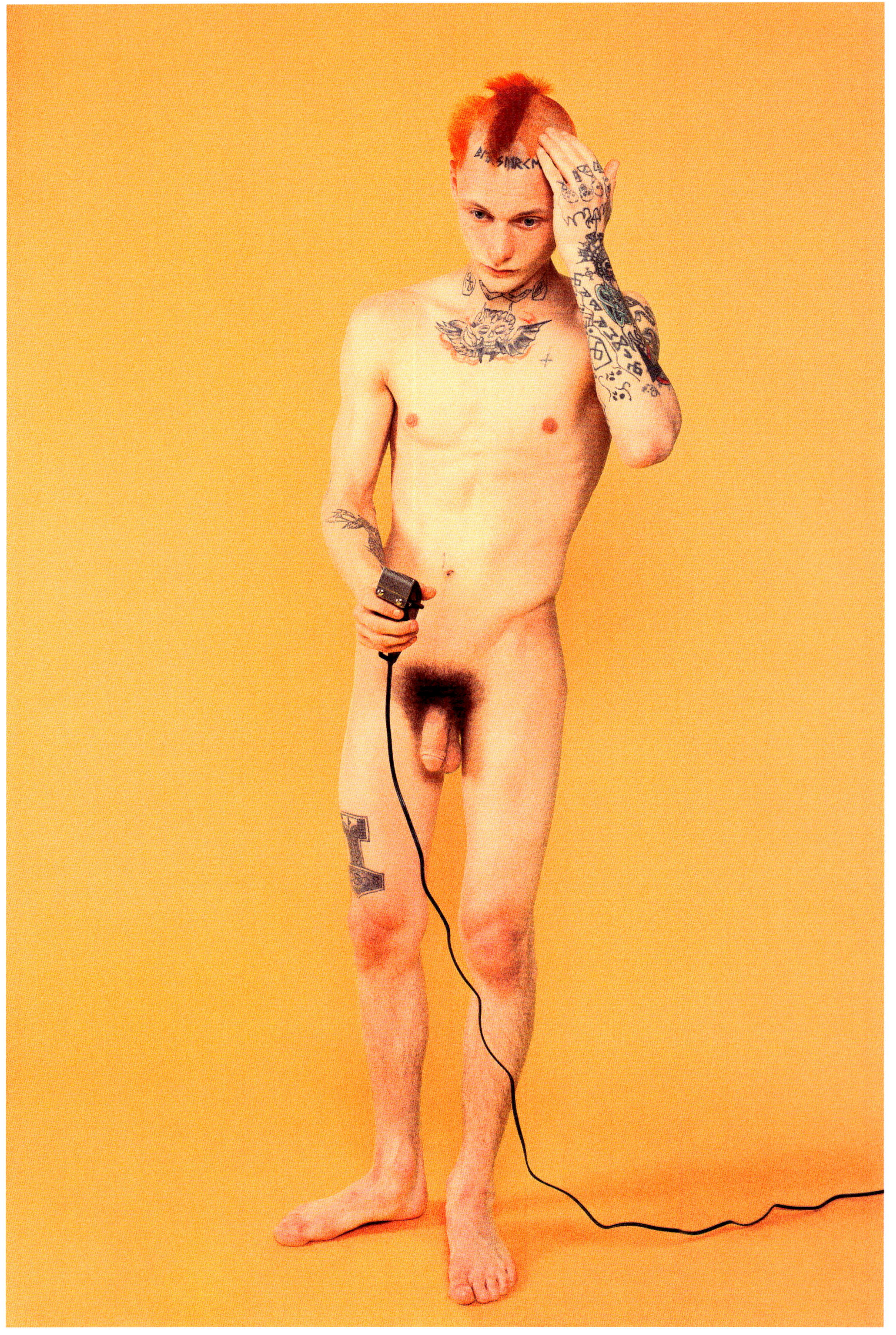

Jasper, April 2010

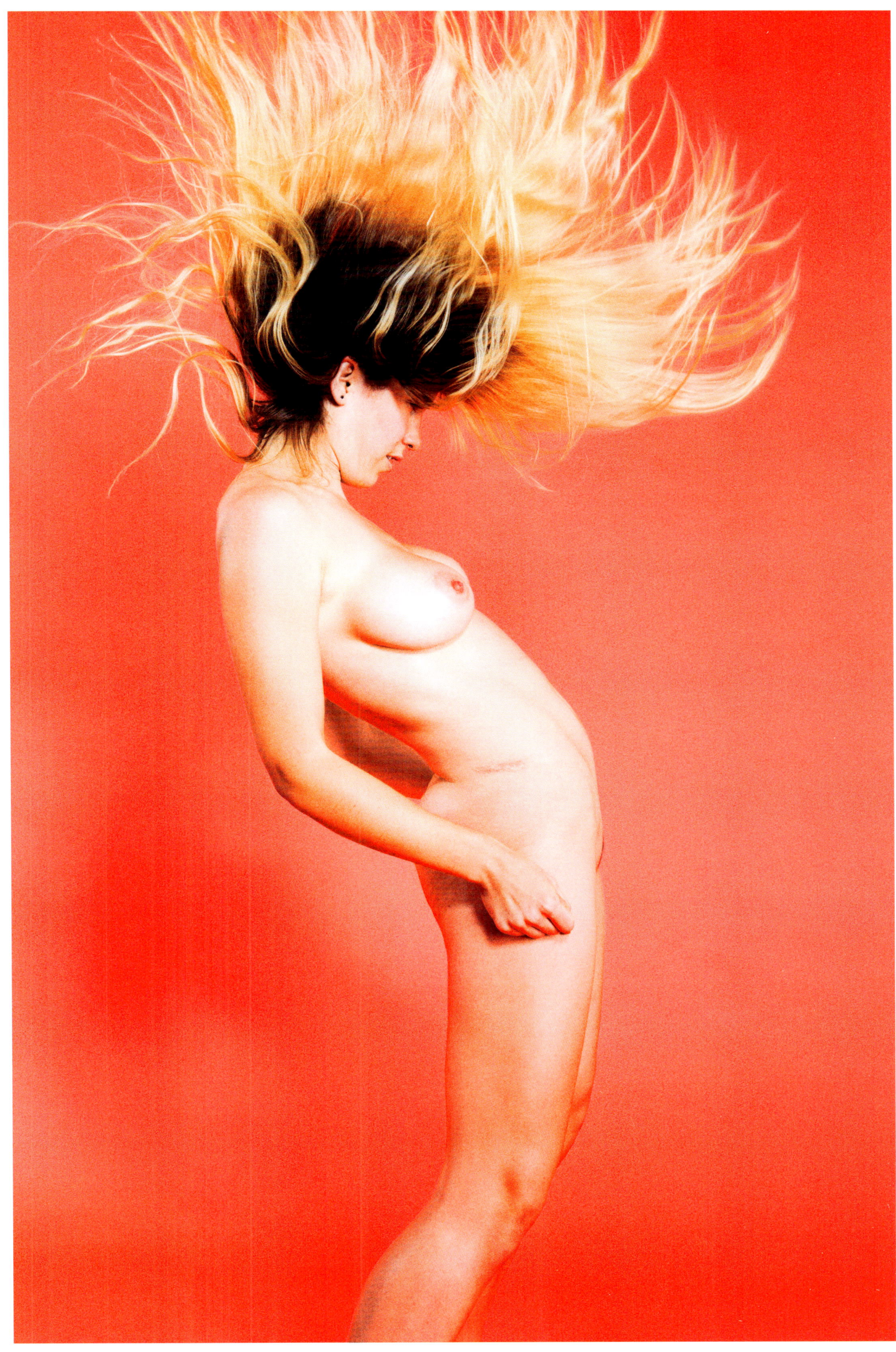

Alexandra, December 2014

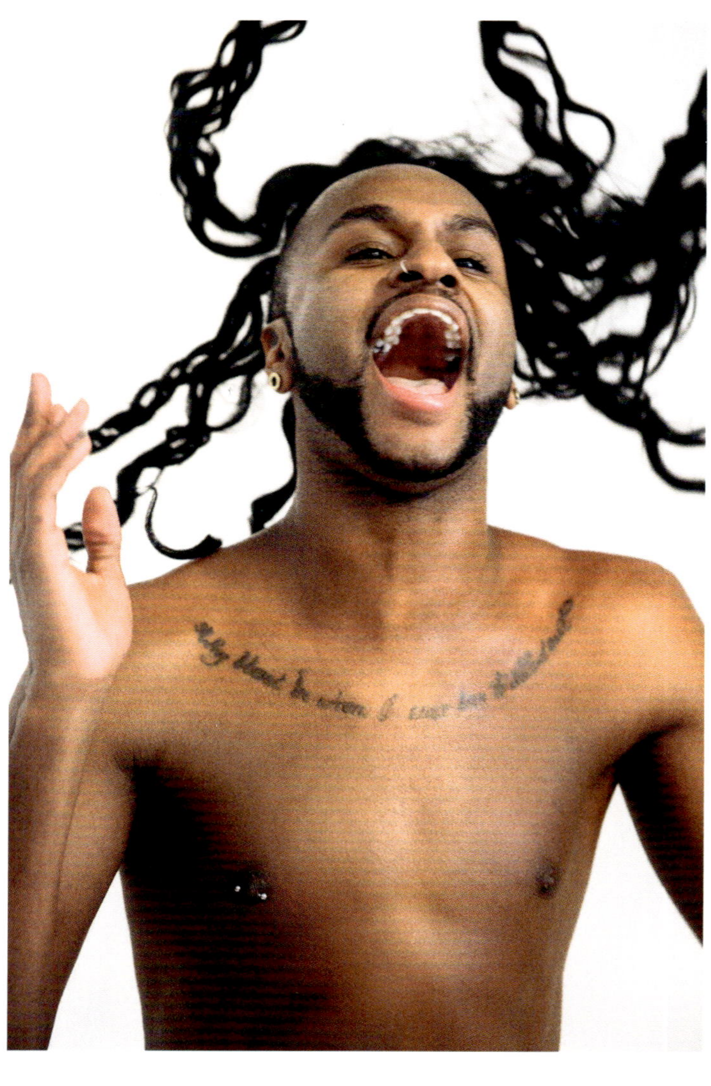

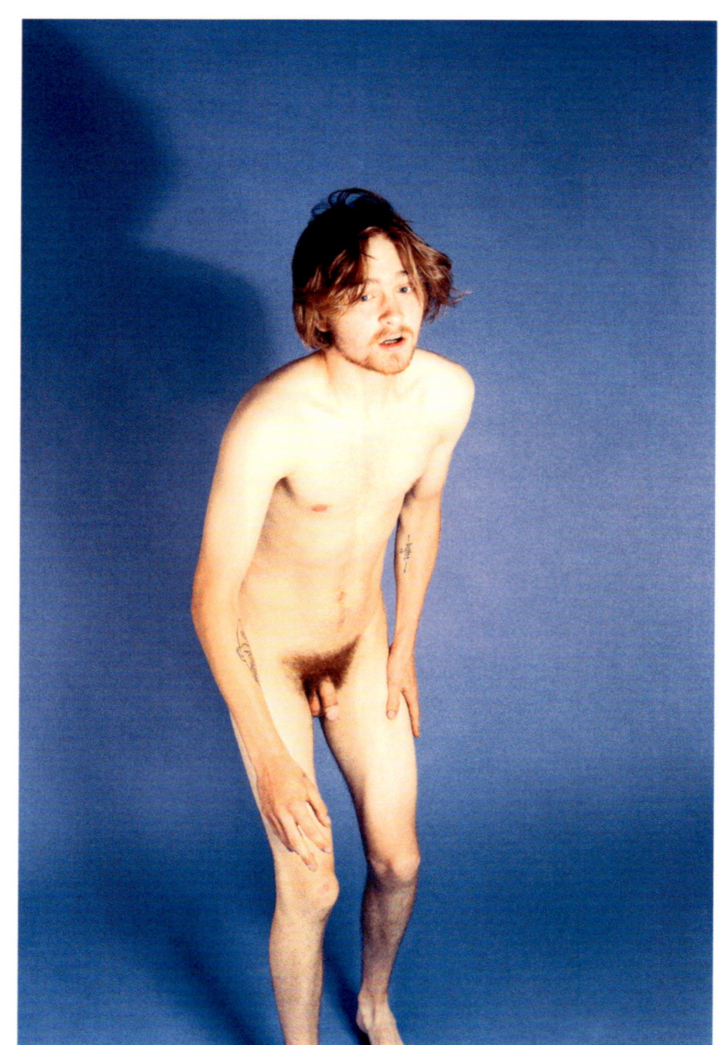

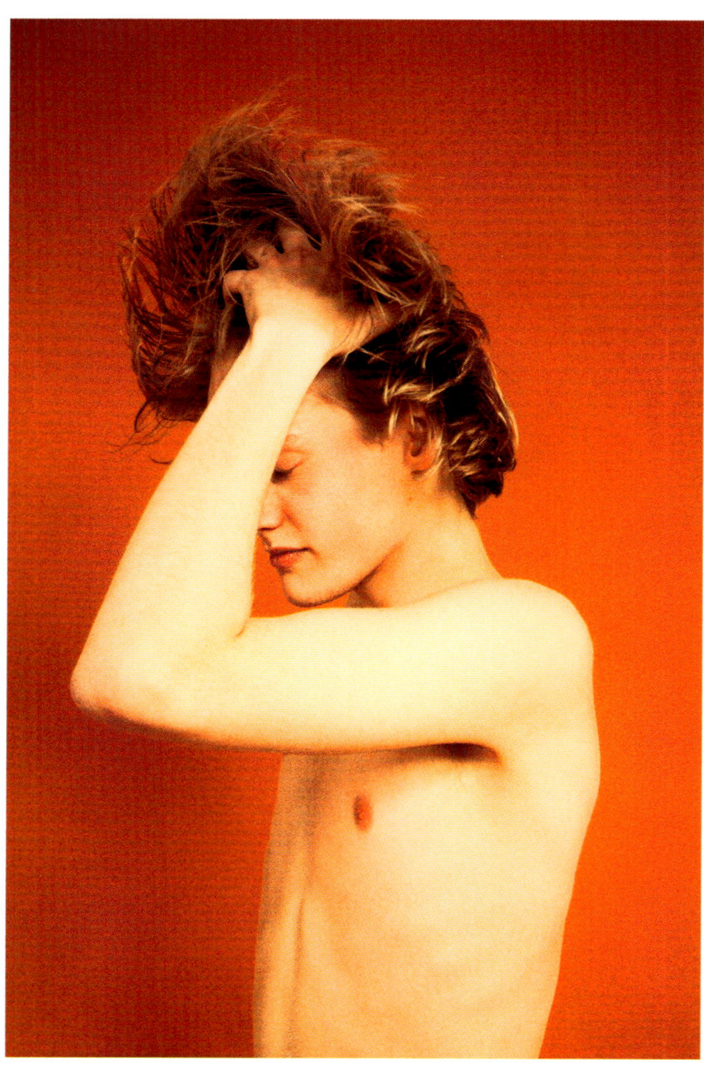

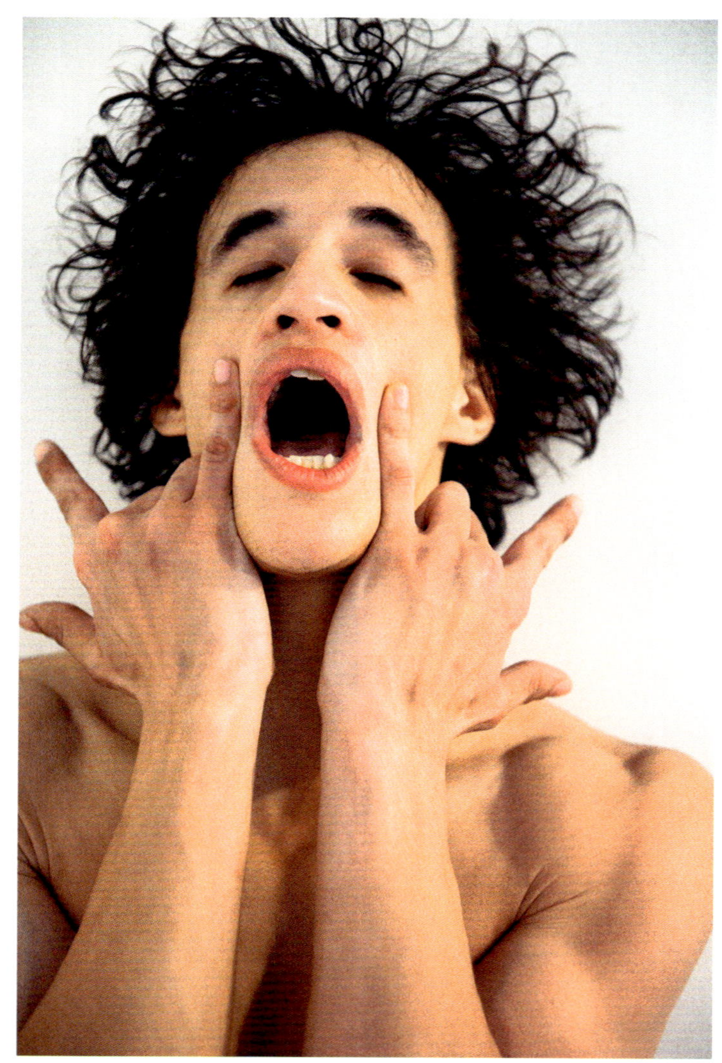

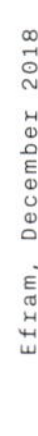

Beaujangles, December 2018 Cheney, April 2012 Aske, January 2012 Efram, December 2018

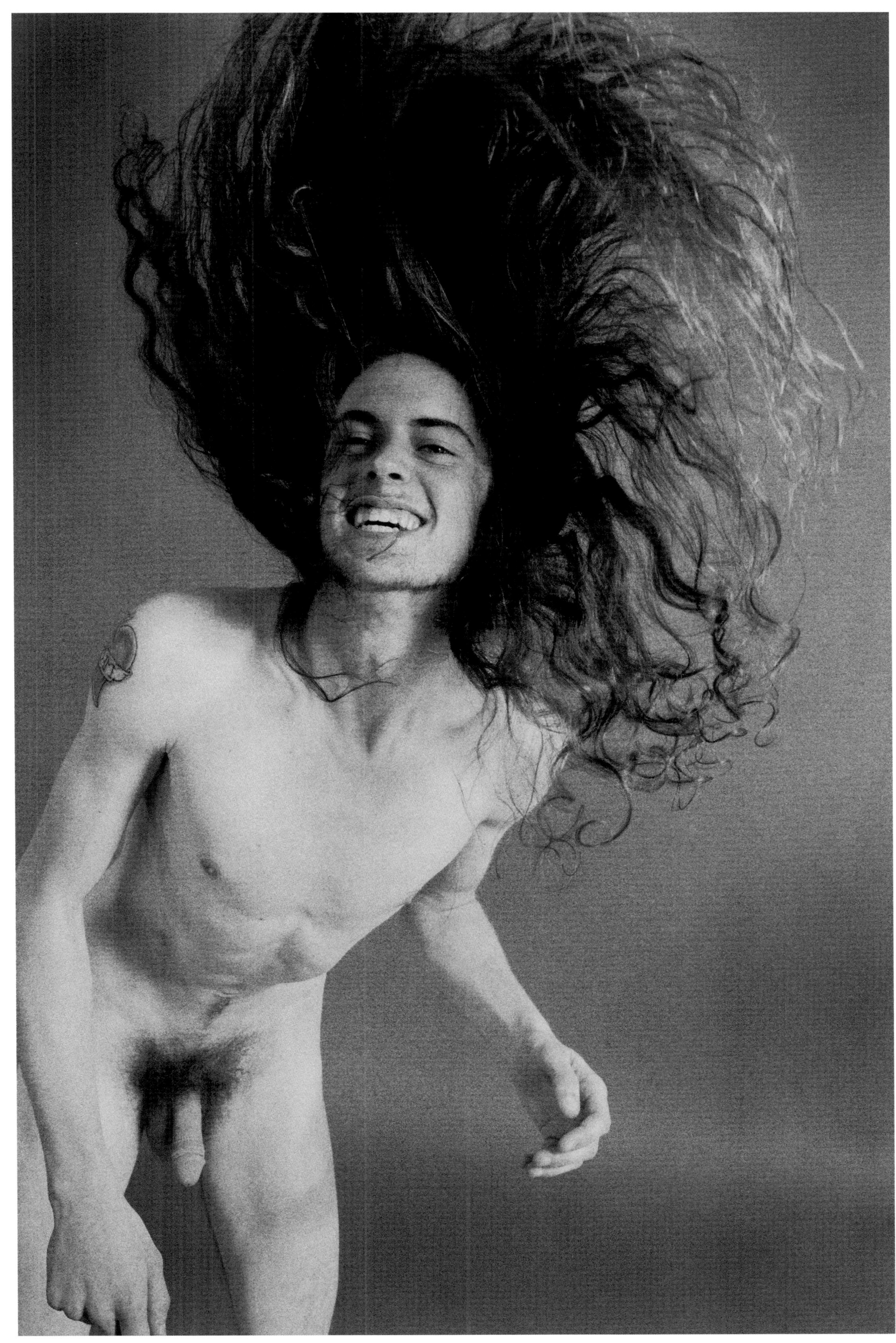

Cory, April 2013

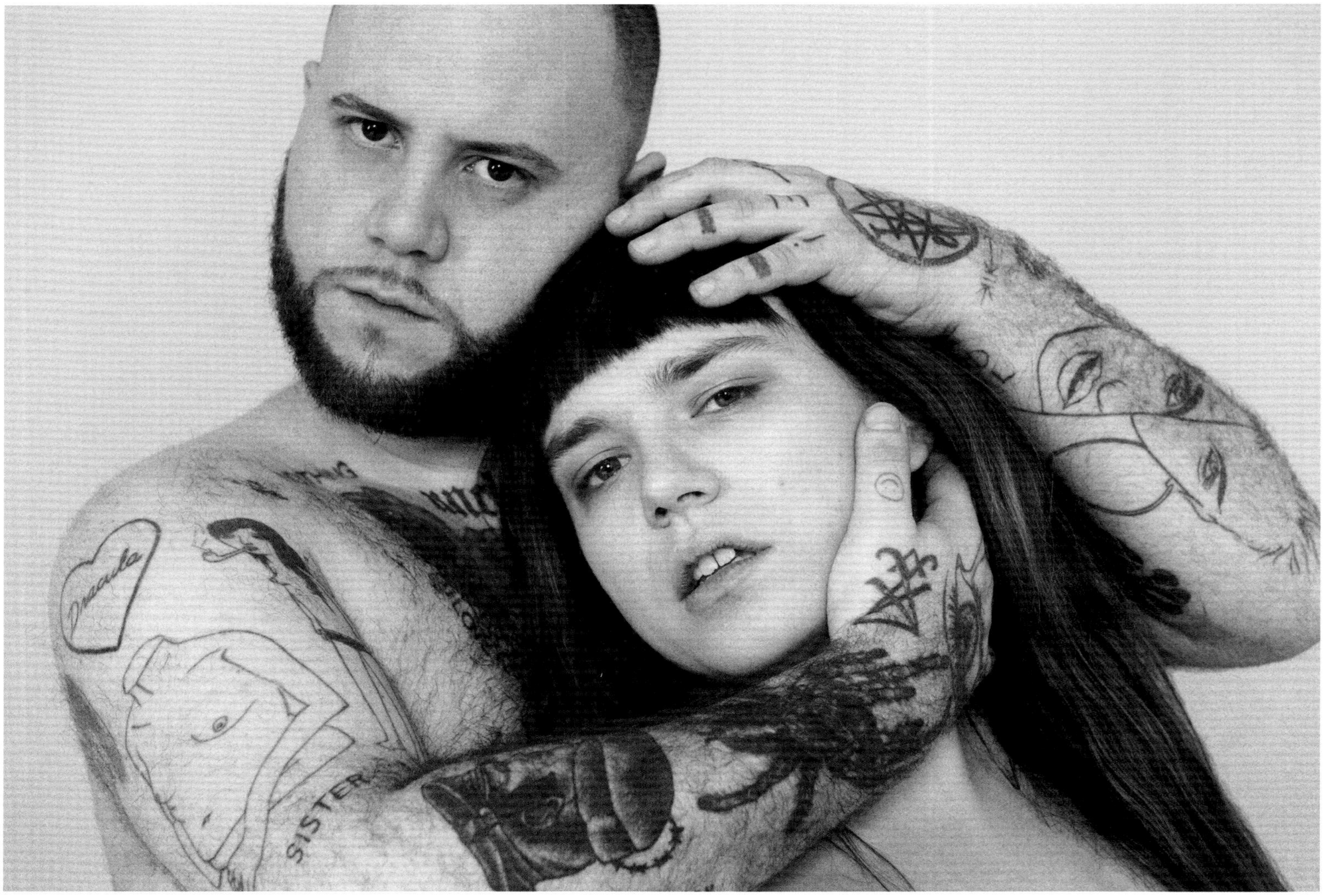

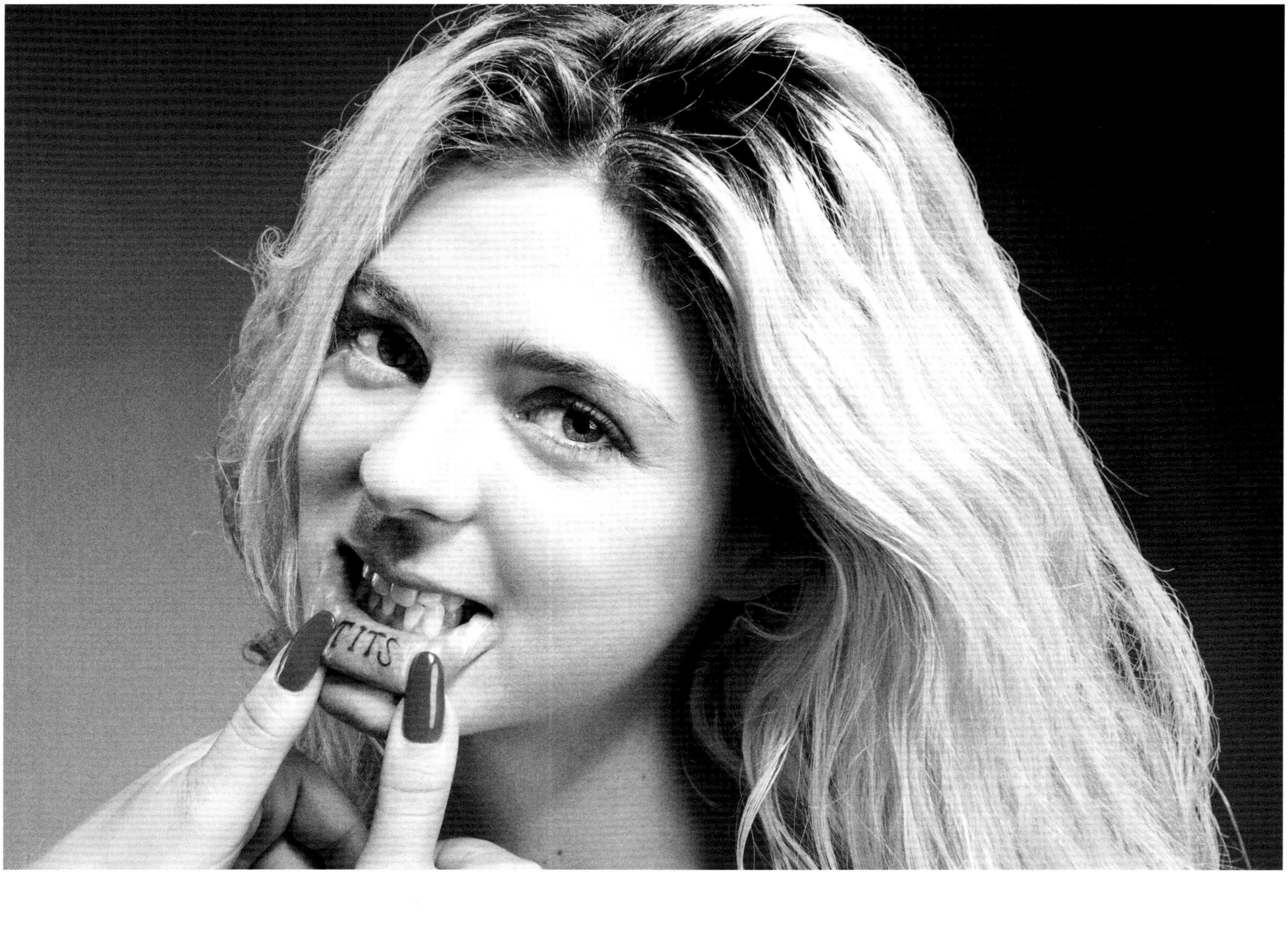

Jake & Macy, January 2017

Lauren, September 2015

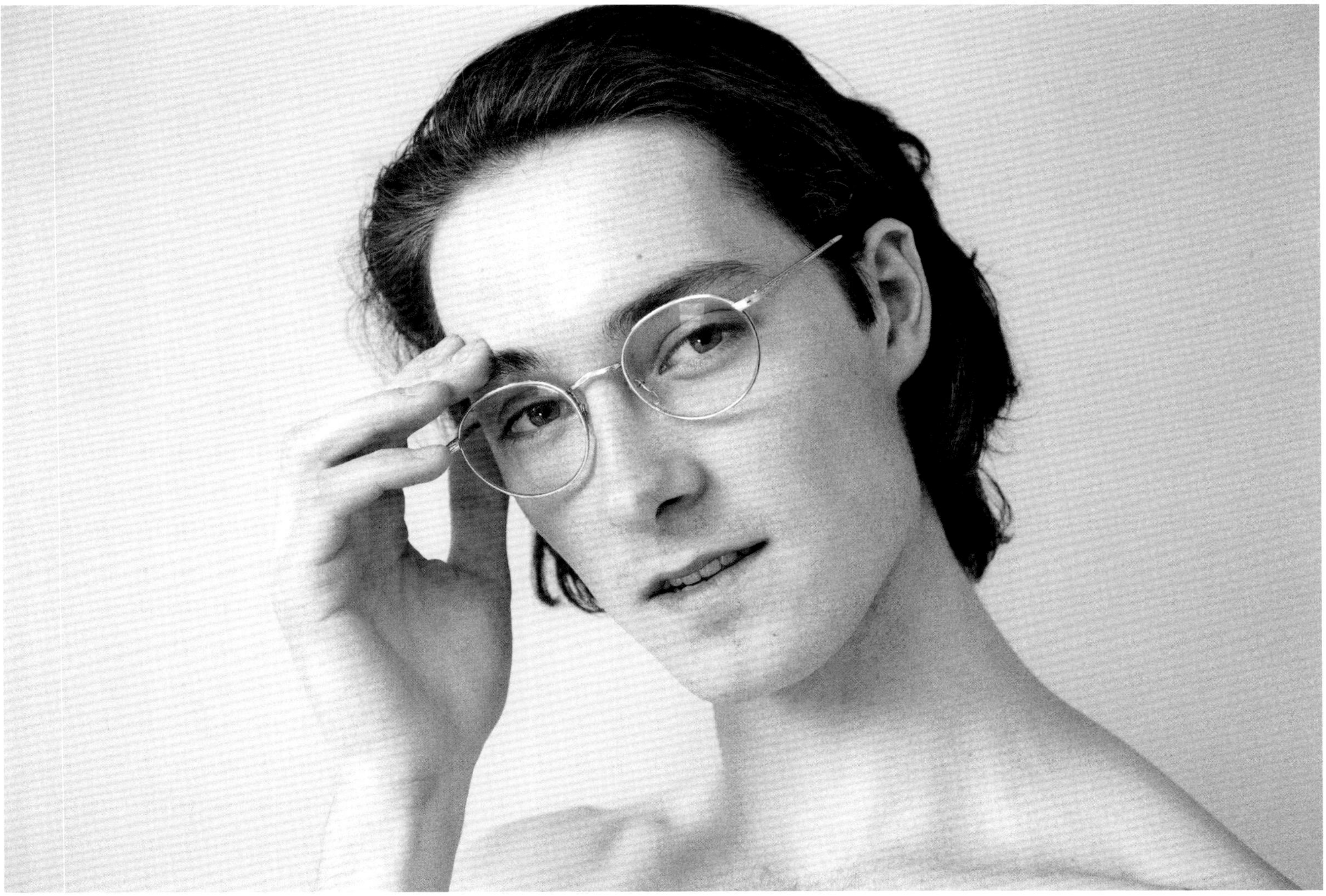

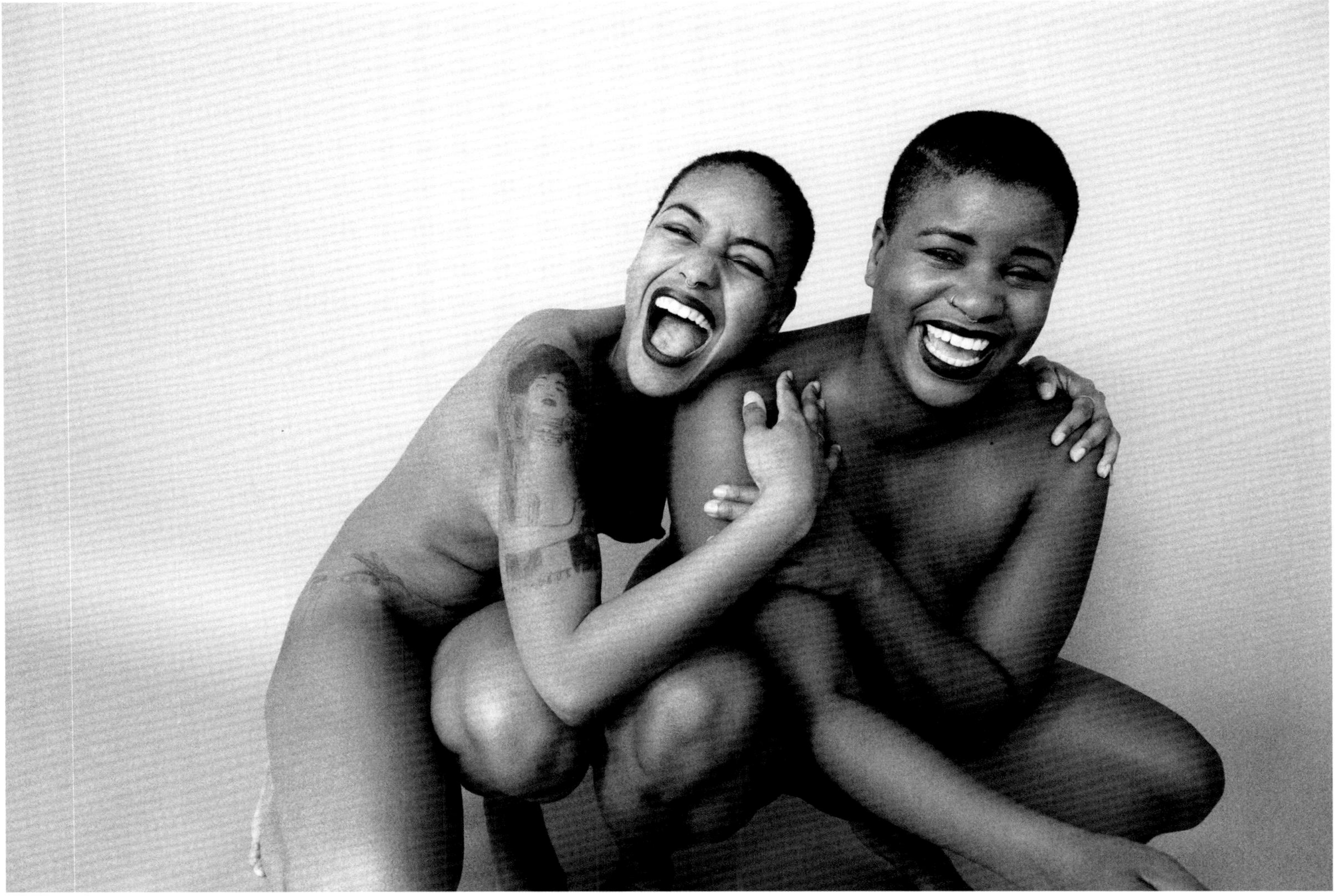

Sam, December 2016   Lorelei & Ericka, January 2017

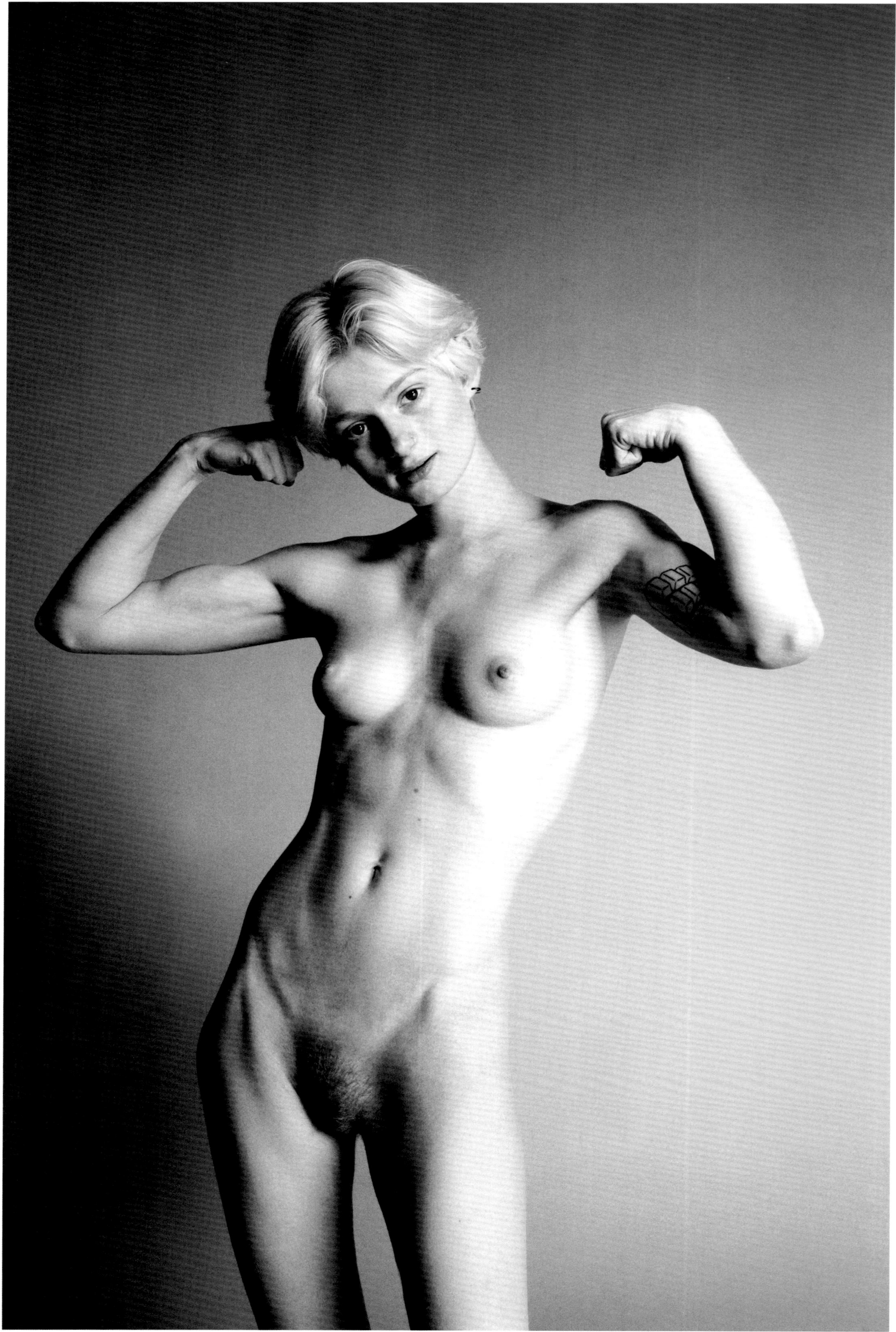

Lily, June 2015

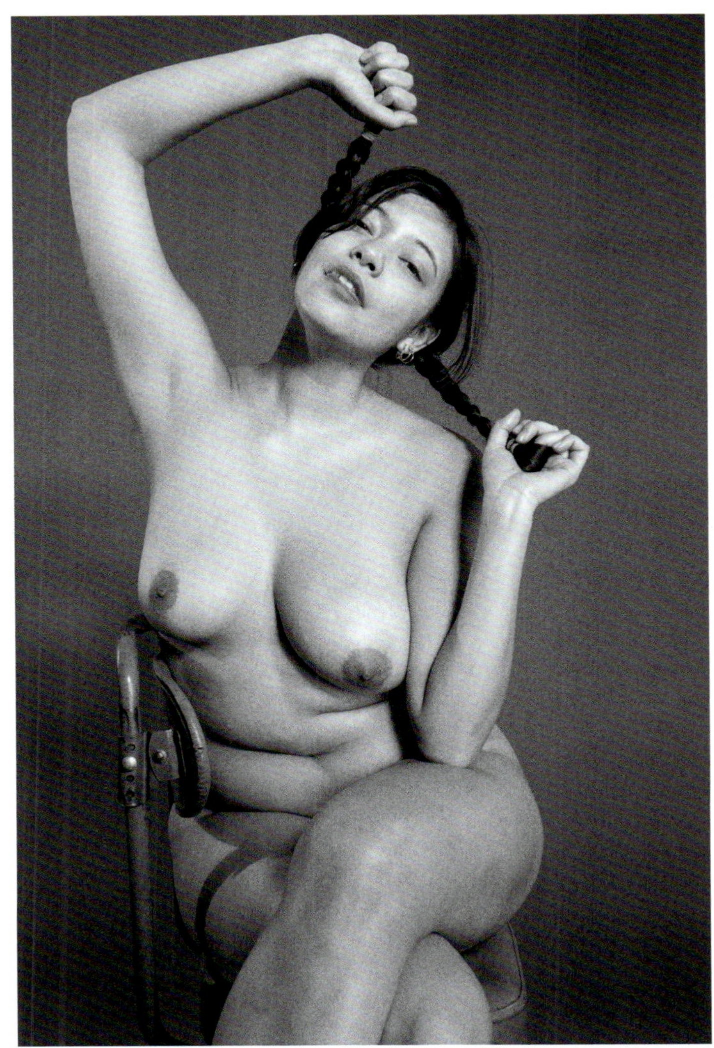

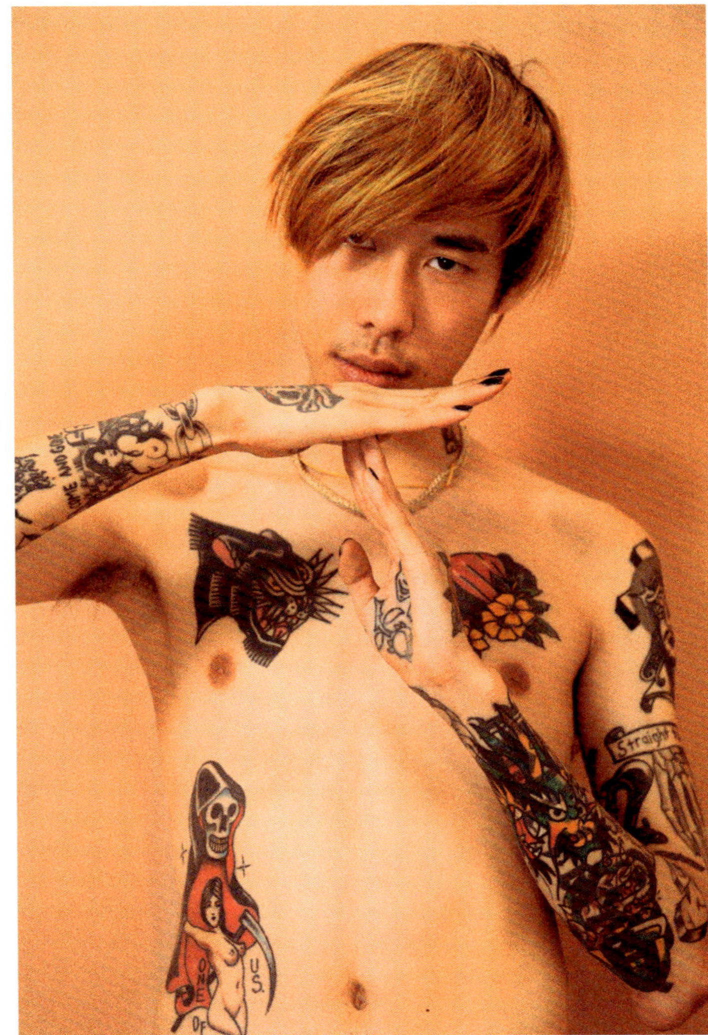

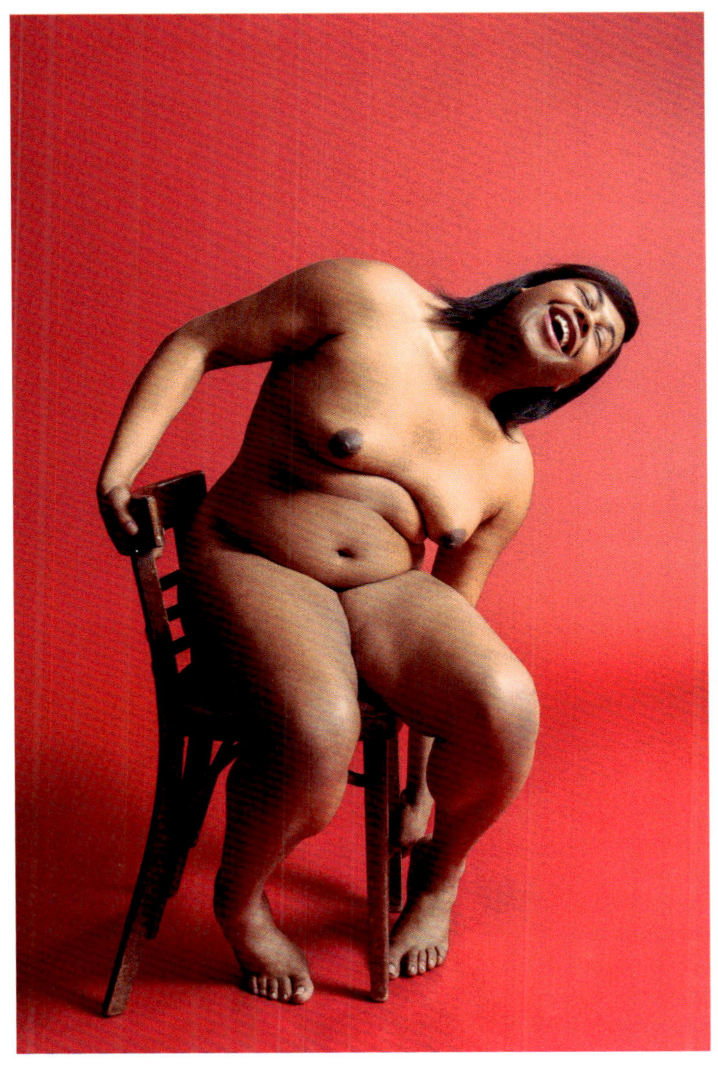

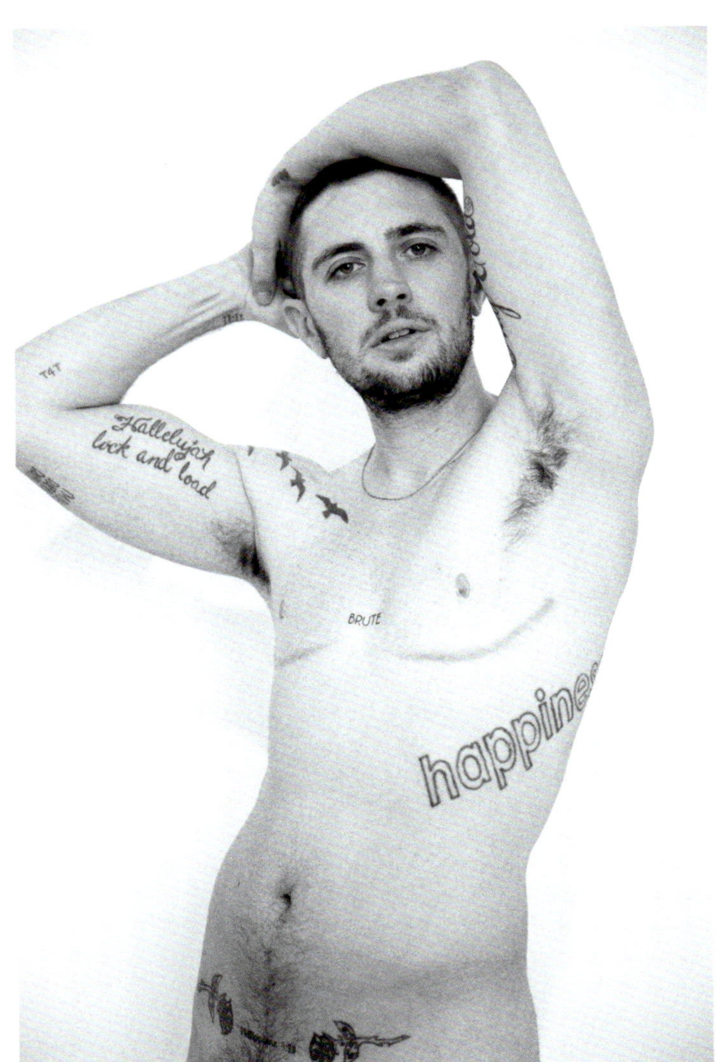

Naomi, March 2014   Eric, November 2016   Catiriana, February 2016   Sawyer, December 2018

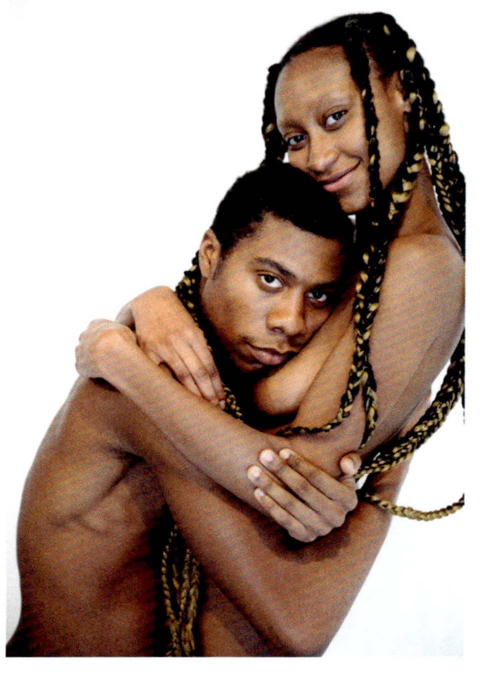
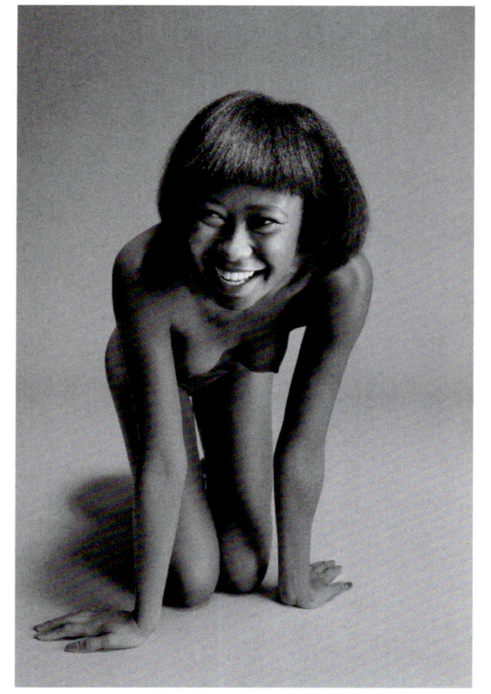
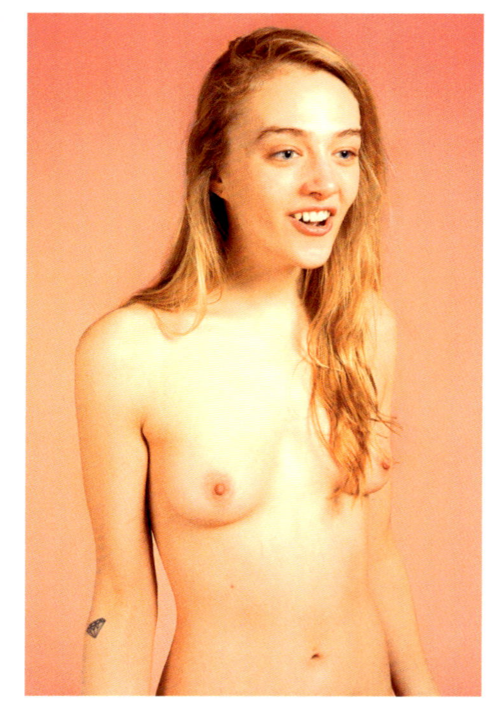
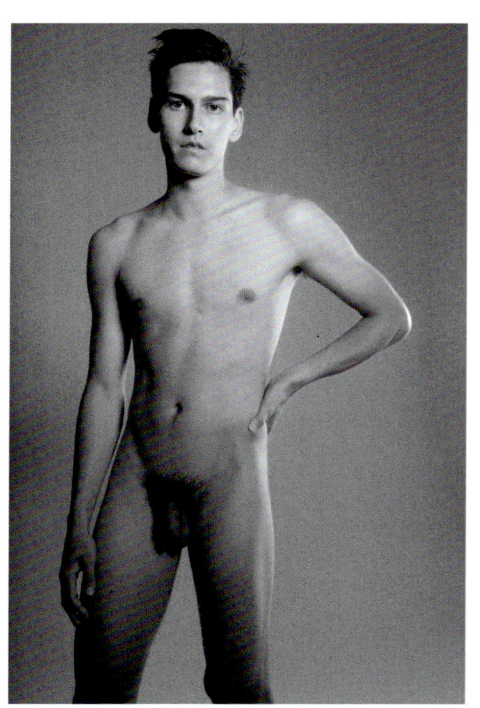
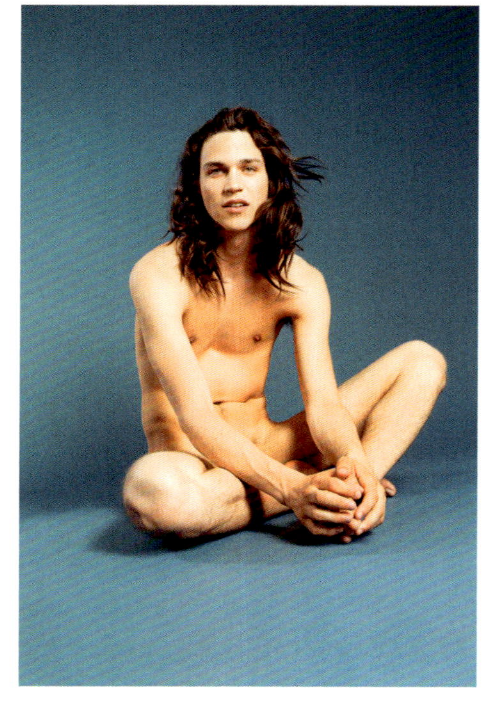
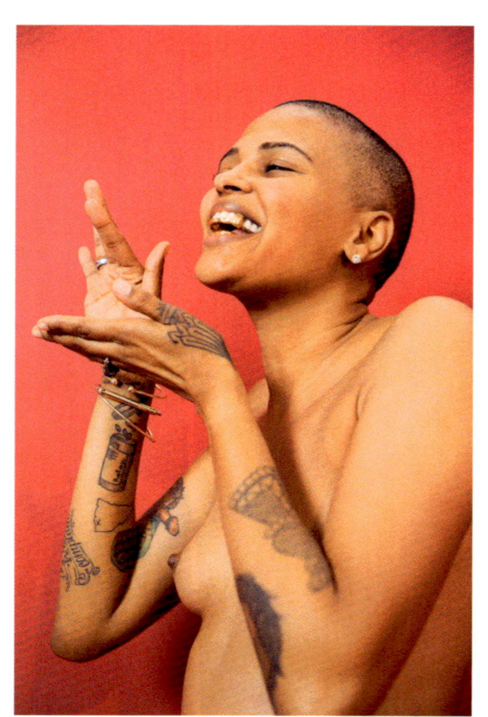
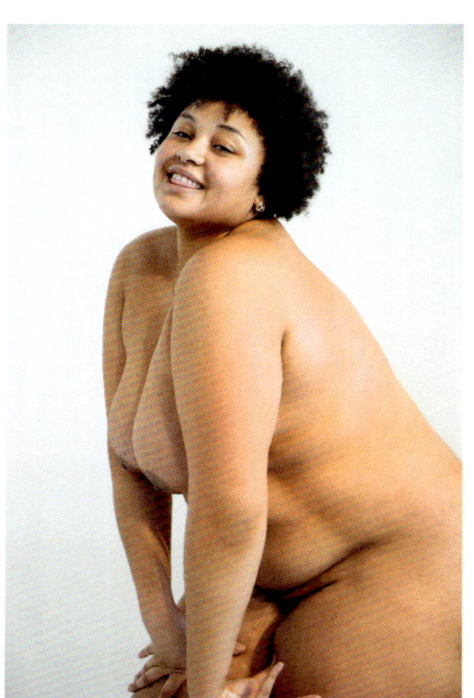
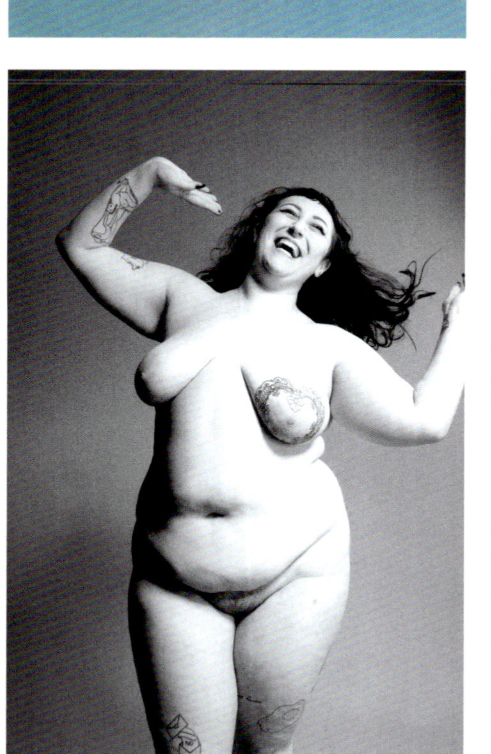
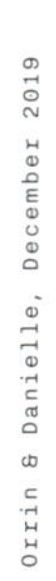

Orrin & Danielle, December 2019 Fleurjedye, September 2015 Caitlin, January 2012 Maxime, July 2015 Miles, June 2011 Matt, October 2010 Ariel, December 2018 Annie, December 2015 Crystal, November 2016

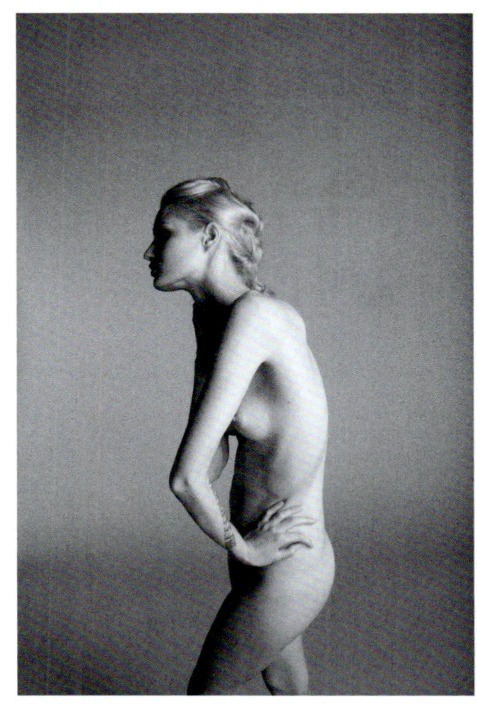
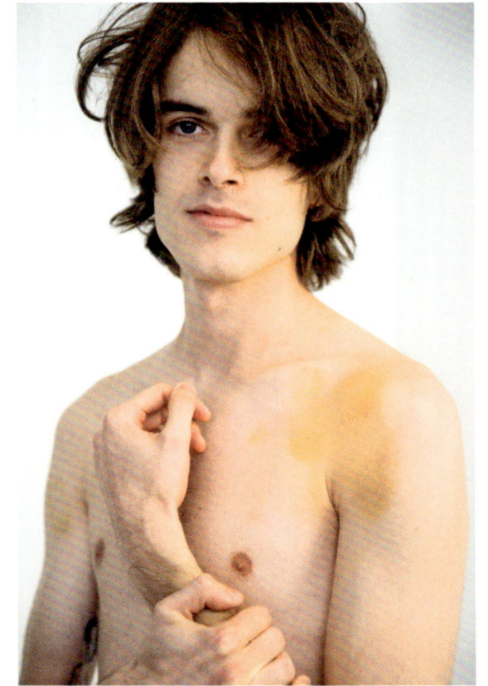
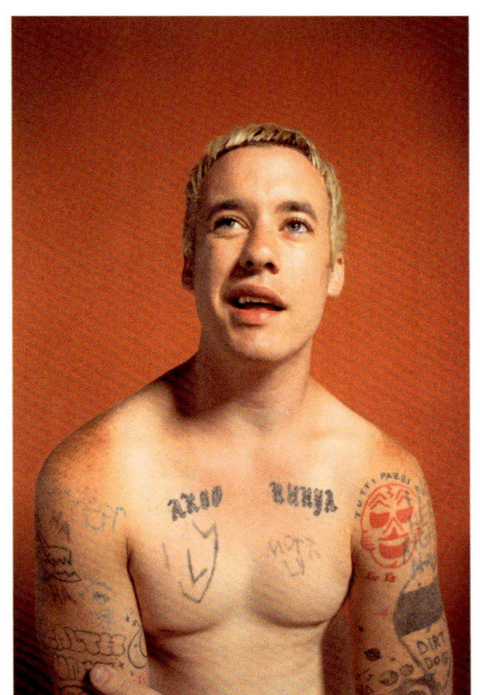
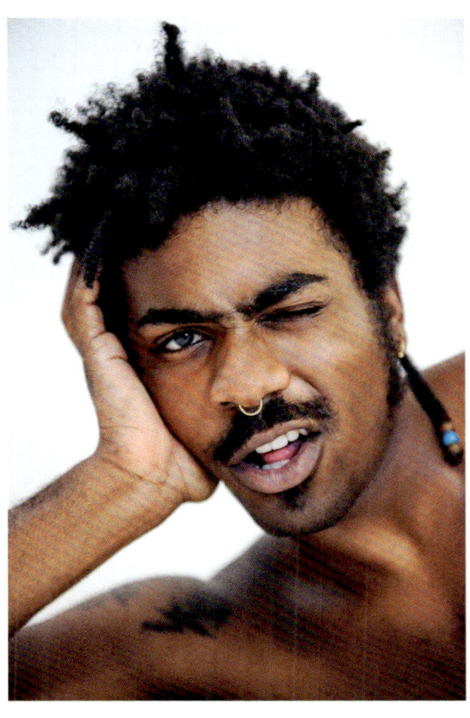
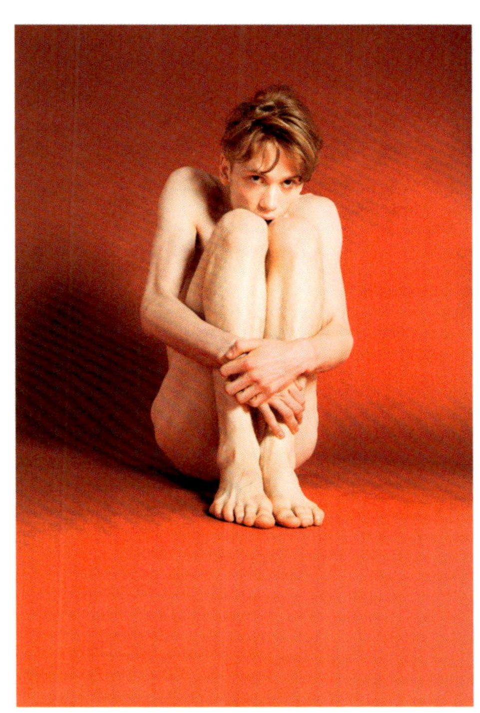
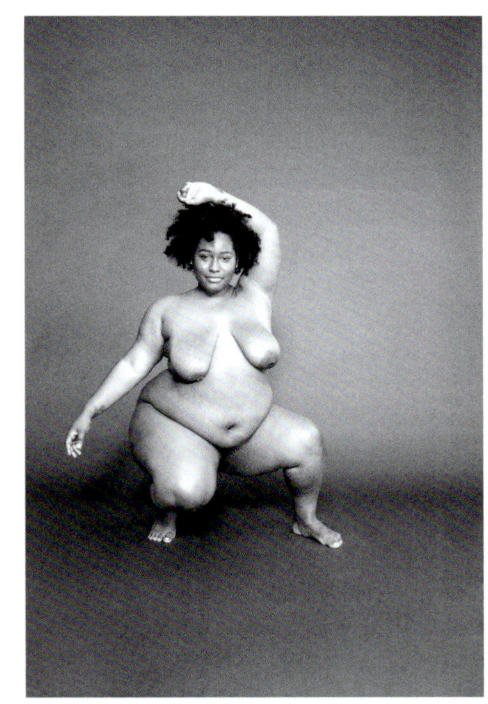
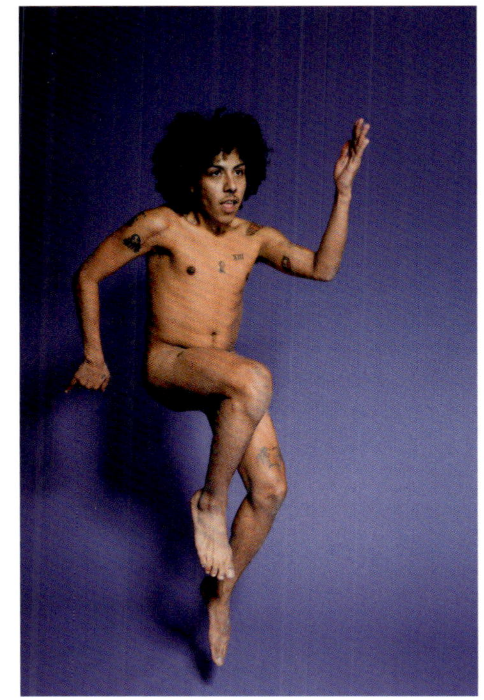
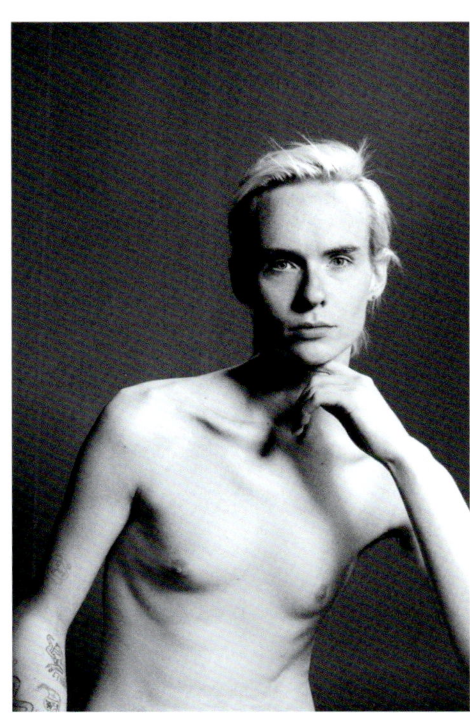
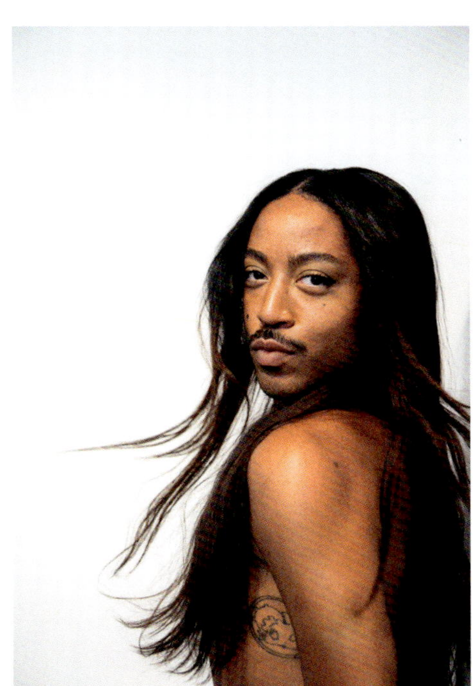

Erika, July 2012 Pedro, September 2018 Rick, July 2012 Brandon, October 2019 William, December 2012 Champale, April 2016 Pat, January 2016 Zac, April 2015 Jeffrey, October 2019

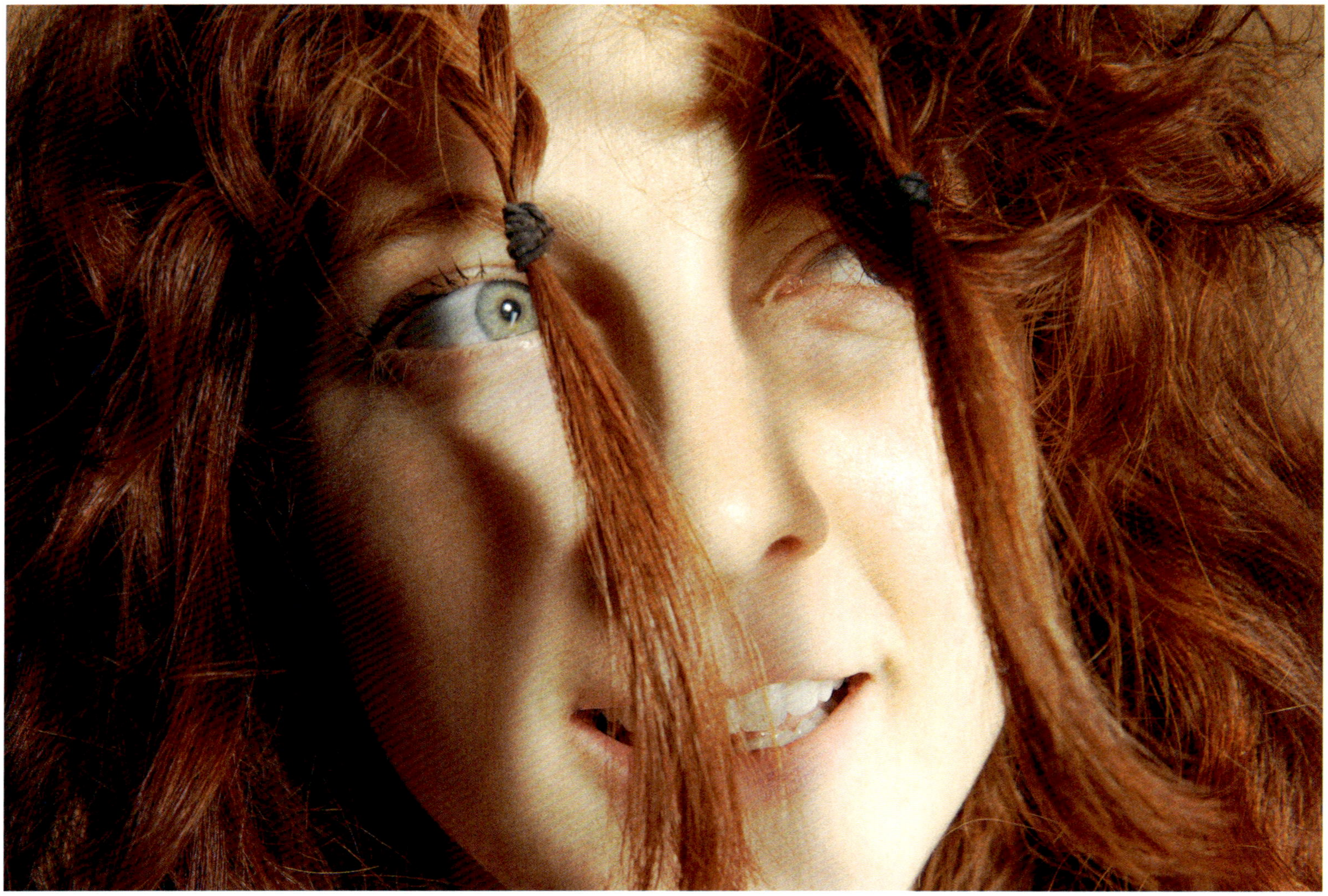

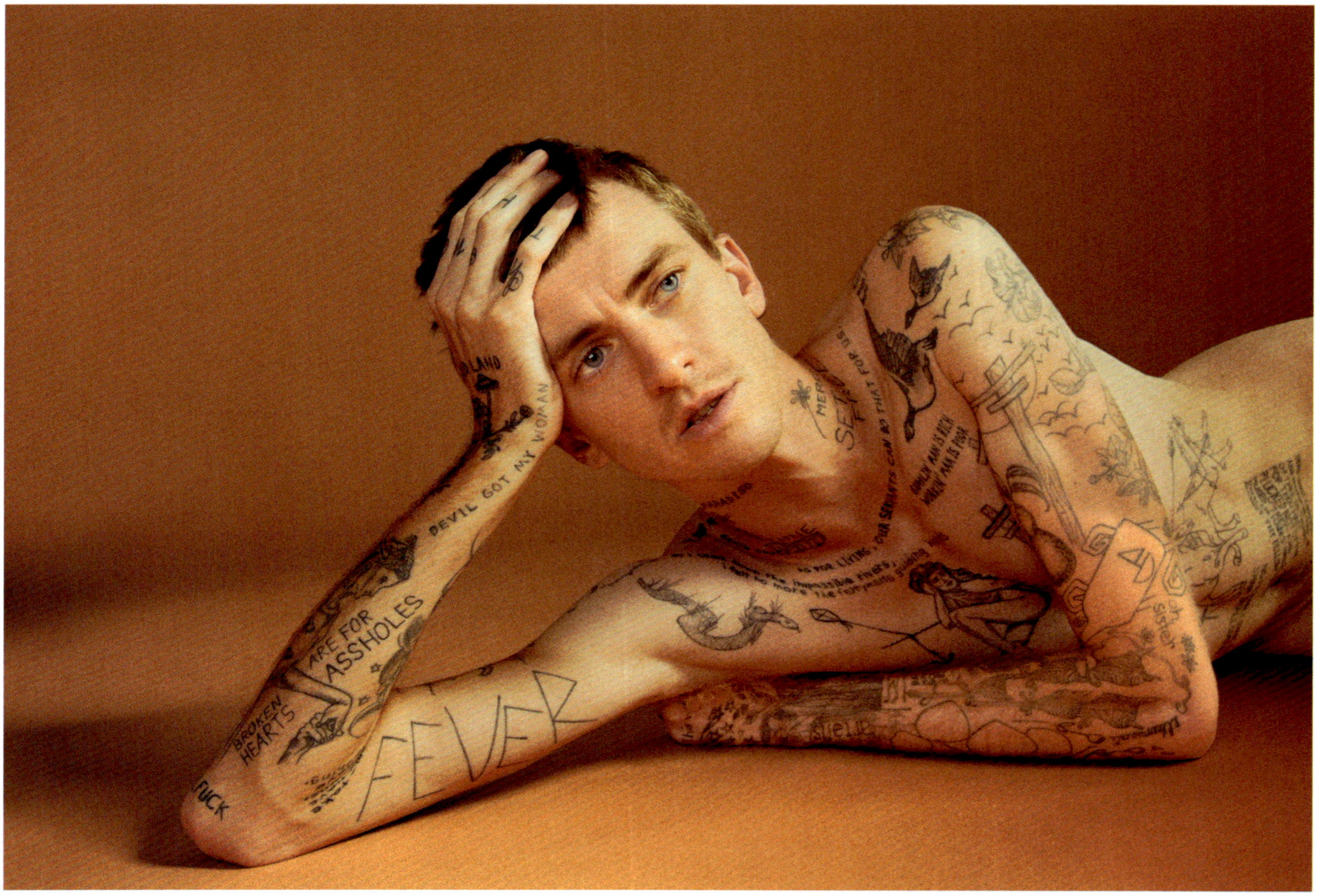

Emily, November 2015   Kensie, August 2012

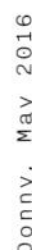
Donny, May 2016

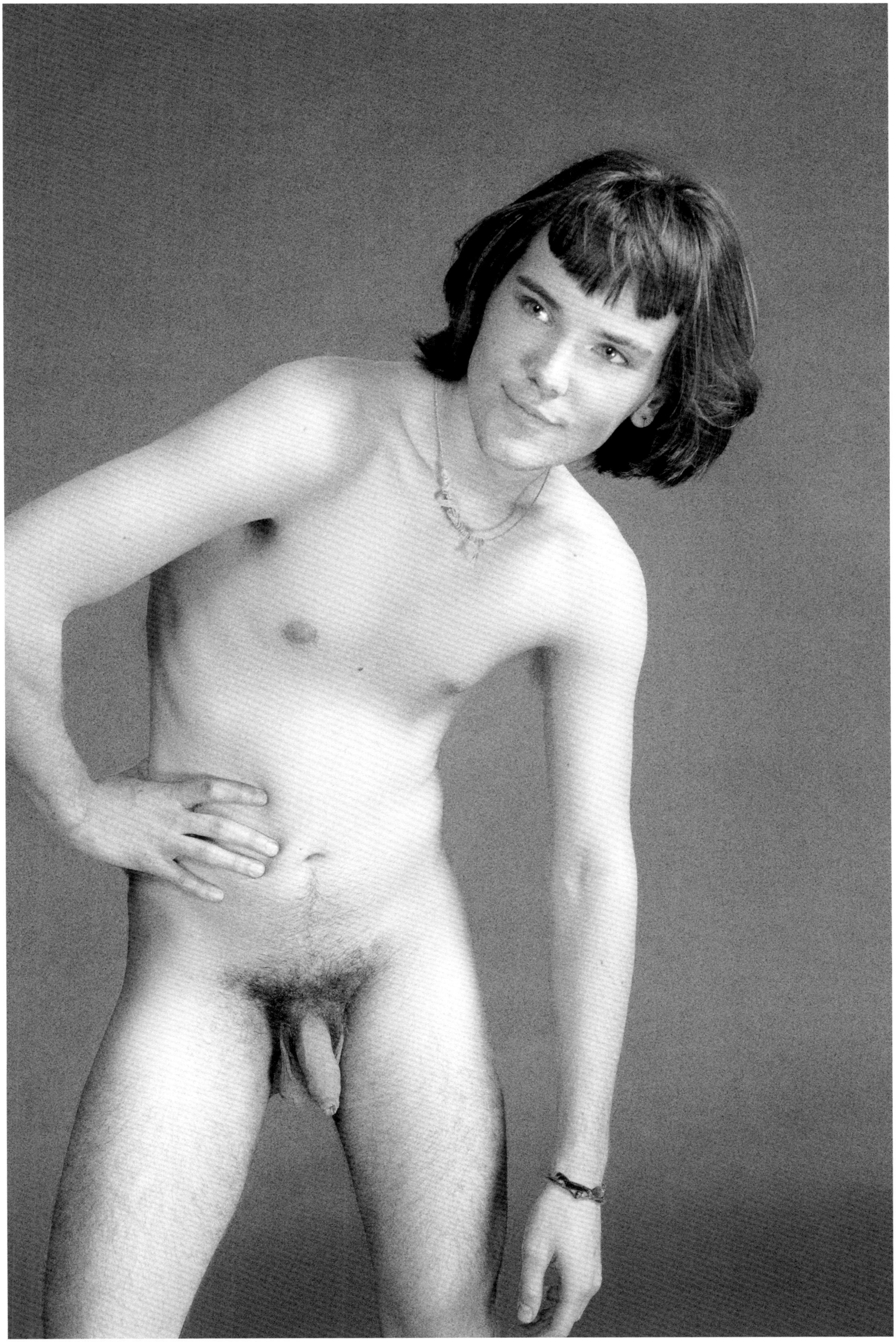

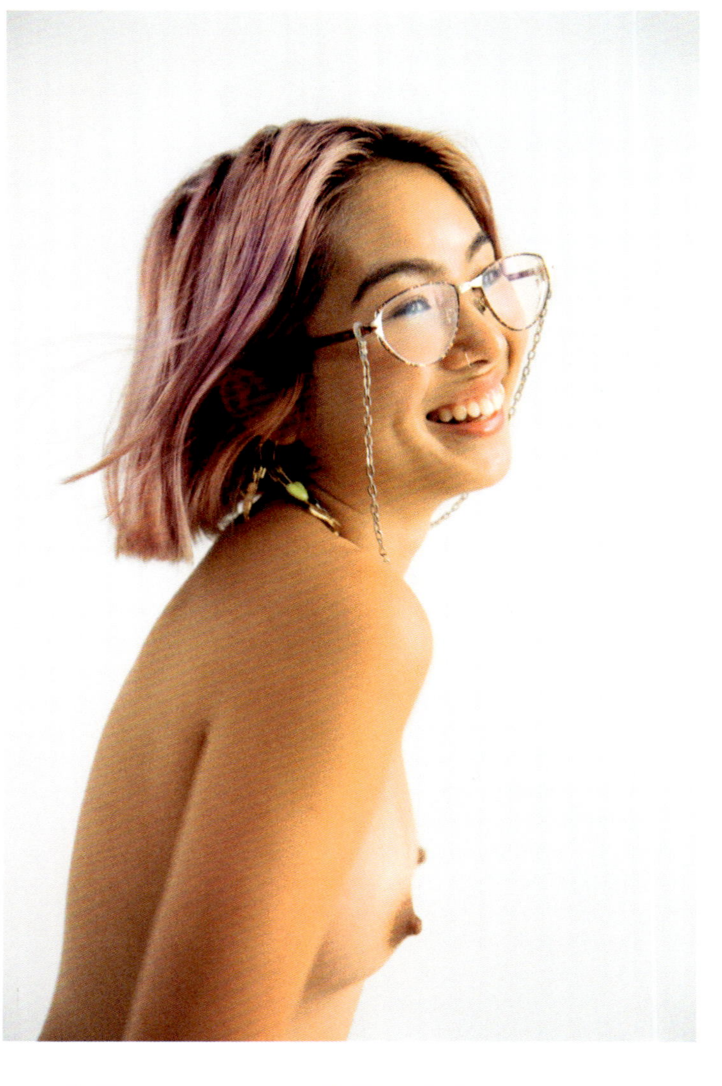

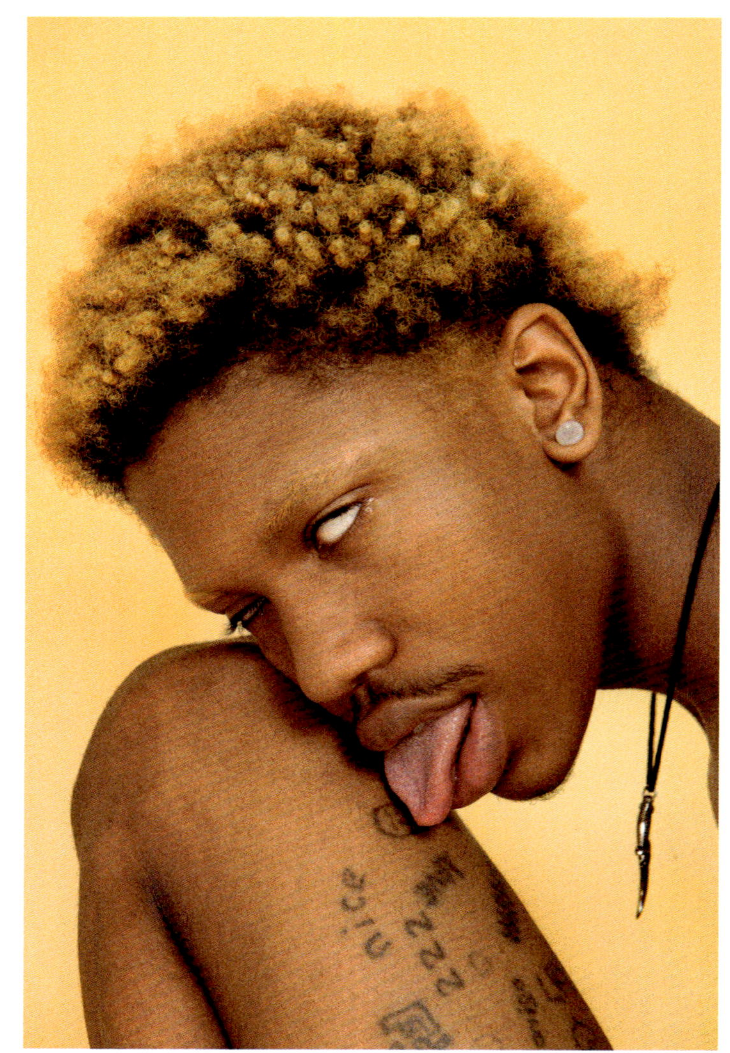

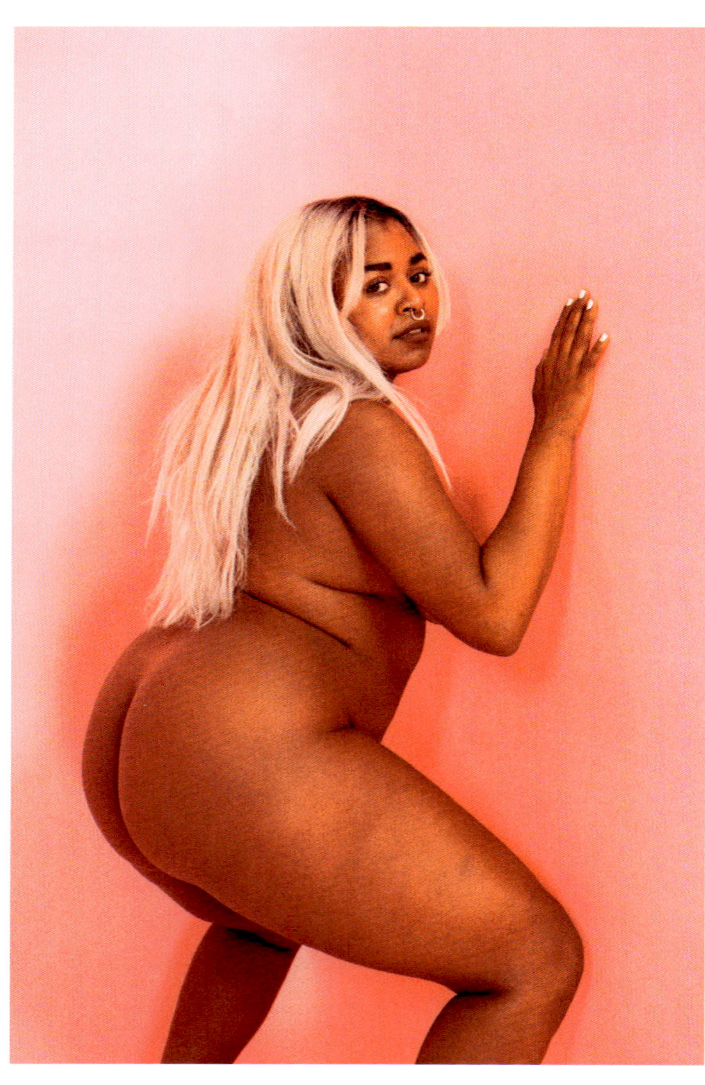

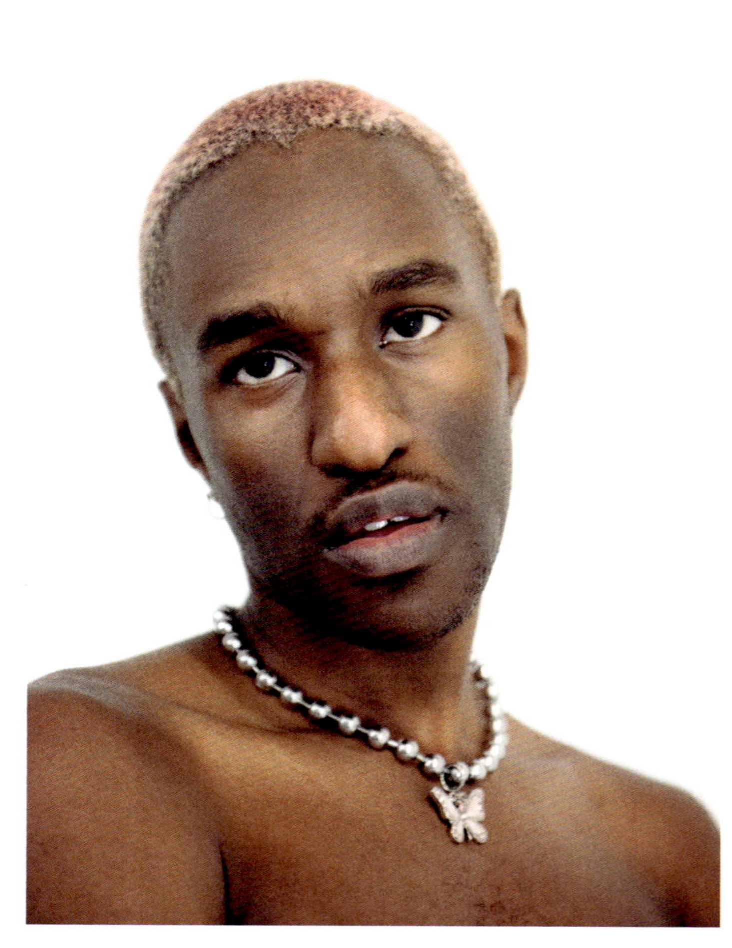

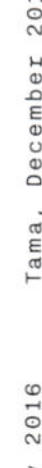

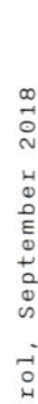

Carol, September 2018 Tariq, July 2016 Andisa, May 2016 Tama, December 2019

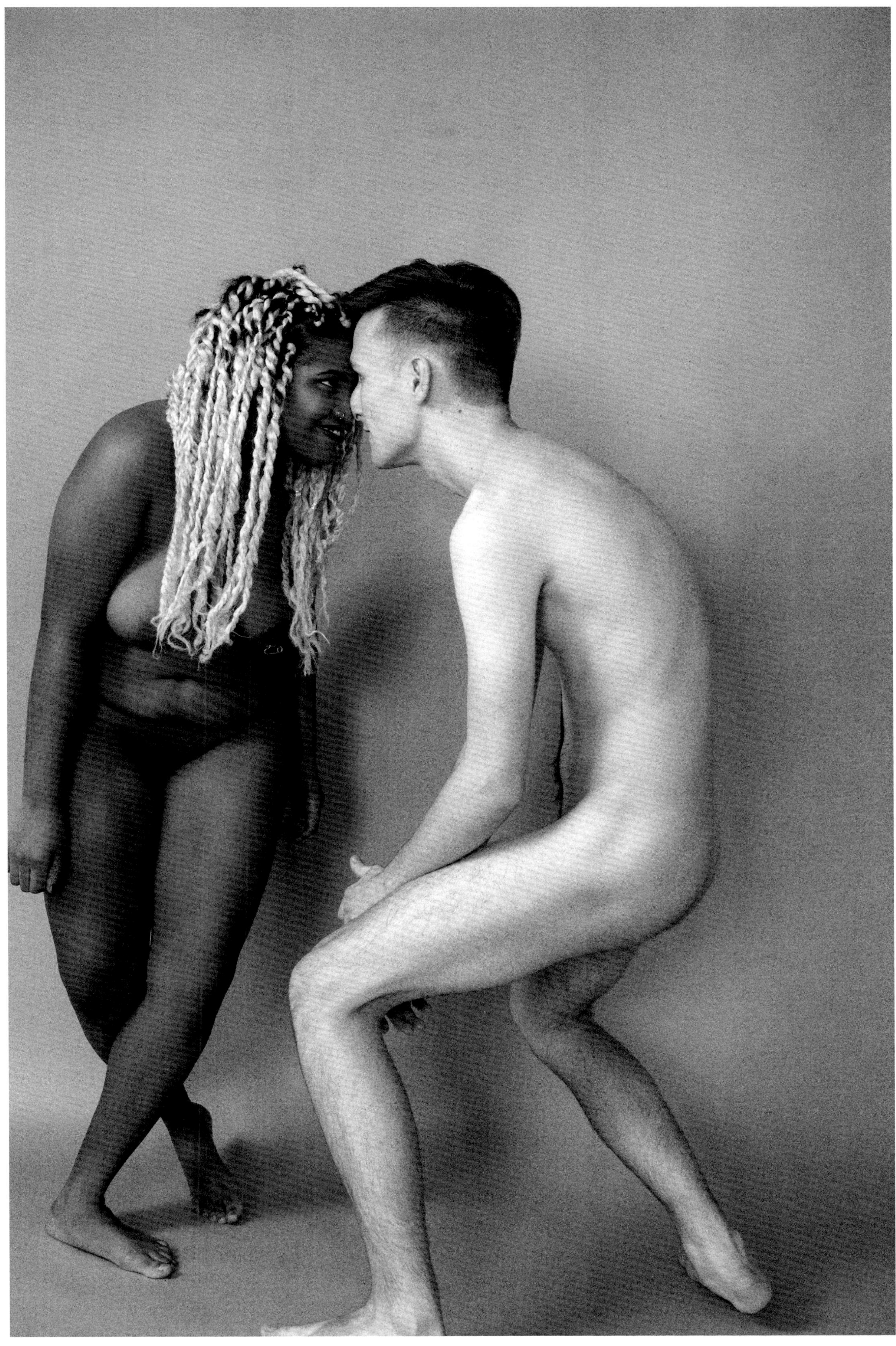

Daiju & Cooper, January 2017

I started getting tattooed when I was thirteen years old.

I wanted my skin to be my yearbook in a way, detailing the different chapters, people, and clubs, if you will, of my life.

I was bullied a lot when I was a kid, to the point where I found more value in being dead than going to school. When I was thirteen, this really popular kid became friends with me. He was sixteen, really handsome, and really good at basketball. He had a really beautiful girlfriend. He was an amazing person, and to this day, I have no idea why he was my friend, which is why I take friendships so seriously now. Sometimes all it takes is one person saying, "Let's hang out," to calm that entire sea of storms happening inside of you. The bullying also kind of subsided because he was so cool.

One night, my friend was taking me to a party. I had never been to a proper high school party before, and I was nervous, but I felt okay 'cause I was with him. We pulled up to another party to pick up his brother and his brother's girlfriend. I ran inside to get them. While I was inside, I heard what I thought were fireworks, but they were actually gunshots. My friend was shot and killed in the car.

I didn't go to the funeral. I heard that people brought Jordans, basketball shorts, and basketballs. I just couldn't face the situation. Instead, I went and got a tear tattooed for him, which I later turned into a cross to commemorate the cross and tear tattoos he had. I was a few days shy of fourteen when I got that done.

I didn't show up for most of my school yearbook photos. But my senior year, my mom wanted a senior photo. They ended up airbrushing my face tattoos out. I look insane. It's so funny. My mom was like, "I feel like that's not even you."

Between eighteen and twenty was when I started to look like I was dipped in a bottle of ink. I had just dropped out of college. I would work and save money to travel to artists who I really loved and artists who were good at tattooing darker skin. I went to Jacksonville, Florida, and to London, Berlin, Hawaii, LA, St. Augustine, Detroit . . . Through those travels, I learned so much about myself.

Eighteen was also my first year of being sober. I started getting the years that I'd been sober tattooed on my face. I see number three on my face in this photo. On the opposite side, there should be a five. When I look at this image and I see the three, I remember how hard it was for me to make it to year two. Now I've been twelve years sober.

Every day is a fight, and so much of that fight is personified through the art of my skin. This photo is almost like another testament to me saying no to the things that were holding me back and working against me. It's incredible to see this photo and remember there was a time when I was confidently saying no. It inspires me to keep doing so.

I feel like I'm always battling something, even if it's not my own fight. There's that dual consciousness where saying no to one thing is an adamant yes to another. And that's how I am when it comes to community.

I feel like the call of community is something that we all should answer, no matter what that looks like. I really feel like we all are multiple tools inside of a toolbox just waiting to be used. Being able to bake a cake can be activism because that cake can be used to feed three or four people who maybe can't afford cake. Being able to braid hair can be activism. You can help someone who is experiencing houselessness and may need their hair braided for a job interview.

I have confidently accepted the call of community, and I never know what that looks like on any given day. There are moments where I sometimes end up going into debt because I am last minute buying a flight to a place that I've never been to, to go and protest with kids, or to hold a memorial for one of the girls who have been killed. I don't know if that's the healthy way to do it, but it is a radical way. I feel like I don't know much, but I'm learning every day, and that is enough for me to keep taking these risks.

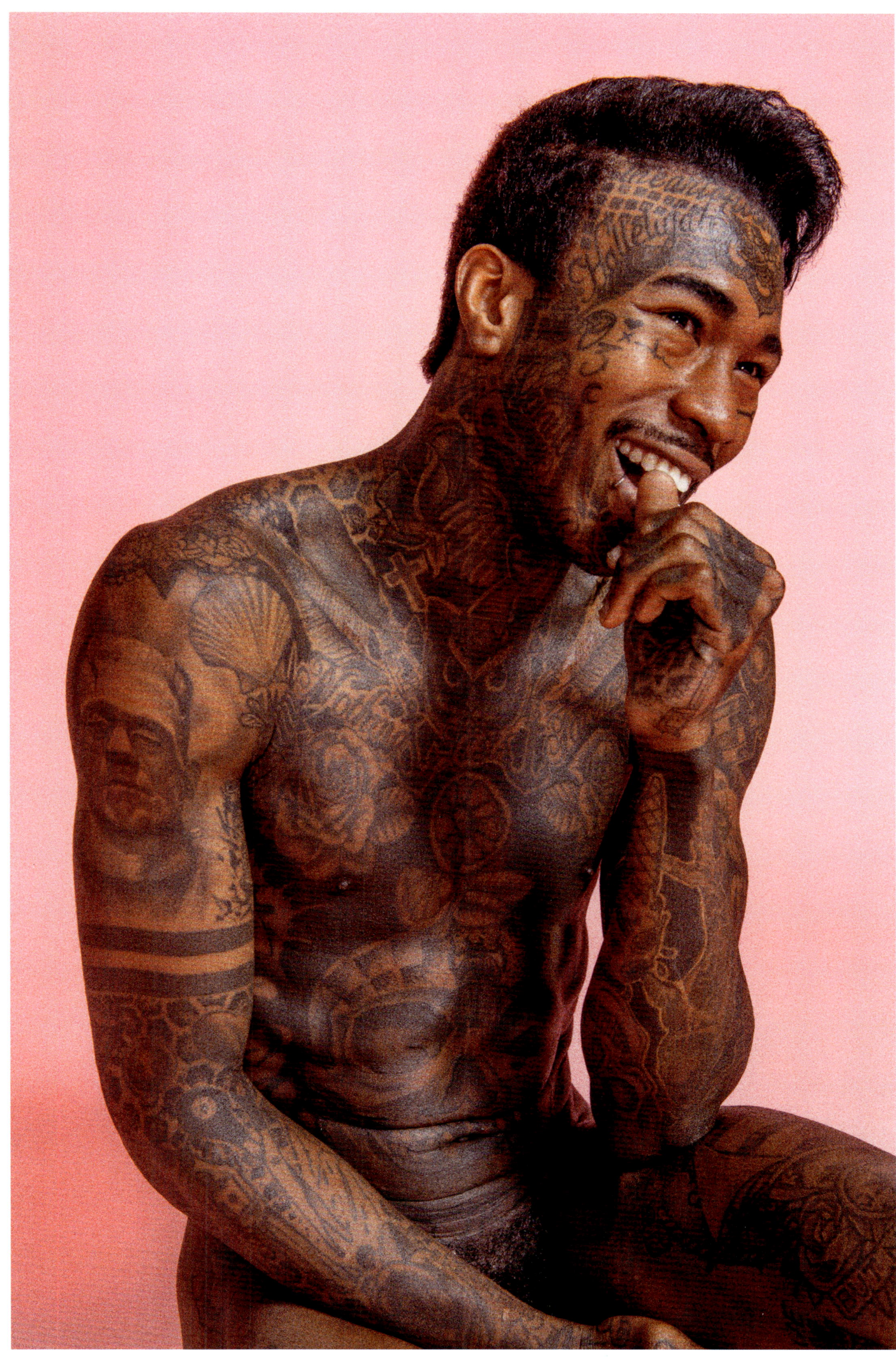

Yves, April 2016

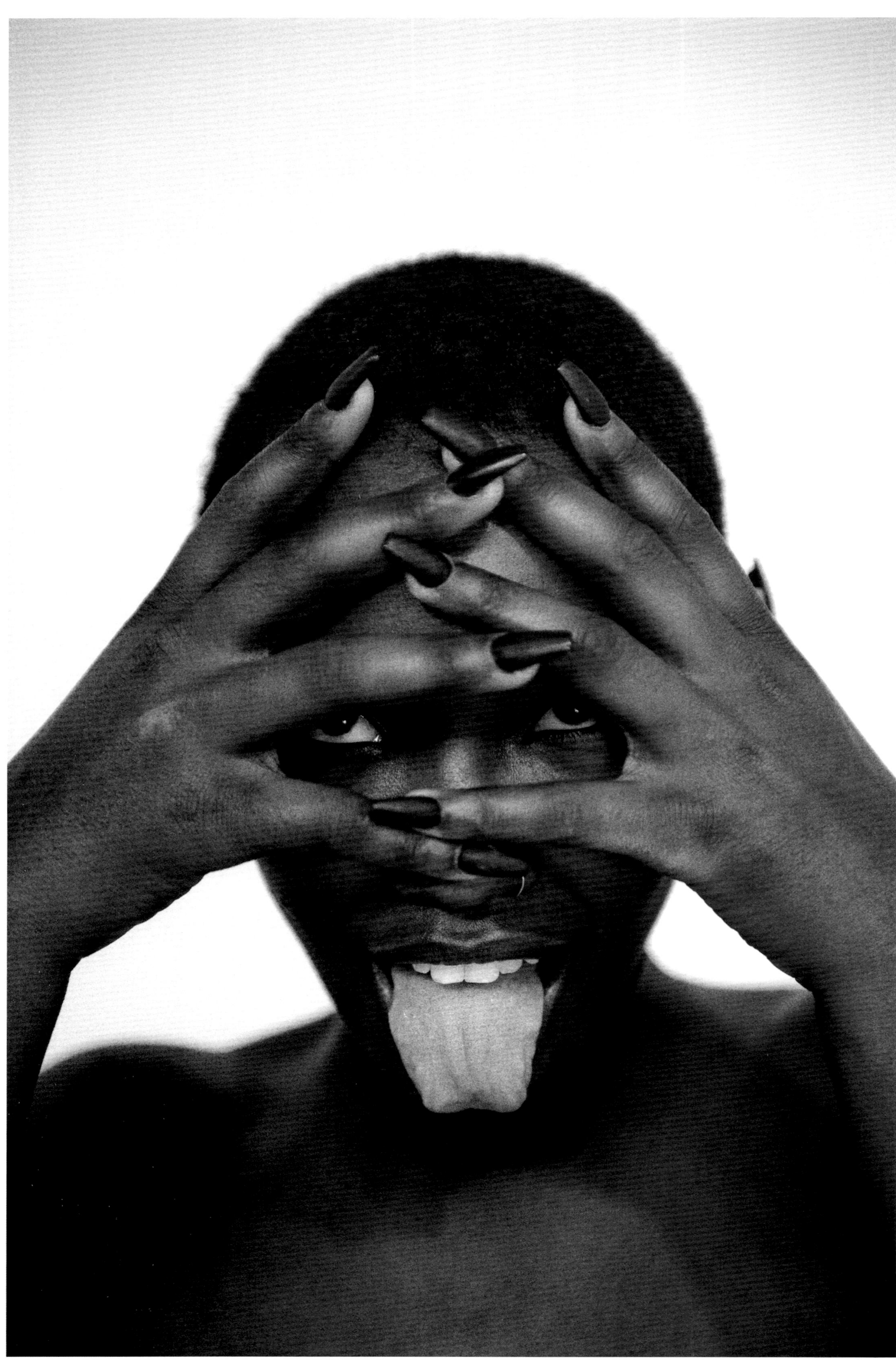

Nyla, October 2019   Ratio 3, San Fransisco, 2013

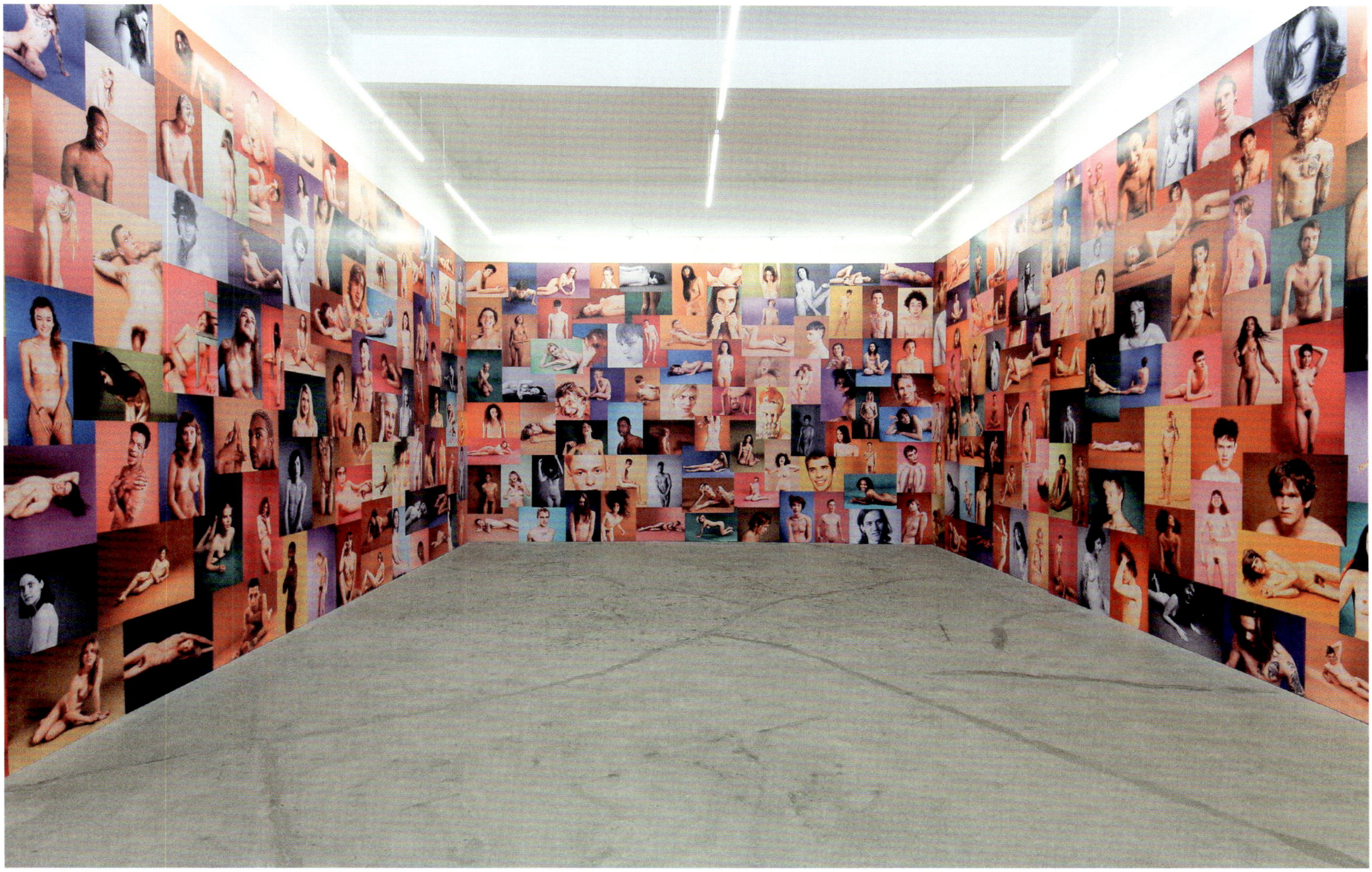

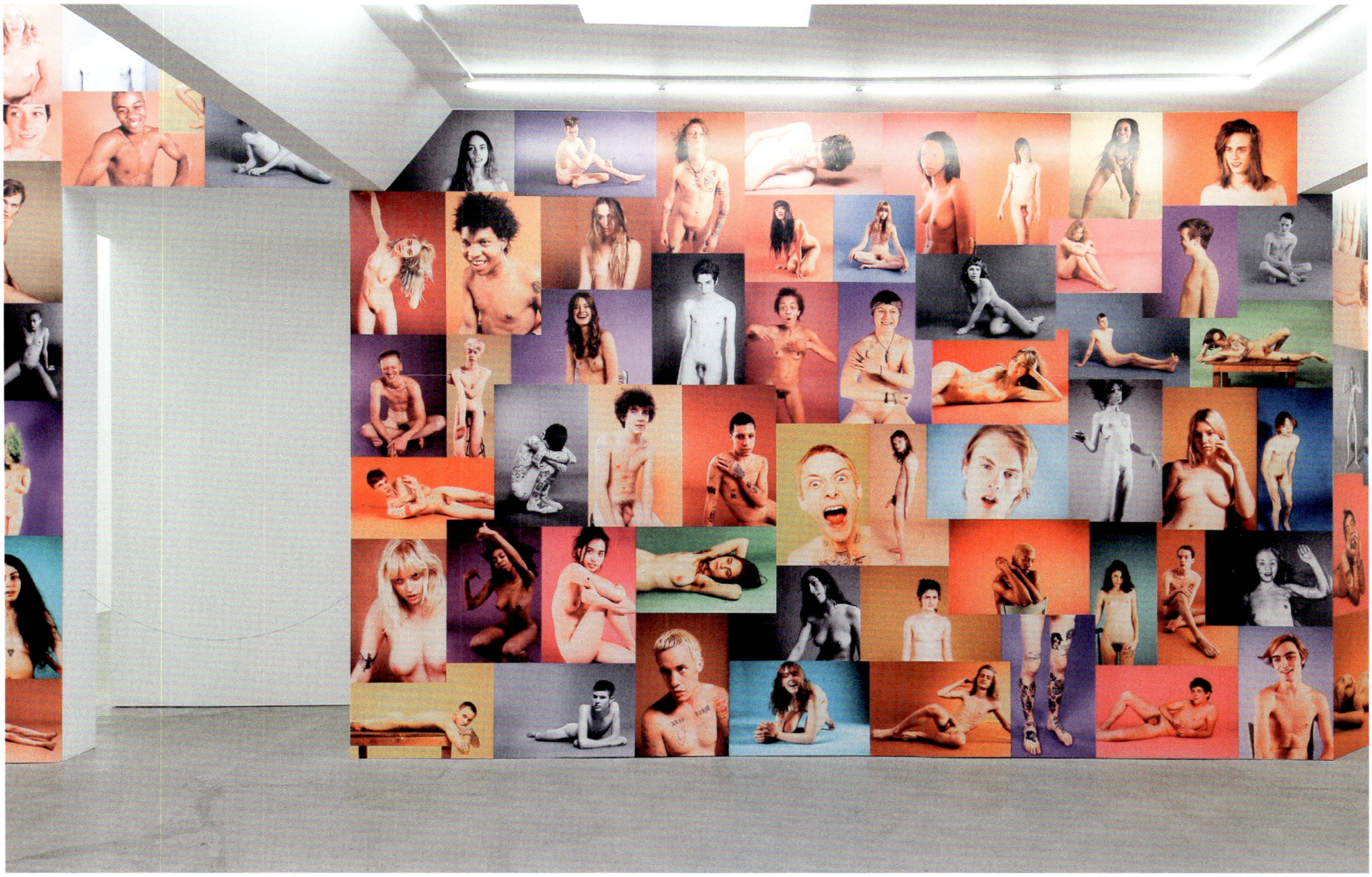

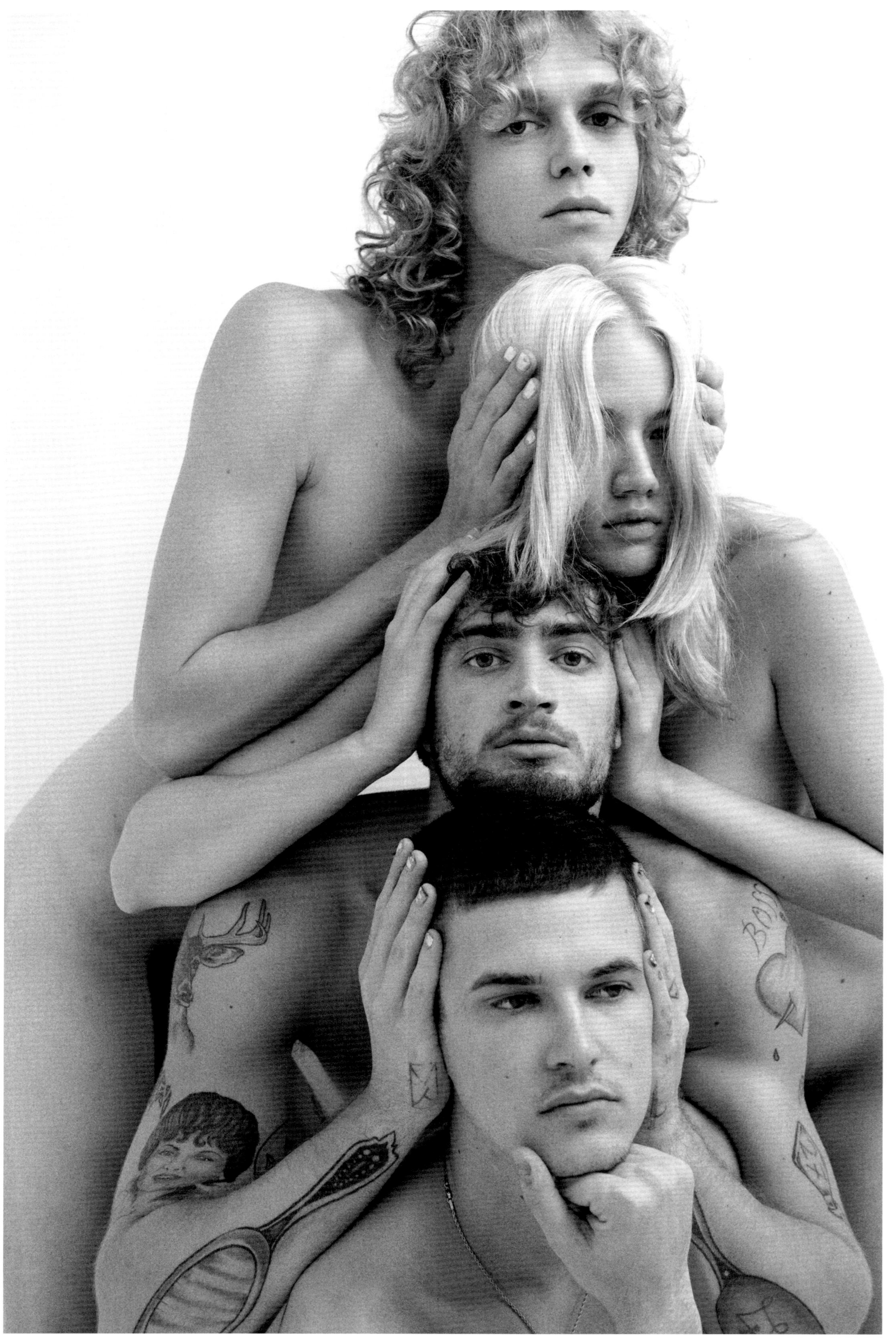

Brett, Lillian, Brody, & John, July 2017

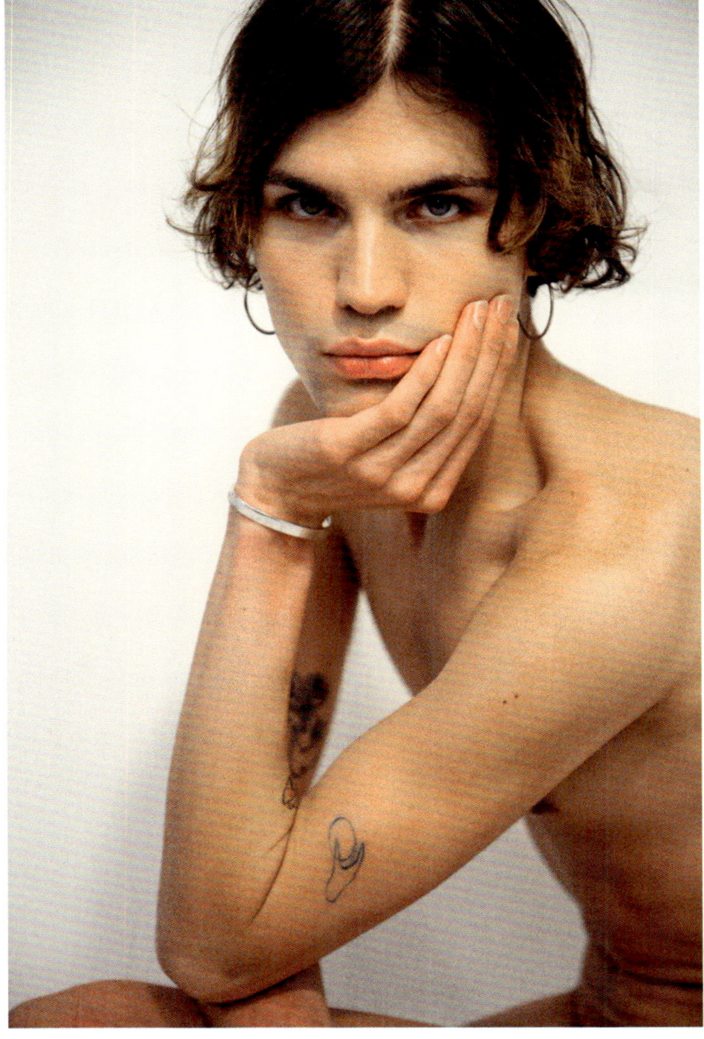

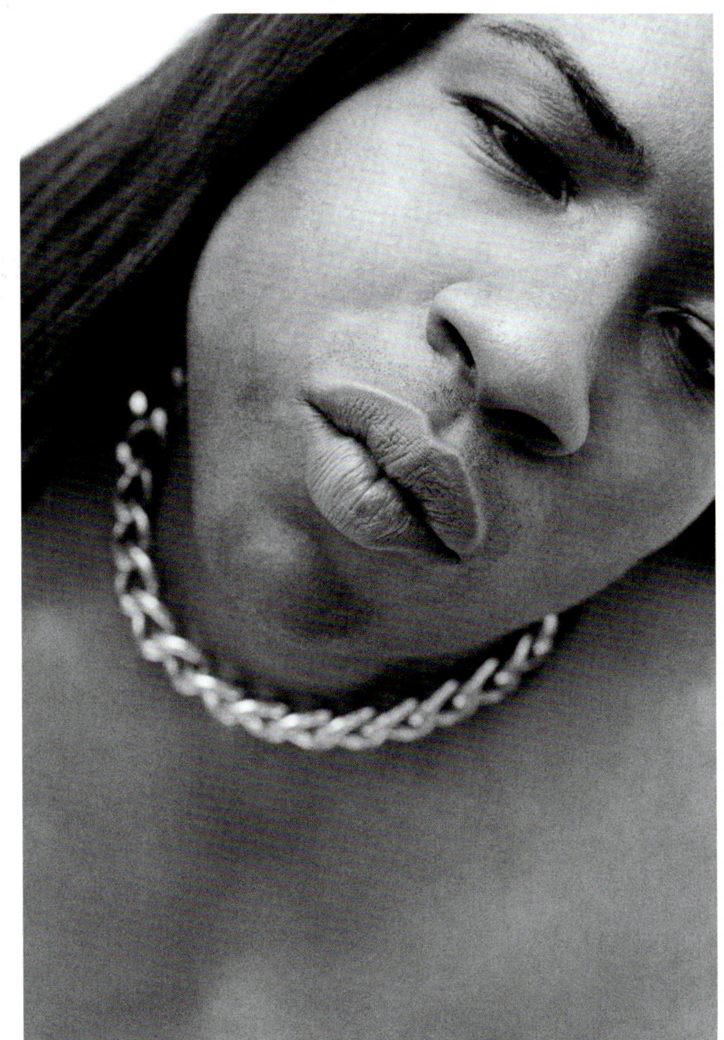

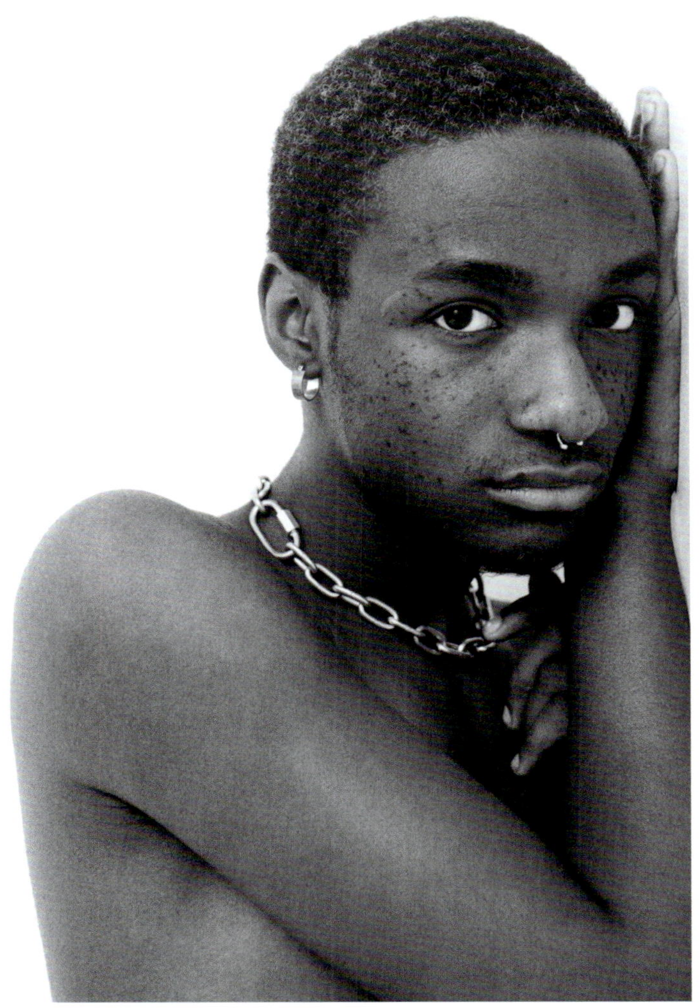

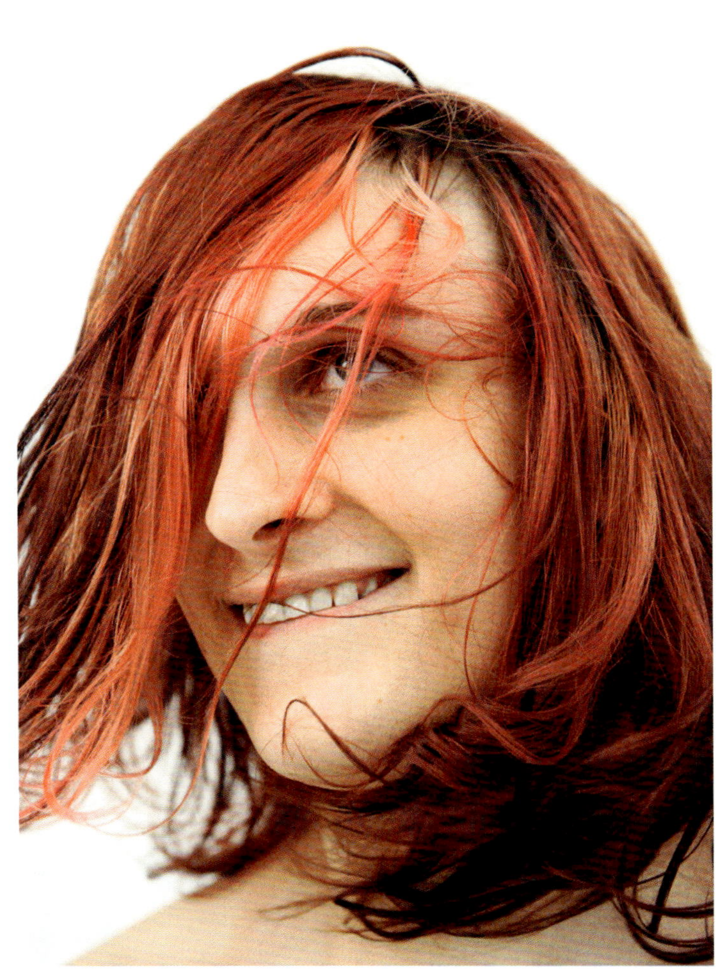

Neve, September 2018 Rahrah, June 2017 Jason, June 2017 Audrey, June 2017

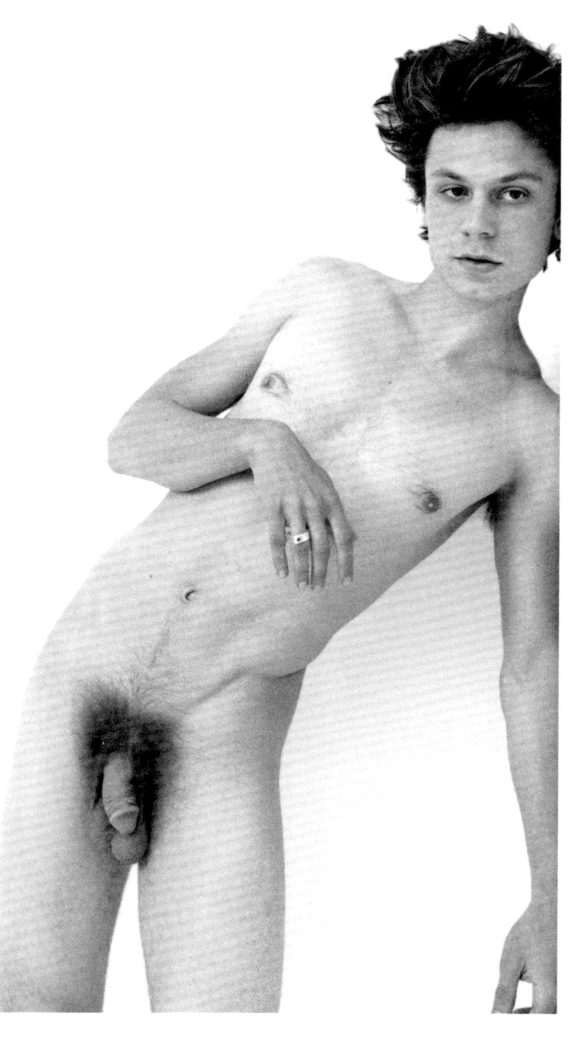

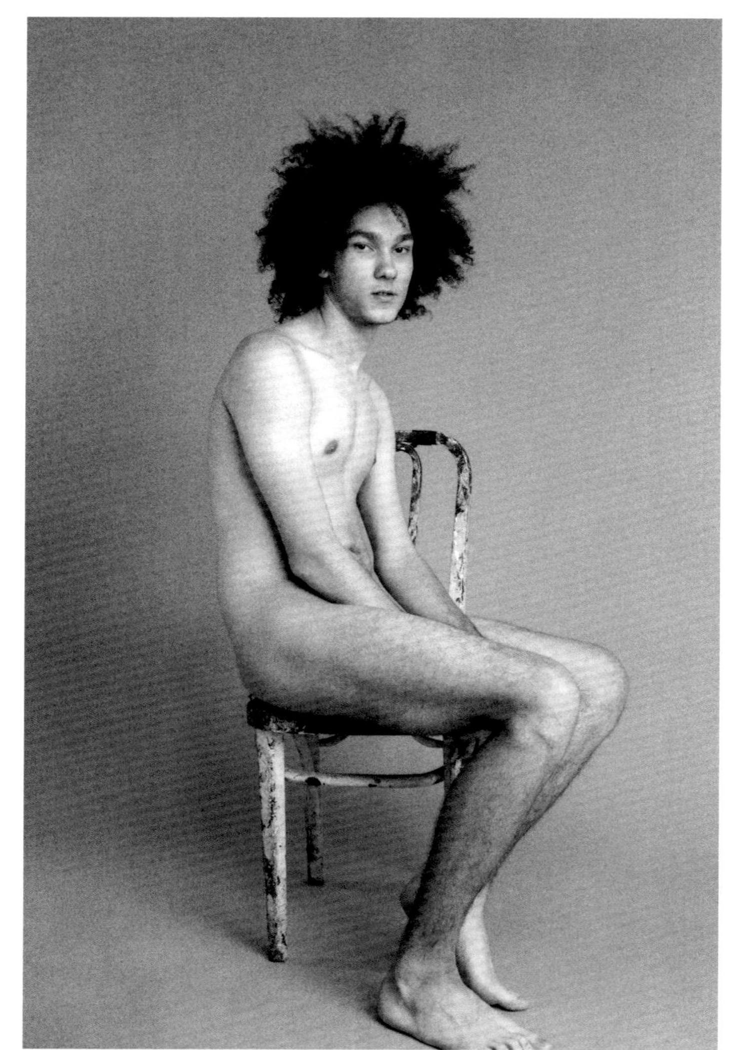

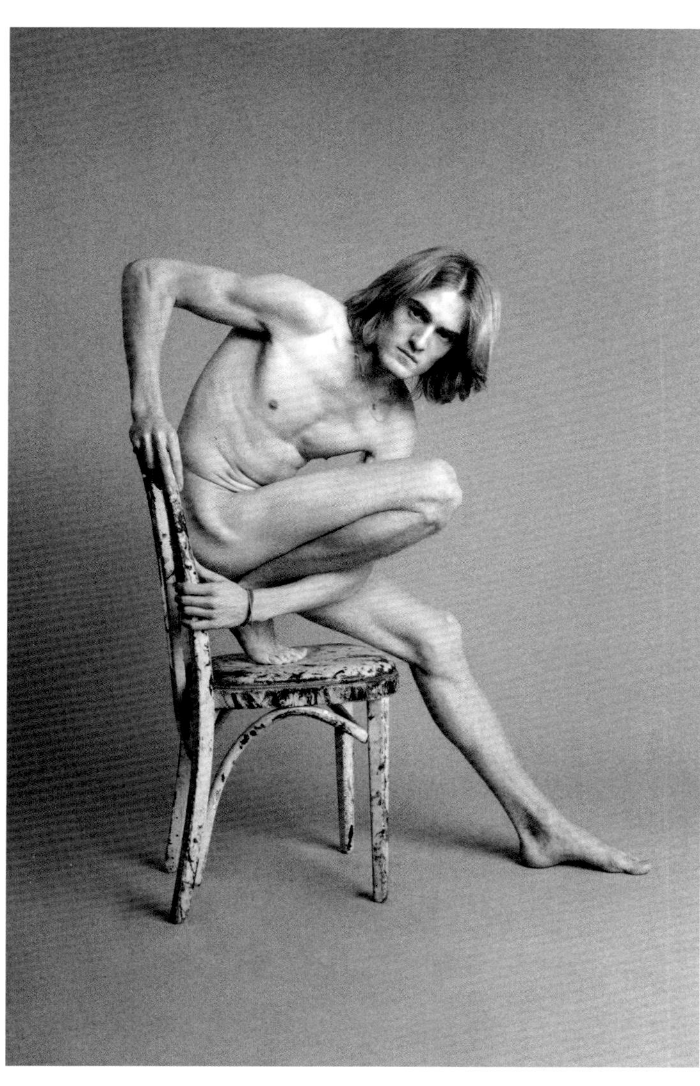

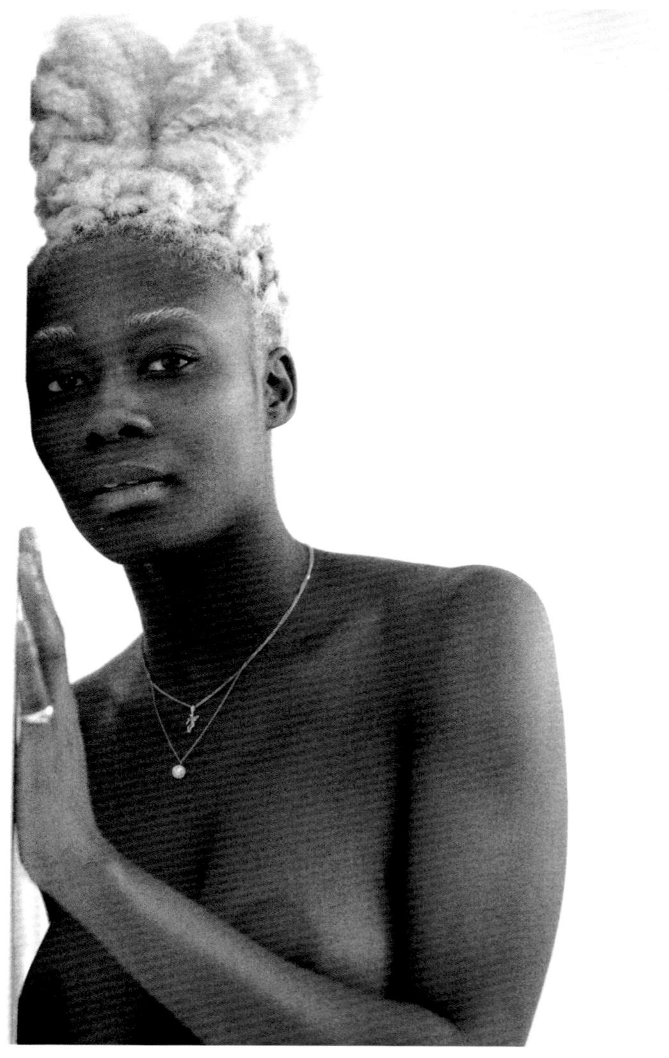

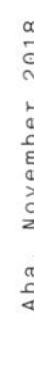

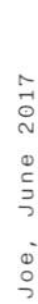

Joe, June 2017 Ben, February 2015 Sam, February 2015 Aba, November 2018

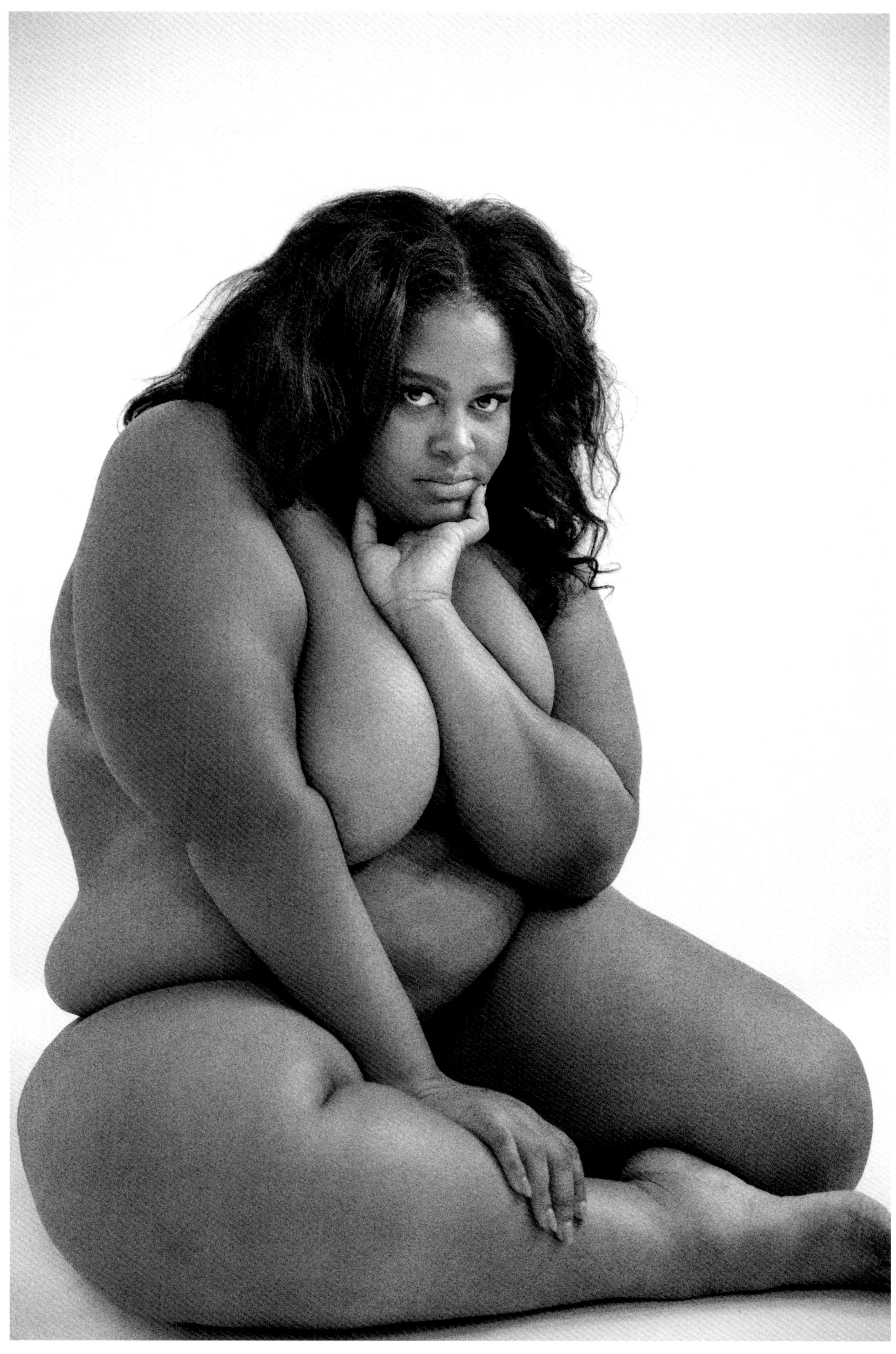

Germany, November 2018

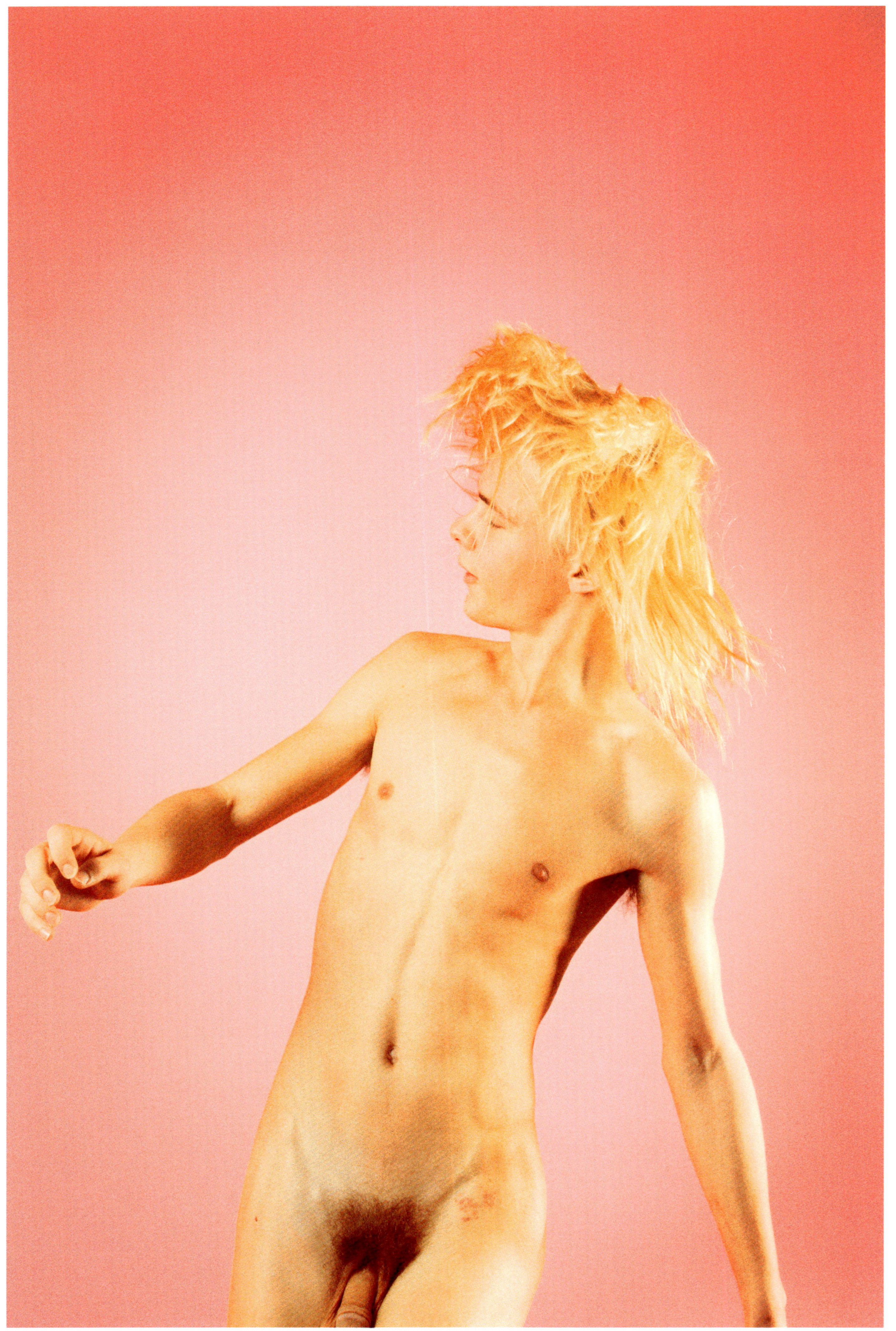

Dakota, November 2011

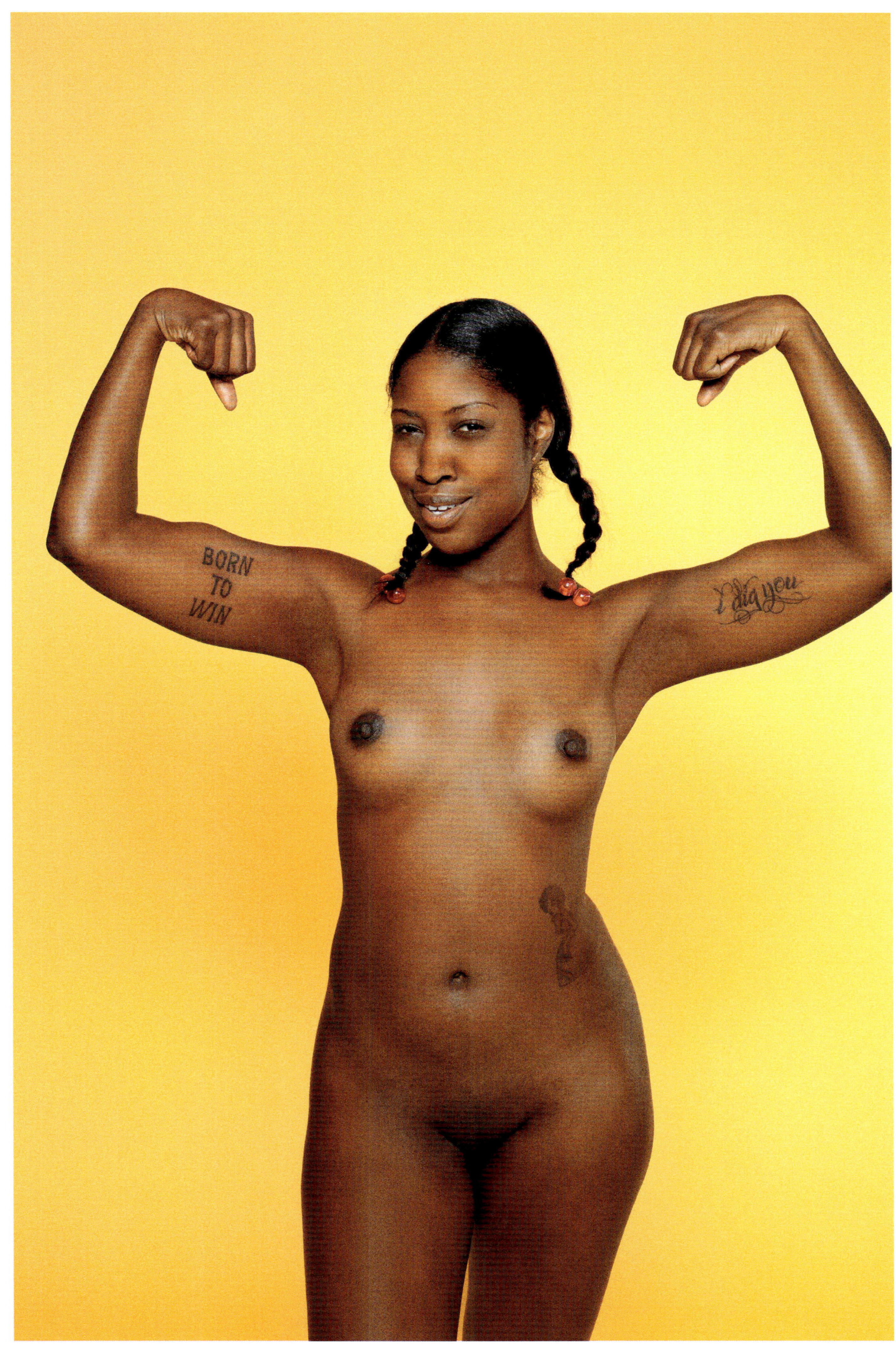

Bridgette, November 2009

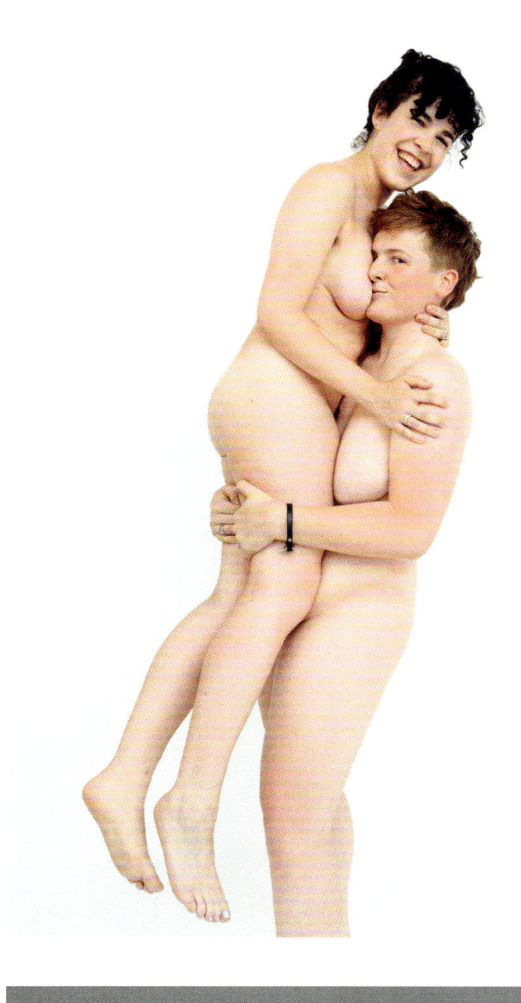

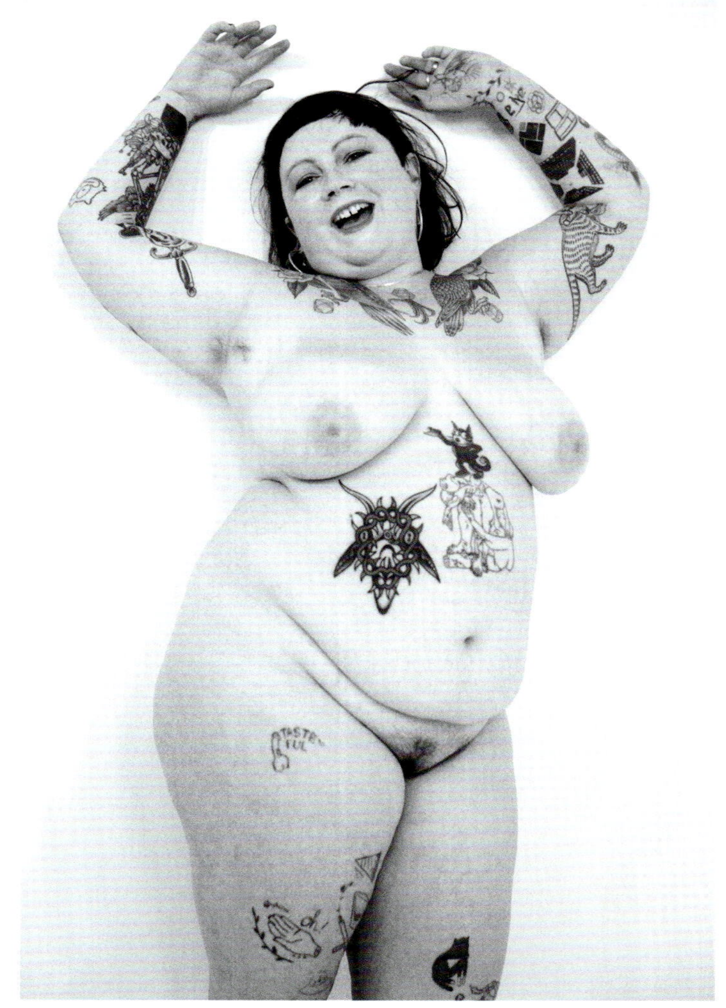

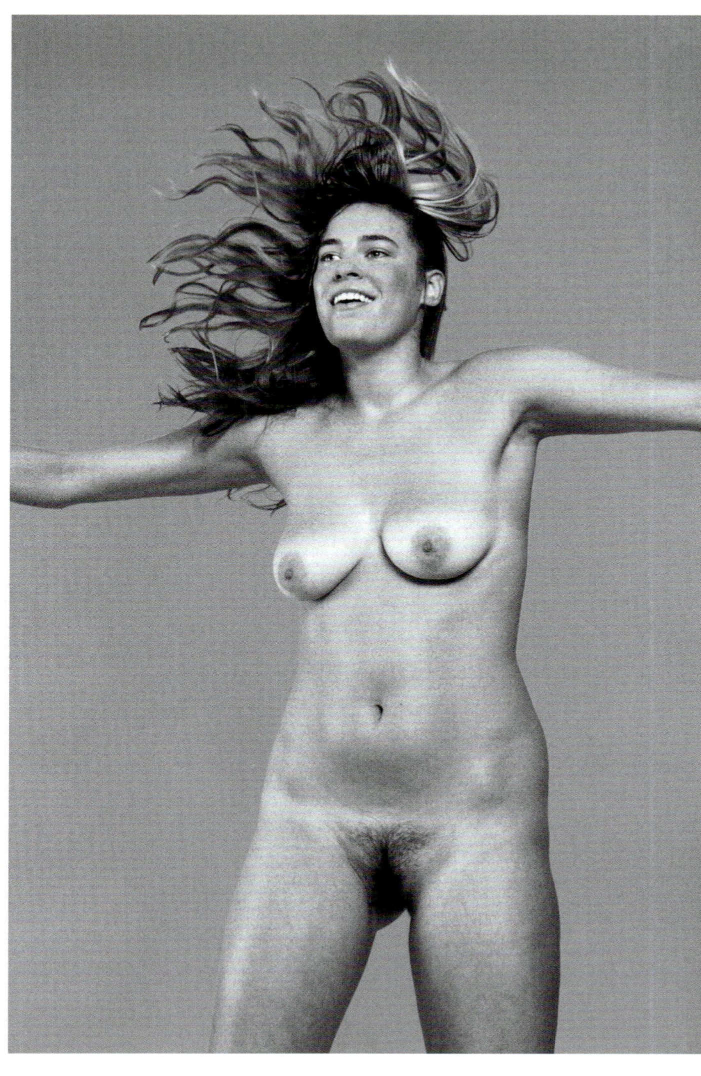

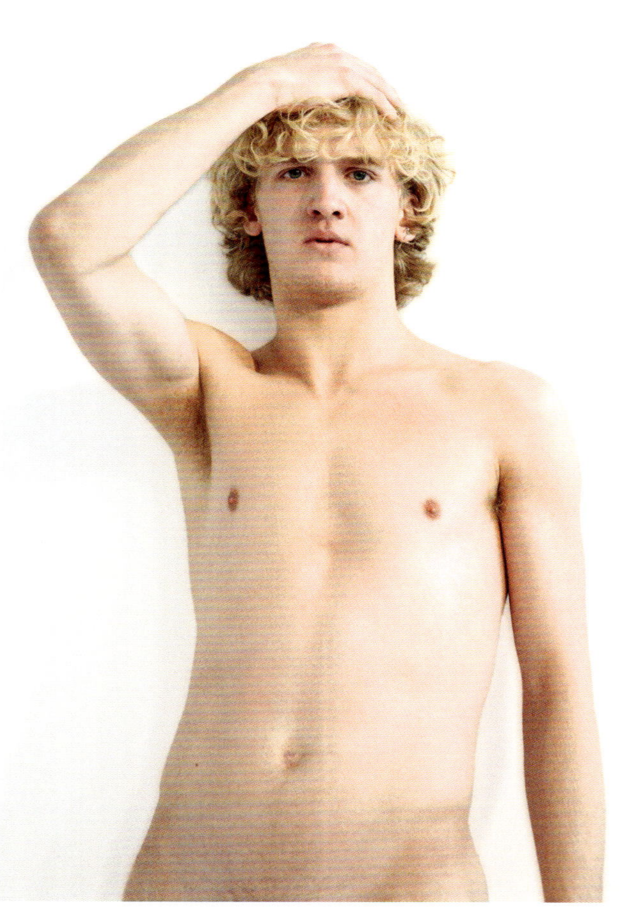

Becca & Allison, June 2017   Zan, November 2018   Amy, April 2010   Jack, November 2018

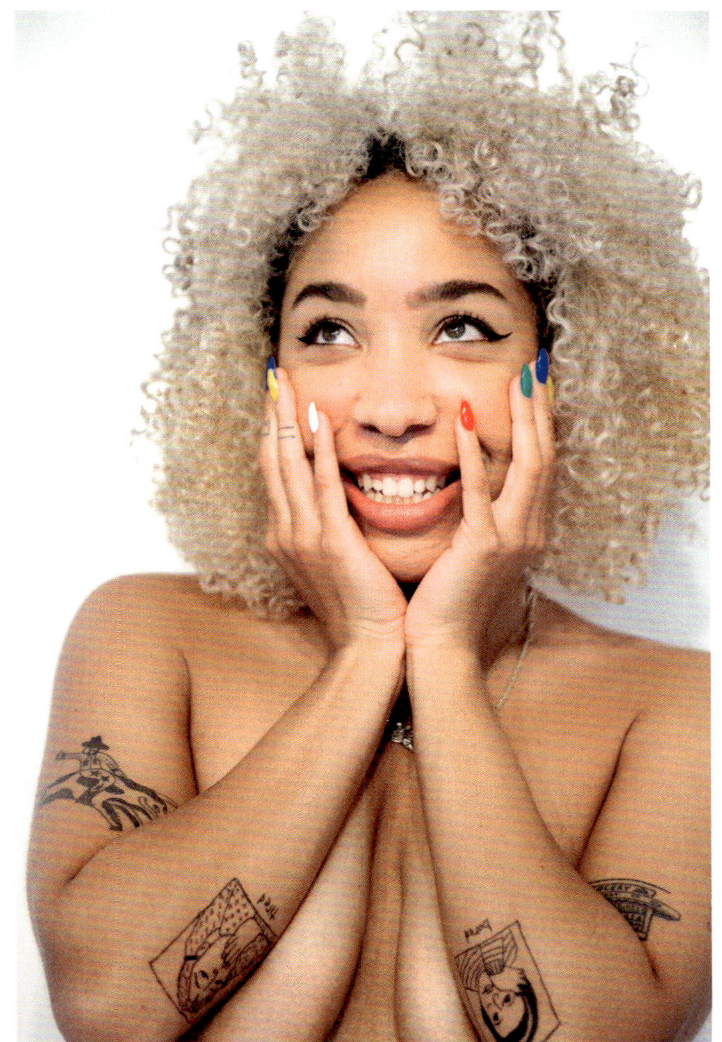

Kelly, October 2019

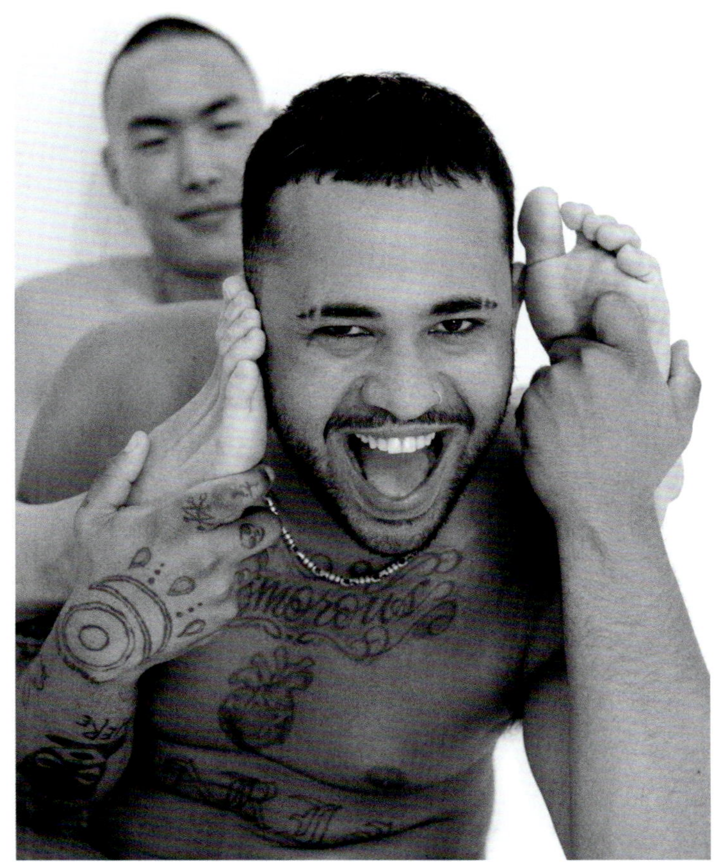

Robot & David, December 2019

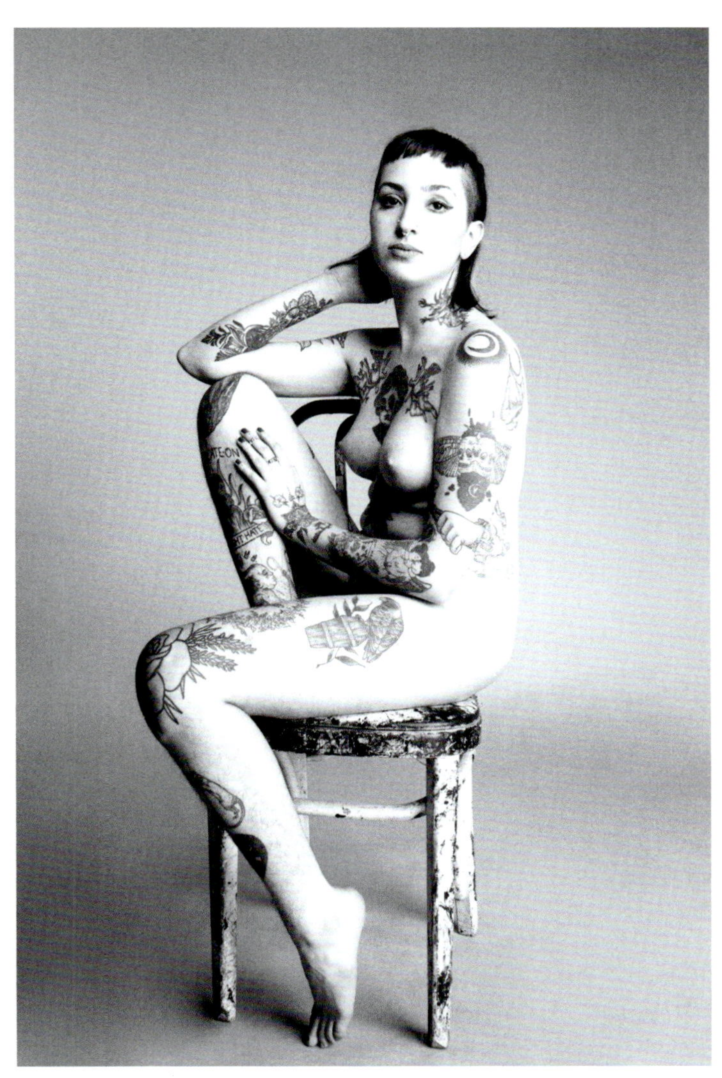

Francesca, January 2015

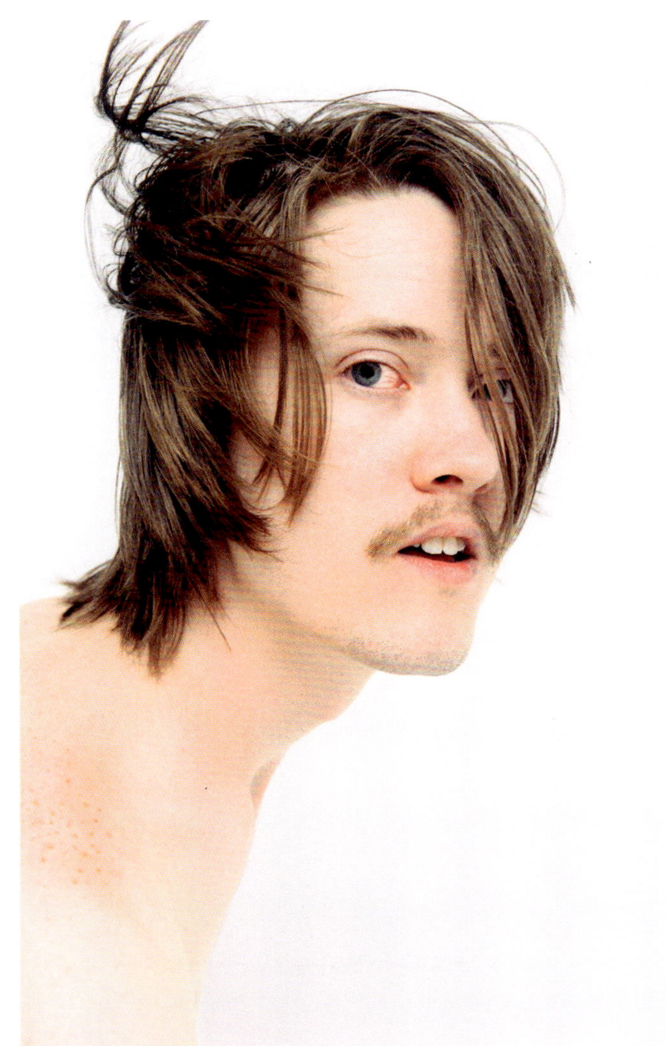

Taylor, June 2017

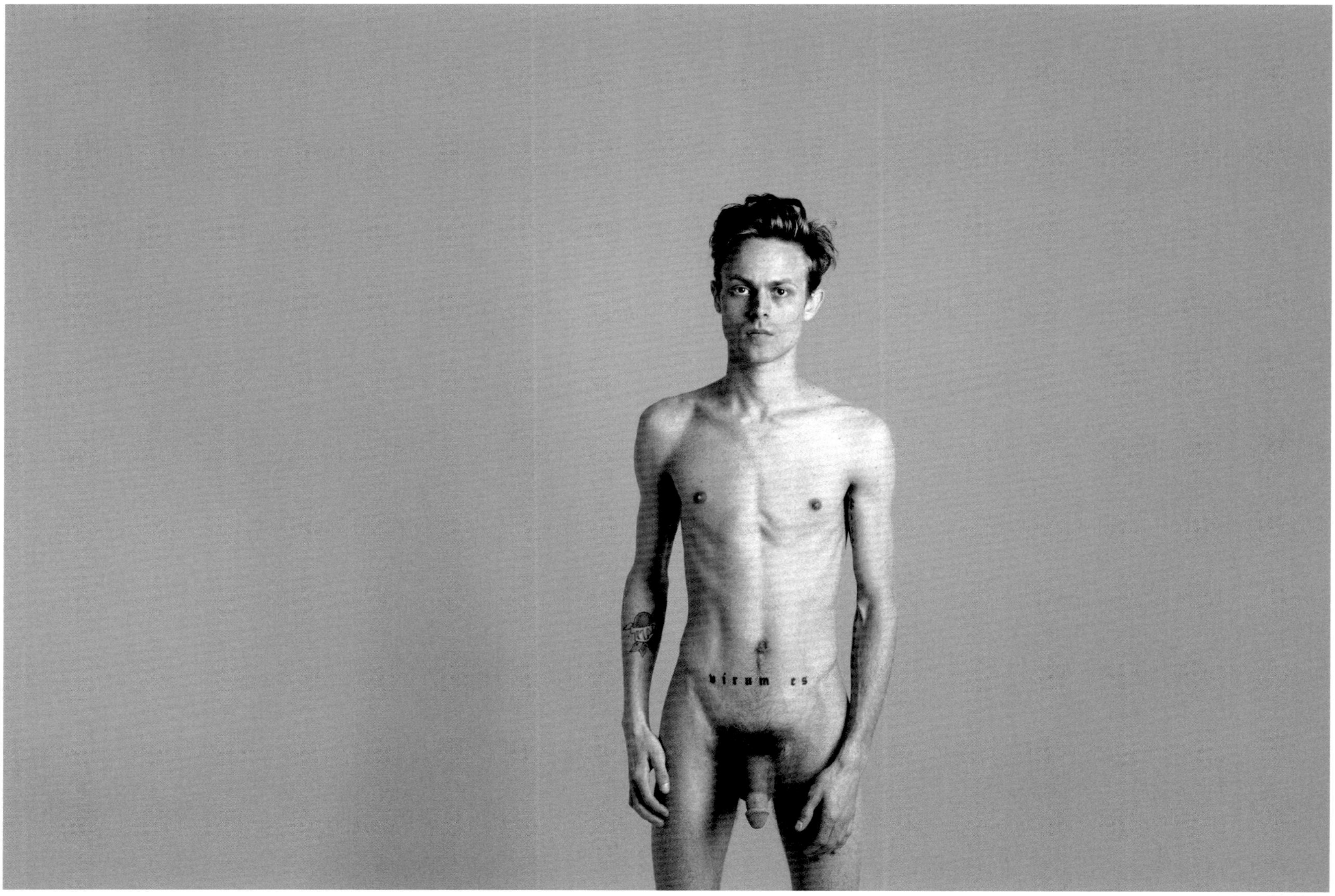

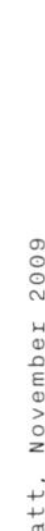
Matt, November 2009

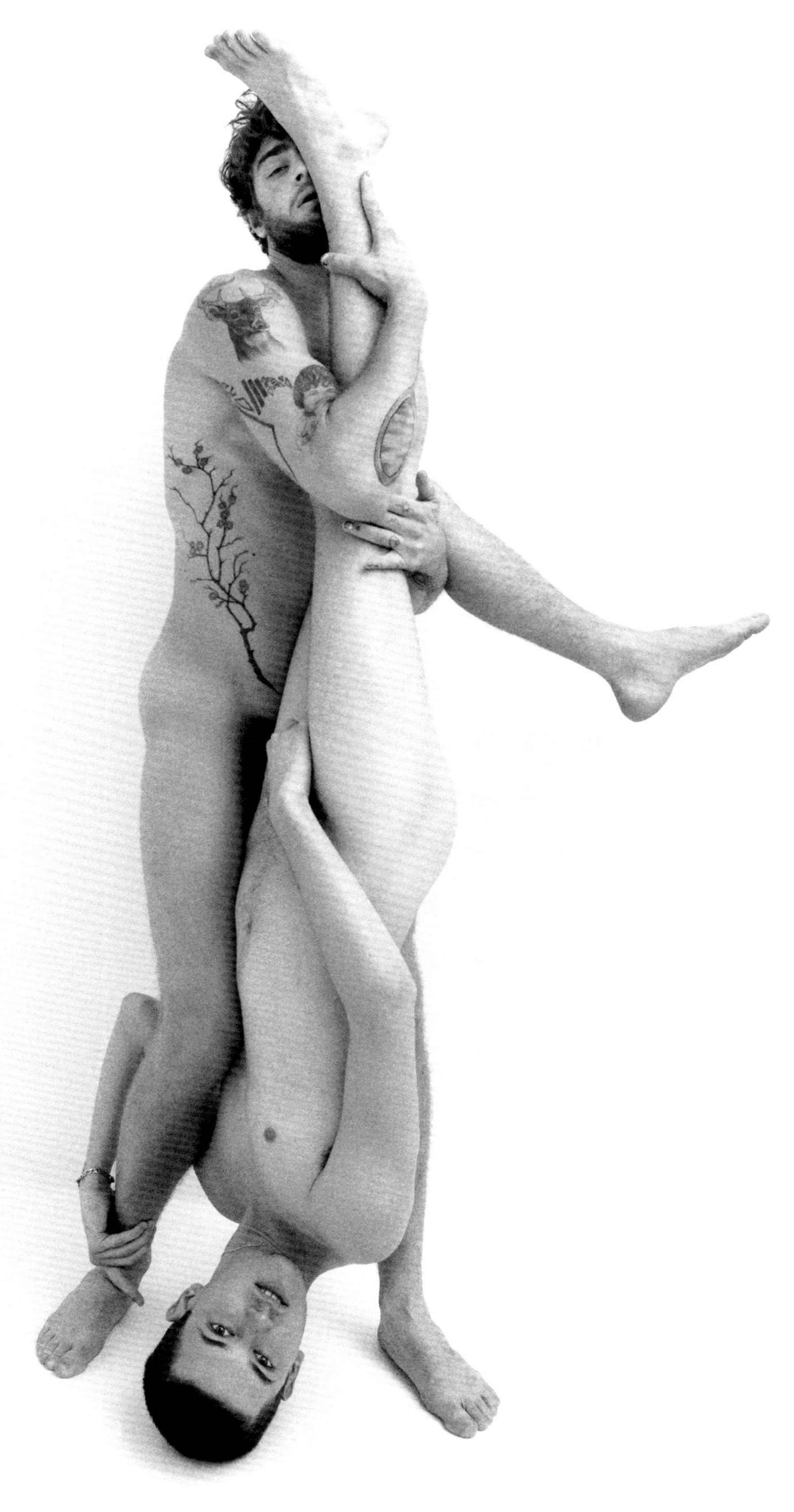

Brody & John, July 2017

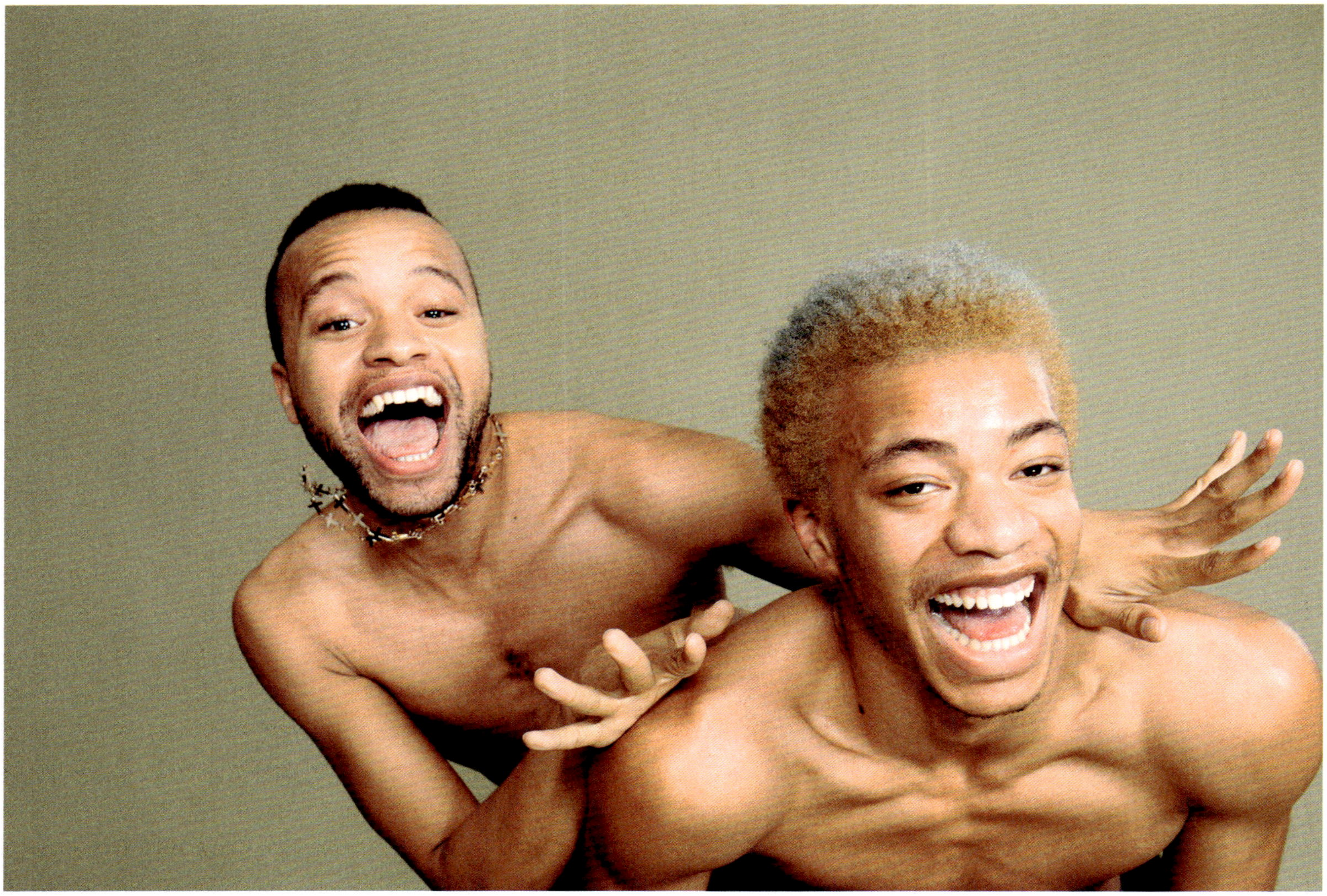

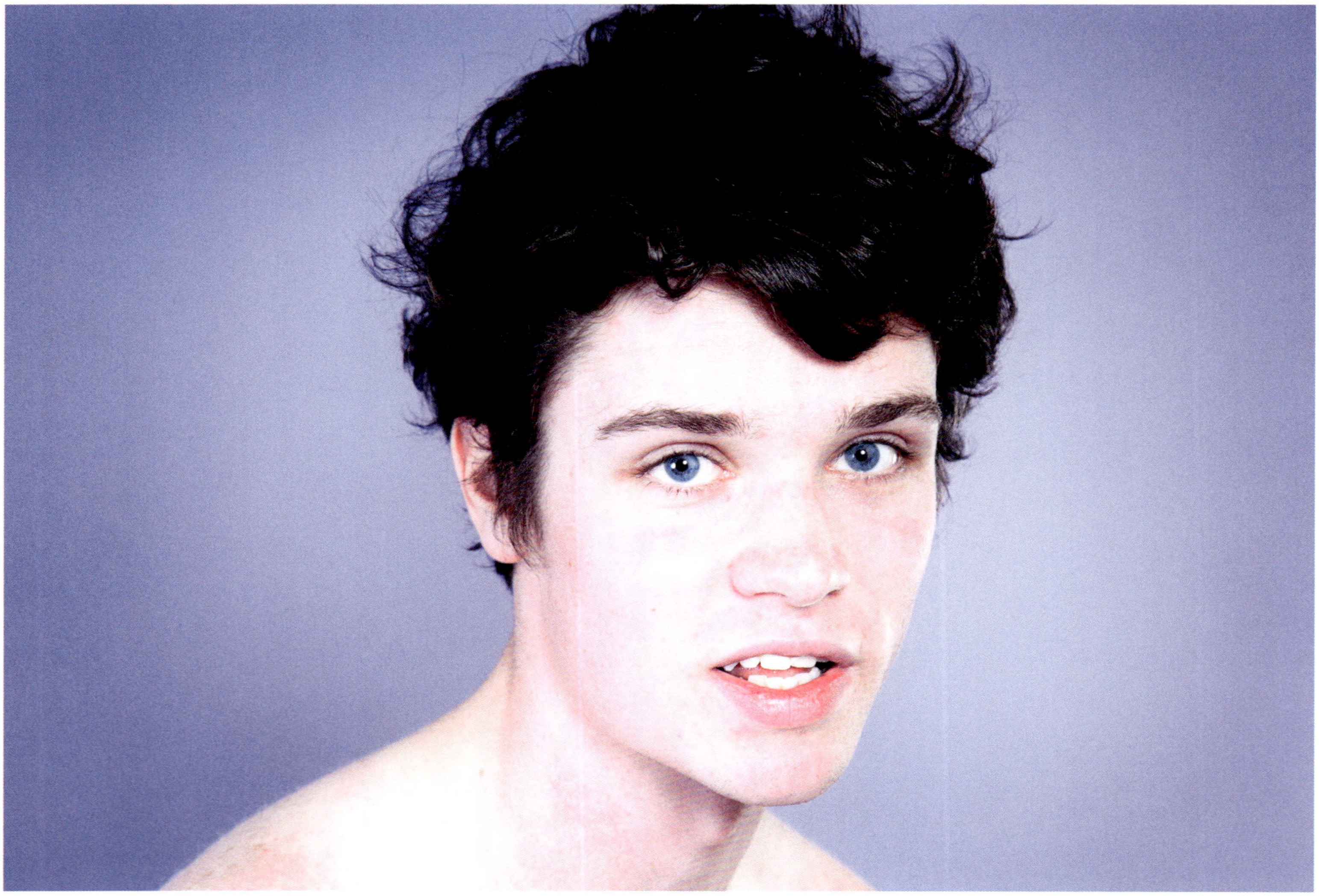

Terence & Gabriel, April 2016

Finnegan, November 2013

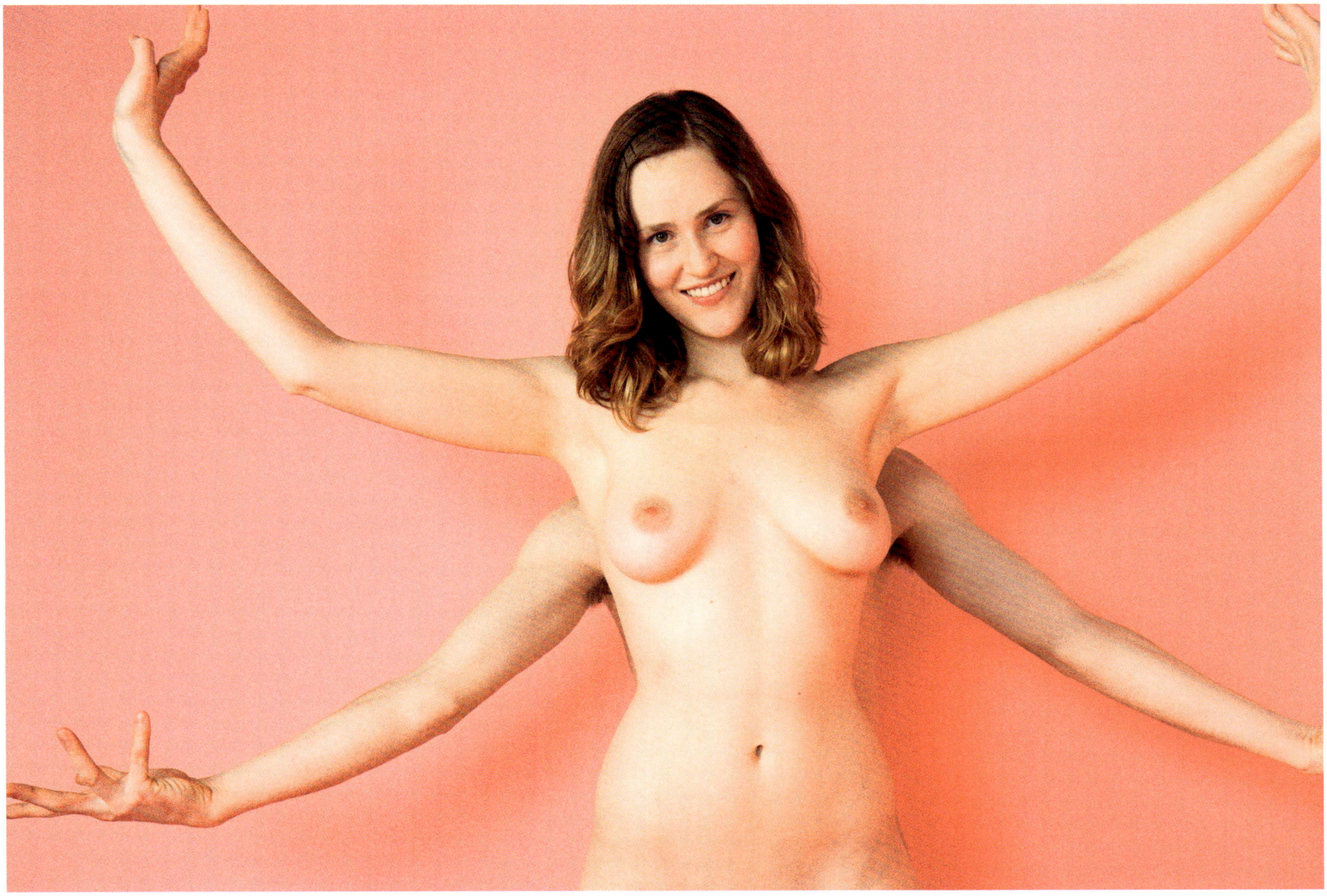

Nellie & Paris, January 2017

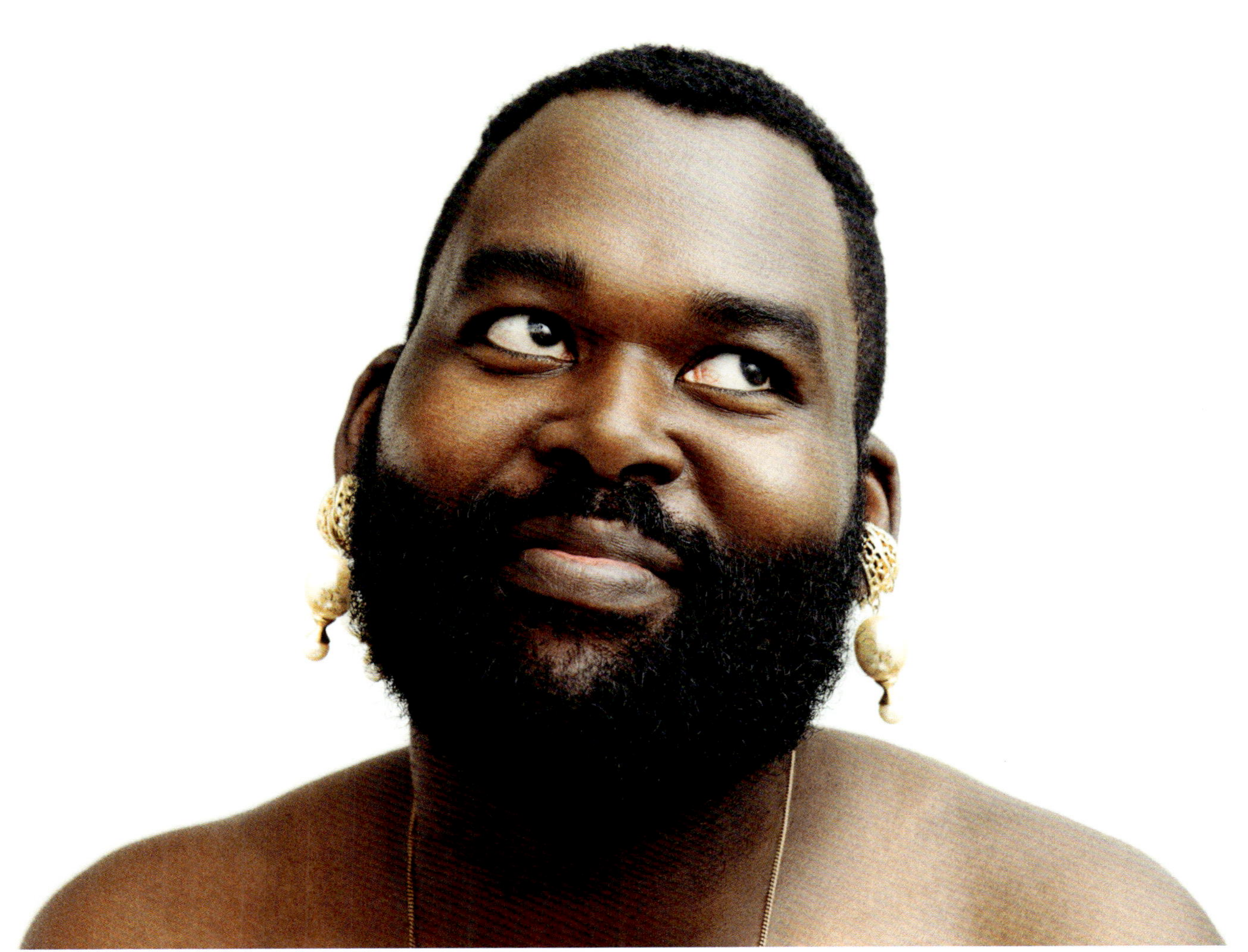

Max, July 2017

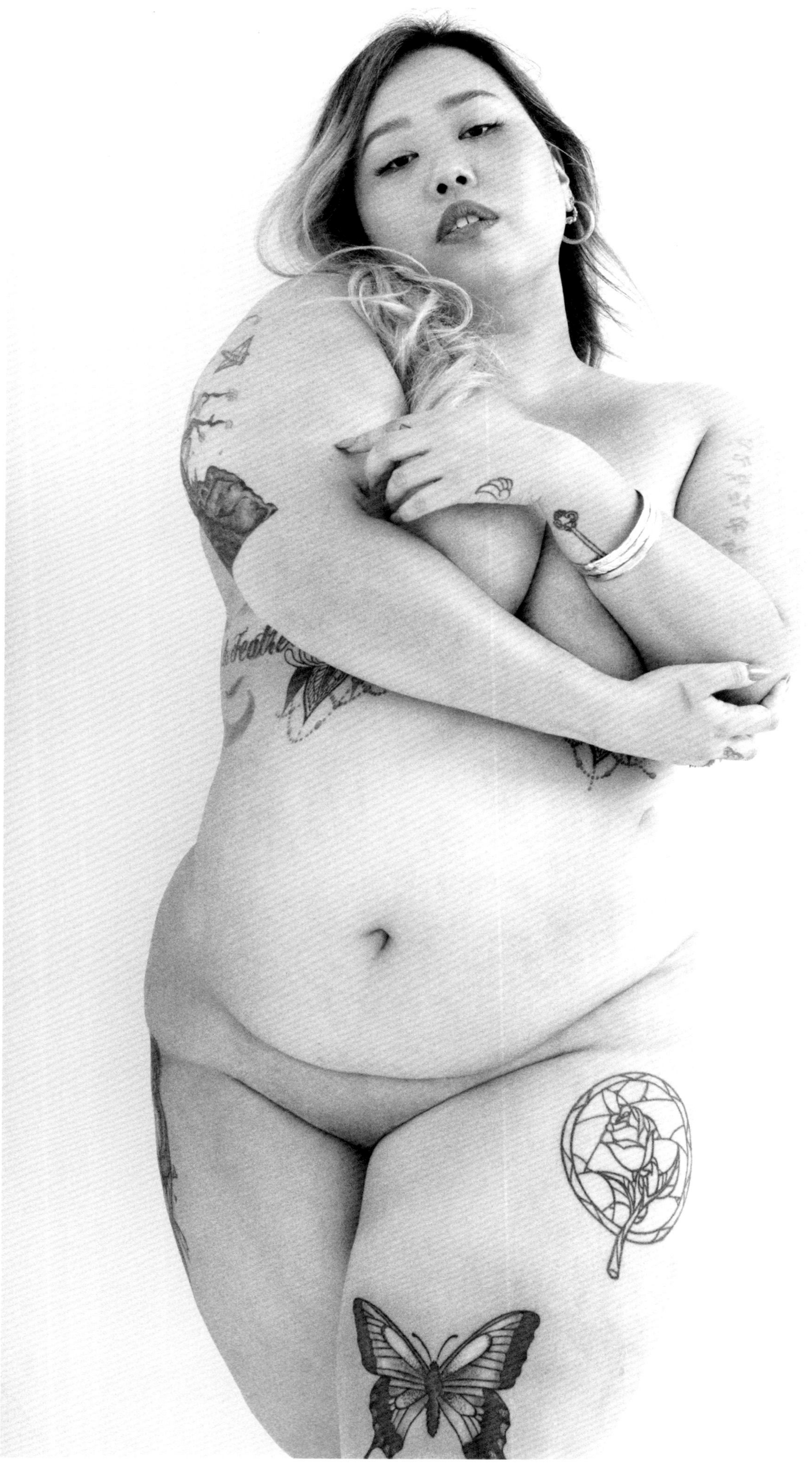

DiDi, July 2017

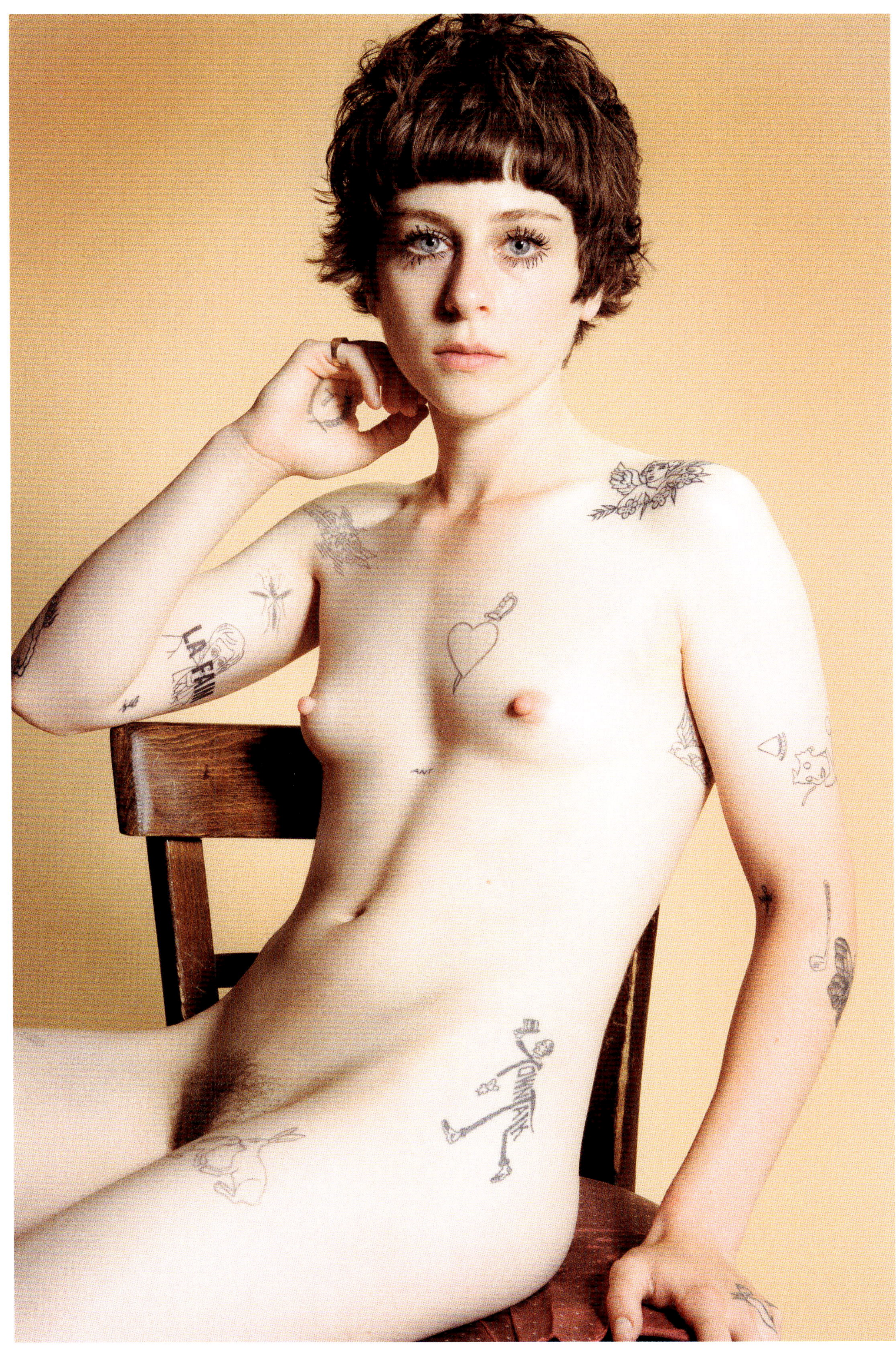

Sophie, June 2015

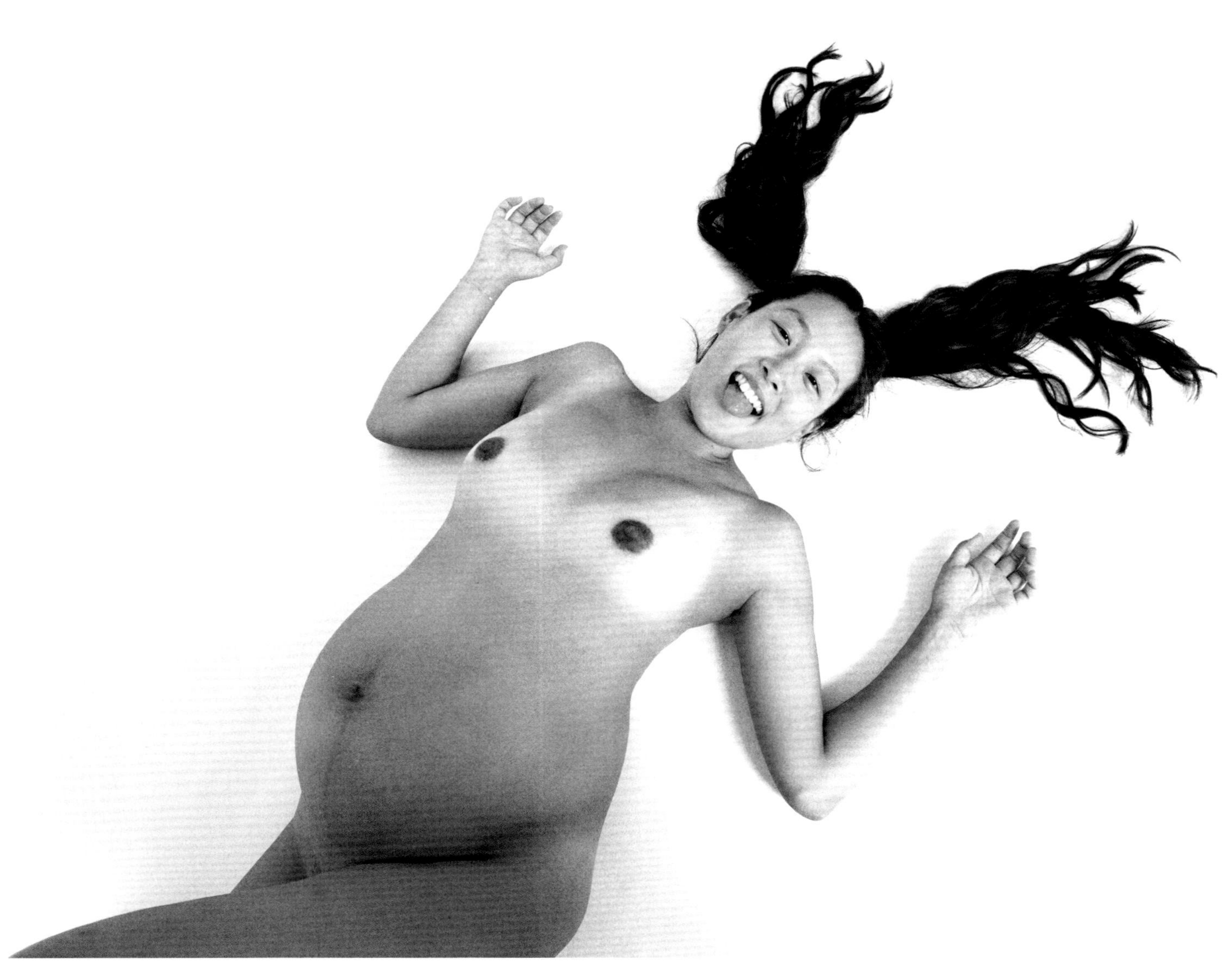

Maia, October 2017

When Ryan asked me to come by, I was *so* pregnant. Nima was a really heavy, big baby. This is TMI, but at that point in my pregnancy, I couldn't control my bladder. I was peeing myself almost every single day. I was at a point where I didn't even care. My pants were always wet! This is something new moms or pregnant moms don't talk about but because of the pressure of the baby on your bladder, you often don't even feel it come out. During the shoot, I was like, "Don't pee yourself, just *don't*."

Then Ryan asked, "Can we put your hair in pigtails?"

I never wear pigtails.

But once he asked and I put my hair up, I was like, "Okay, cool. I have no idea what this photo is going to be." It was a nice way to give in.

I think two days later, I gave birth.

Three months later, my family ended up living in the same building as Ryan's studio.

At the time, I didn't have many mom friends. And as an identity, "artist mom" wasn't really a popular thing. I remember feeling like I had to get back in the studio ASAP or I was going to lose myself. If I were to do it again, I would take a longer break; at three months, they're still so tiny and attached to you. I remember having my son strapped onto me going to gallery walk-throughs and working on-site with artists.

I was also working as the director of a nonprofit called Wide Rainbow, an after-school art nonprofit serving different organizations around New York. We would invite artists to lead workshops in partnership with organizations like the Women's Prison Association on the Lower East Side, Girls Club New York, and shelters.

Being a parent really does bleed back into your art practice. It's hard but it's also expansive in a way that I can't compare to anything else, in terms of how much I've learned, especially about myself. I'm interacting with this new human being who's a mirror to me but also, in and of itself, a unique person. There's a sense of surprise at every corner. Acceptance becomes a big thing. There are things you can't change, and there are things you can. Also, through my son, I feel more accepted, which is very bizarre 'cause he's like a little person, but it plays a huge part.

I love having Nima in my studio. He walks around and he knows what my sculptures are called. He'll be like, "Oh, are you making another Bondage Baggage?" He wants to be an artist. He's like, "When I become an artist, can you work for me?" I'm like, "Yes, I will work for you. Give me a job."

I just joined the board of a really incredible nonprofit called Artists and Mothers. It's a grant for artists who are mothers that's given directly to caregivers of the children, so mothers can go work in their studios. I remember when I was a new mom, wishing there was an organization that would prioritize this.

All the organizers are also artist moms or moms in the creative art world. It's this artist-mom community trying to figure it out together. How do we support each other during challenging phases? How do we even ask for what we need?

When Nima came along, I think everyone was like, "How is Maia going to do it?" Or [my partner] Peter, who's, like, an aging skater from the downtown community? He had never held a baby before. I think people were legitimately surprised by how much fun we had as new parents despite the challenges.

From the moment Nima was able to prop his head up, Peter would plop him onto the front of his bike. From the time he was three months old, Peter was biking him all over the place every single day. All the skaters hung out with him. There was a baby in the scene now, a really chunky baby. It's like a whole new generation appears, and you just have to accept it 'cause everyone is getting older.

I'd be pushing Nima in the stroller, and these downtown hipster kids, like the Supreme skaters, would be like, "Hey, Nima, what's up?"

The moment he started fist-bumping Supreme skaters, I was like, "We have to get out of here. We have to leave the city."

Now we're away from it, in simple suburbia. That's our way of being like: Just be bored, run around, be with kids. You can discover all that other stuff later.

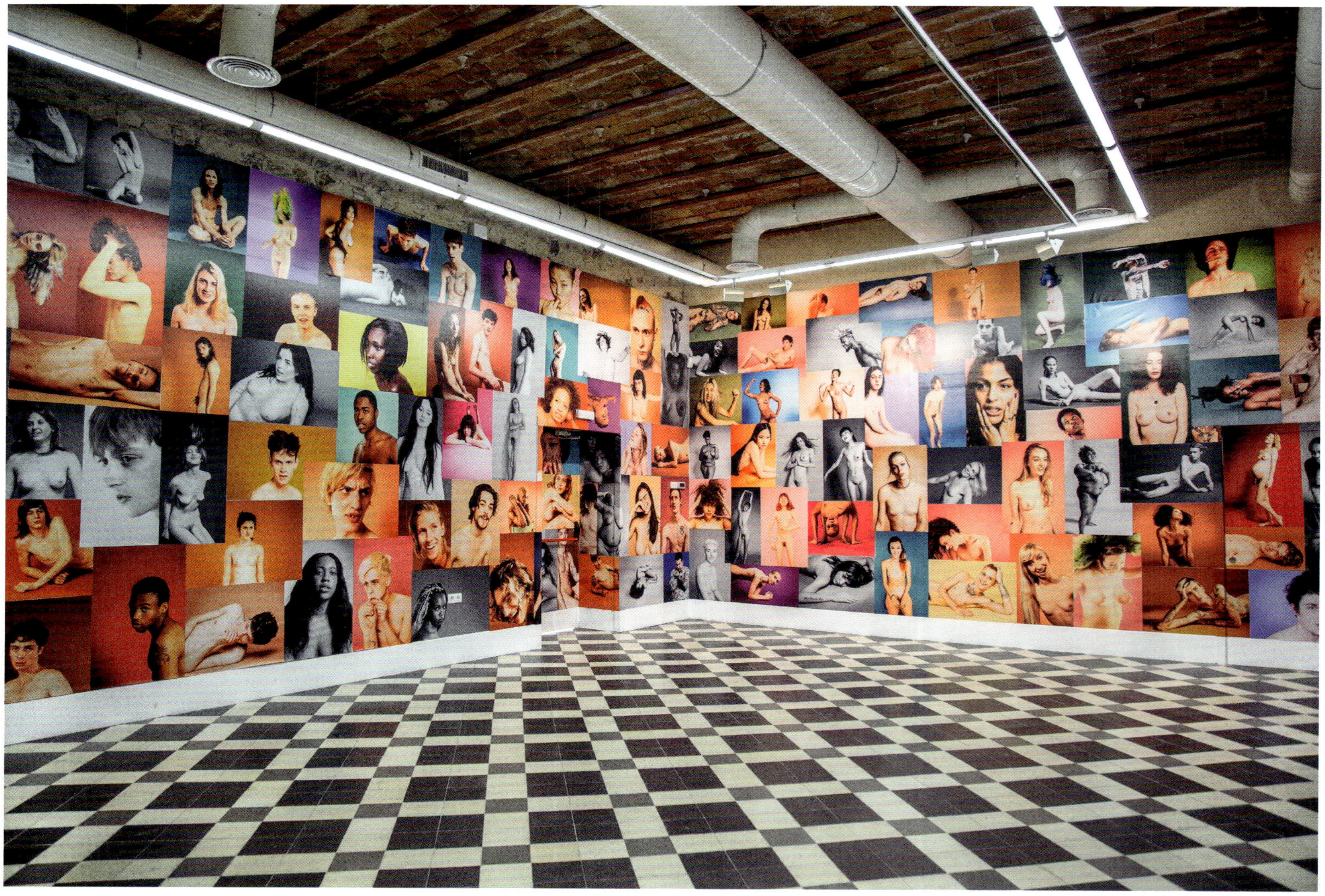

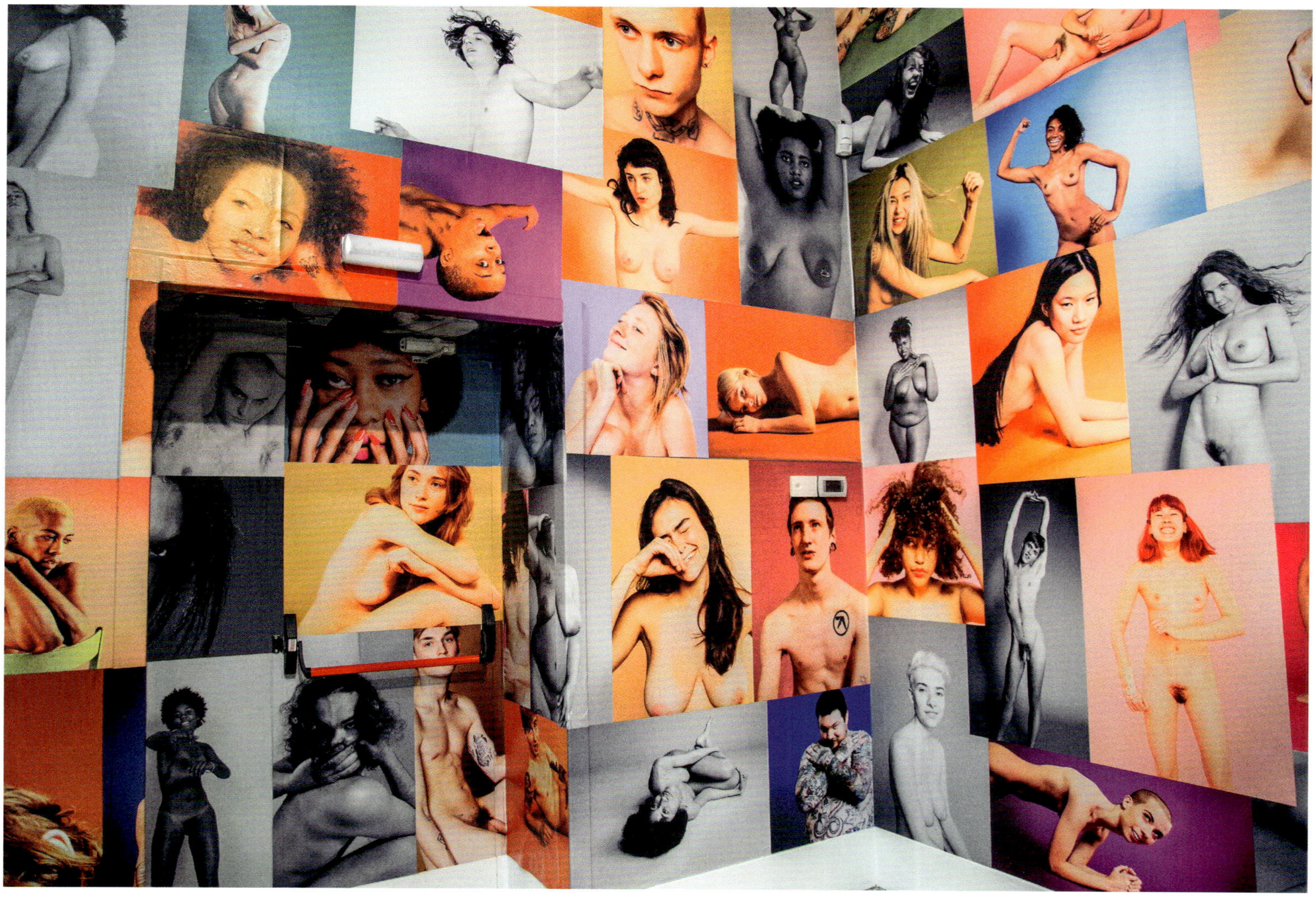

La Termica Museum, Spain, 2017

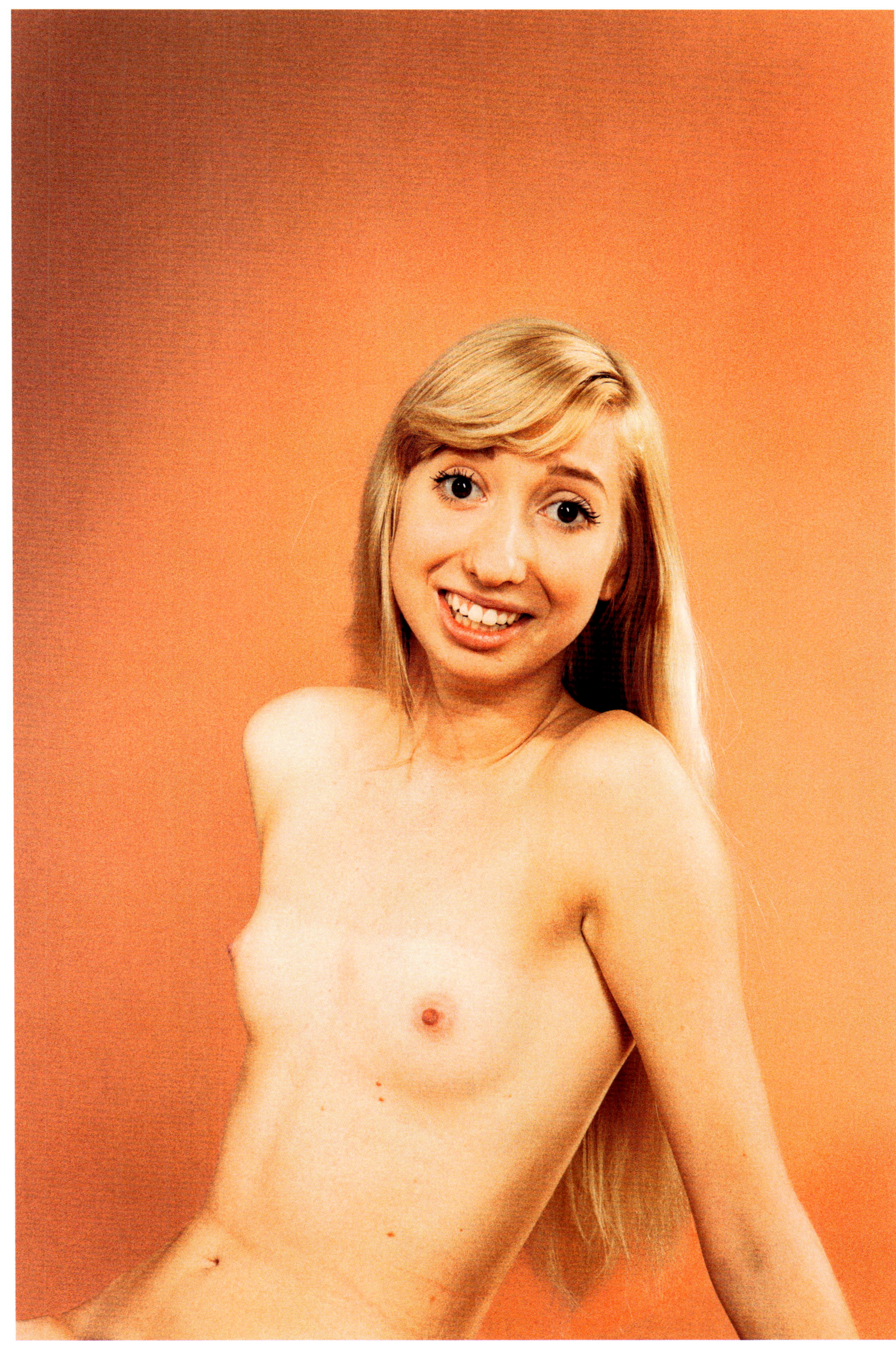

Elle, June 2011

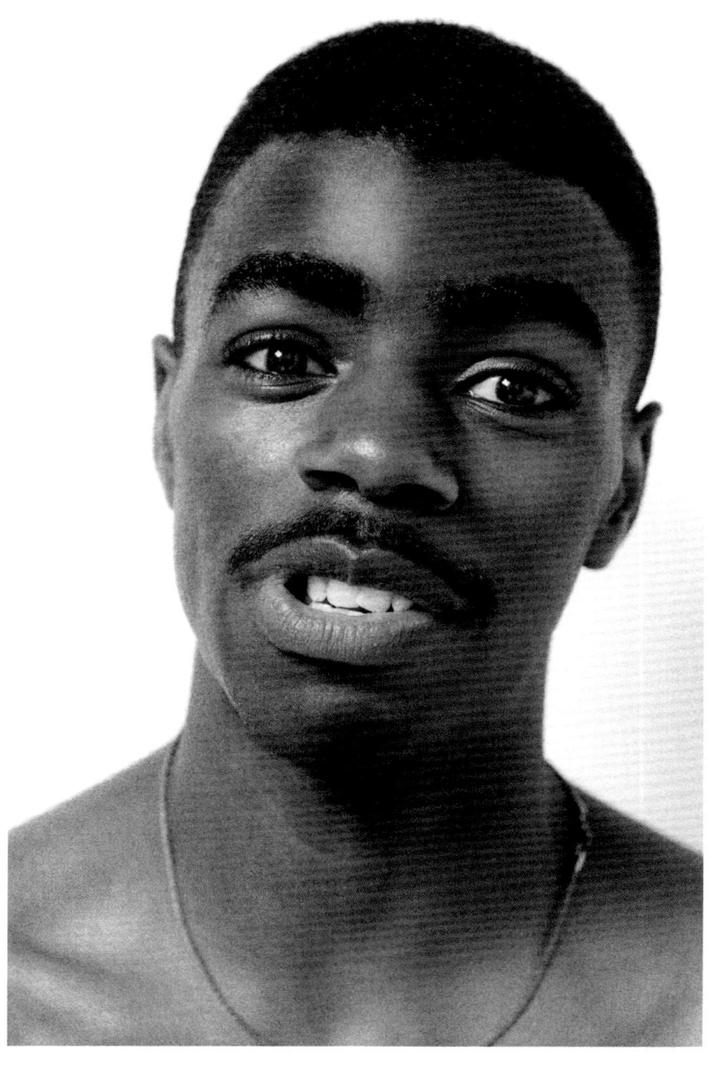

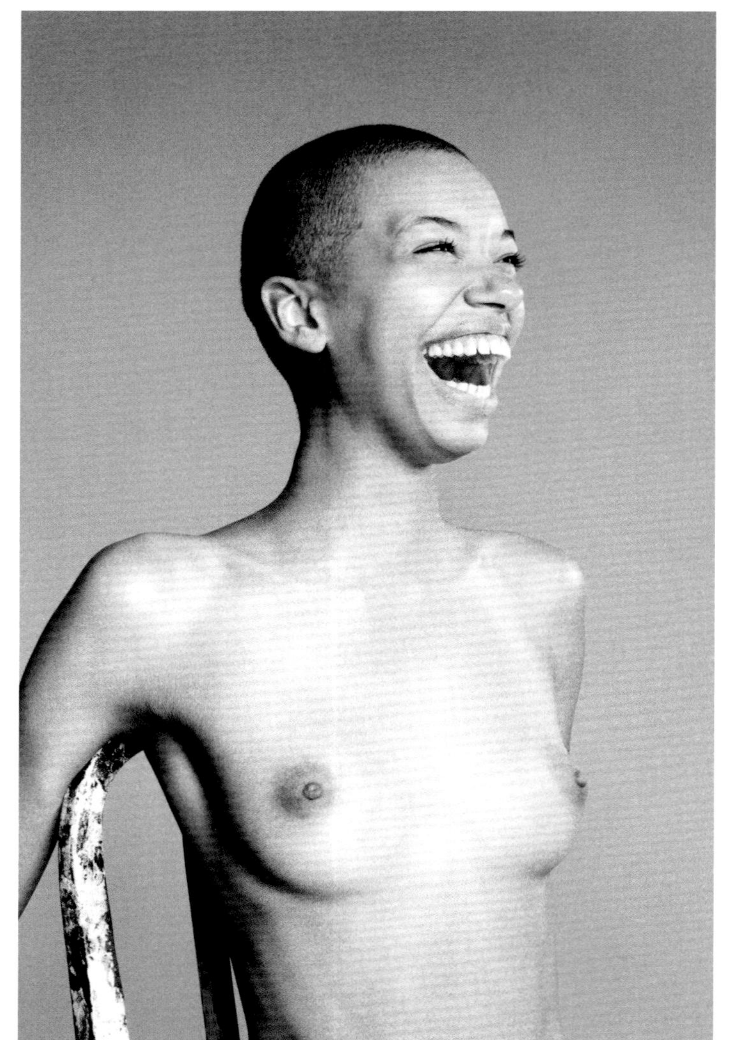

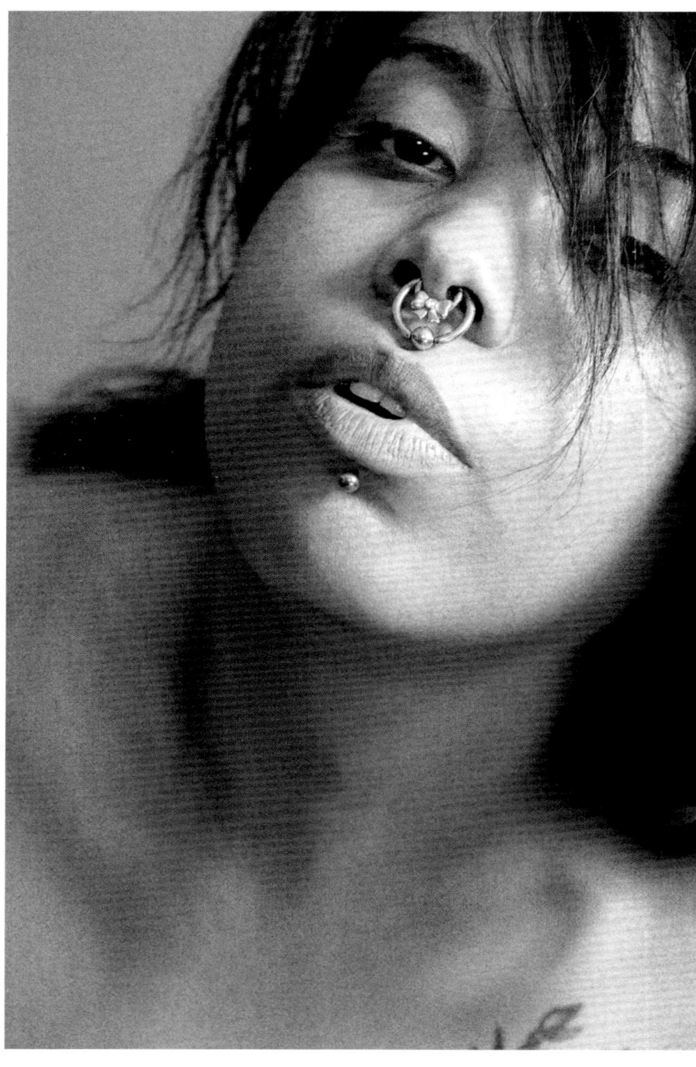

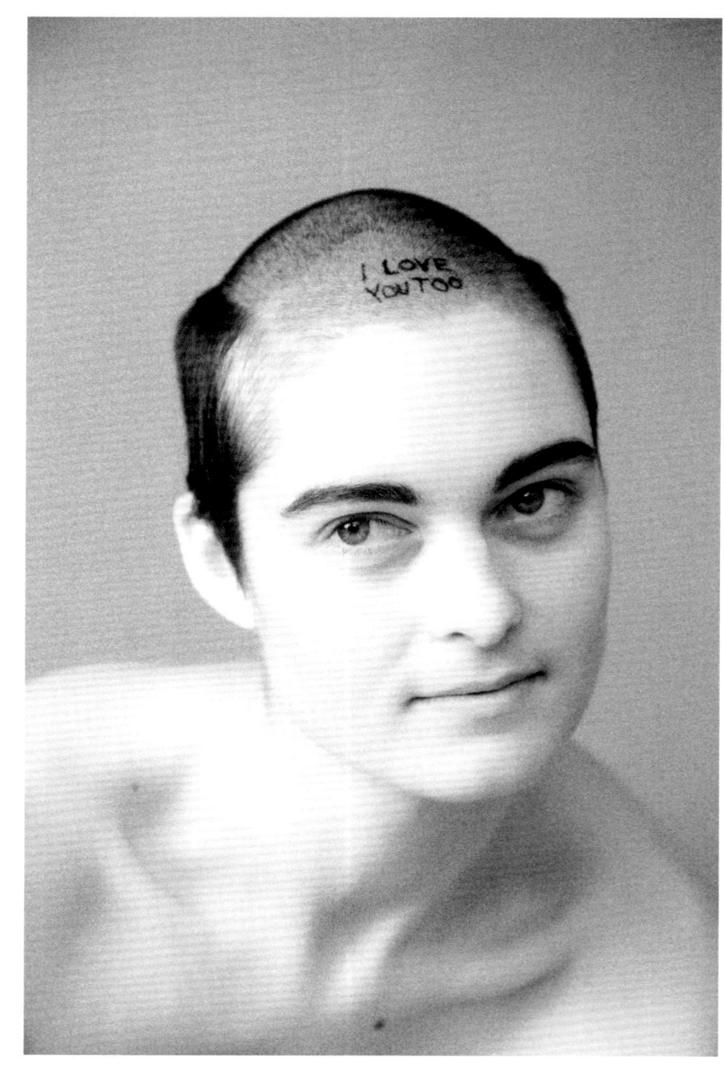

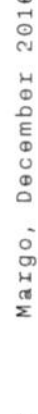

Tyrell, April 2017 Theresa, July 2015 Aeon, April 2016 Margo, December 2016

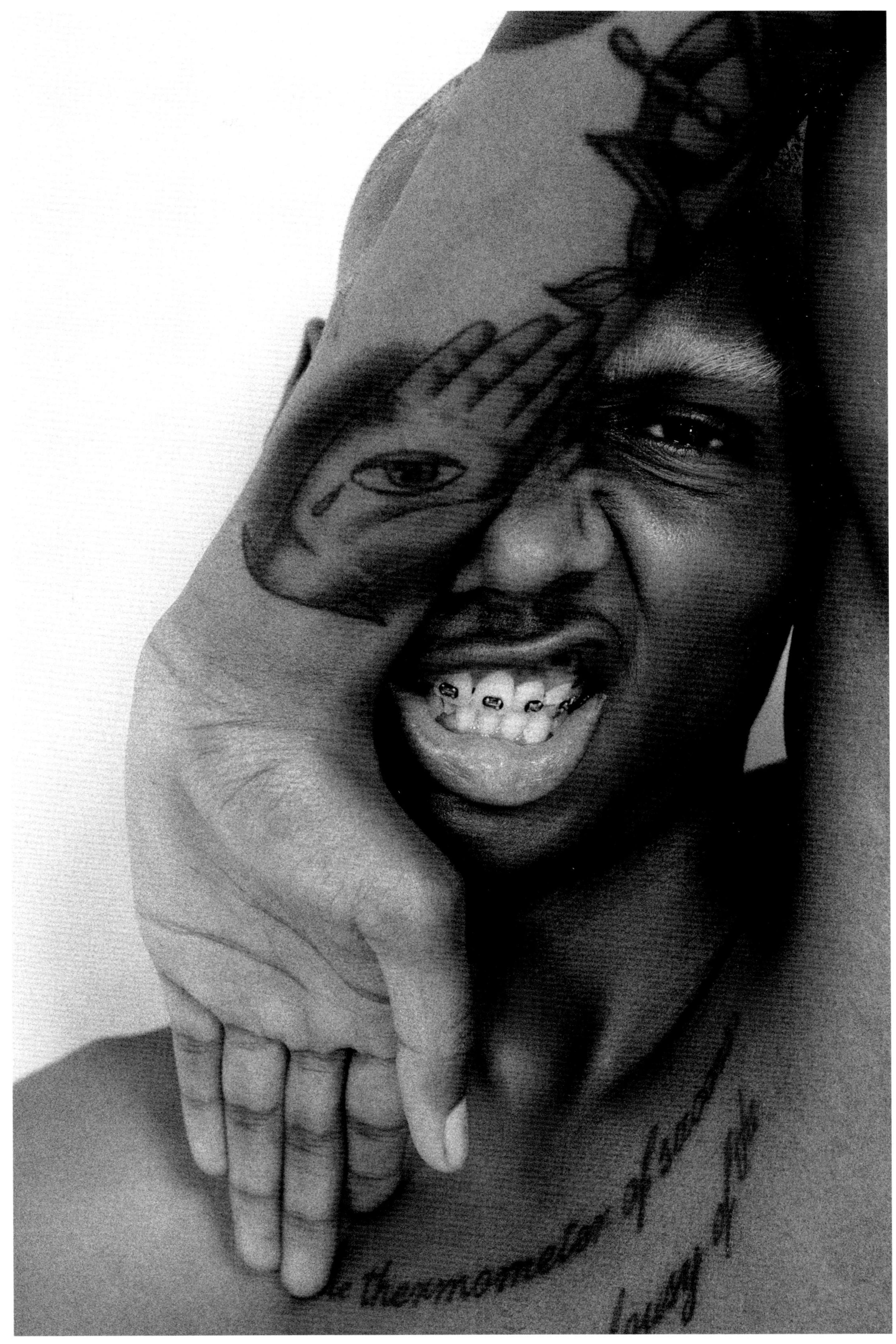

Blayke, July 2016

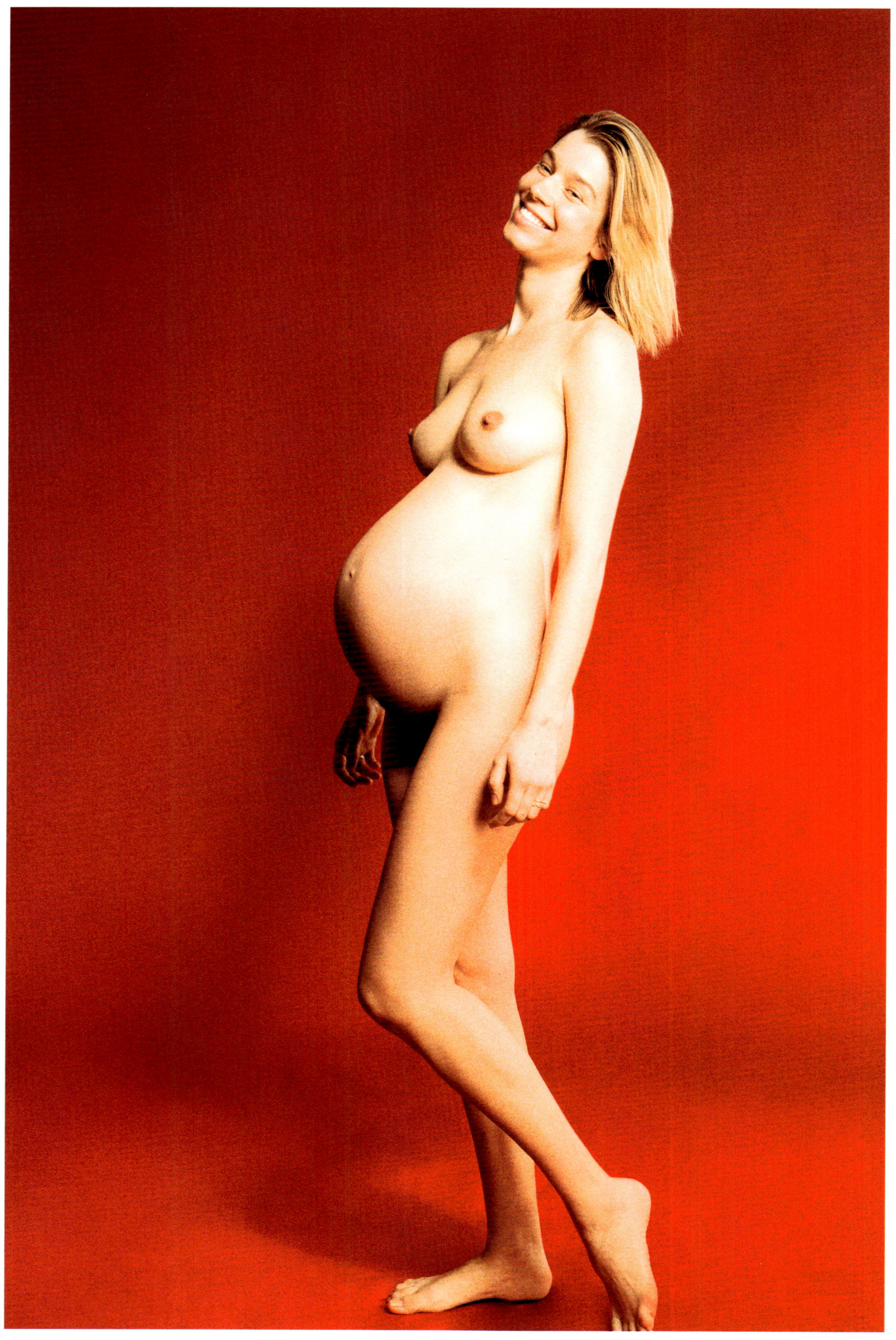

Mollie, January 2014

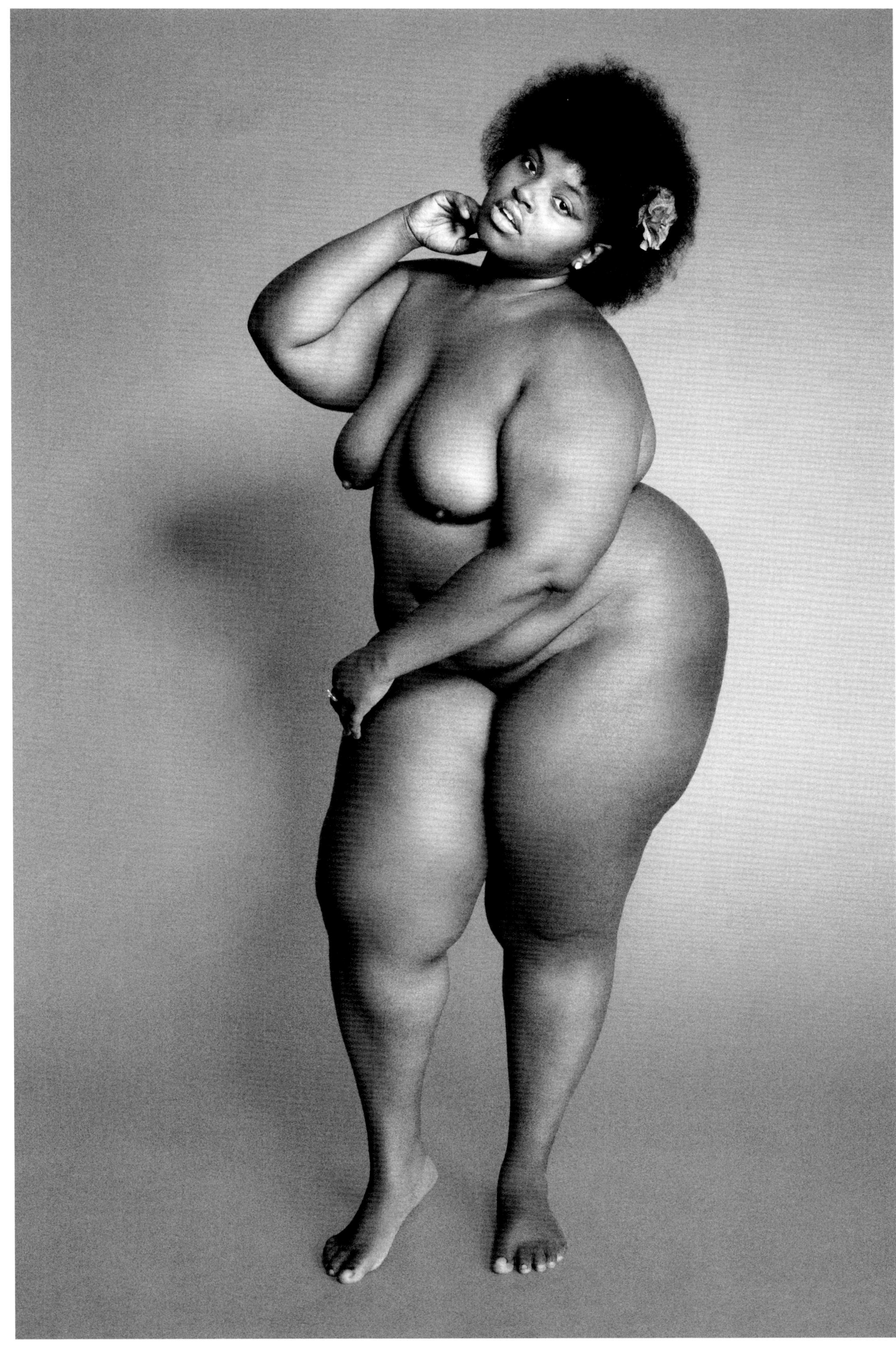

Marilyn, October 2015

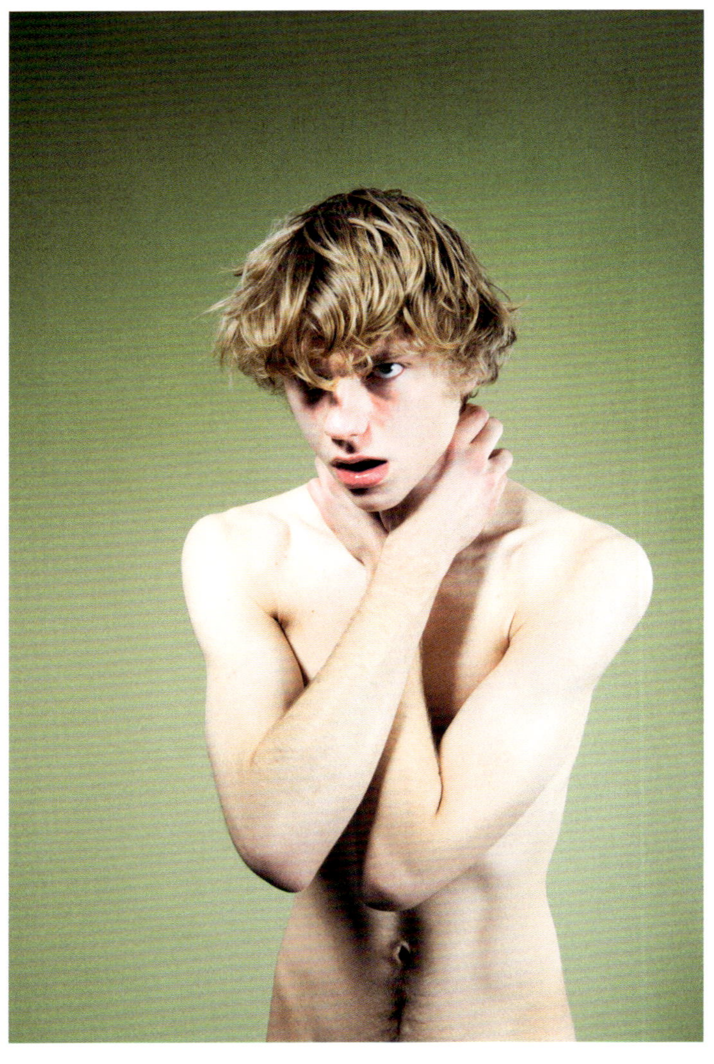

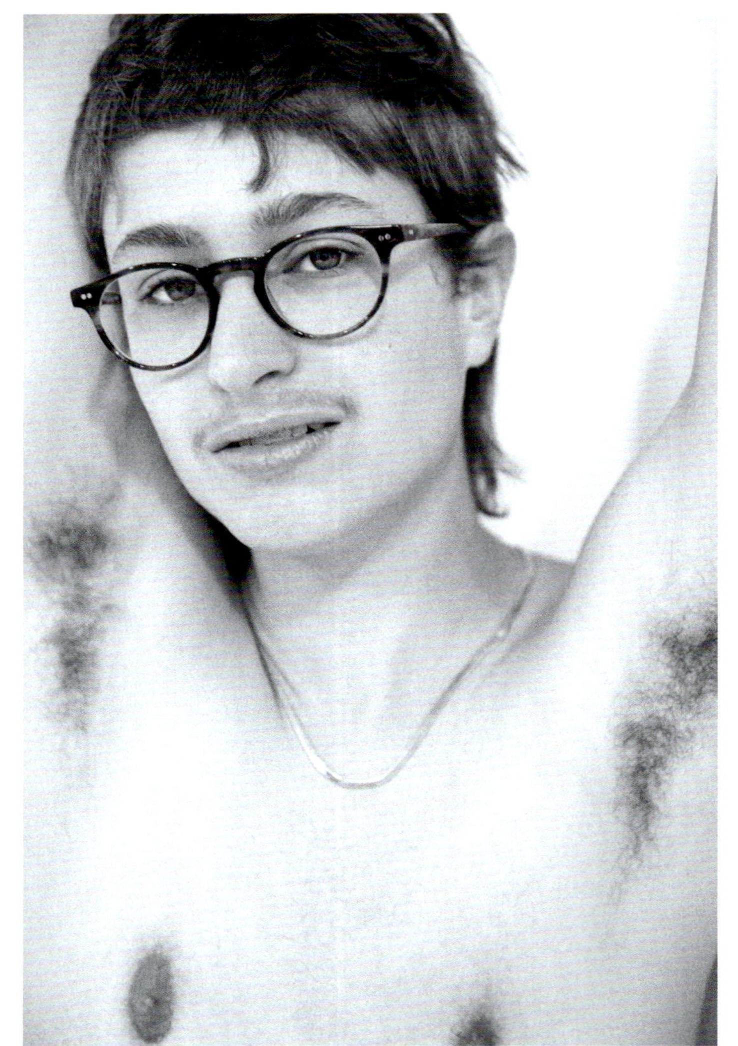

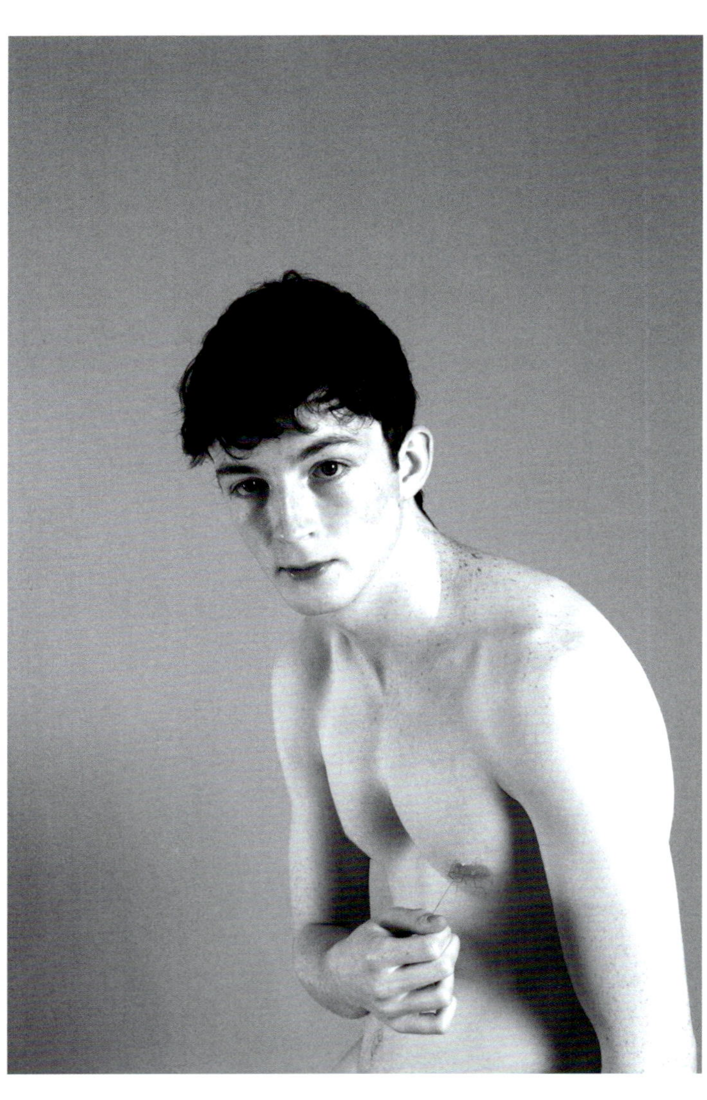

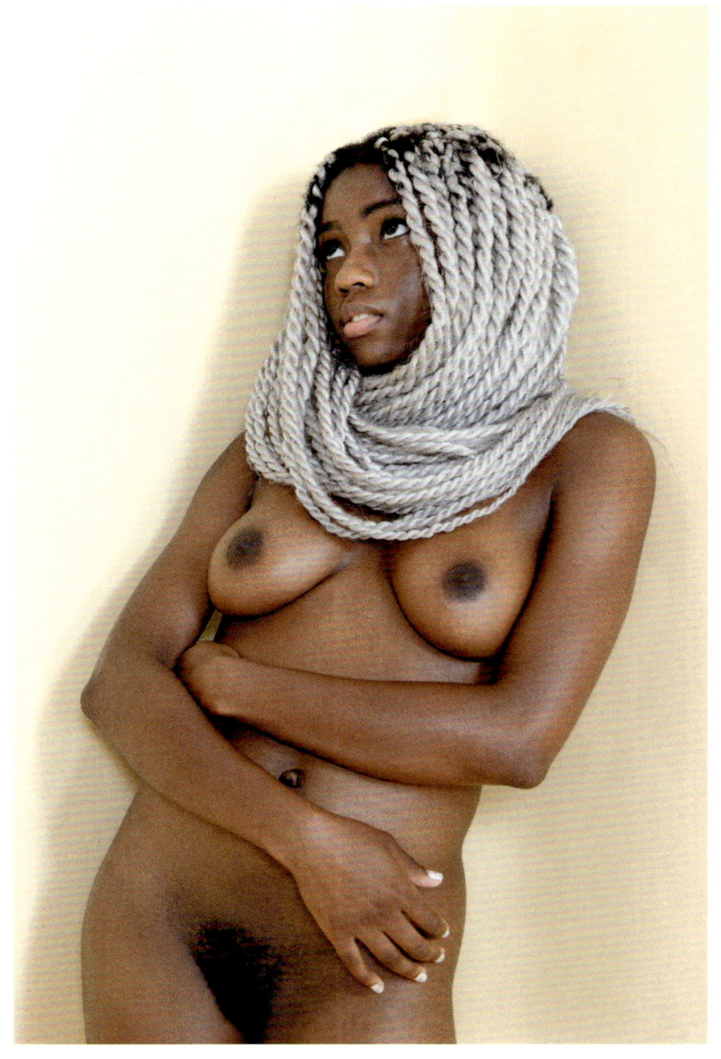

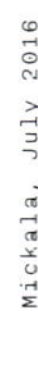

Gabriel, December 2014

Angal, February 2019

Mickey, September 2011

Mickala, July 2016

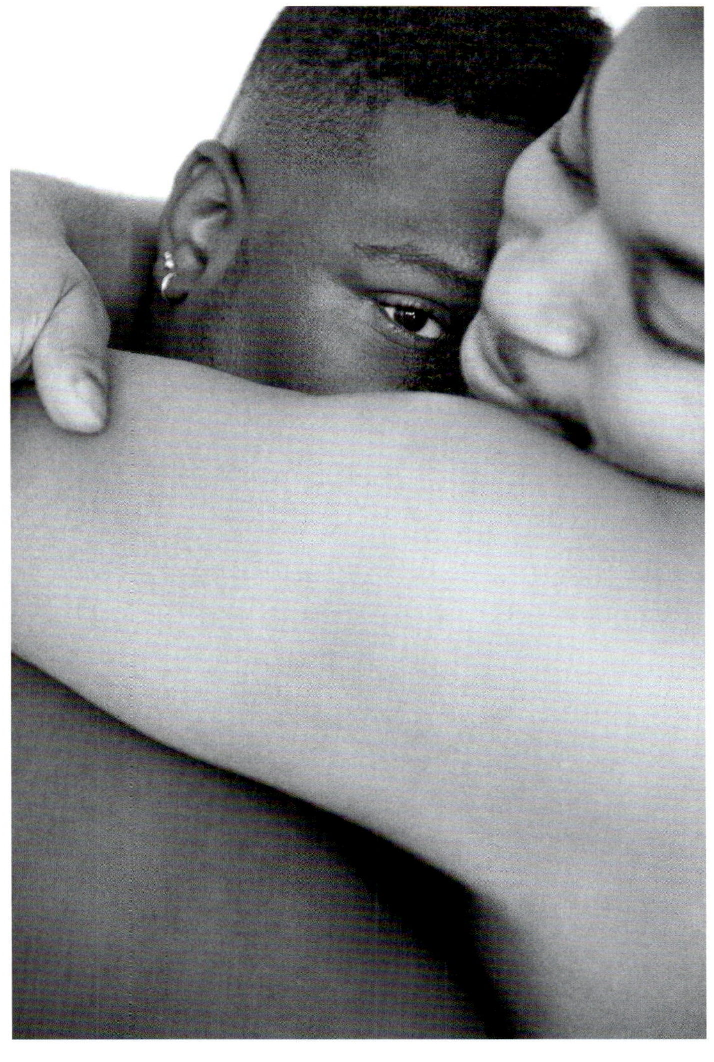

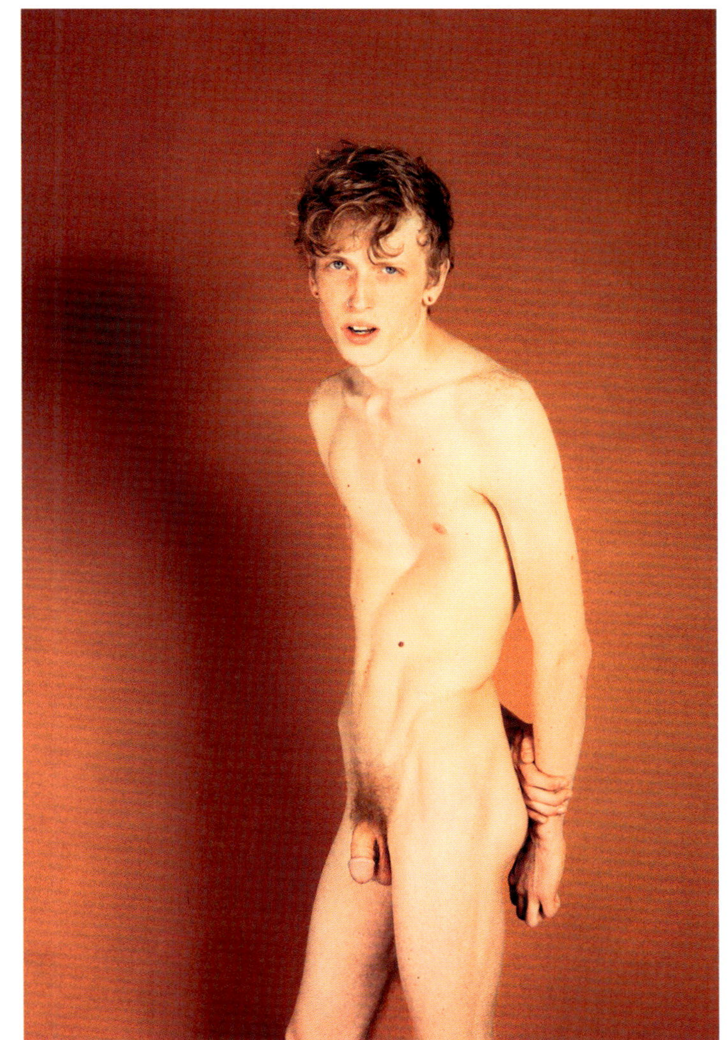

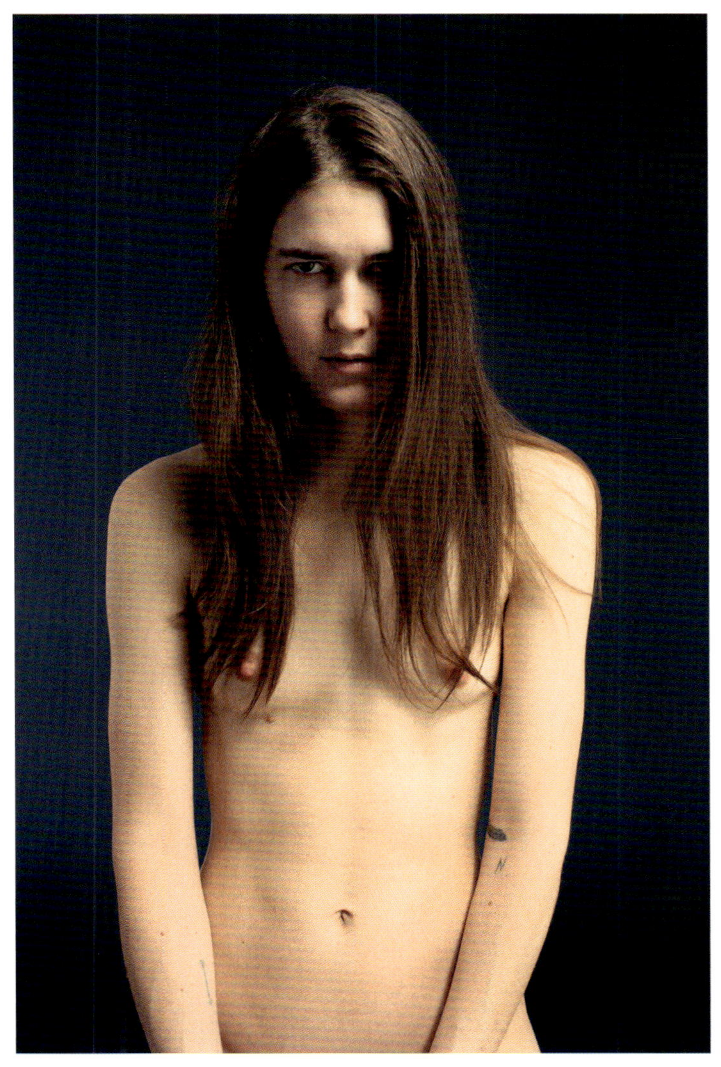

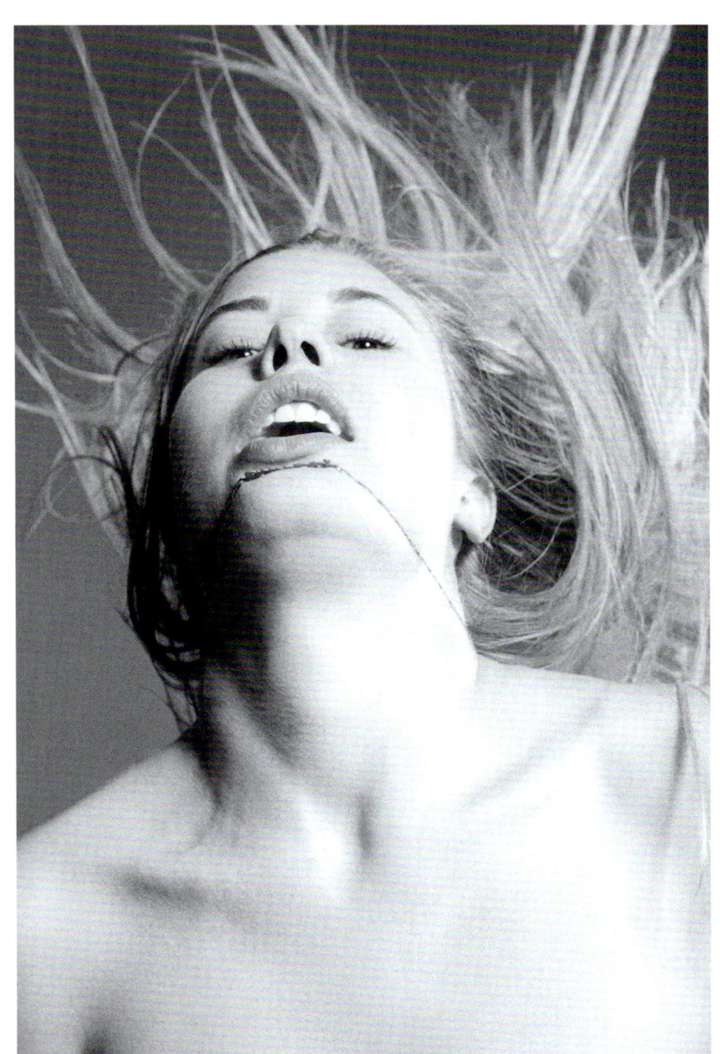

Tevin & Jaquan, October 2019 Patrick, April 2012 Eliza, January 2013 Kira, July 2015

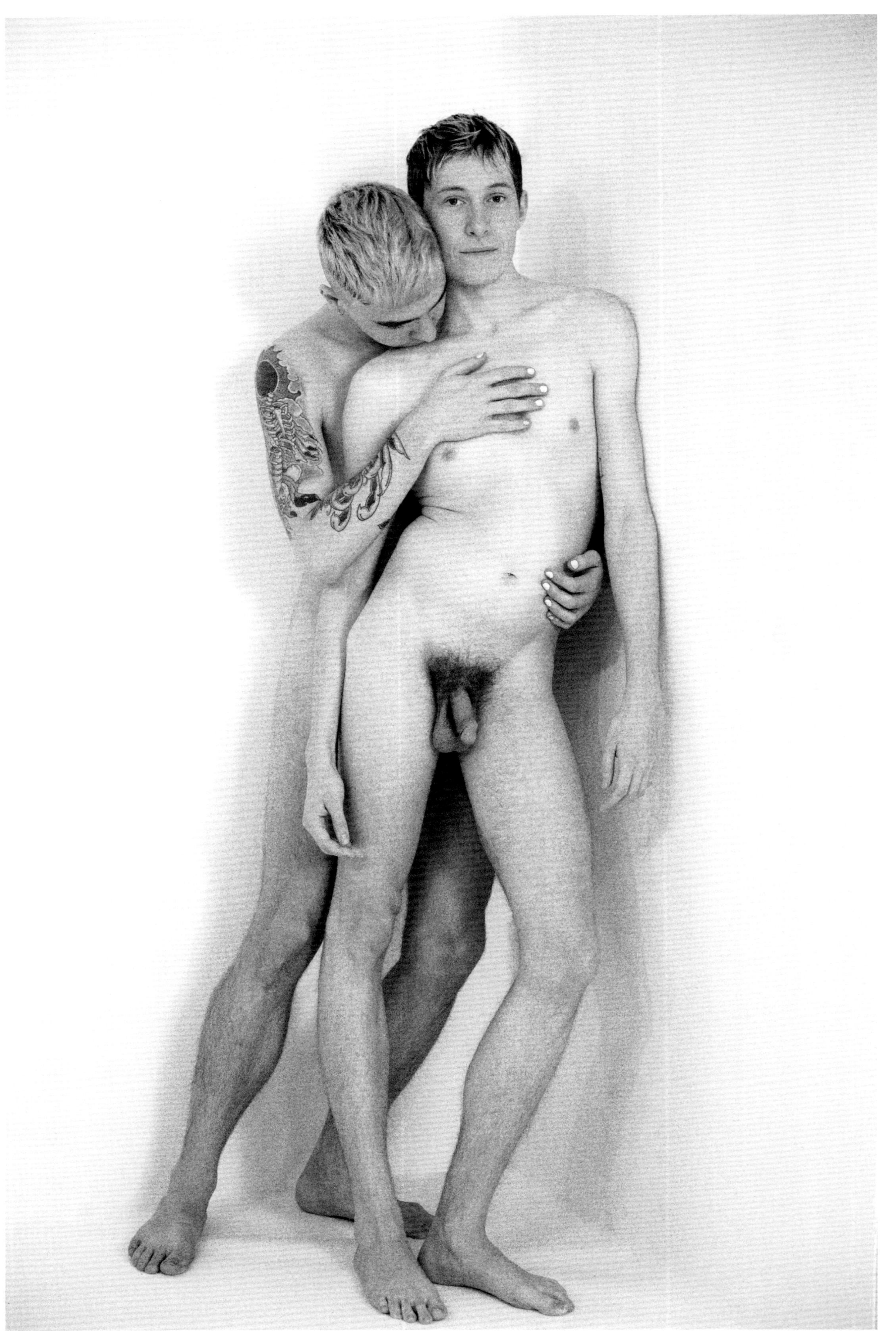

Colin & Justin, December 2018

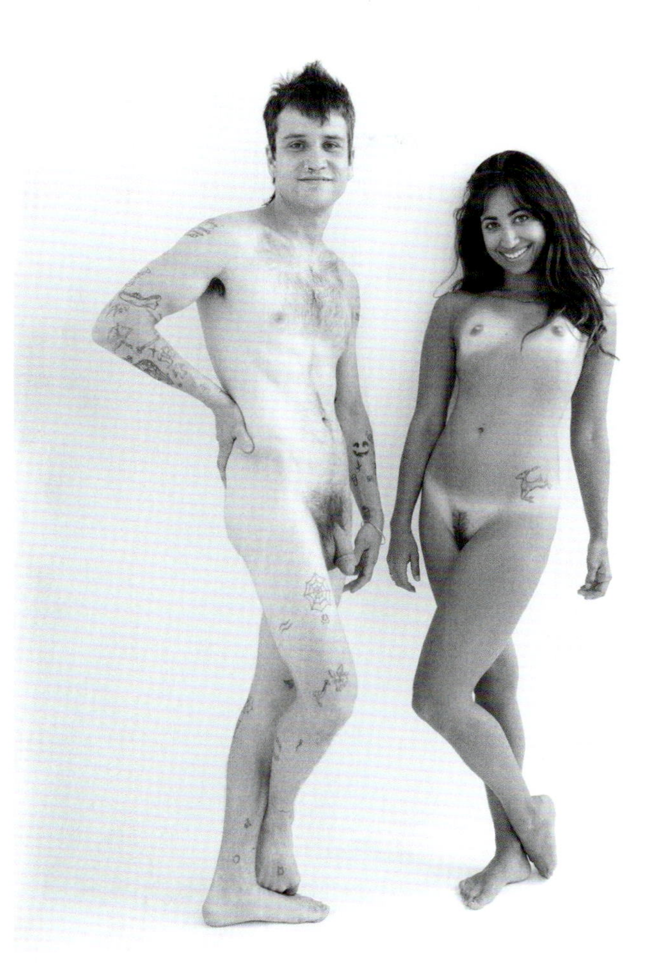

Annapurna & Danny, August 2017

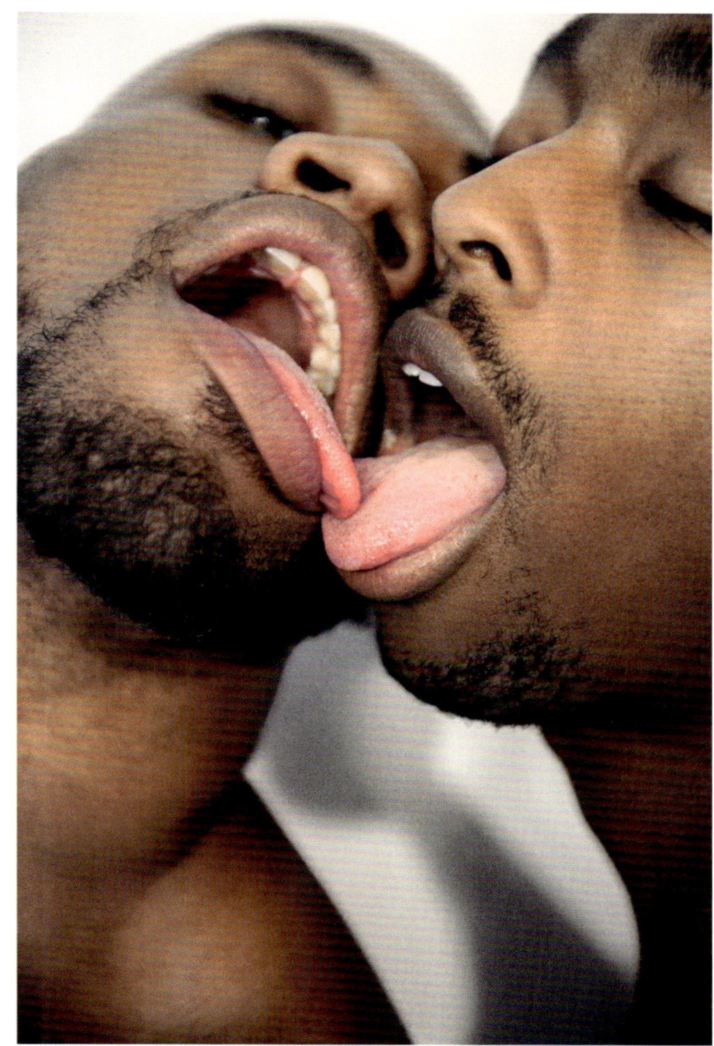

Kadar & Myles, October 2019

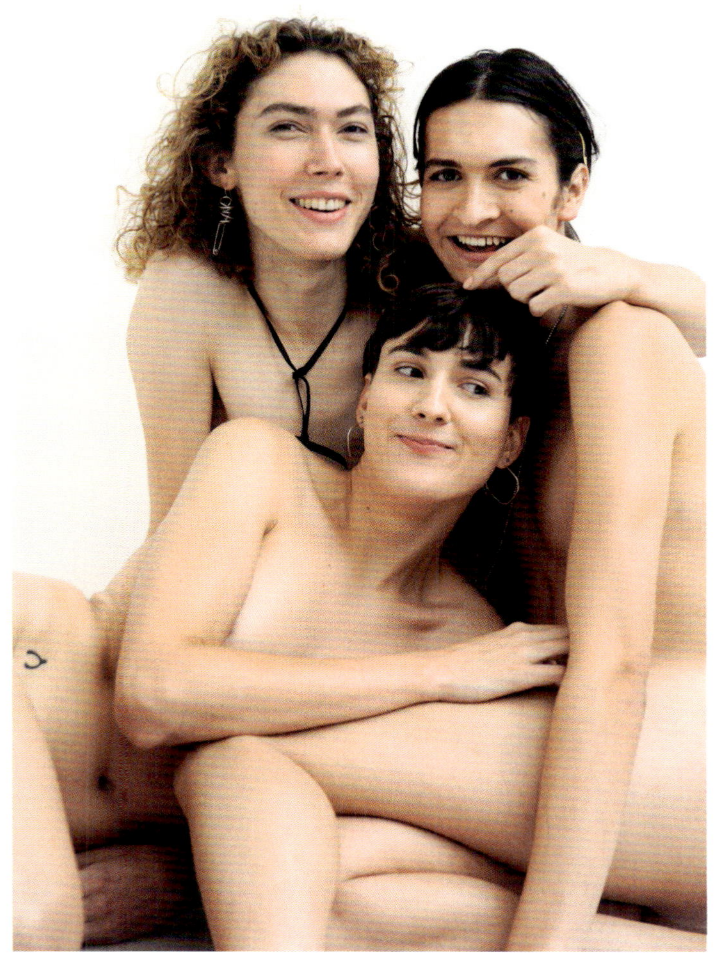

Cloe & June & Miles, July 2017

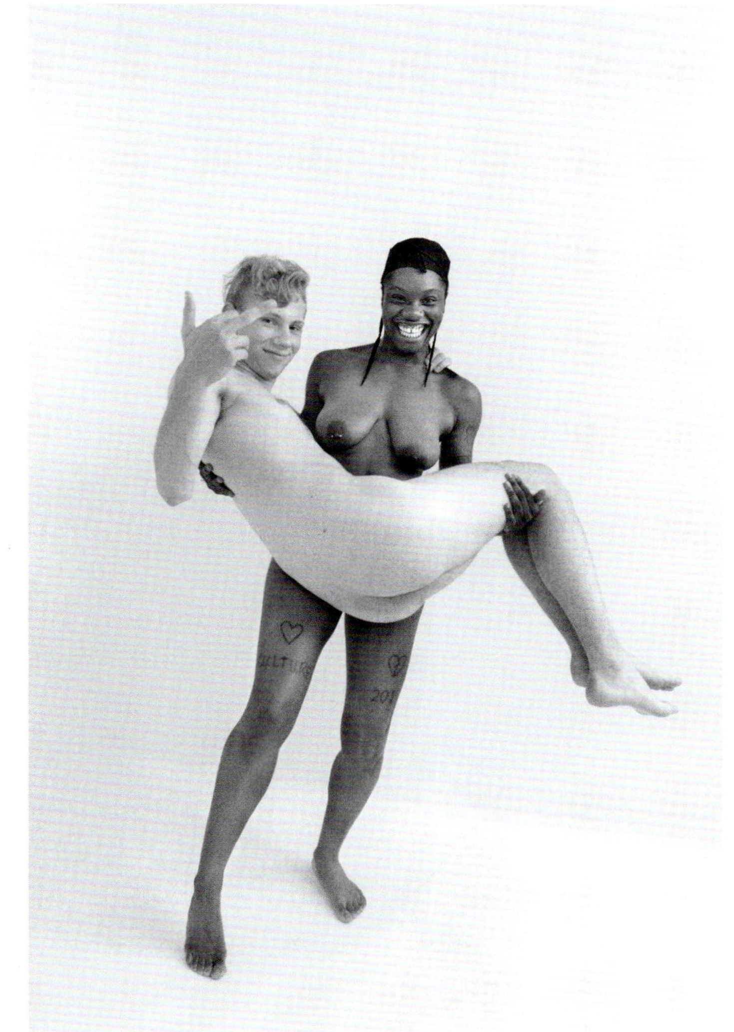

Rock & Tim, July 2017

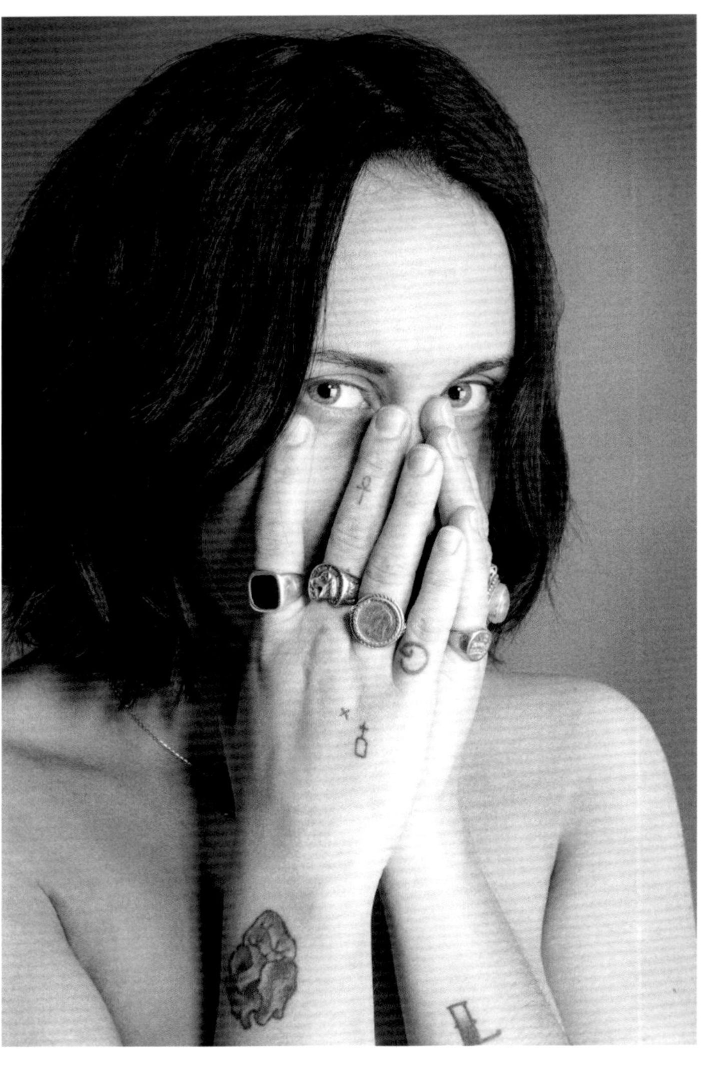

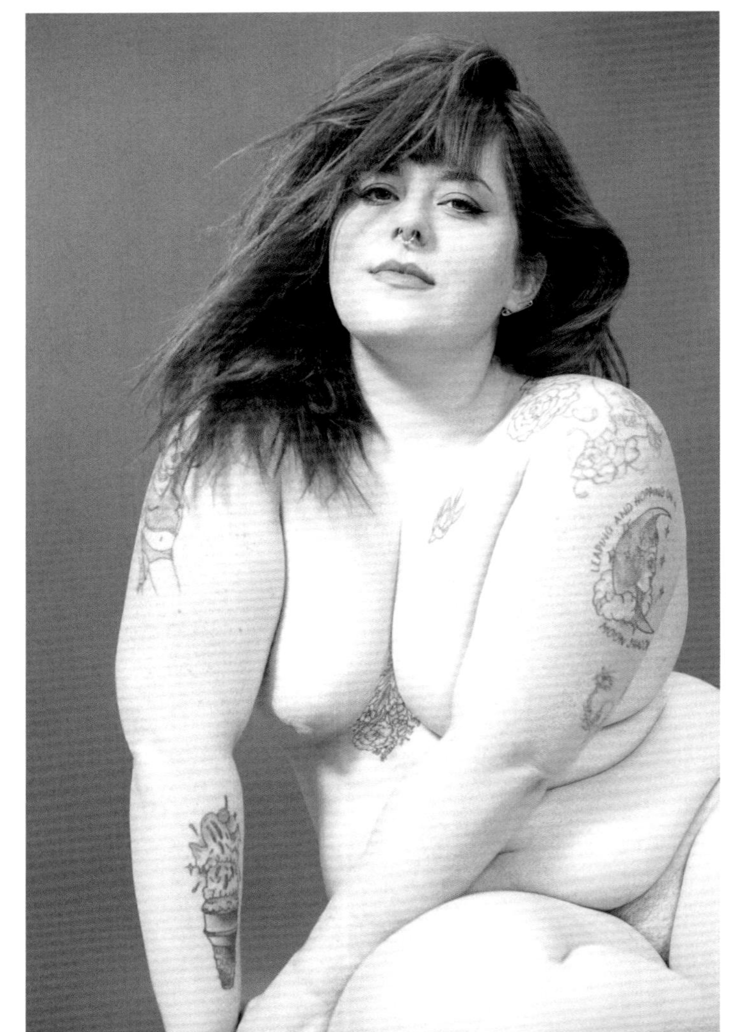

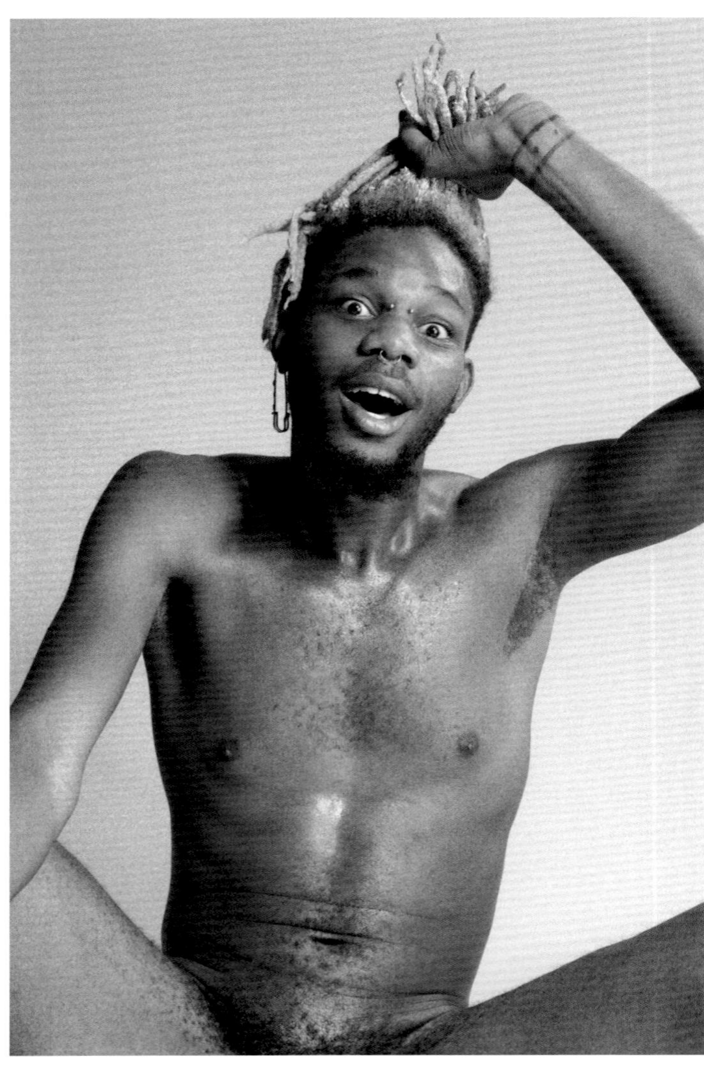

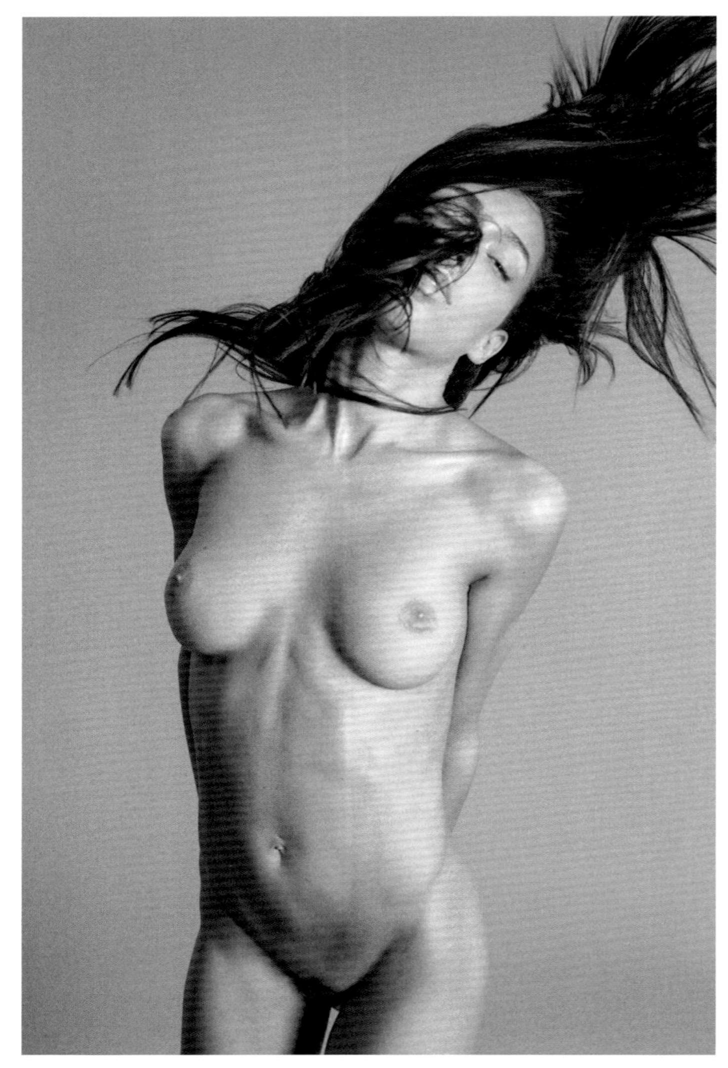

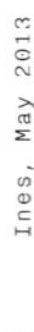

Antonia, December 2015 Corine, November 2016 Kendario, September 2015 Ines, May 2013

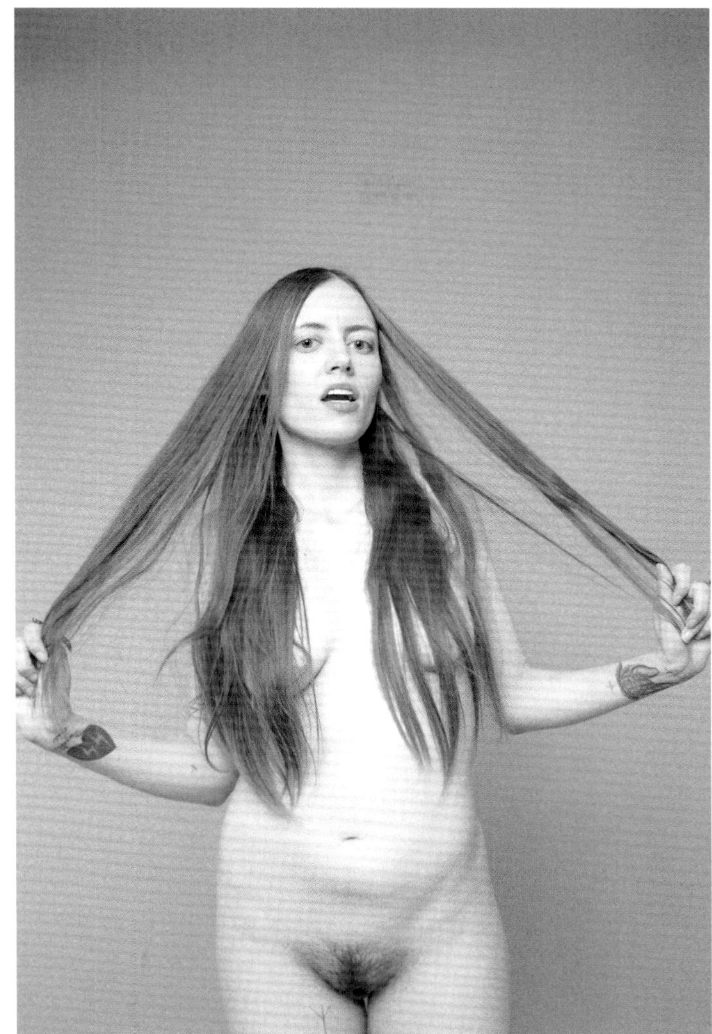

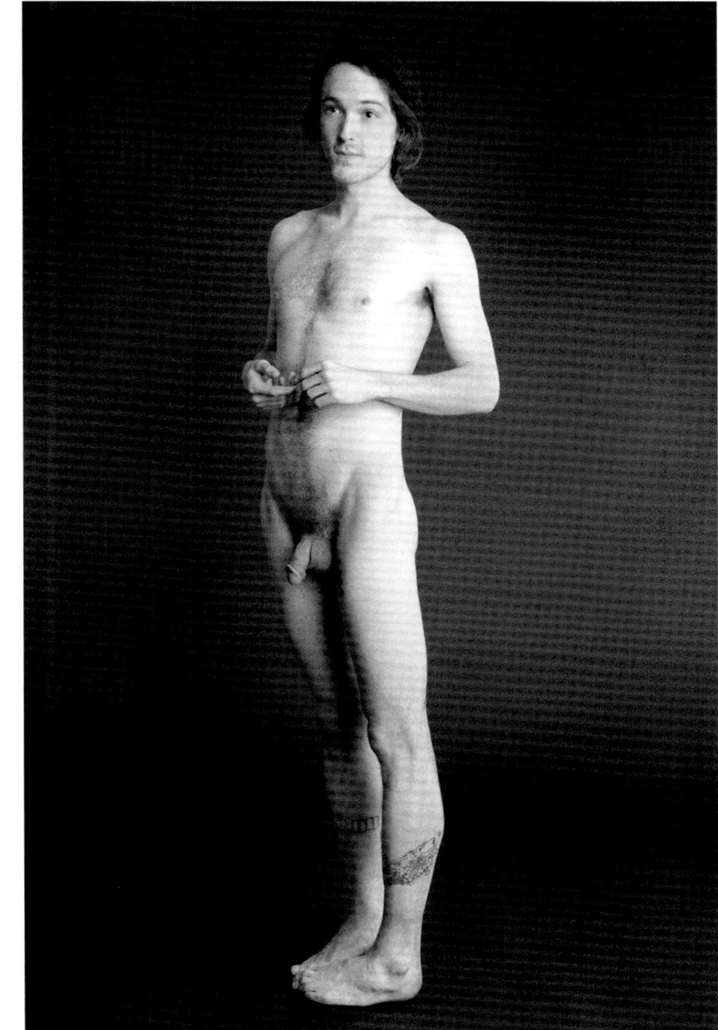

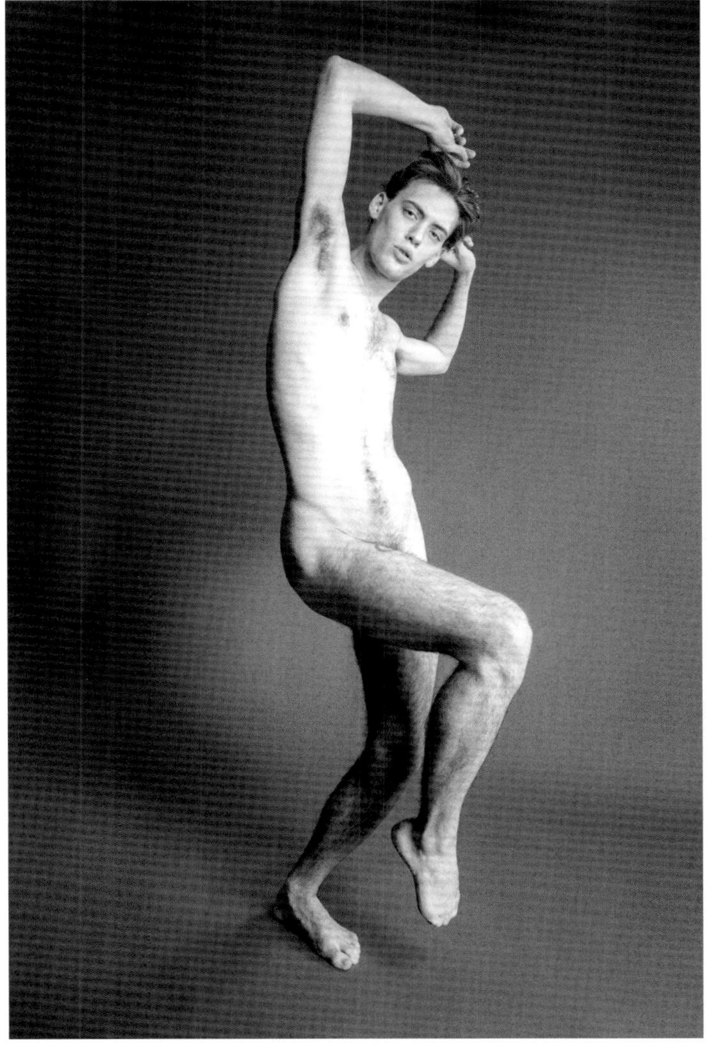

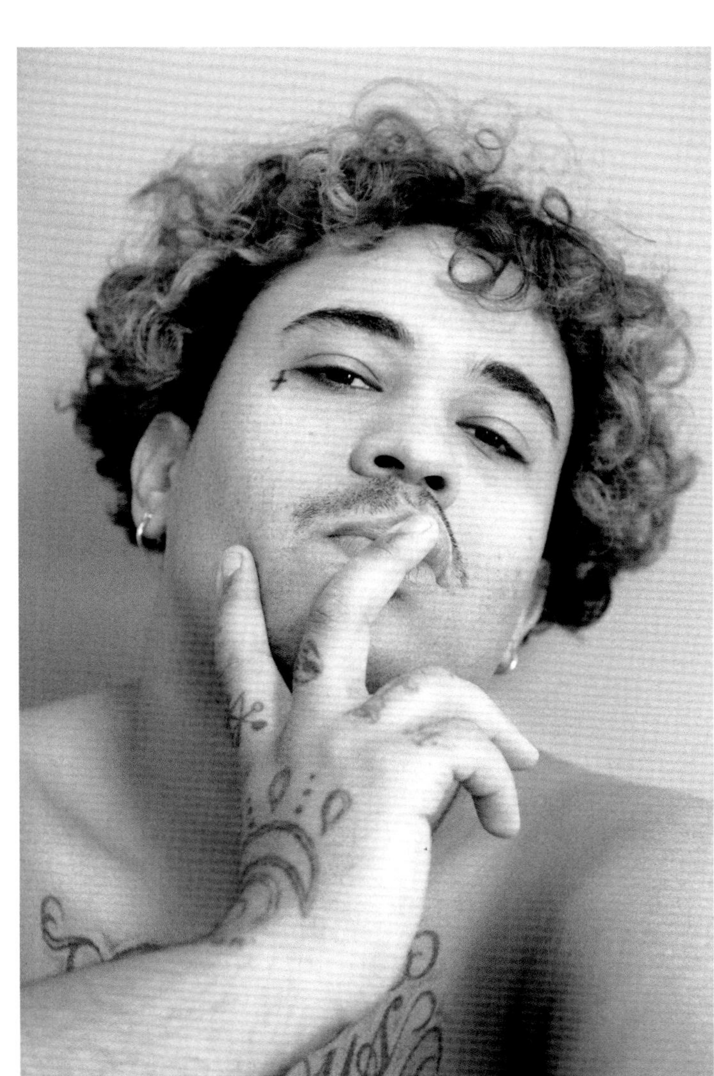

Kendra, May 2011 Pat, January 2014 John, January 2016 Robot, November 2016

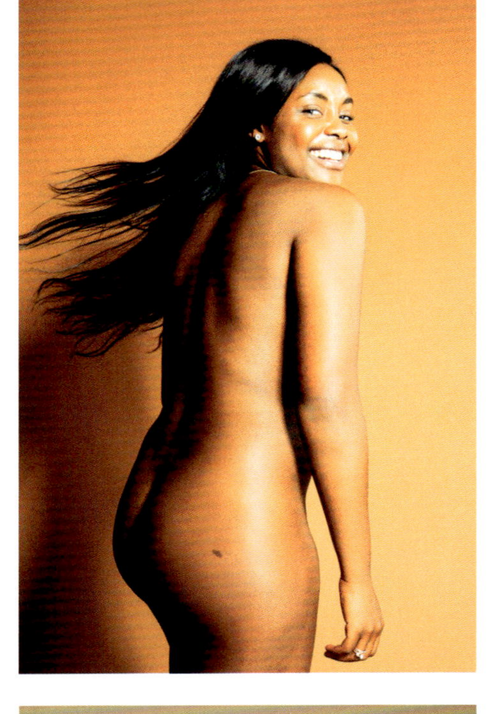

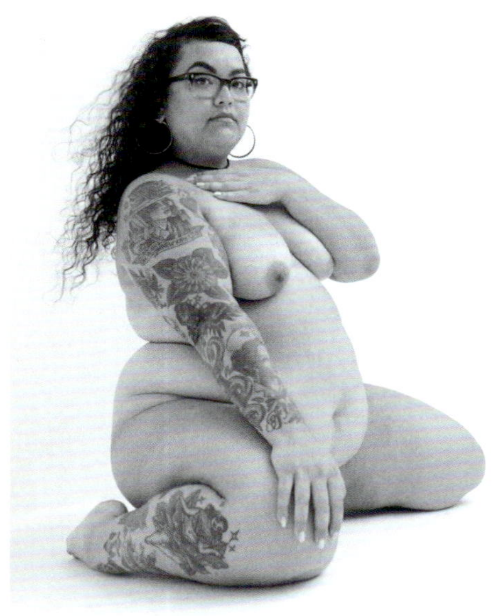

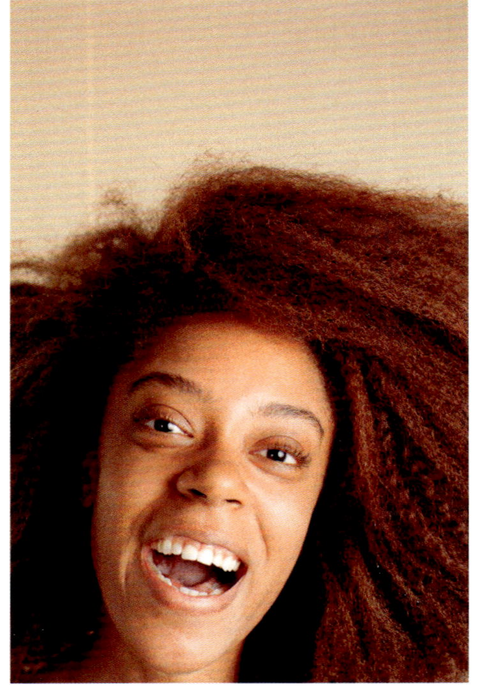

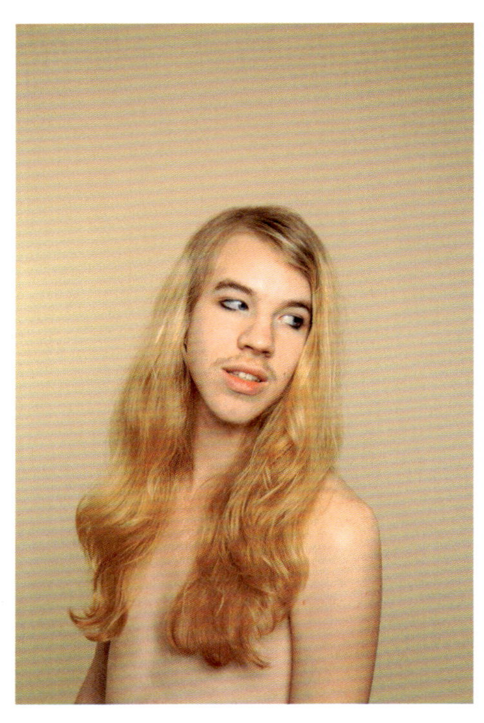

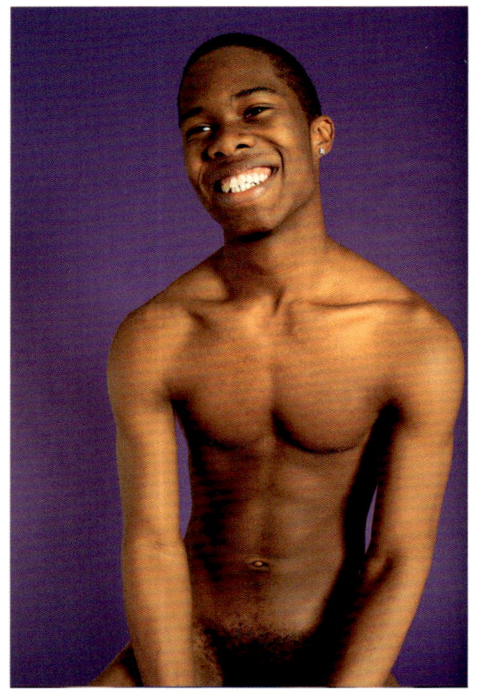

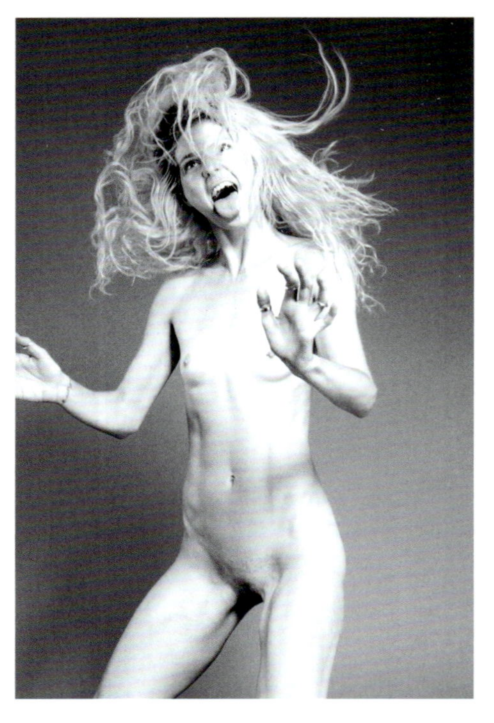

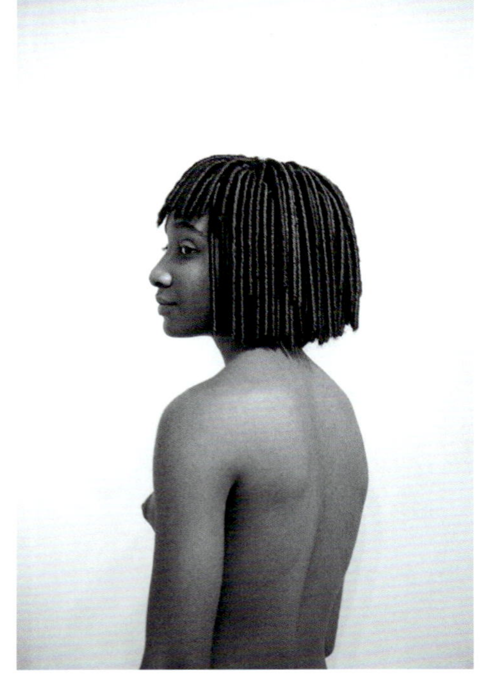

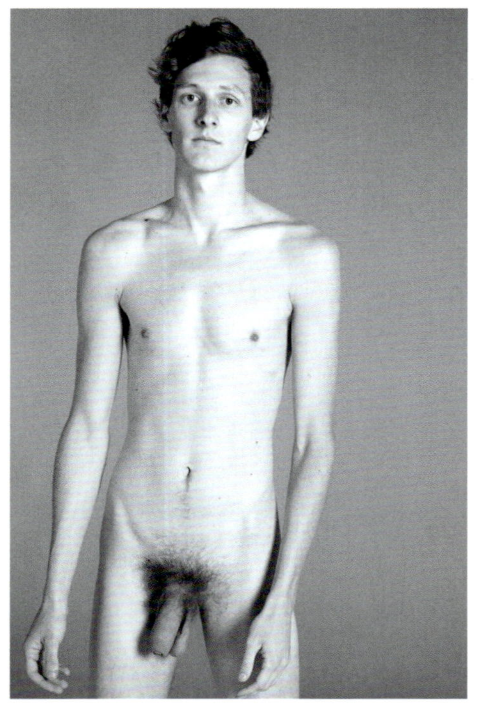

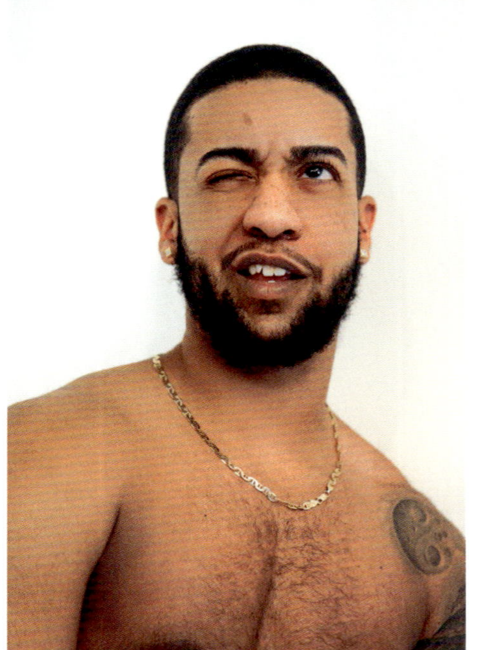

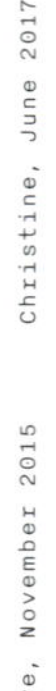

Inye, November 2015   Christine, June 2017   Keondra, September 2010   George, November 2010   Rhamier, December 2012   Lauren, September 2015   Aroma, October 2018   Casey, May 2000   Draxton, February 2019

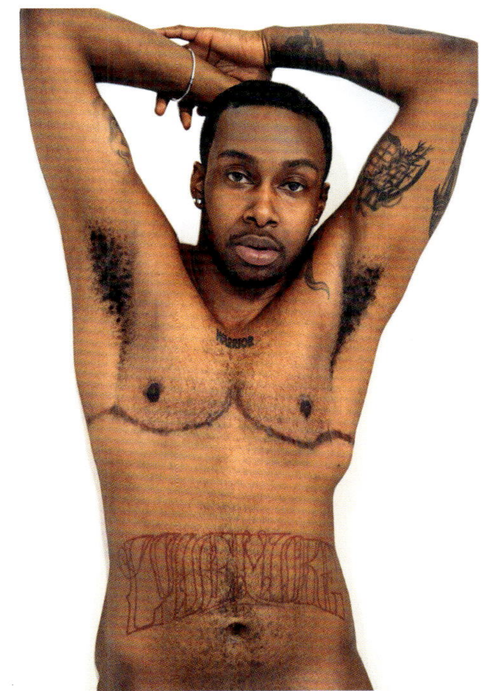

Paul, October 2012

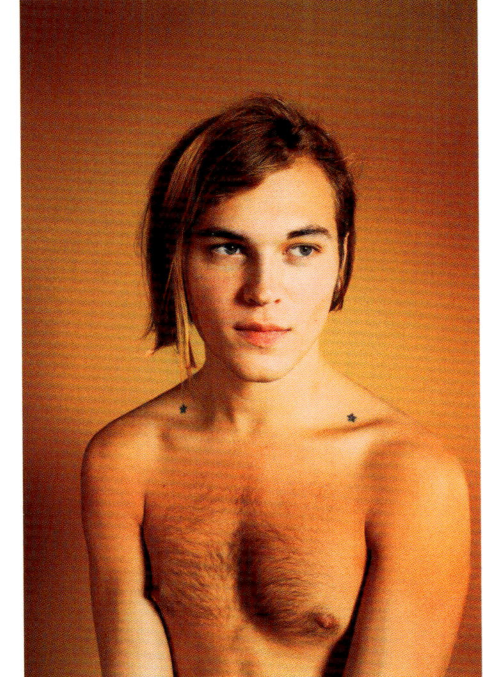

Nelle, December 2014

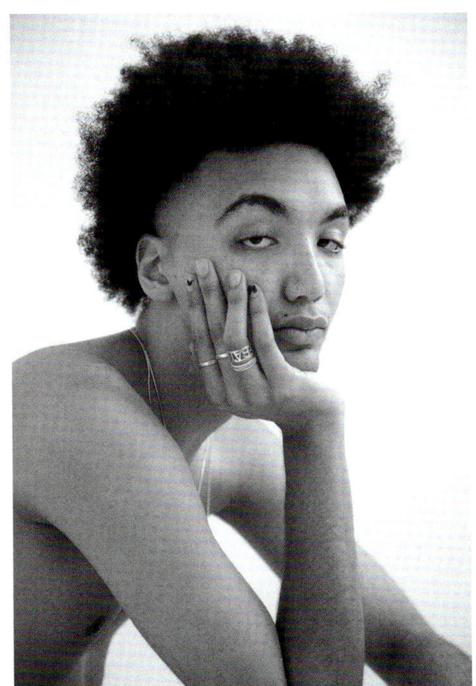

Marshall, October 2015

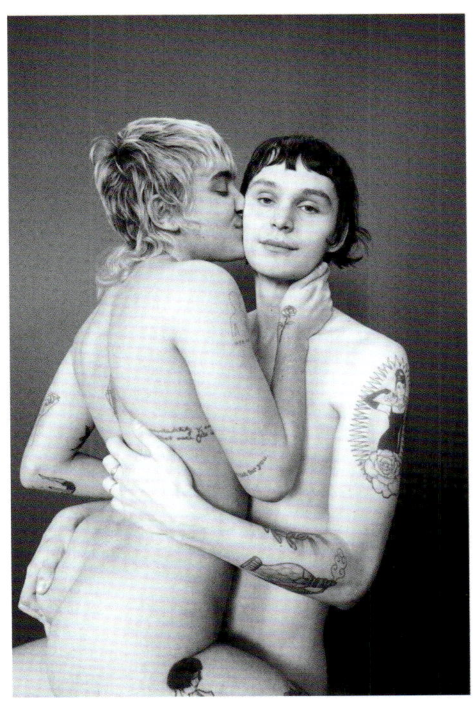

Mars & Coco, January 2017

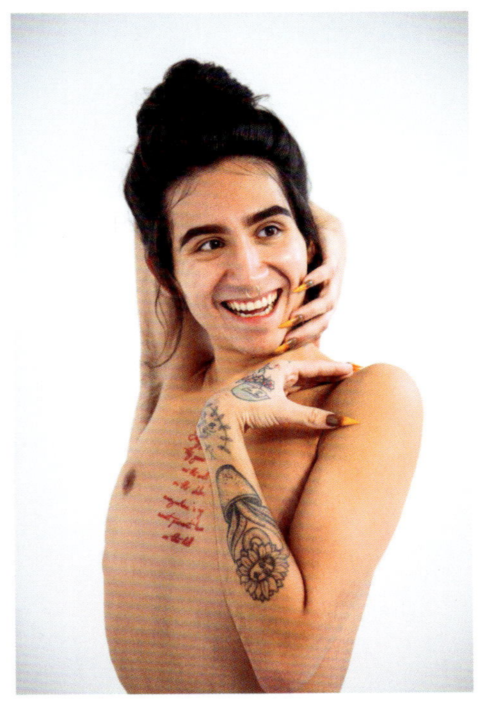

Amarilla, October 2018

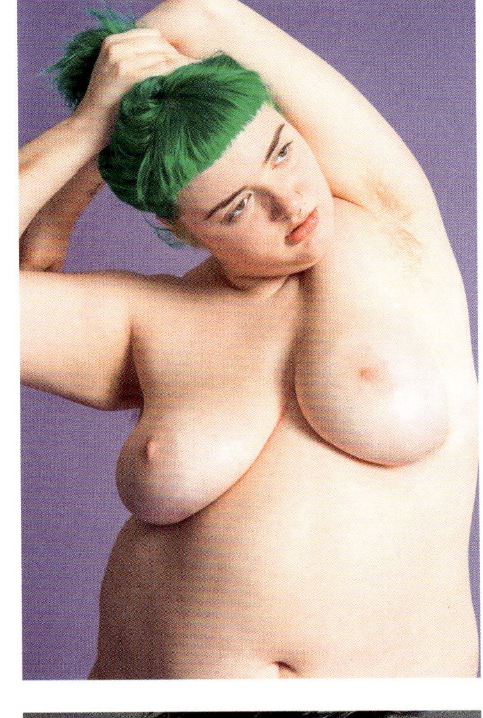

Gillian, February 2016

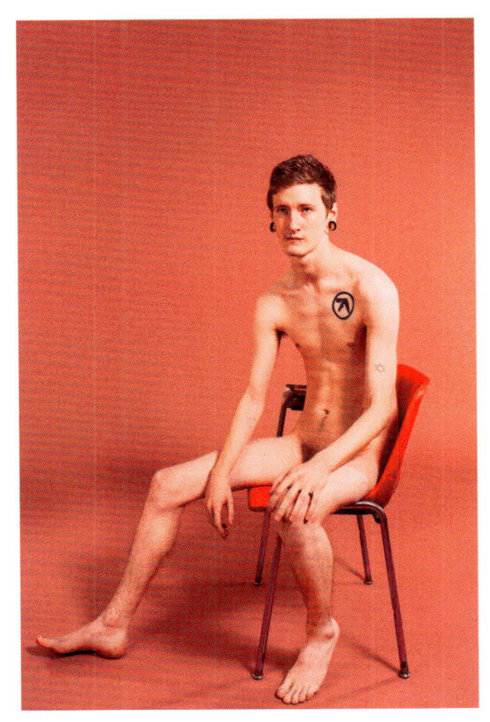

Tashan, February 2019

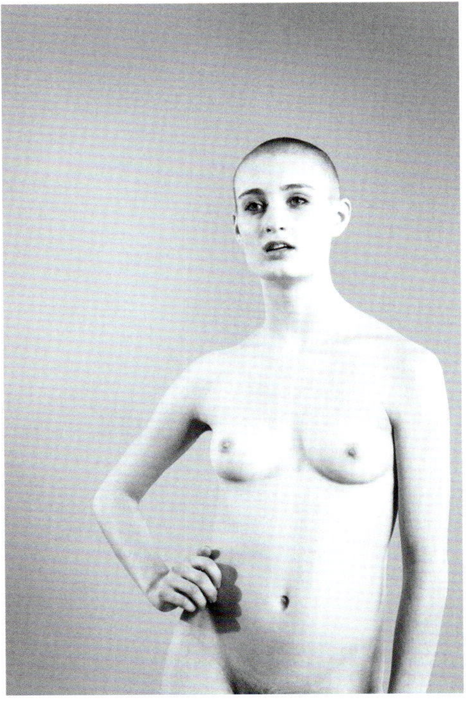

Mike, October 2012

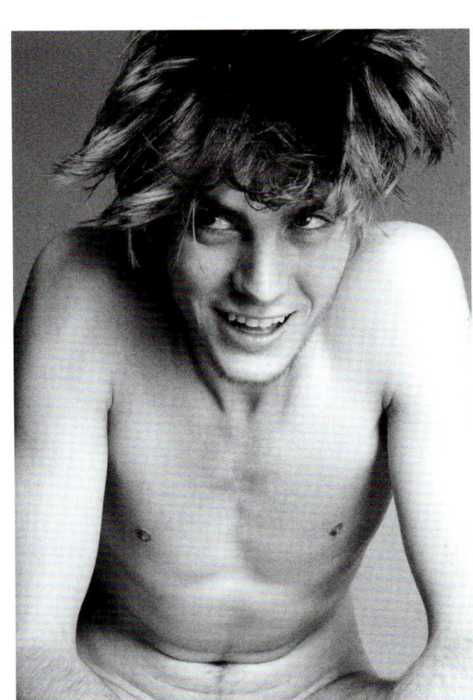

Noah, September 2018

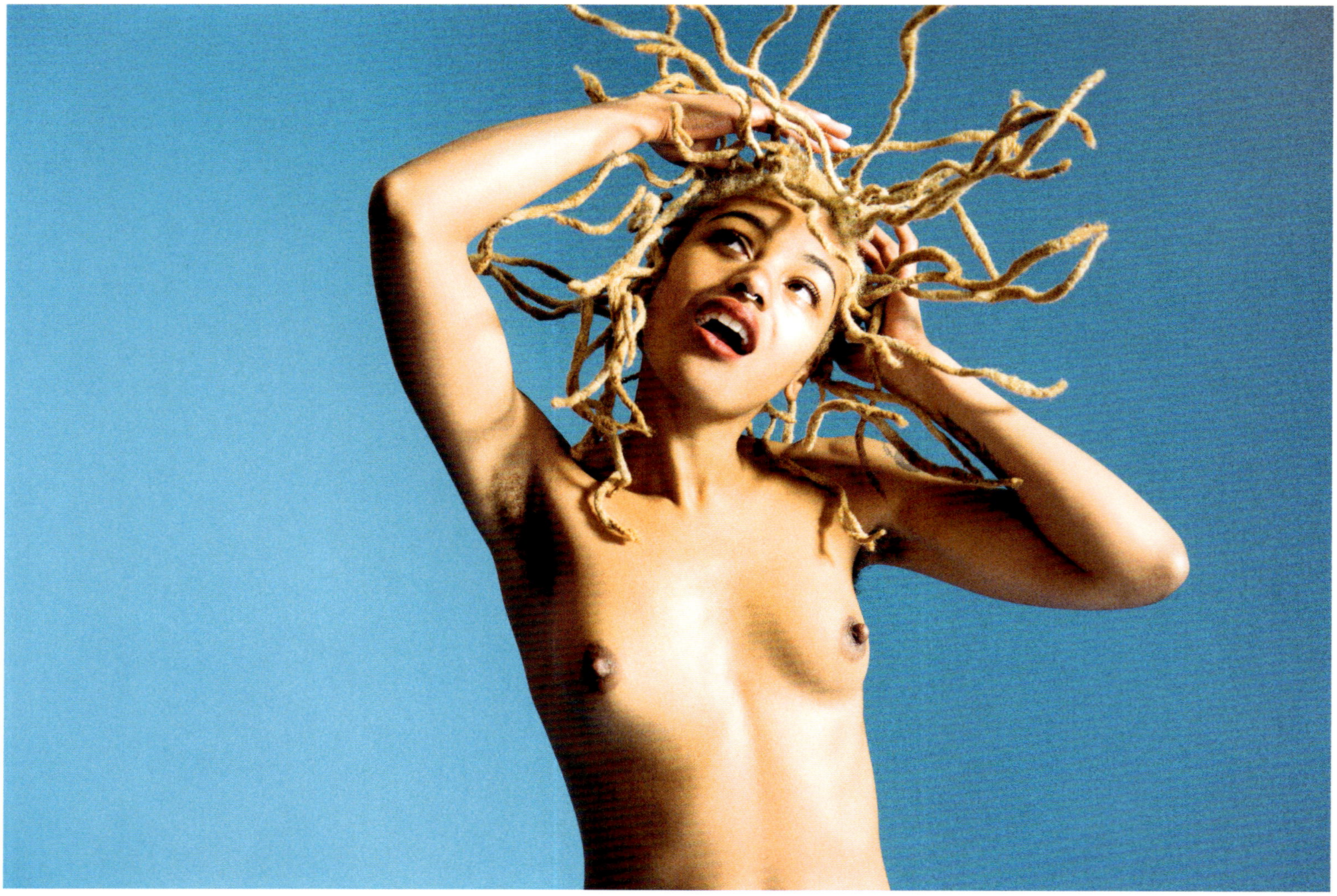

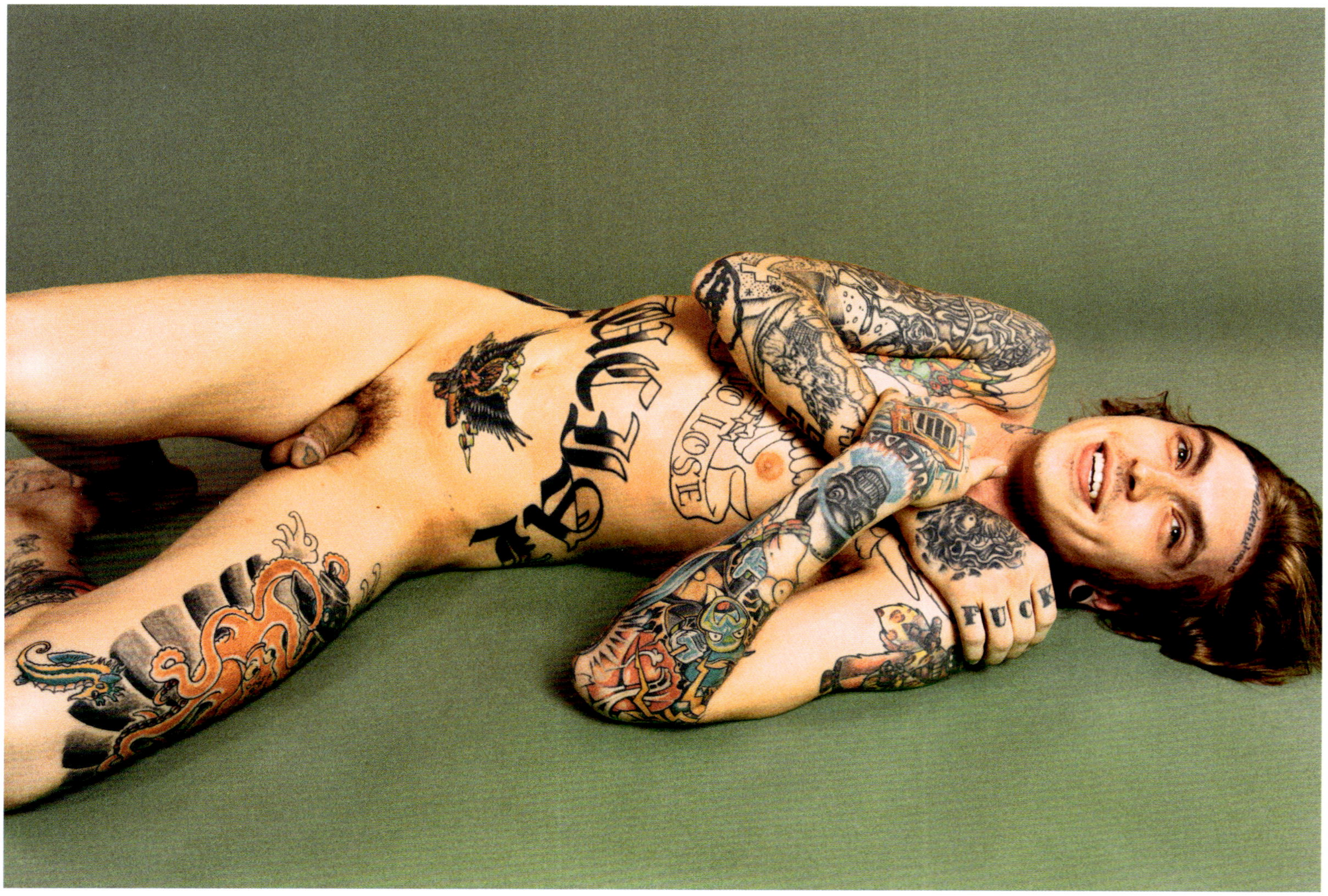

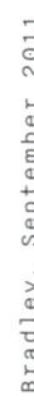

Lorelei, March 2016

Bradley, September 2011

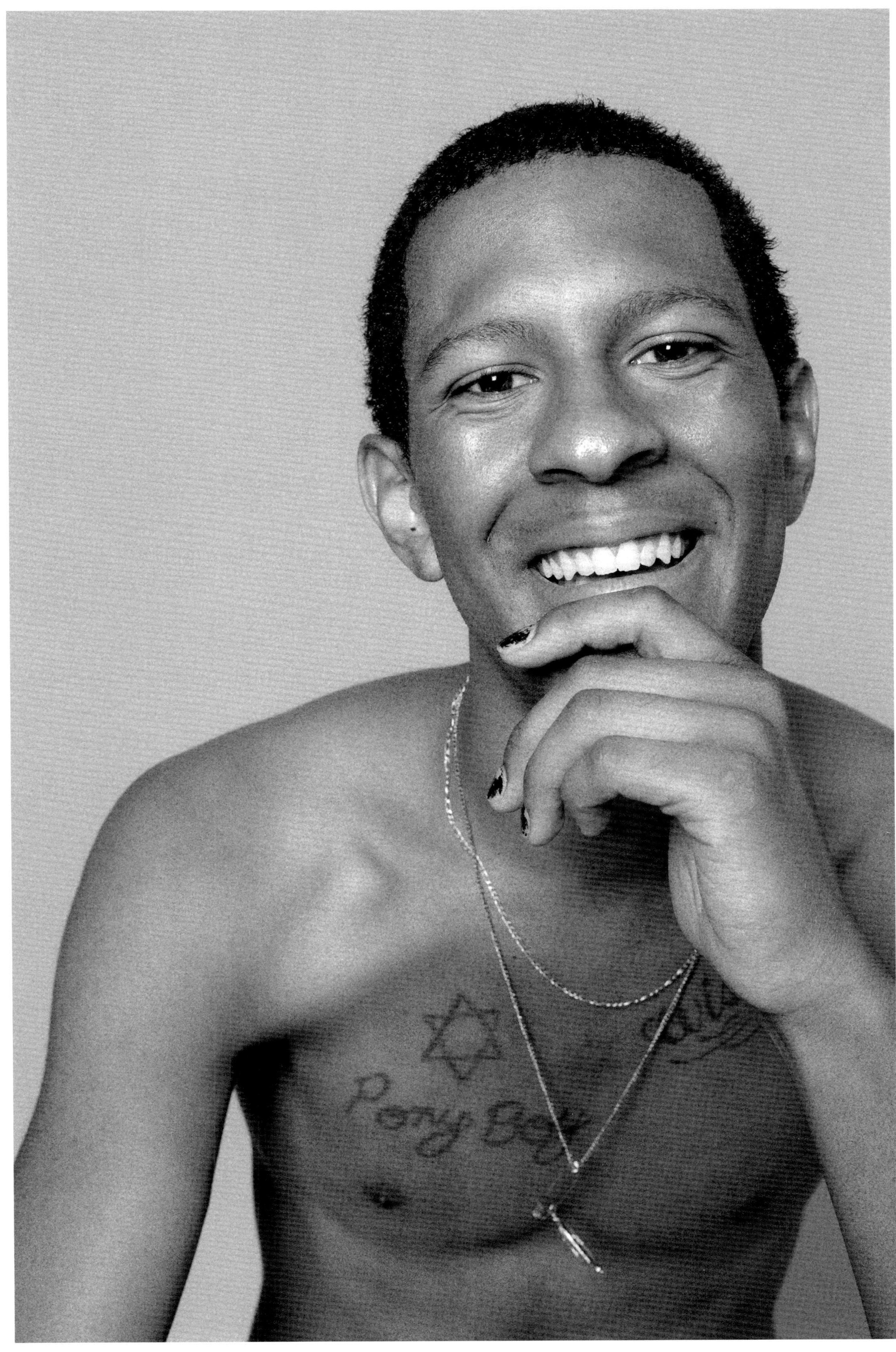

Mykki, August 2009

Right before this shoot, I'd spoken at a protest in Times Square with Gays Against Guns. It was in response to the Thousand Oaks mass shooting. When I was protesting or doing something political under the Trump presidency, I'd usually wear the matching pink eyeliner and kippah you see here.

My chosen family son, Timothy, had just moved to New York. It was literally his first day in New York. Timmy came to meet me at the protest, and I had already planned to go see Ryan afterward so I brought Timmy with me. When we showed up, there was such a community feel in the room, with a bunch of folks hanging out in the little kitchen area next to the studio. I introduced Timmy to Ryan. "I hope it's okay that I brought Timmy, my gay son." Ryan's response was, "Oh my God, of course." I knew that it would be.

Ryan and I became close when I was doing a lot of street activism with this group I founded in 2017 called Voices4. We were taking direct inspiration from other New York-based queer activist groups, specifically Queer Nation, Gays Against Guns, and ACT UP. Ryan had a connection to ACT UP and New York street activism through his brother. He saw what we were doing, and I think that drew him in. We'd been friends before but that's when we started working together.

Ryan and I often collaborate on direct action activism, which is when you see there is a problem and you're finding creative and meaningful ways to point that out or provide a solution. A protest or rally is a really good way to do that. With these very physical gatherings, communication becomes really important. That's something that ACT UP really understood. You need soundbites and images that a) articulate what you're trying to say and b) are compelling.

Now that we have social media, we can tell the stories from within the movement. Images are tools of communication that can spread a message really, really fast. If you can get the right image, it will be reflected and shown all over the world. That's why having a photographer like Ryan within the movement is so extremely powerful. His photographs are so beautiful and let's be honest, he also has a high profile. We can leverage his name and photos to achieve our community-organizing goals. For example, there are certain key publications that may normally pass on covering a protest but they will absolutely cover it if Ryan is giving them the photos.

I've said before that "Queer people anywhere are responsible for queer people everywhere." It's always been my dream to help create a queer community that reflects that ethos. What that means is: across any and every gender, racial, class, religious, identity, and international lines, queer people, simply by virtue of being queer, have an obligation to show up for each other. If you are a gay man, that means you have an obligation to show up for trans women. If you're an American queer person and persecution is taking place in Chechnya, you have an obligation to show up for queer people there. This is one of my core beliefs, and I know that Ryan believes it too.

I'm so grateful for this photograph and shoot. A different photo we took that day went on to become the author photo of my first book.

It's also important to mention that my hair looks amazing. It looks so good, it's almost offensive. Not only is it the best that my hair has ever looked, it might be some of the best anyone's hair has ever looked. God shines on the gays.

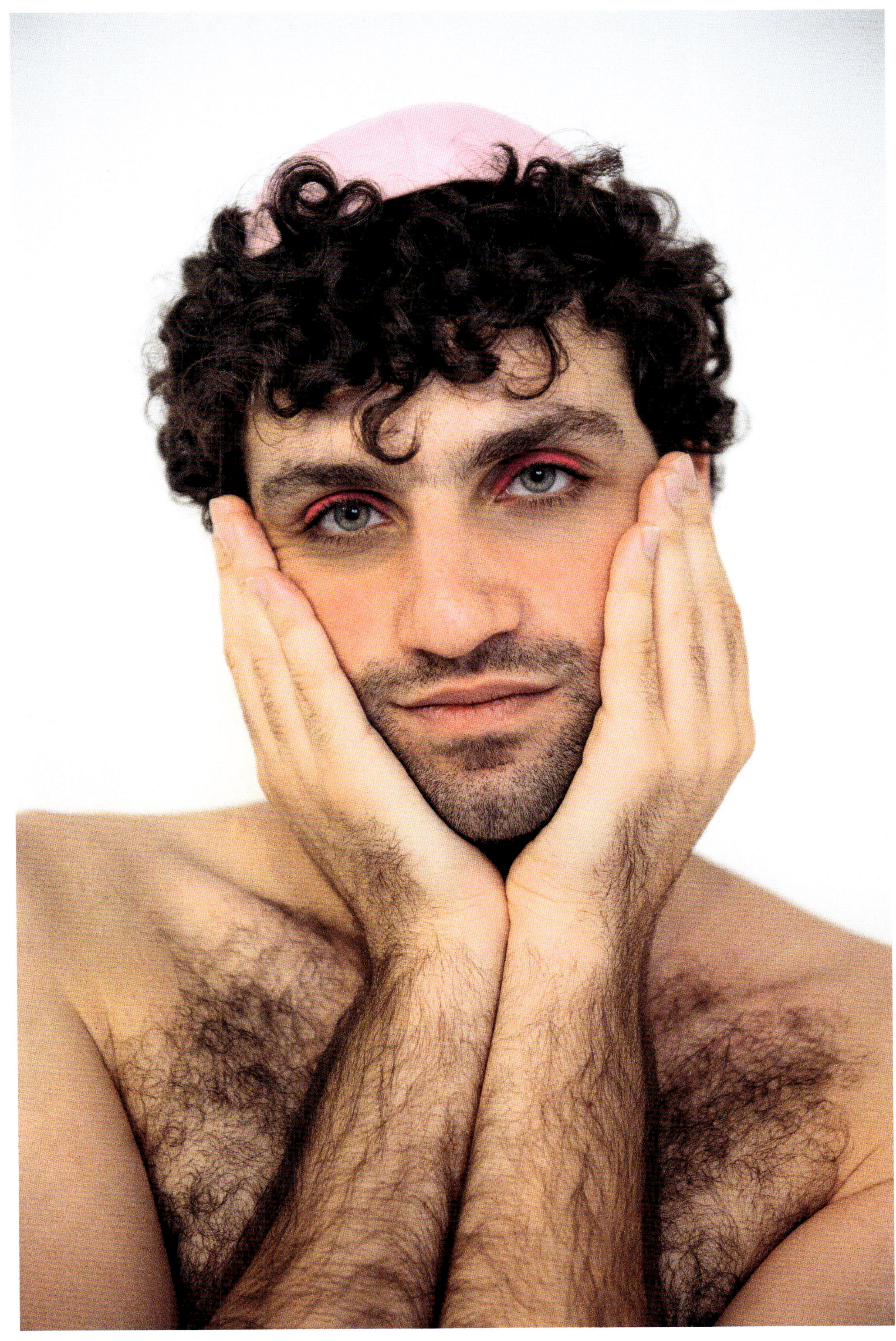

Adam, November 2018

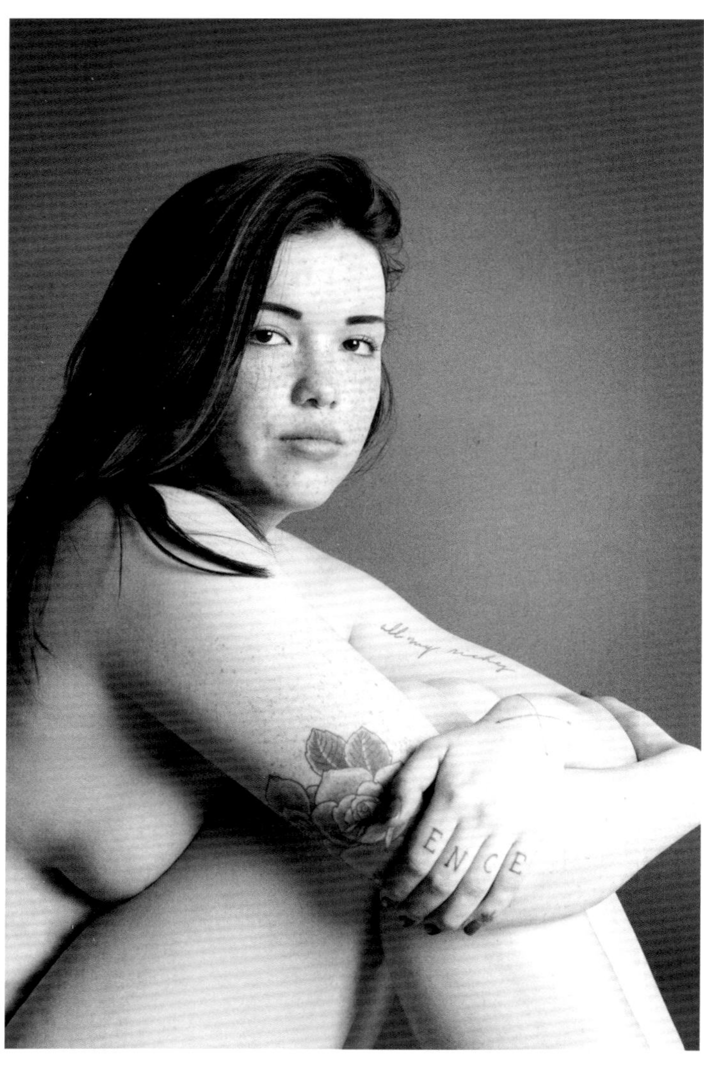

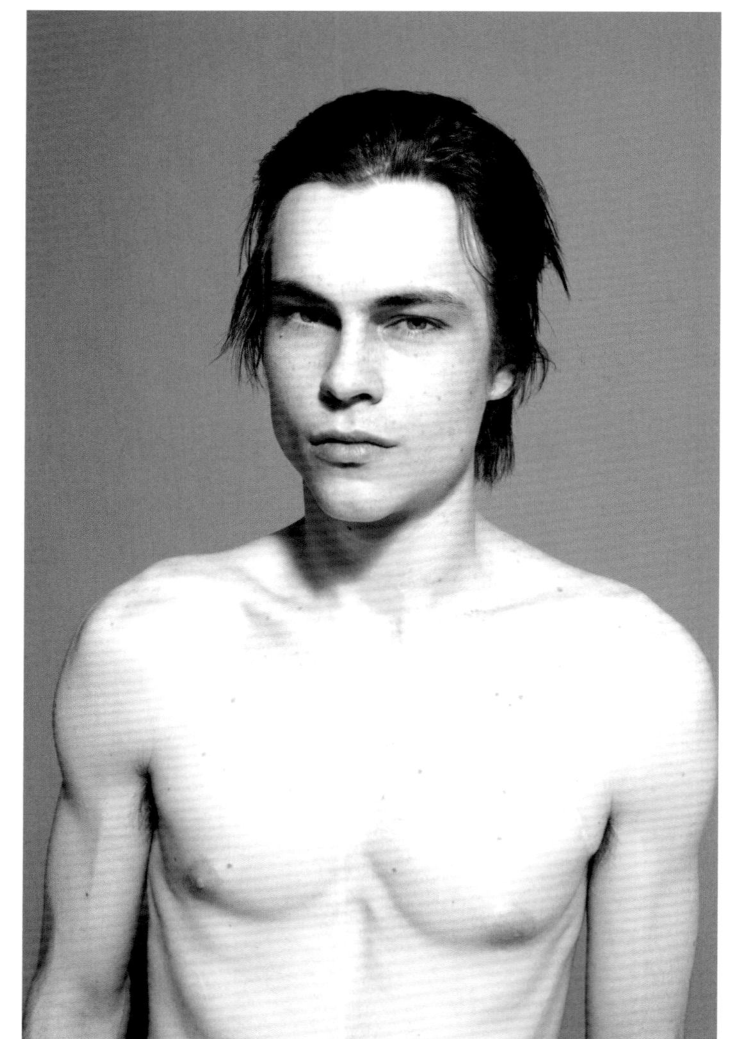

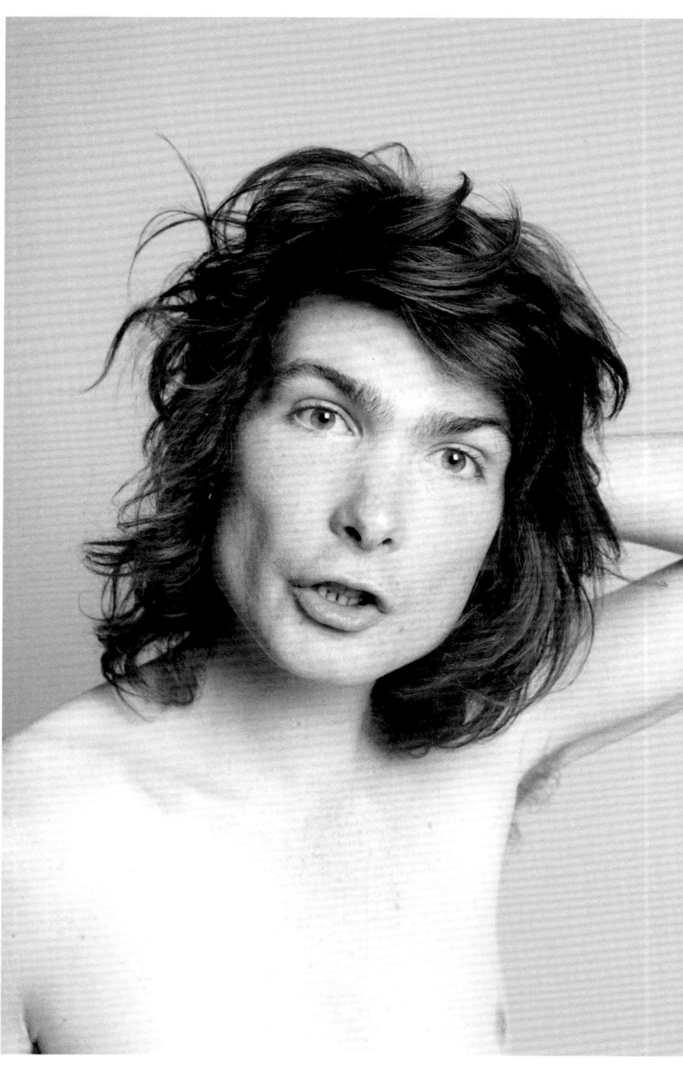

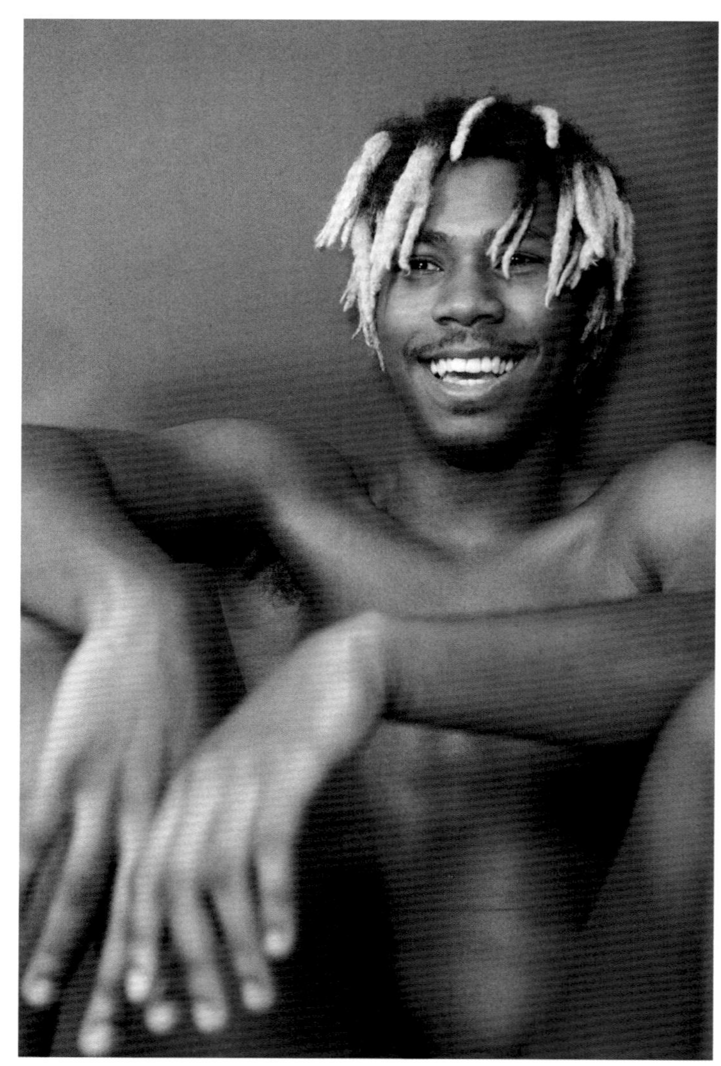

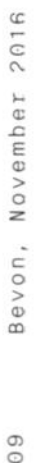

Tessa, April 2014 Jackson, April 2008 Chris, March 2009 Bevon, November 2016

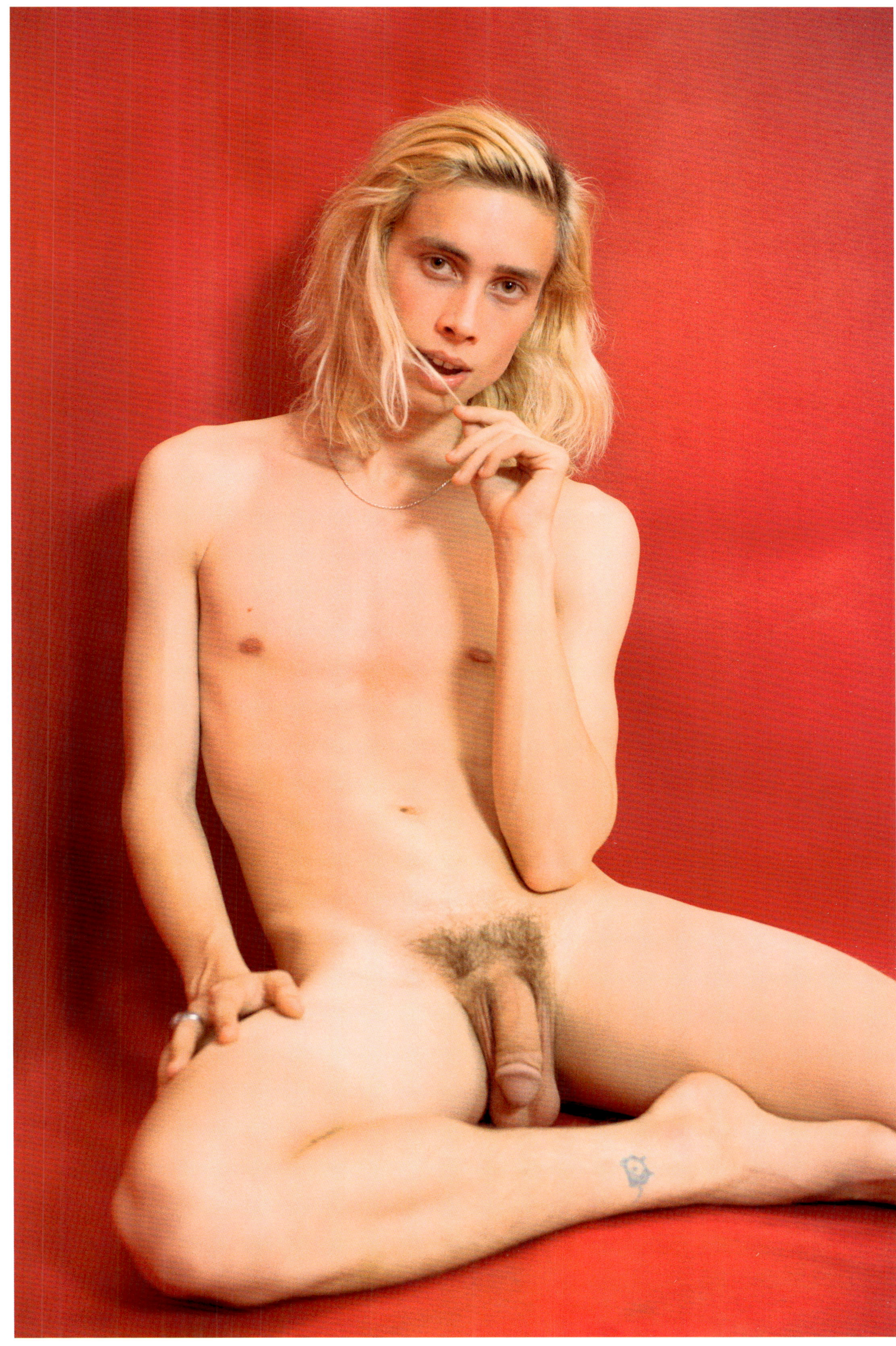

Carl, November 2016

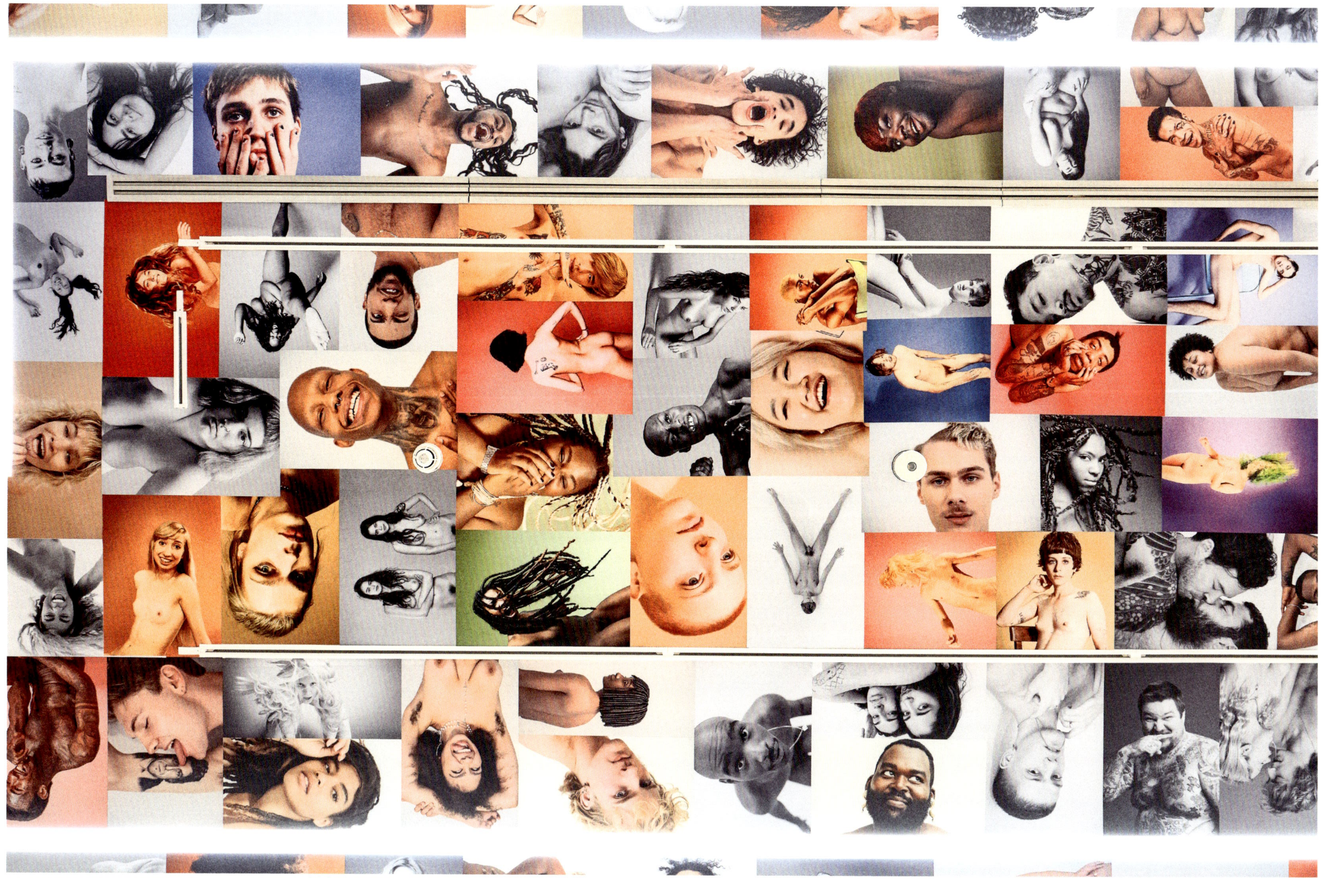

Pretty Free, Marlborough London, 2020

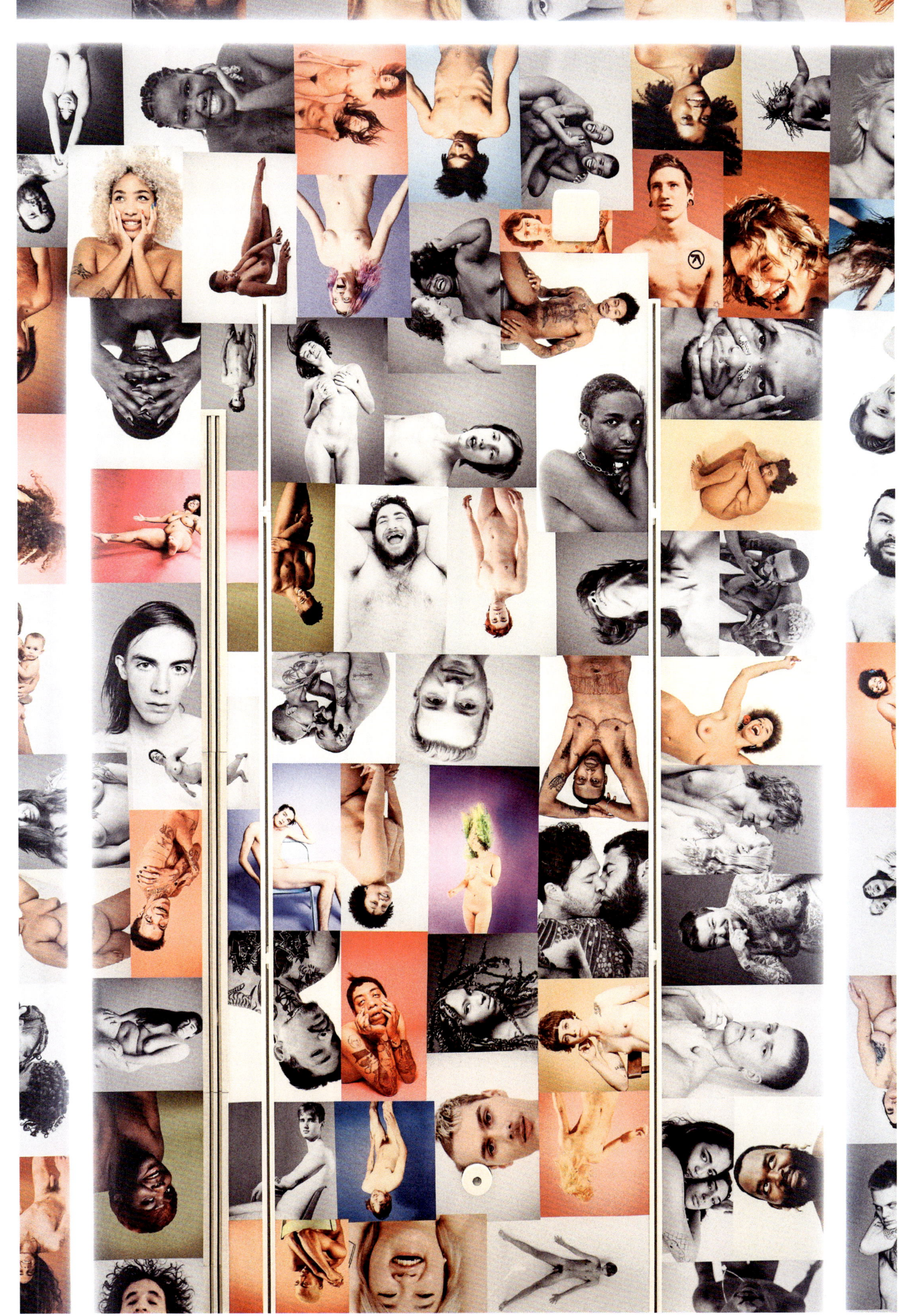

Pretty Free, Marlborough London, 2020

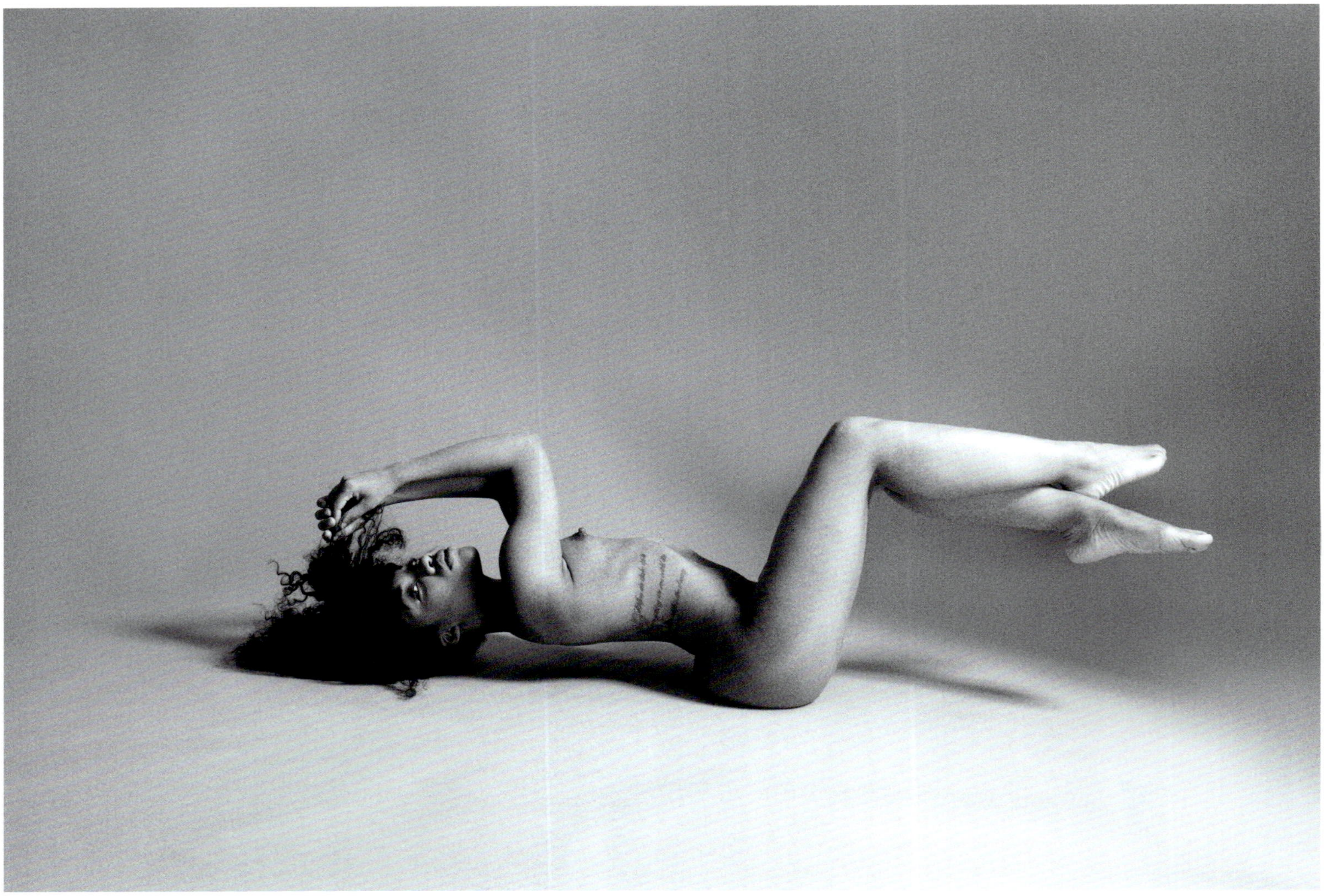

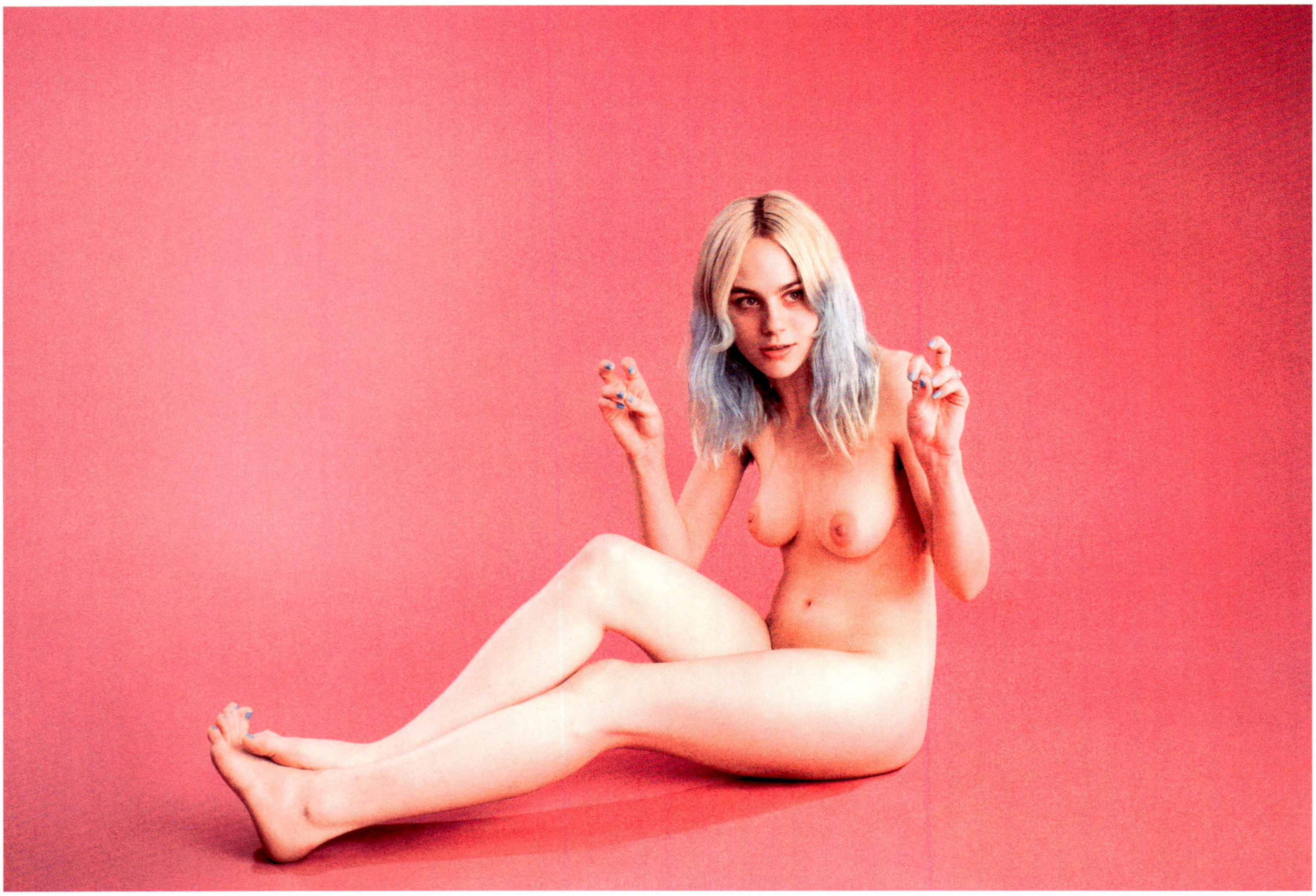

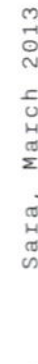

Morgan, March 2016   Sara, March 2013

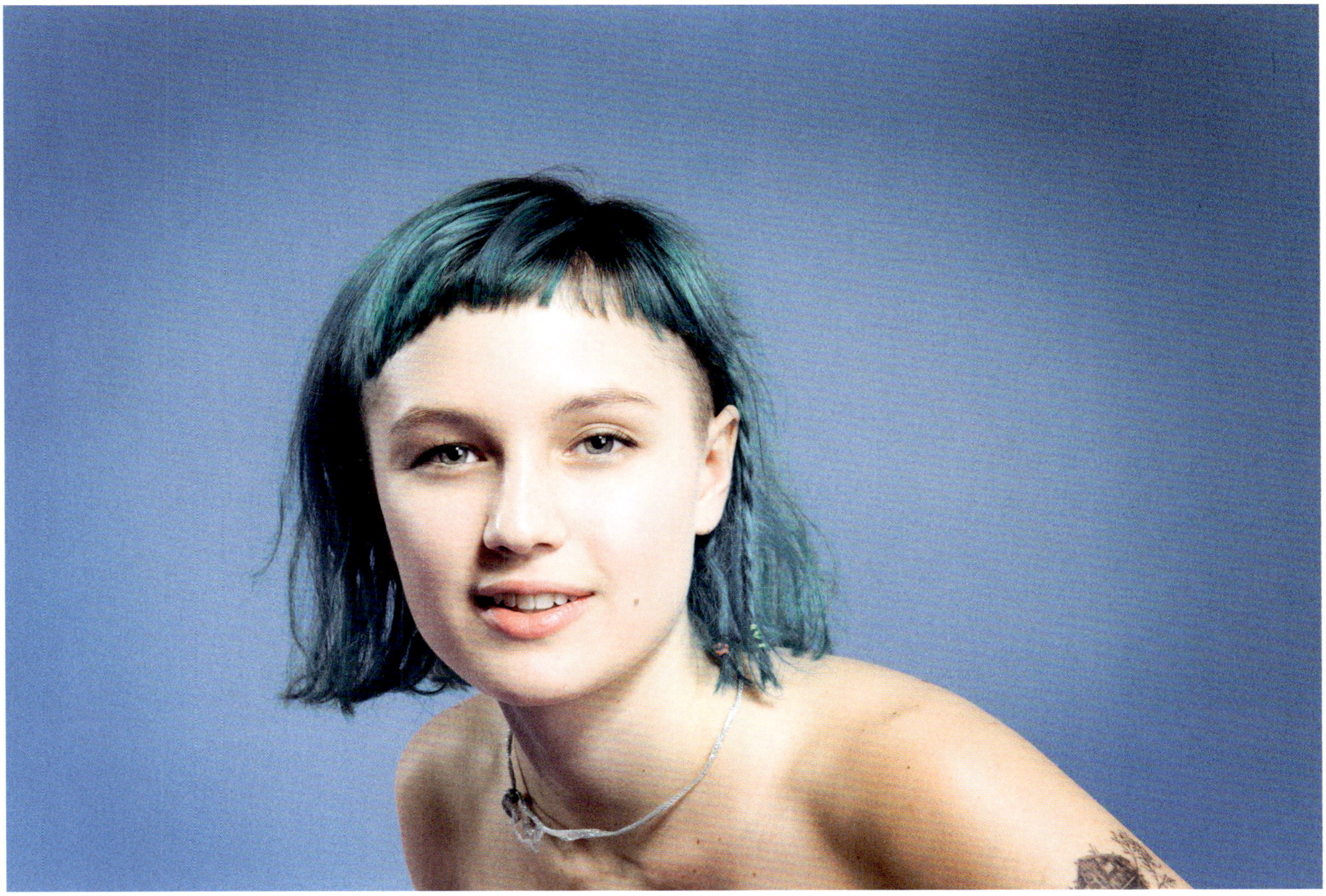

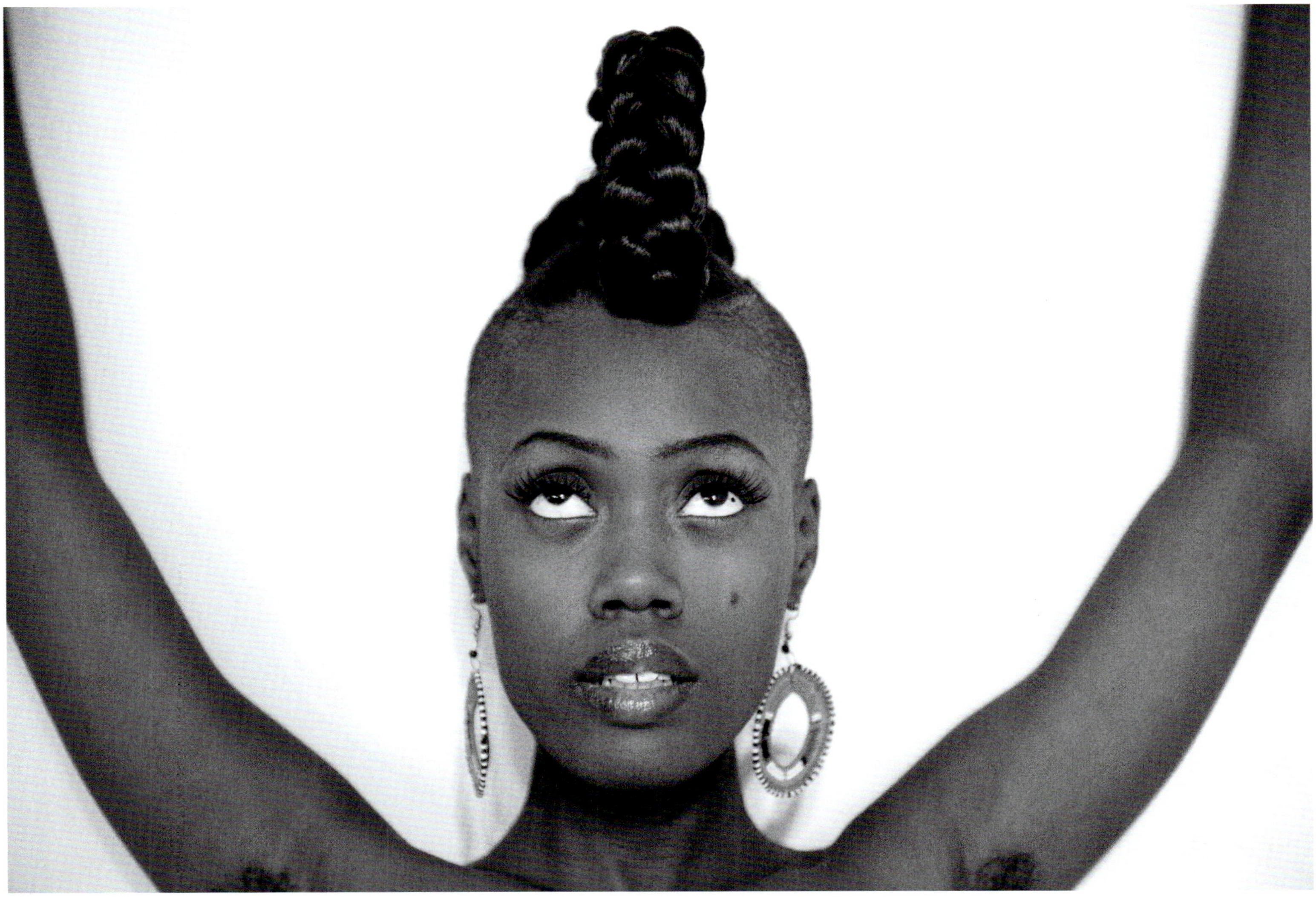

Rebecca, December 2014

Terry, October 2018

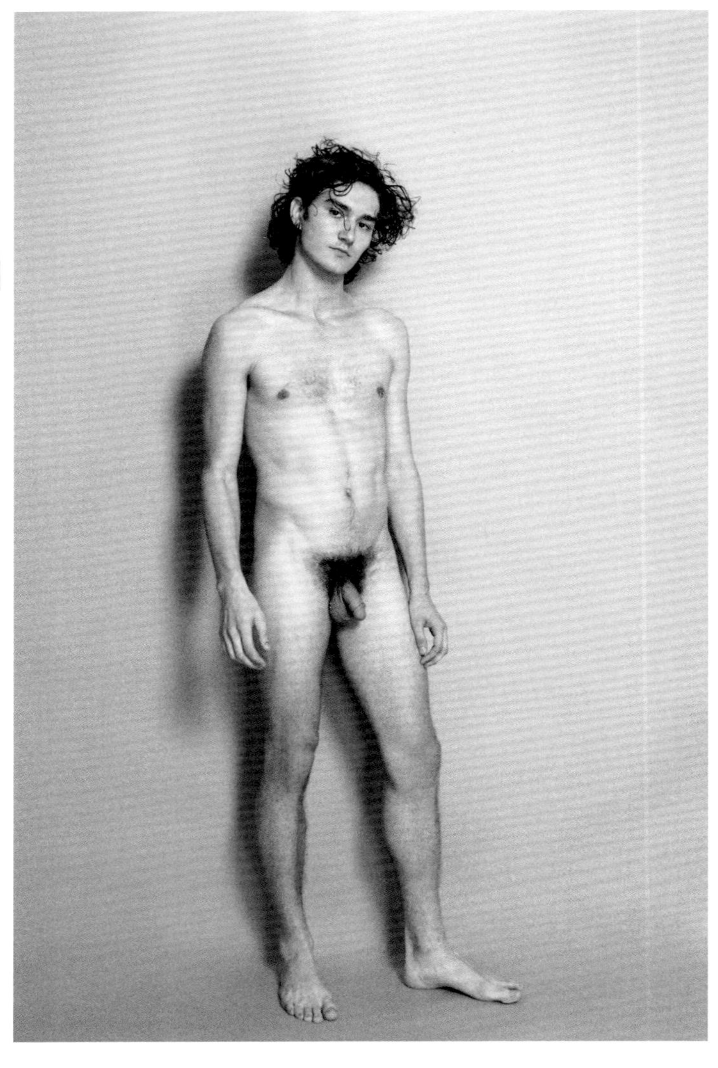

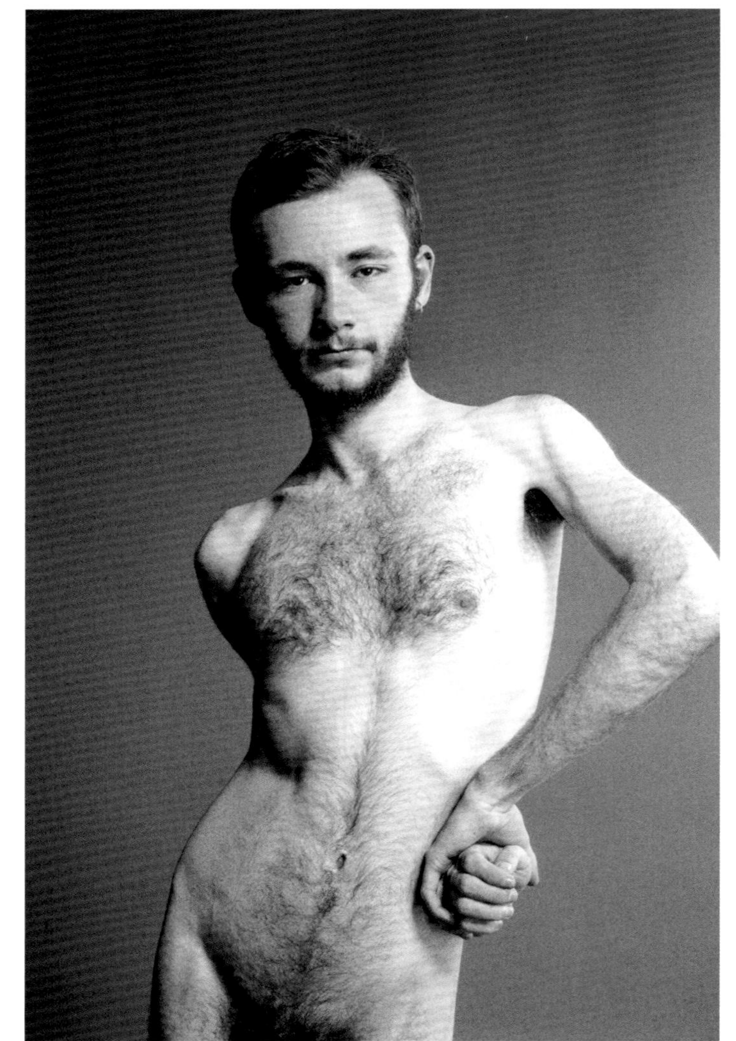

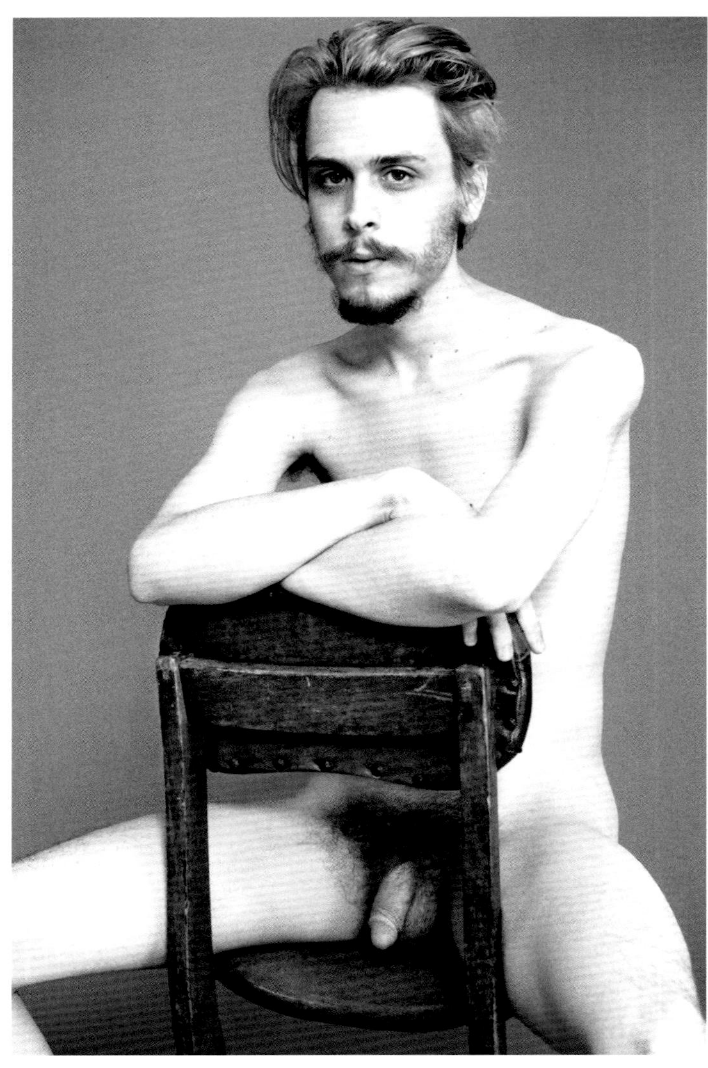

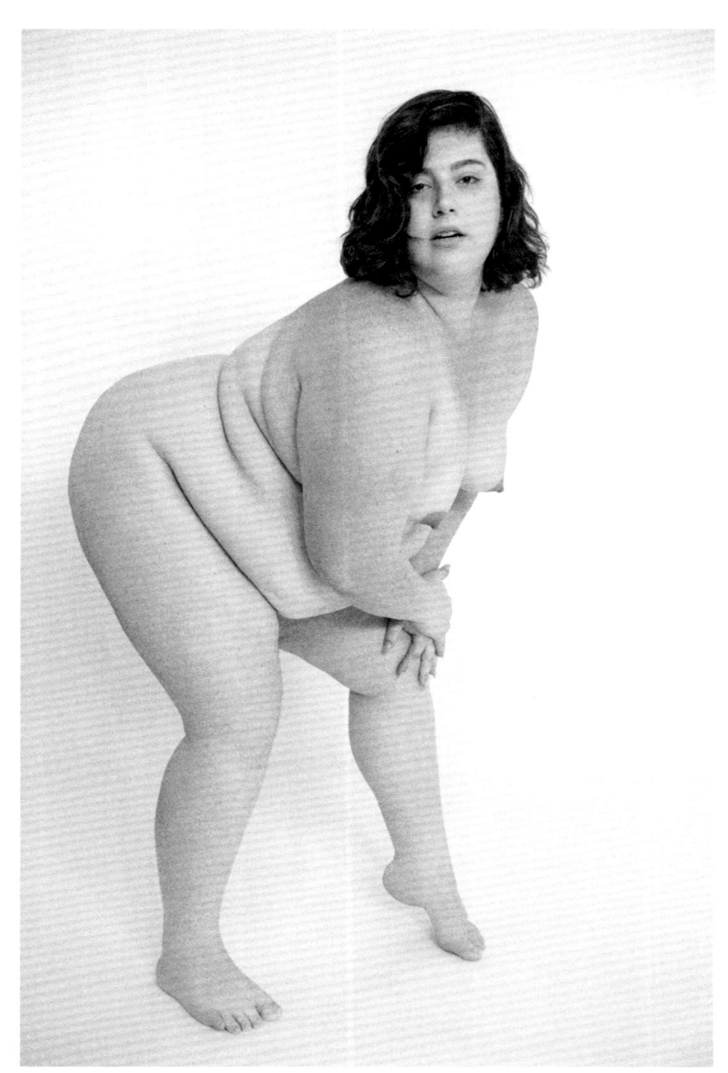

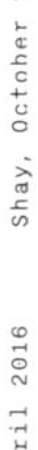

Austin, September 2016   Taylor, April 2015   Christian, April 2016   Shay, October 2019

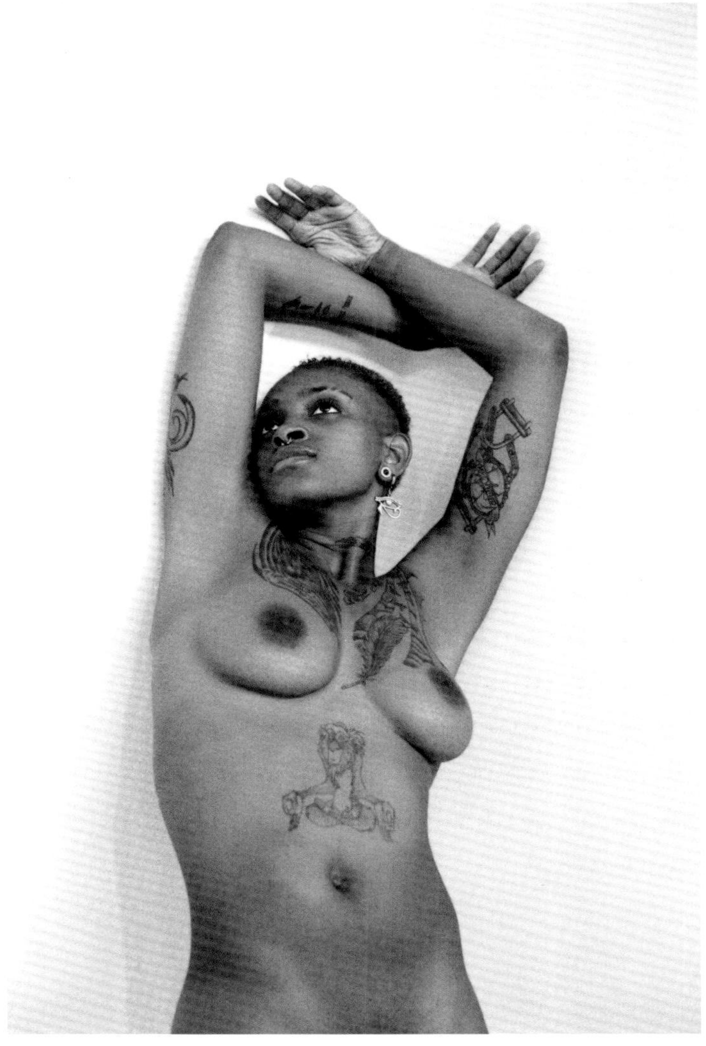

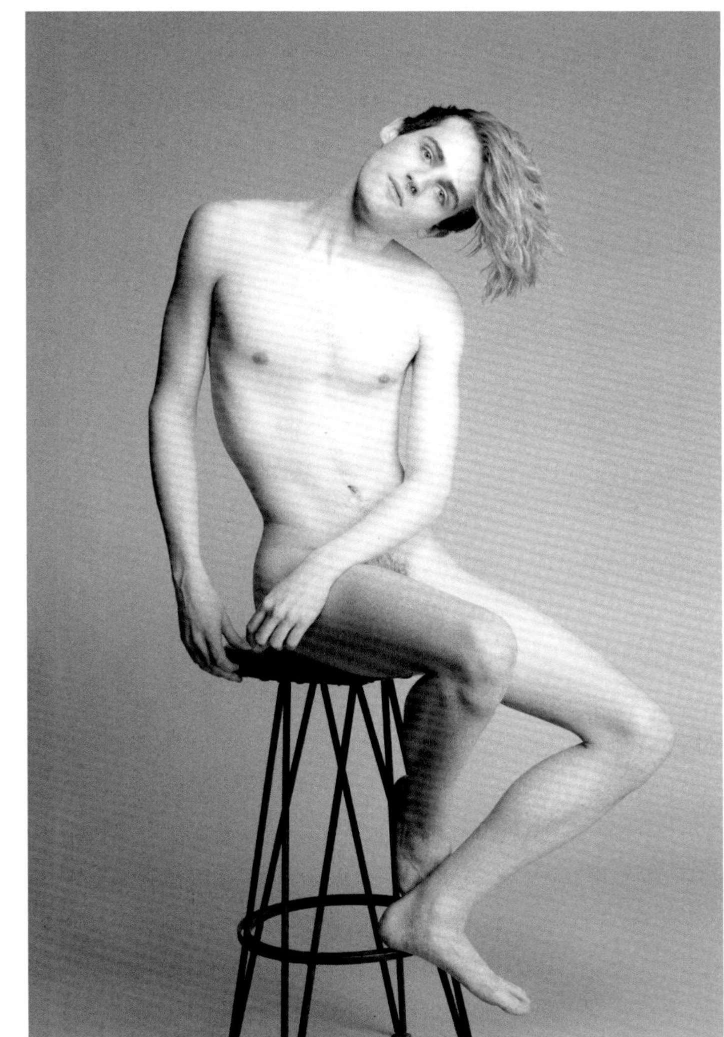

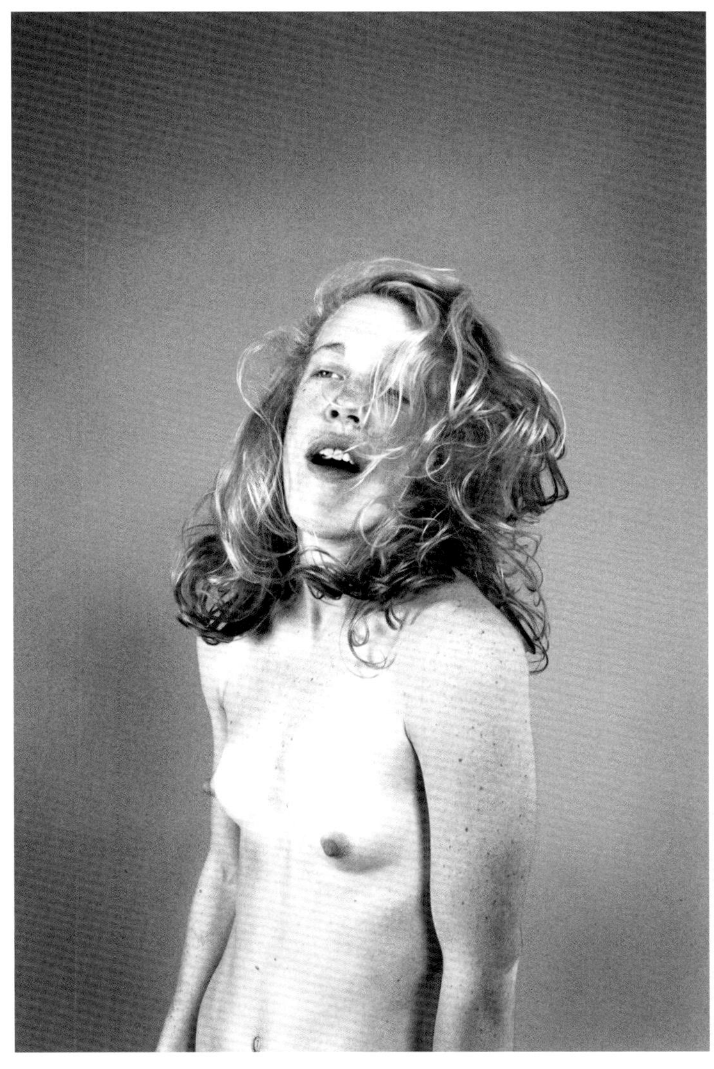

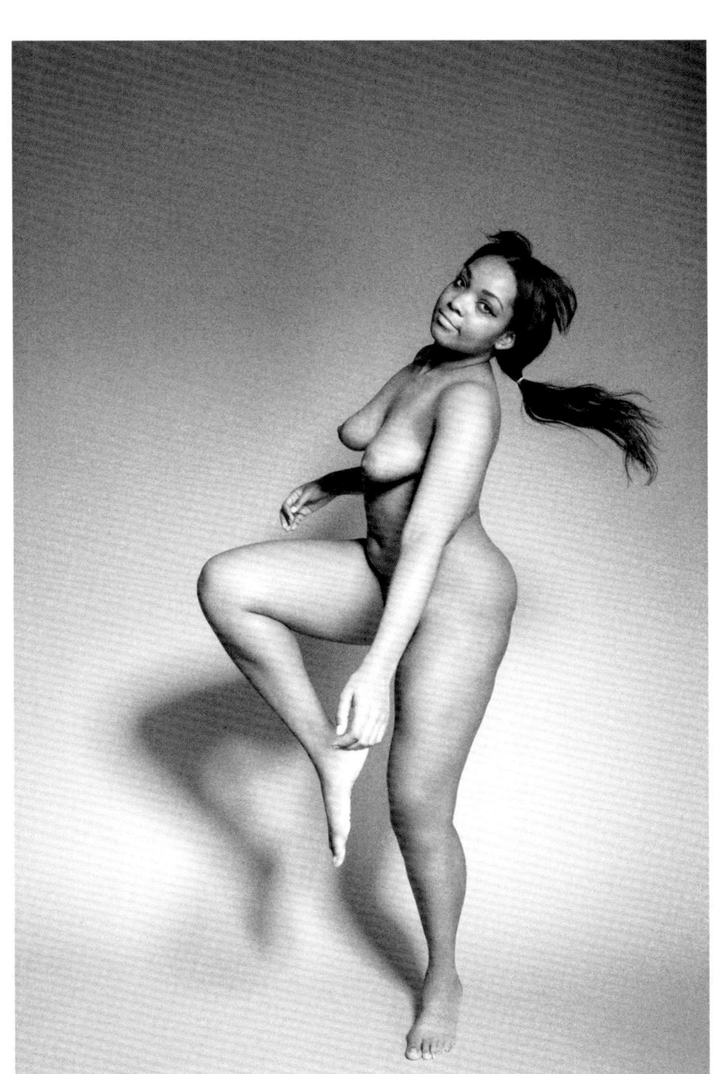

Lia, October 2019 Mark, February 2014 Sarah, October 2012 Tyler, December 2015

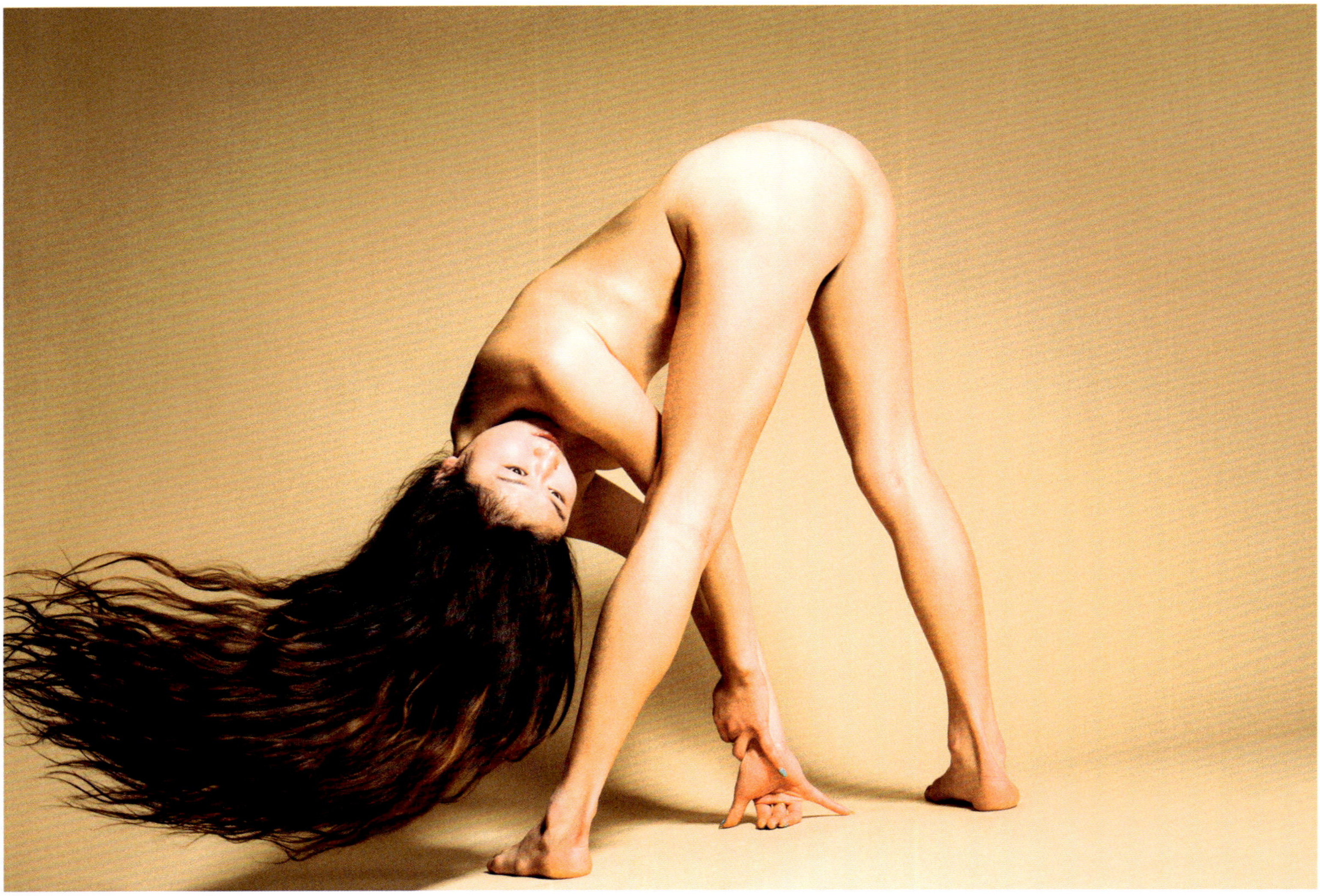

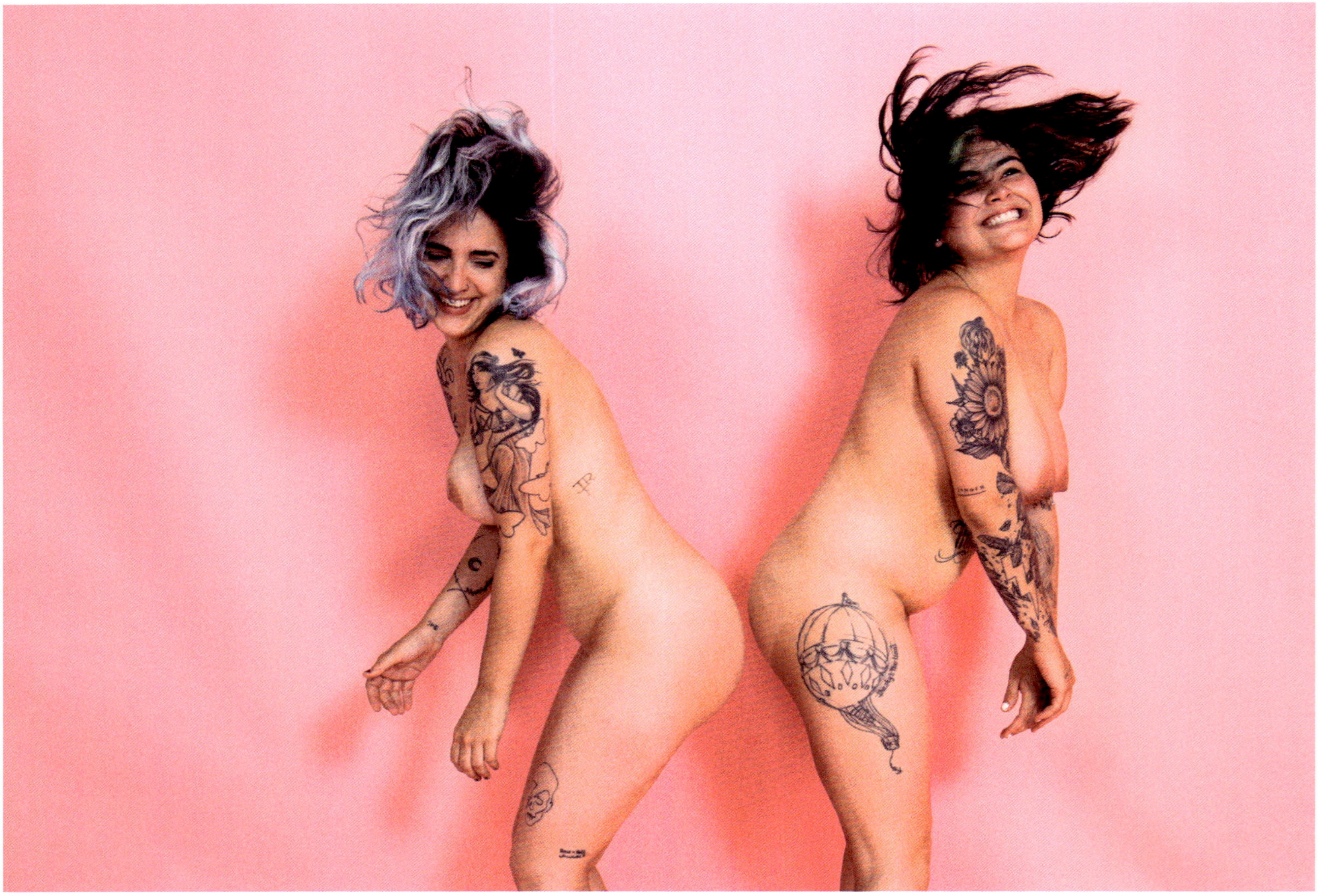

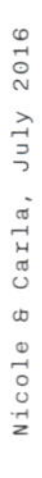

Lee, January 2016

Nicole & Carla, July 2016

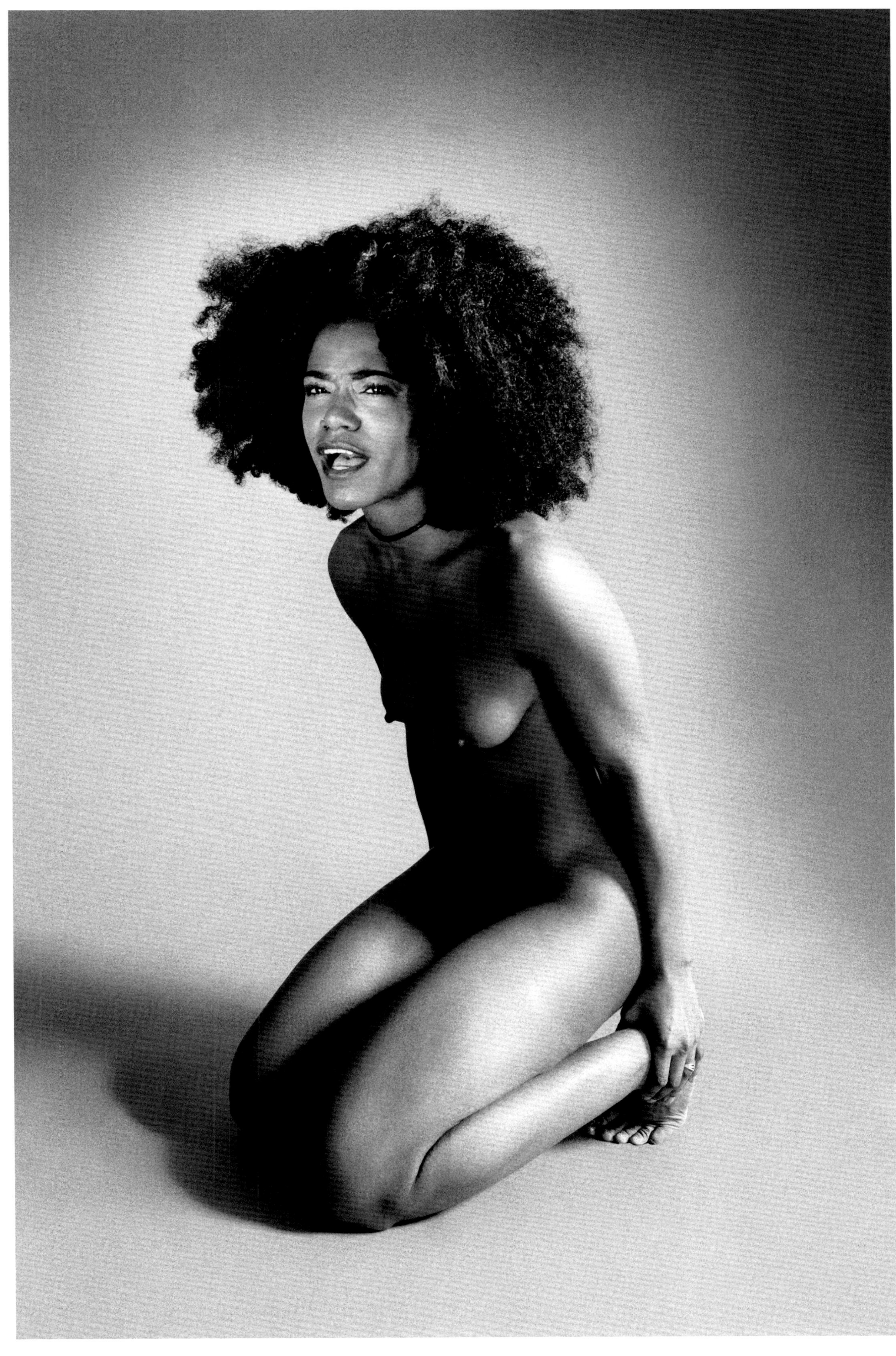

Jade, March 2016

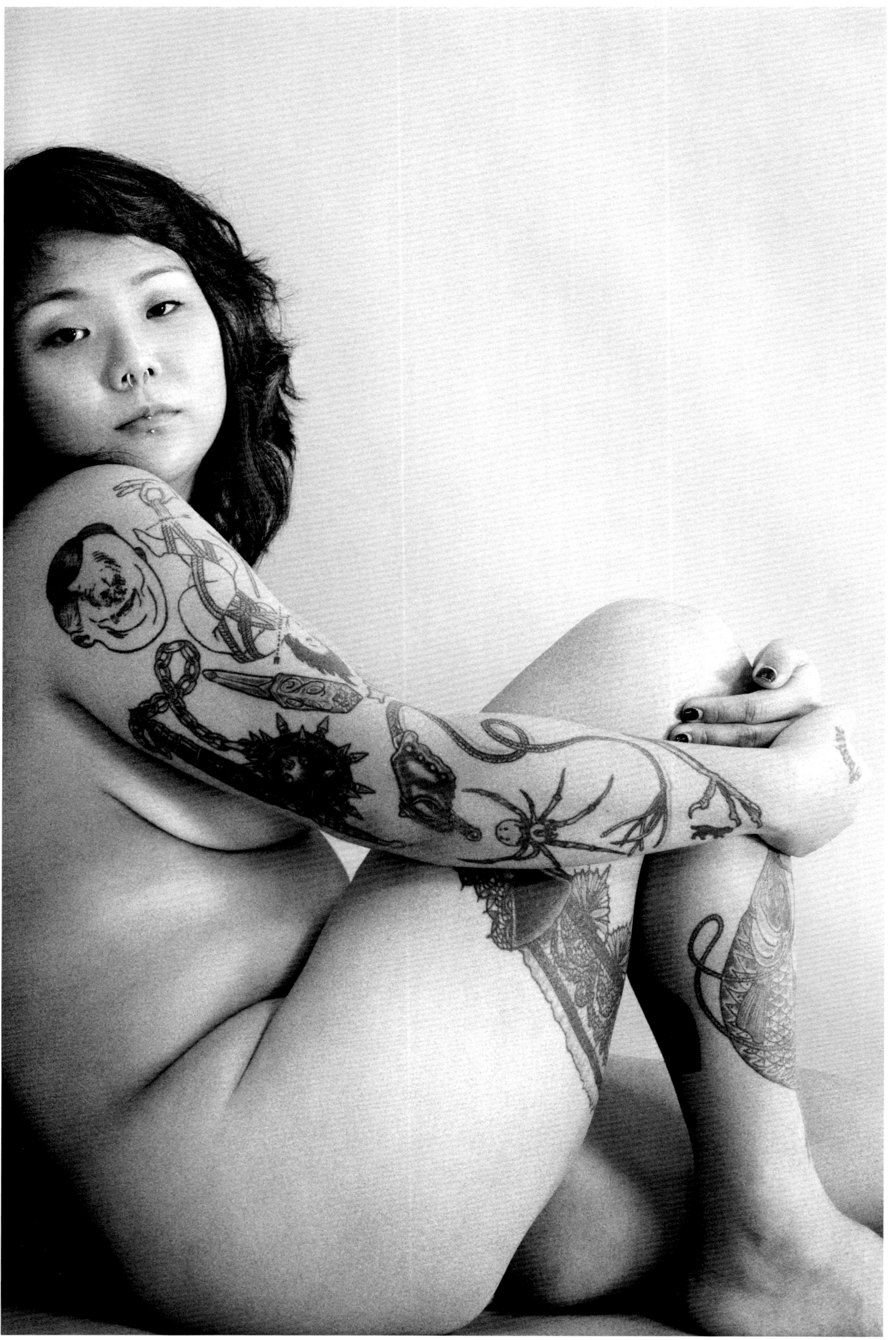

Jinhee, November 2016

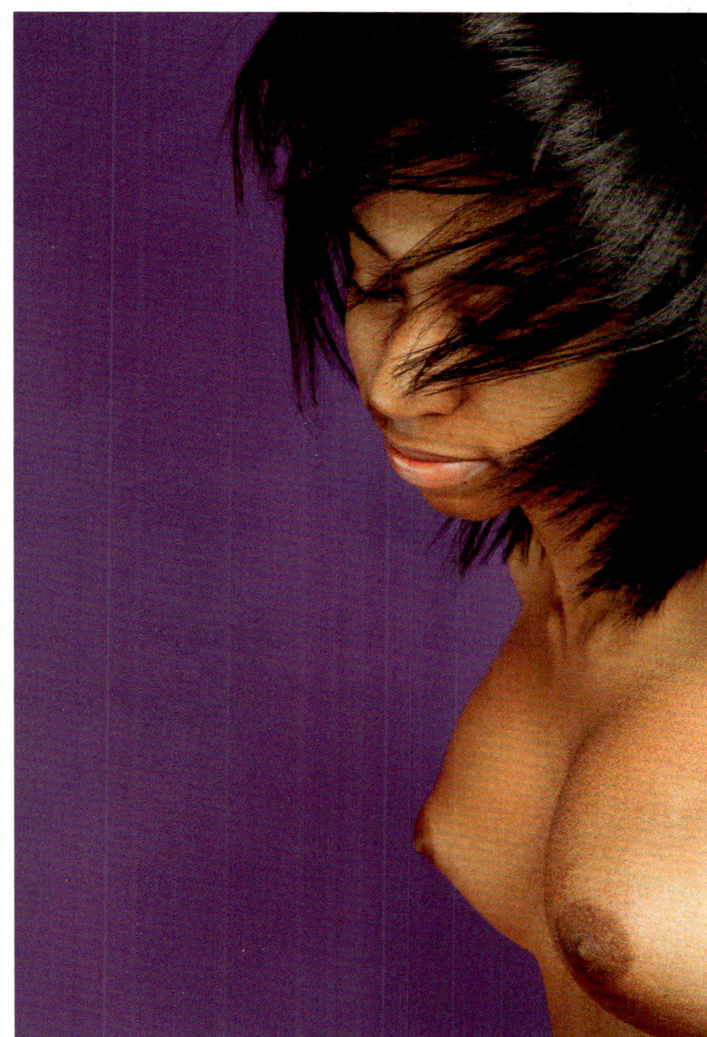

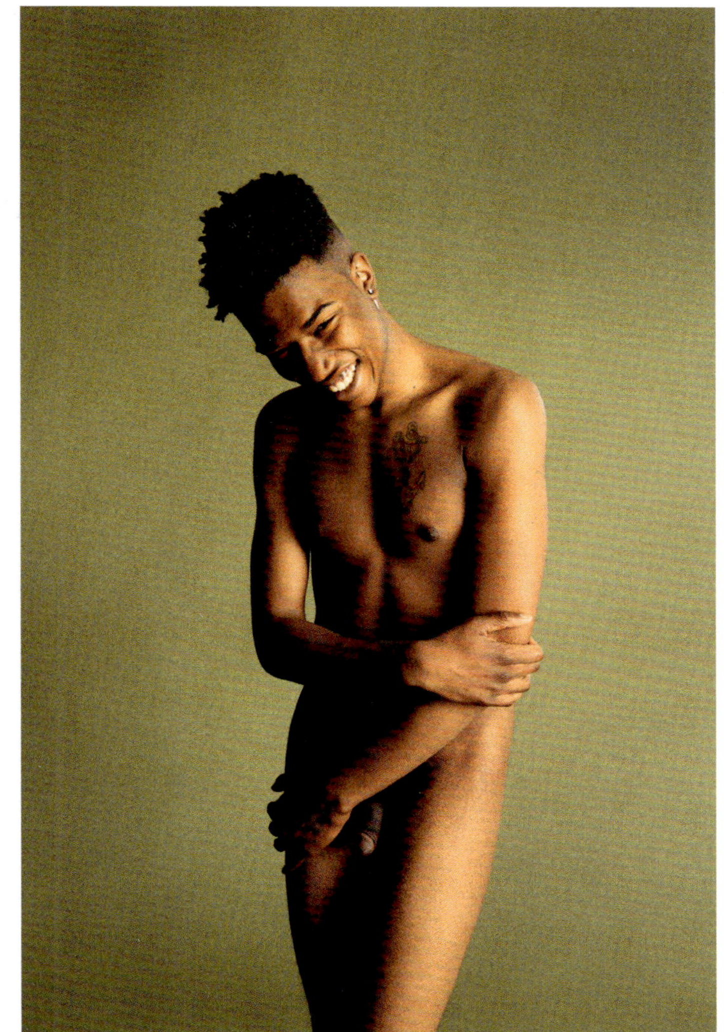

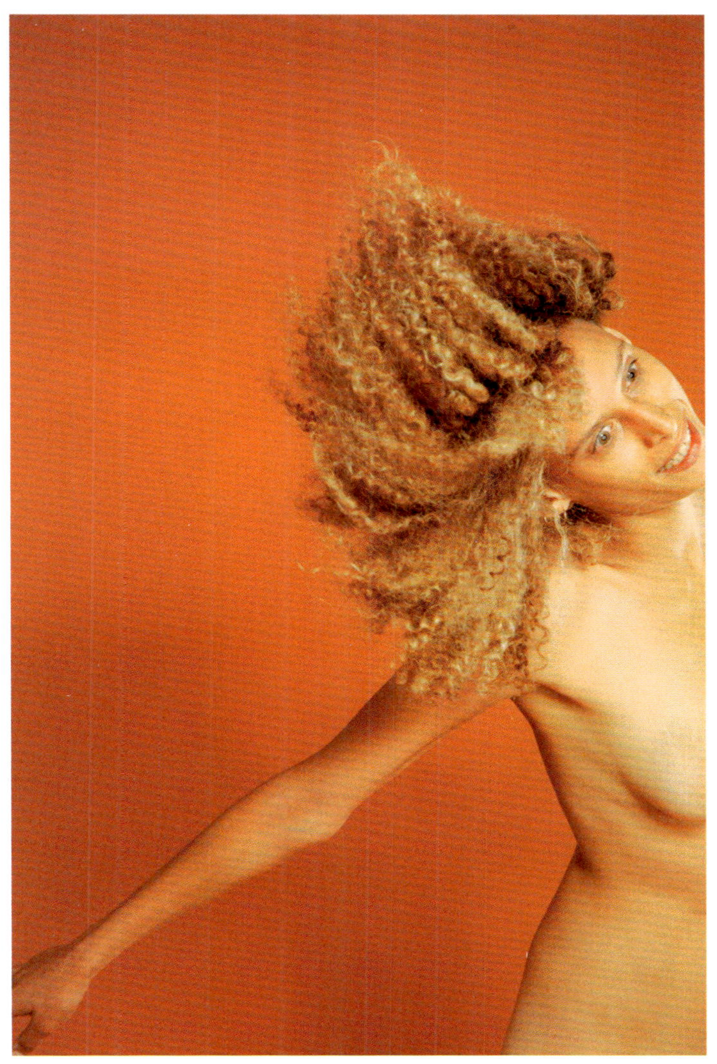

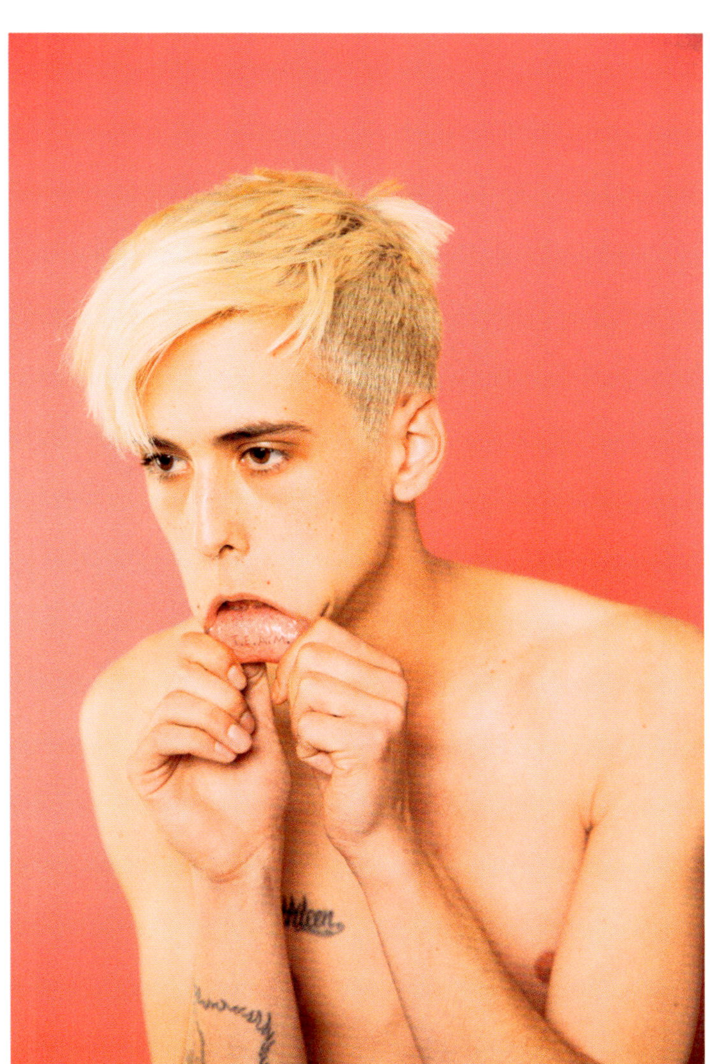

Perris, February 2012   Desmond, August 2014   Ludamilla, August 2012   John, April 2011

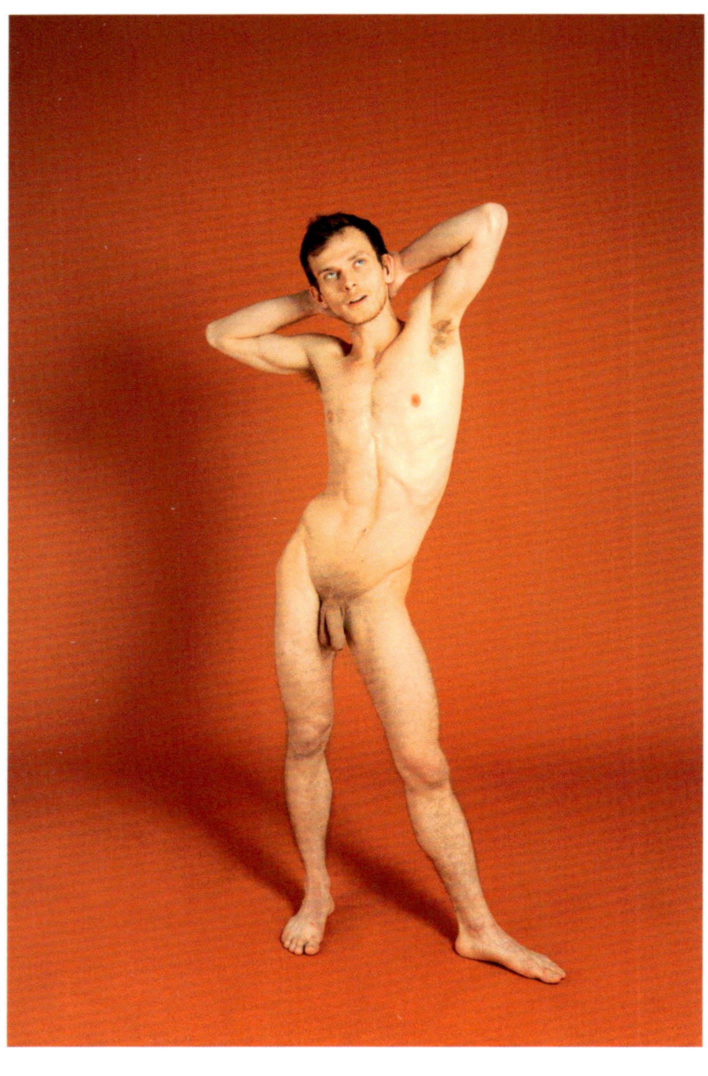

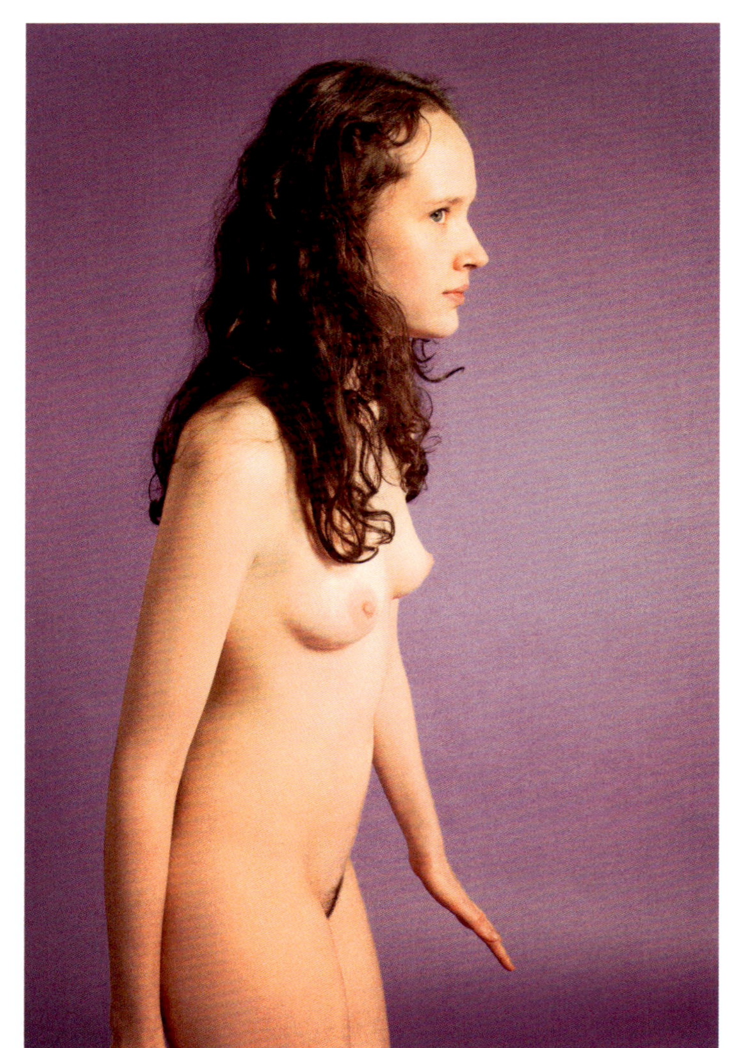

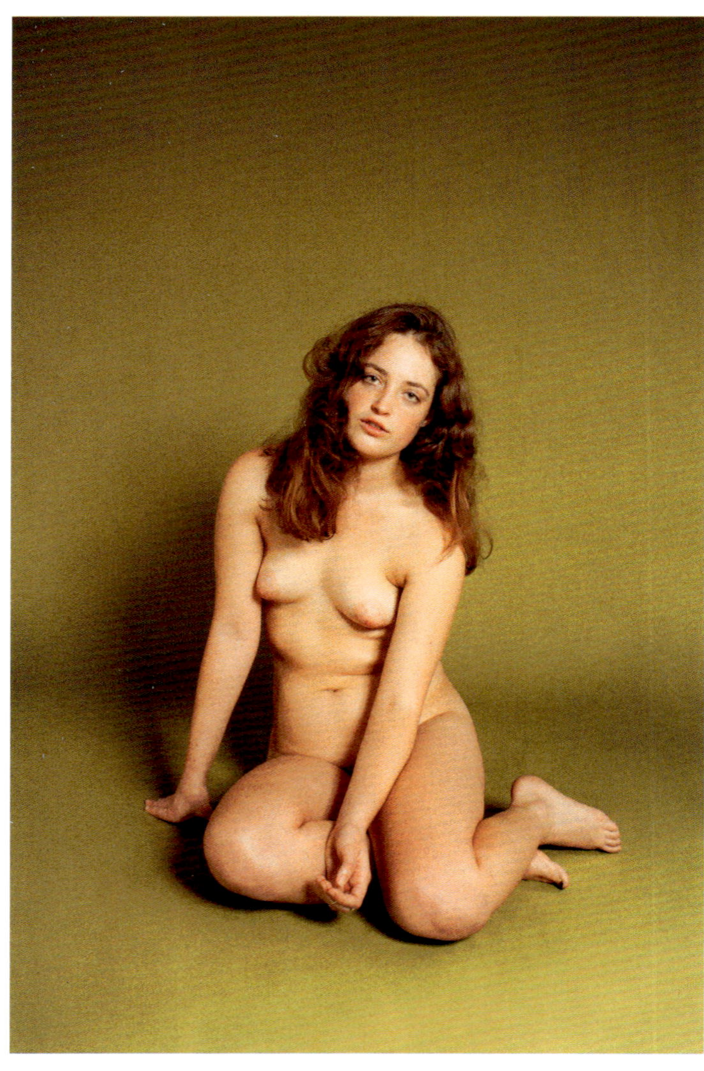

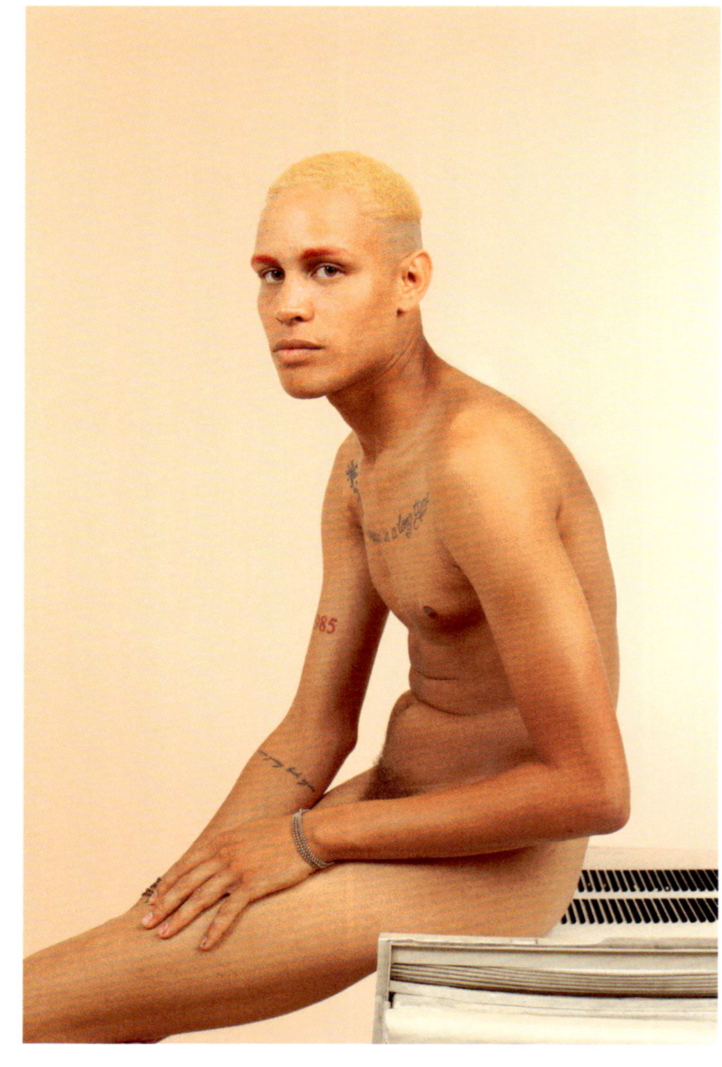

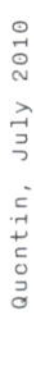

Joseph, June 2012   Charlotte, April 2013   Kelly, October 2012   Quentin, July 2010

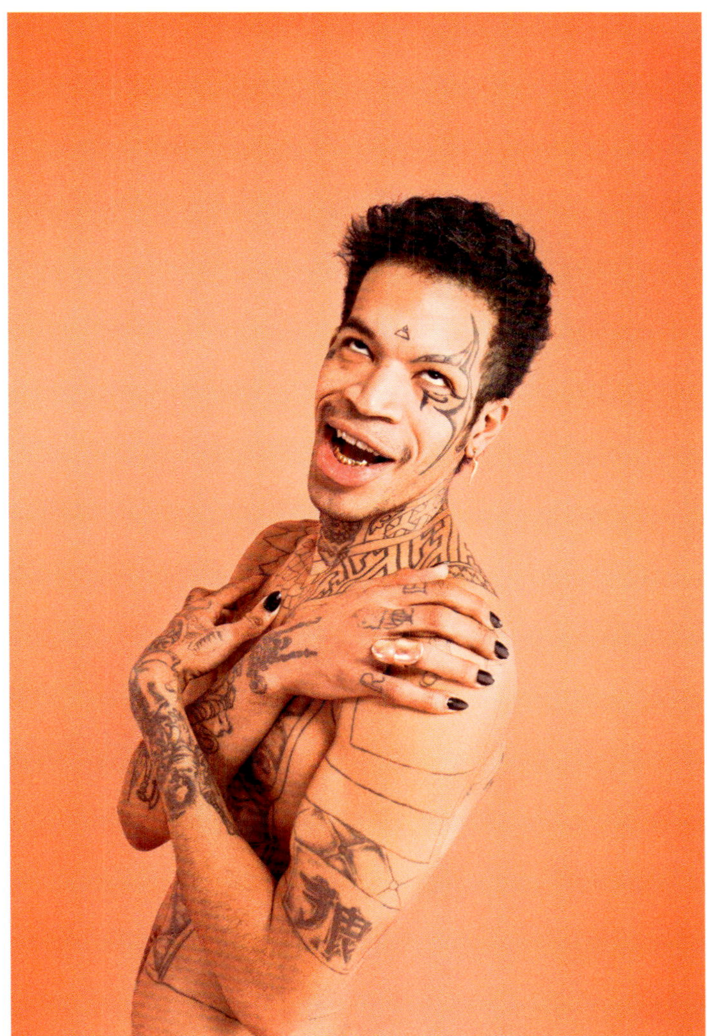

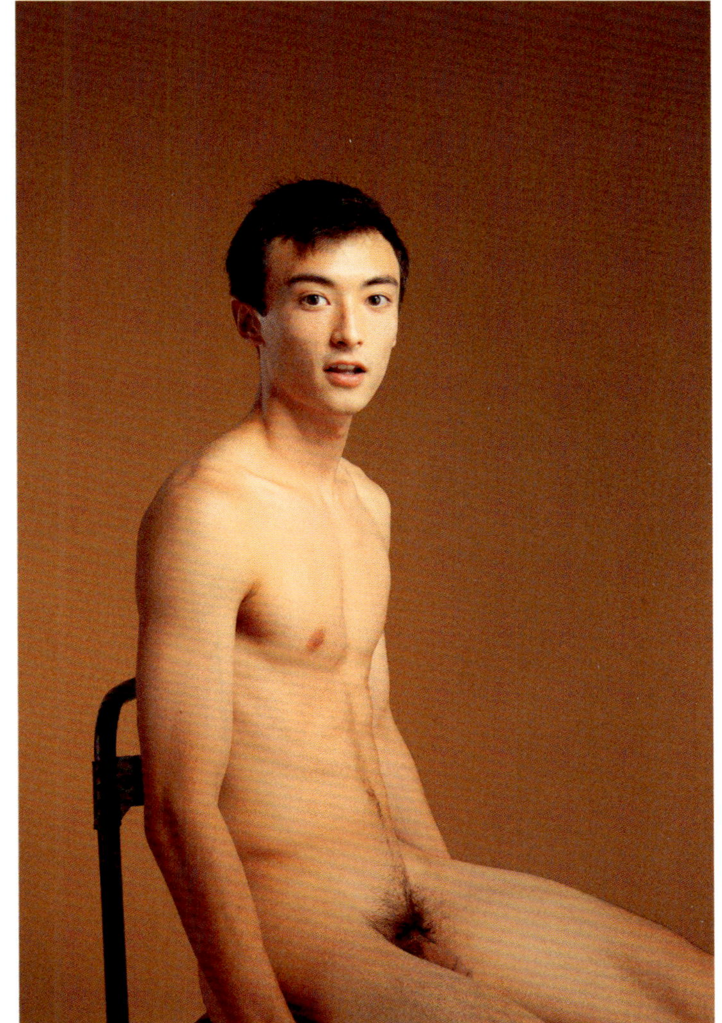

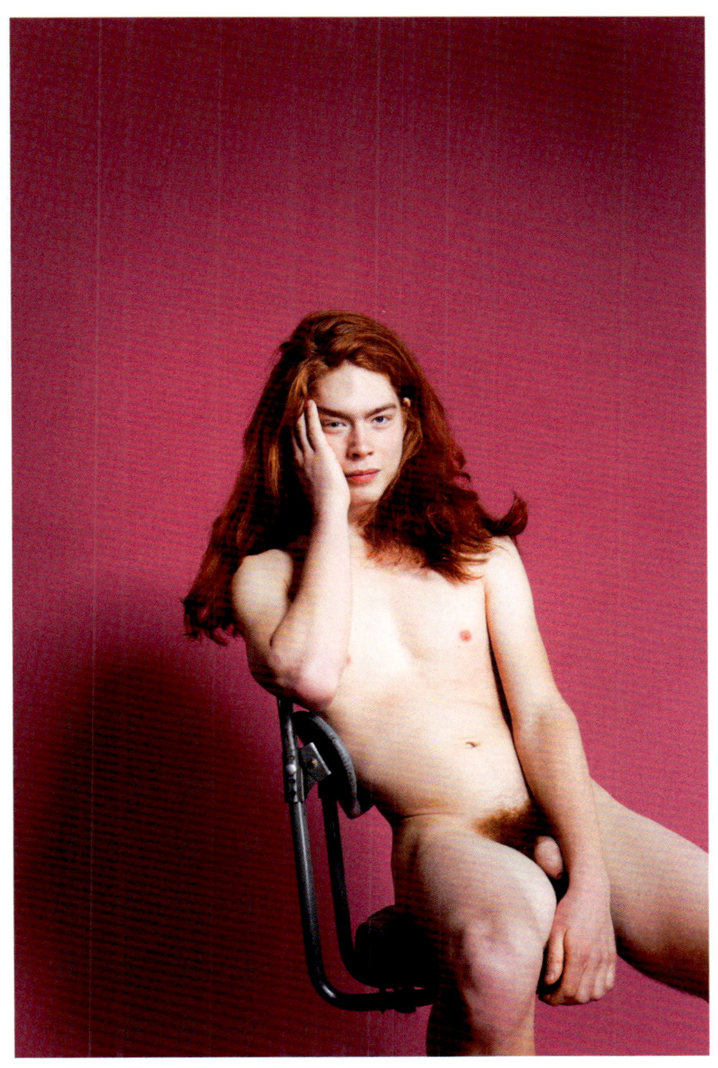

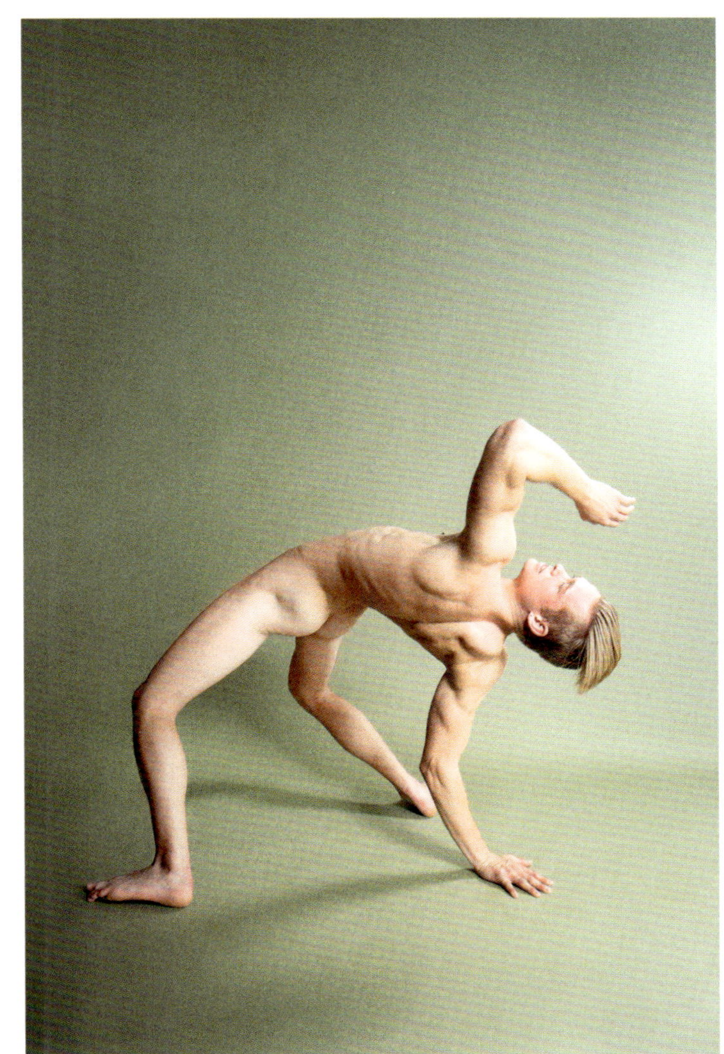

Logan, March 2013 Alex, August 2012 Mato, December 2014 Will, December 2015

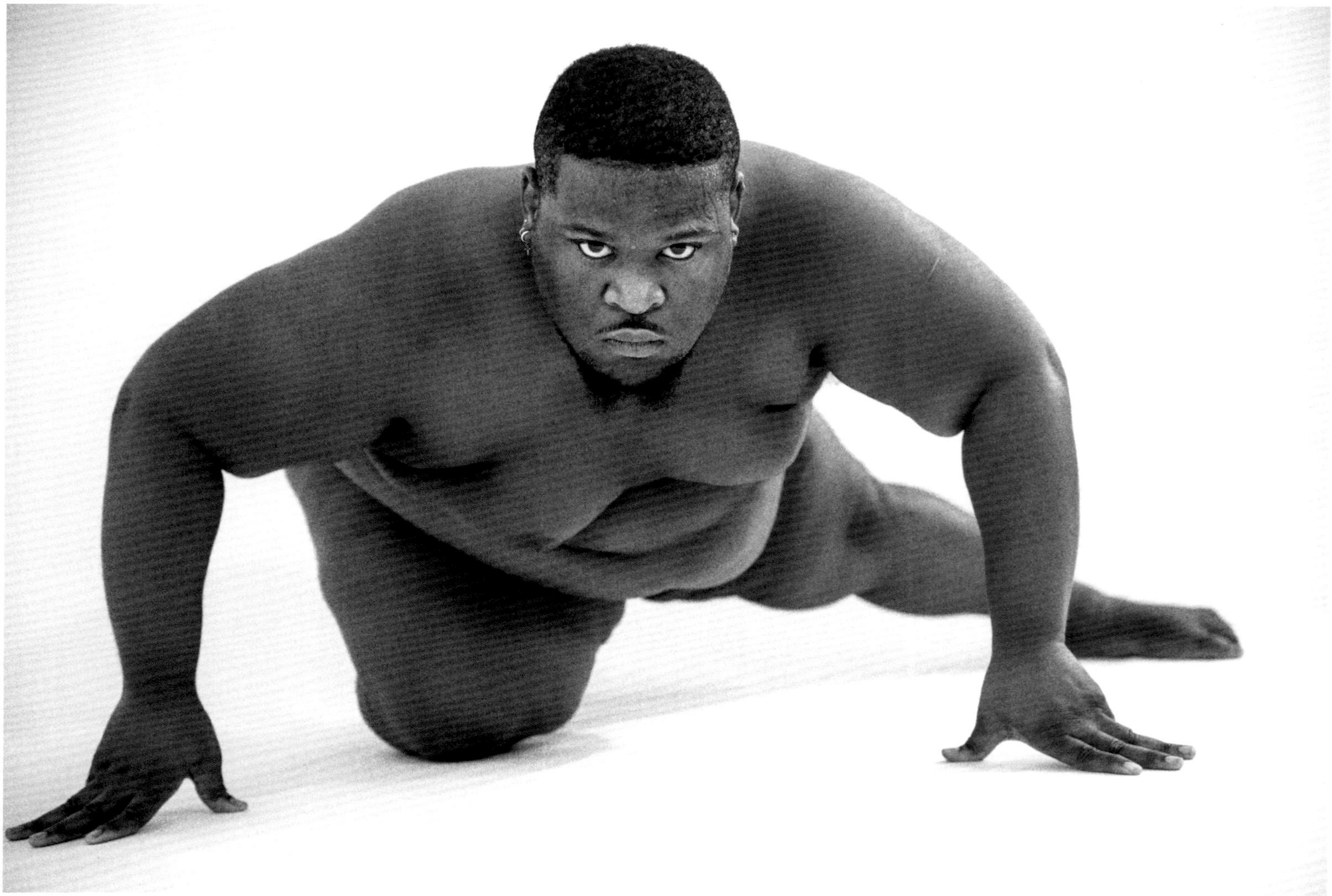

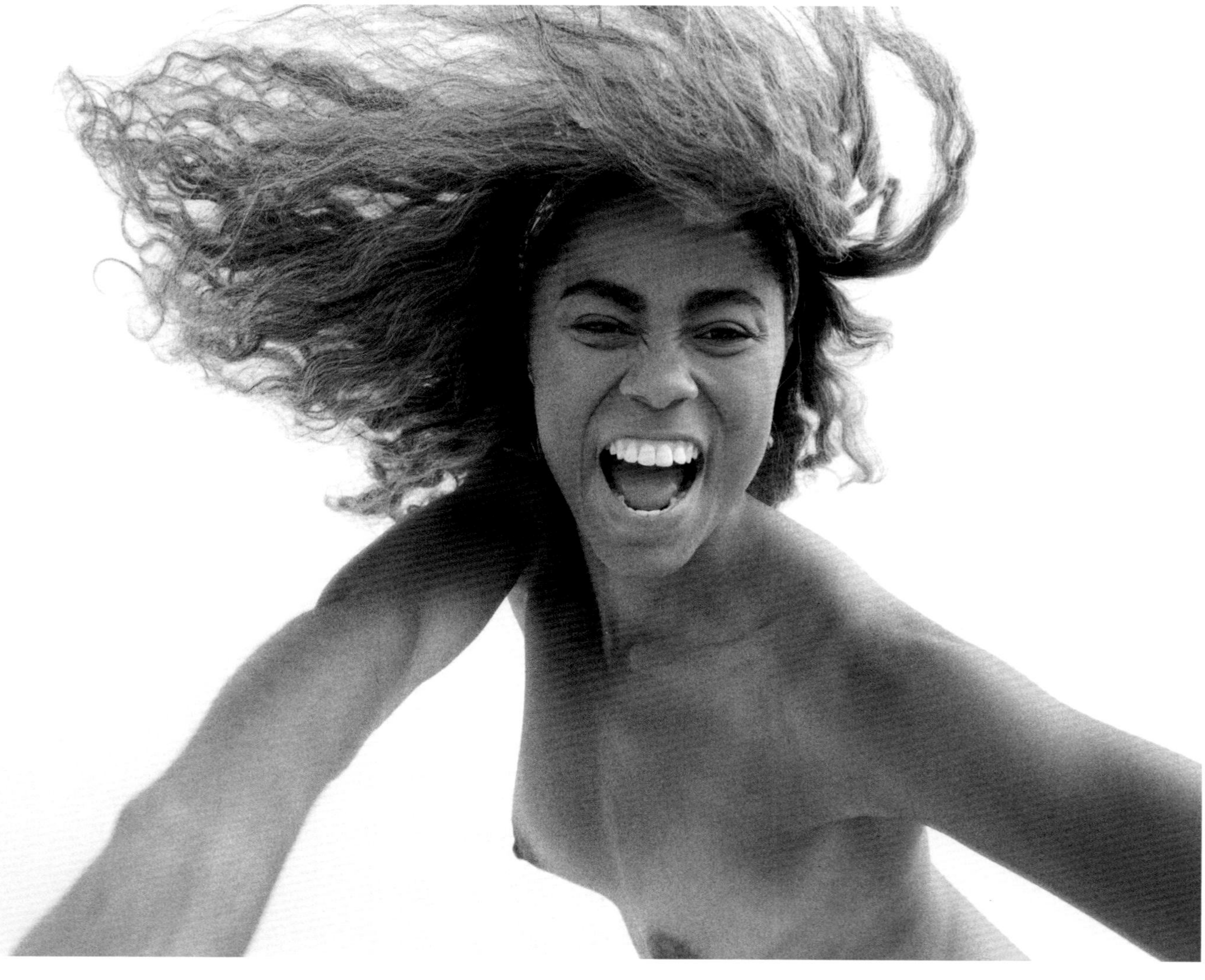

Tevin, December 2018

Devie, September 2017

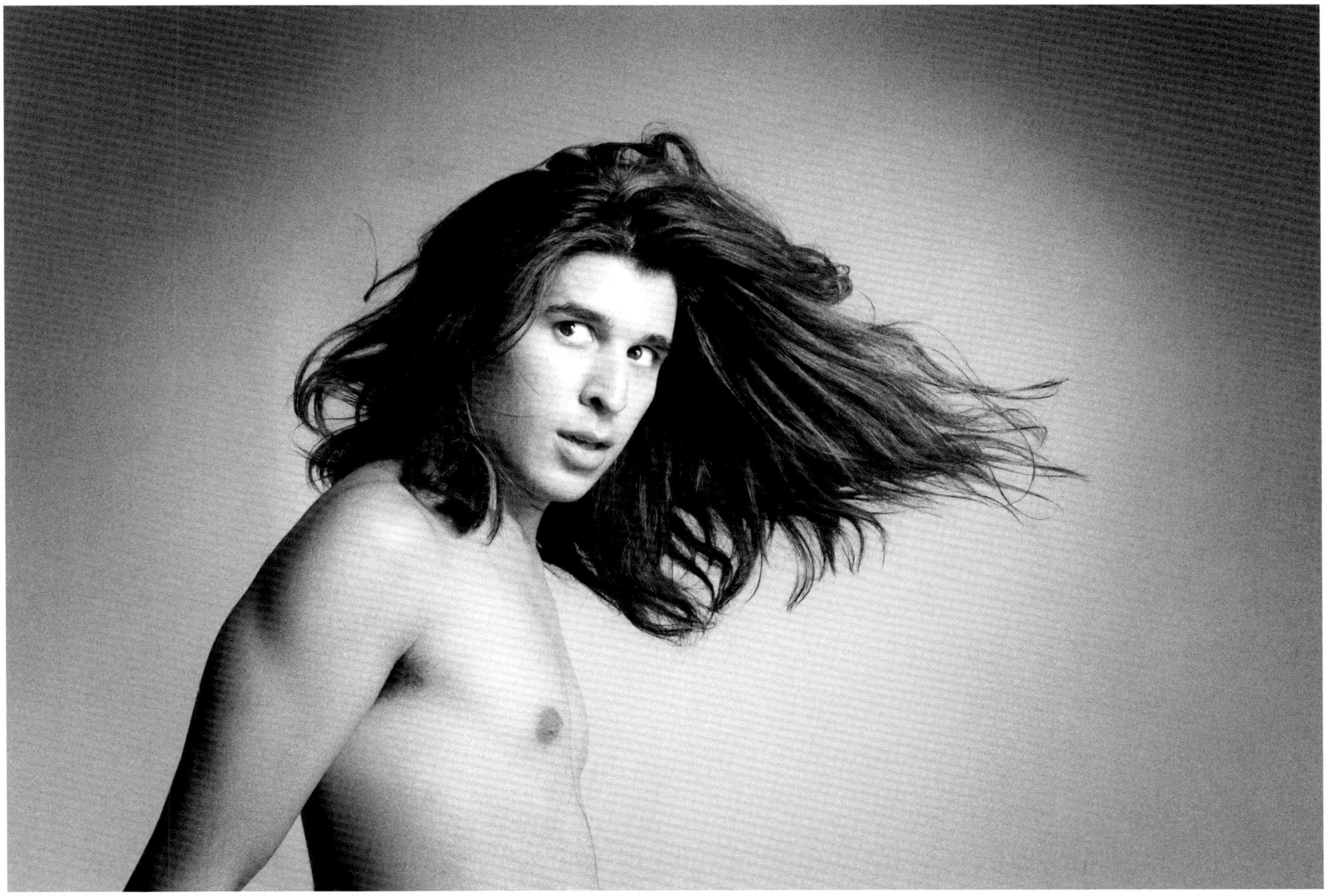

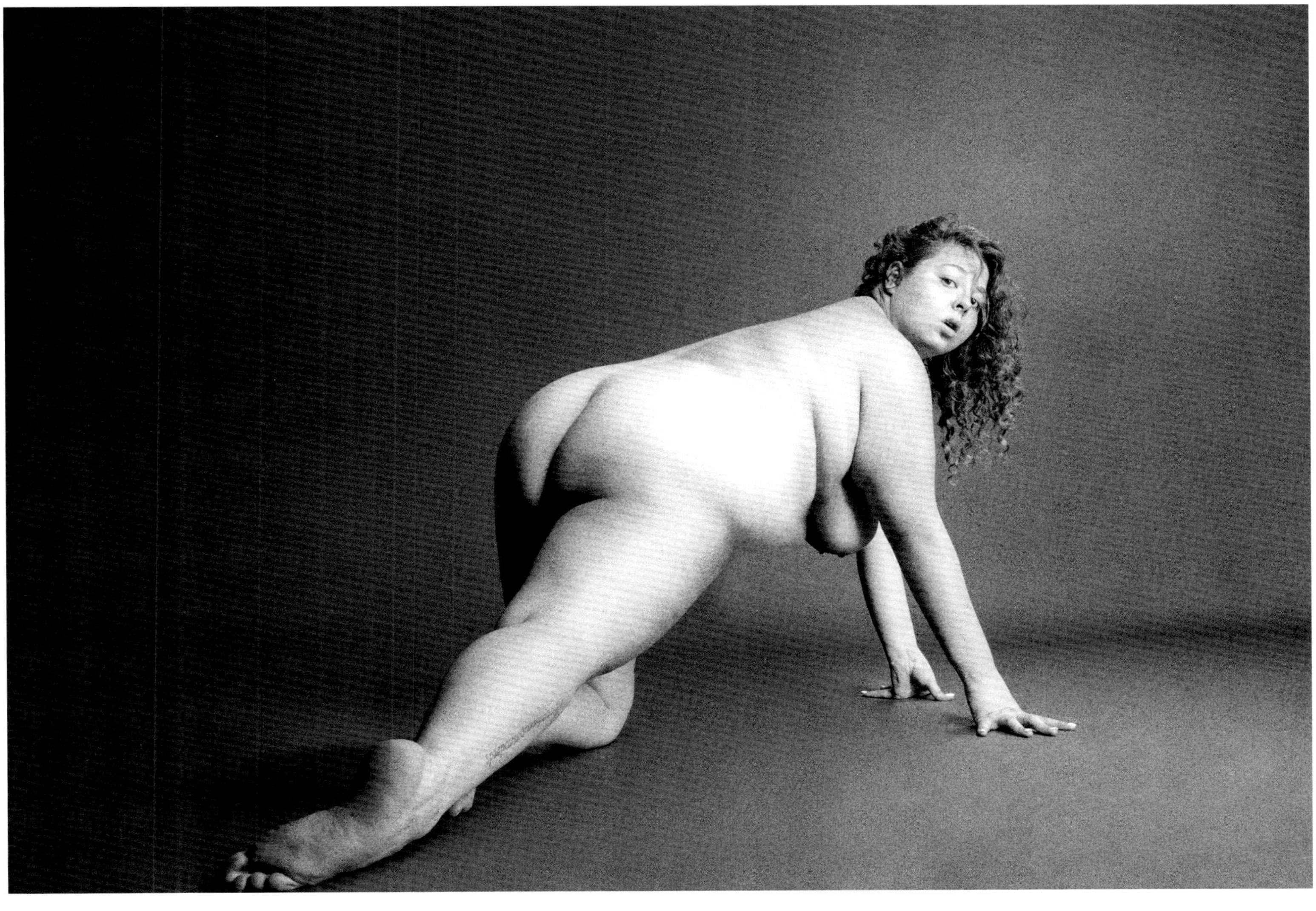

Jose, March 2015

Jewelz, December 2015

It's weird seeing my body with comparatively few tattoos. I'm so covered now: full back, all of my chest, my neck, my arms. I must have over one hundred tattoos, but I don't think about them so much as individuals. I see a total composition and spaces that I need to fill in. I see the negative space. Getting tattooed was something that I was super interested in from a young age. I grew up going to an all-girls Catholic school. We had a uniform and a really strict dress code. We couldn't dye our hair, we couldn't get piercings. I was desperate for just an ounce of bodily autonomy. So as soon as I turned eighteen, that week, I got my first tattoo. It was the first time I'd experienced being able to make a choice for my own body that couldn't be taken away by someone else.

The permanence felt really important; it was unable to be reversed by an external party. Getting tattooed also felt important to me as a way to express my gender. When I was that young, I couldn't necessarily access other types of gender-affirming care, but I was able to access getting tattooed, getting piercings, whatever.

As I got older, I started seeing more and more people relating to getting tattooed in the same way that I did. So I started tattooing, wanting to provide that experience. I was bad at drawing and had little interest in the more artistic element of tattooing. I just knew the process and intimacy of being able to go to someone who you feel comfortable with, or share an identity with, while getting tattooed.

I've been tattooing full-time for roughly nine years now. I do a lot of figurative work that I've described as really gay woodcuts. I also do super big animals and wiggly, loose-line drawings. This photo was taken around the time that I moved into my first tattoo studio. I was working alongside other artists, leaving my little bedroom, trying to take it more seriously. That was a cool time for the industry in general. There were a lot more DIY, self-taught, and queer tattooers starting to gain recognition. Suddenly, all of these spaces popped up with a much more diverse roster of artists doing their best to provide a more comfortable and trauma-informed environment for clients.

Trauma-informed tattooing can be as basic as asking before you touch someone or checking in throughout the process. It's about acknowledging that your client is not a canvas; your client is a person with a body and a history, and they might have emotional or physical needs during the session.

Everyone says tattoos are addictive. At least half of my weeks are always scheduled with returning clients, so there might be something to that. There's the physical sensation and the euphoria you get from the endorphins and the adrenaline. There's the power of changing your body in a way that you have control over.

With tattoos, I feel like people always say, "Oh, what is it going to look like when you turn fifty?" I always think, if a tattoo is the thing that I like least about my body when I turn fifty, then that's awesome. That means I'm doing great in terms of overall self-esteem. Also, if I turn fifty, that's really awesome. What a blessing to be able to age.

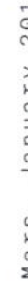

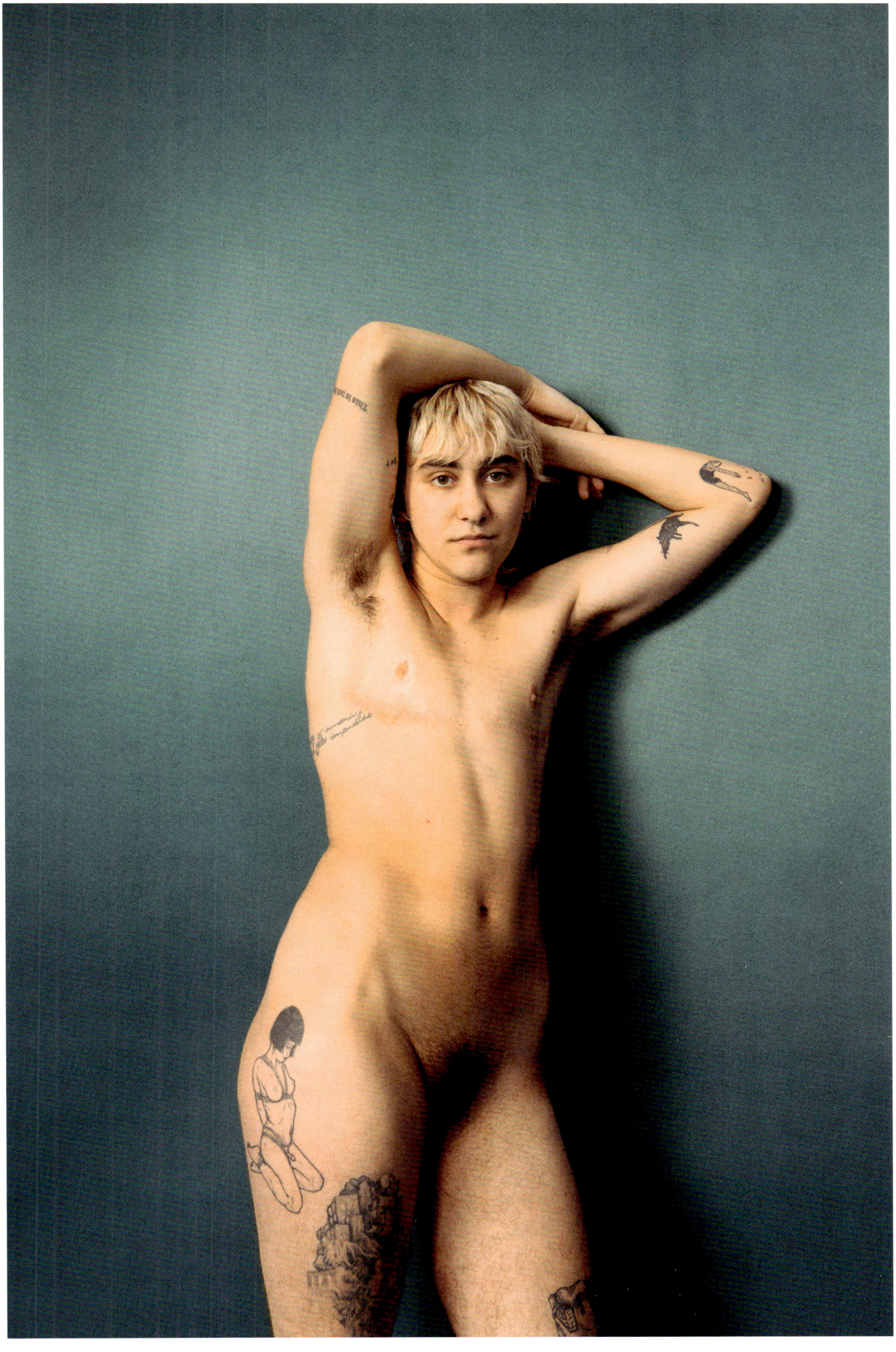

Mars, January 2017

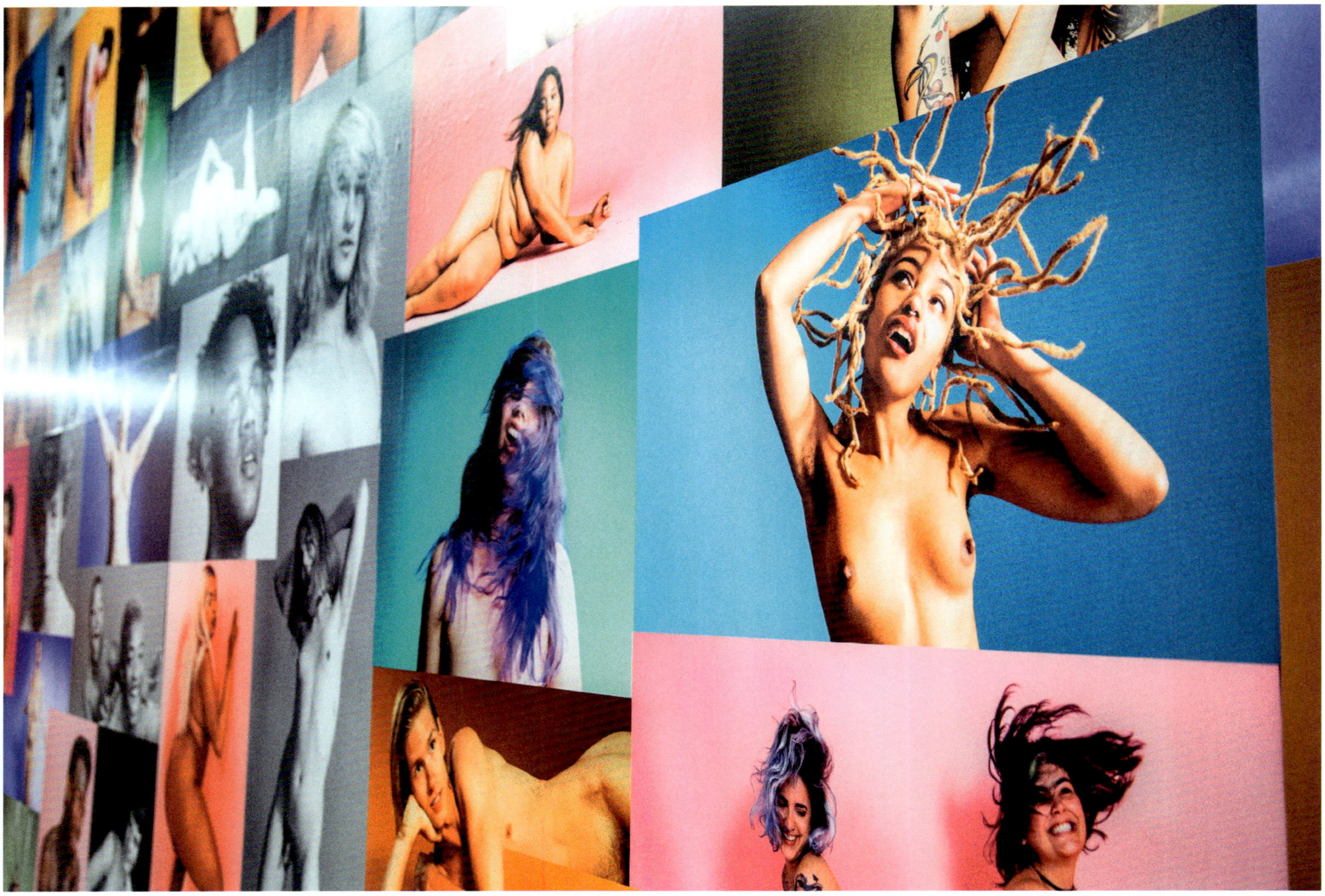

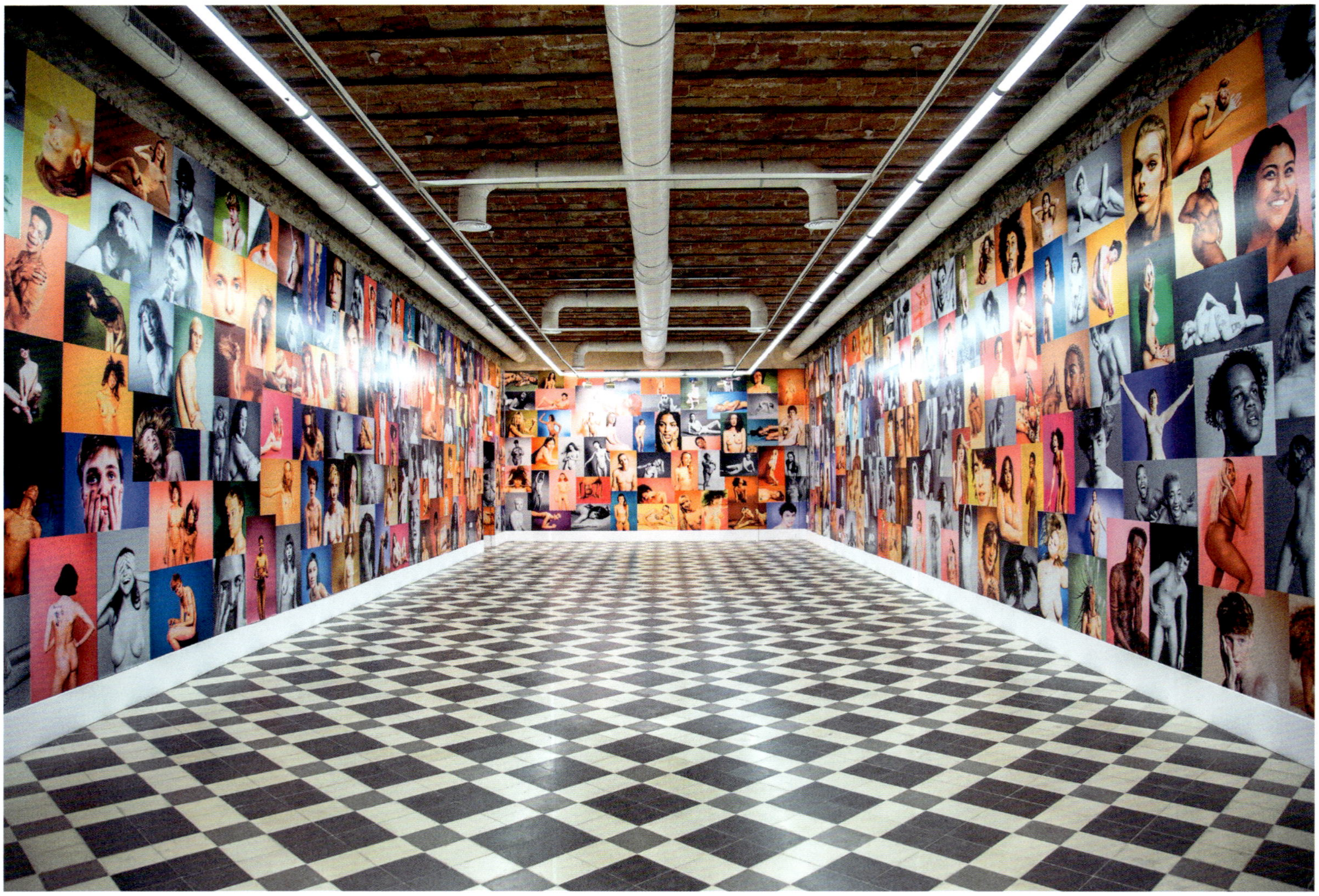

La Termica Museum, Spain, 2017

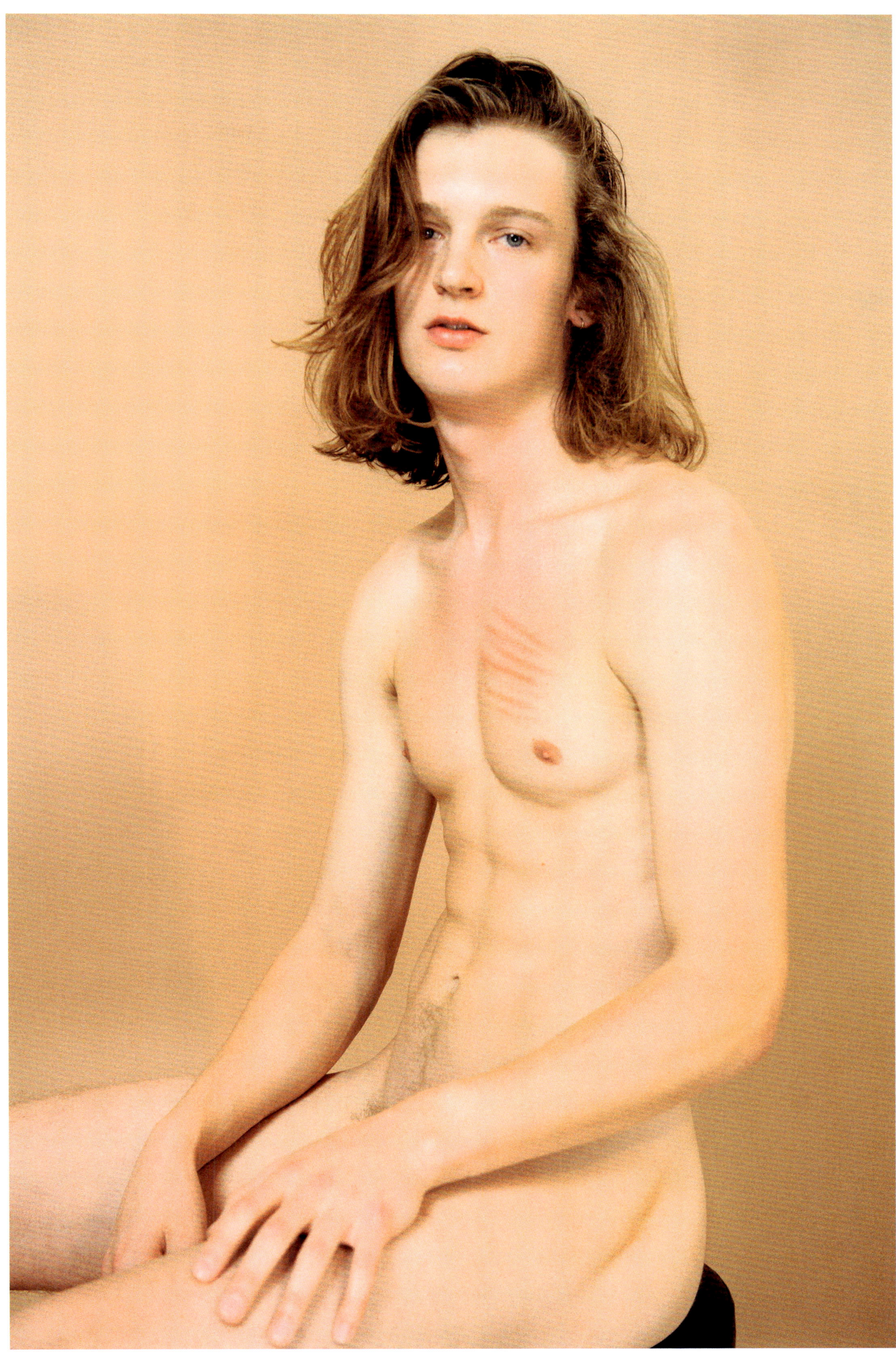

Sam, November 2016

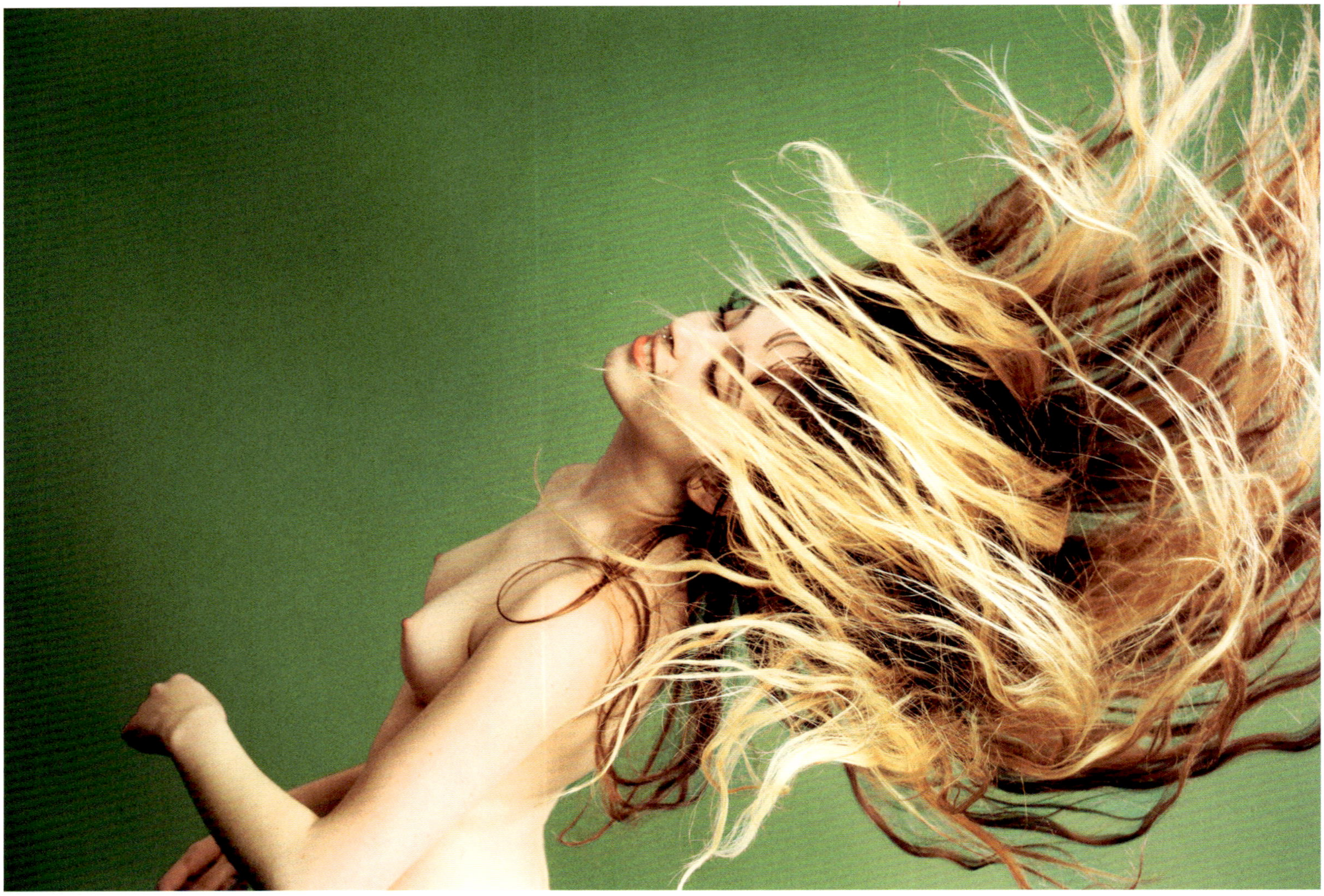

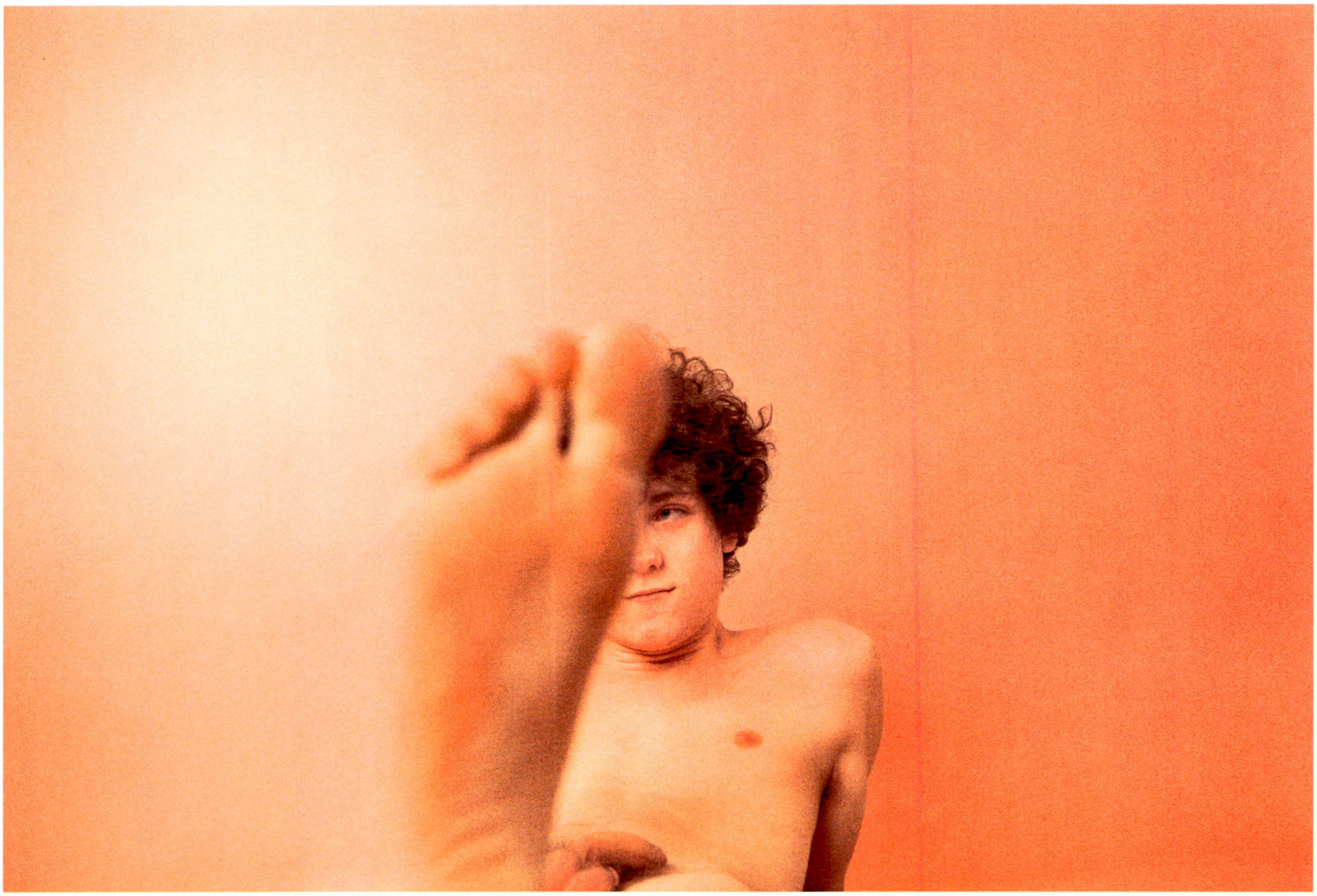

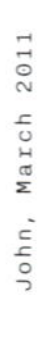

Nika, May 2014

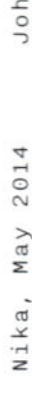

John, March 2011

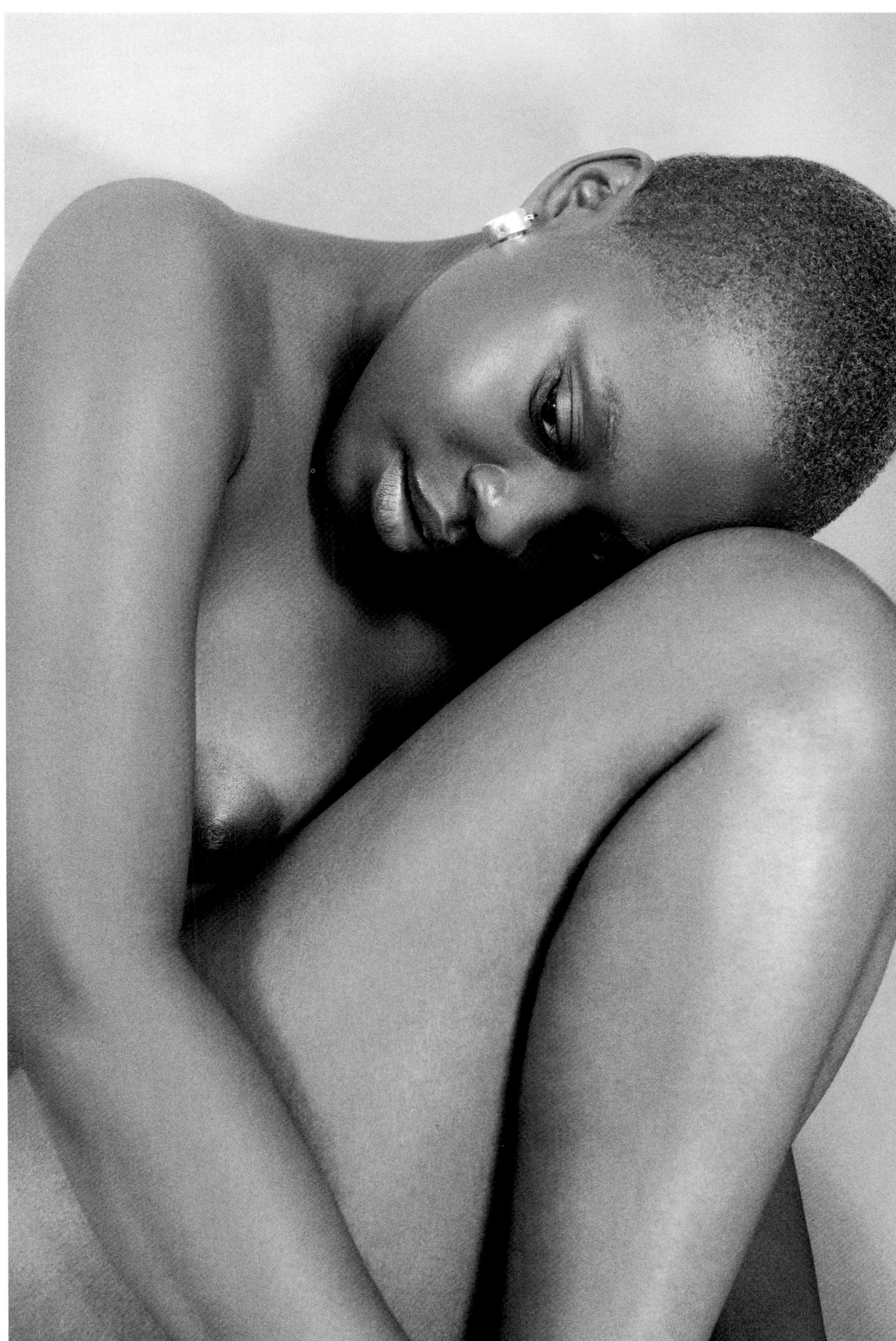

Satori, September 2016

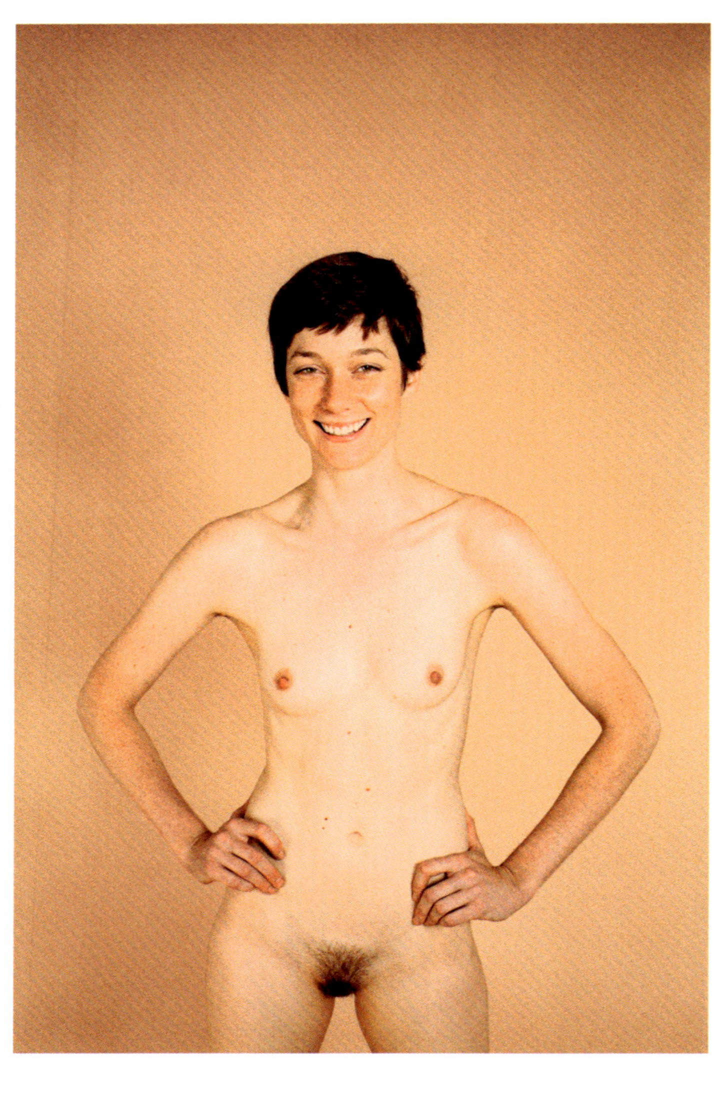

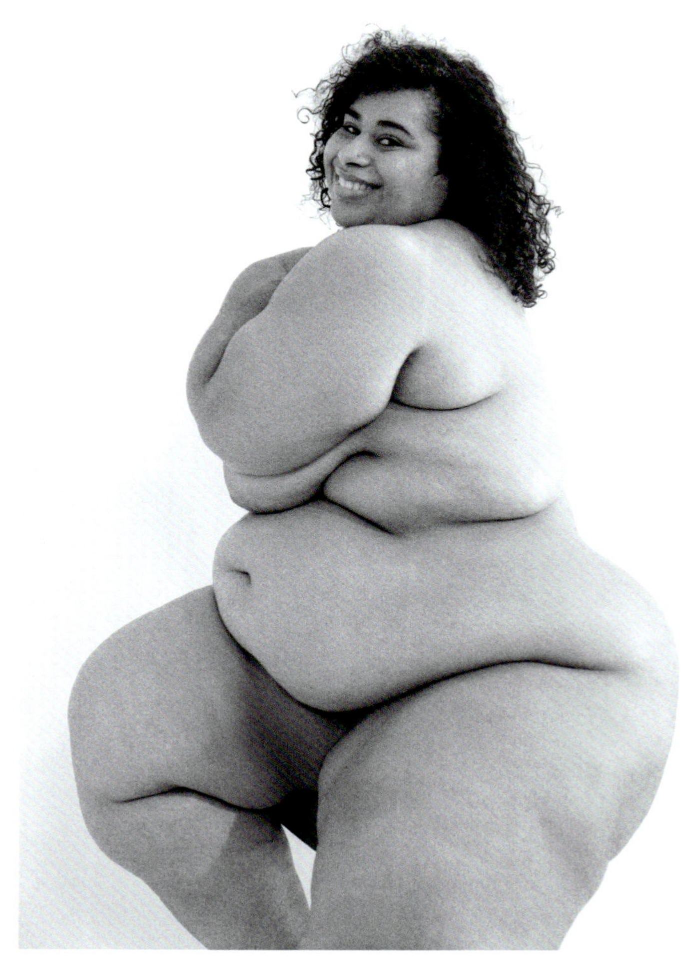

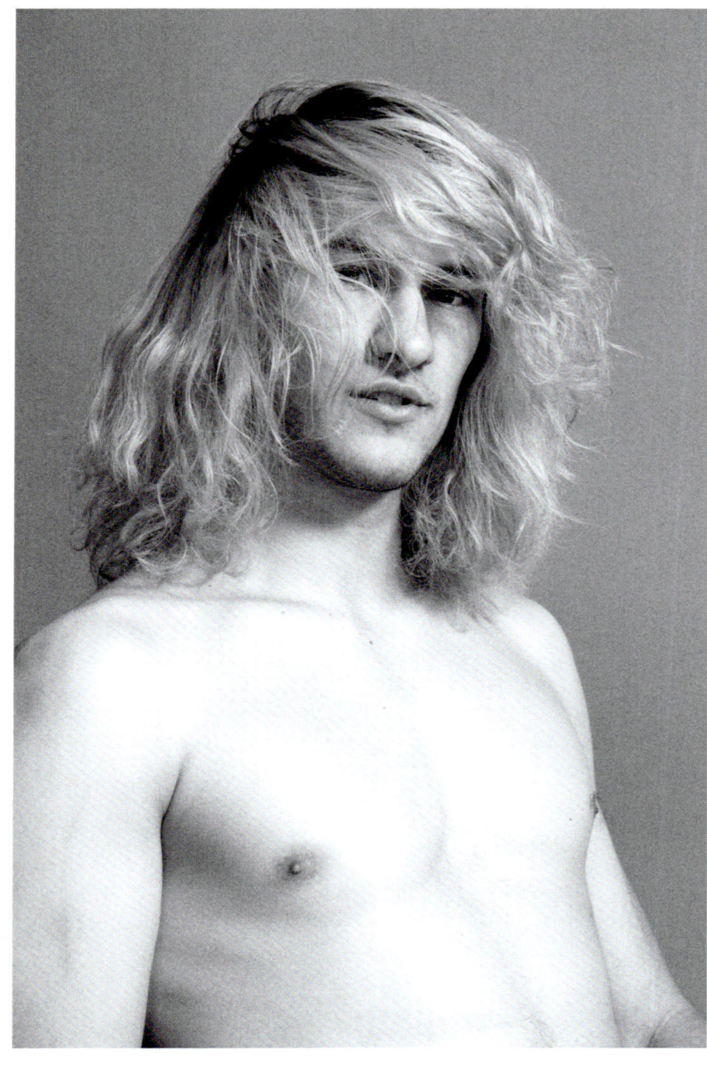

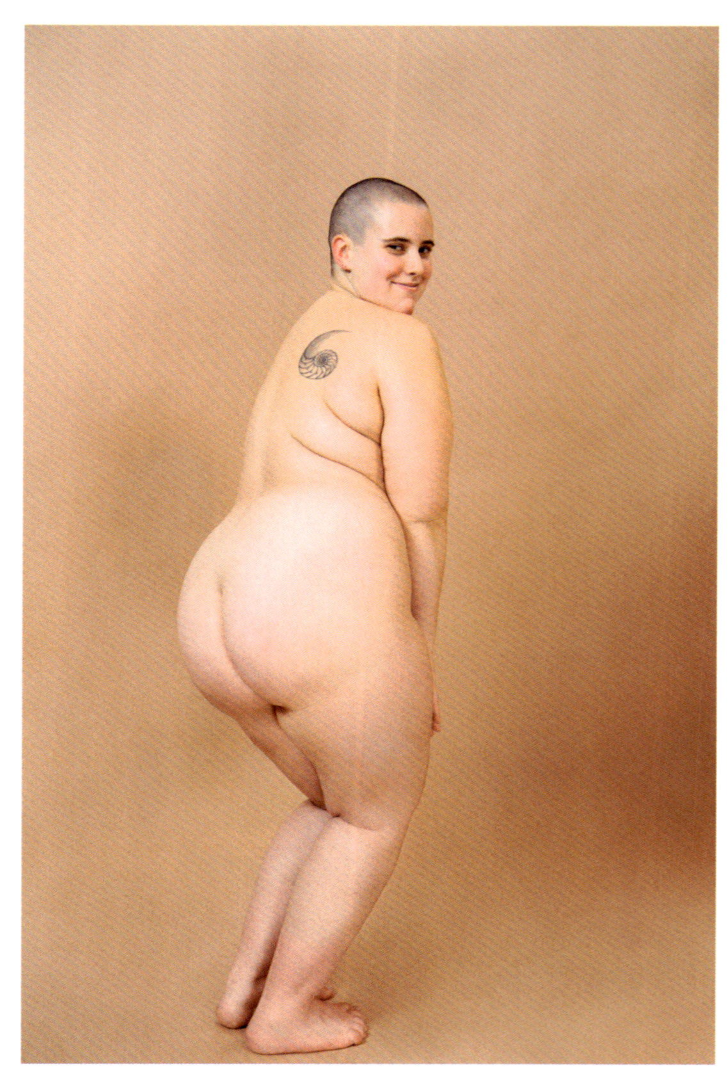

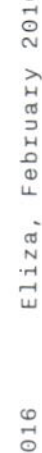

Mary, October 2012   Kimbree, December 2019   Matt, April 2016   Eliza, February 2016

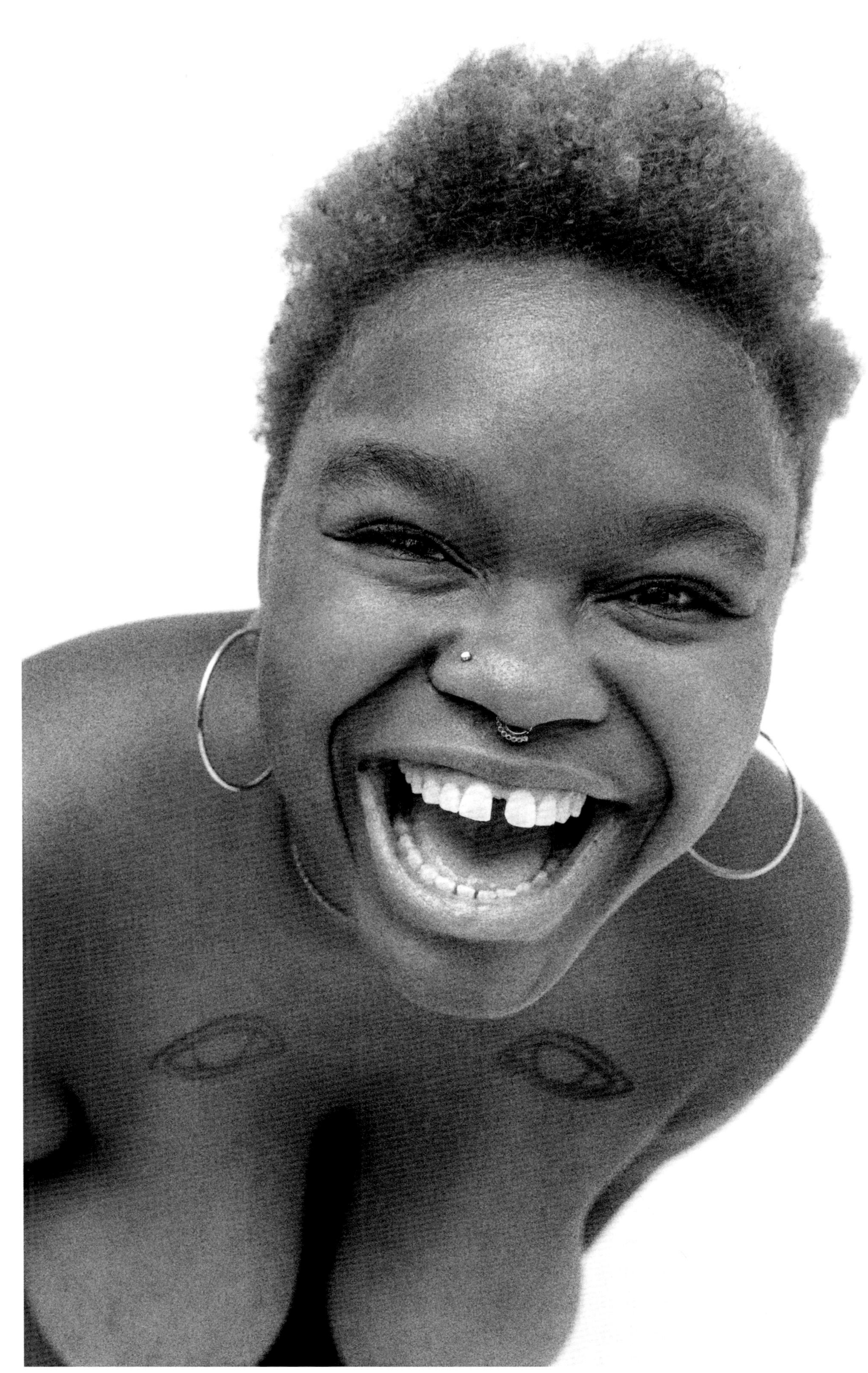

Jenne, June 2017

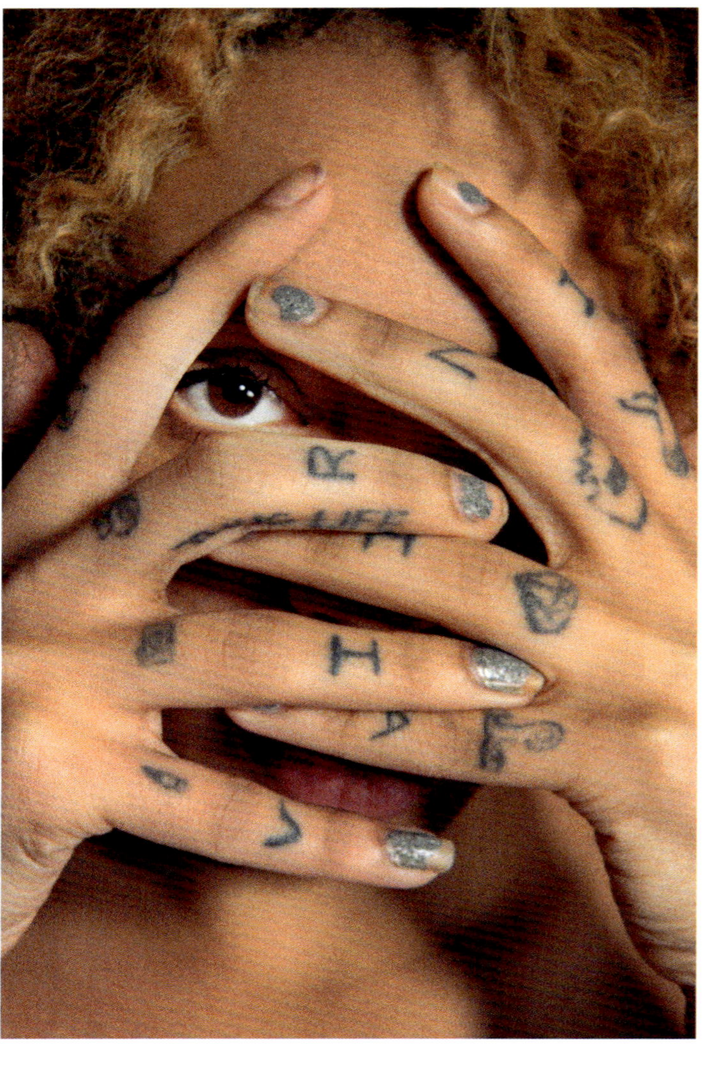

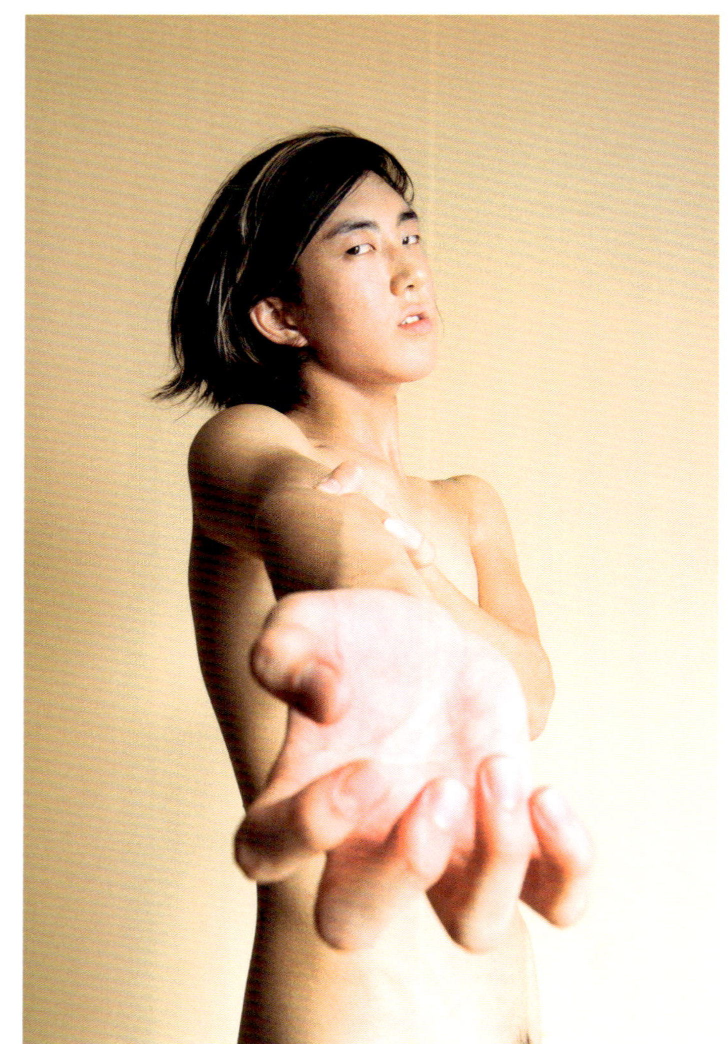

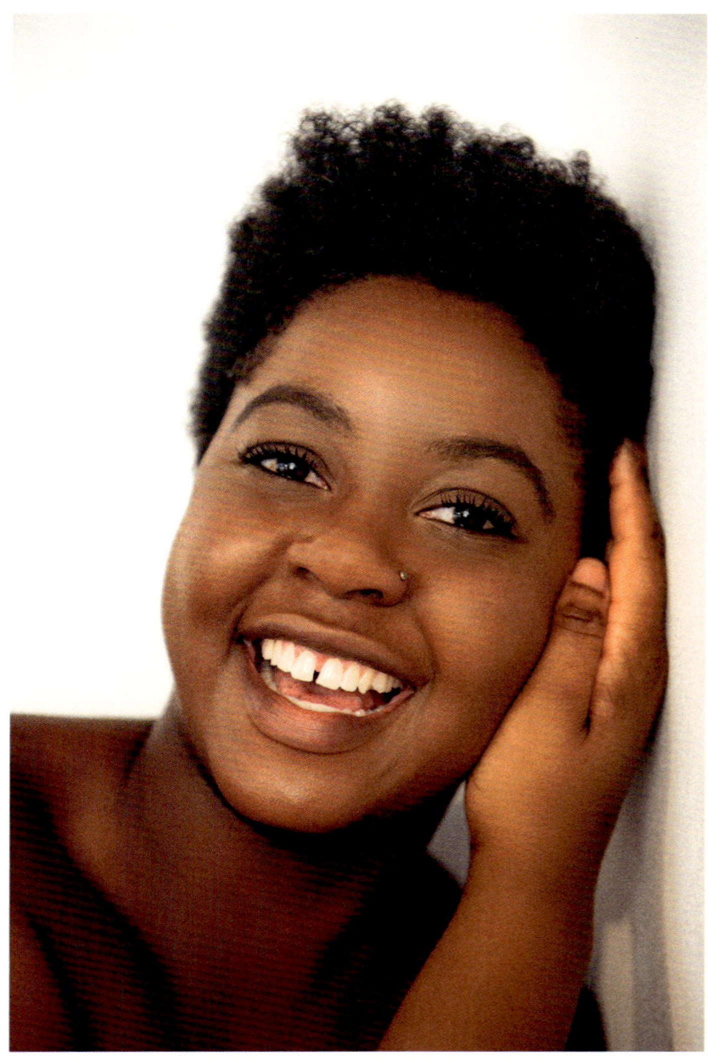

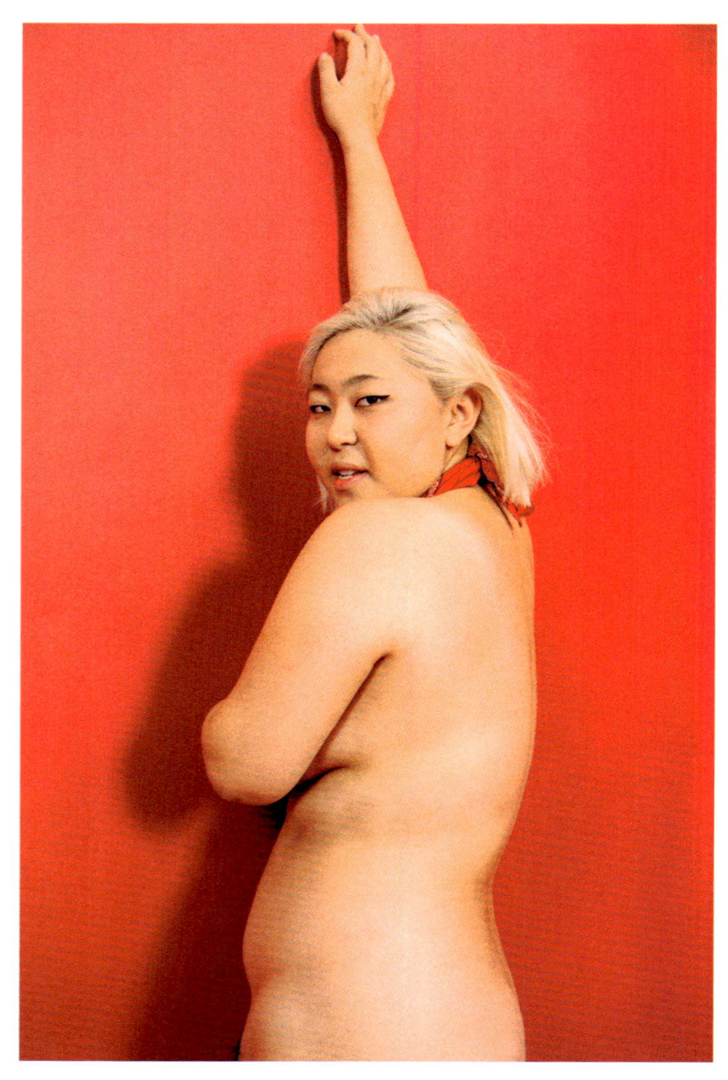

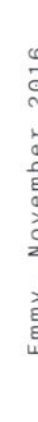

Keyona, January 2016   Sebastian, September 2015   Ife, September 2018   Emmy, November 2016

Brandee, February 2012

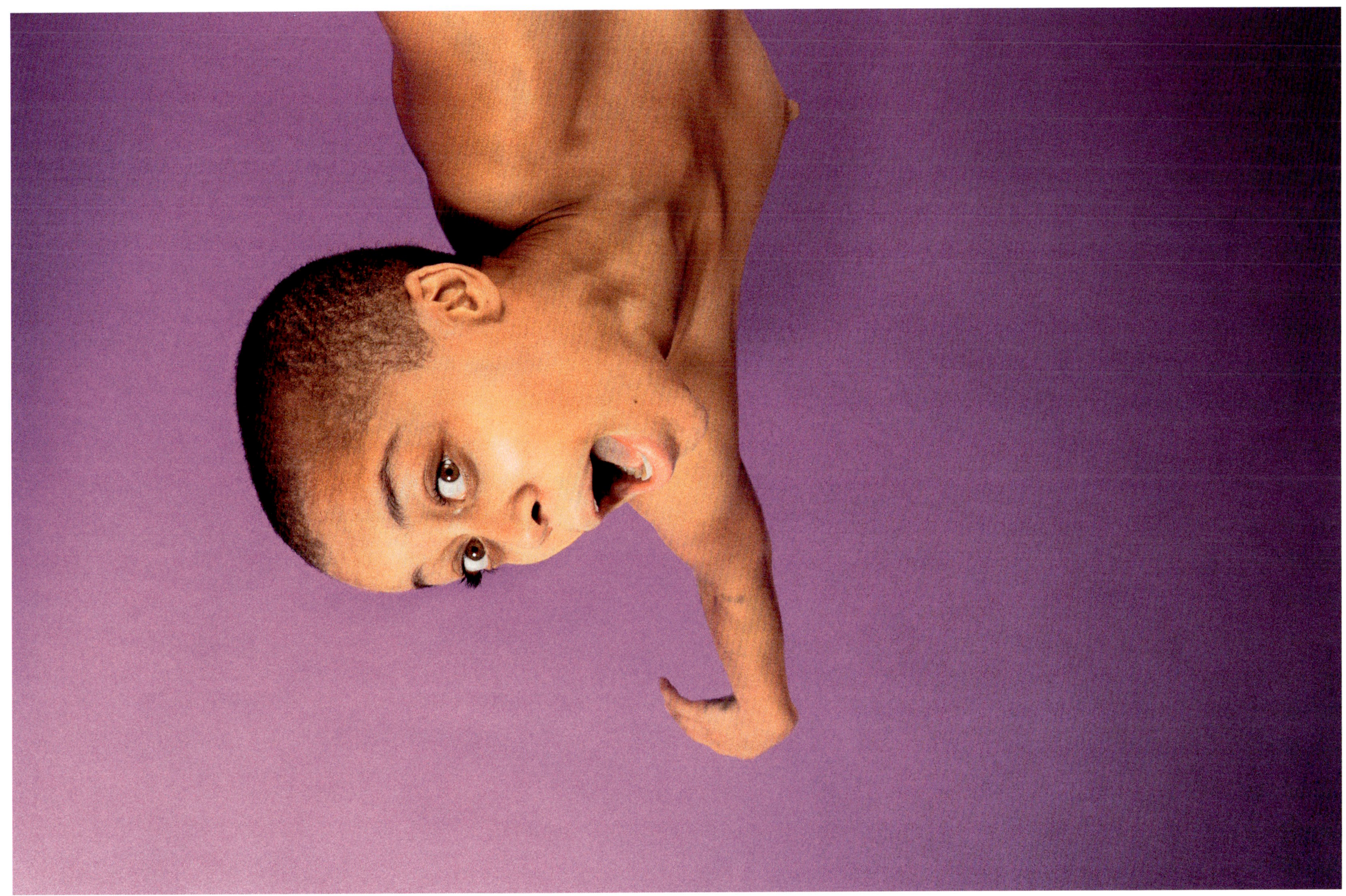

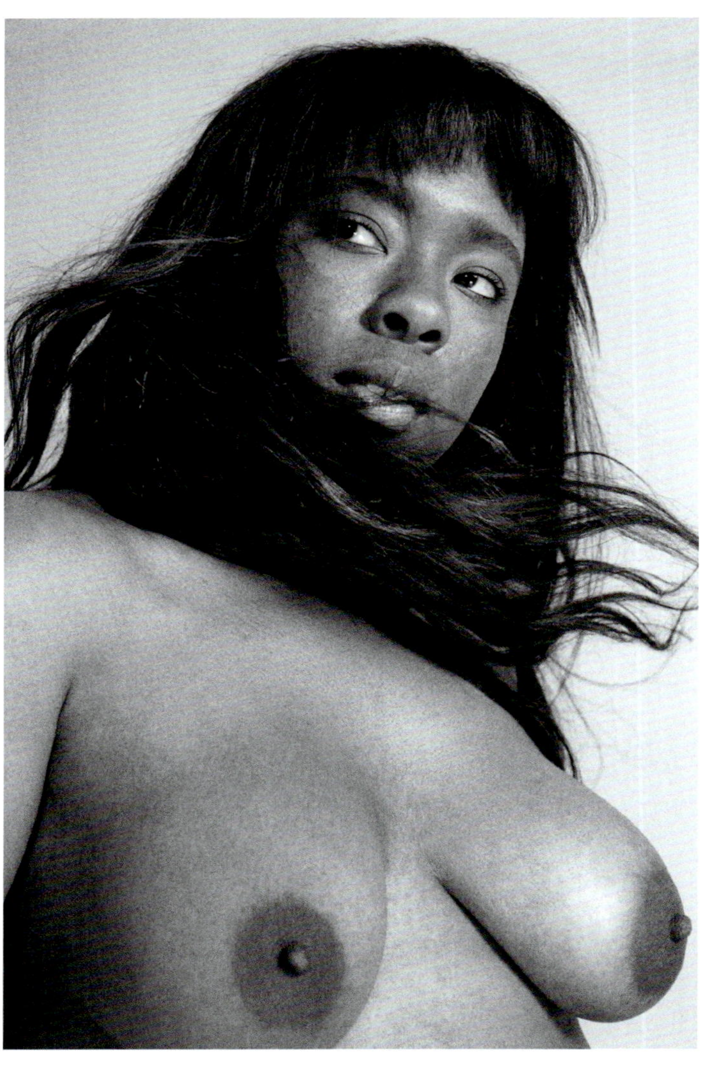

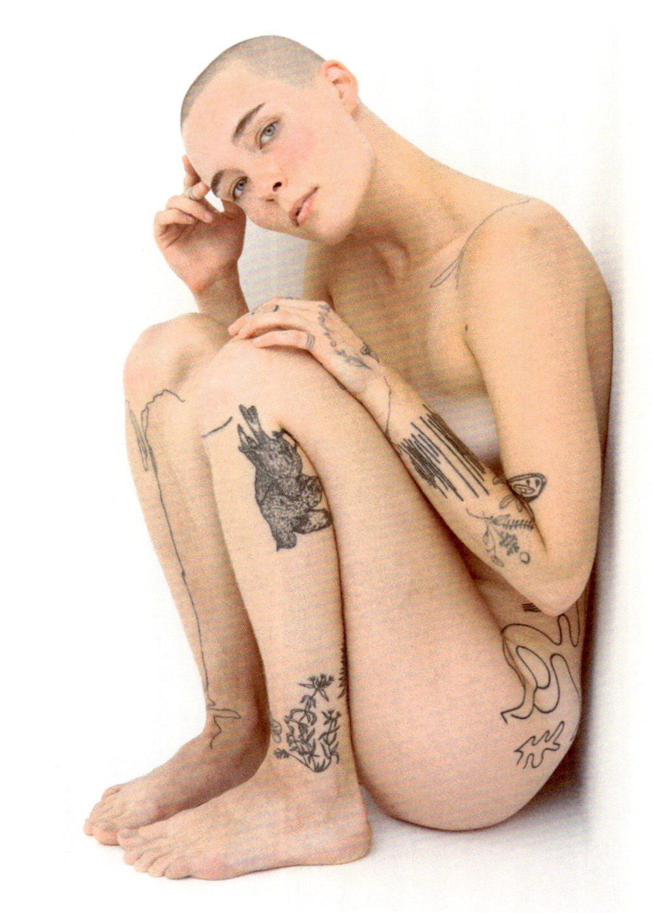

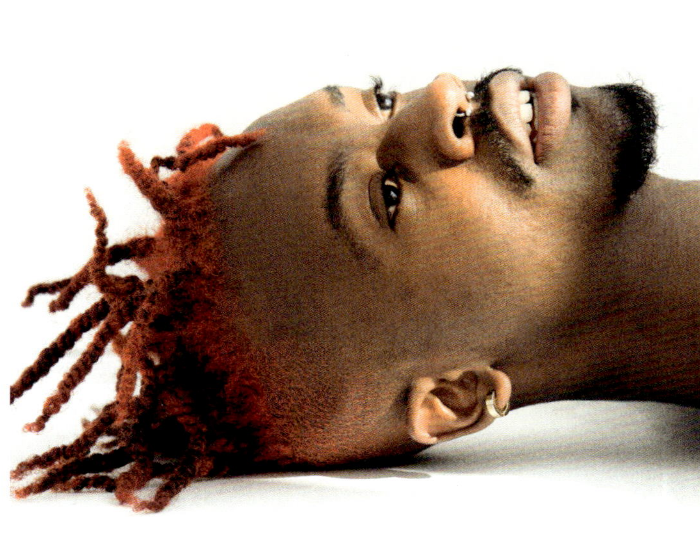

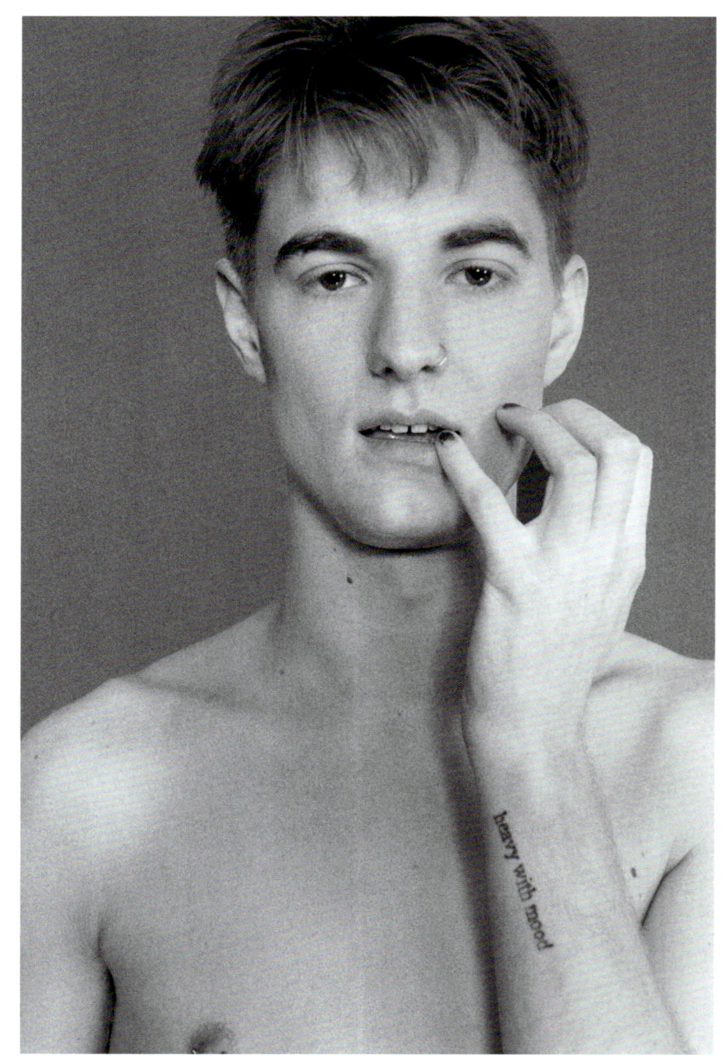

Michelle, 2016 Krista, September 2017 Edvin, September 2017 Walker, April 2016

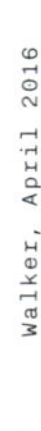

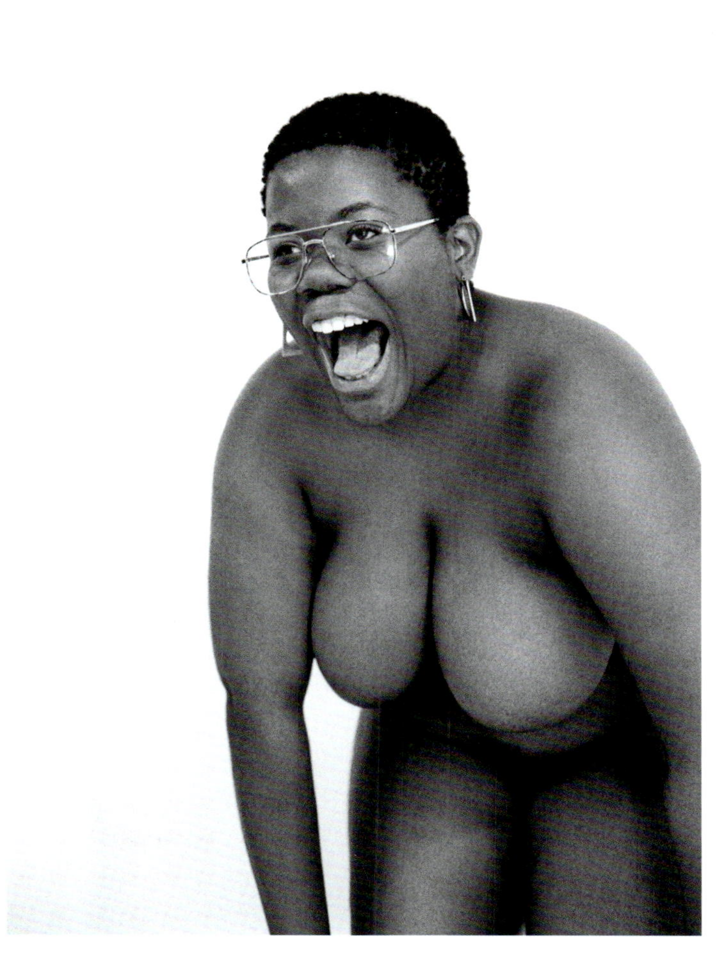

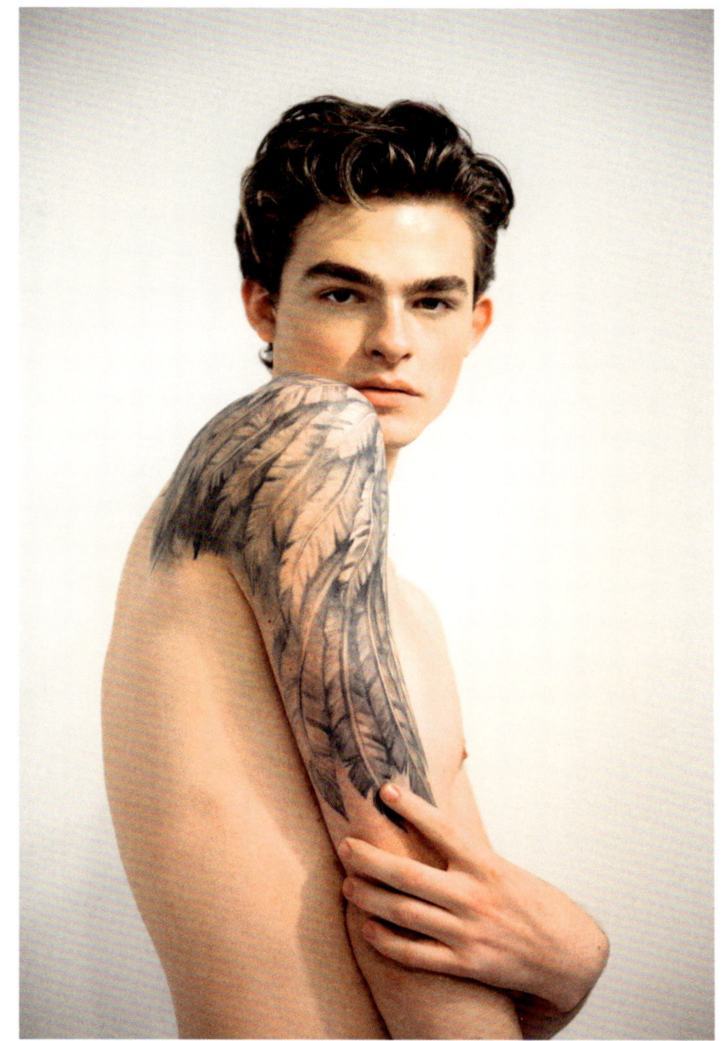

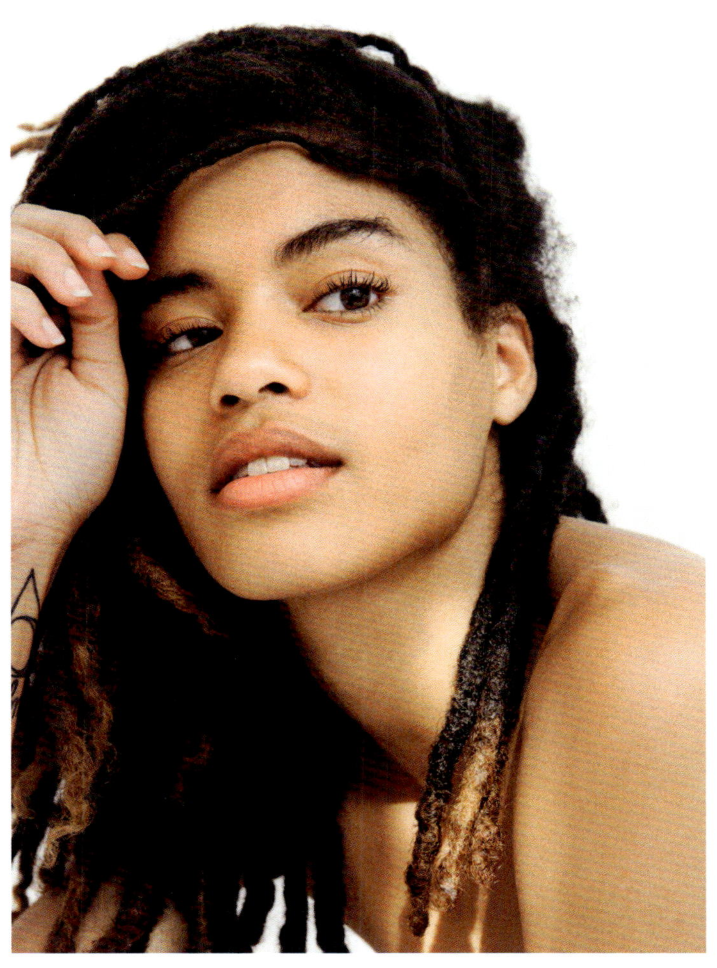

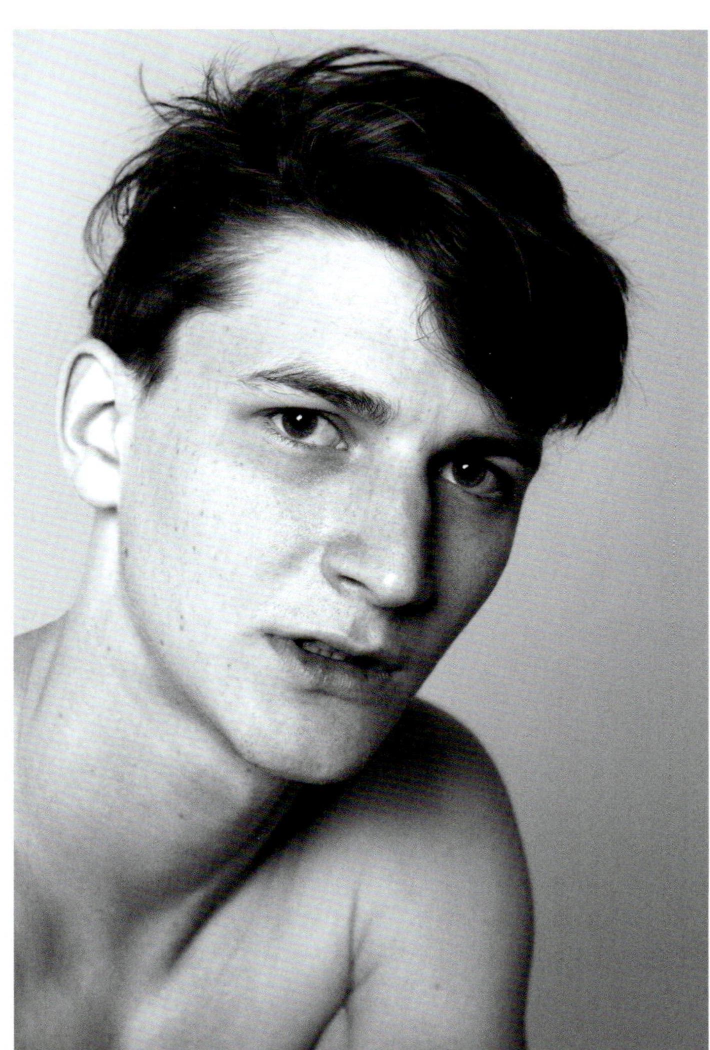

Madelynn, December 2019 Jesse, October 2018 Dina, September 2017 CJ, January 2010

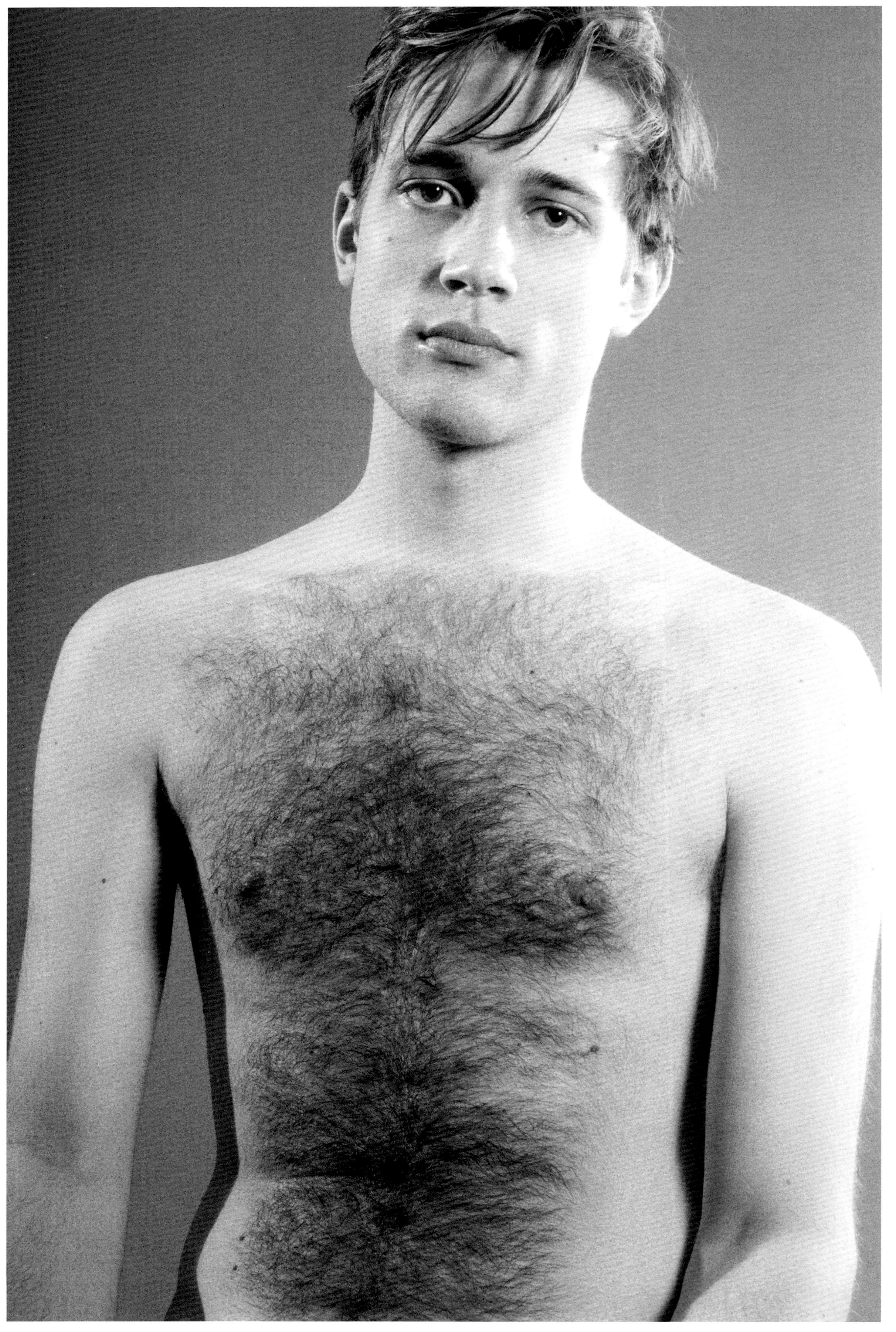

Lucas, July 2015

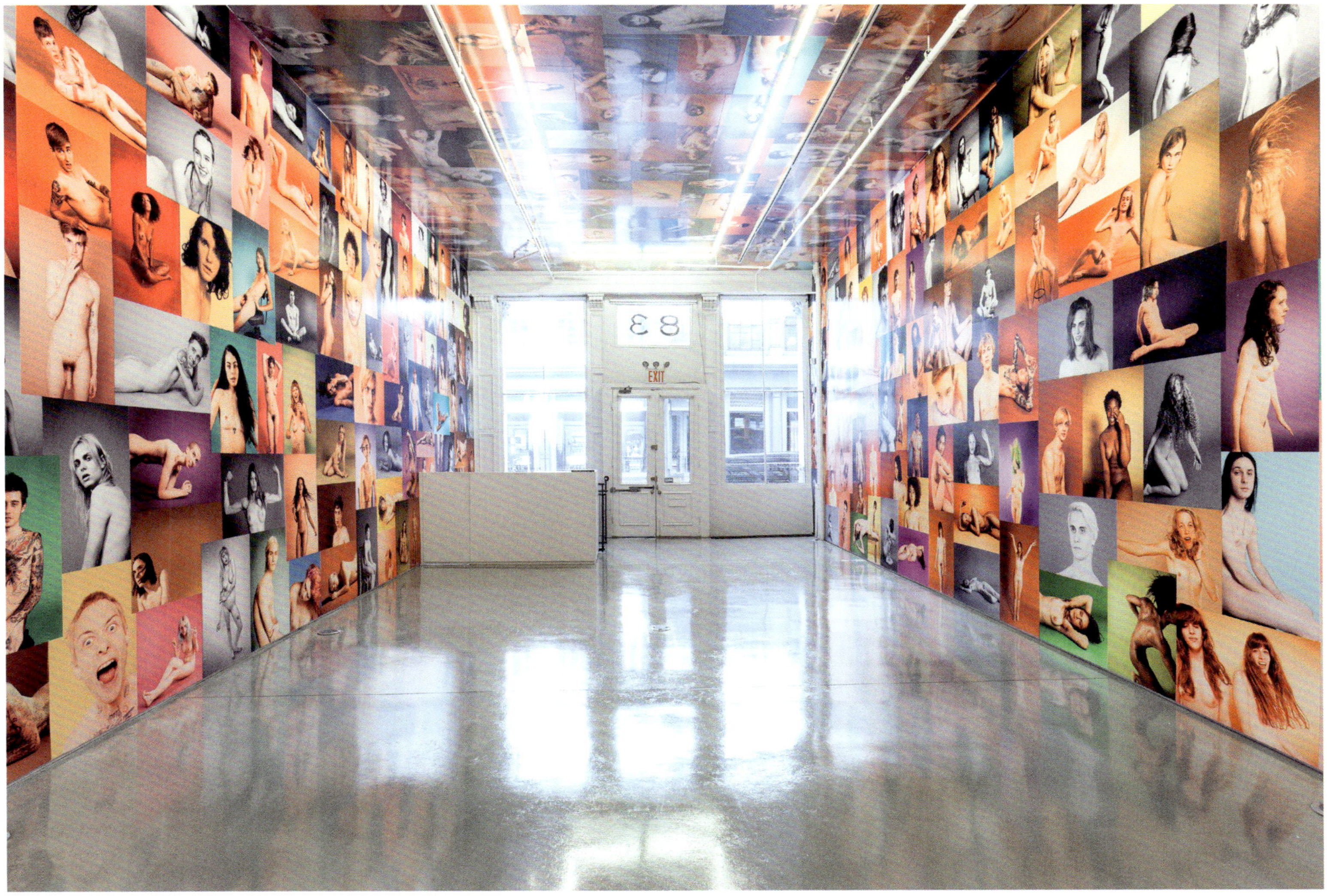

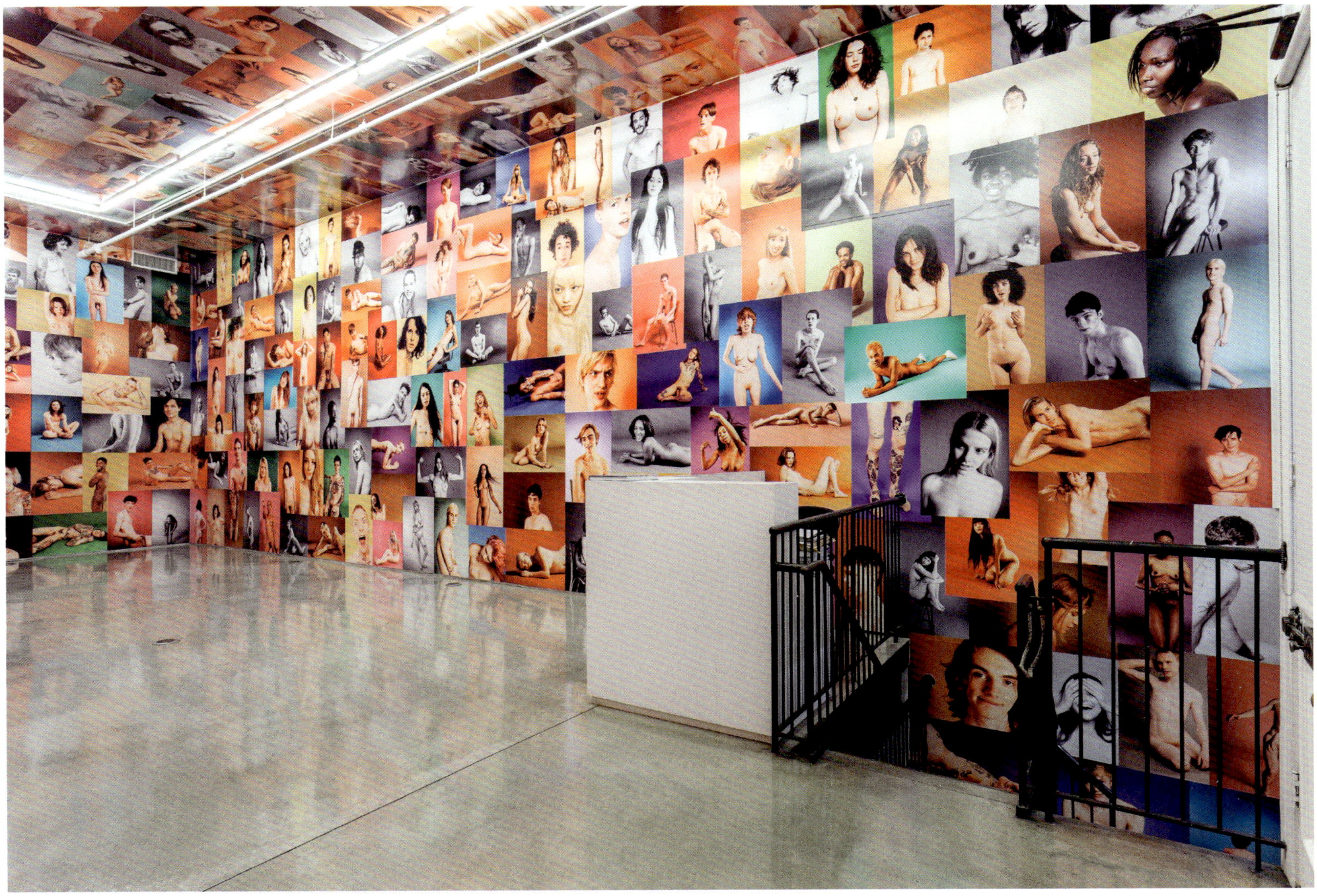

83 Grand Street Gallery, NYC, 2014

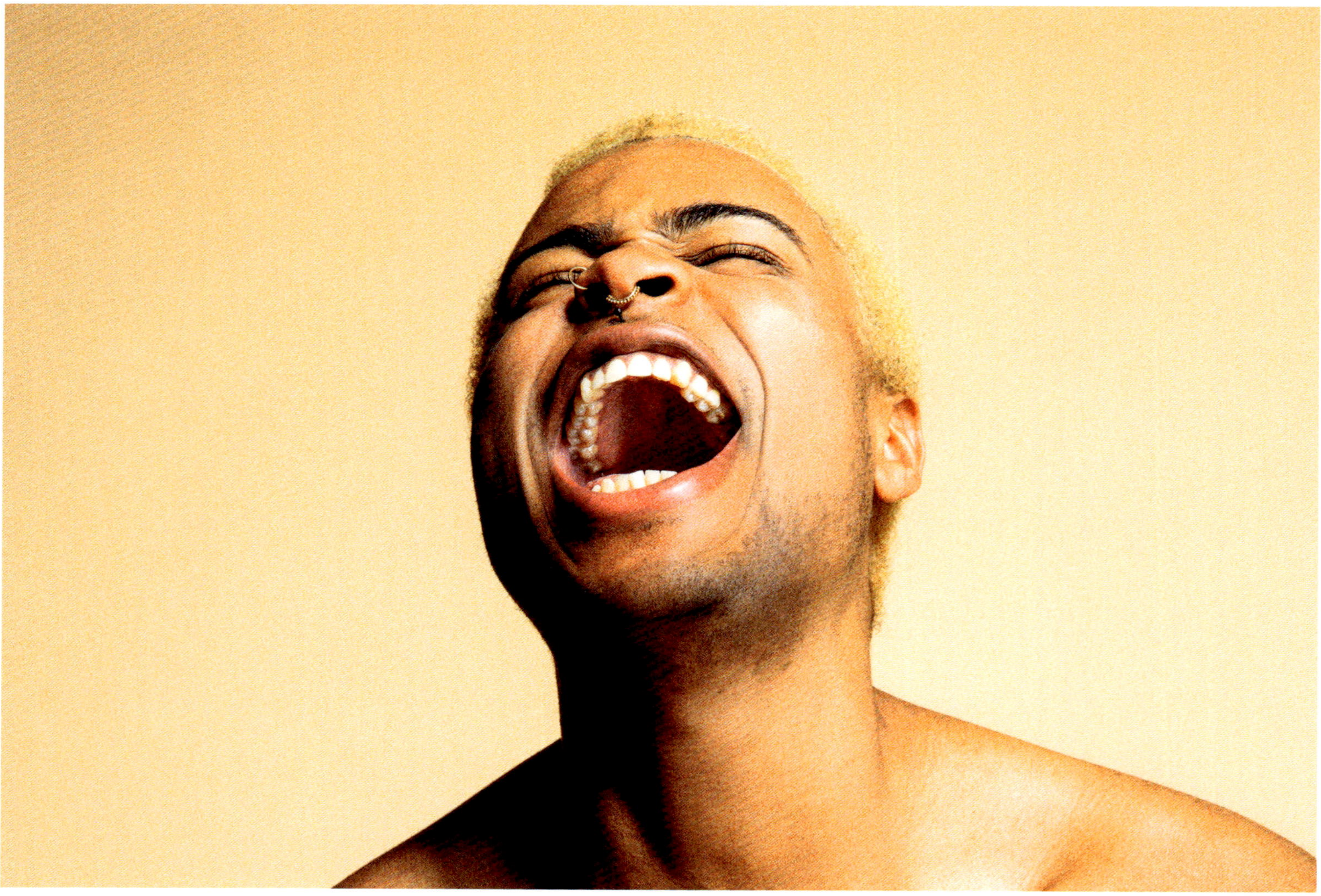

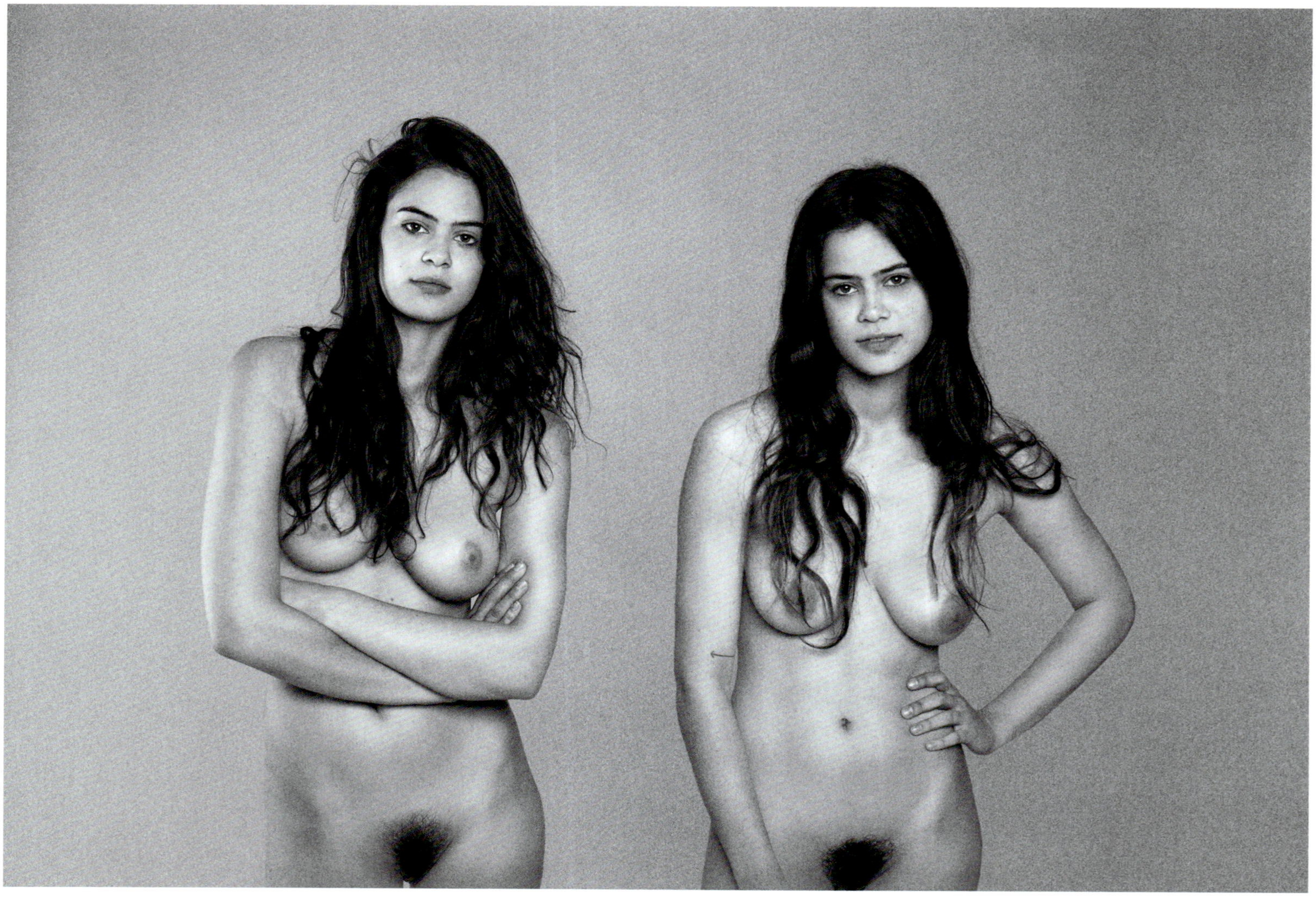

Spencer, October 2015

Lexie & Rachel, April 2010

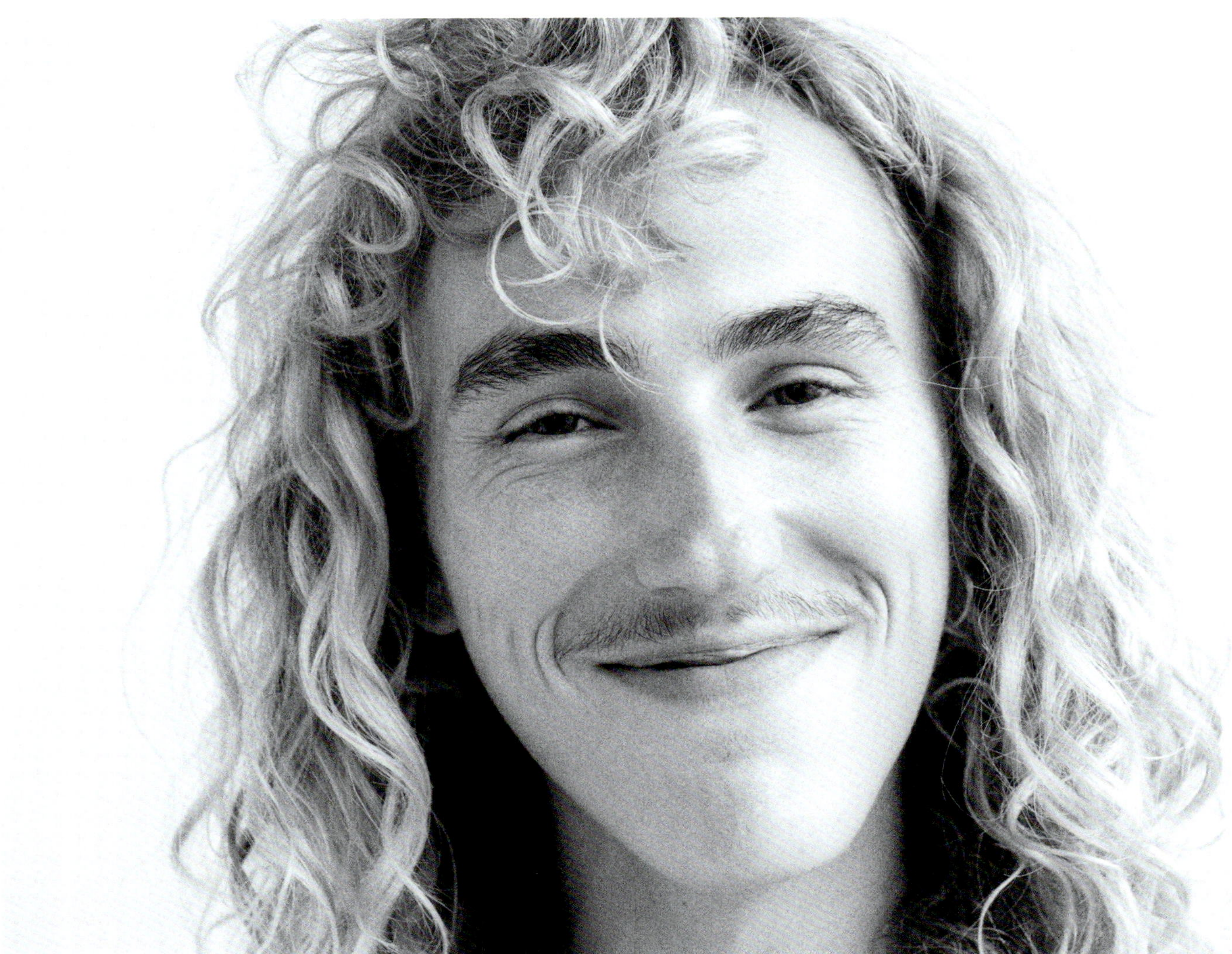

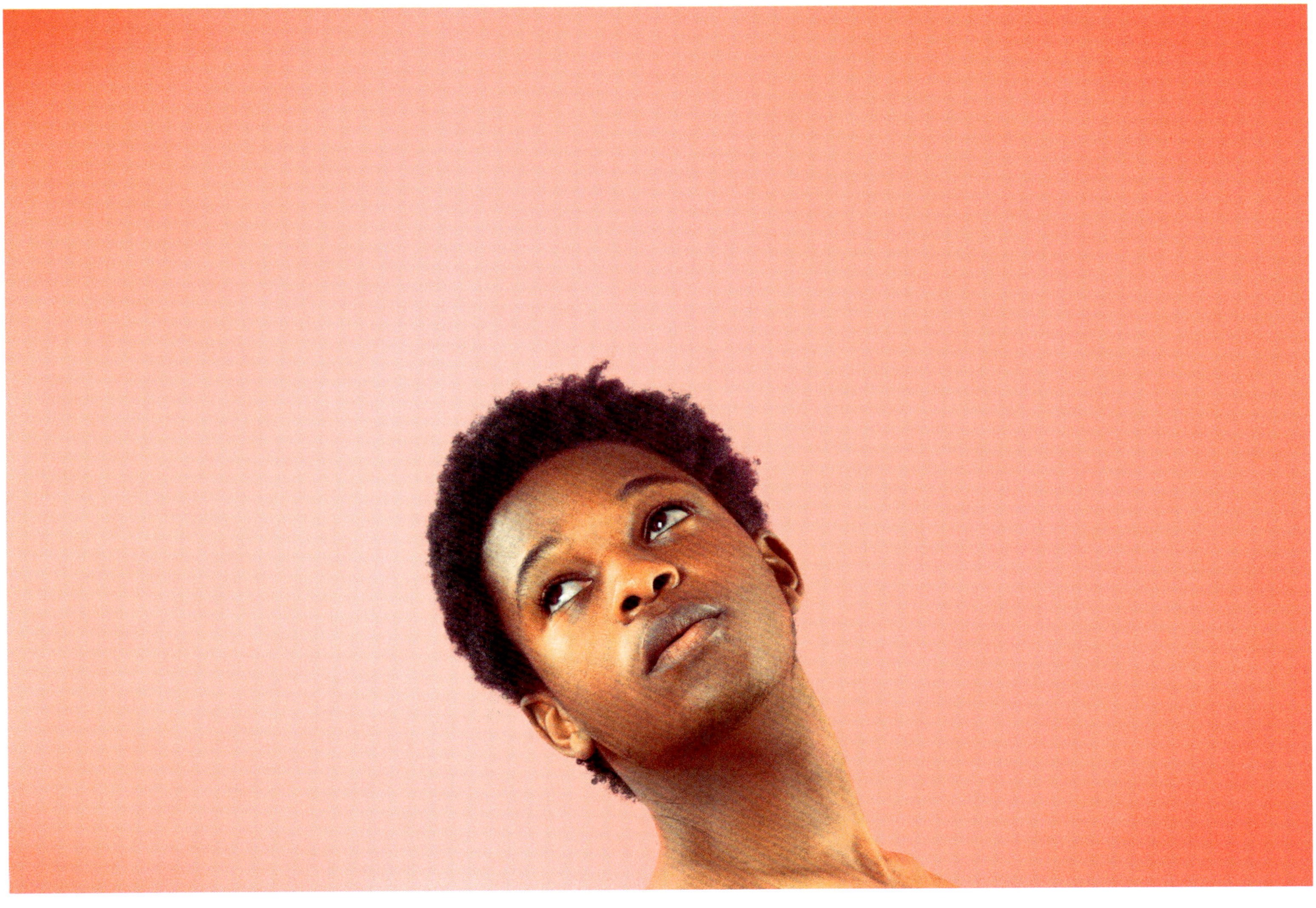

Dustin, July 2017   Marcel, November 2011

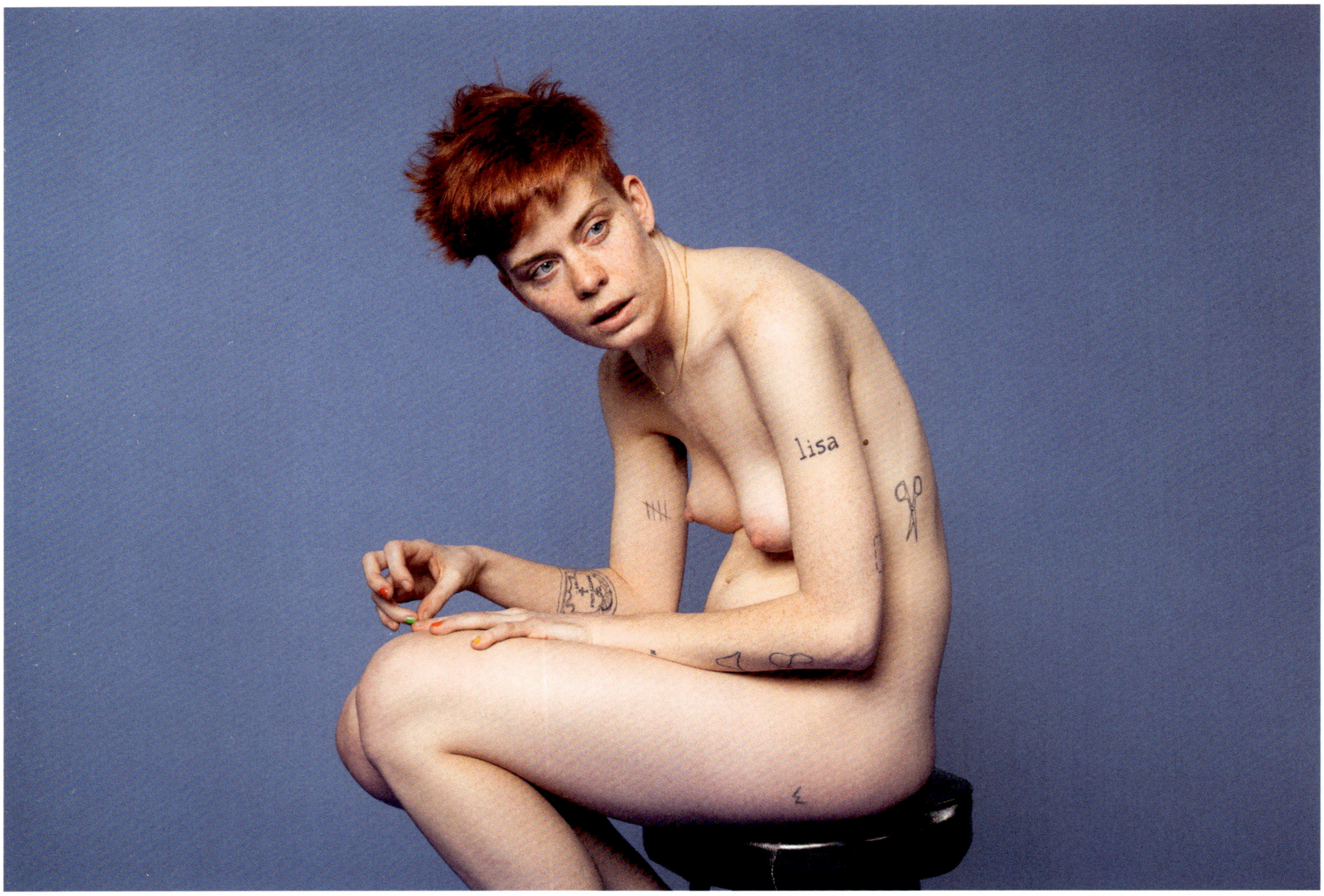

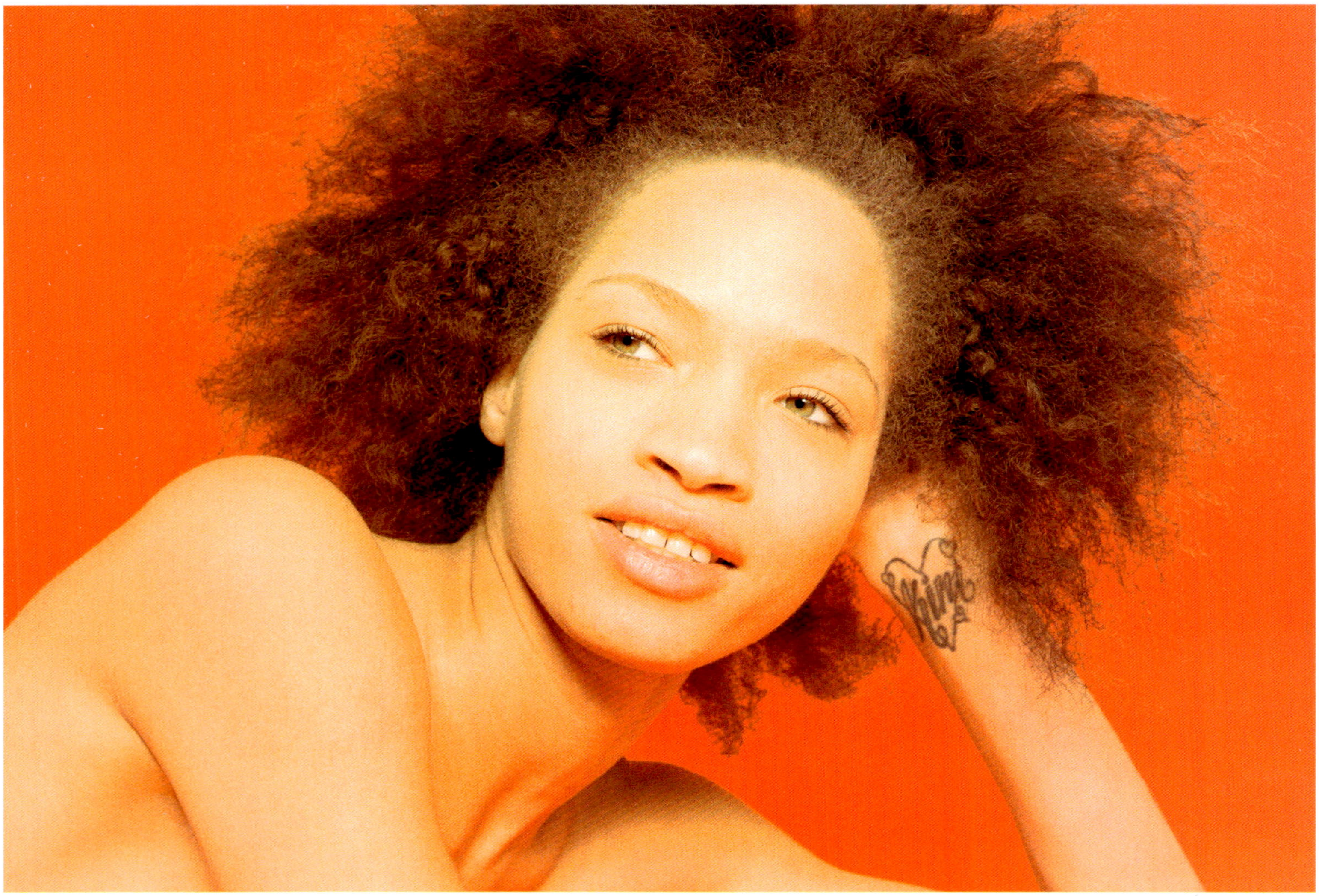

Vala, April 2011

Devan, January 2014

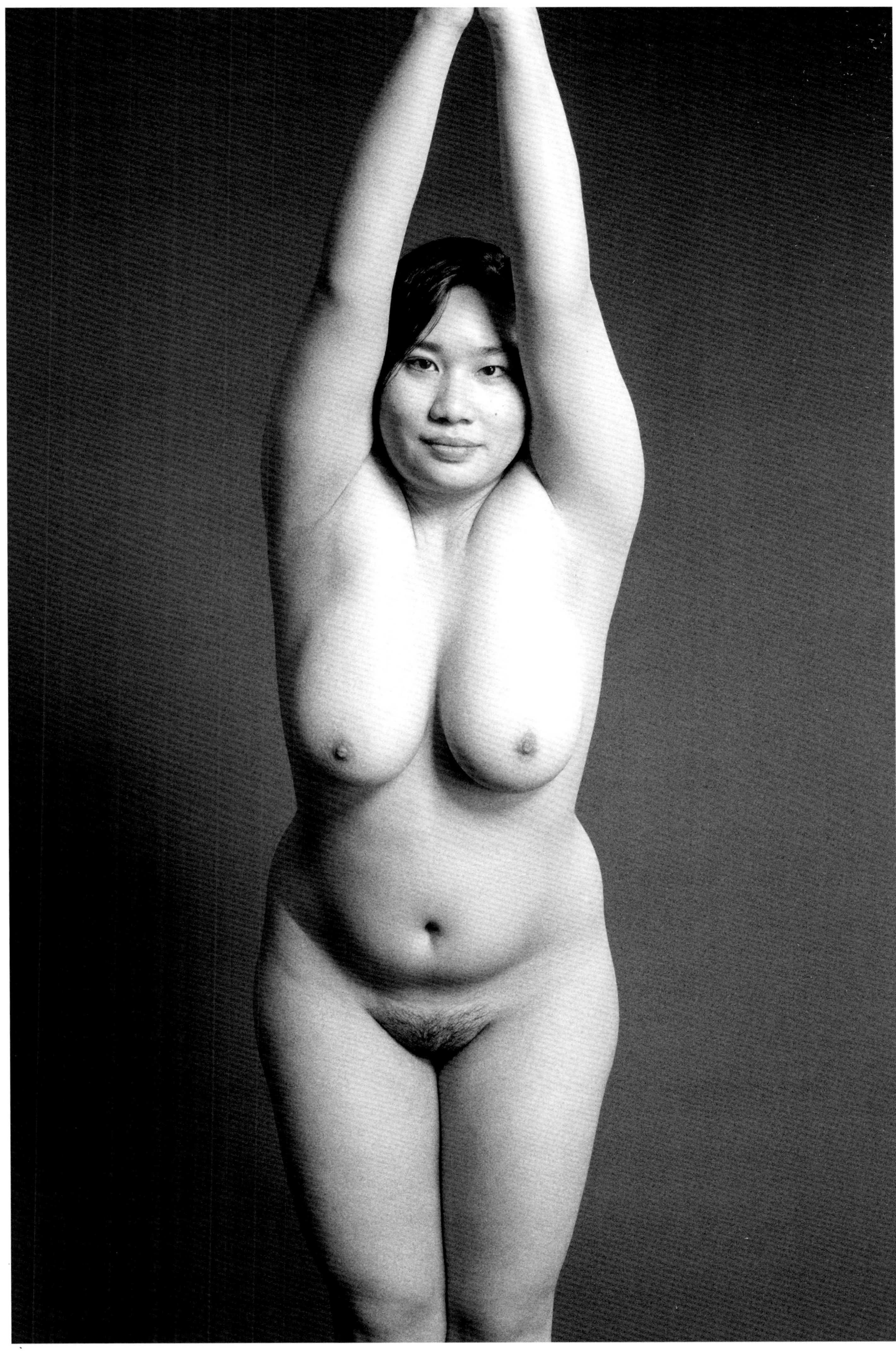

Anna, October 2015

Ryan gave an artist talk my first year at Yale. He visited my studio, where I was showing my CripFag series, and a friendship budded up from there.

The CripFag series is about my journey as a disabled gay man and my sexual awakening after sustaining a spinal cord injury when I was twenty-one. The work reclaims two derogatory terms, cripple and faggot. It's a love letter not only to myself but to my community as well.

When I was in the hospital and rehab, I quickly realized that my medical professionals were ill-equipped to talk about sexuality and especially with me as a gay man. I had all of these questions: Can I bottom? Can I top? How can I safely do these things because of my injury and my new body? Since I don't have feeling in certain areas, how can I safely be penetrated? Can I penetrate? What does this look like? Everyone kept walking around the questions and deflecting. "Oh well, talk to your doctor," one would say. "Oh, well, talk to this person," the doctor would say.

My sexual education was left up to me. I spent about a year at home at my parent's after my accident, and then I went back to school. That's when I started experimenting with my body, trying all these sex toys and different things. After I had kind of figured out my body and learned to own my sexuality, I started creating the work that I wanted to see in the world. There's such a lack of visual representation of disability and sexuality made from the point of view of being disabled.

When these portraits were taken, I was in my second and last year at Yale grad school. I traveled into the city with my roommate at the time. We took the train from Yale, got some food, and met up with my friend Benjamin Fredrickson, who is in one of the photos with me. Then we went to Ryan's studio. This was before the Covid-19 lockdown. It was cool to see the studio.

Ryan and I work pretty similarly. We both work with a creative group of people who understand our vision. Last June, I photographed Ryan. I was commissioned by NYC Tourism, and we were both at the Queer Liberation March and photographed each other, which was really fun.

In undergrad, I had already started honing in on my photography skills. I fell in love with four-by-five large format: the detail, the color, and the quality of the image you can get. The color darkroom was my favorite. Since then, I've been a quality whore. I have a tattoo of a four-by-five on my chest that you can see in this photo. It was actually a four-by-five naked self-portrait that I'd traced. It's got the notches and everything.

Around the time these photos were taken, my first Instagram account was deleted after [the art critic] Jerry Saltz found my work and posted it on his Instagram. People were going to my account and tagging me. I was getting more followers but then people were also reporting many of my images. I lost that account. I remember when I first met Ryan, he posted snapshots of my work and ultimately his posts got taken down as well.

Even though I do the same amount of self-censoring as anyone else, I'm not allowed to post my own work. Art institutions and galleries can. When I was in a show in New York, the gallery and I posted the same image of my work. It's an image of me, reclined, in my apartment. It looks like I'm sucking this guy's dick. His butt is towards the camera, and I'm looking at the camera. I censored the image when I posted it. Then the gallery posted the whole image; there were no repercussions for them. But when I shared that photo on my story, it got my Instagram deleted for the second time.

Instagram tries to silence people like me who are making work about sexuality, especially if they can't make money off of you, if you don't have a big platform. It's challenging because this creates missed opportunities since museums and galleries are also interested in showing work that boosts their engagement. I'm being erased from the story of not only disability but of queer voices as well.

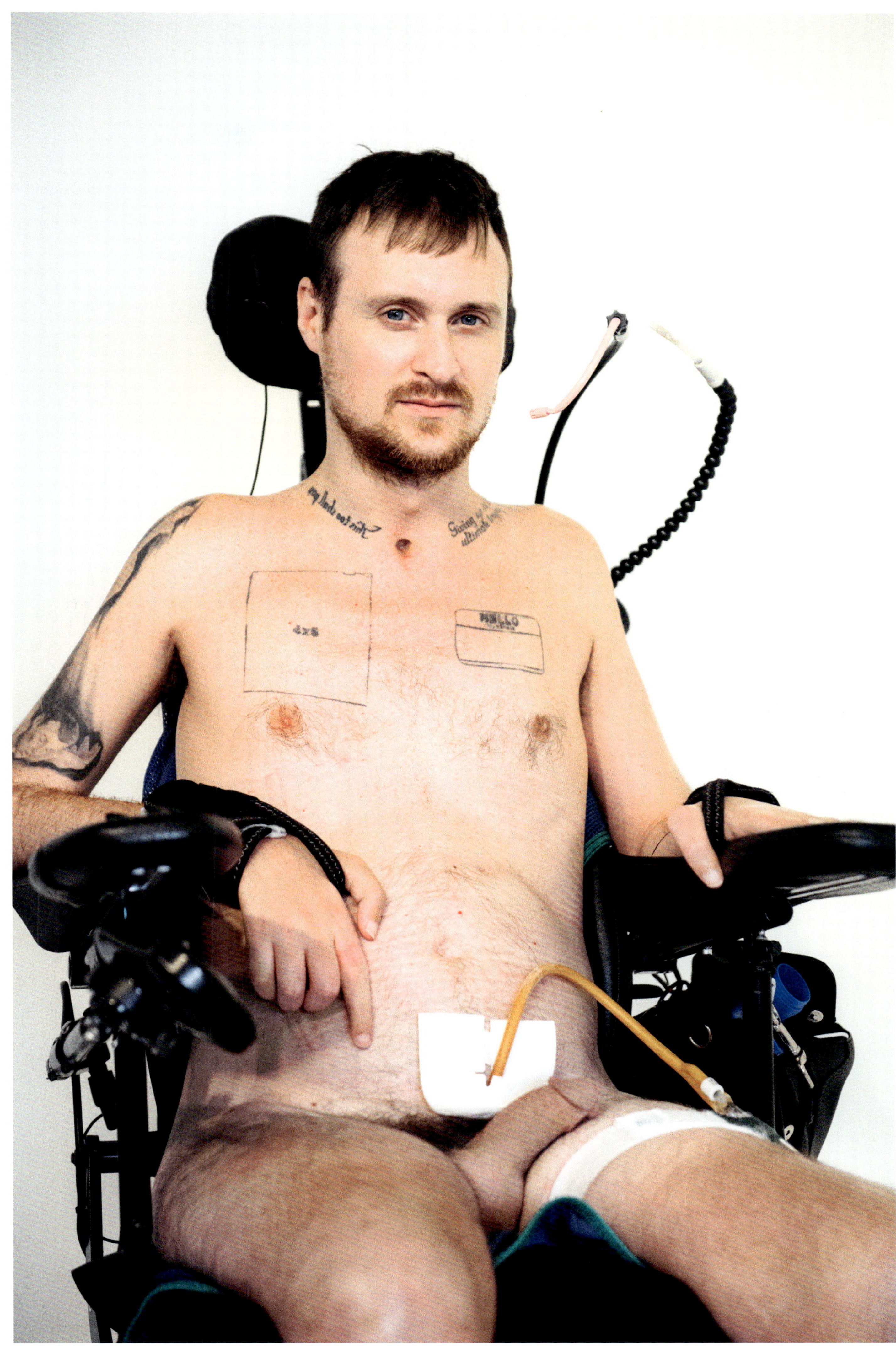

Robert, October 2019

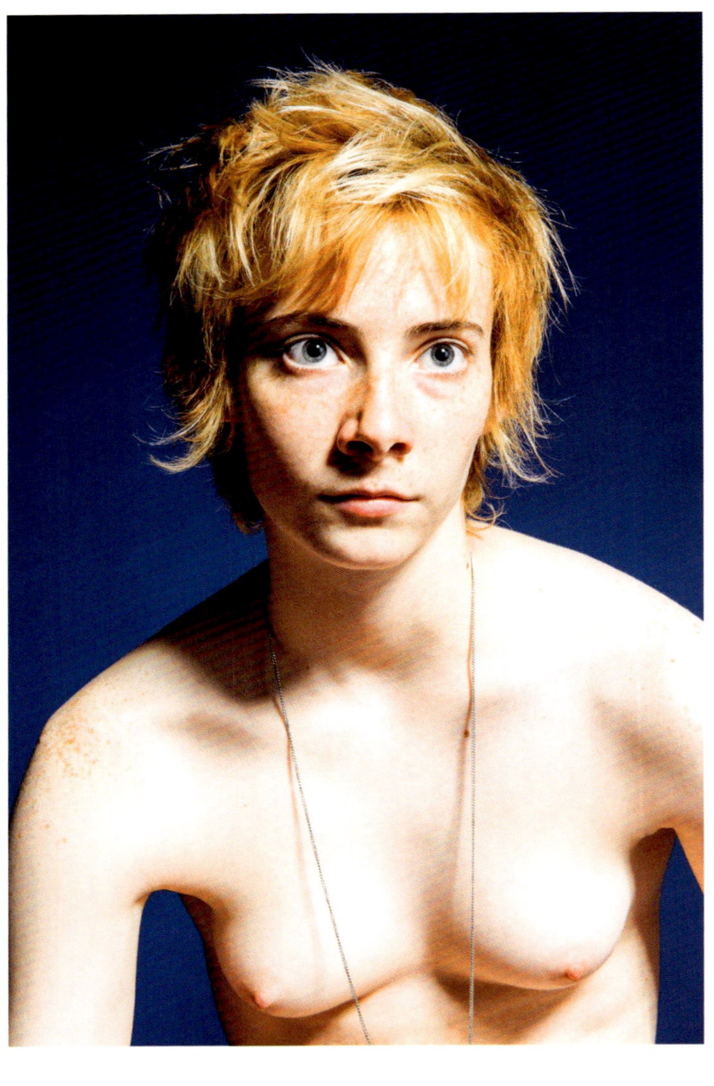

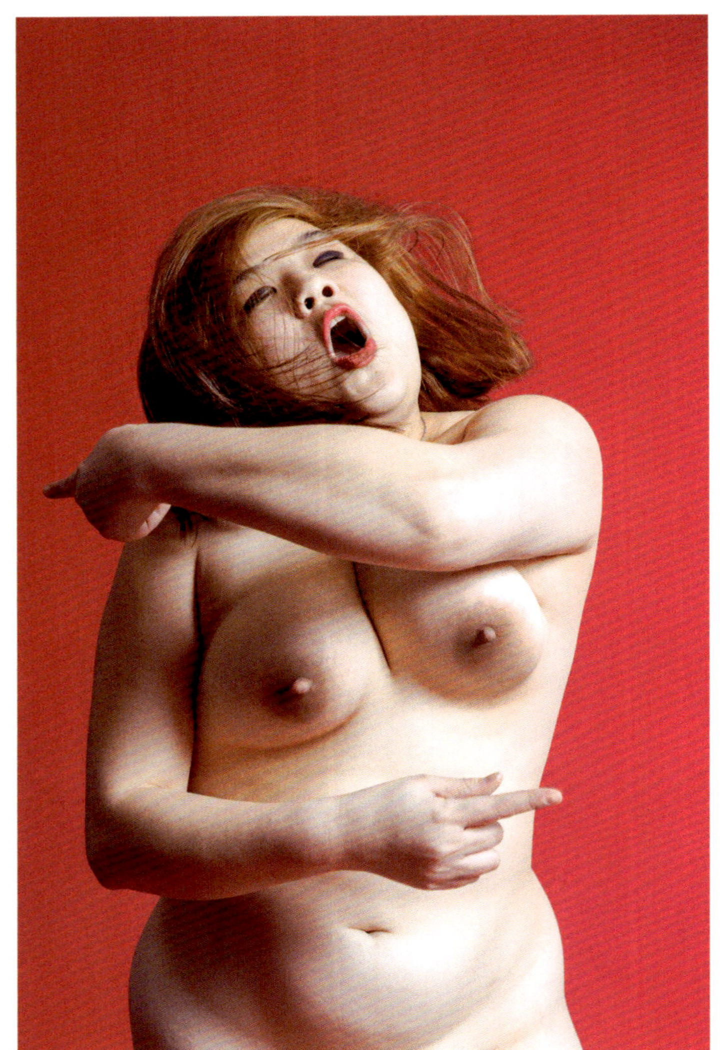

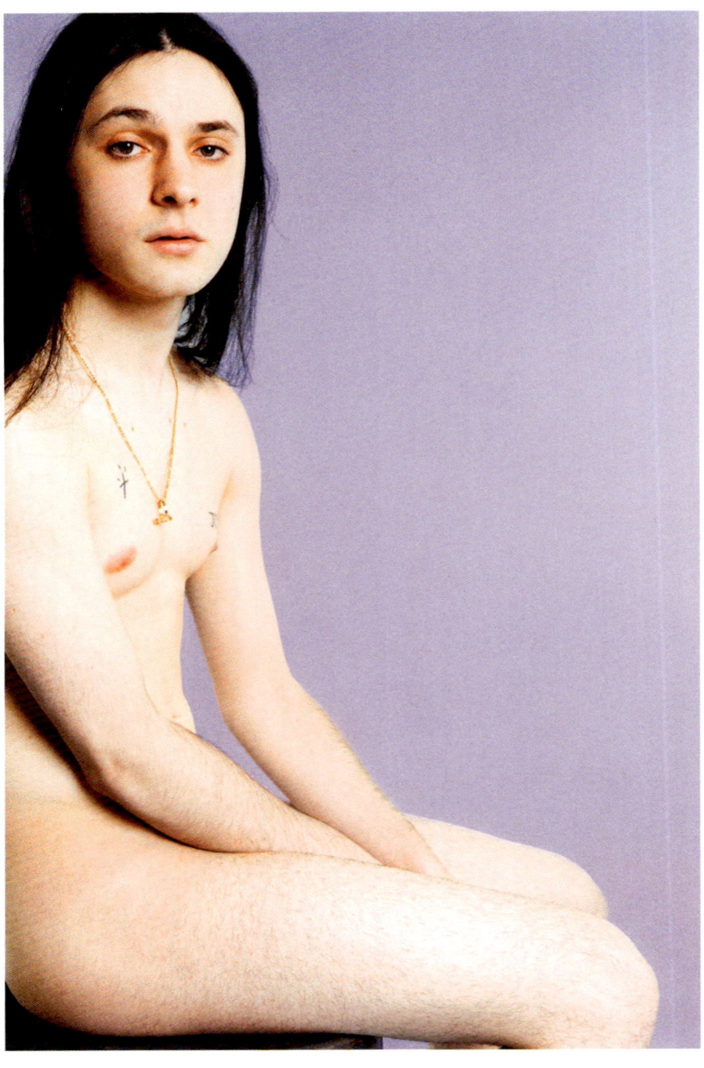

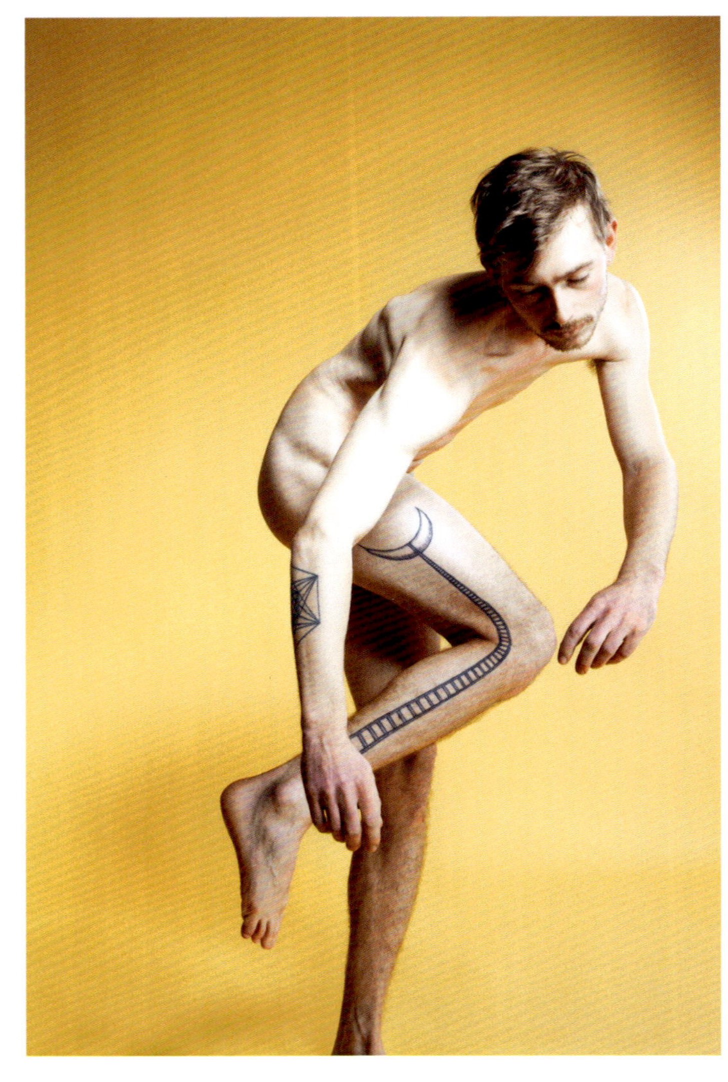

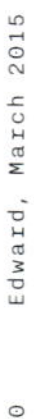

Grace, December 2015   James, February 2010   Joe, December 2010   Edward, March 2015

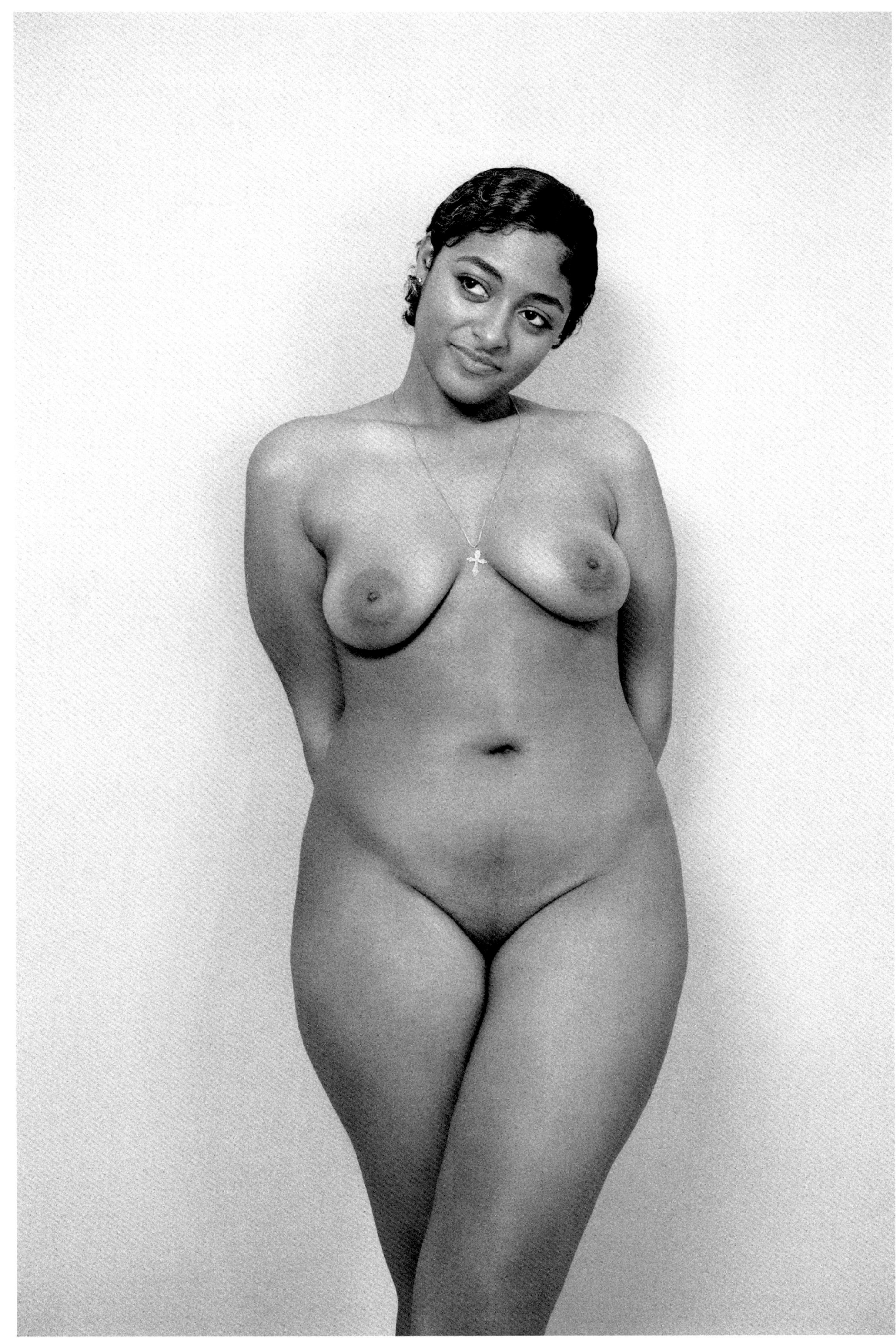

Waverly, November 2016

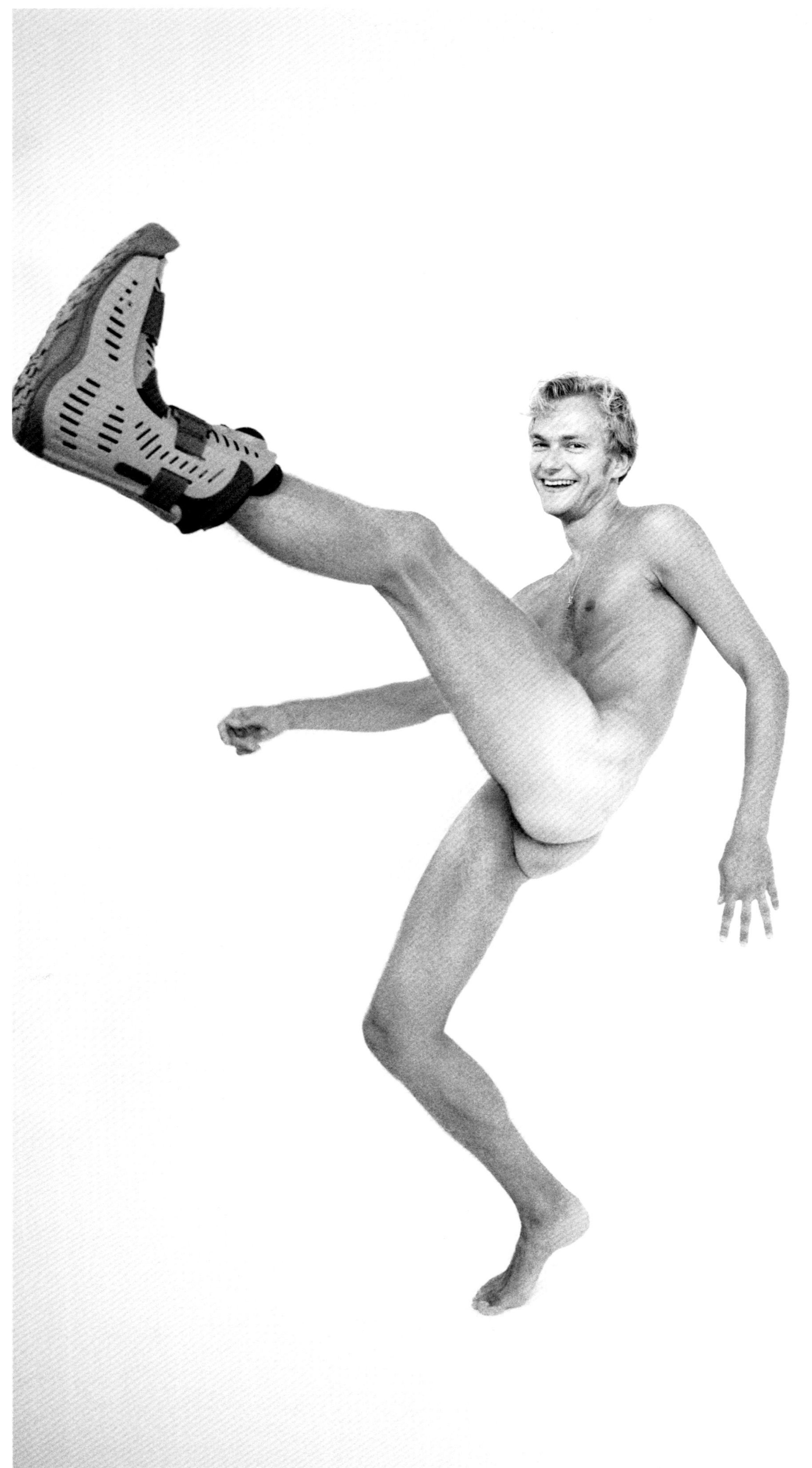

Gabriel, October 2019

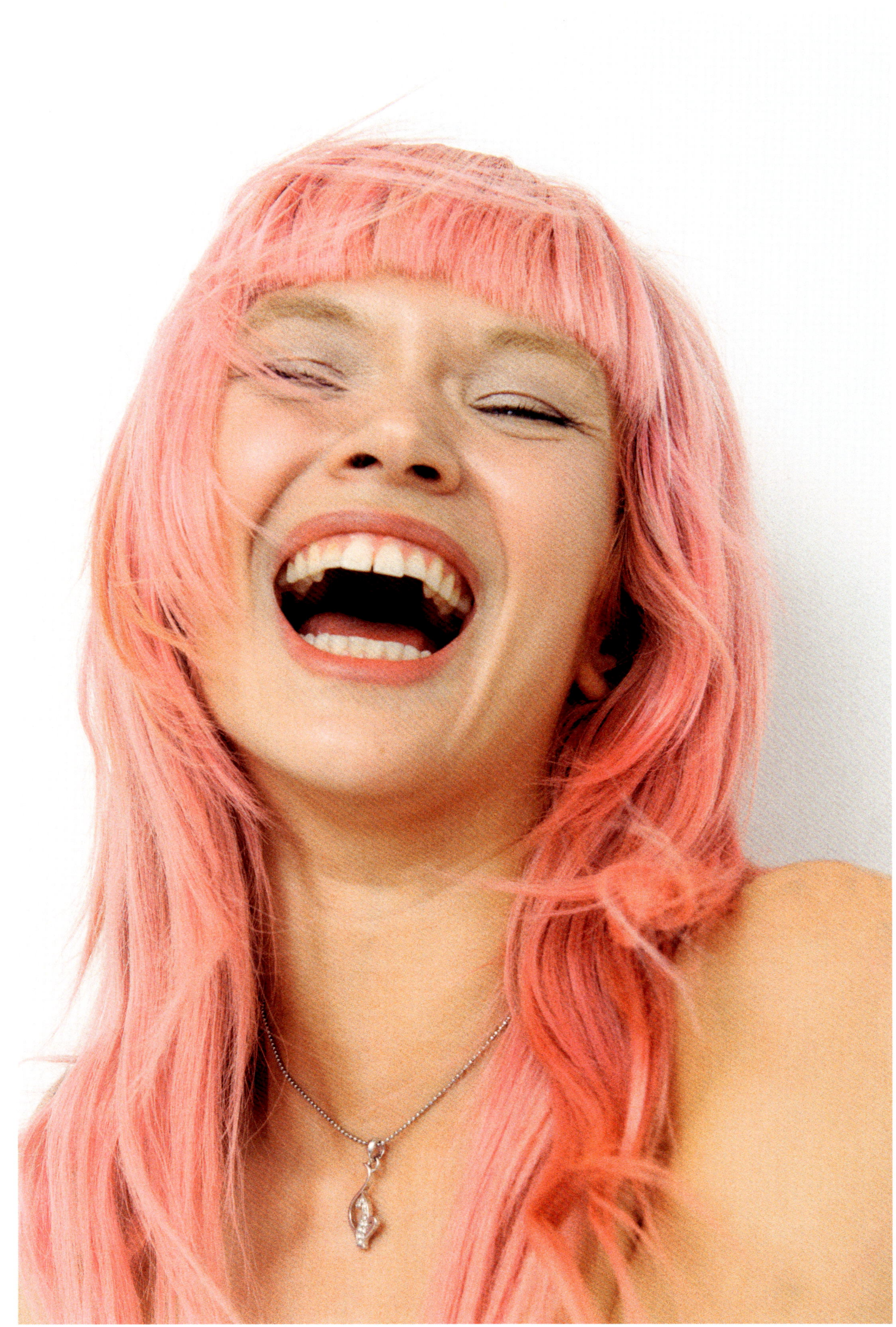

Vega, June 2017

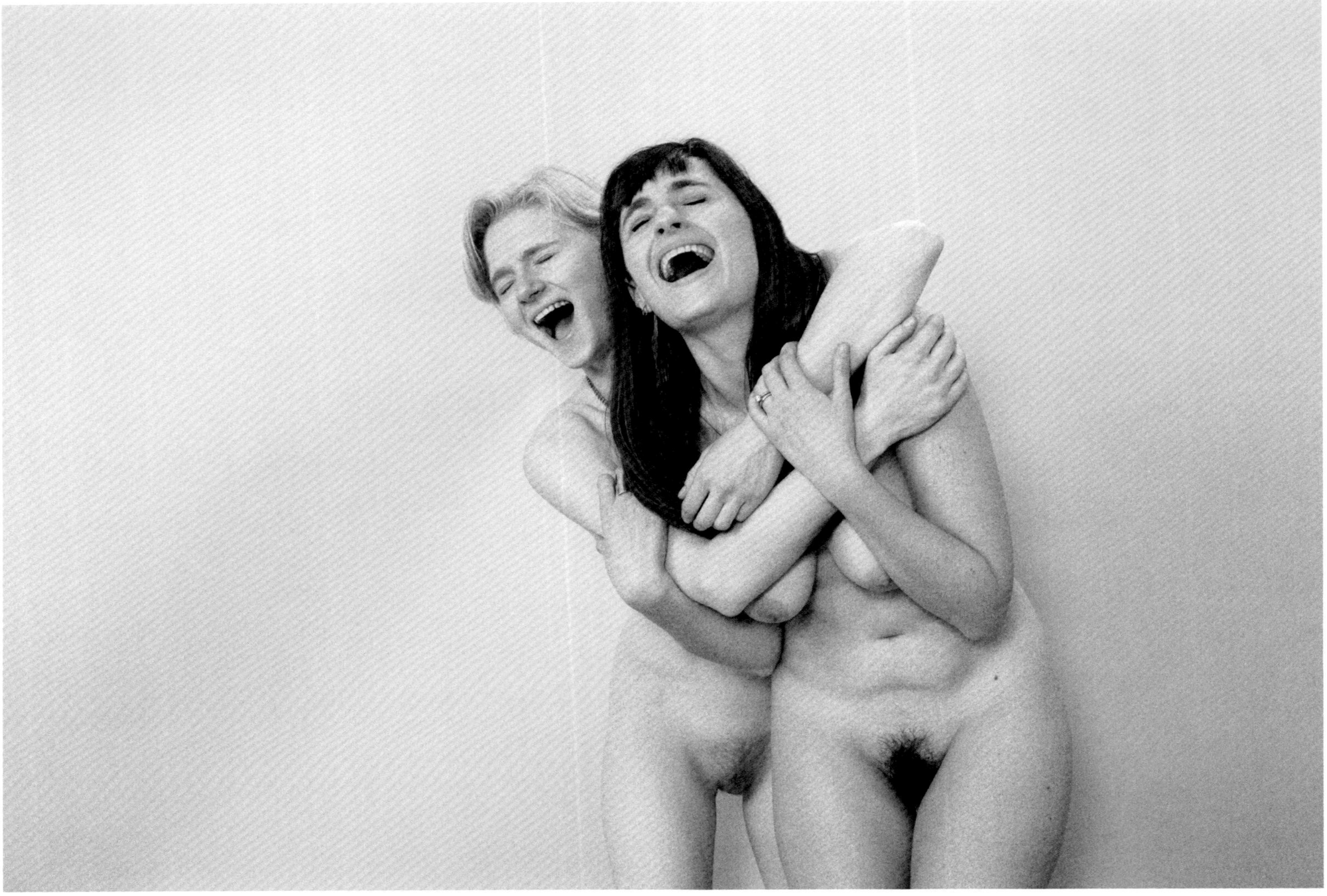

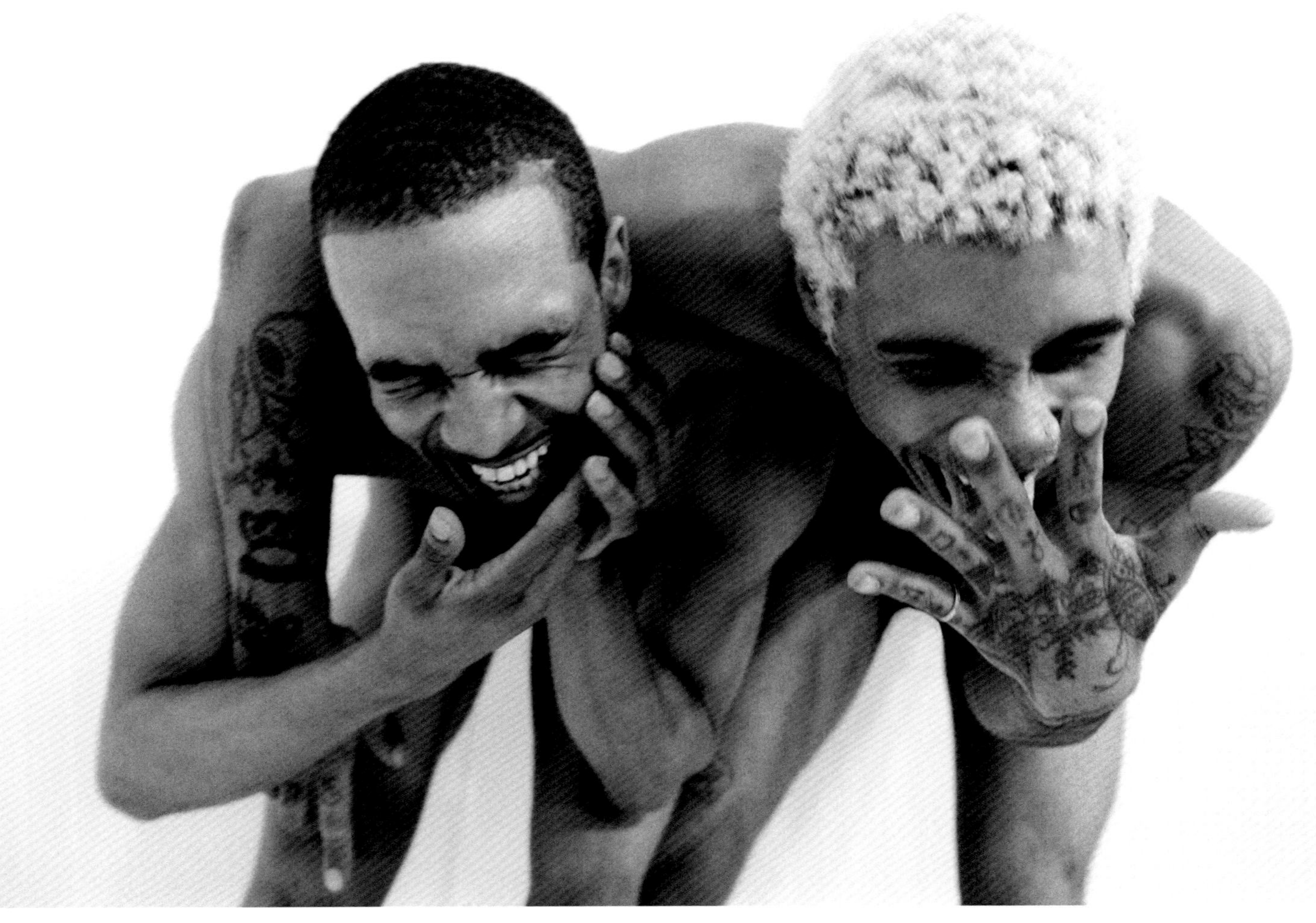

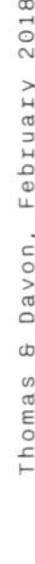

Lily & Britt, January 2017

Thomas & Davon, February 2018

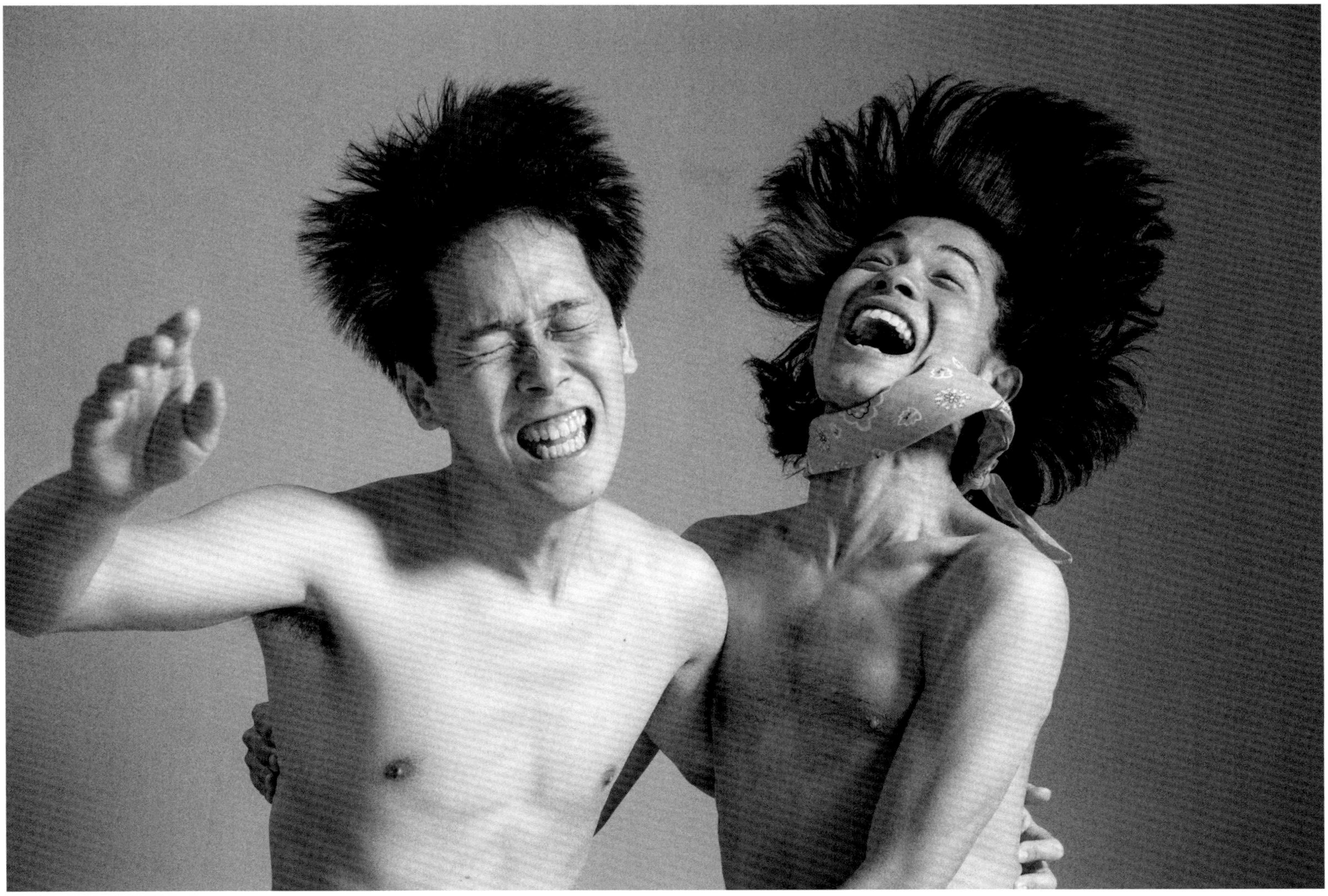

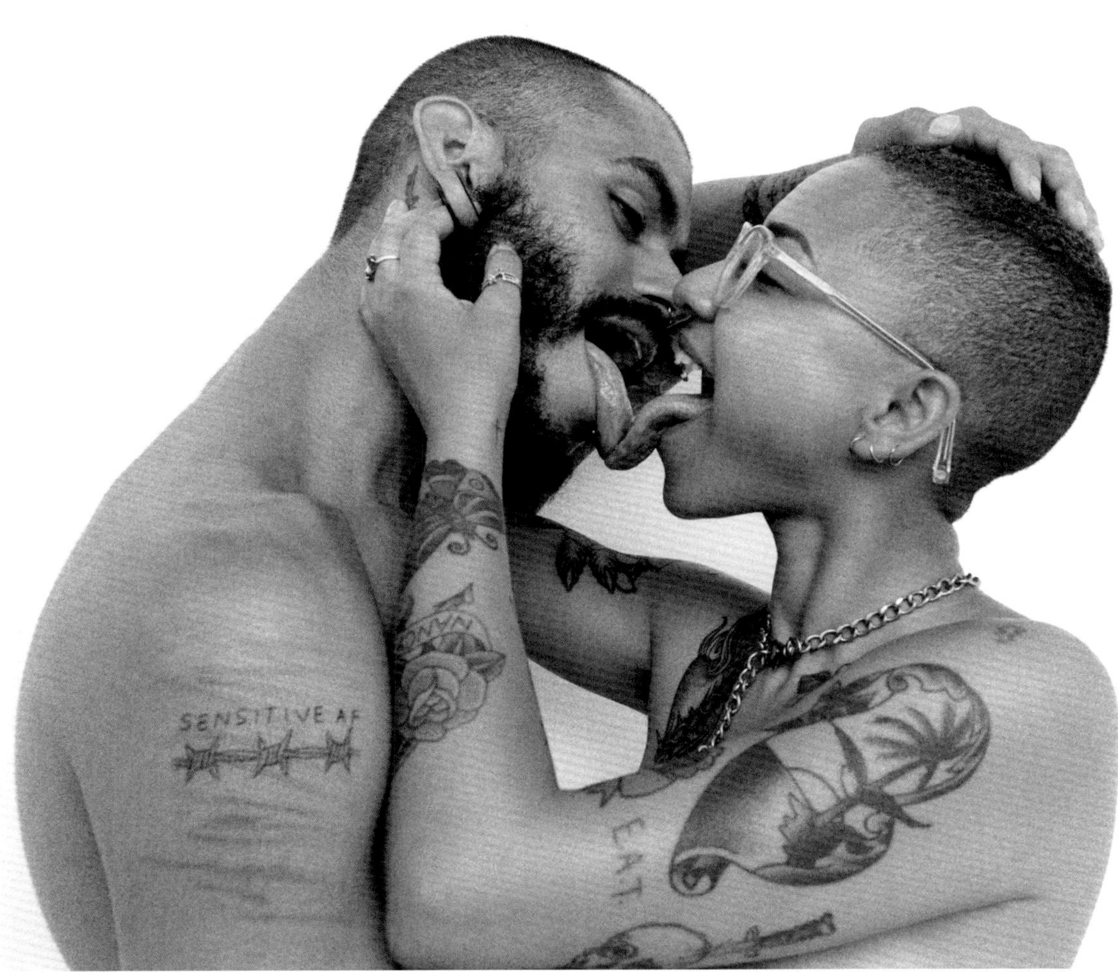

Miyachi & Daiki, March 2016   Alys & Adrian, June 2017

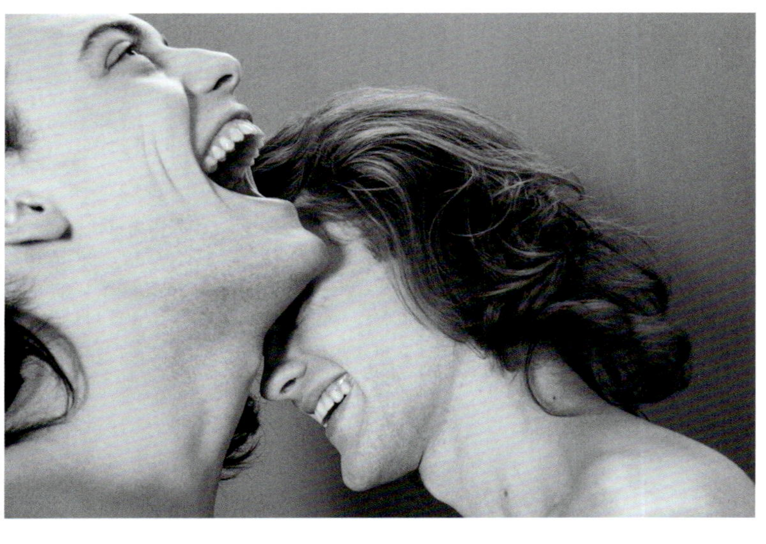

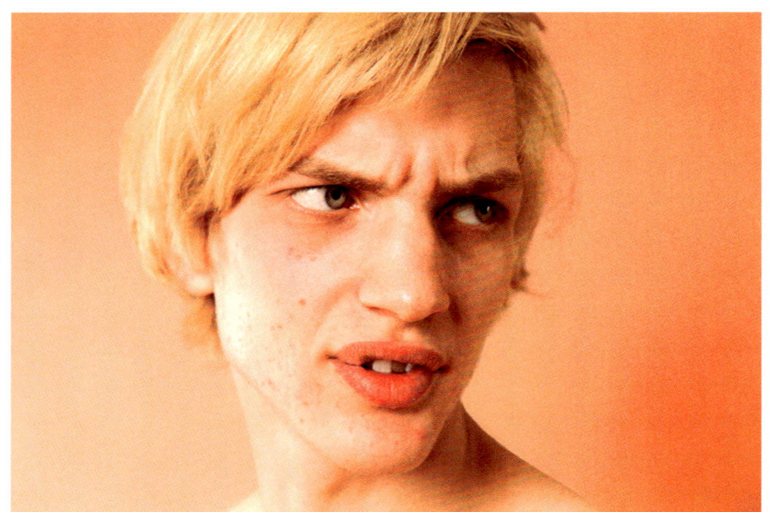

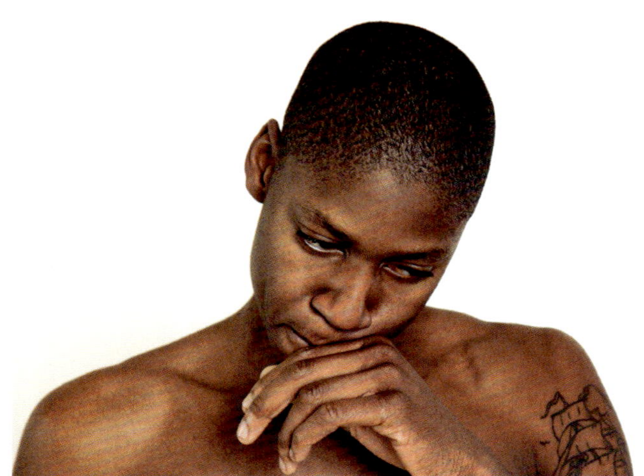

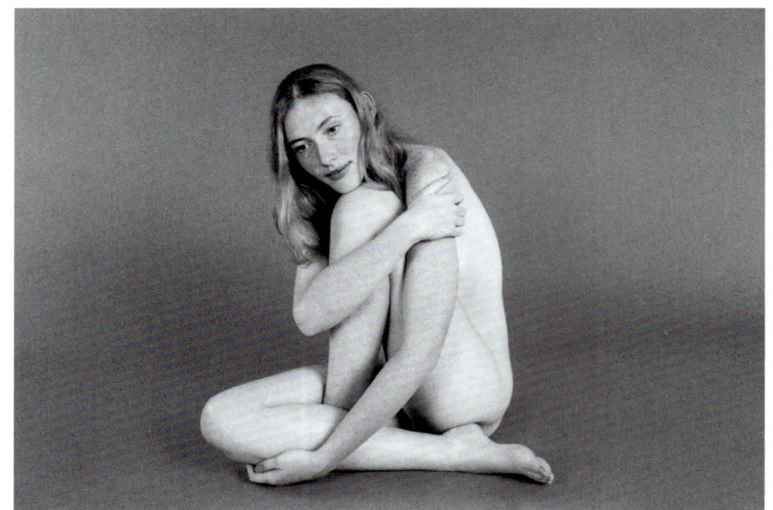

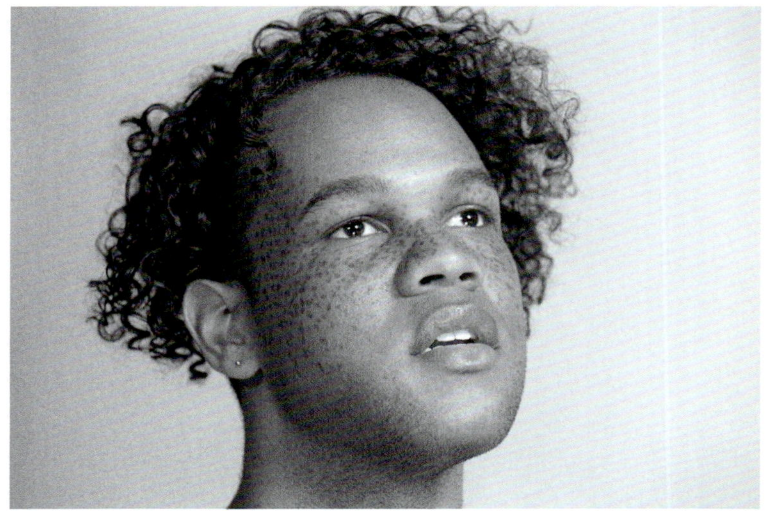

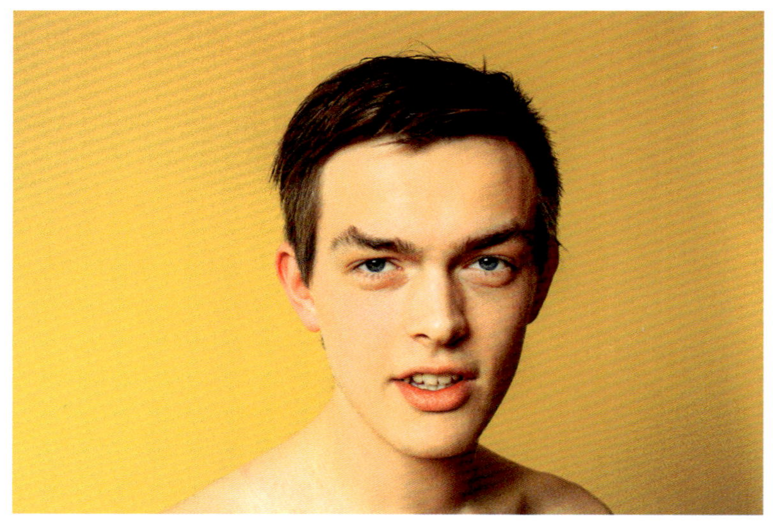

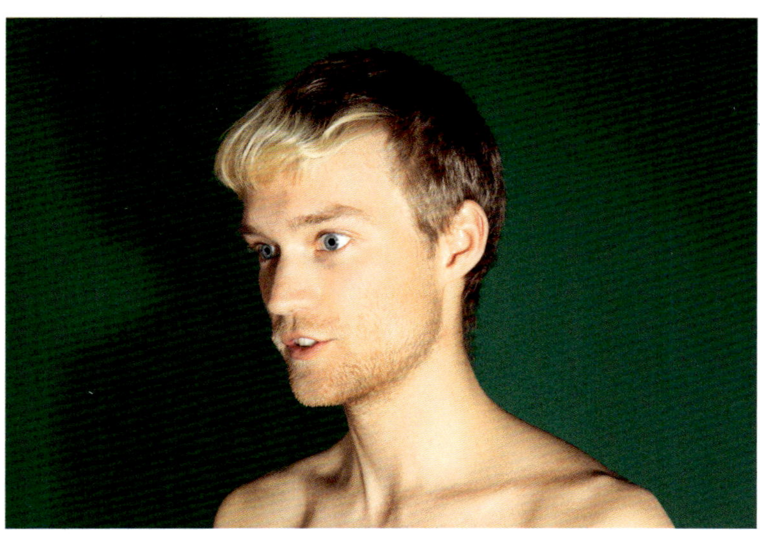

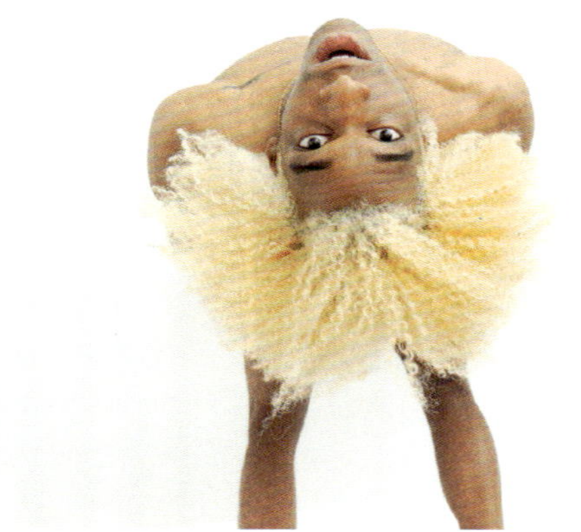

John & Daniel, January 2017 Paul, March 2011 Alex, November 2010 Aine, September 2011 Jordan, May 2016 Alex, January 2010 William, April 2012 Shane, June 2017

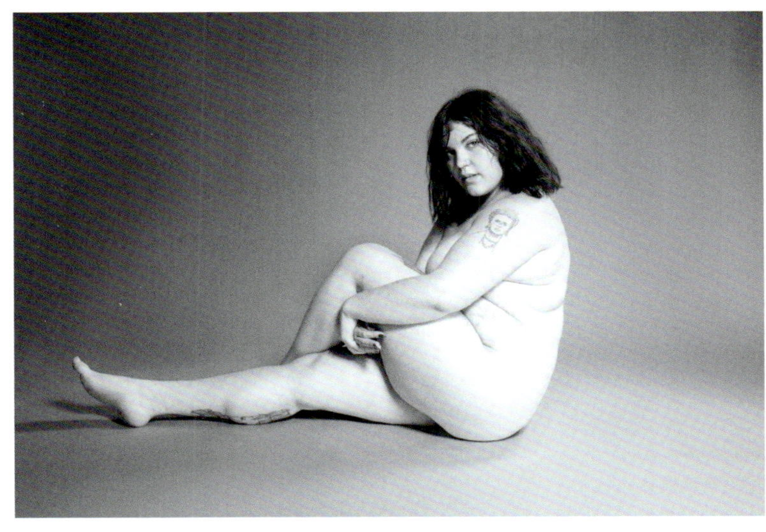

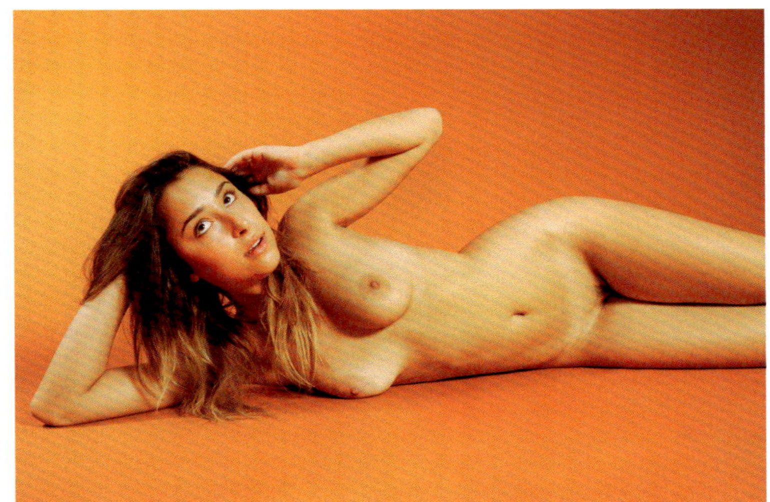

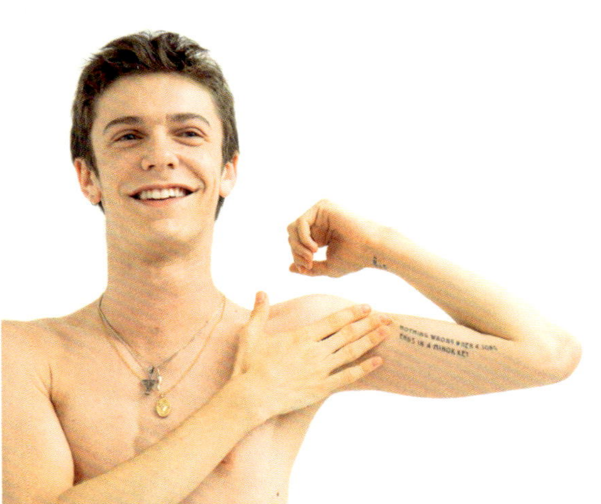

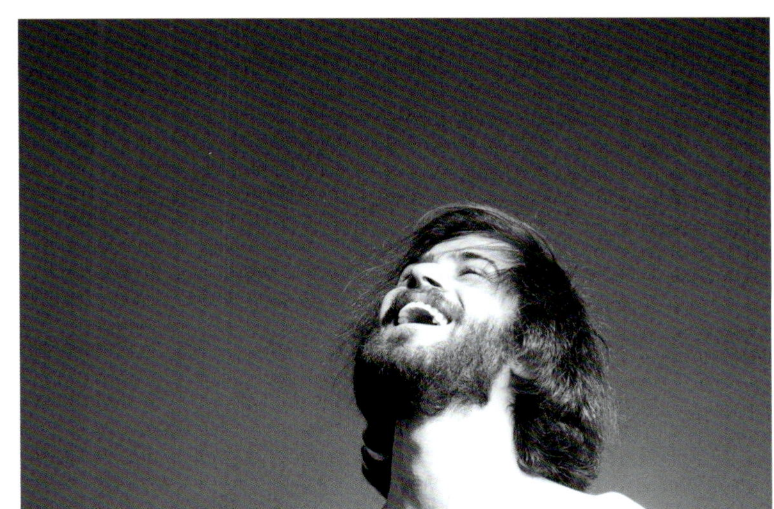

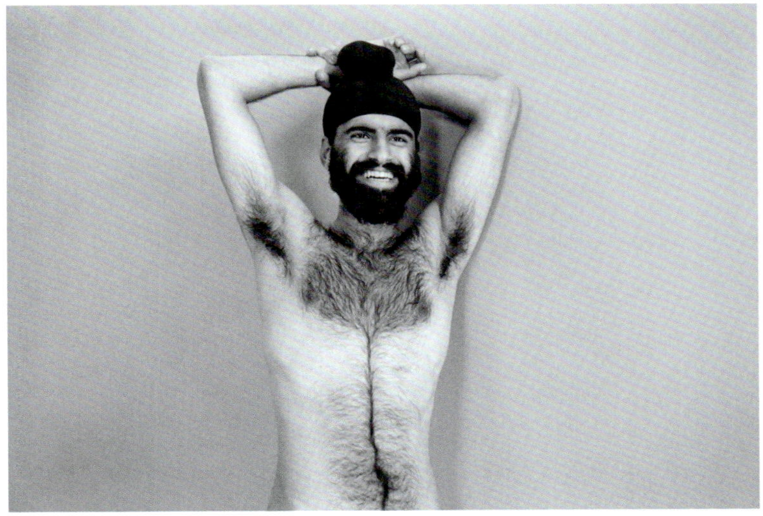

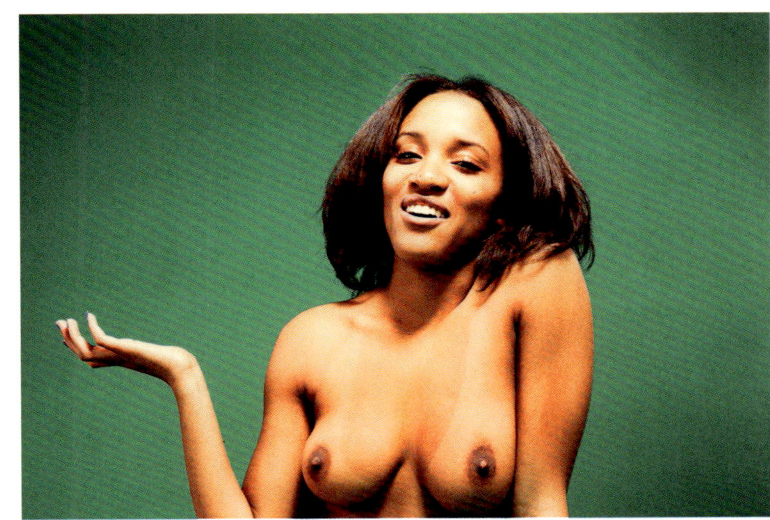

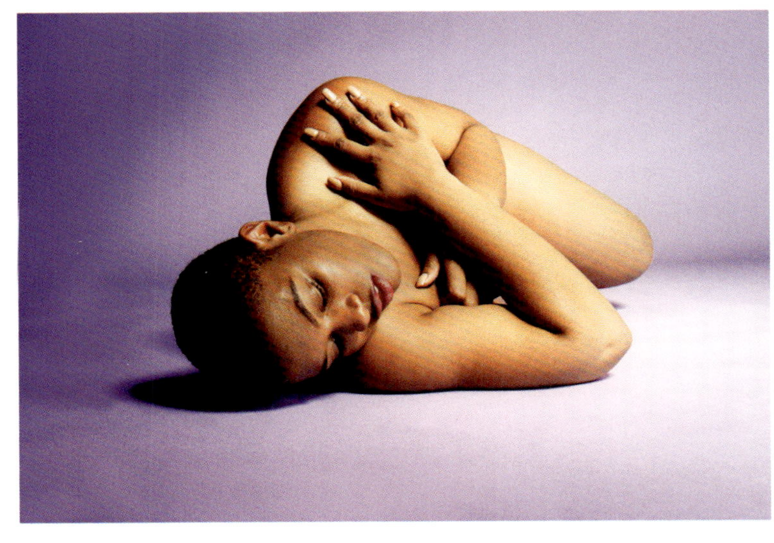

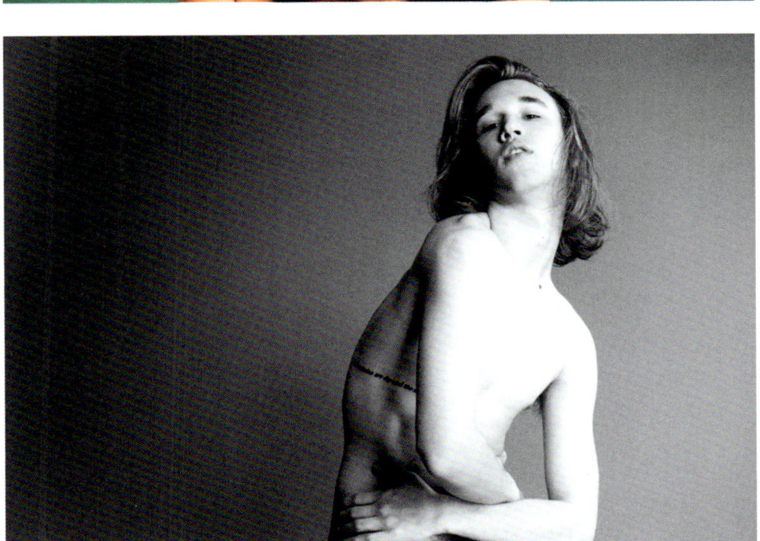

Taylor, October 2015   Chloe, June 2011   Ben, July 2017   Francisco, March 2015   Harry, November 2016   Talia, April 2012   Lovette, January 2015   Samuel, April 2015

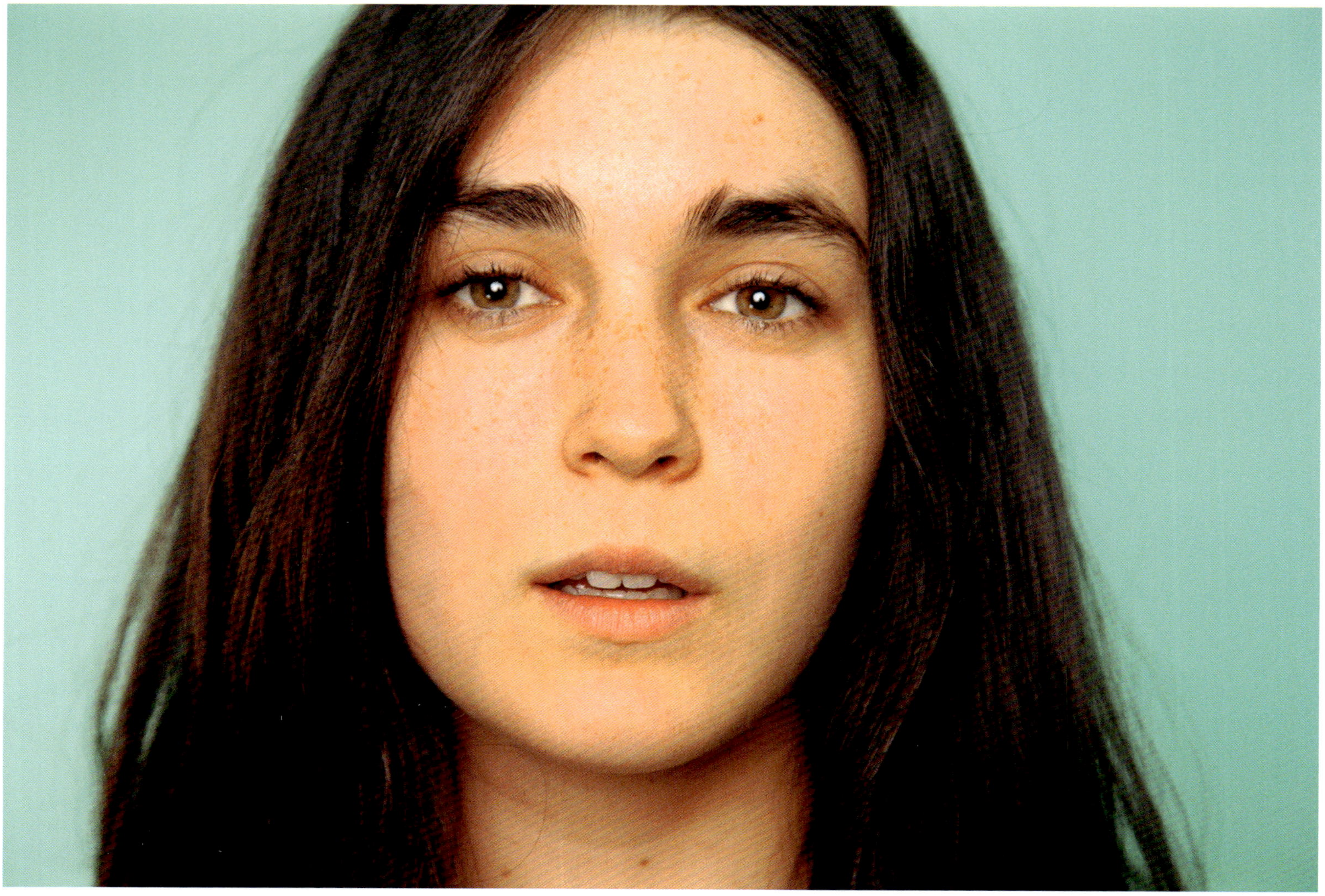

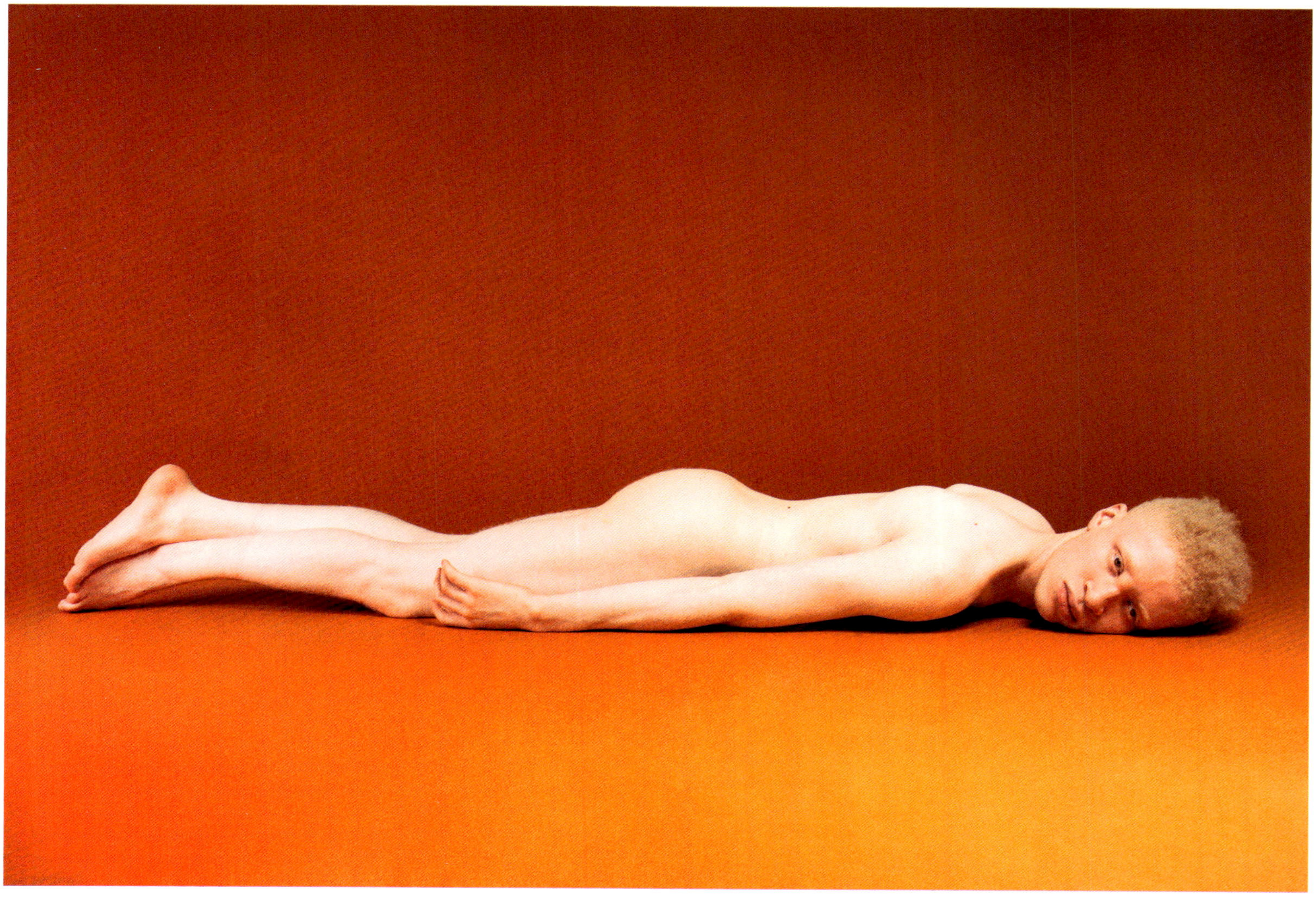

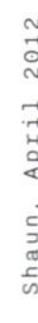
Mara, January 2011 Shaun, April 2012

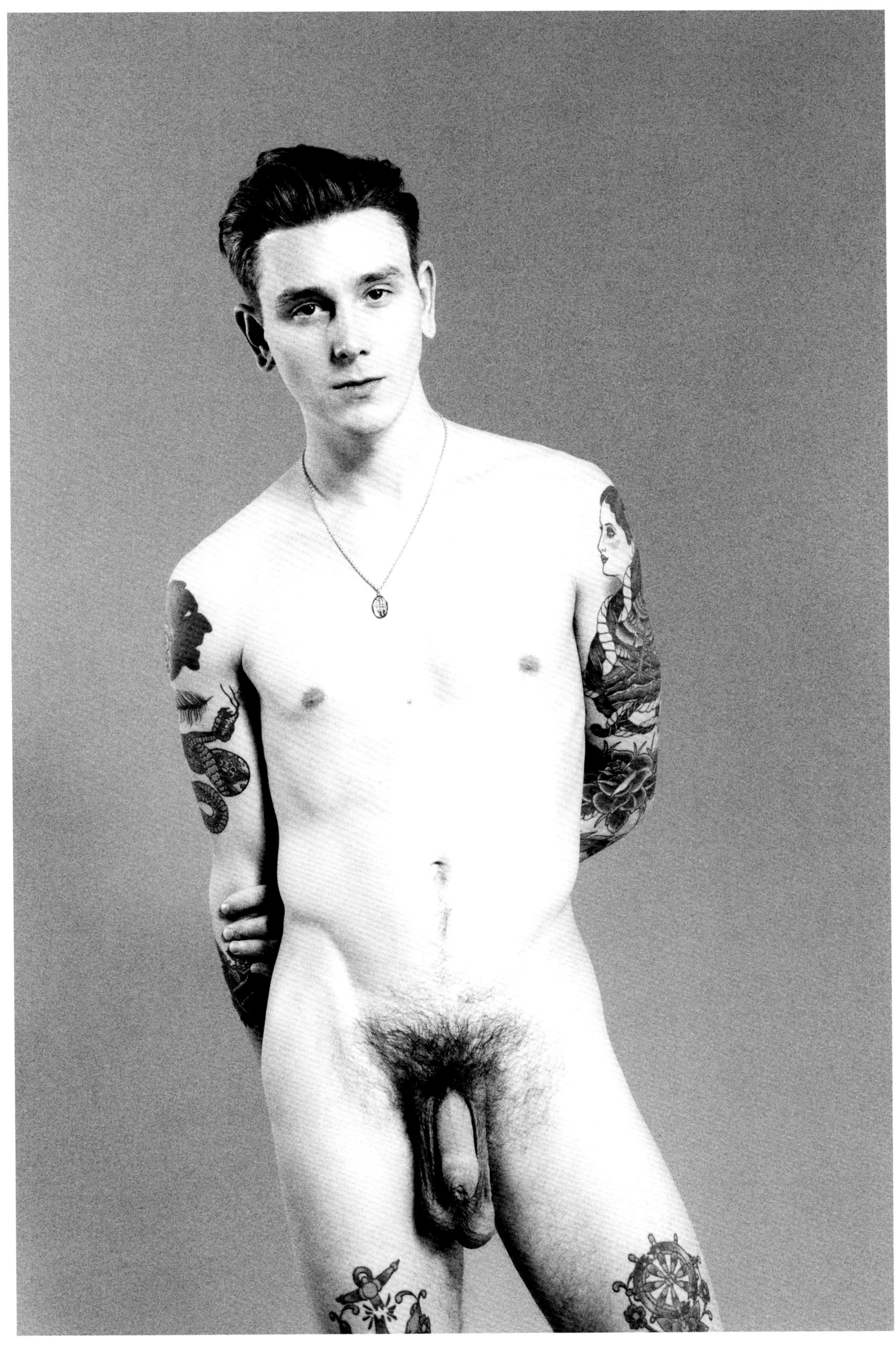

David, December 2014

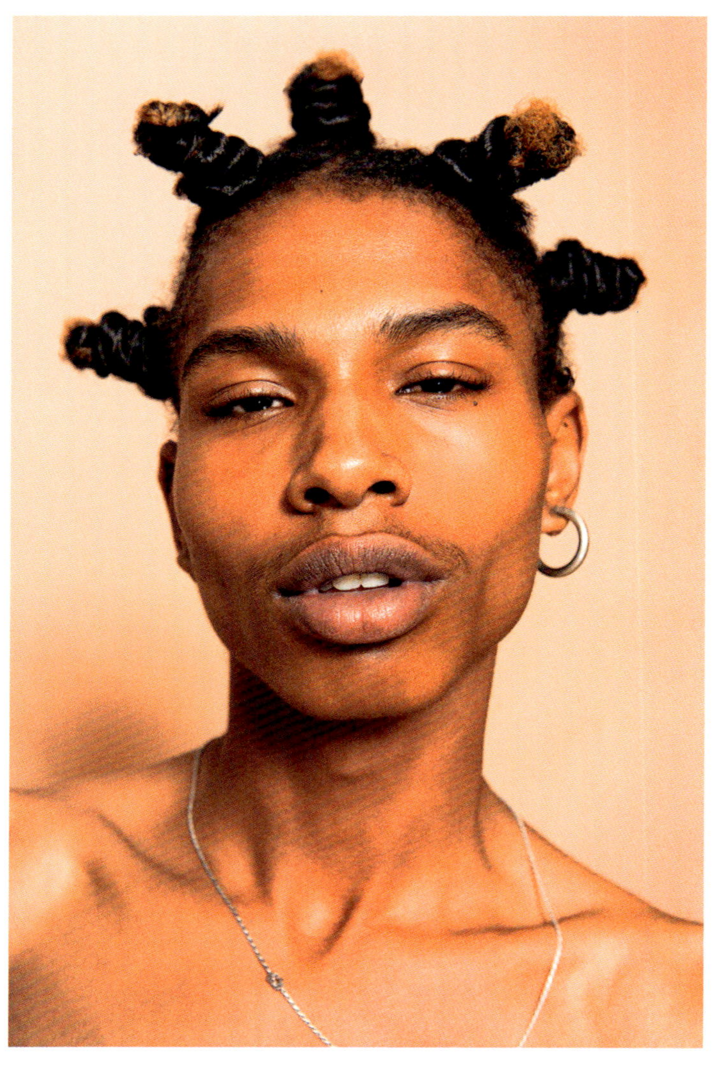

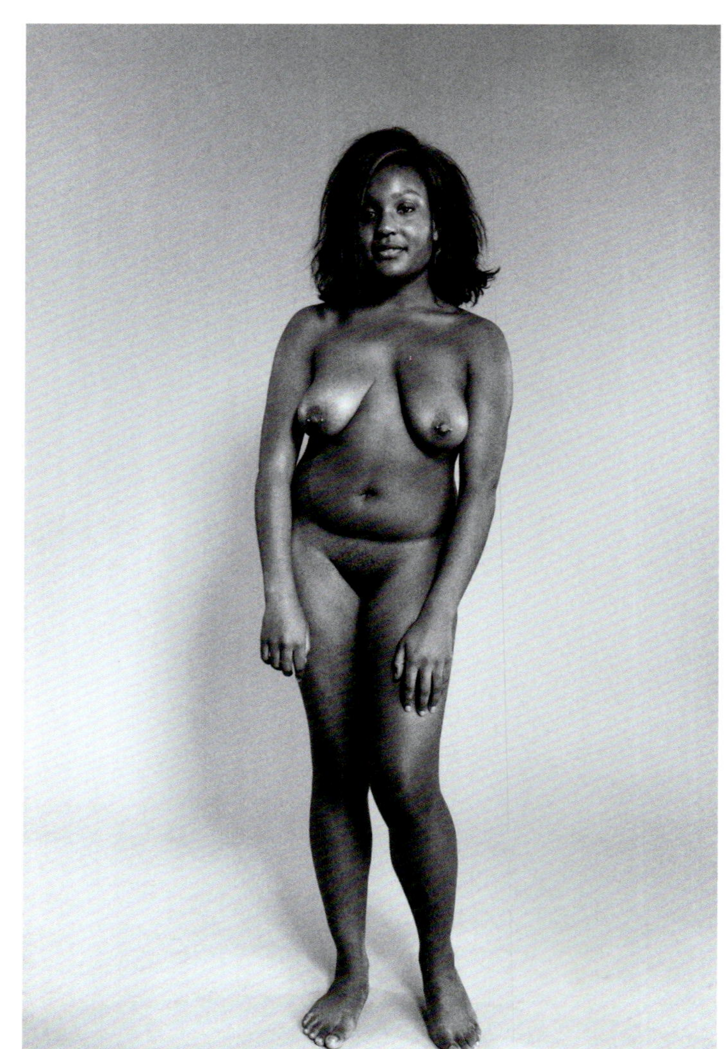

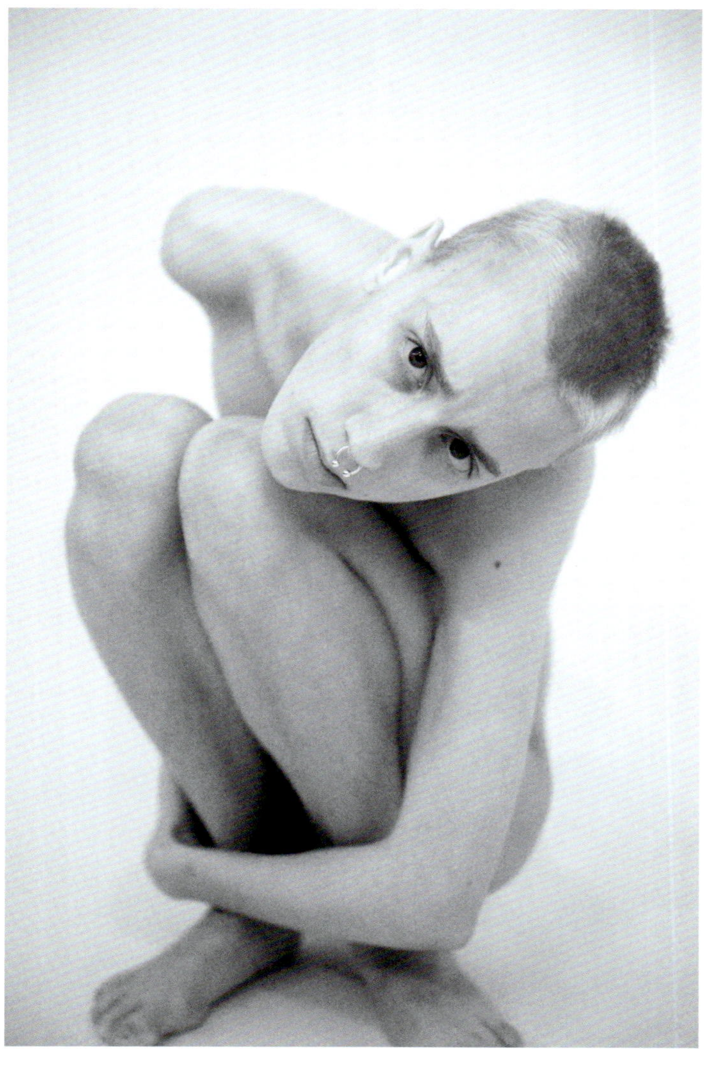

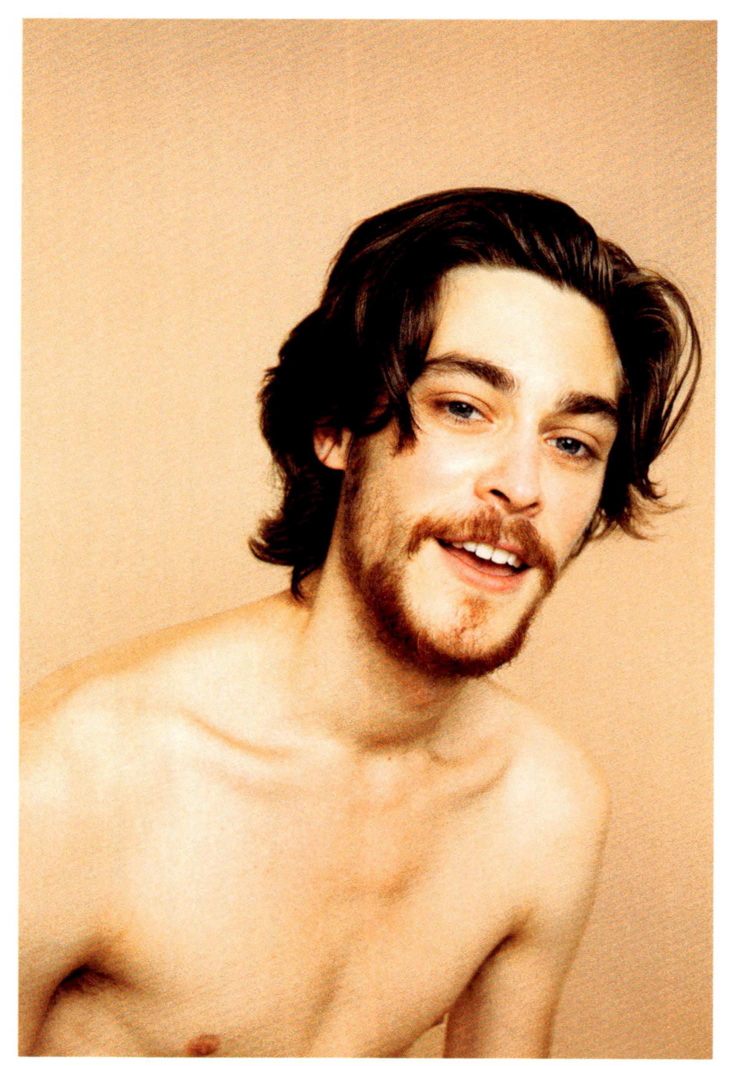

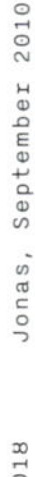

Tawan, September 2016   Alaina, December 2014   Ox, December 2018   Jonas, September 2010

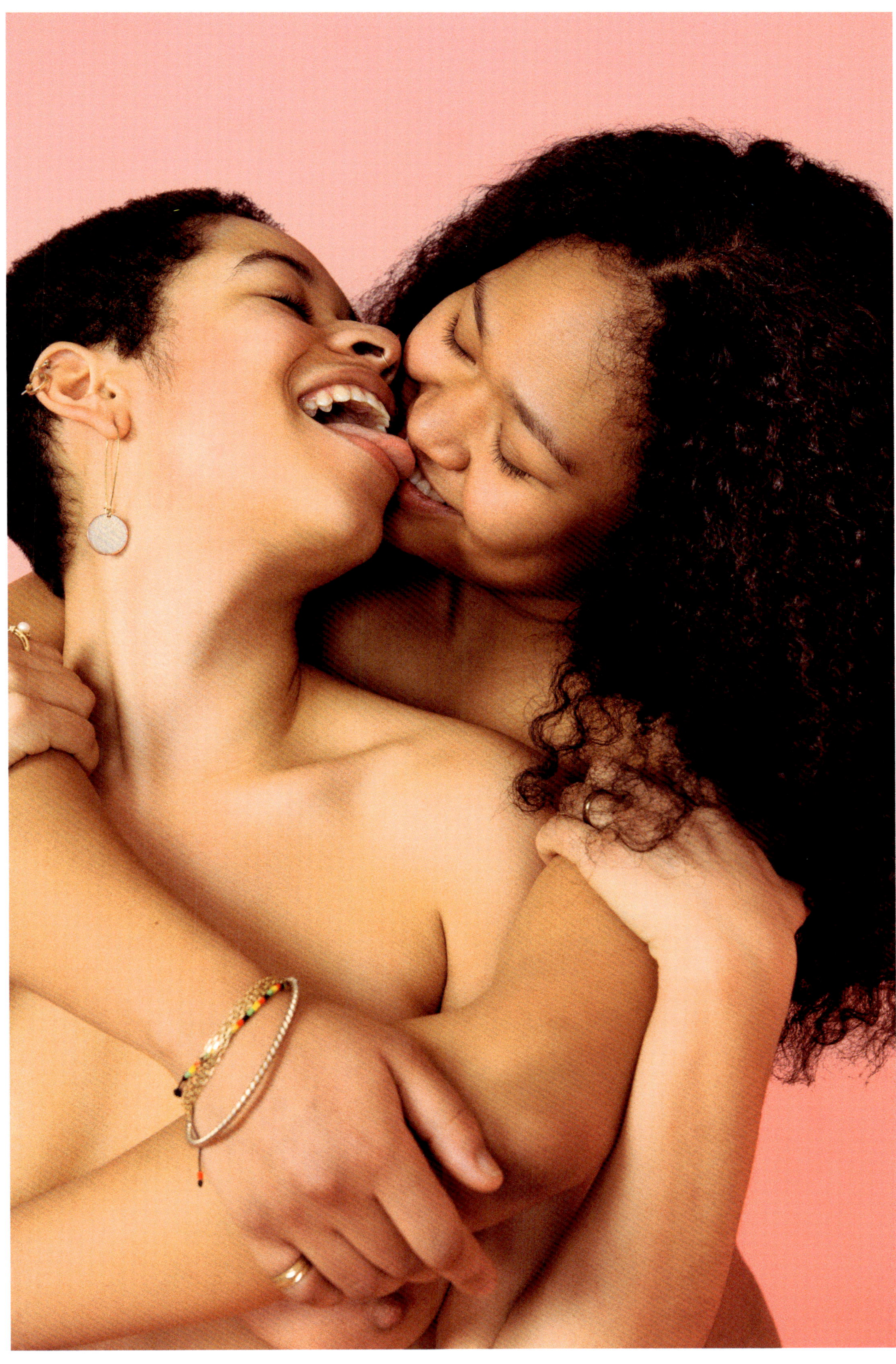

Sasha & Chloe, January 2017

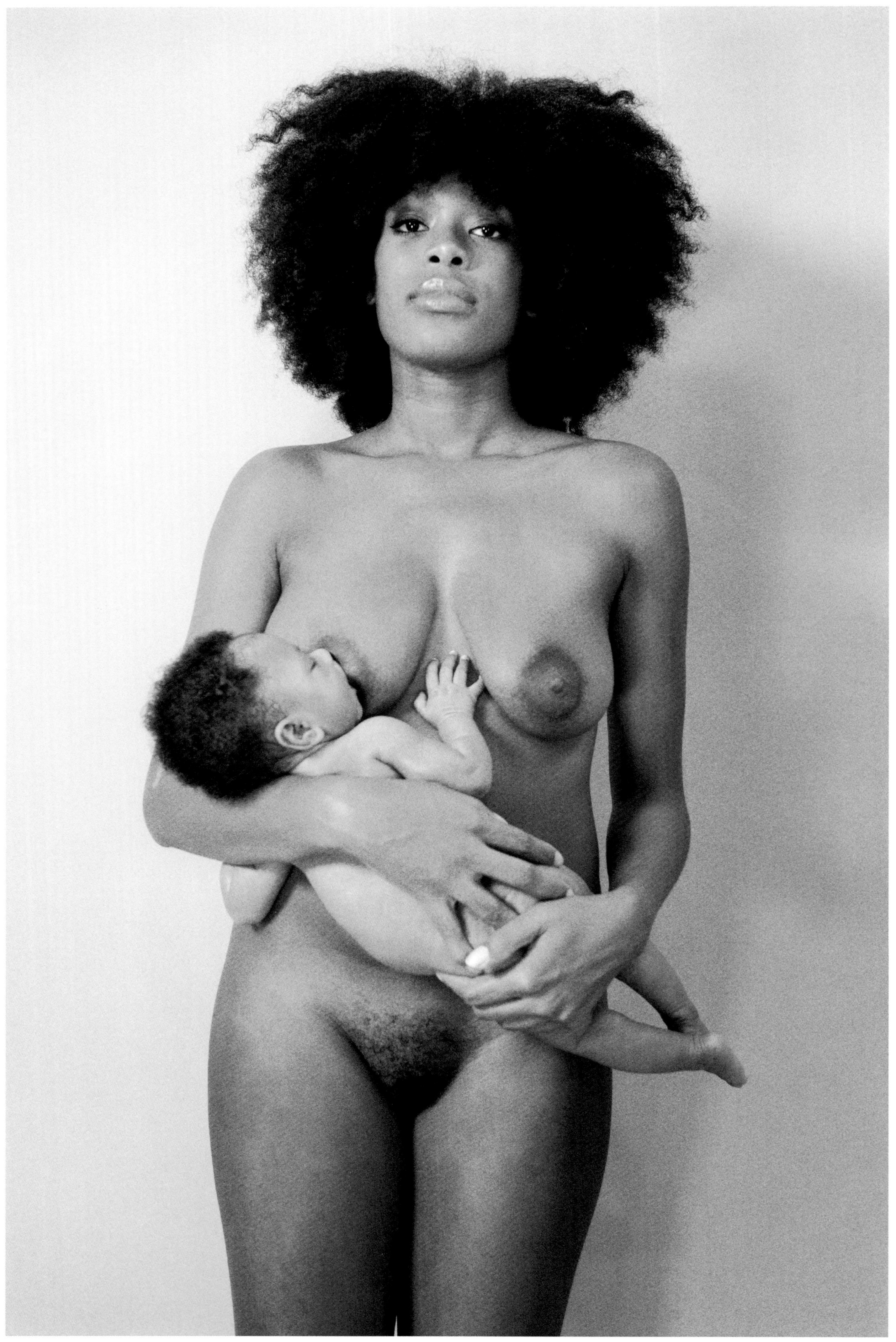

Alexis & Auset, November 2016

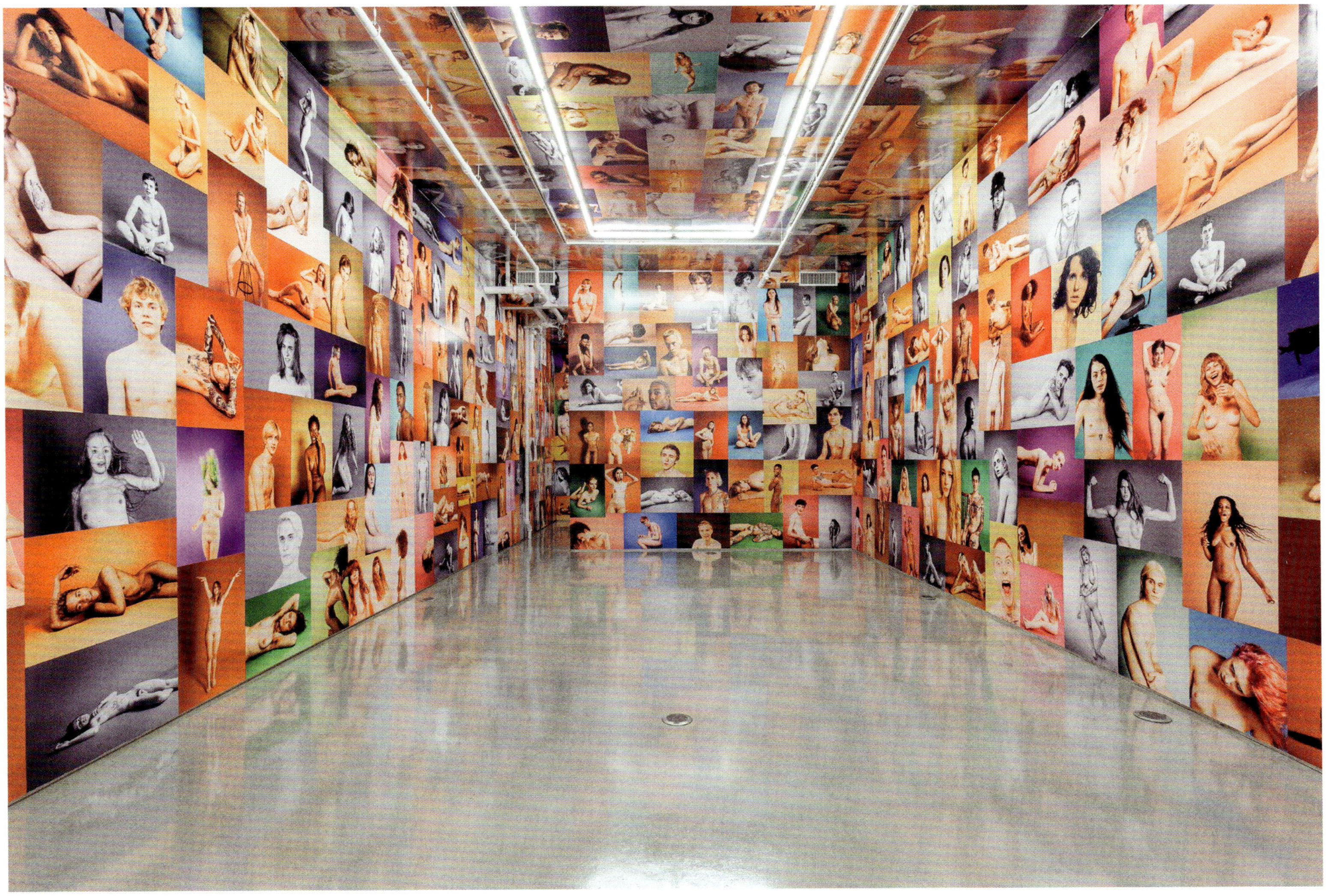

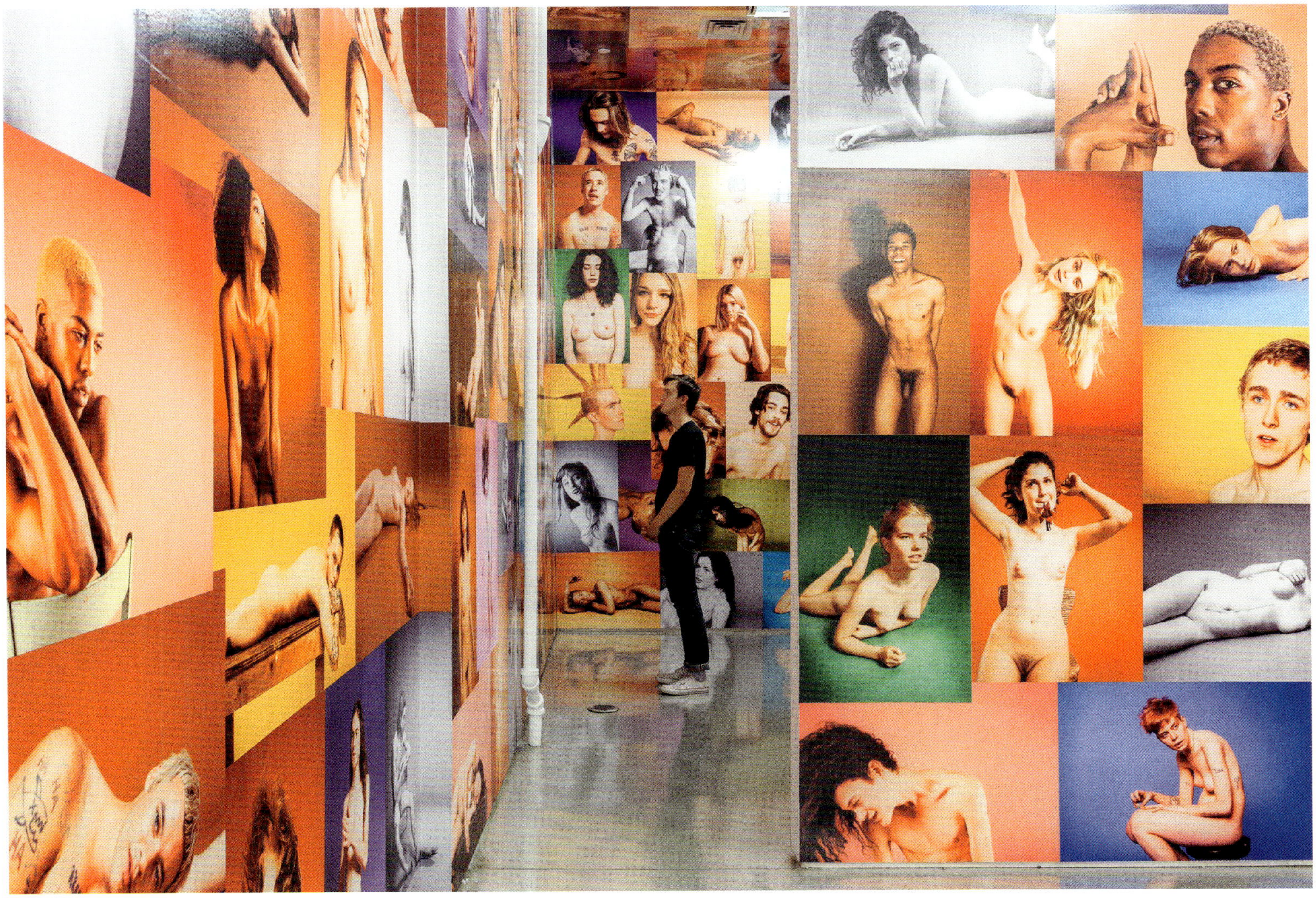

83 Grand Street Gallery, NYC, 2014

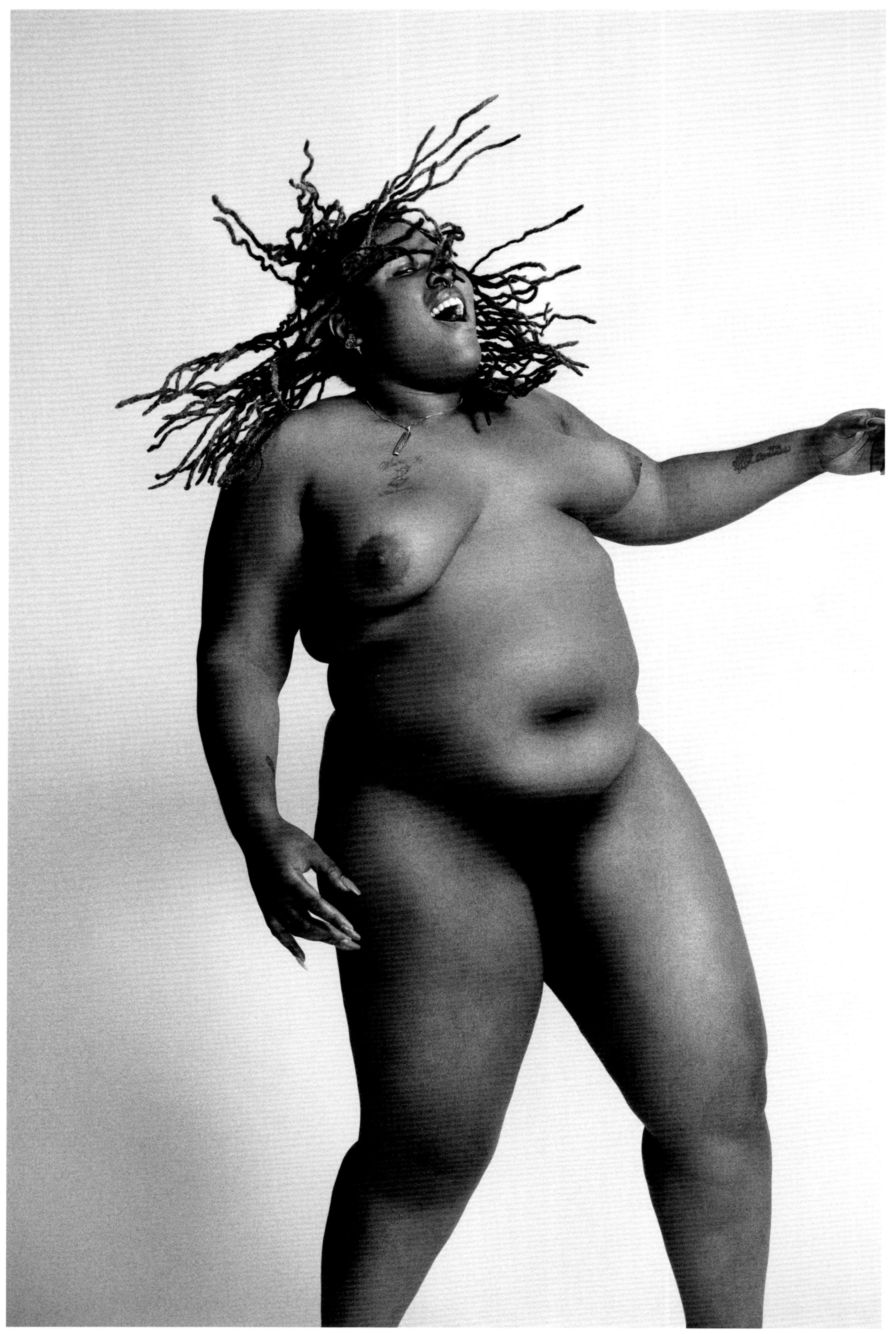

Apyphanie, May 2016

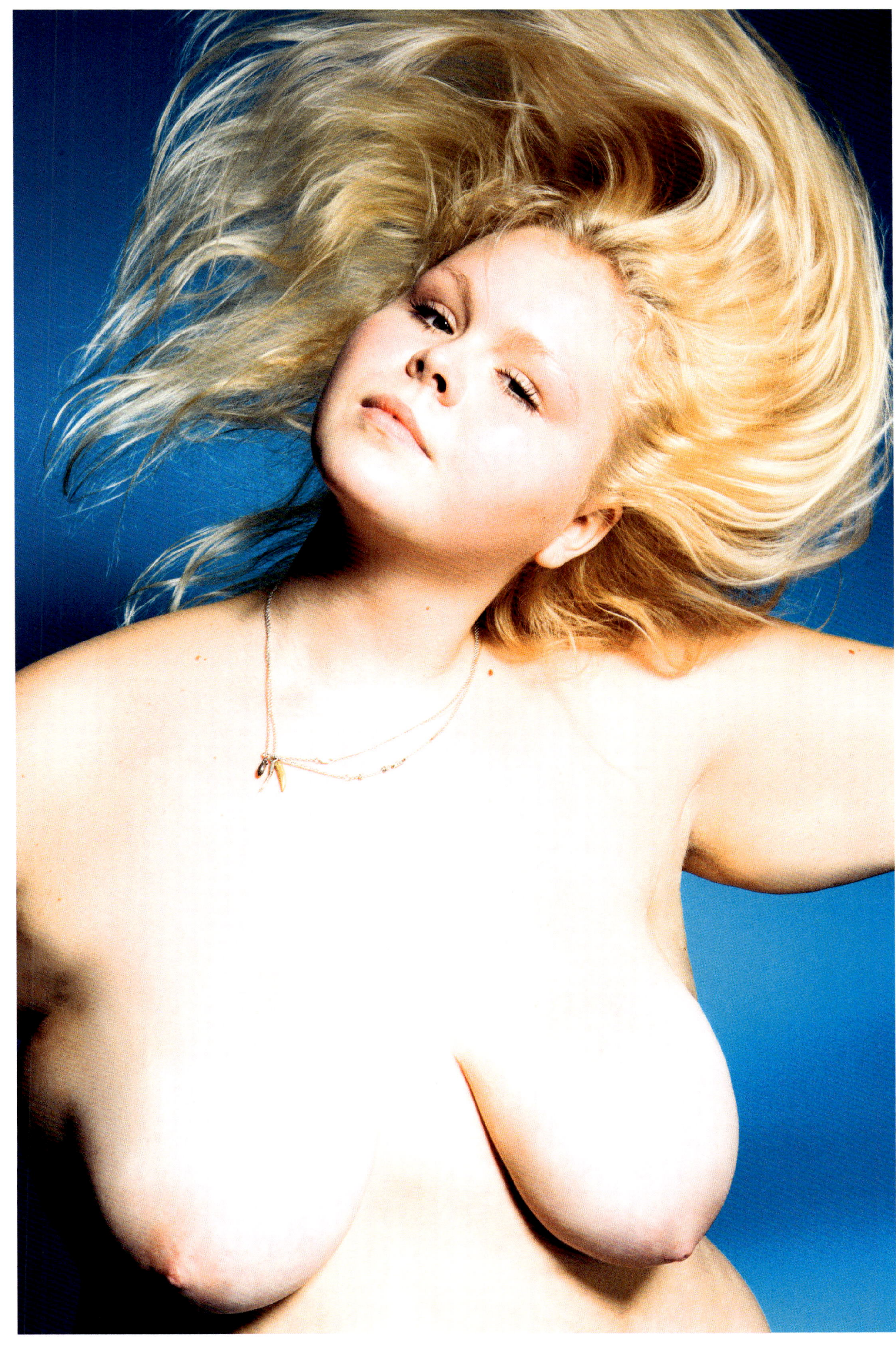

Agusta, December 2015

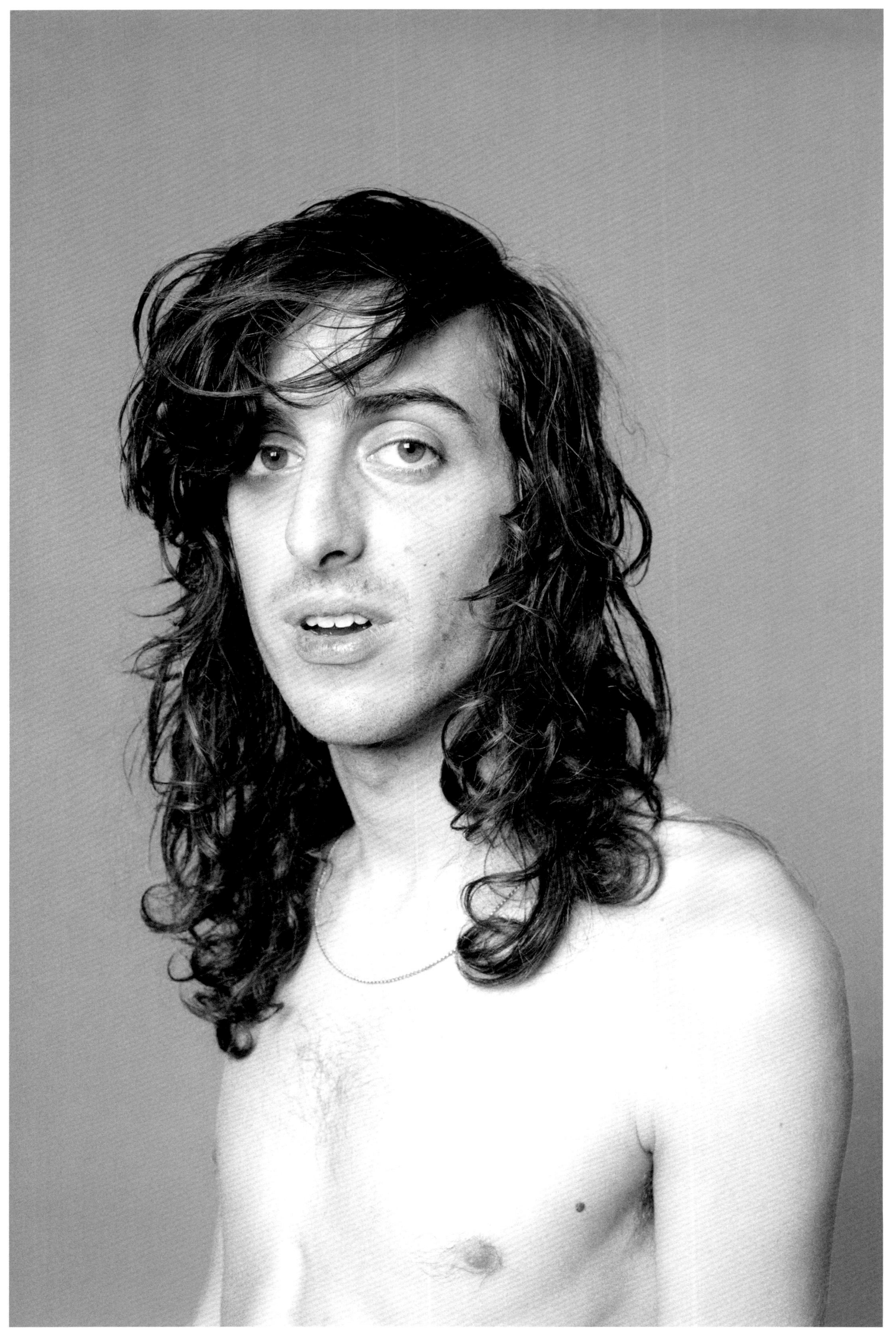

Hamilton, August 2009

I was twenty-two in this photo. I had just started doing lab work and scientific research at a university in Philadelphia. This was around the same time that *Vice* was skyrocketing into a new realm of success. There was a lot of partying. And there were certainly a lot of people using drugs.

In mainstream publishing back then, there was still the standard, square, scaremongering approach about the dangers of drugs and drug addiction. Even places like *Rolling Stone* were running scare stories of one kind or another. And then there was a libertine, ultra-hedonist approach that was probably exemplified by early *Vice*, where there was a kind of romanticization of people who had really excessive boundary-pushing drug use behavior. I was neither of those things. I felt that there had to be something in between, where you could have an appreciation of the power of drugs and of the joy and the fun associated with them, but also appreciate their toxicology, history, and chemistry. The influx of funding at *Vice* made it possible to pursue this. I started by writing a column. Then I pivoted to video [with *Hamilton's Pharmacopeia*].

Just fifteen years ago, it was considered very weird and novel to do what I was doing. Like, "Oh my god, there's a guy and he's only studying and reporting on drugs. That's crazy." As if it was such a fringe topic when, for better or worse, drugs are one of the most consequential influences in our society. Drug overdoses are one of the major causes of death among young people. The use of antidepressants is widespread. Drugs were never a fringe topic, there was just a lack of seriousness and carefully considered analysis.

That's changed. Drugs and especially psychedelics have gone from a bizarre thing to report on to being endlessly discussed and studied by so many new labs. Ketamine was recently approved as a treatment for treatment-resistant depression by the FDA. Current projections suggest that both psilocybin and MDMA will be clinically approved next year. There's a long history to psychedelics—it's not like this began in 2009—but we can trace the "psychedelic renaissance" to around this time.

A major shift has been towards the ketamine orientation of our current moment, which is emblematic, I think, of the isolation and atomization of people. At a time when people are working from home and in ways where they don't have actual physical contact with anybody else, ketamine almost seems like the perfect embodiment of that experience, where you go entirely within yourself and disconnect yourself from other people. I don't necessarily think that's a good thing. In fact, it's potentially a very bad thing, but it's also just an extension of the cultural climate.

In the same way that there's this reverberation between drugs and culture, there's also that exchange between art and culture. Looking at this photo, it's funny. The long hair was a brief phase for me. I feel like a lot of men had long hair then because that was the Ryan McGinley style. Ryan's work was so influential, it was almost like he was changing the ways people were behaving. Well, who's even to say? Everyone around me was, in some way, at least one degree of separation from Ryan. I was living with one of his models. It's impossible to know if they inspired Ryan McGinley, or he inspired them—there was this constant interplay.

There is something strange about seeing so many people you know being converted into fine art. It's nice, and I'm grateful it happened. This is Ryan's vision of what he found beautiful in New York and within a scene of creative people. I appreciate that he used real people with interesting stories. There's a whole world in each of these people.

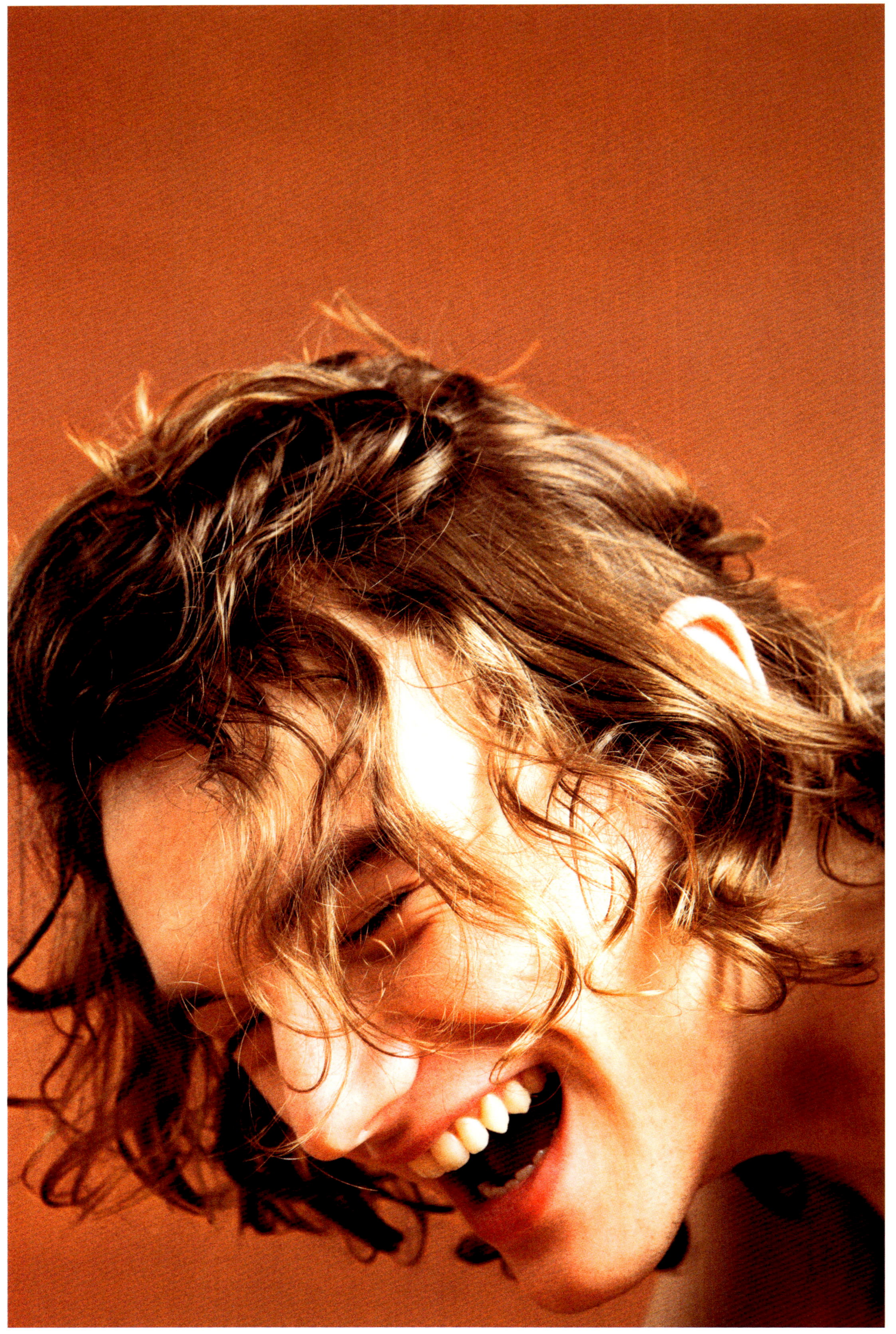

Richard, November 2011

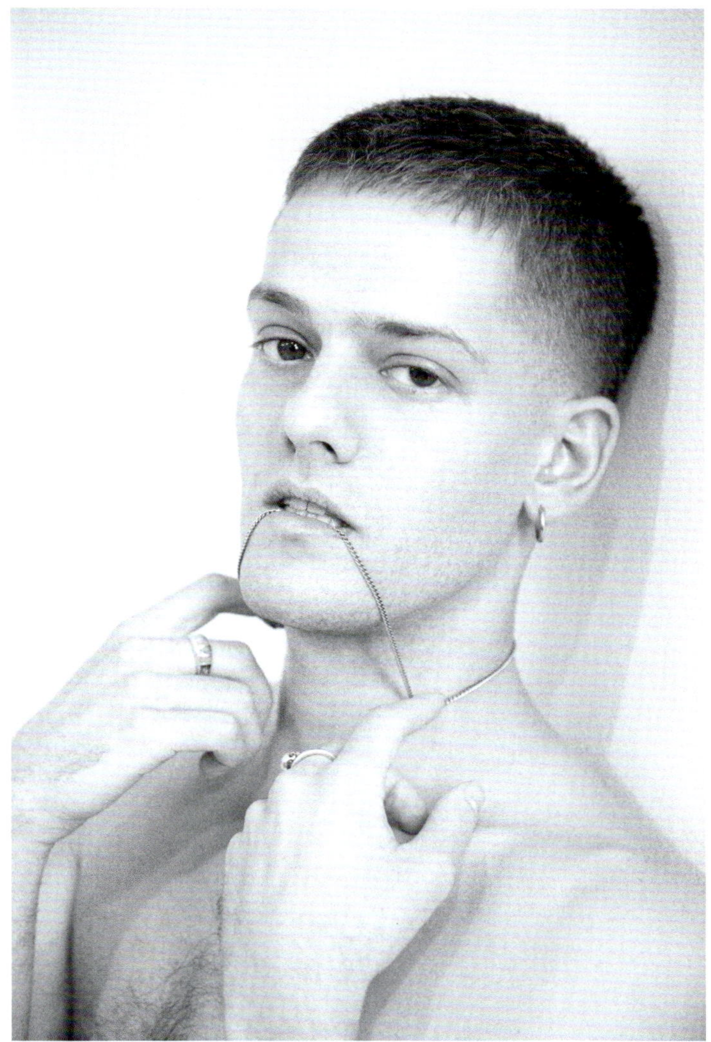

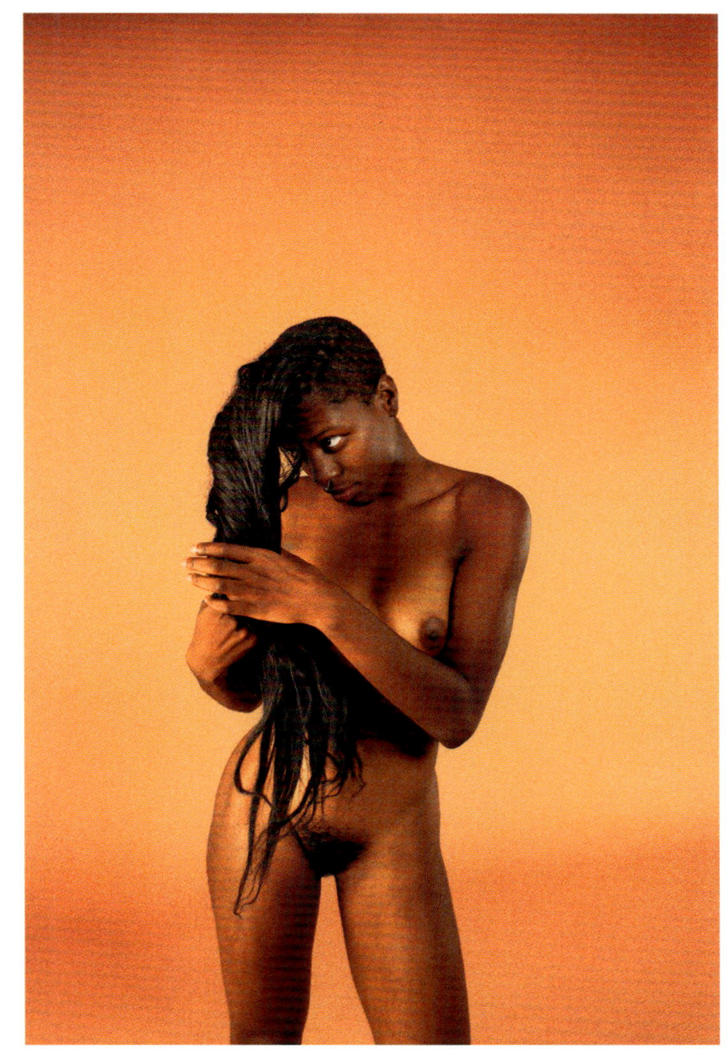

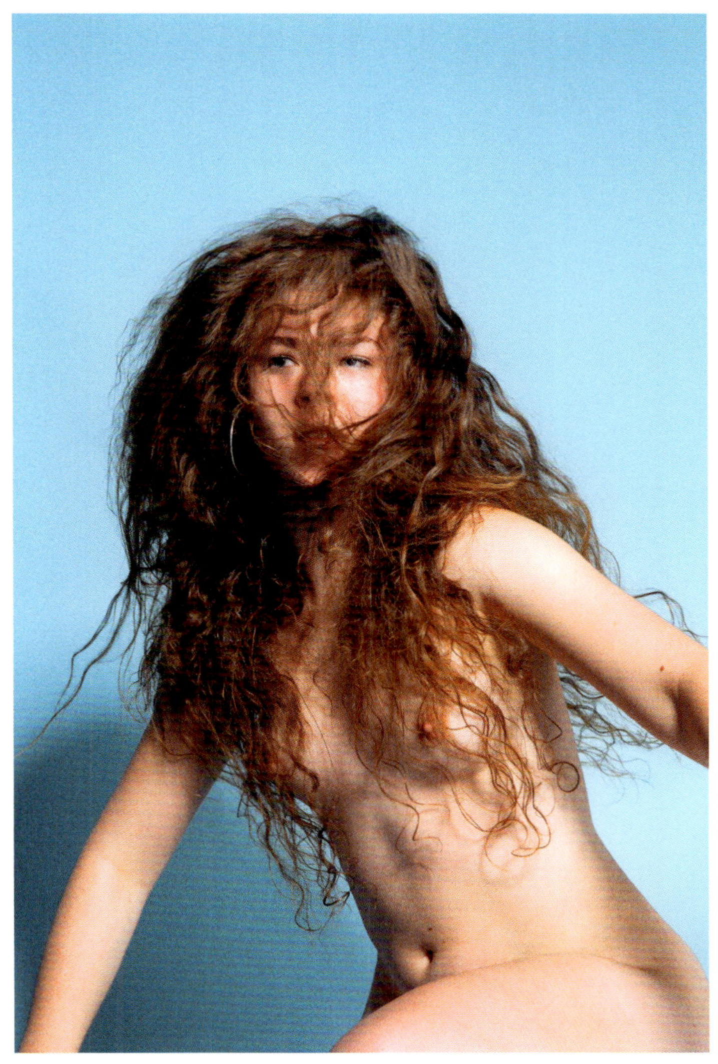

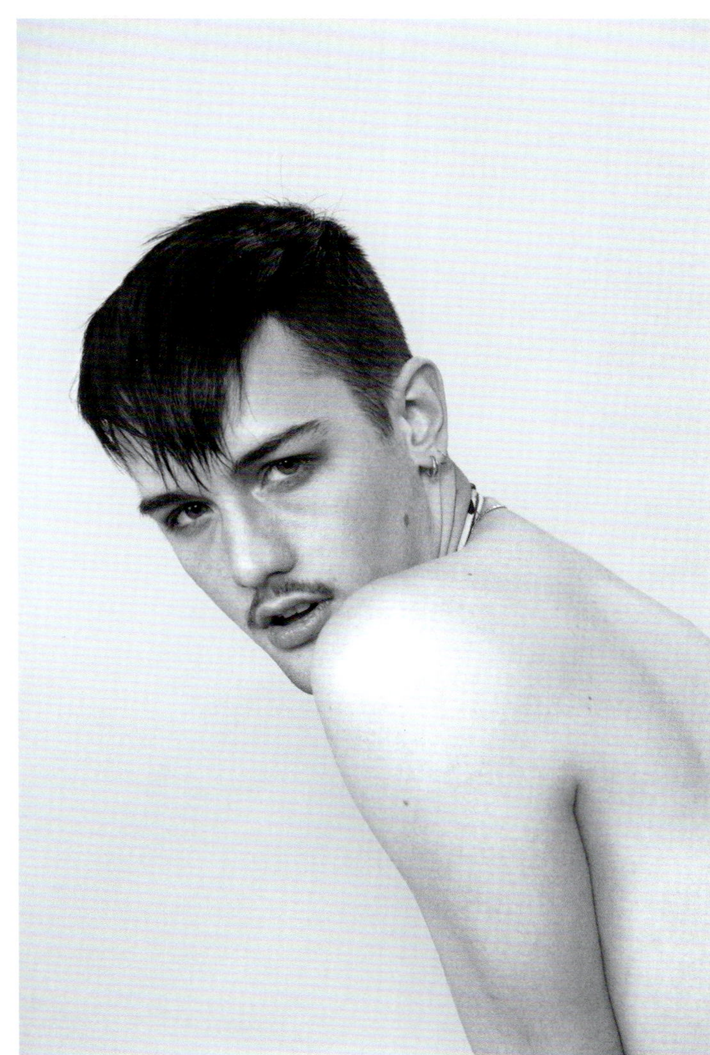

Jacob, December 2018   Devin, October 2012   Annabel, October 2015   McLayne, January 2017

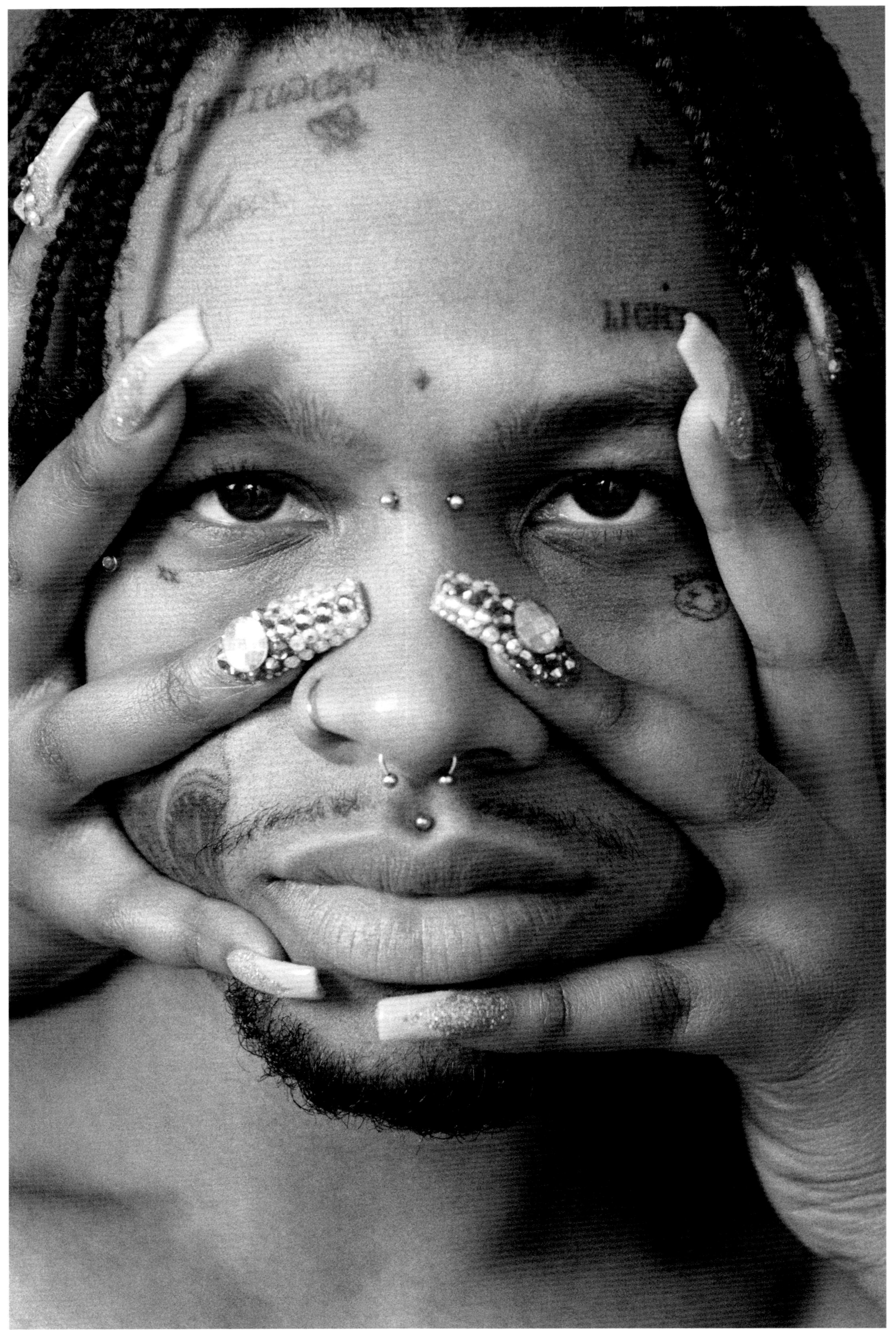

Rad & Raisa, January 2017

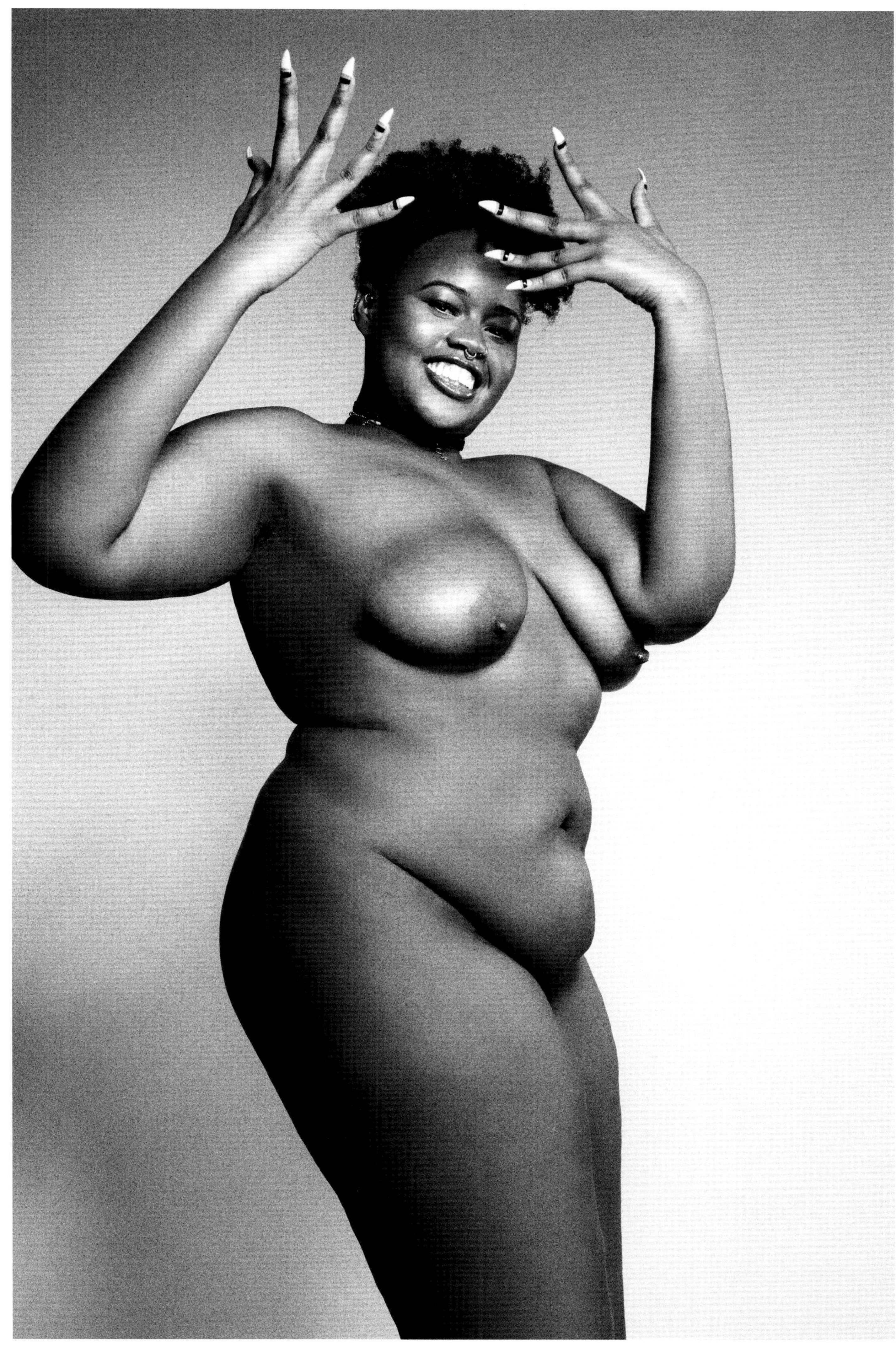

Raisa, April 2015

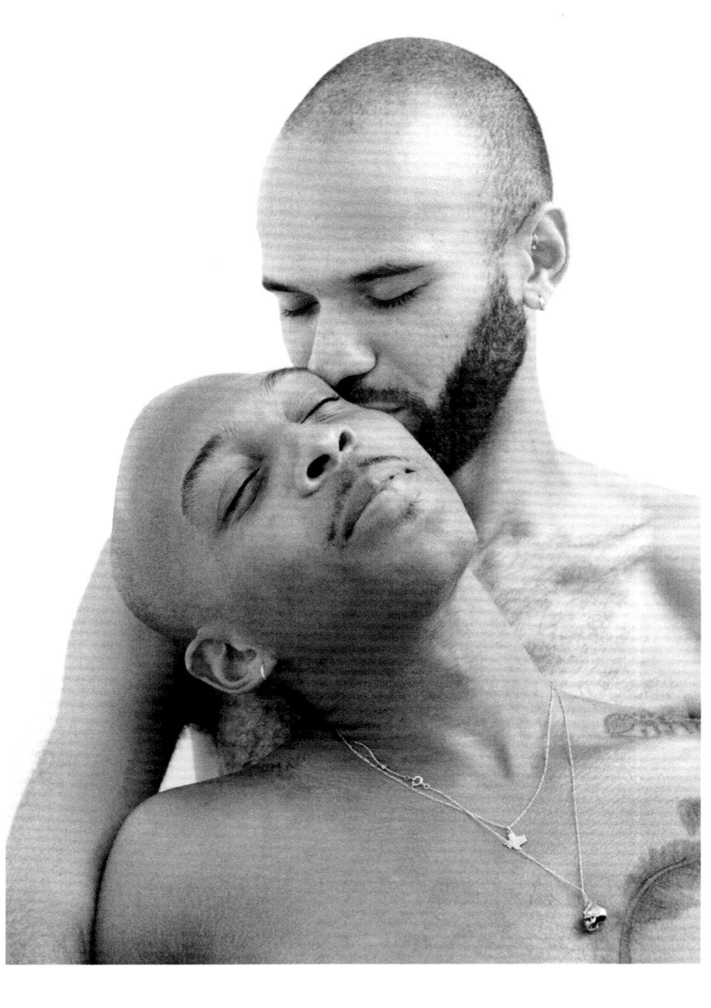

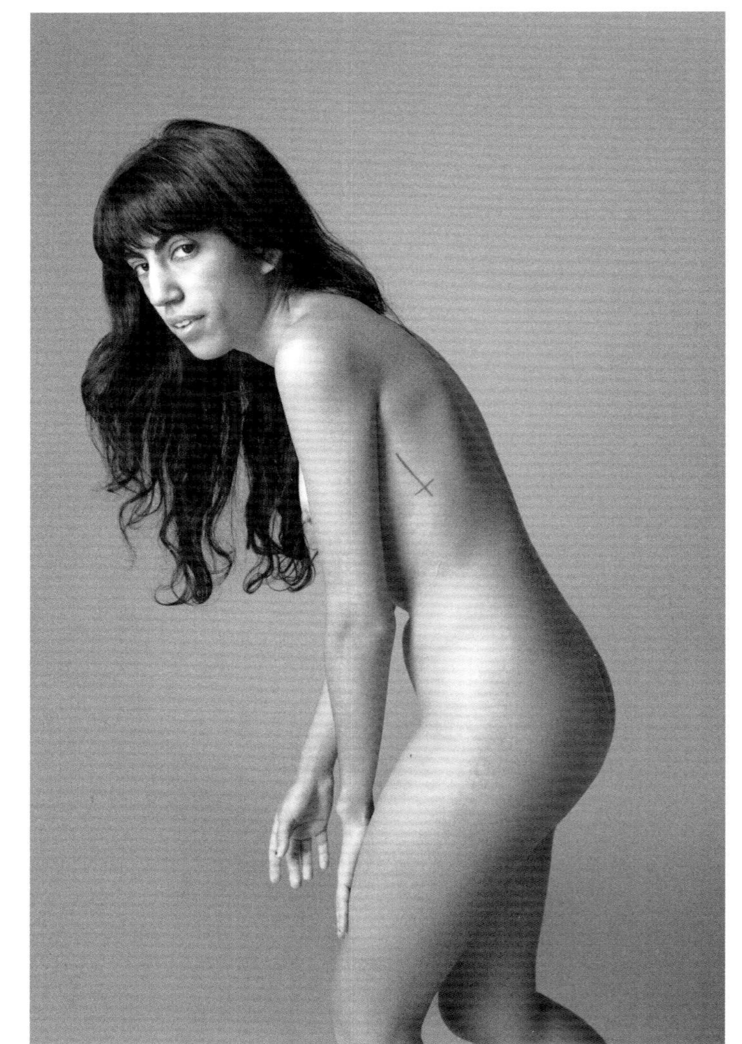

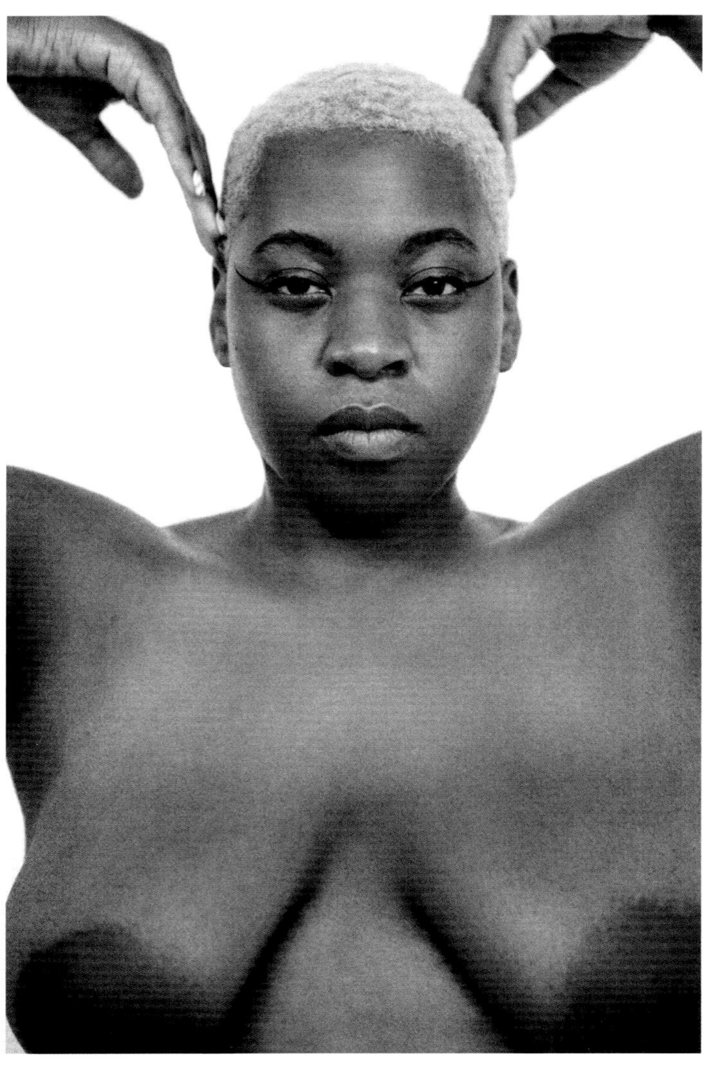

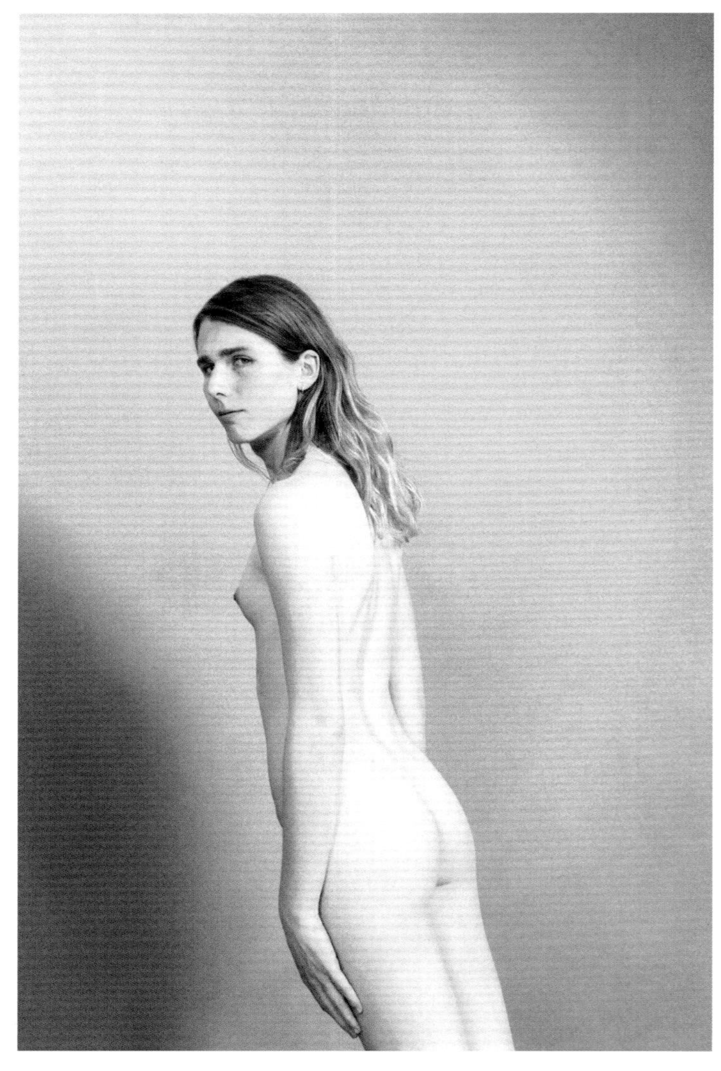

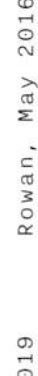

Ashton & Ty, September 2017   Irina, November 2008   Getty, October 2019   Rowan, May 2016

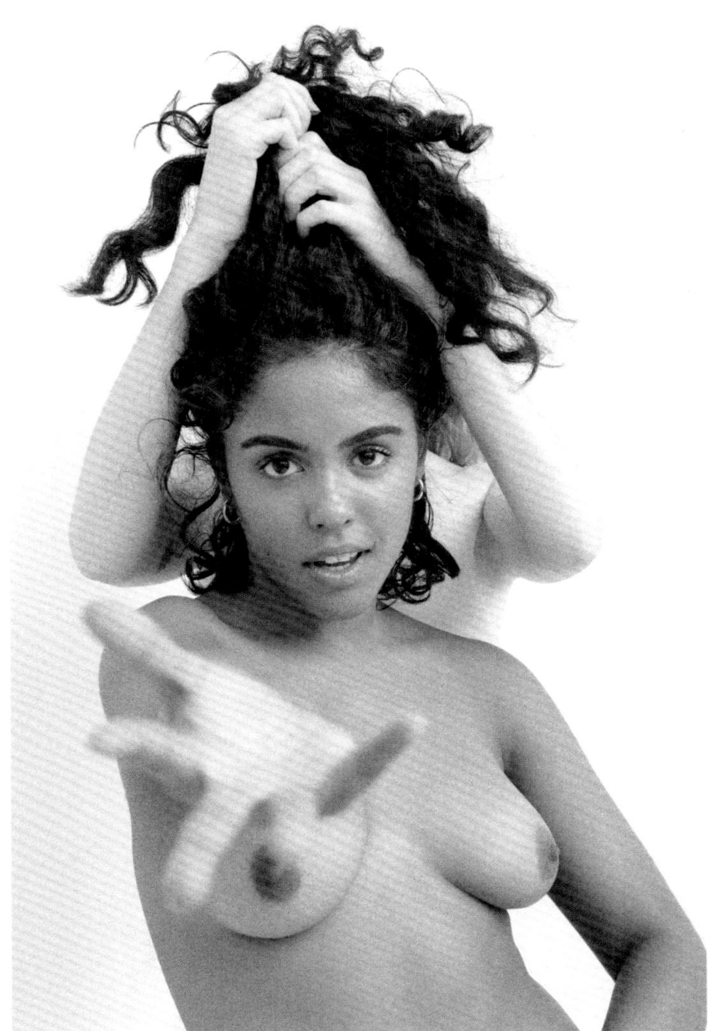

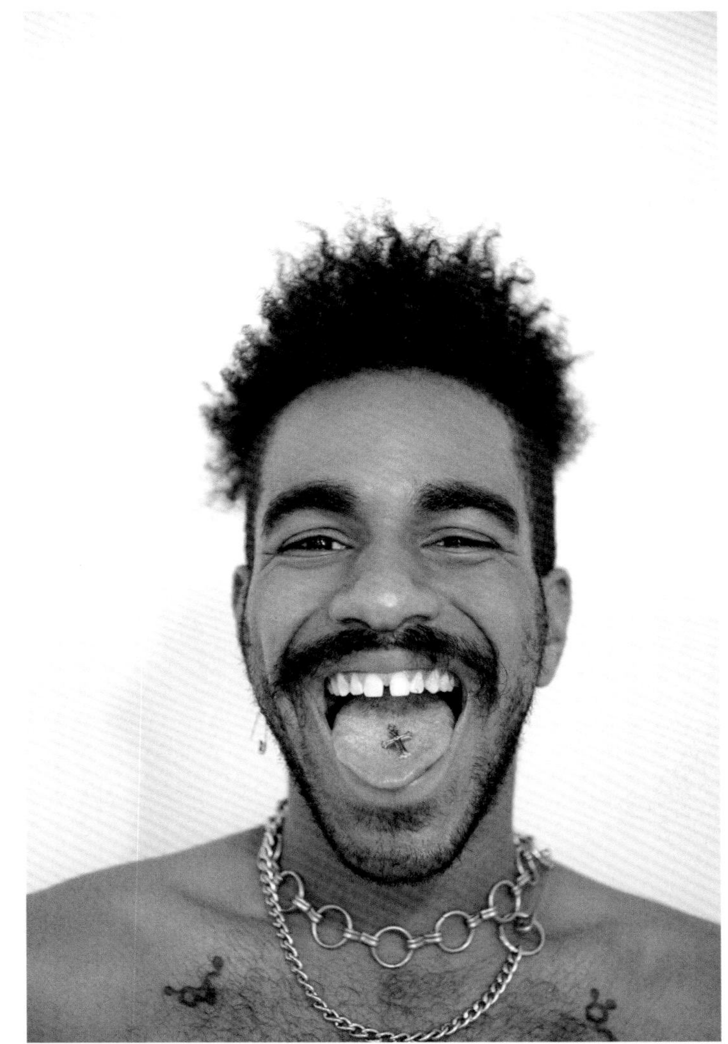

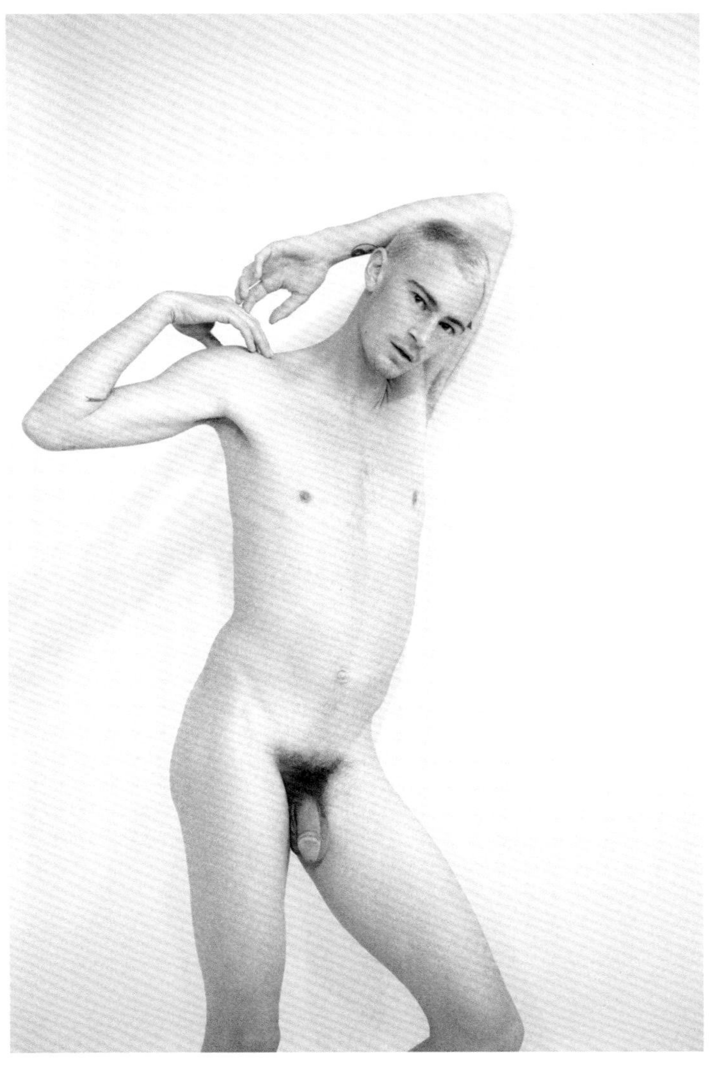

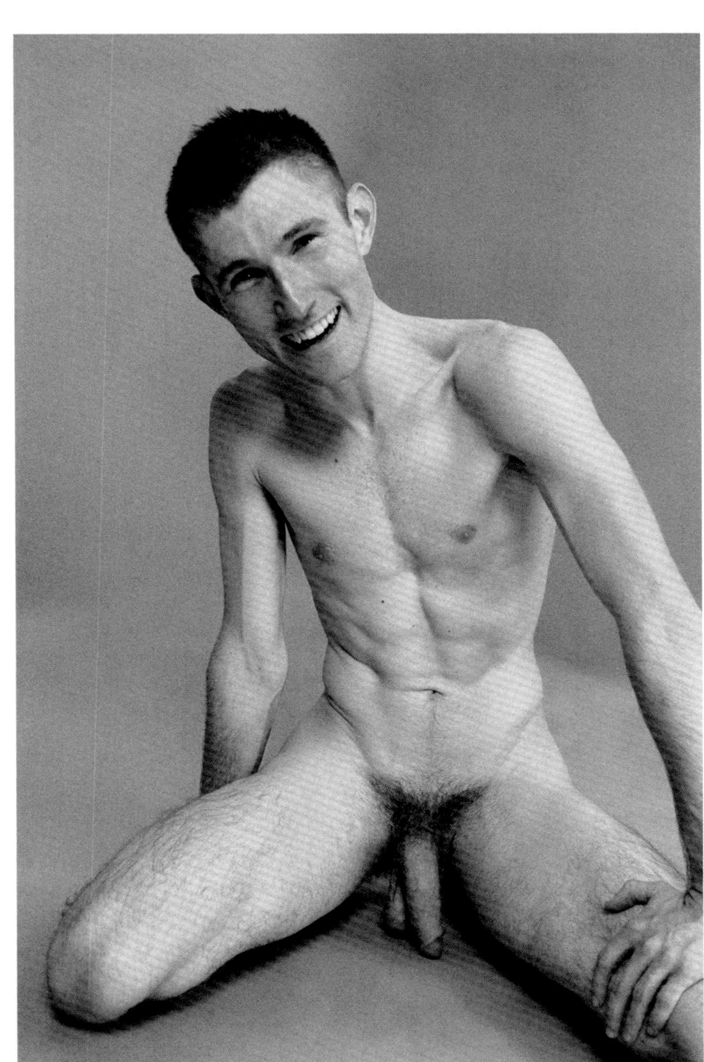

Sabrina & Maggie, July 2017   Shaitique, December 2018   Max, November 2018   Les, November 2016

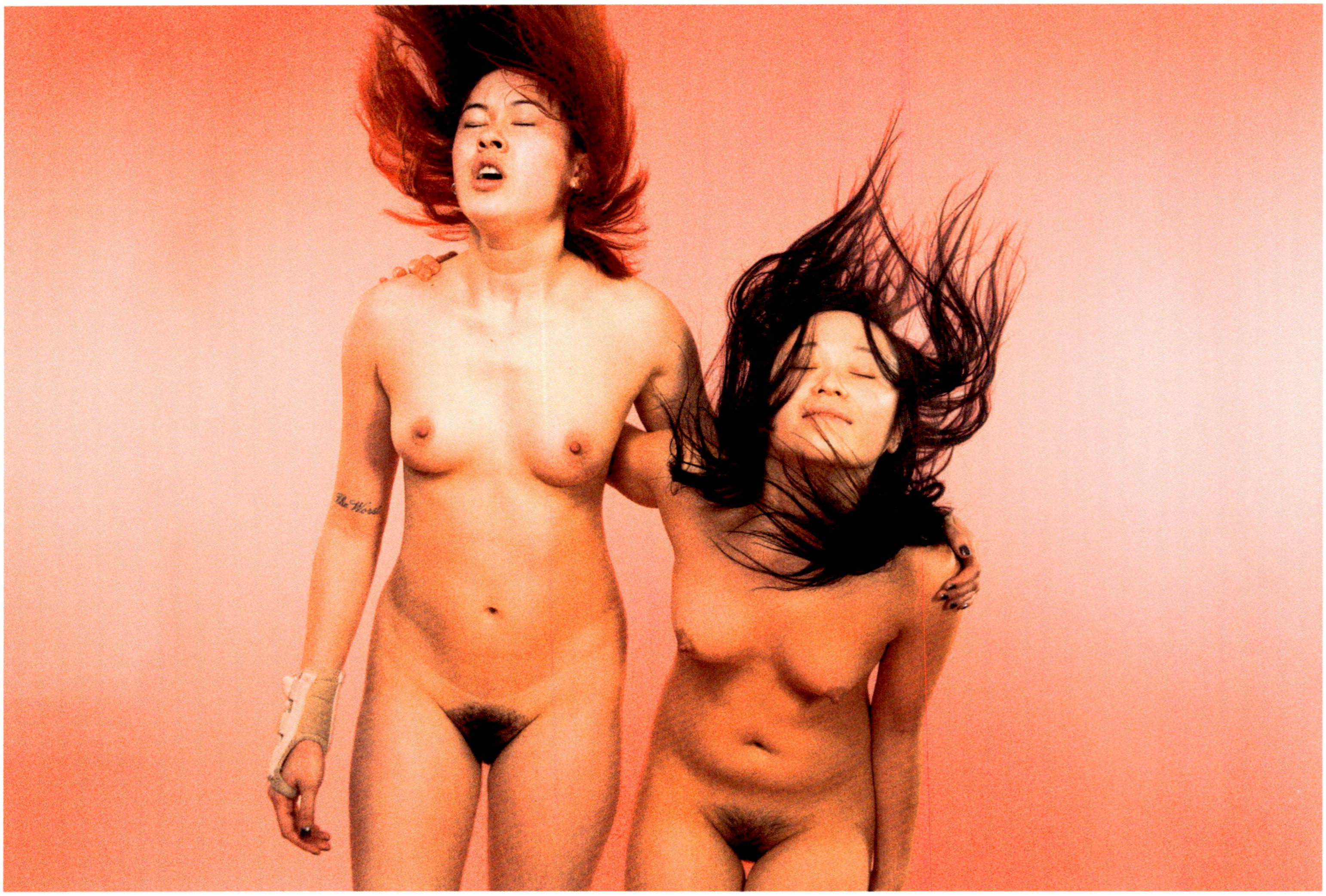

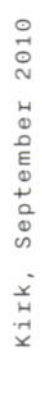

Erin & Suede, March 2011

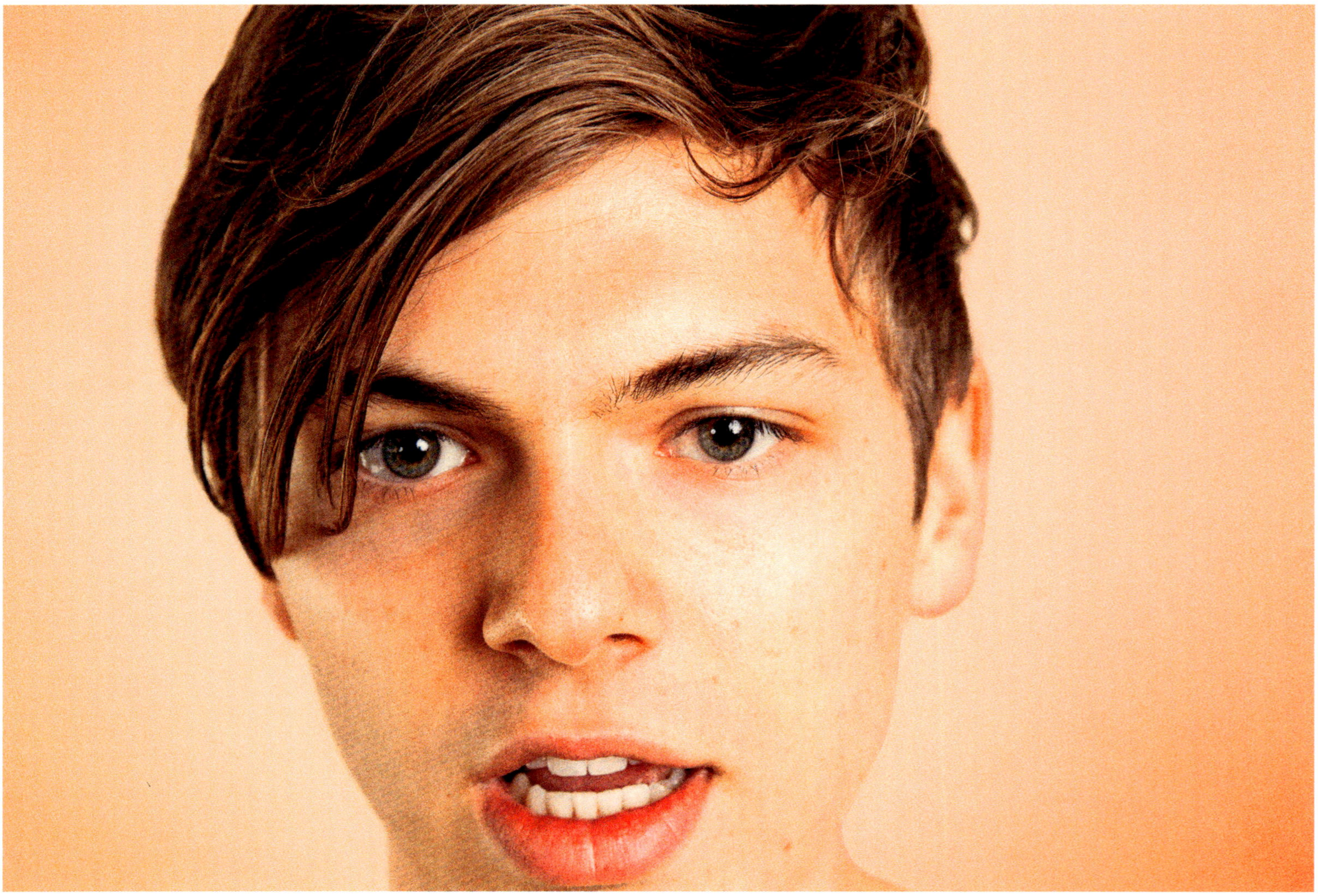

Kirk, September 2010

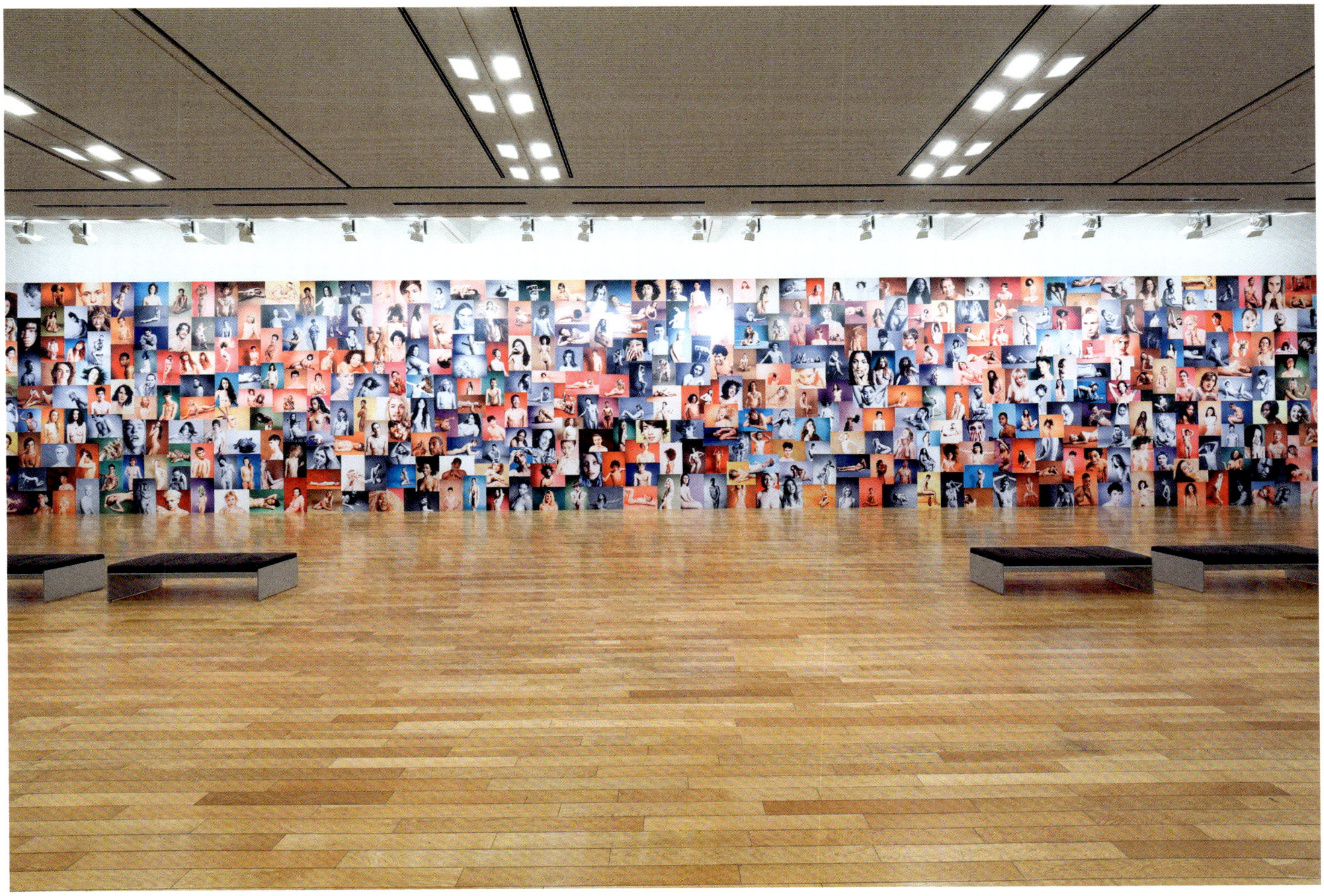

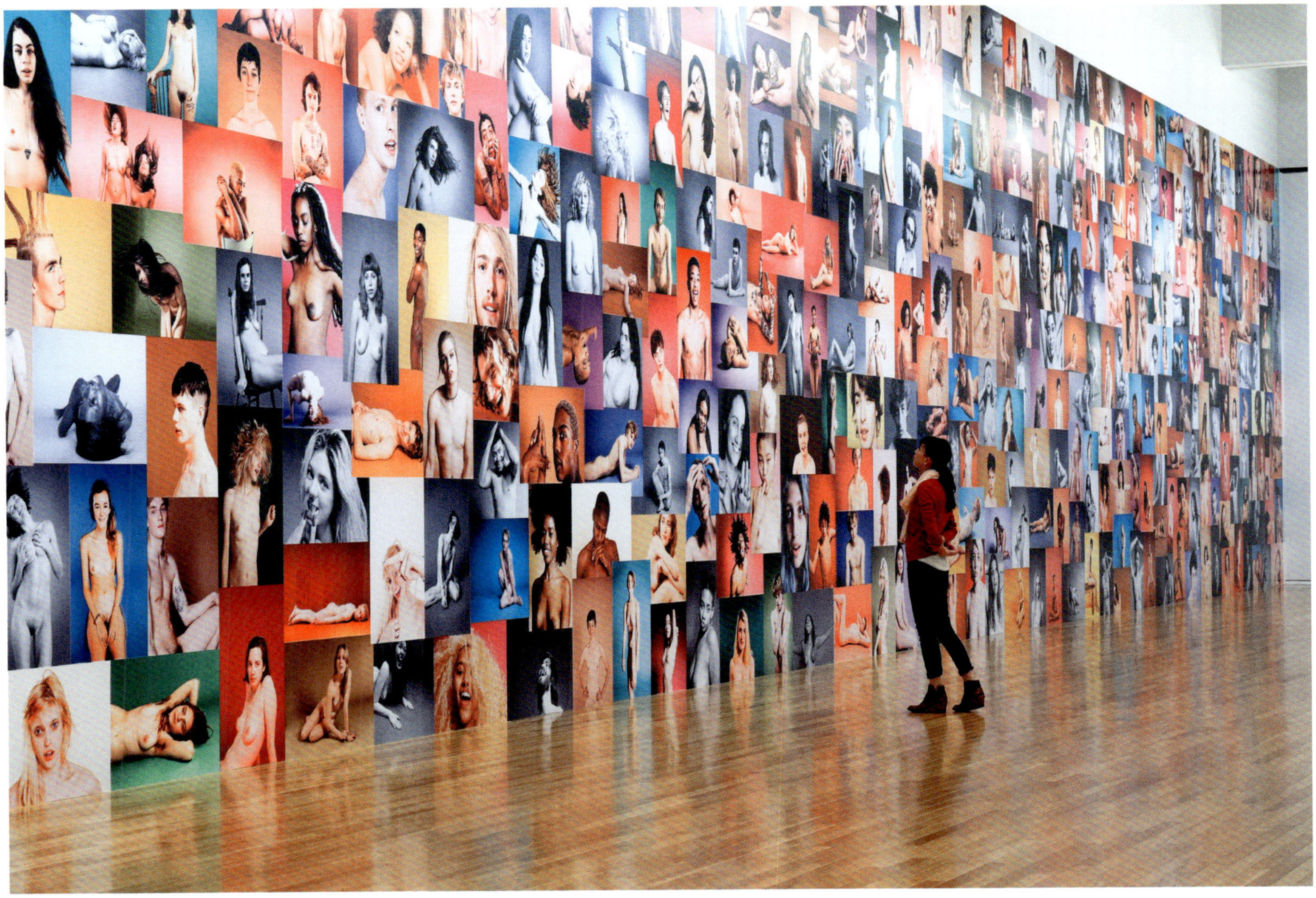

Body Loud, Tokyo Opera City Museum, Japan, 2016

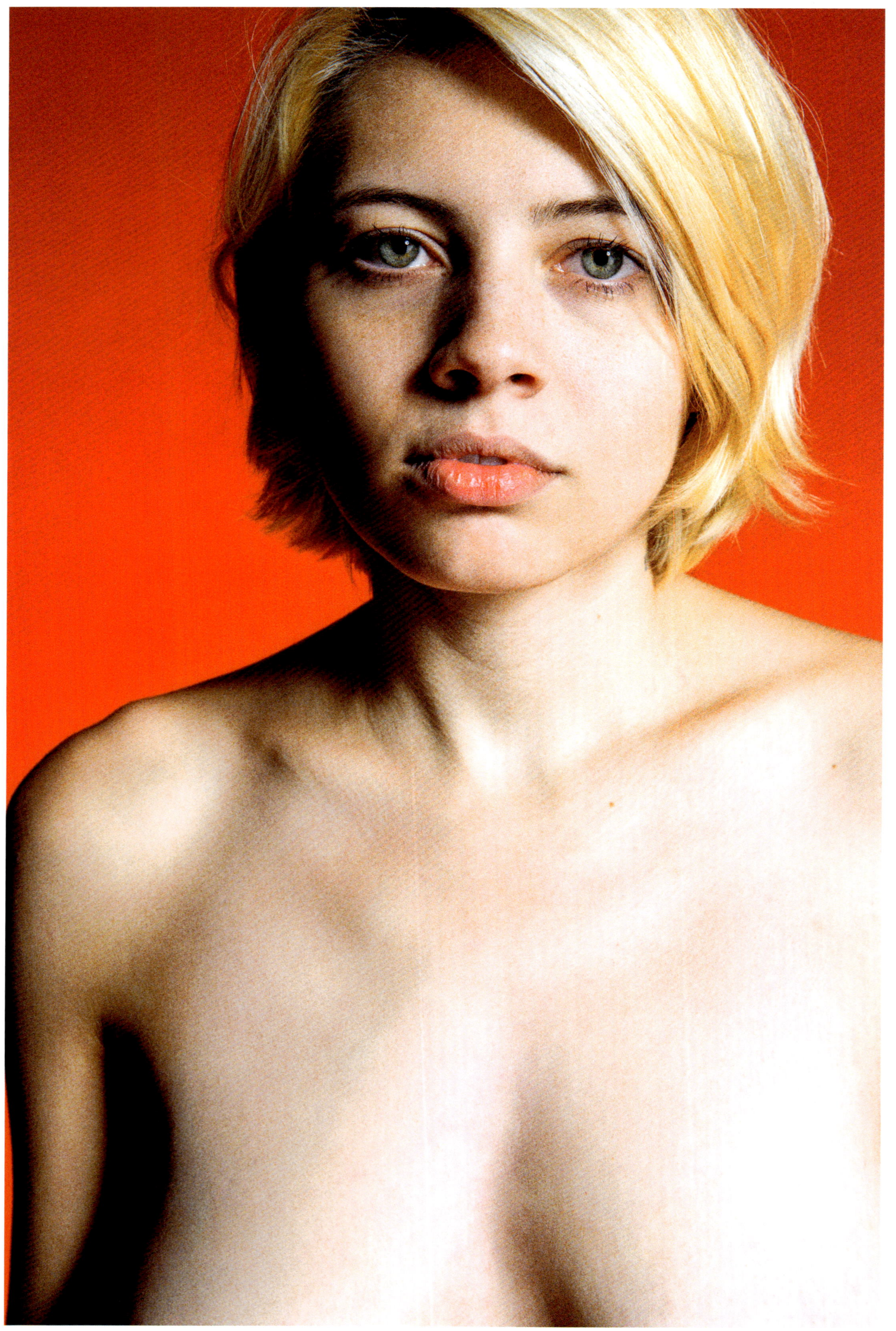

Jessi, October 2015

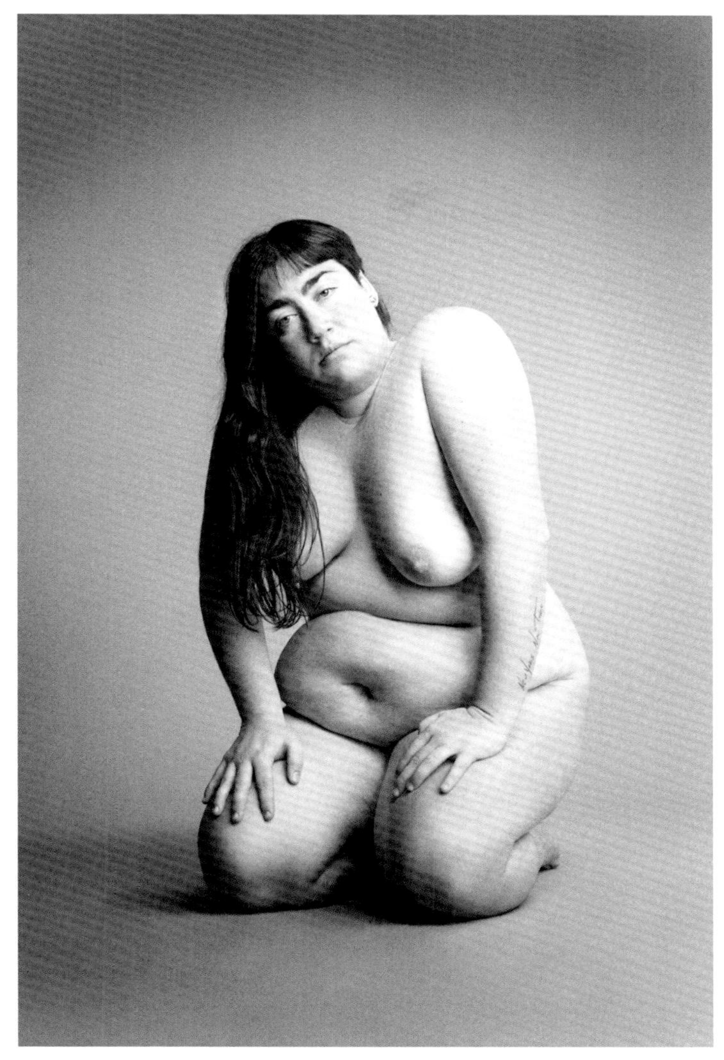

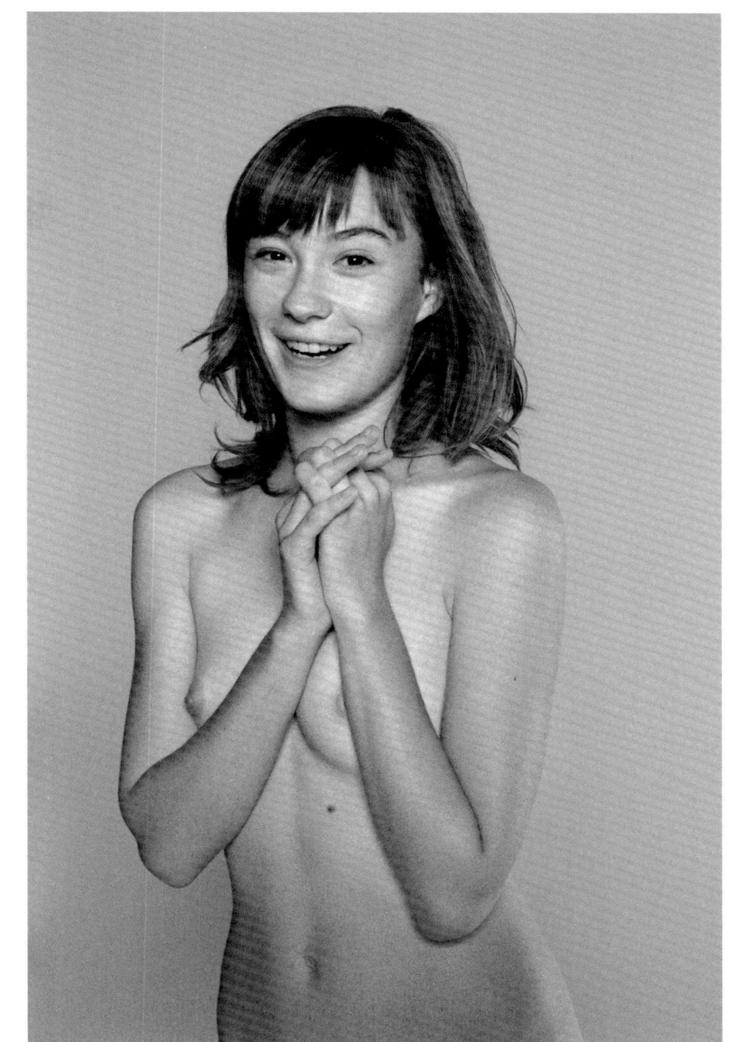

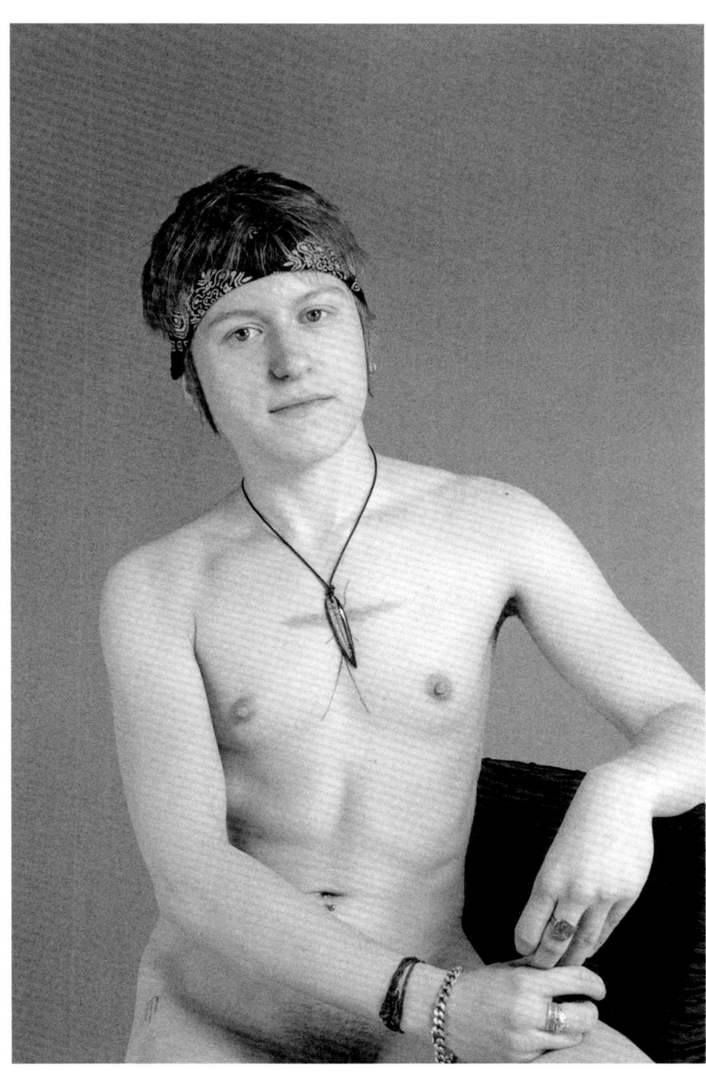

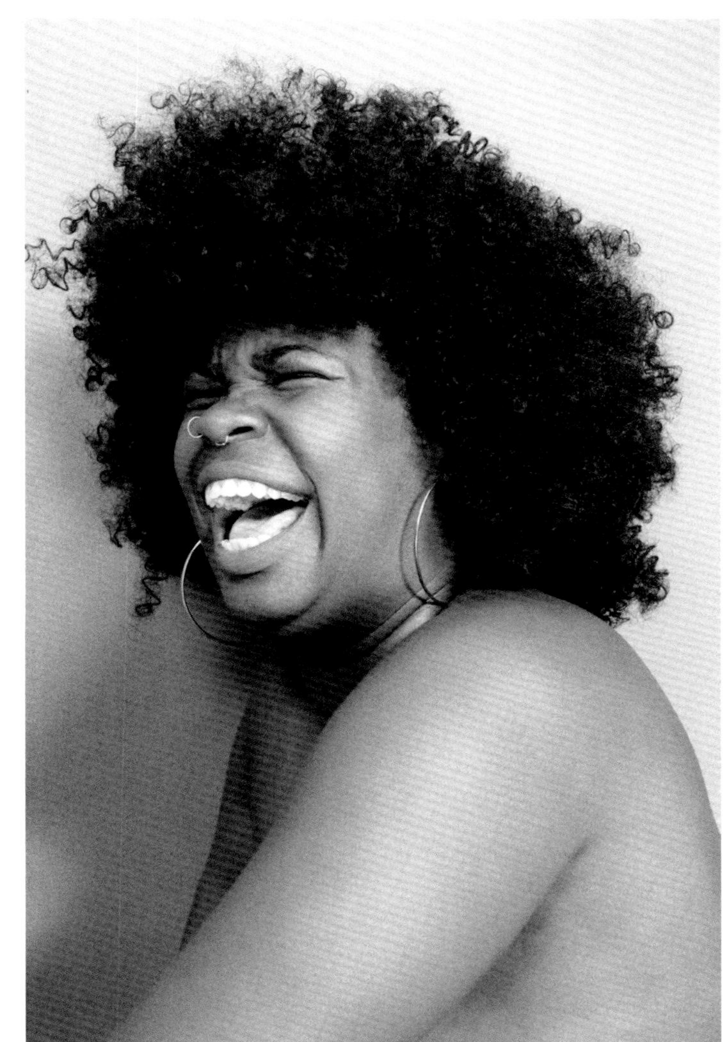

Jennifer, January 2015 India, September 2009 Shay, February 2012 Brittani, September 2016

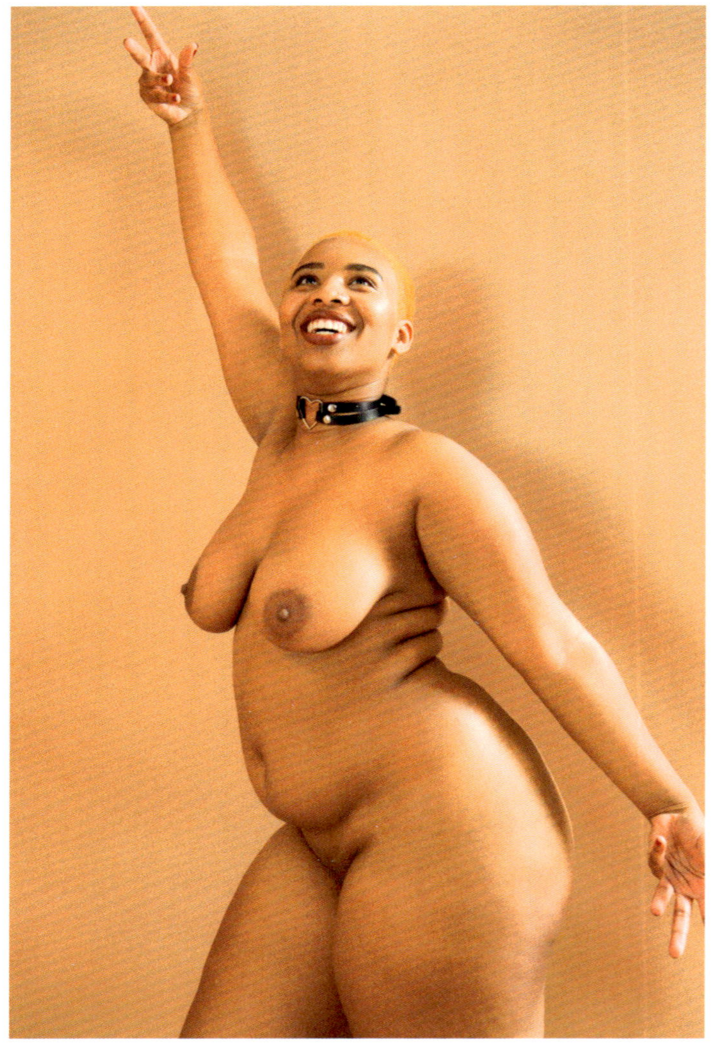

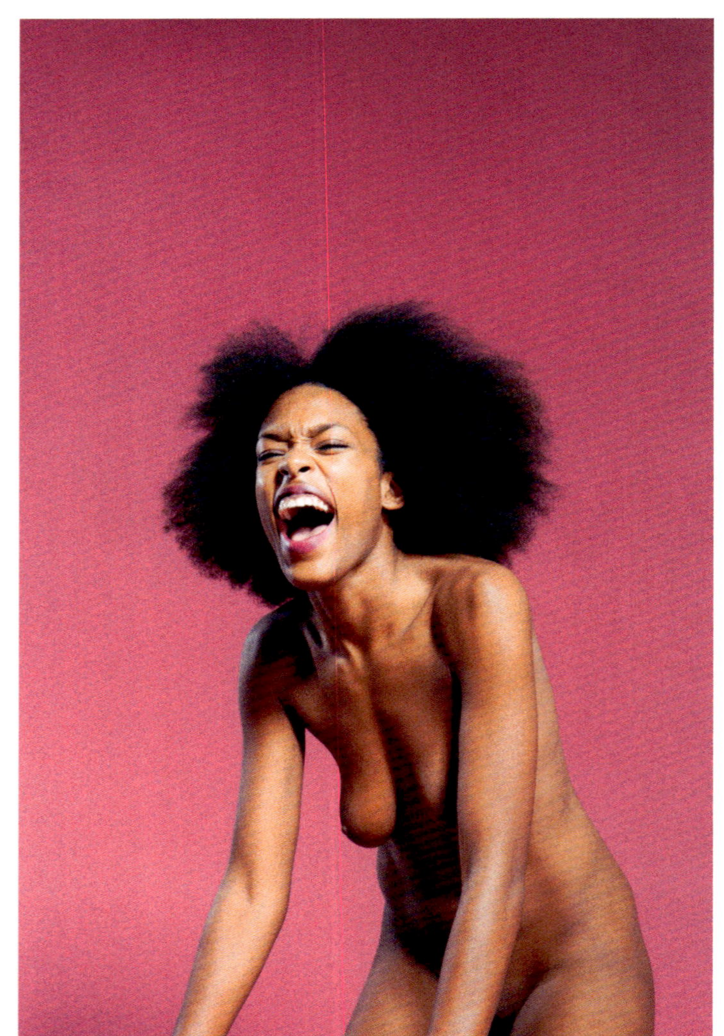

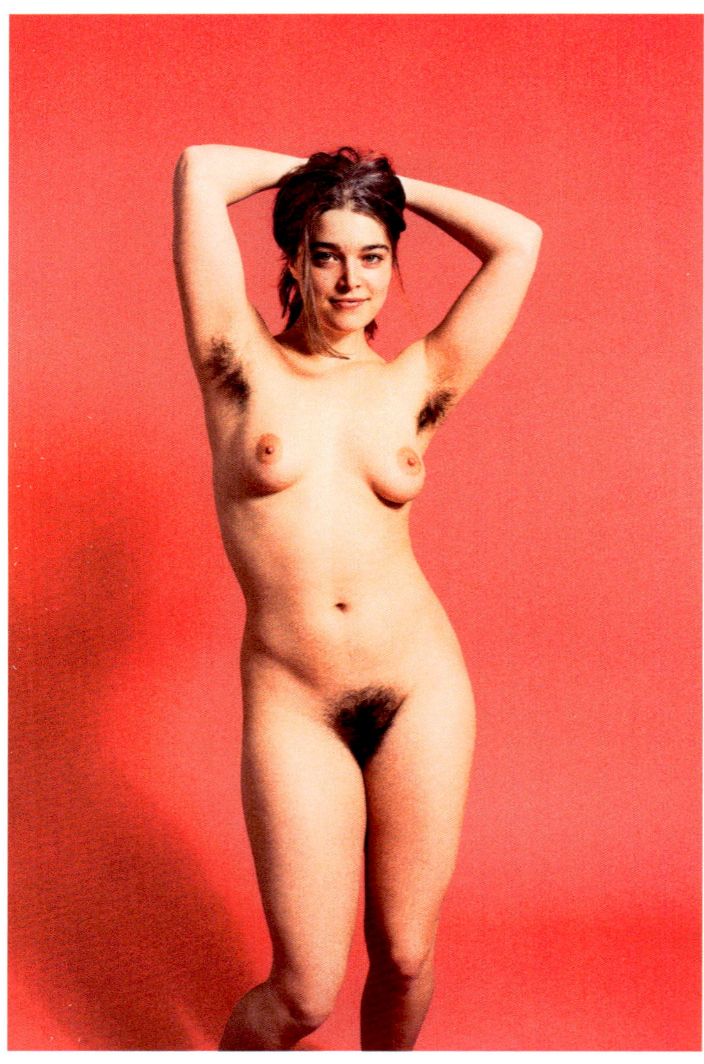

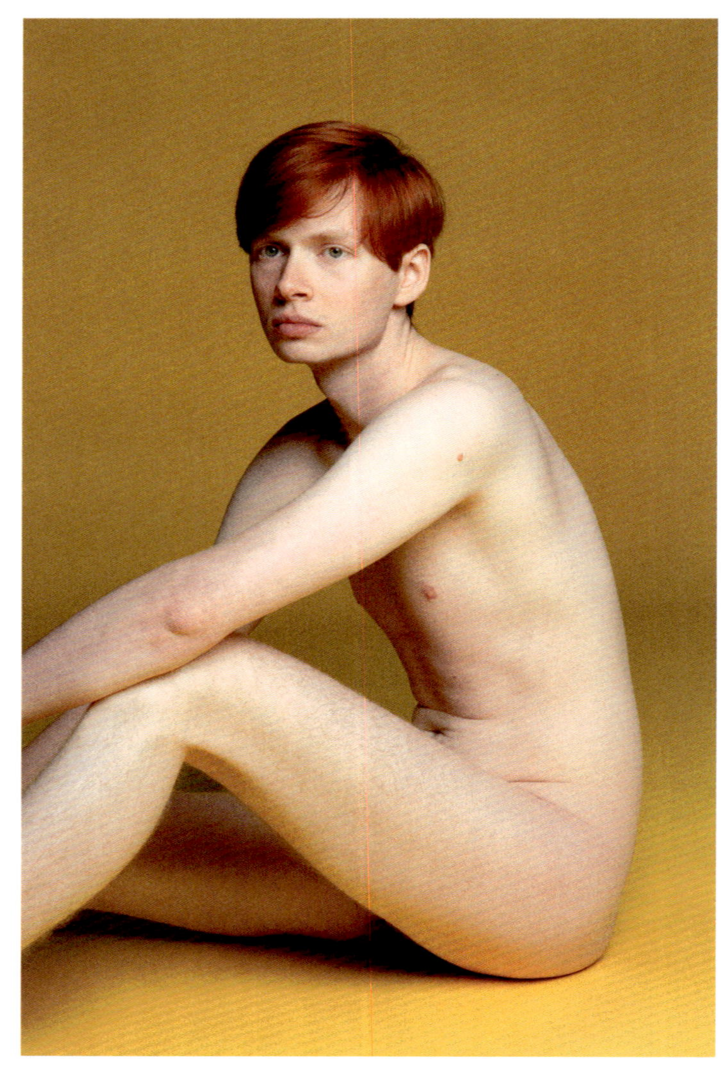

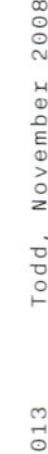

Wisdom, September 2016 Alexis, December 2014 Elise, April 2013 Todd, November 2008

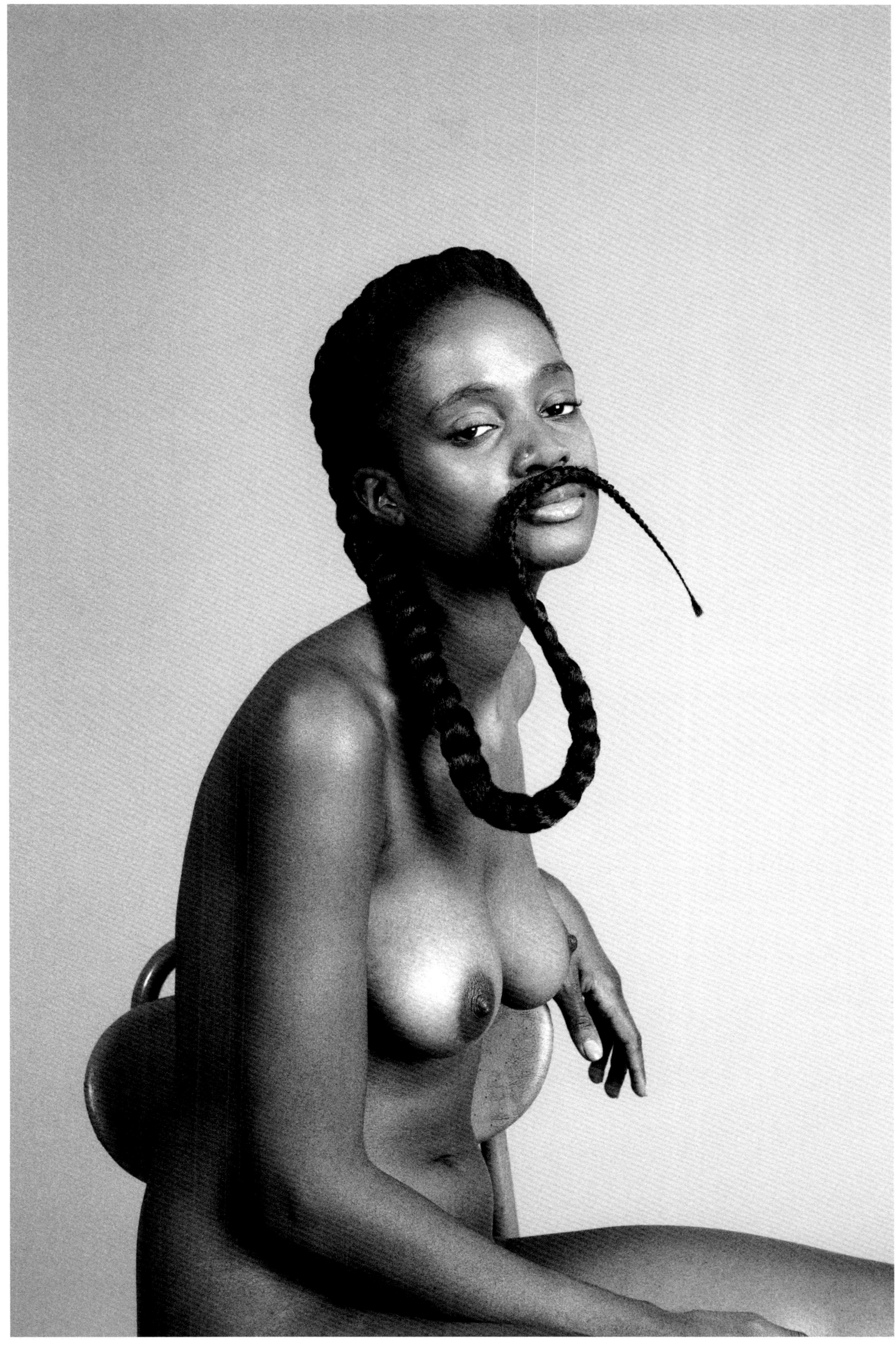

Valerie, December 2014

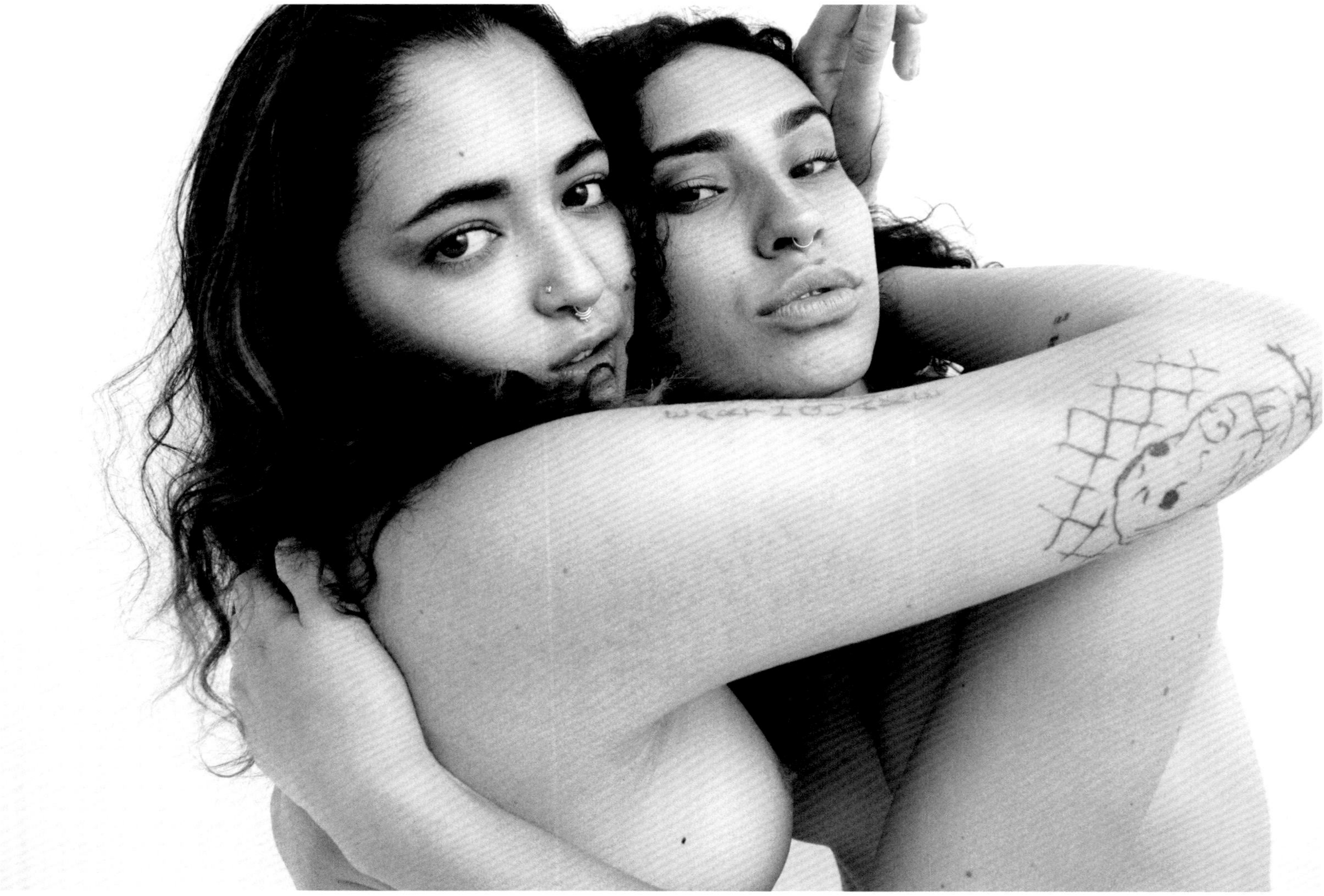

MeiMei & Gabrielle, June 2017

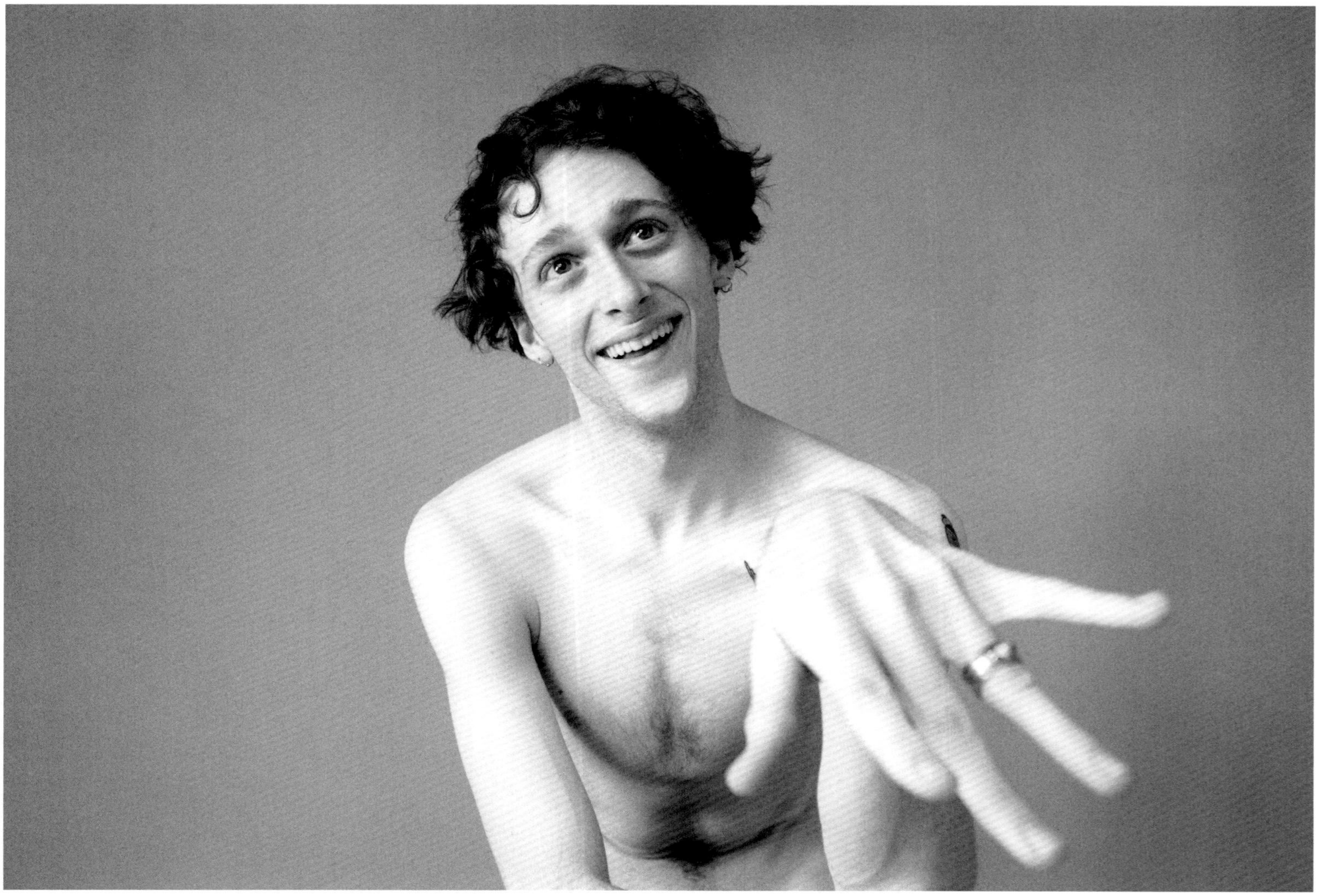

Adam, December 2016

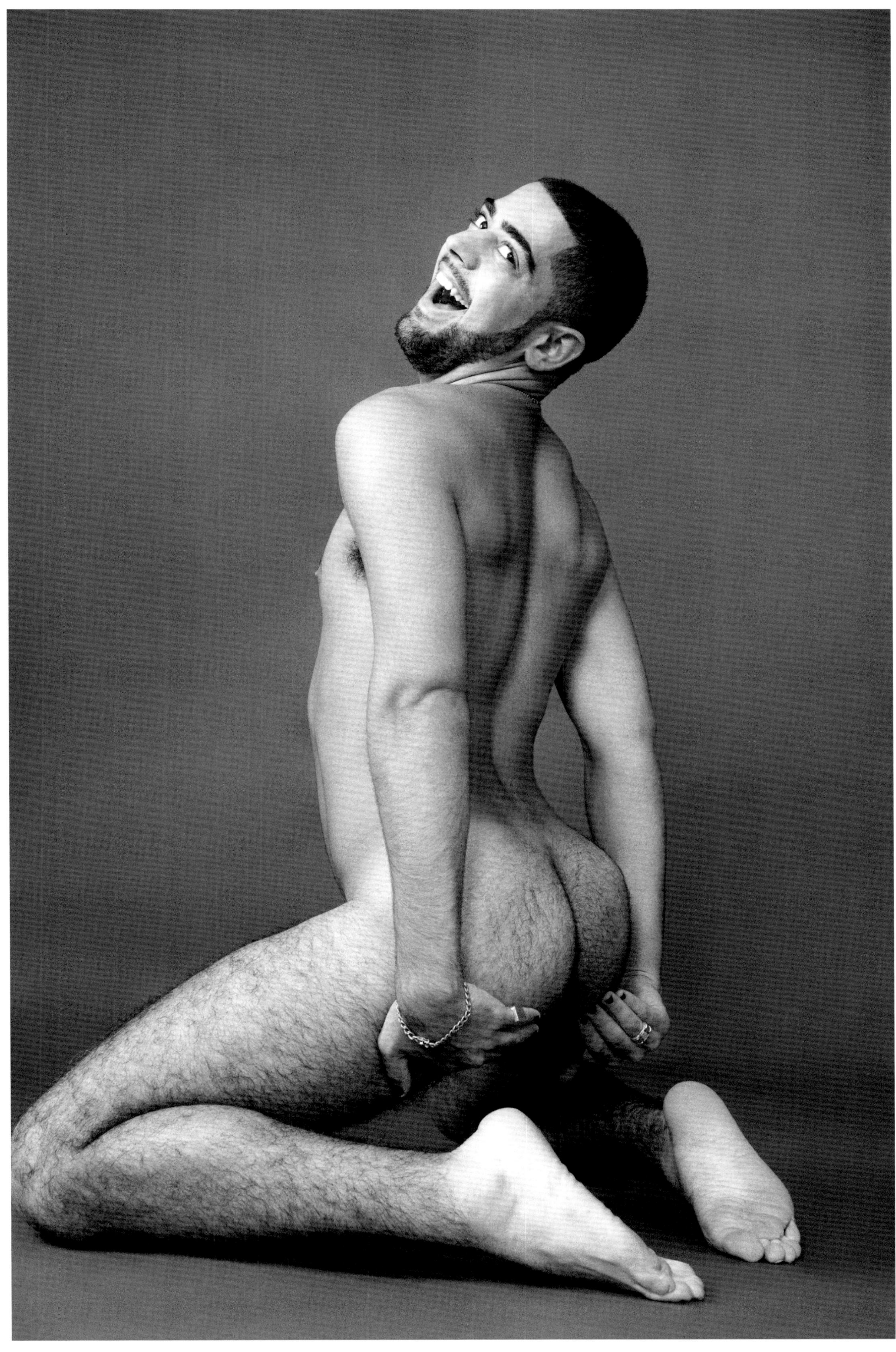

Matheus, January 2017

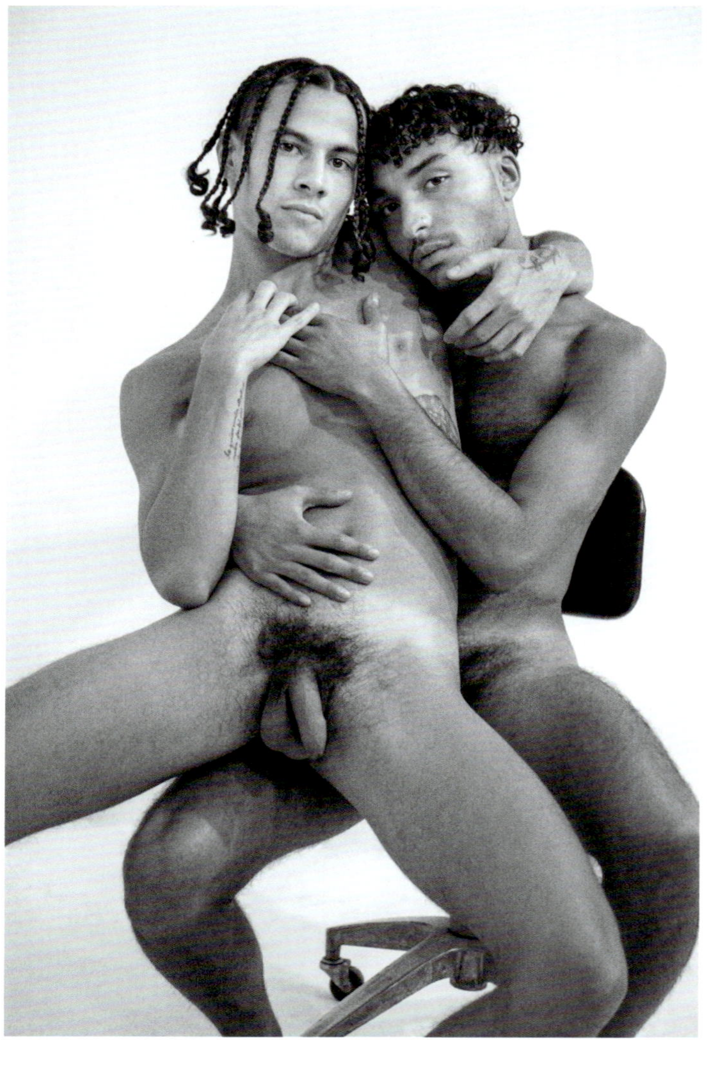

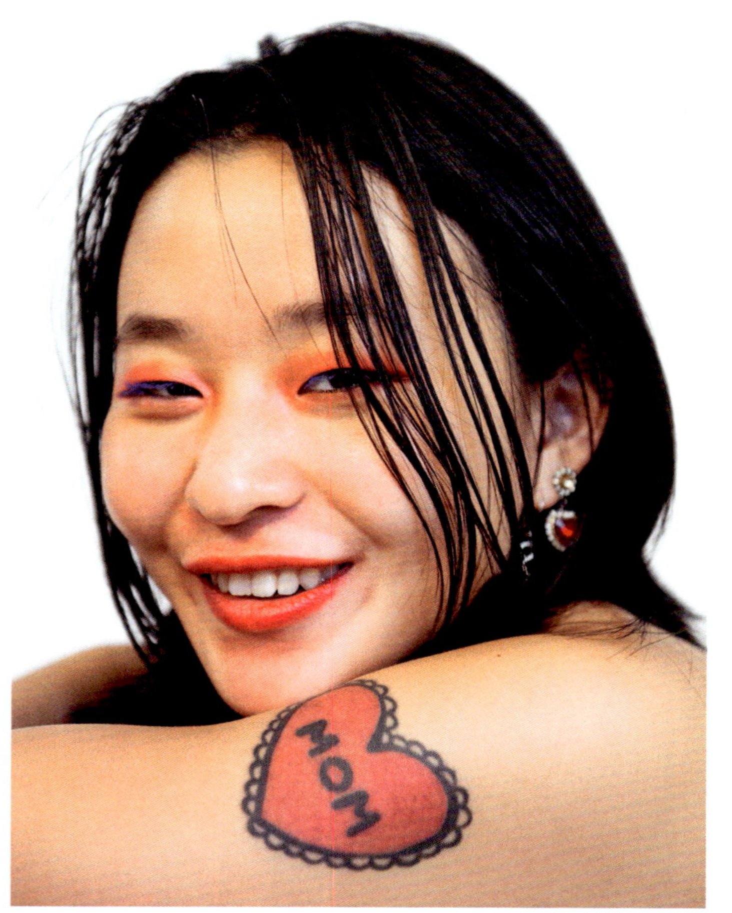

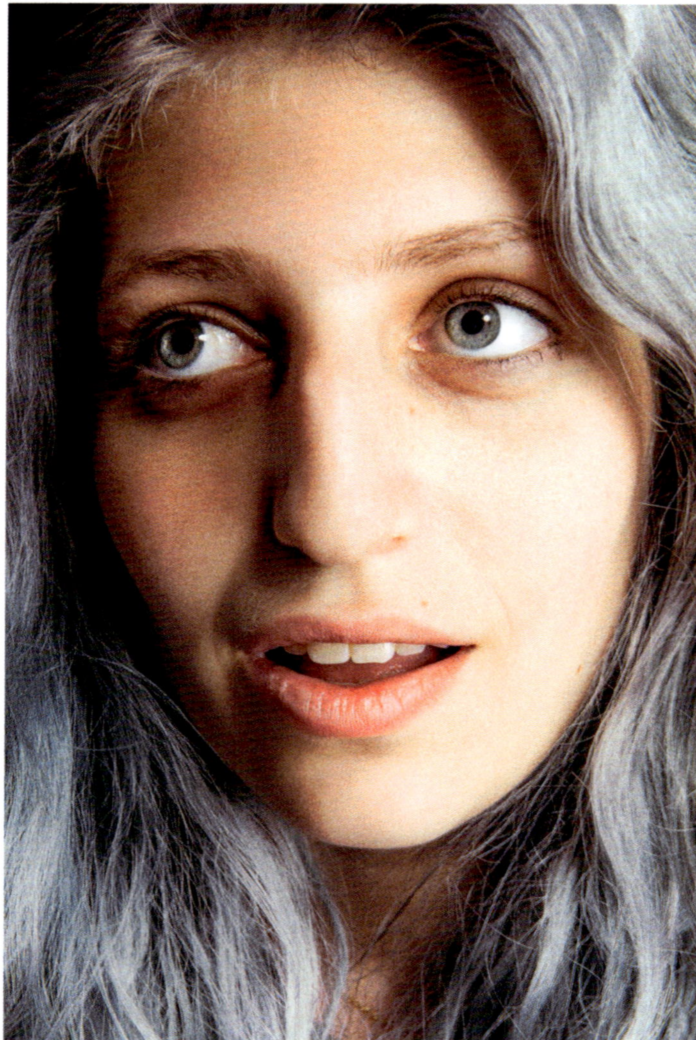

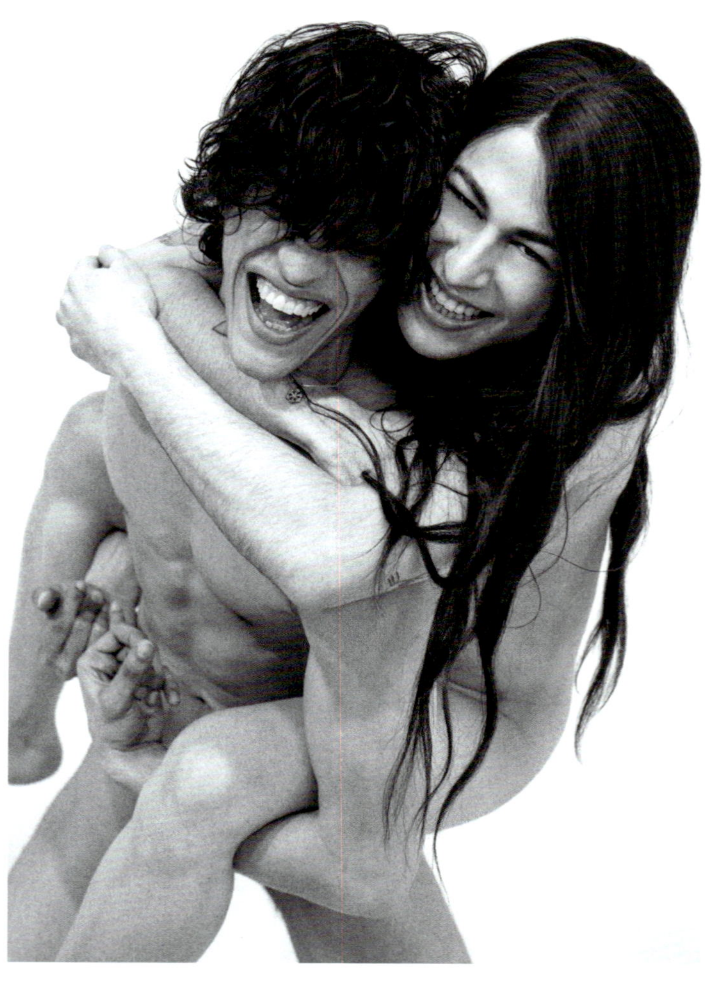

Gabriel & Goyin, February 2019   Sonia, November 2018   Jessica, September 2015   Efram & Richie, February 2019

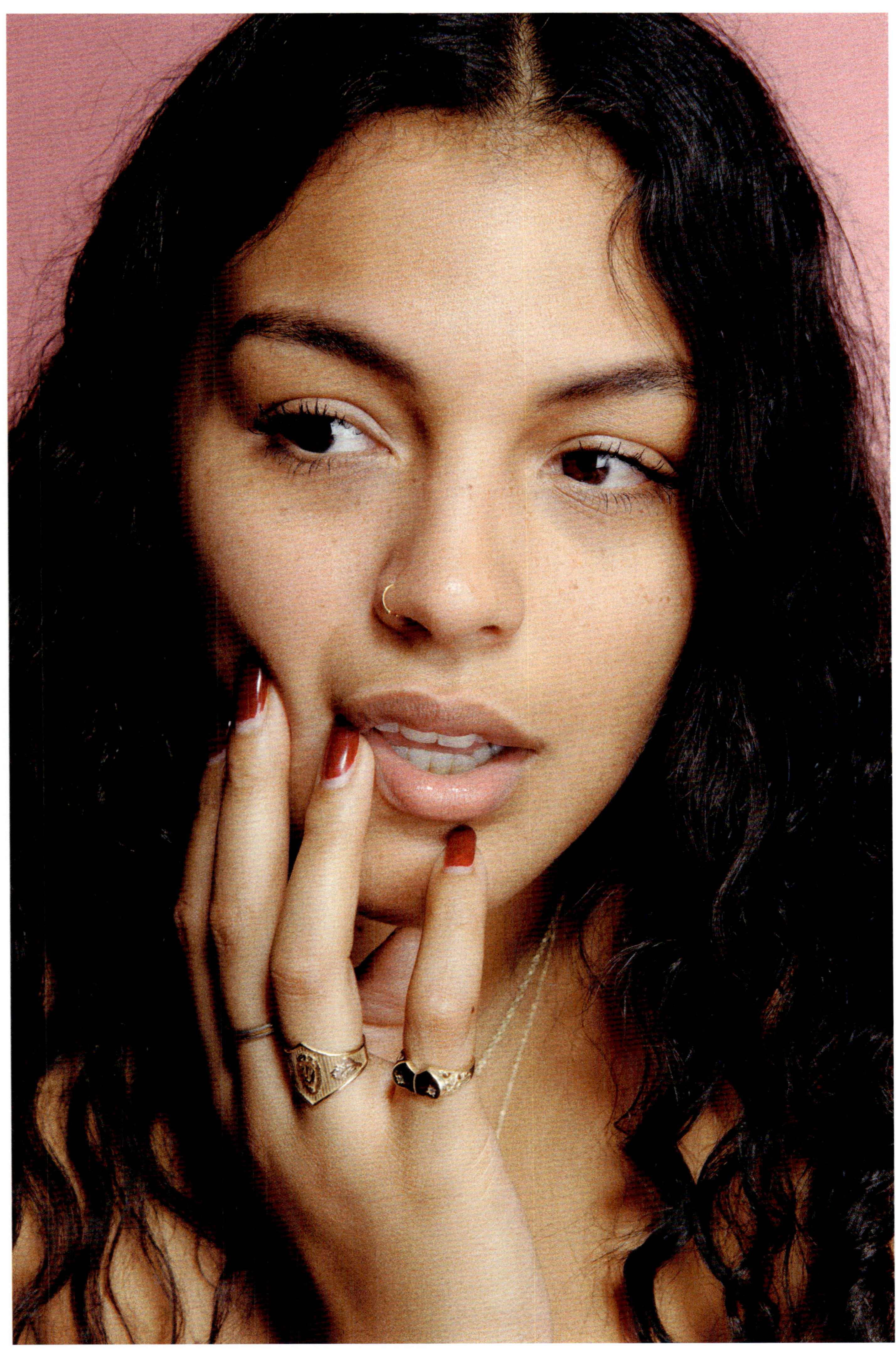

Paloma, December 2015

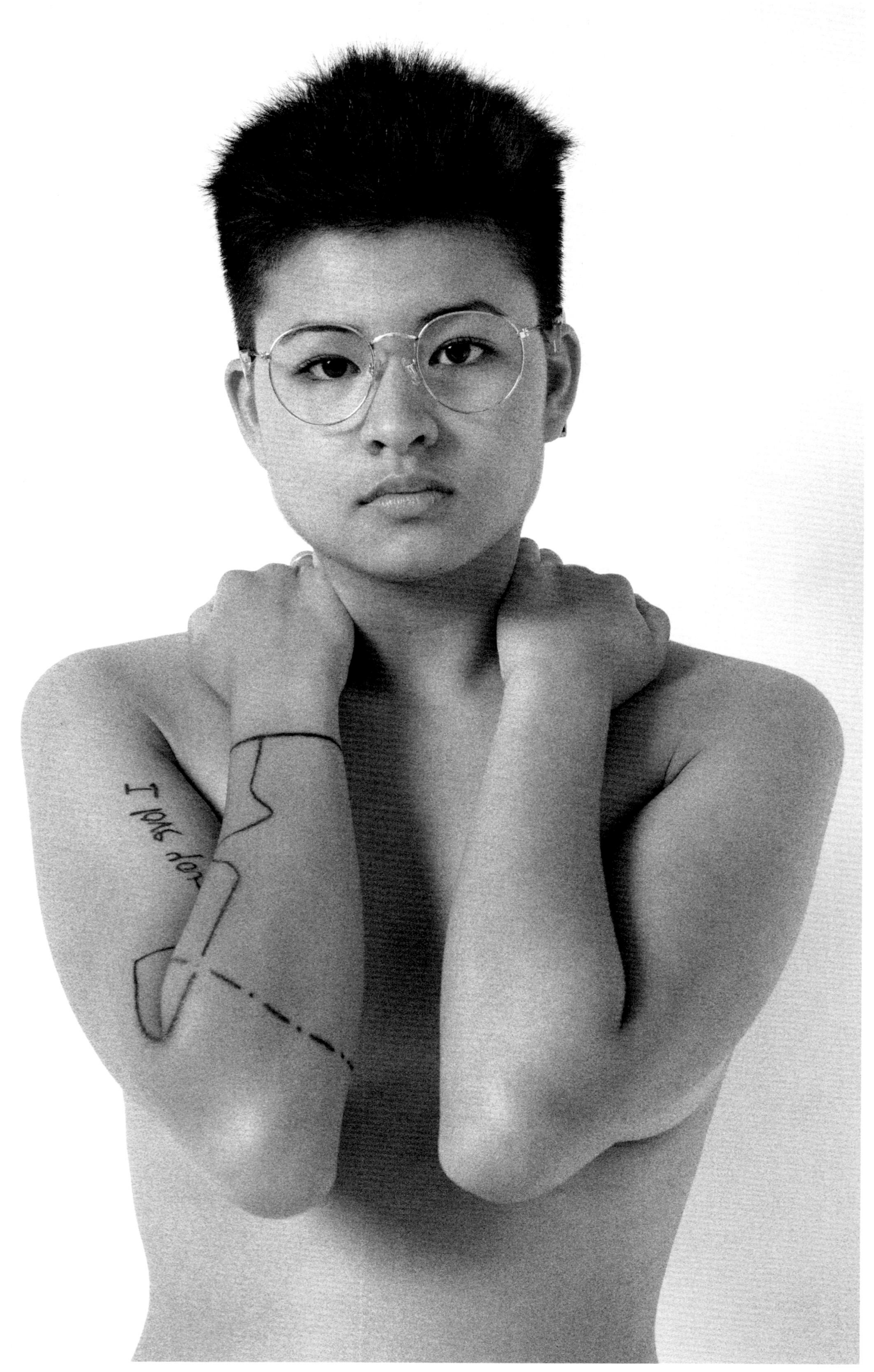

Chella, April 2017

CHELLA MAN

I was new to Ryan's work. I was honestly new to everything because I grew up in a conservative town in central Pennsylvania and there was a lot that I never was exposed to.

There was something about his energy that I felt I could trust.

It was a vulnerable shoot. I hadn't been in front of the camera much at that point, which is wild to say now. Being naked on camera is something that I wouldn't bat an eye about now, but back then, it was like, "Whoa, this is so vulnerable," especially as a trans individual.

Twenty seventeen was a whirlwind of so much love, beauty, pain, and culture shock. Having moved from the small town where I grew up to New York, I felt like I had time traveled thousands of years into the future and into a different dimension. I had been deeply depressed in central Pennsylvania. I worked very hard academically to graduate high school early as a junior because I couldn't stay one more year. It was a survival thing to go to New York and being there saved me for a multitude of reasons, and this shoot with Ryan really captured the beginning of it all.

There was so much love because I was in love. I was falling in love not just with one person, but a whole community and the culture and the liberation that existed in the city.

But also, this was when Donald Trump was elected president. I was balancing this euphoria of liberation and culture shock while feeling so many constraints and frustrations with the state of the world. I felt, frankly, very helpless. It was everything all at once.

I remember learning what the word *artist* was and realizing, "I guess that's what I am." Before then, I was just creating things that felt good. I was doing what that word meant, and then I discovered the word.

My own art practice is perpetually expansive. I lean towards whatever medium will best convey the message I'm trying to share, whether it's drawing, painting, experimental performance art, or directing films, as I am now. The commonality between everything is this continuous discarding of binaries and categorization.

All of my work, at its core, is about this idea of the continuum, which is life beyond binaries of gender, race, sexuality, disability, or even morality and ethics. It's analyzing the balance of language itself, how language is so helpful, but also constraining at the same time. We internalize so much of the connotations attached to certain words within social constructs of ableism, transphobia, racism, etcetera. At its very core, though, it's all just feelings and our spirits or souls. Sometimes you don't need language.

My art mentors are my friends, the people that I'm surrounded by, like MaryV, my partner of five years. We both mentored each other. Or Ryan and my friend Christine Sun Kim, who is a deaf Asian artist. You don't really have to be a mentor in art to be a mentor for art. A lot of the people who have taught me about my practice would never identify as artists.

I often go back to that Spider-Man quote, "With great power comes great responsibility." I never thought my life would be this way, and I'm deeply, deeply grateful and feel a lot of responsibility and passion to alchemize my status into something that is beneficial for all. There are so many people who deserve to be recognized and uplifted. In my current and future projects, I'm just trying to kick the fucking door down a little because it's so hard to even get your foot in the door as a disabled person, a trans person, a person of color, or a young person. I help uplift others in my community with my platform. That's what Ryan is doing, too, with this book.

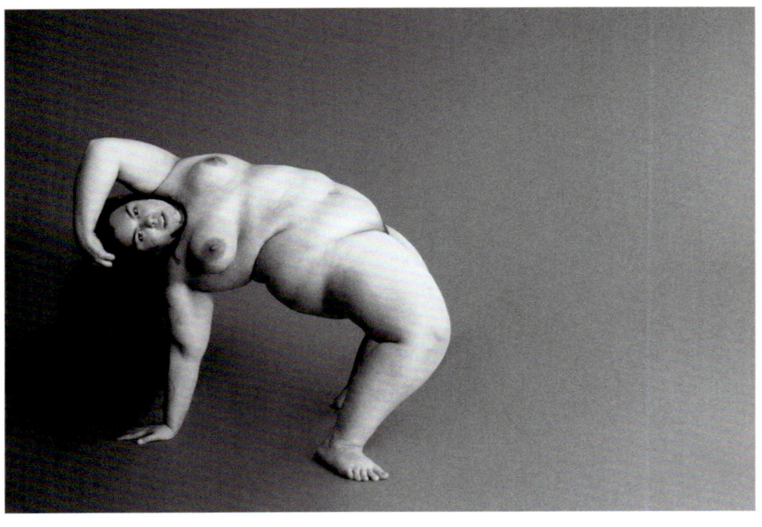

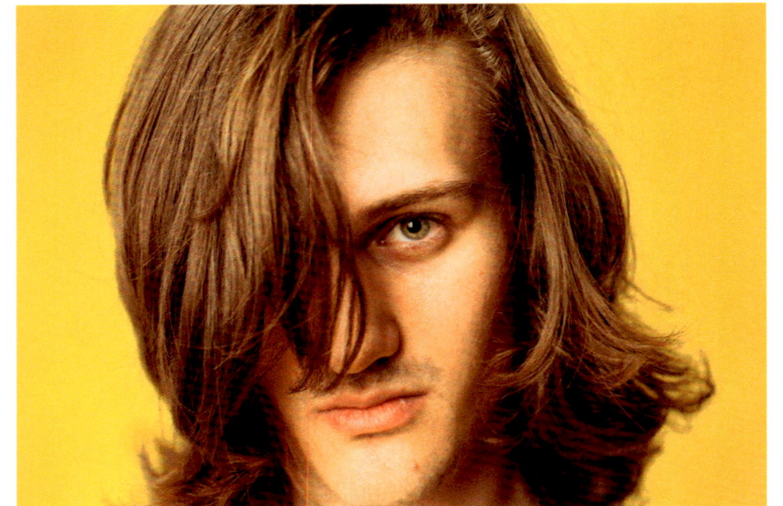

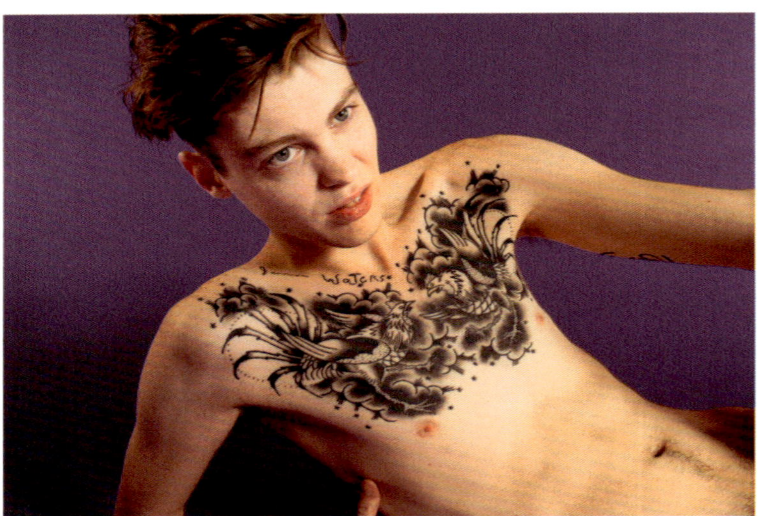

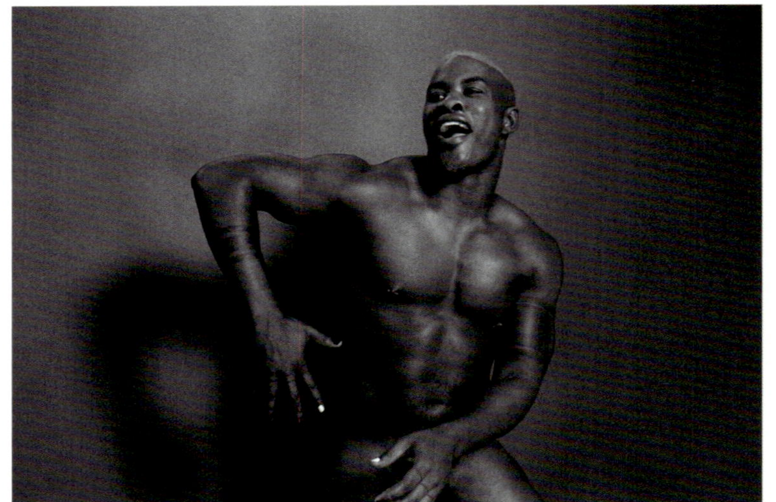

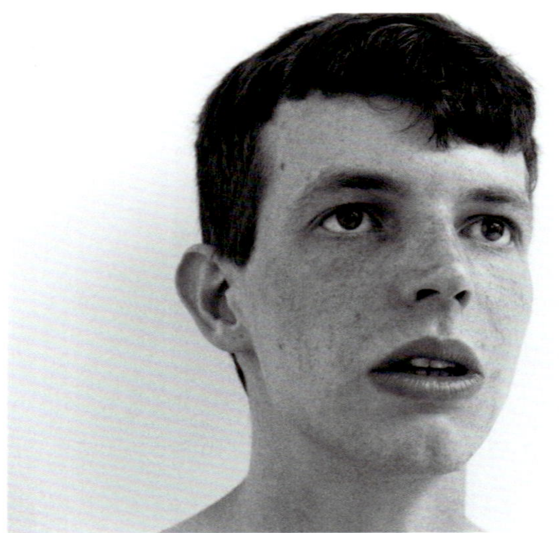

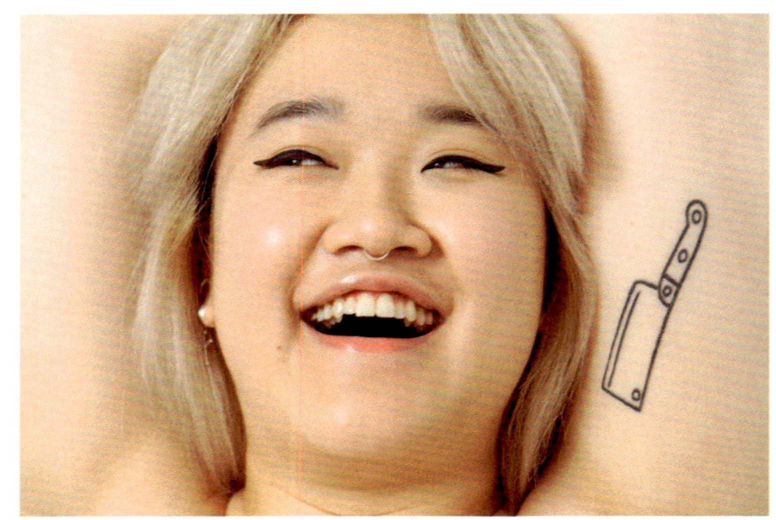

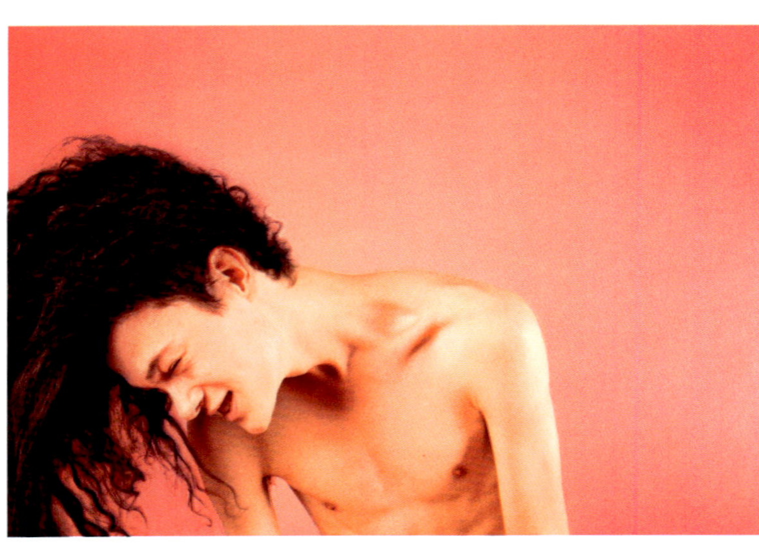

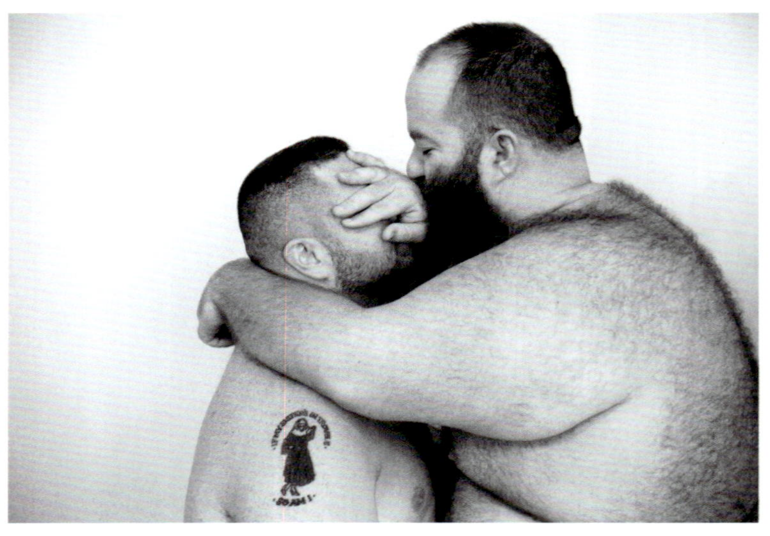

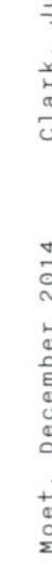

Moet, December 2014   Clark, July 2010   Shane, December 2012   Vandawn, September 2016   Ryan, July 2017   Nancy, April 2017   Chris, December 2011   Dusty & Shane, November 2018

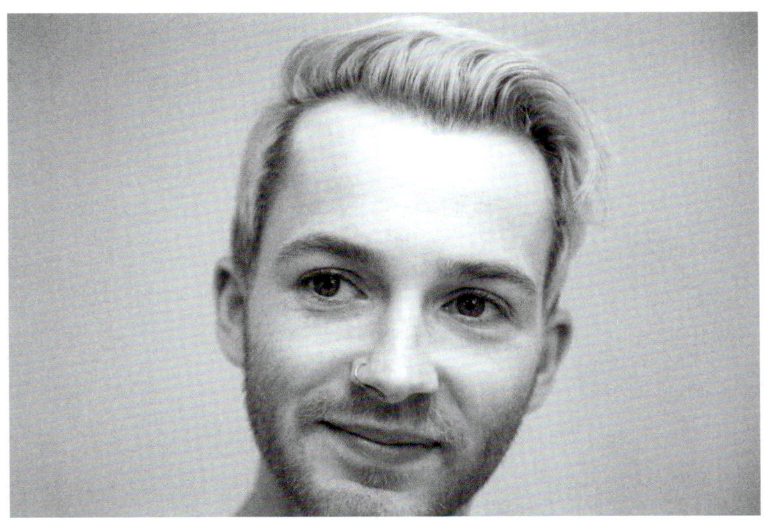

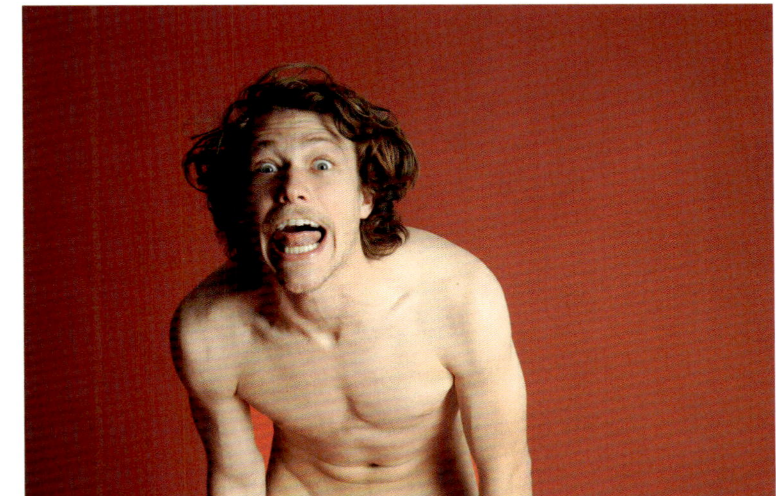

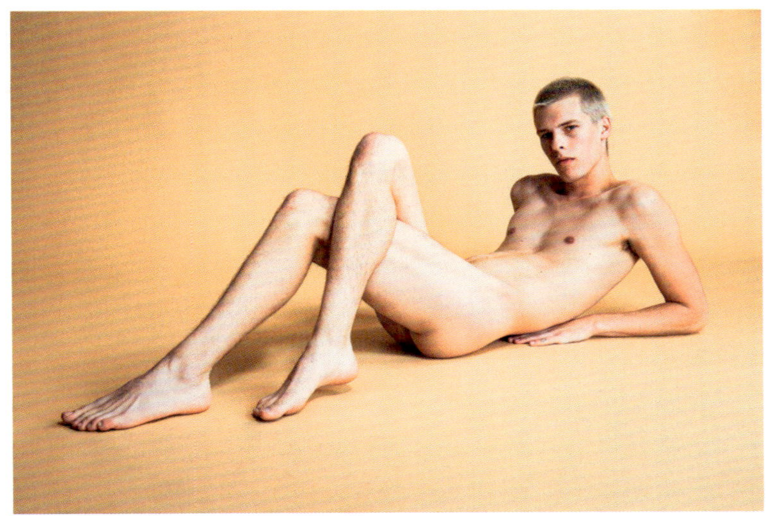

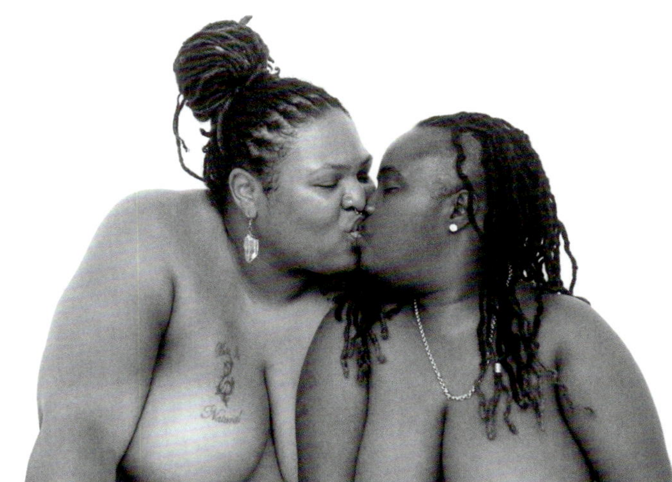

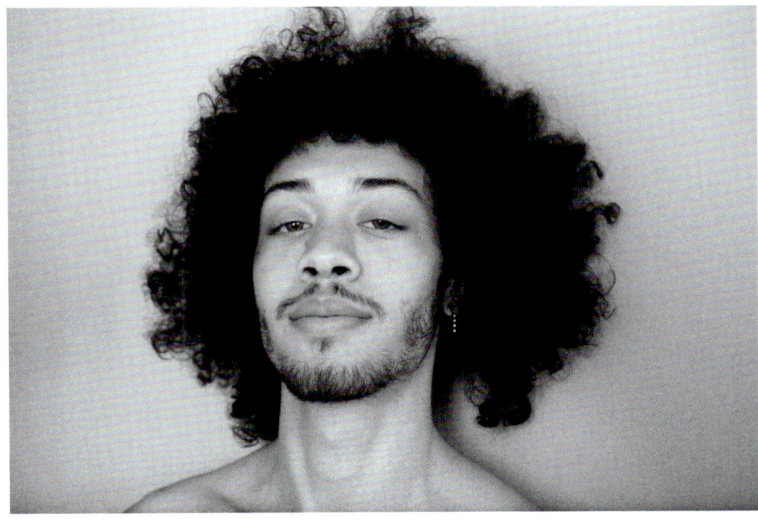

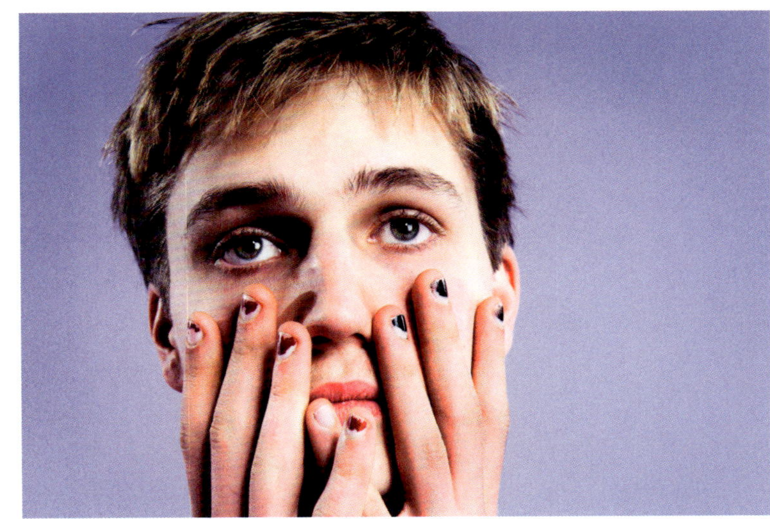

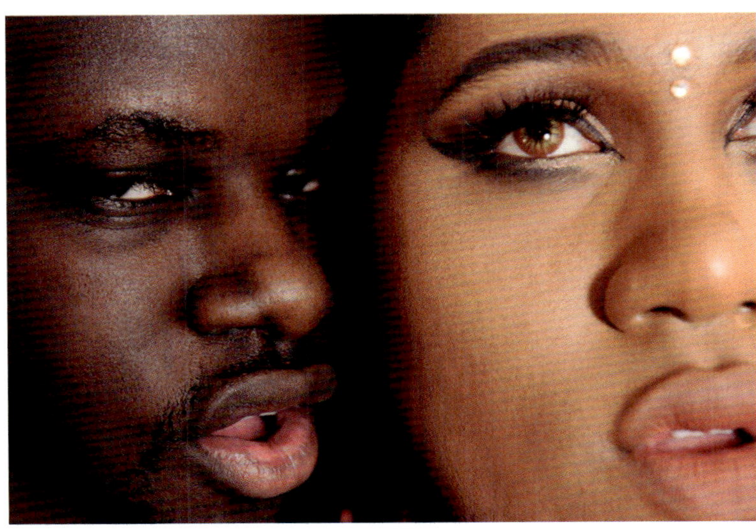

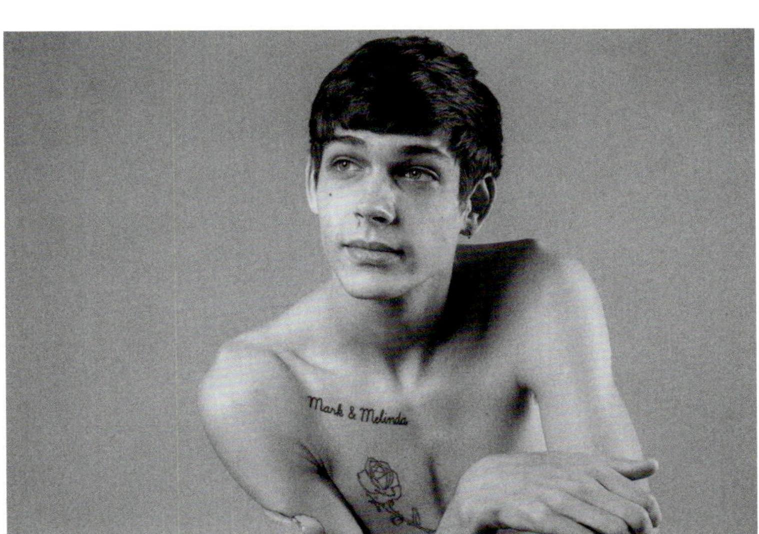

Brian, September 2018 Buster, May 2014 August, October 2015 Apyphanie & Dani, July 2017 Taevon, December 2016 Liam, December 2014 Mojo & Terrance, January 2017 Ethan, November 2011

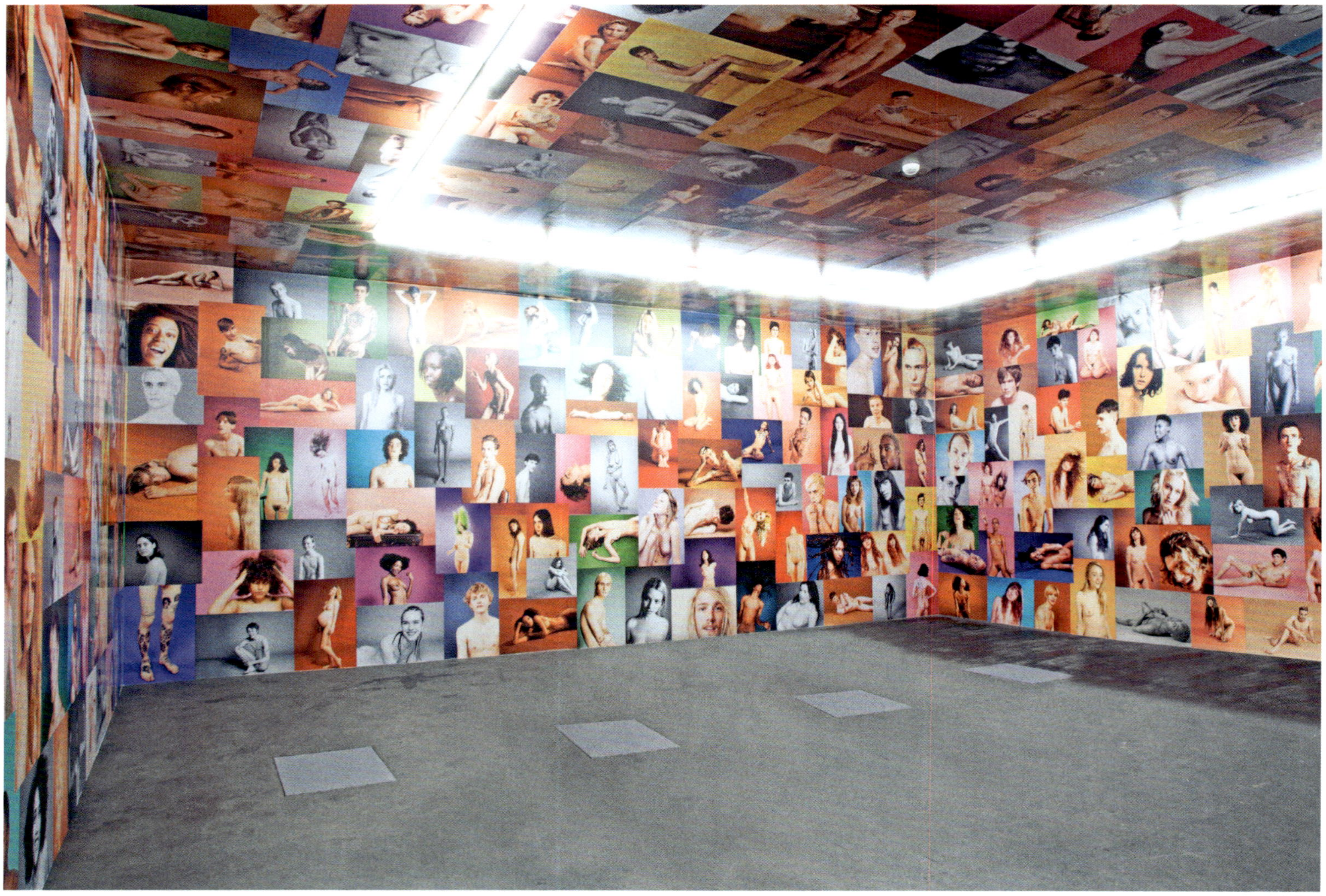

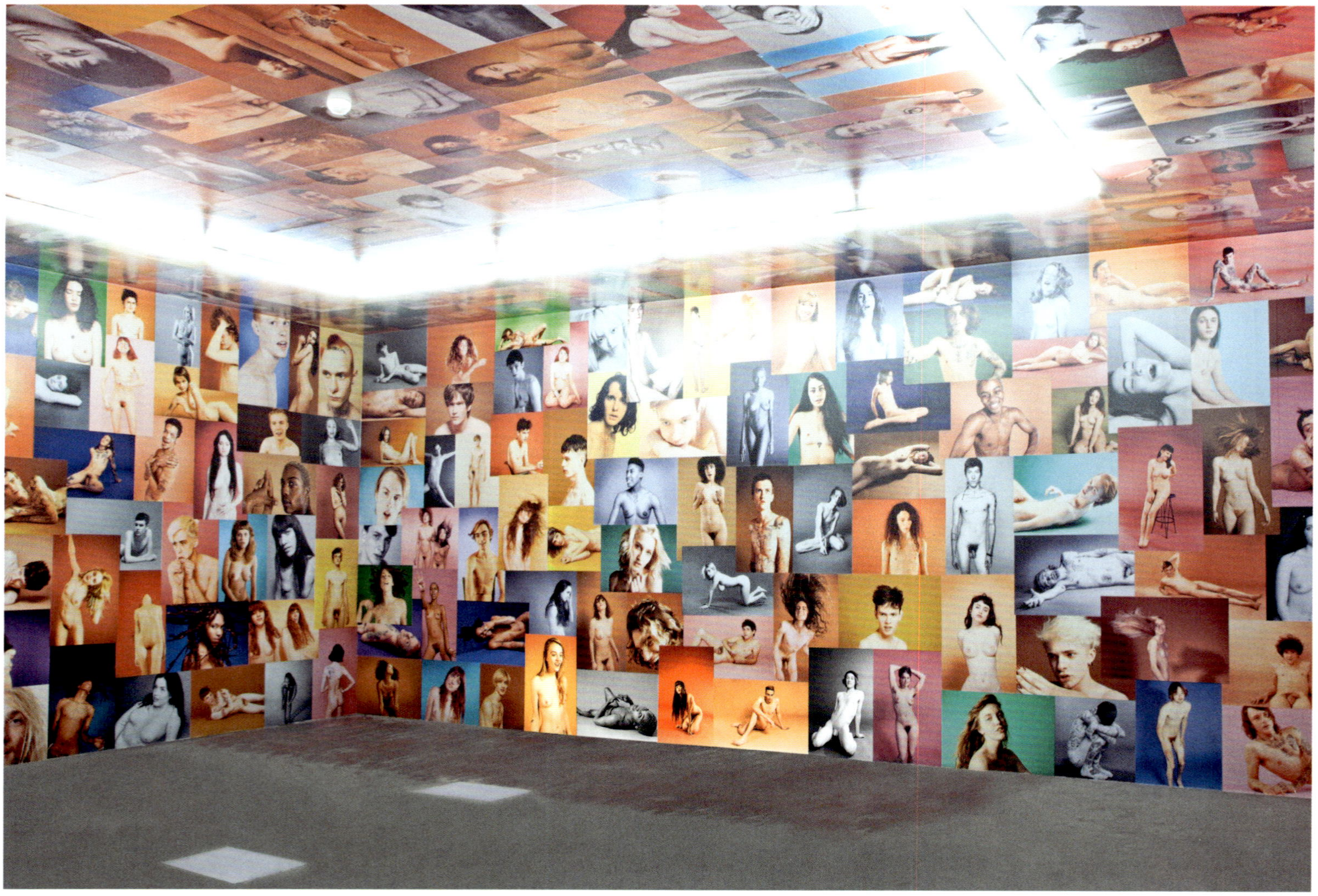

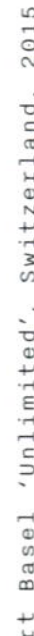
Art Basel 'Unlimited', Switzerland, 2015

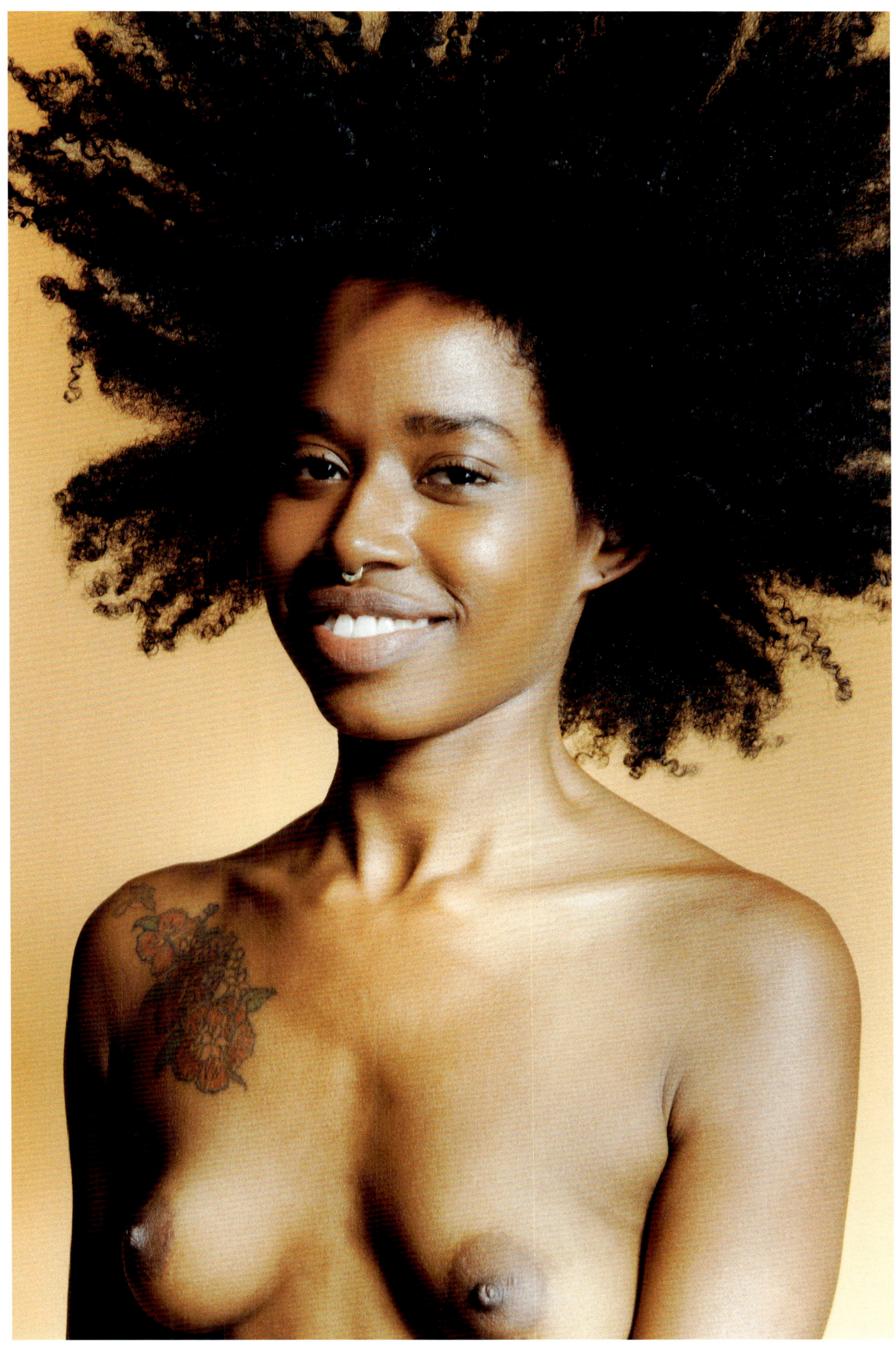

Merie, November 2015

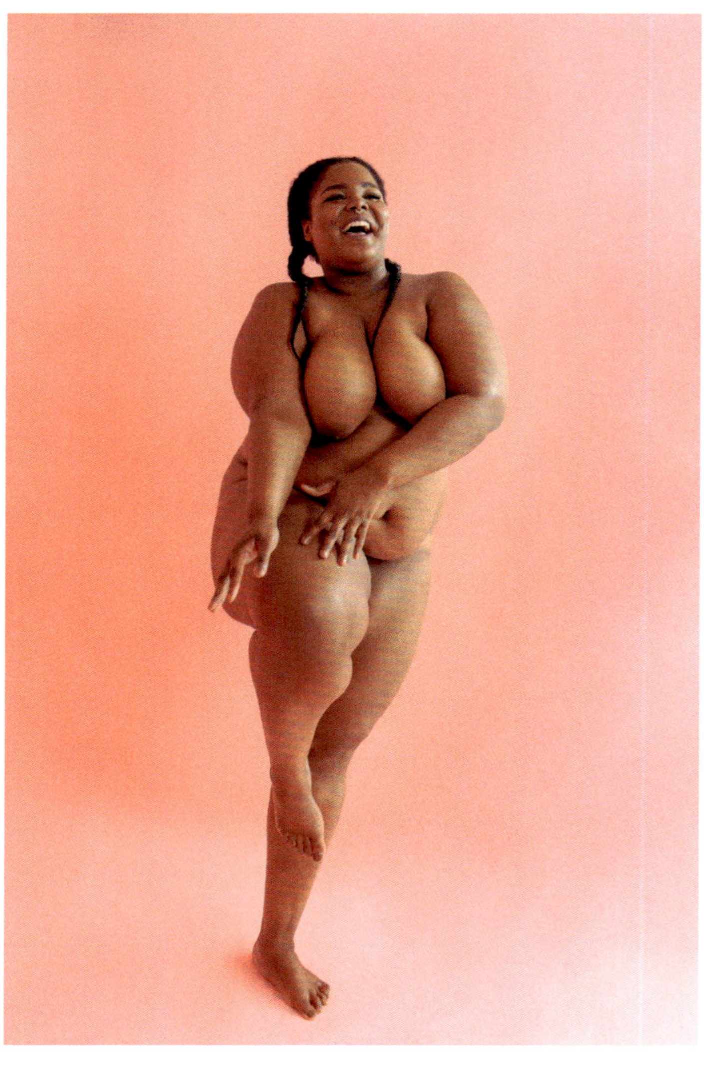

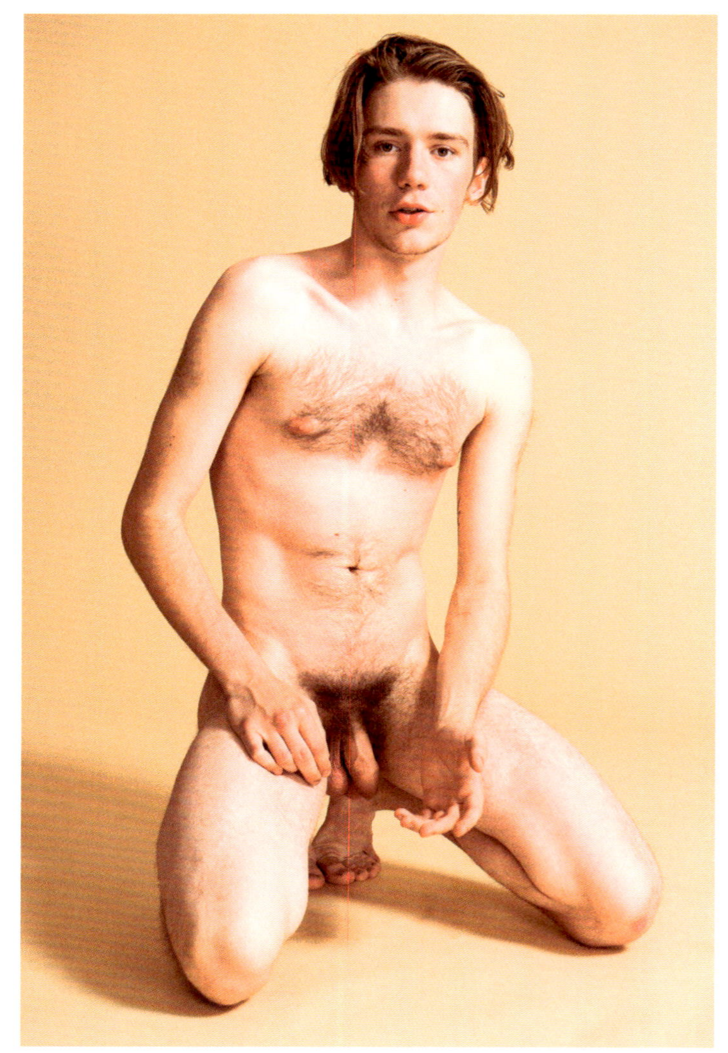

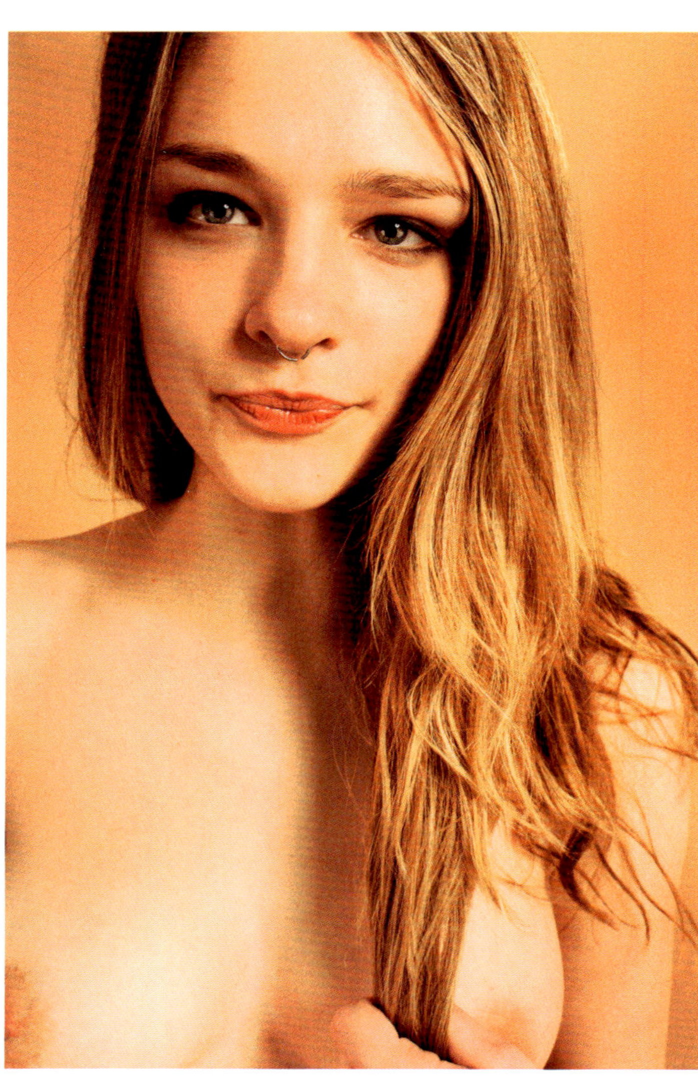

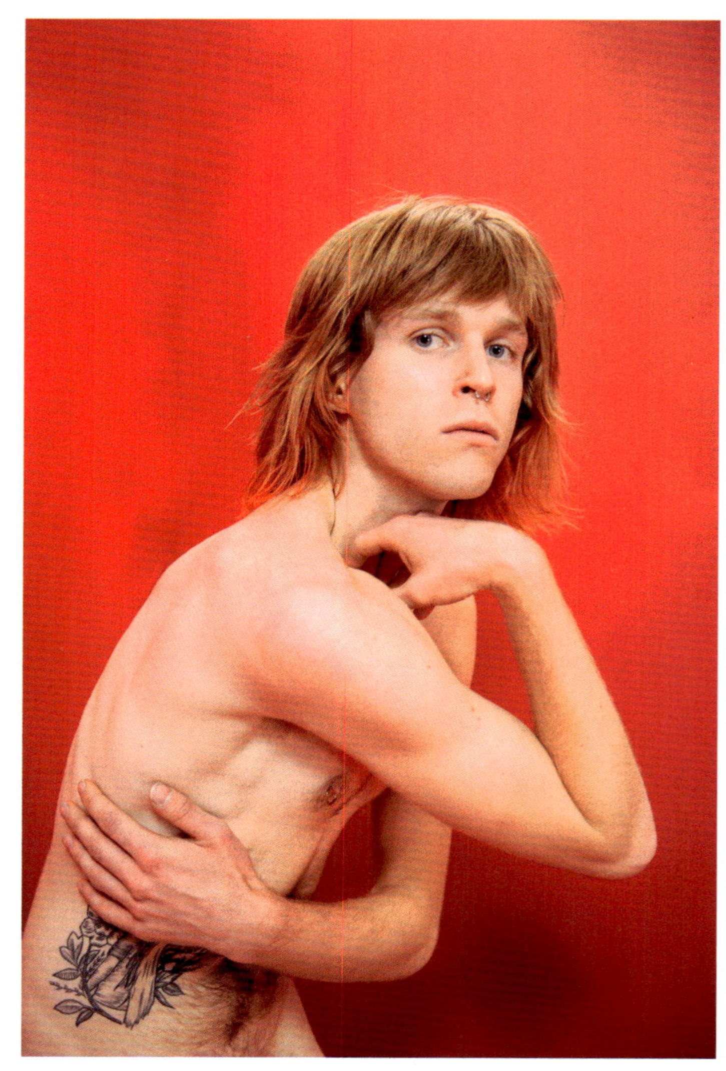

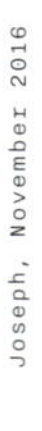

Ashleigh, July 2016 Luca, May 2016 Alex, January 2013 Joseph, November 2016

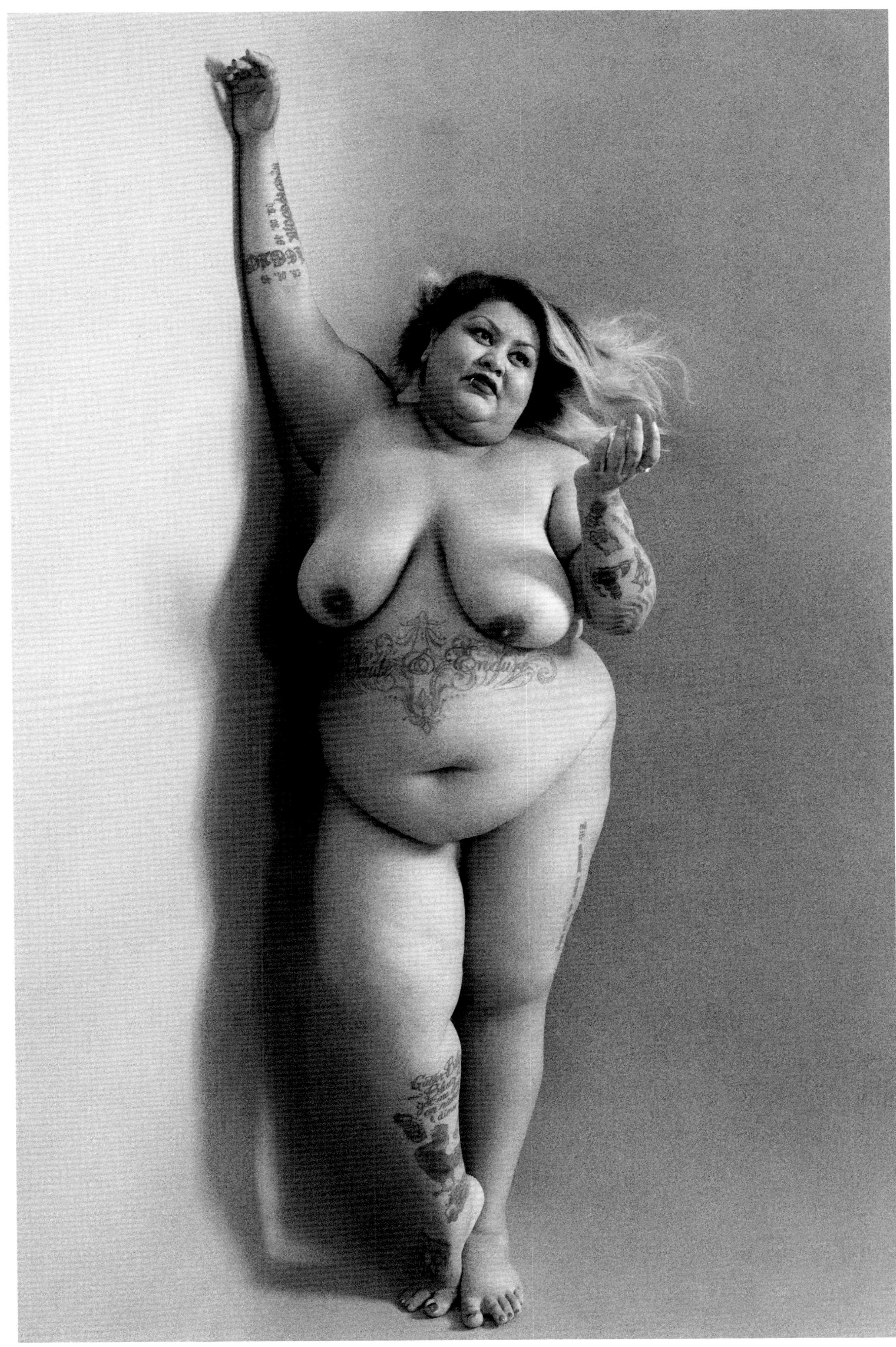

Ushshi, May 2016

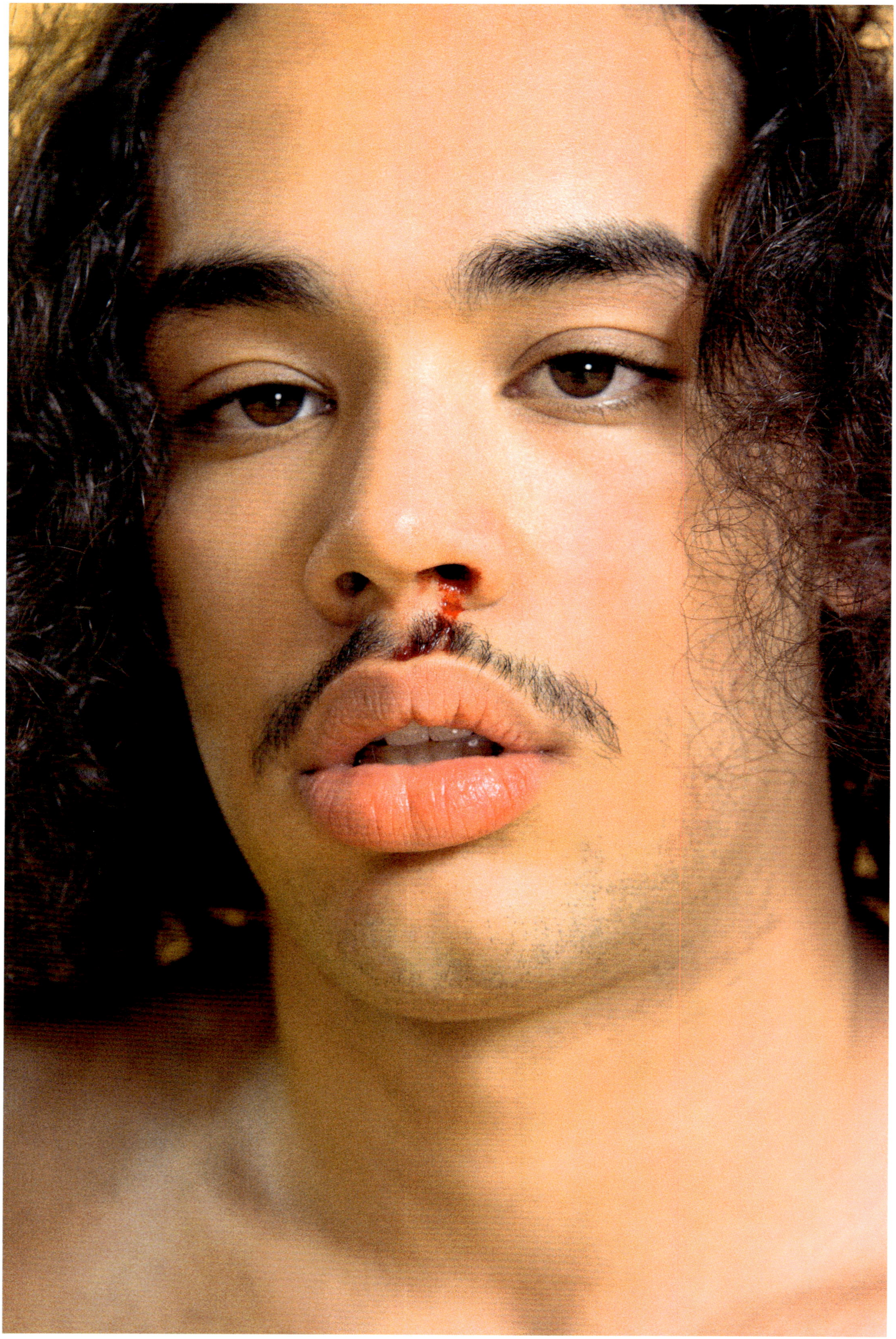

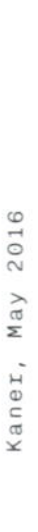
Kaner, May 2016

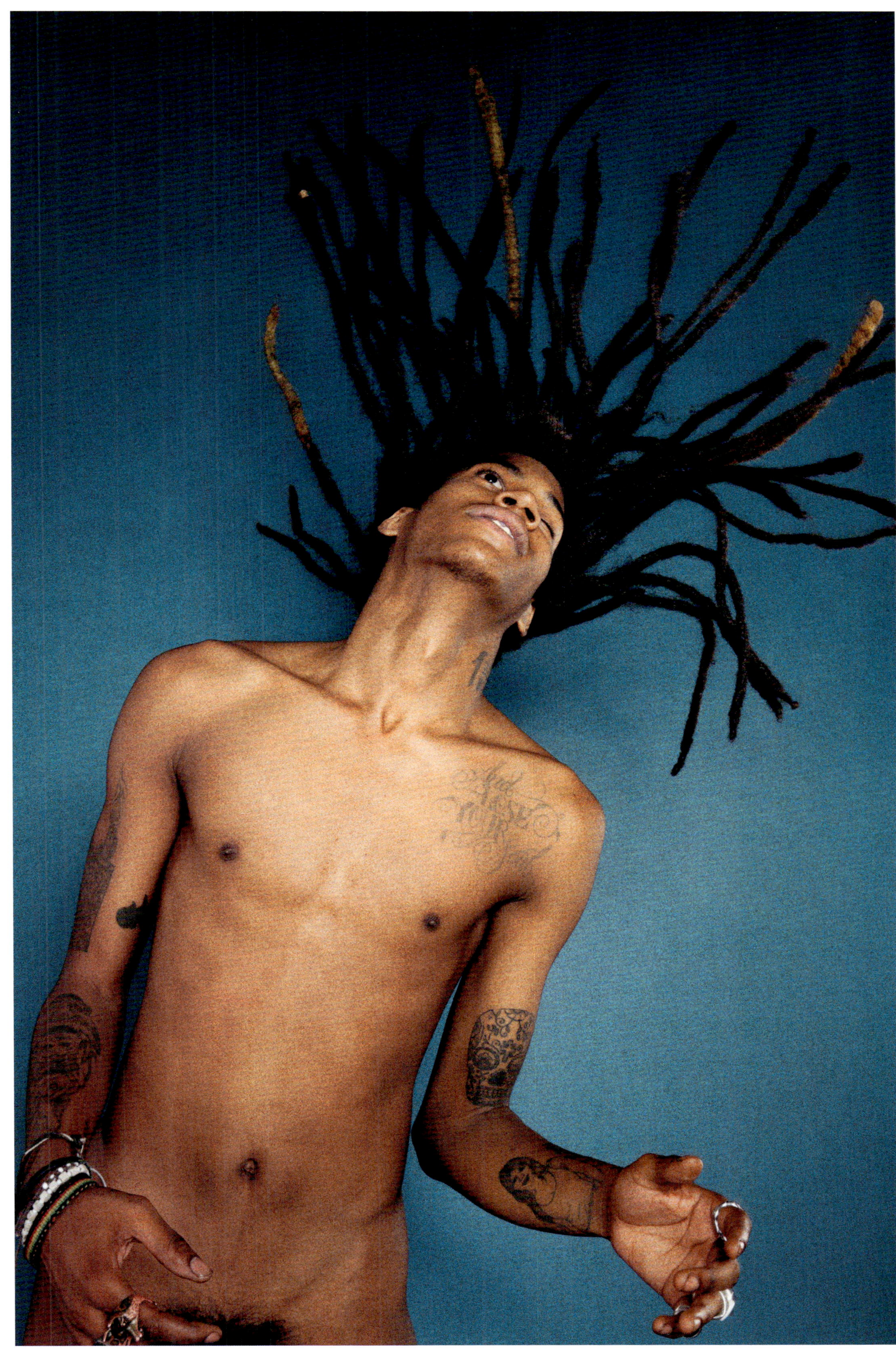

George, 2012

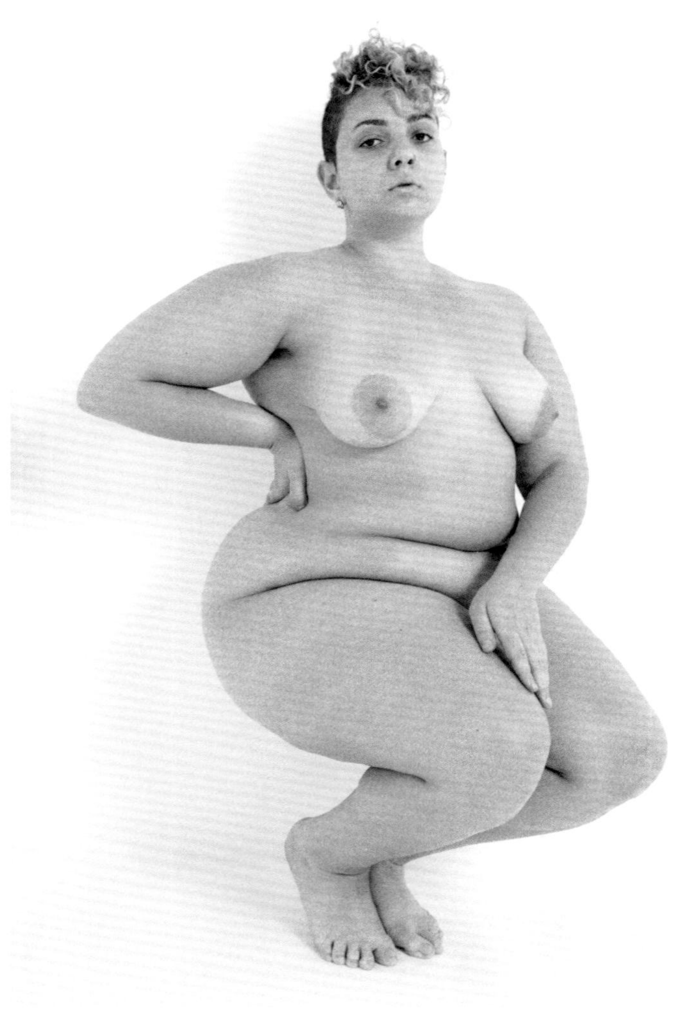

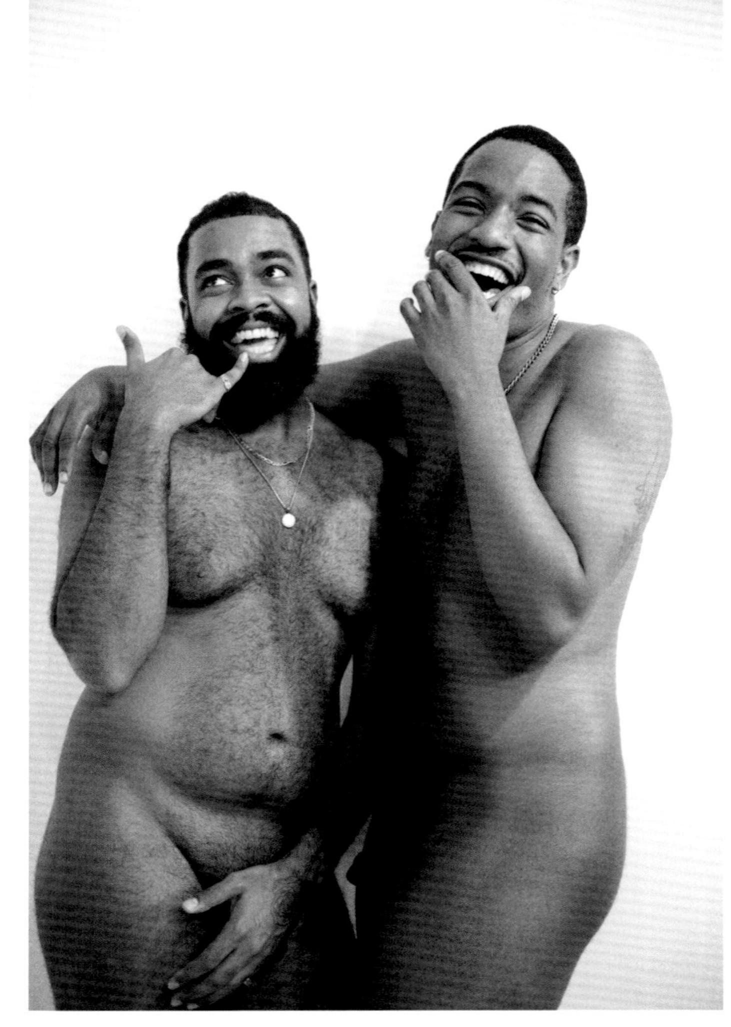

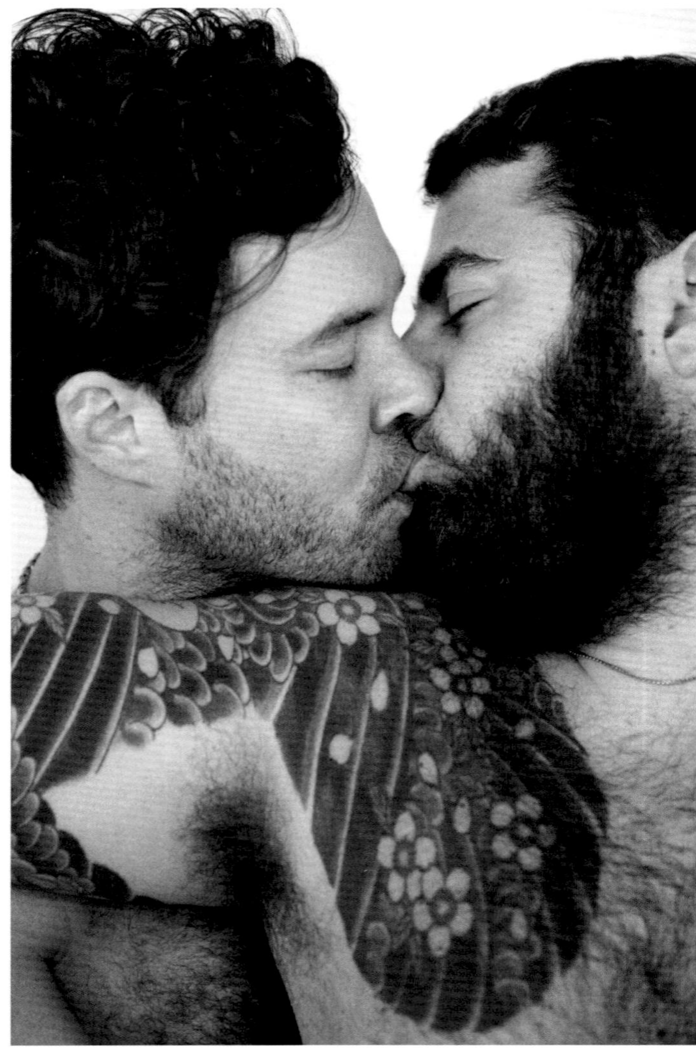

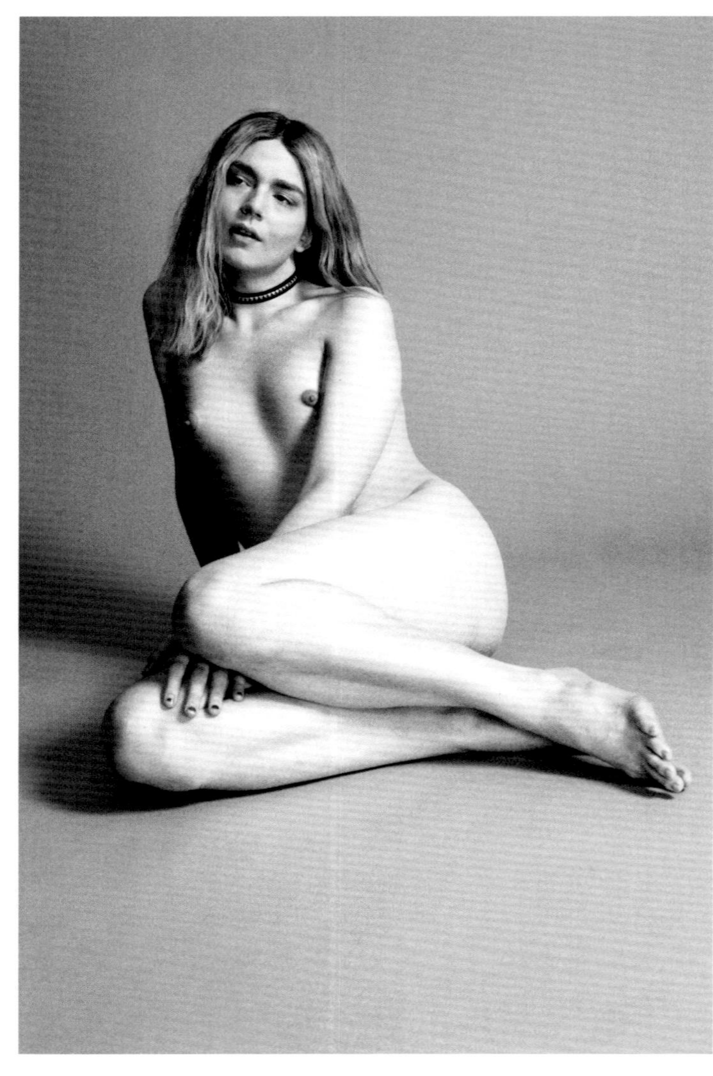

Maya, April 2017 Lorenzo & Milton, October 2019 Nolan & Justin, November 2018 Macy, May 2016

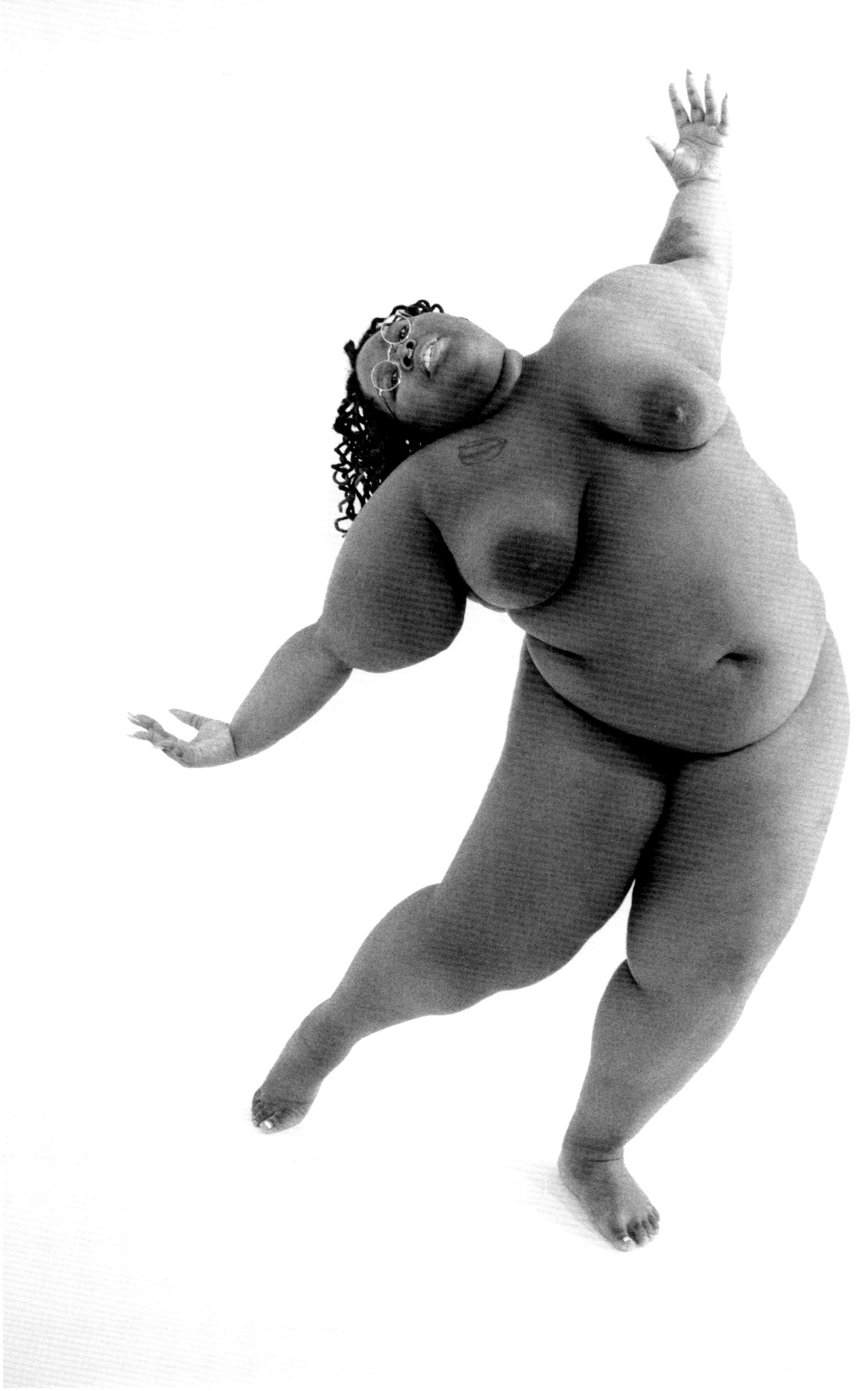

Maya, December 2019

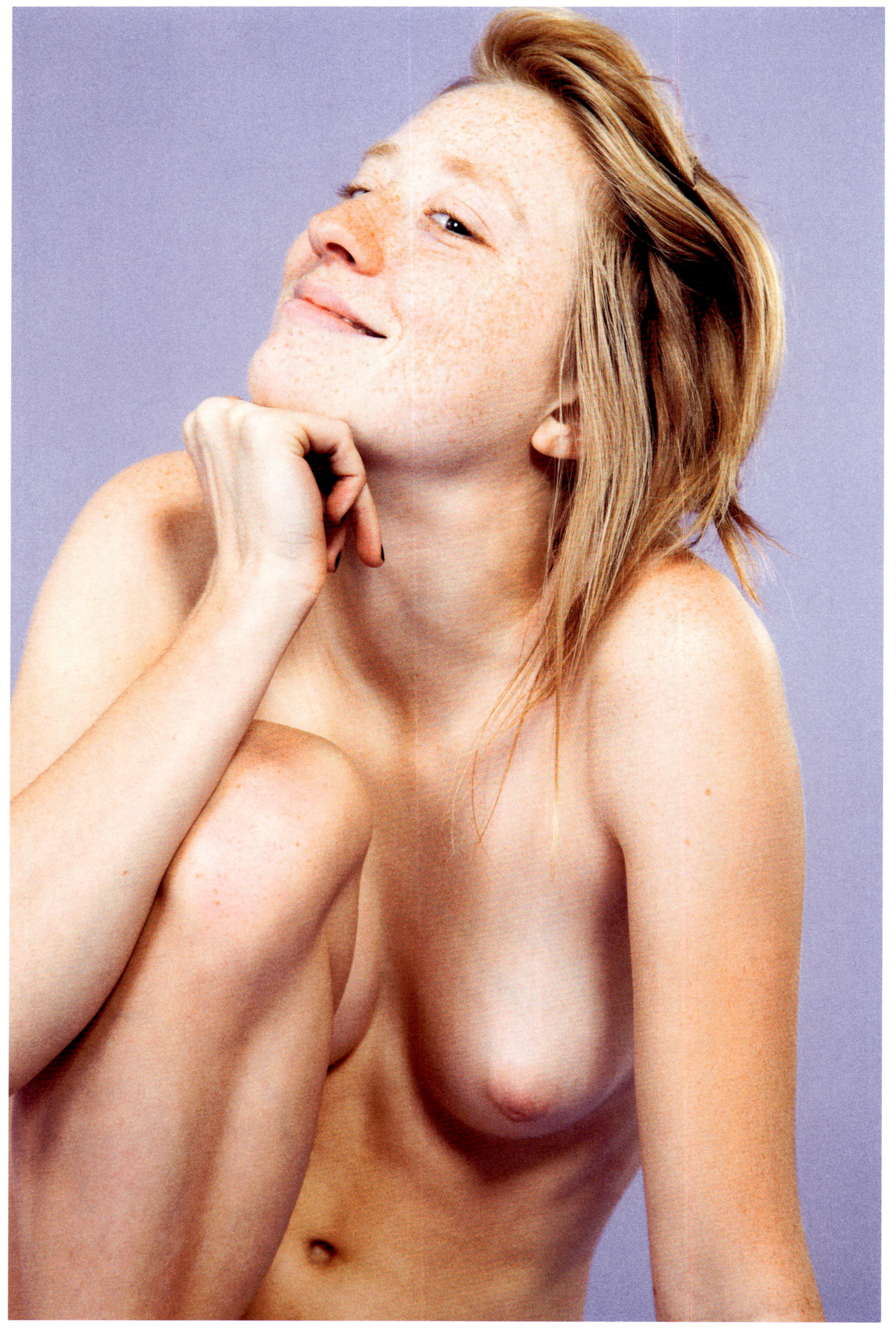

Maren, November 2013

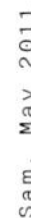

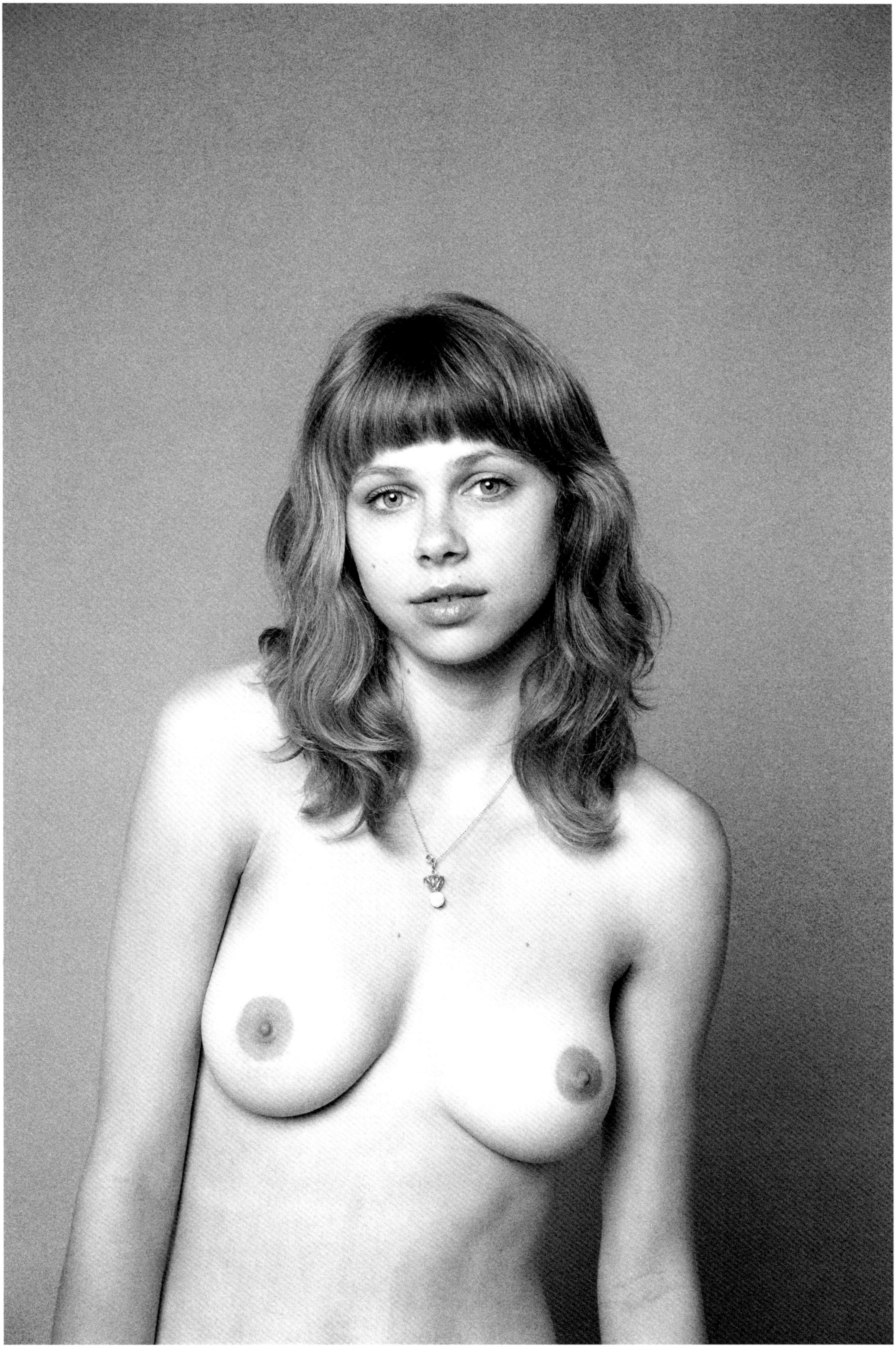

Sam, May 2011

My middle name is Shazam. I despised it growing up. I felt it had this really strong masculine tone and I hated it. As I progressed through high school and college, I started owning the name. I realized that my mom had implanted it into my title. Owning it was an homage to her. I fell in love with Shazam's strength and cultural significance. It's like having a superhero name. It made me feel powerful even in moments when I didn't feel so powerful.

I grew up in Queens. My parents are from Guyana in South America. My home life was very intense. My mom was sick and losing her eyesight. My father had no qualms about putting hands on me and calling me every name under the sun. I give him grace now—grace from afar. I understand how my parents were plucked out of their country and into a completely different world. Everything I did was scrutinized. I wanted so badly just to be free.

I remember coming into the city at twelve and thirteen. At first, it was for education. By fourteen, I was taking the subway to Union Square to hang out with other kids and smoke weed illegally. I was drawn to trouble. My whole life was being a sneak, a freak. I saw doing bad shit as a mechanism to find myself and the city as a place where people come to be their authentic selves.

I was drawn to freak shows. The era of freak shows in New York City is unfortunately dying. You used to be able to walk through these fucking iconic historical neighborhoods and everyone had a story. That might exist at the peripheries, but it barely exists anymore. My youth was the beginning of the Internet, AOL chat rooms, whatever. We were lucky. We could link up and have these really raw, authentic exchanges.

You know when you find your people and you're like, "Wait, we're speaking the same language." You don't have to work to communicate. It's so crazy that my sisters and I found each other in this tumultuous, scary world. When I first met Brianna [Andalore], we were fourteen, fifteen. I was instantly entranced by her aura. The same with Julia [Fox]. Our sisterhood came together organically. We were all social butterflies who loved nighttime festivities. Our bond was strengthened by our love of style.

When I still lived at home, I'd change outfits on the train. It wasn't safe to wear what I wanted to wear at home. I was breaking gender codes and embracing my femininity in sexy silhouettes, makeup, and heels. At the same time, I had this weird ancestral tie to my body hair. It all felt natural to me. It was organic. I didn't have any language for it. It was a physical rush. I was expressing myself. We were all just actively being ourselves at that time. Later, what we were doing became this commodity thing. The commodification of identity, a trend. Exactly what we said we didn't want it to be. Body positivity and gender identity are not trends. This is who we are and we're not going anywhere.

I got sober when I was still so baby, at twenty-one, twenty-two-years-old. I would go to meetings and then hit the club right after. I'm really grateful that my girls and I were going out all the time and having so much fun while I was seeing the richness of sobriety. When I see this photo and the other photos in the book, it's a special moment of looking at baby versions of all of us. I hold these photos warmly to my heart. Ryan is family to me. It's a trusted lens. We really need our tribe, our community, our people to hold our hands through time. We're constantly being reborn.

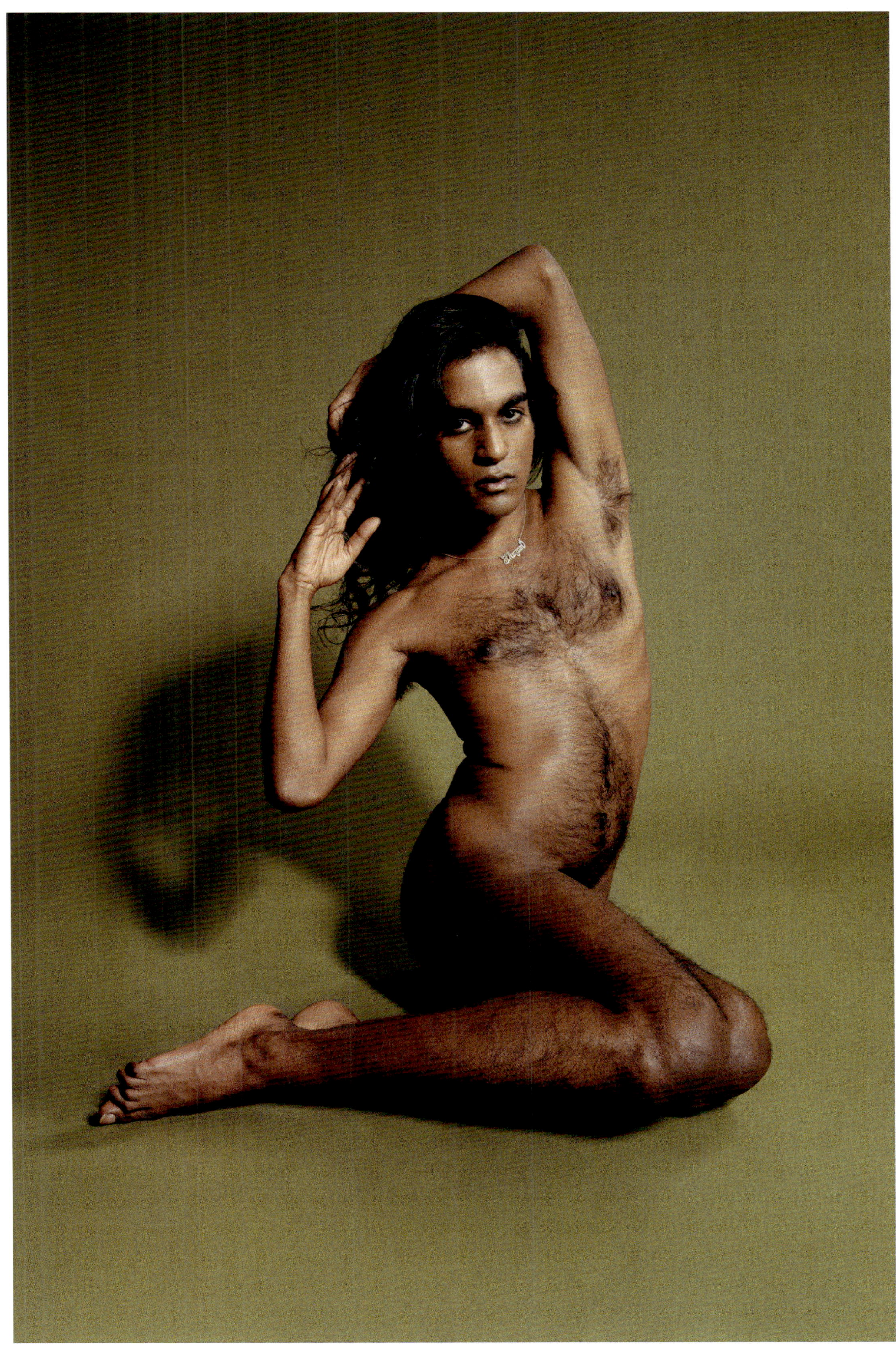

Richie, January 2016

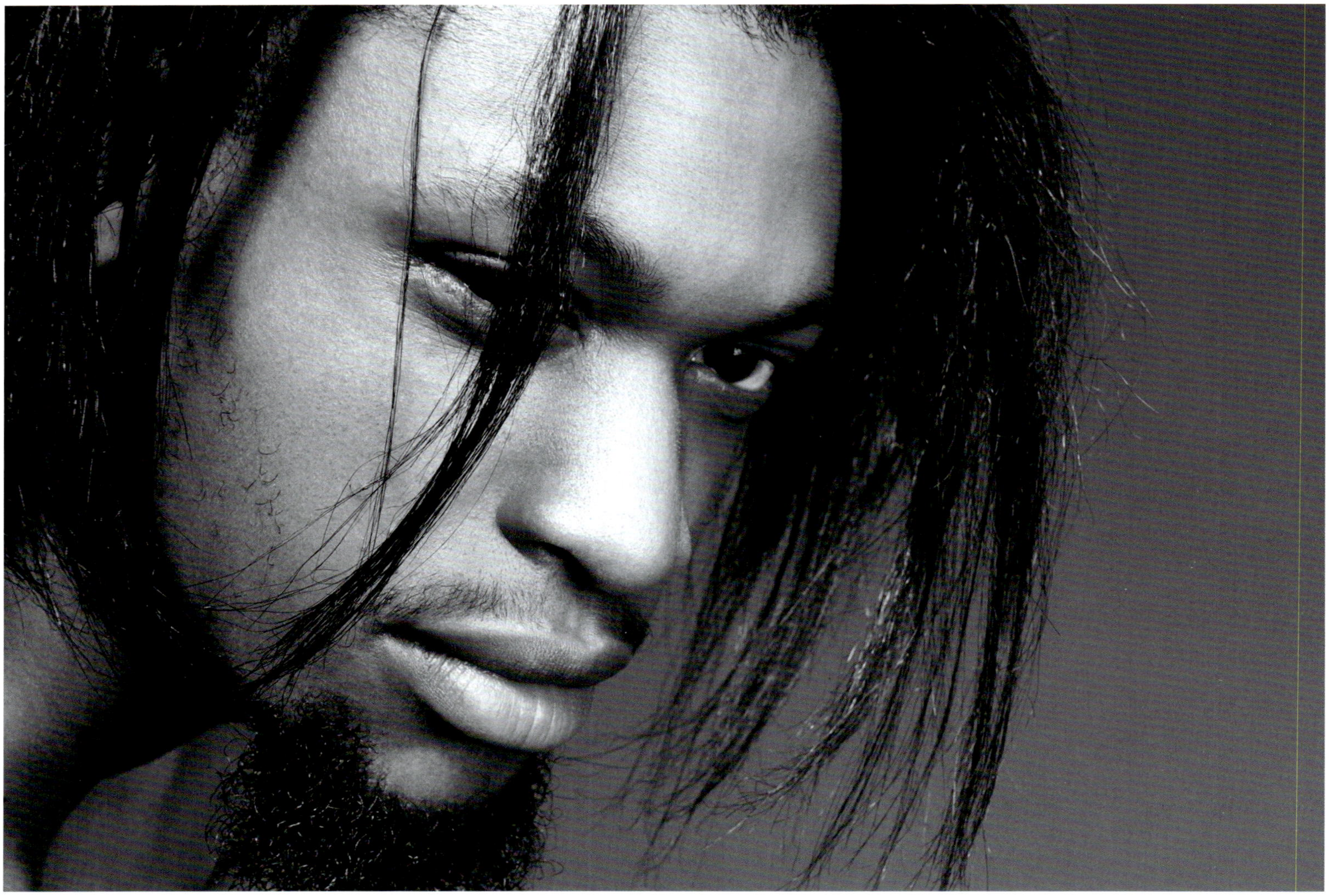

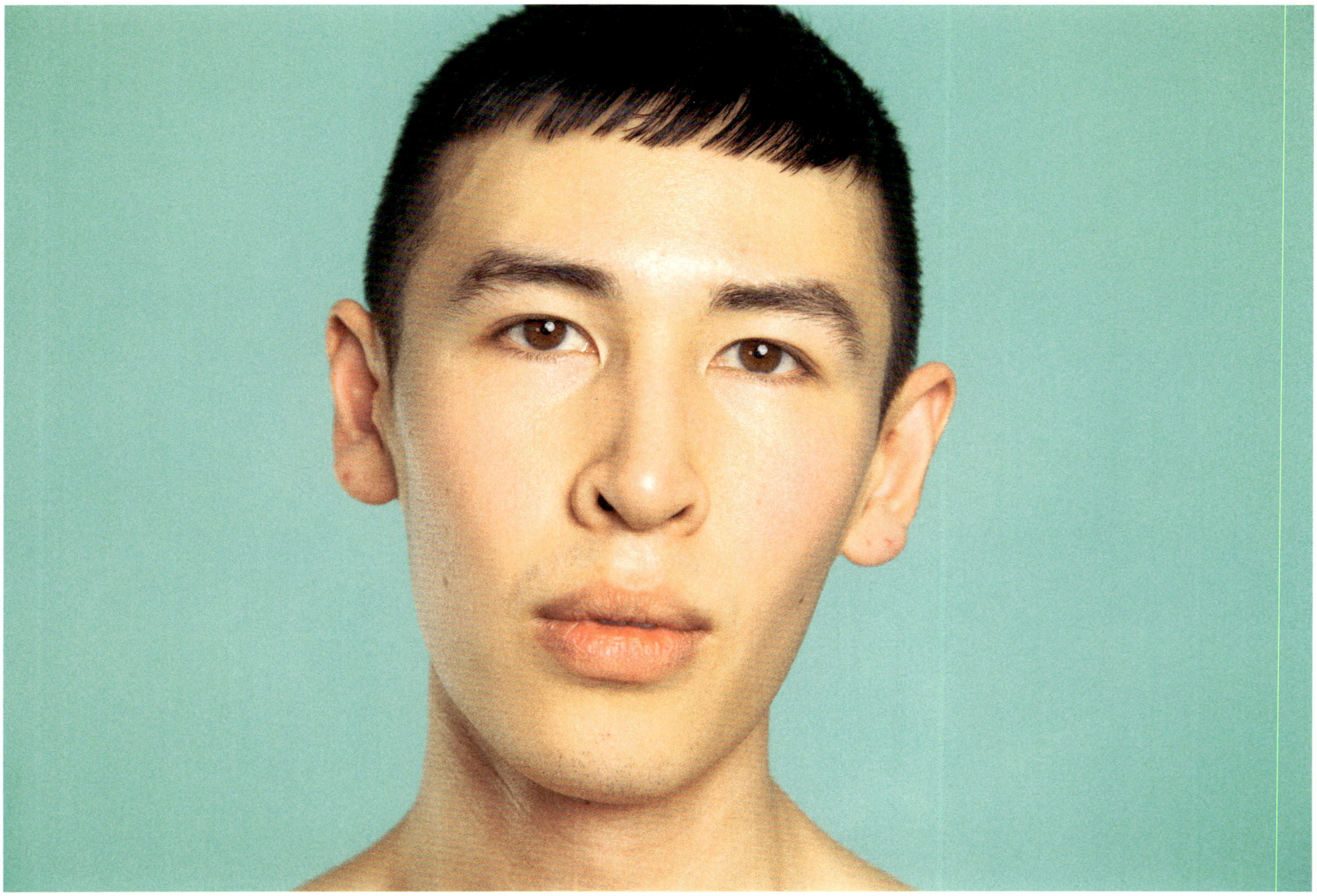

Jarez, September 2015

Winston, January 2011

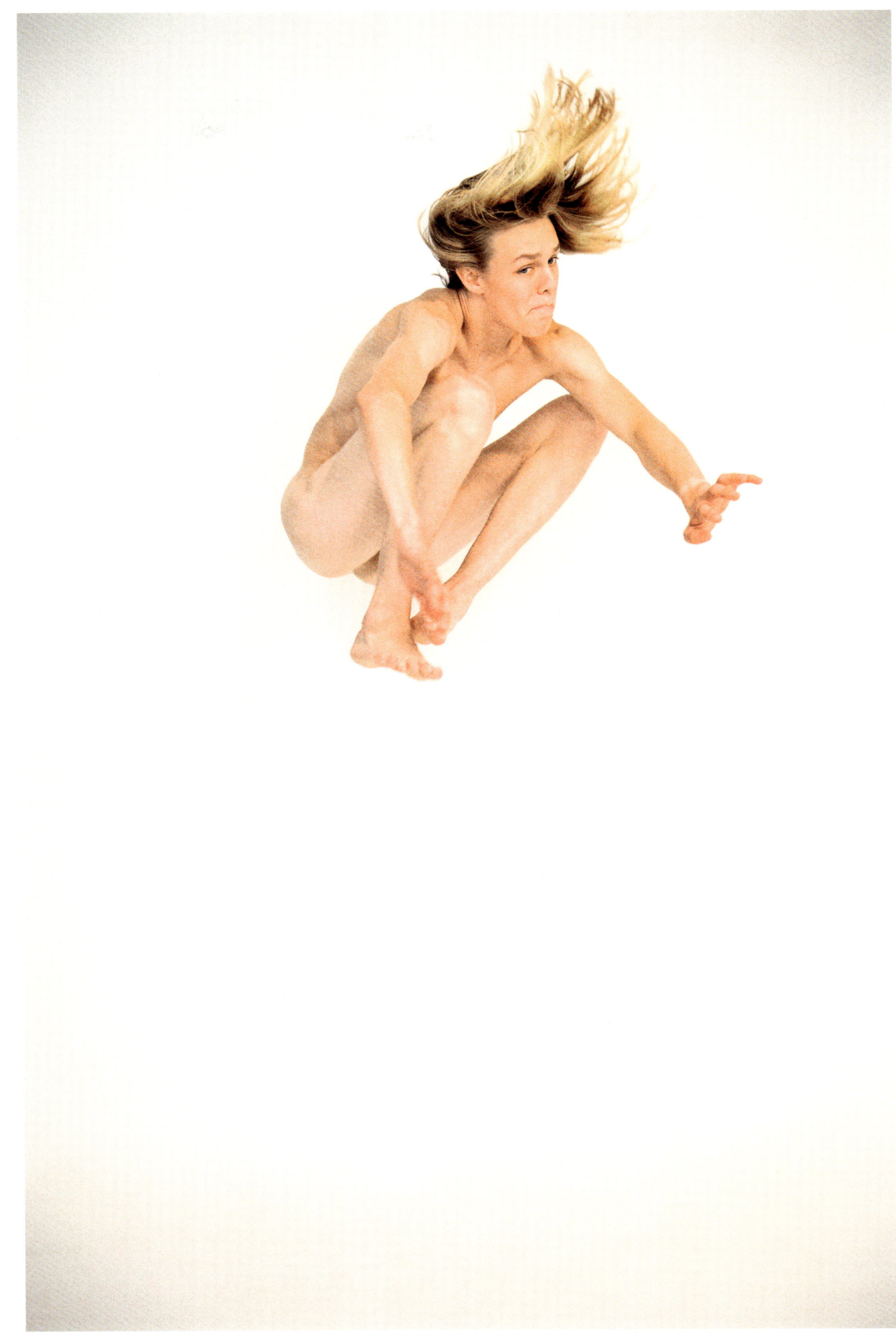

Quinn, September 2018

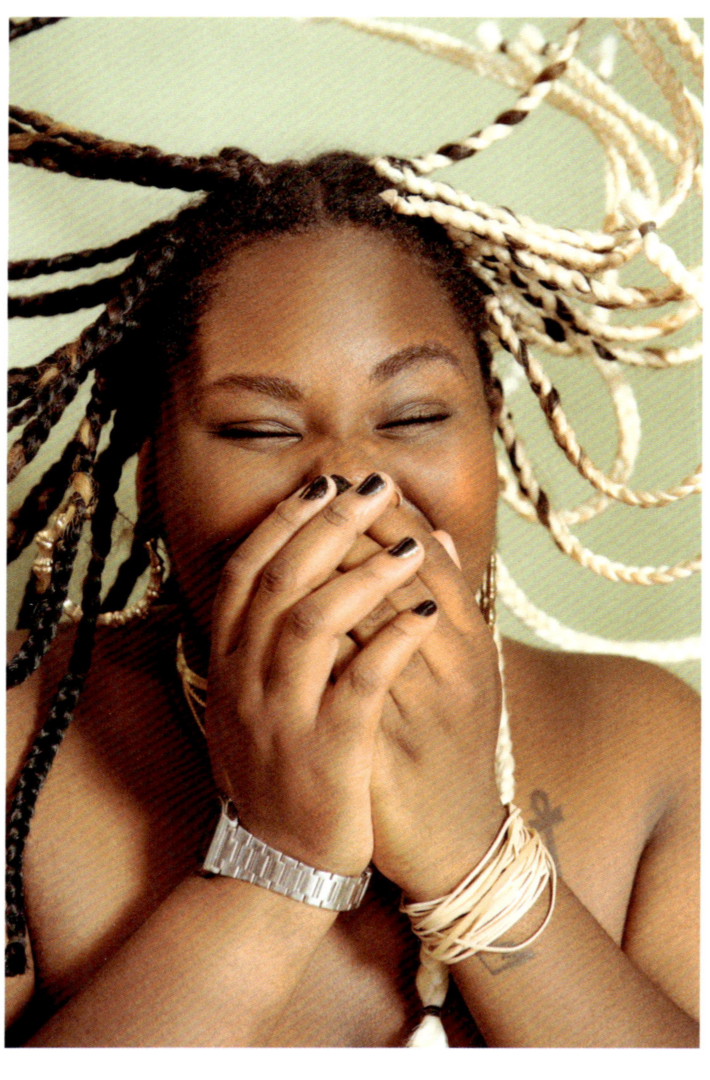

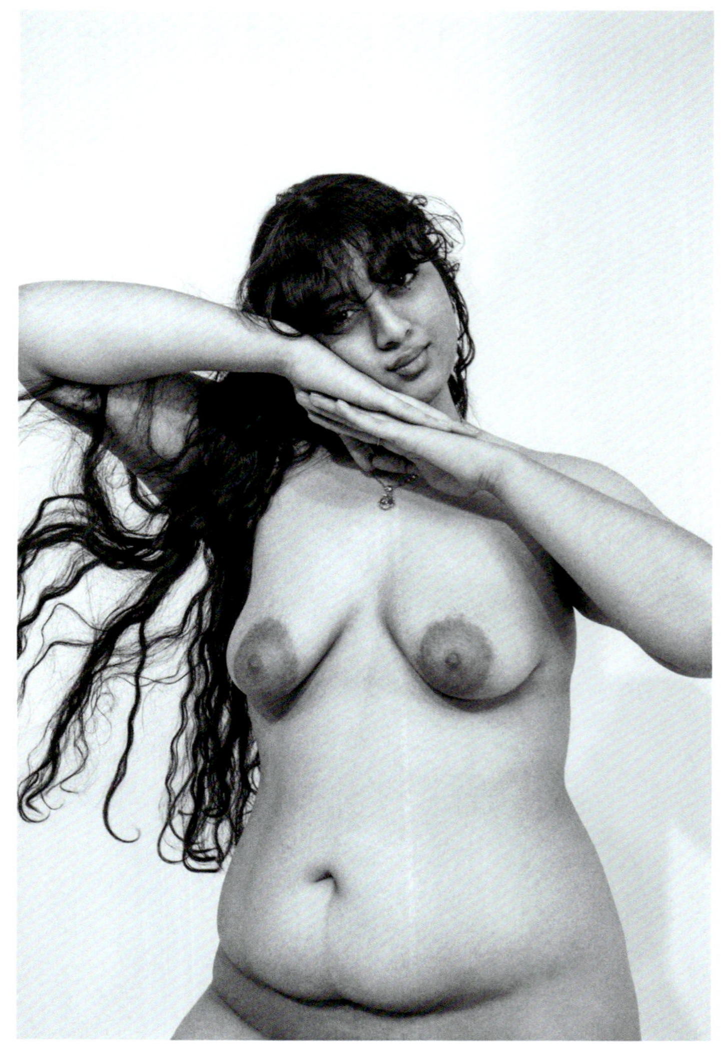

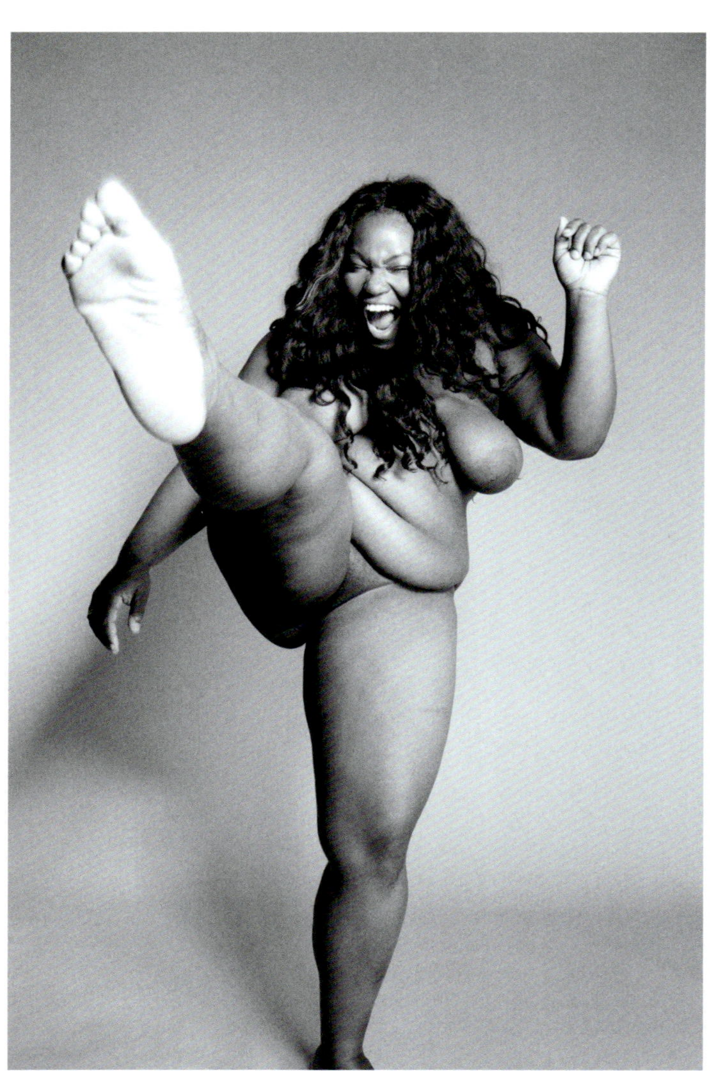

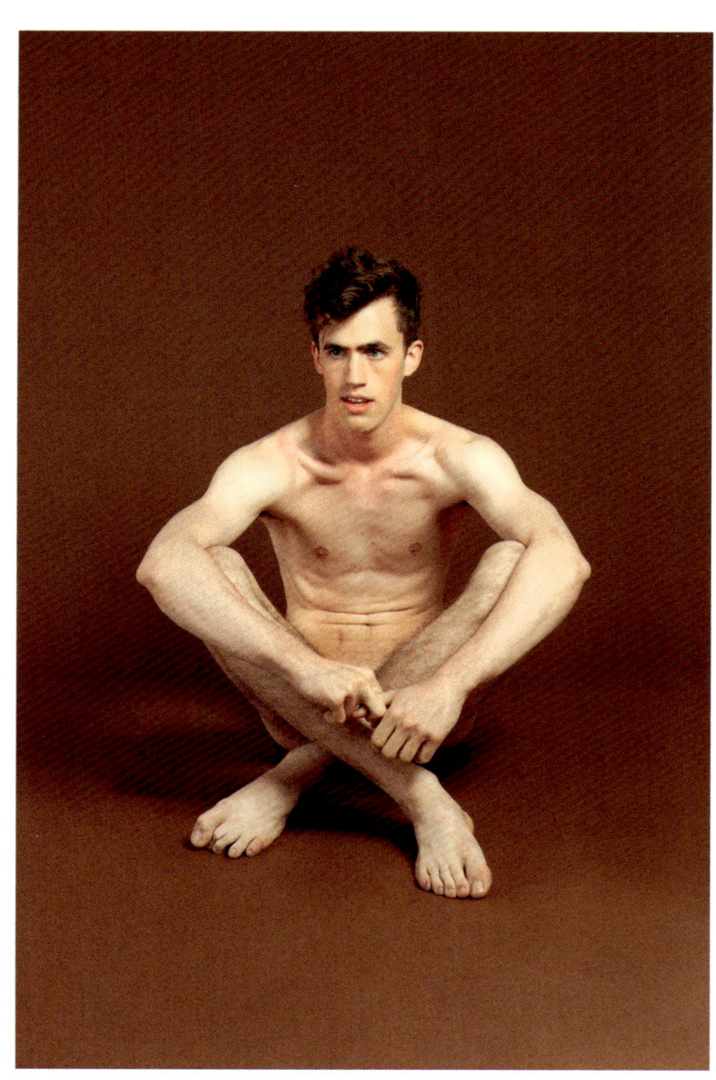

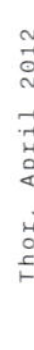

Mykeyla, September 2016 Vineeta, February 2019 Maria, October 2015 Thor, April 2012

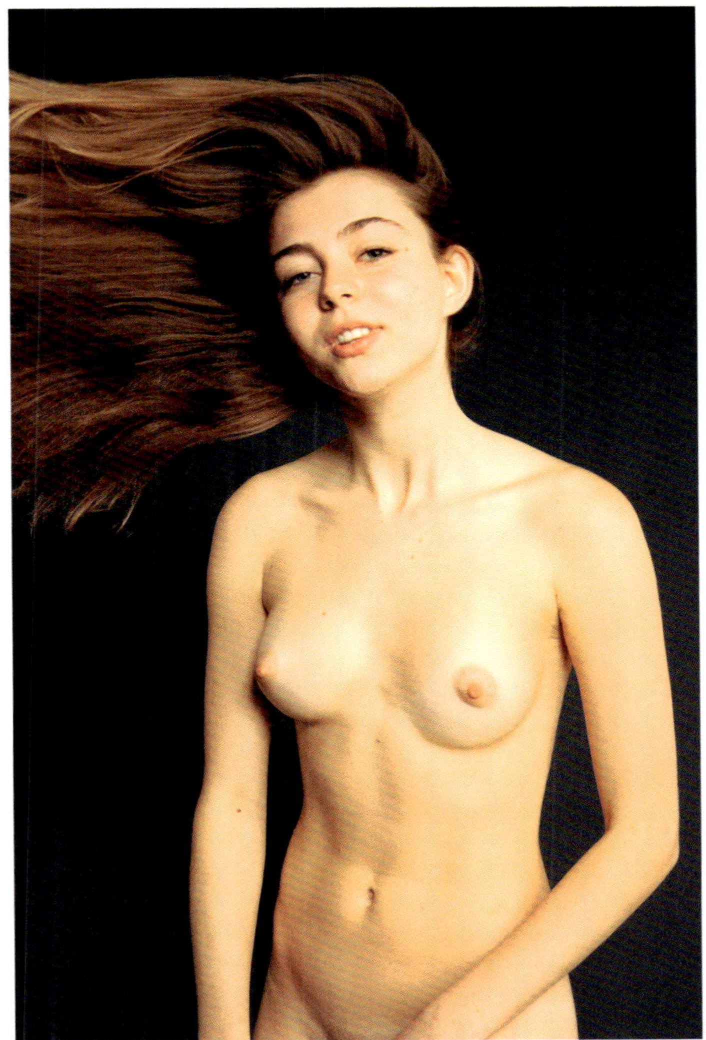

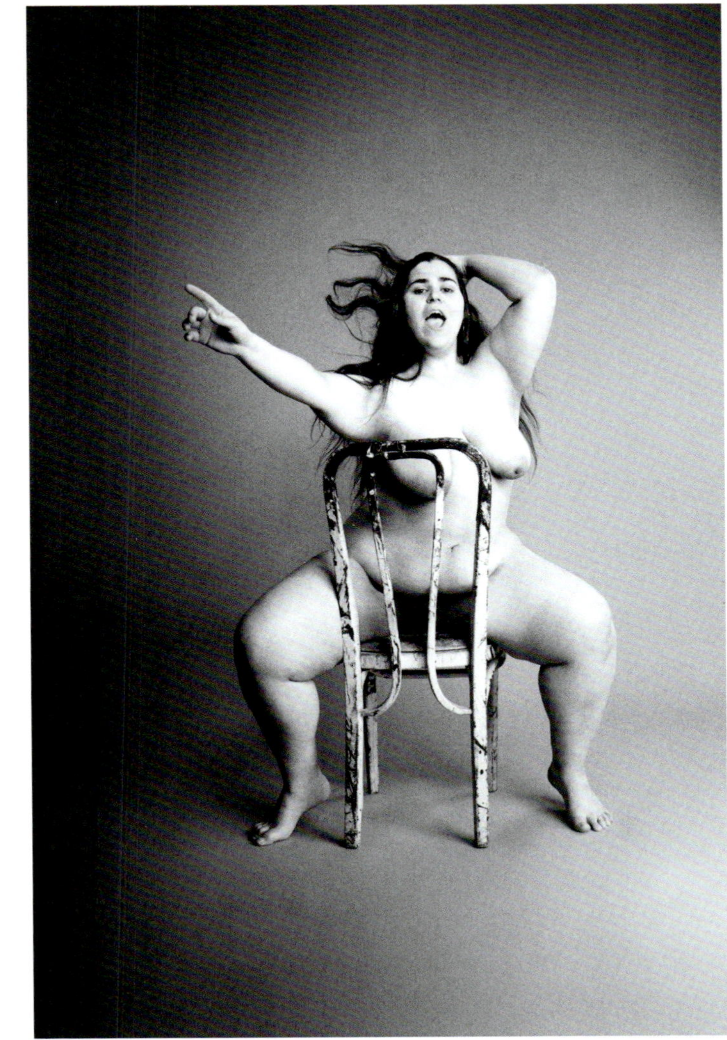

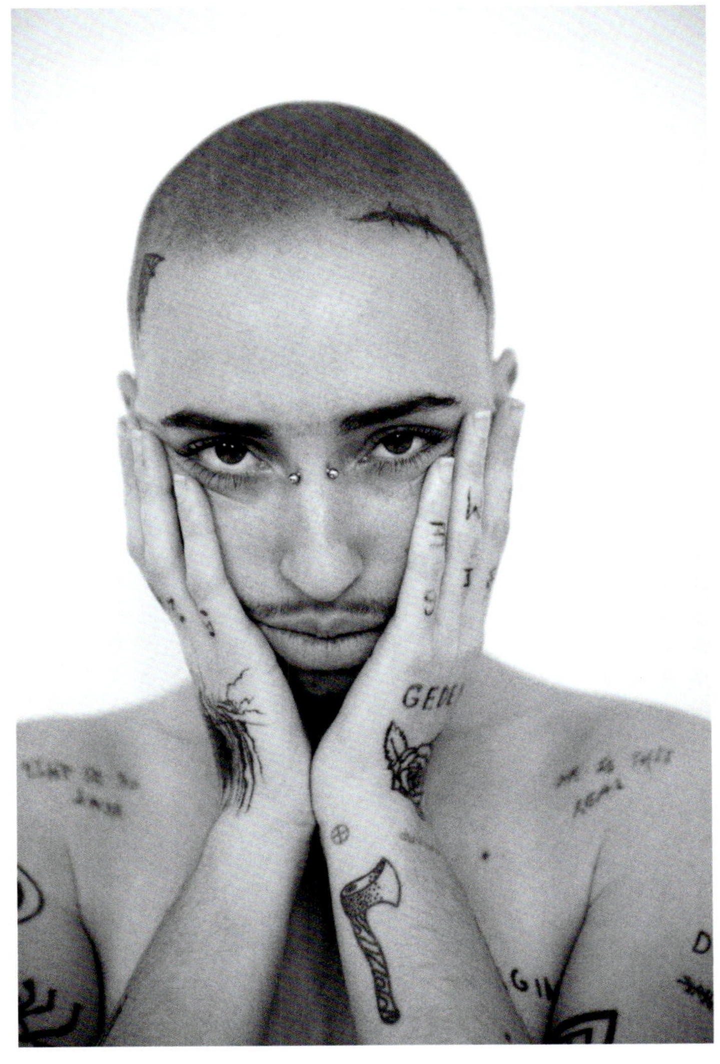

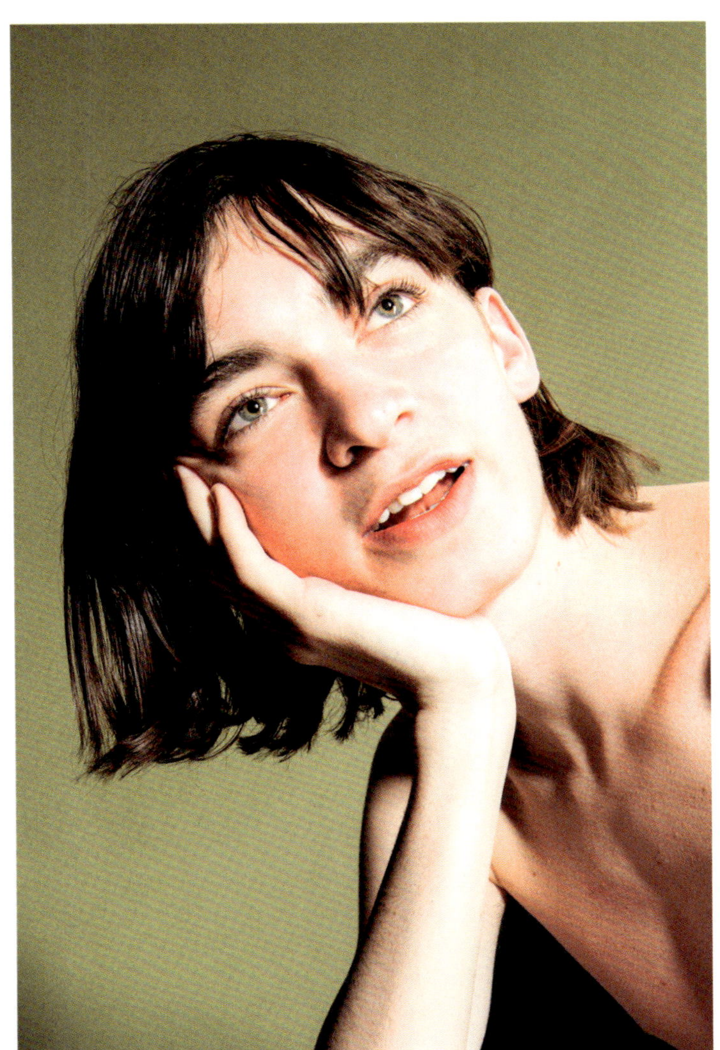

Mirella, January 2014 Steph January 2015 Lux, November 2018 Meetka, January 2016

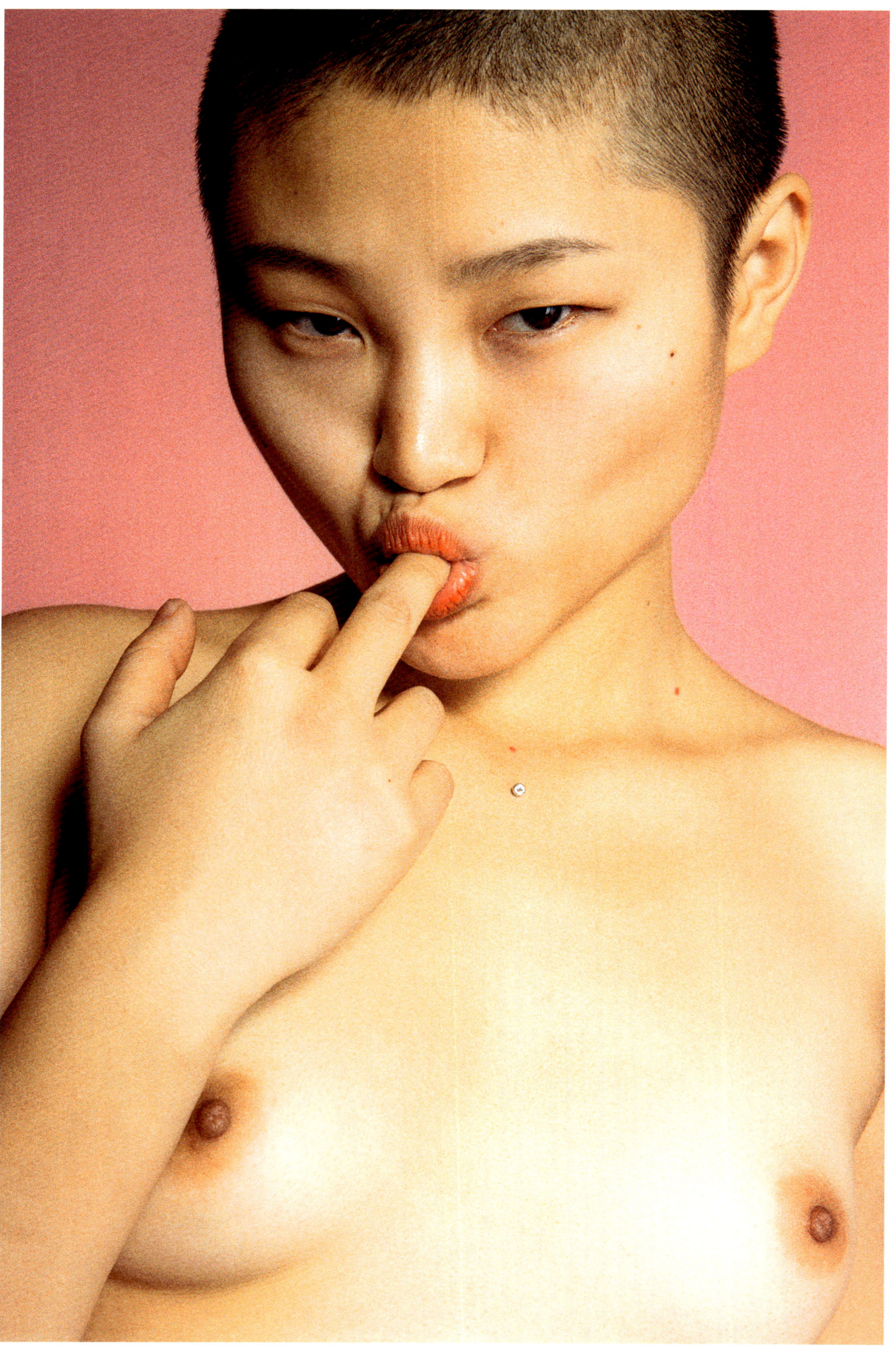

Xi, November 2015

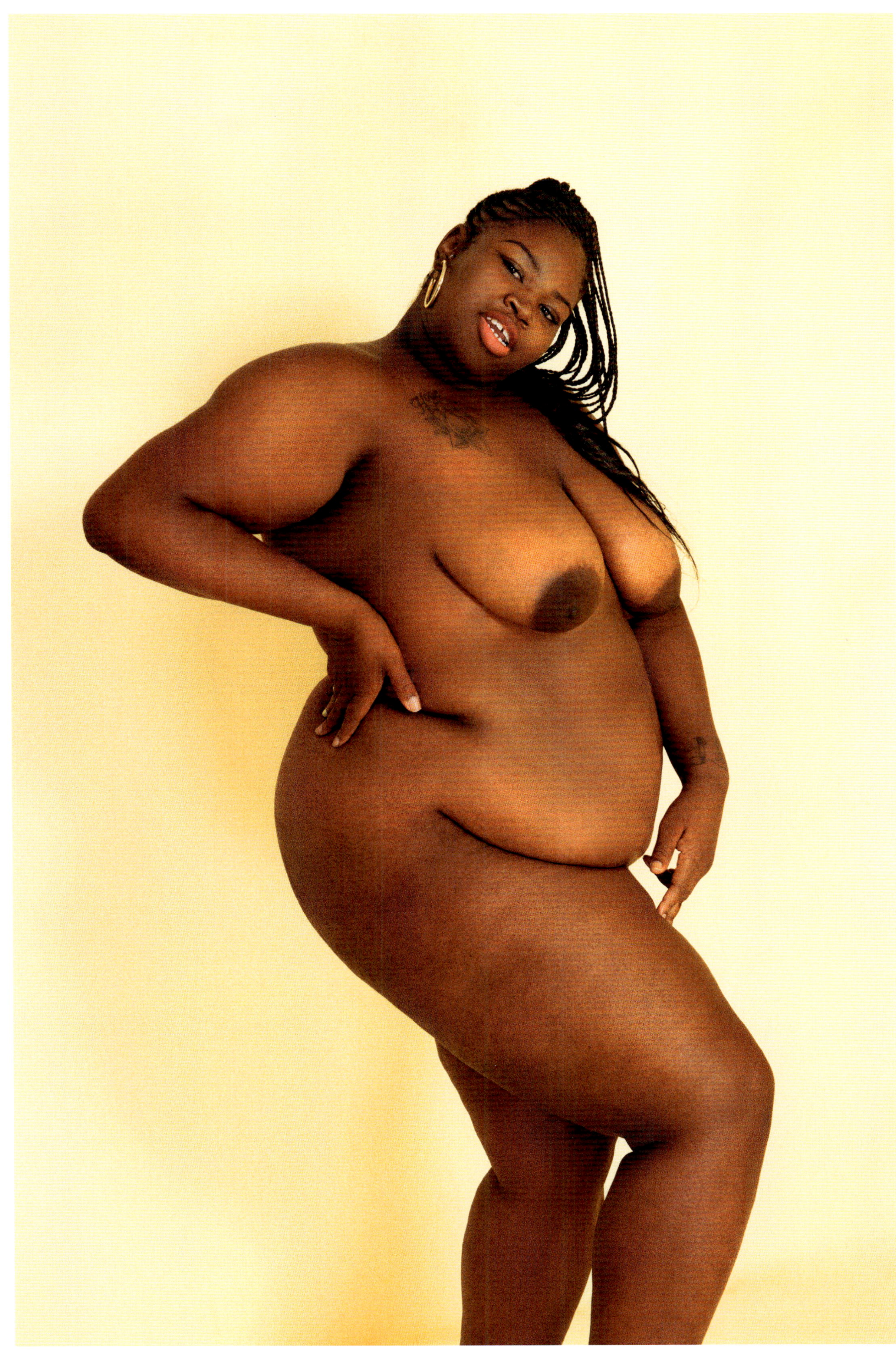

Alisha, July 2016

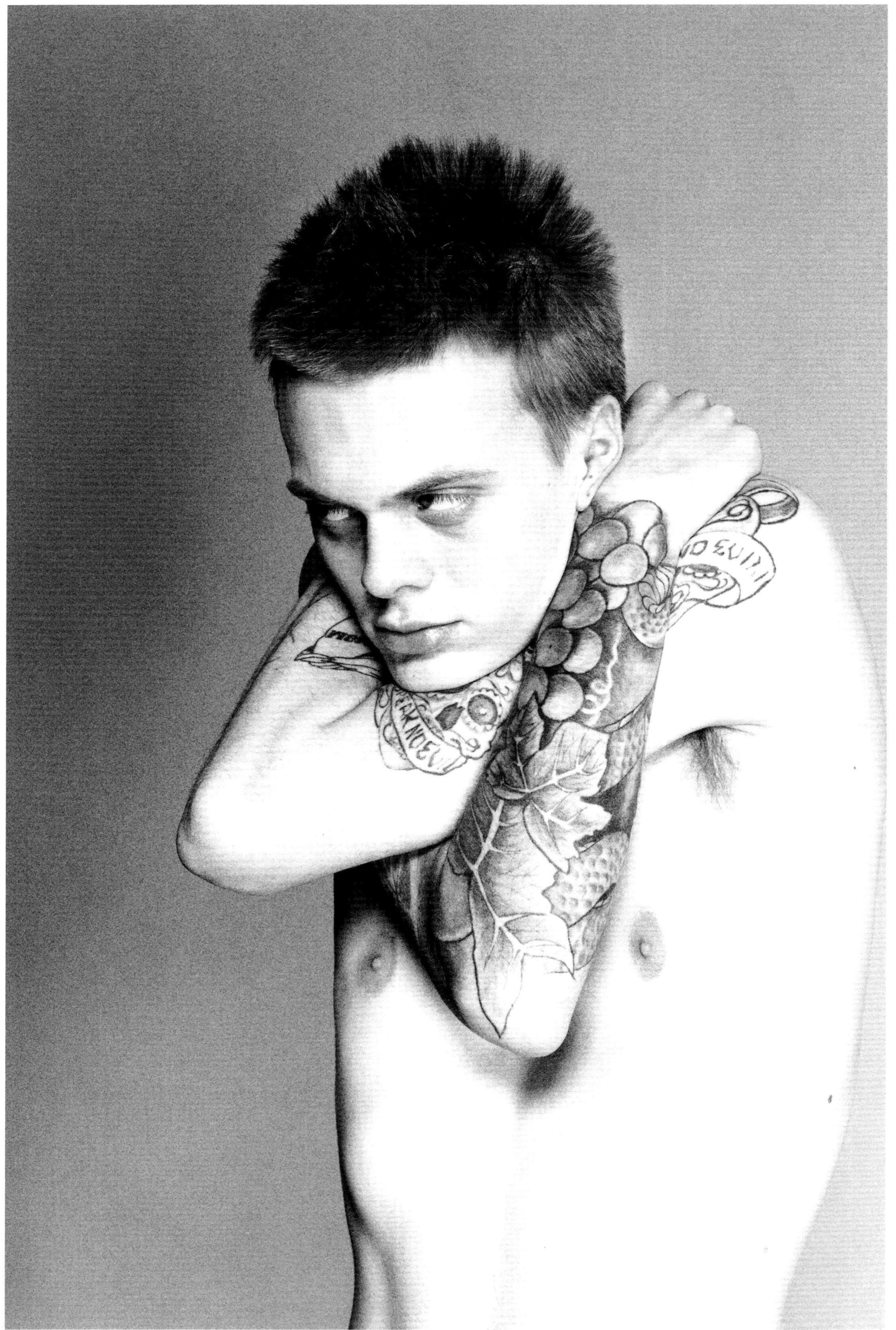

Ian, December 2015

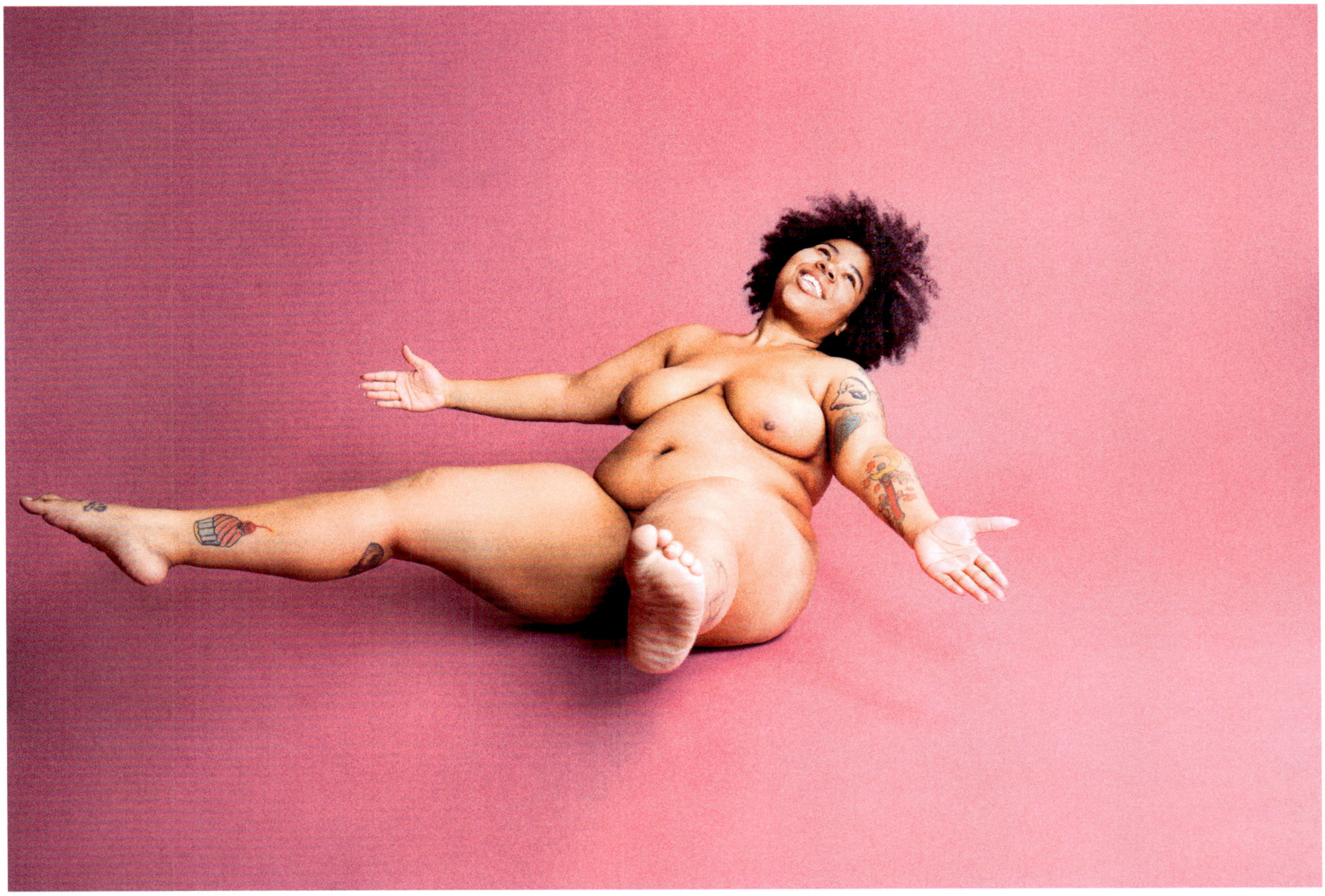

Chavon, October 2015 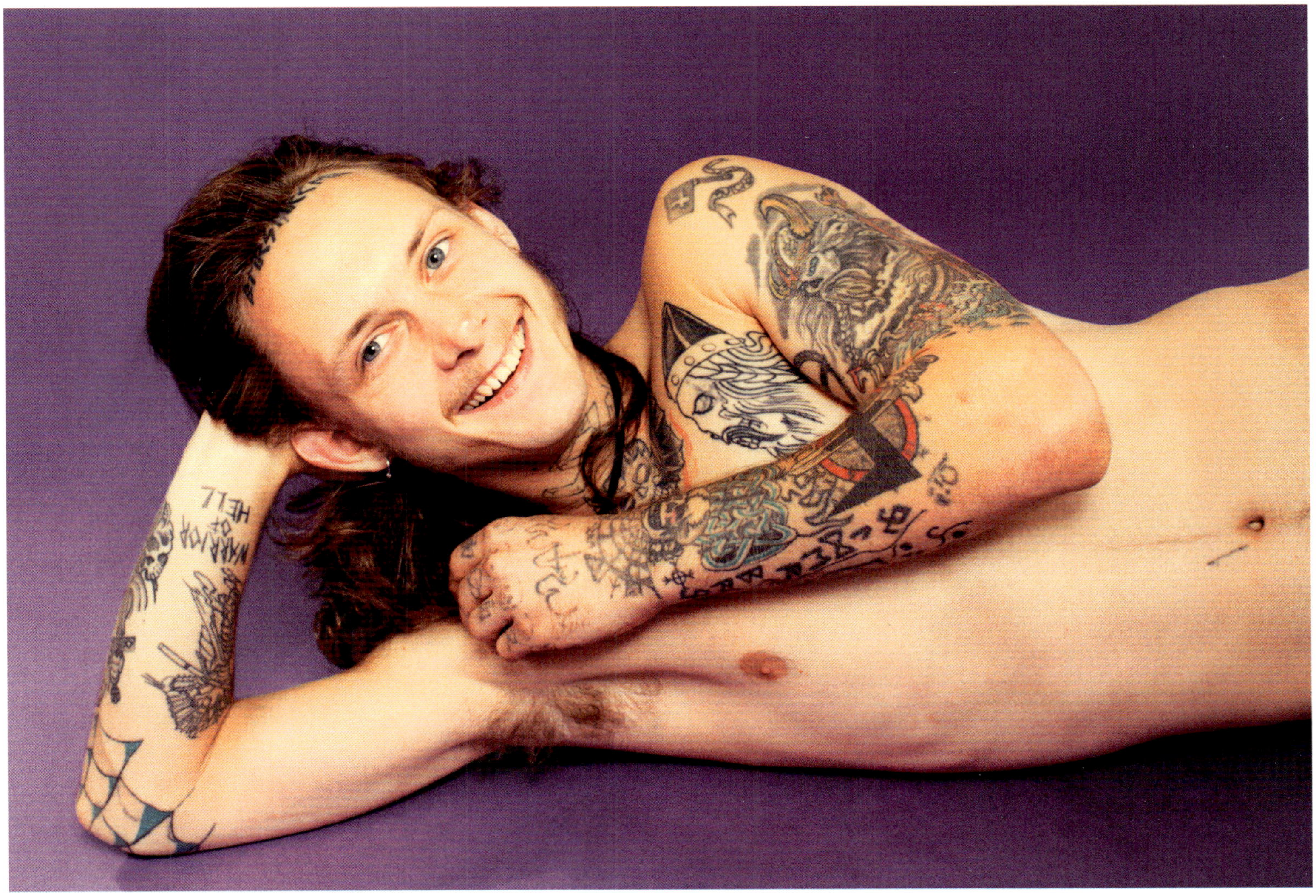   Jasper, September 2013

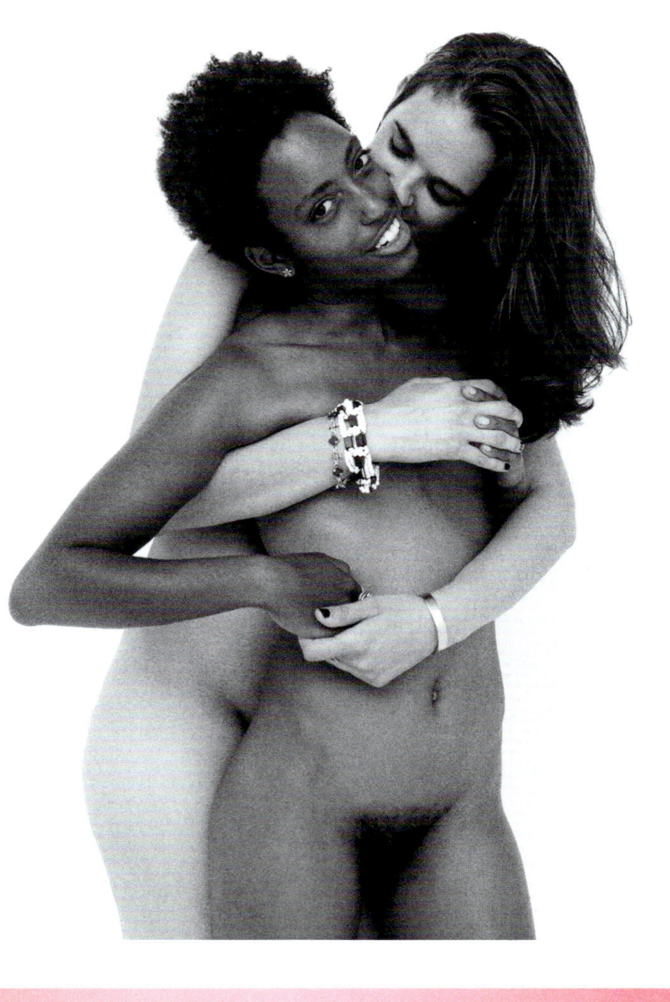

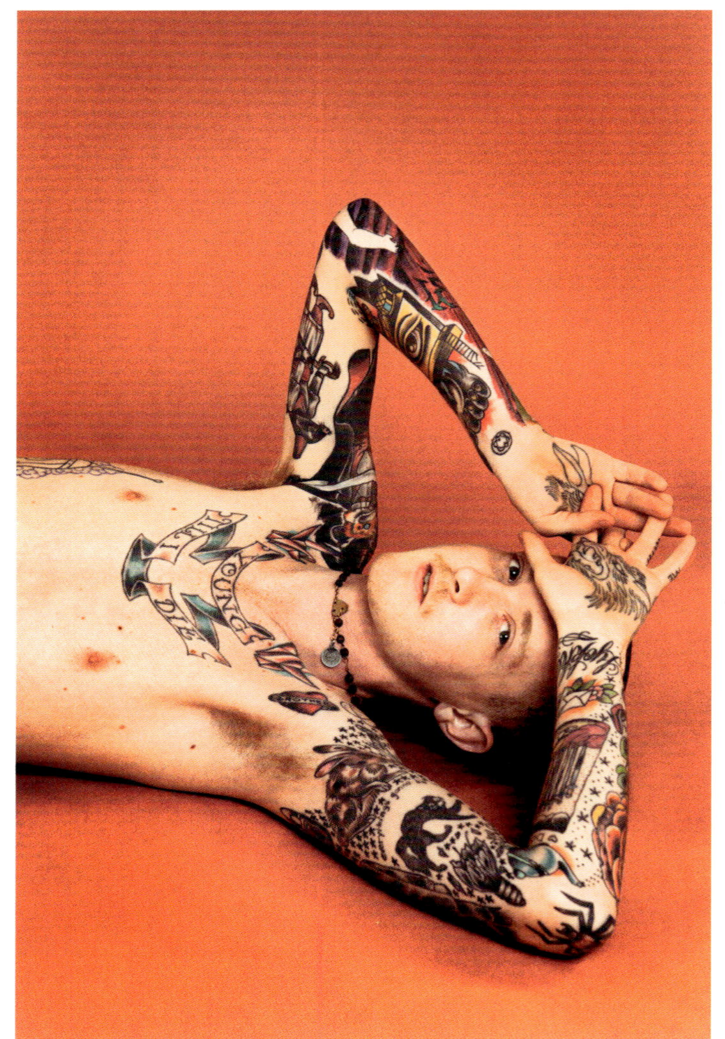

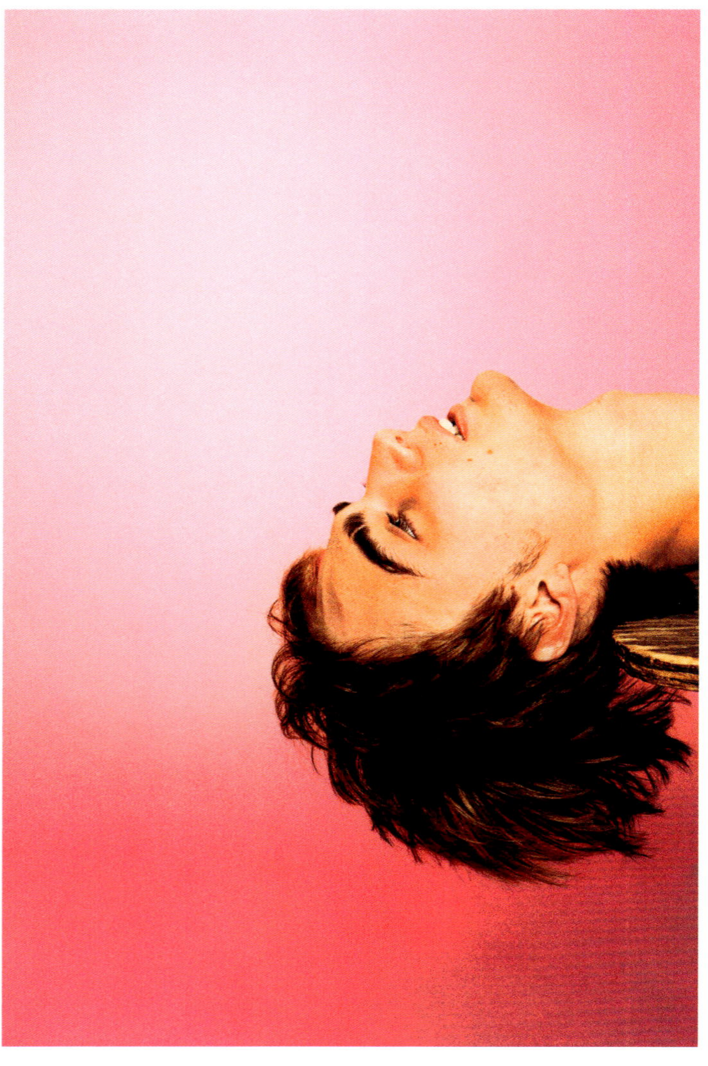

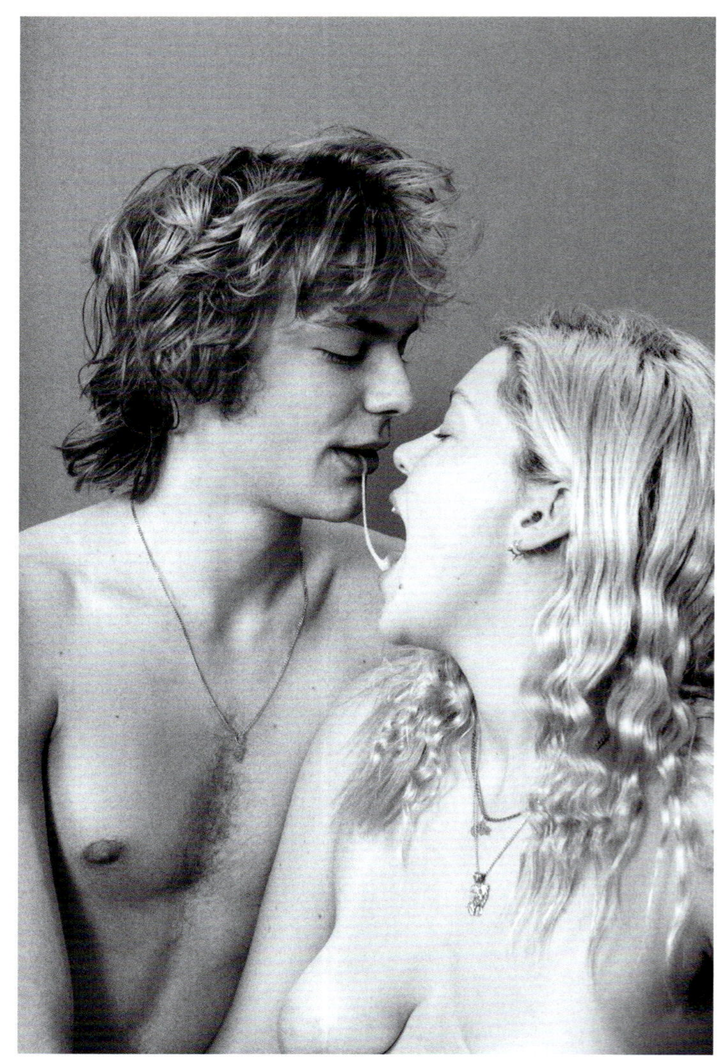

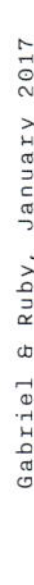

Rowan & Sequoia, June 2017 Matthew, September 2011 Chris, November 2011 Gabriel & Ruby, January 2017

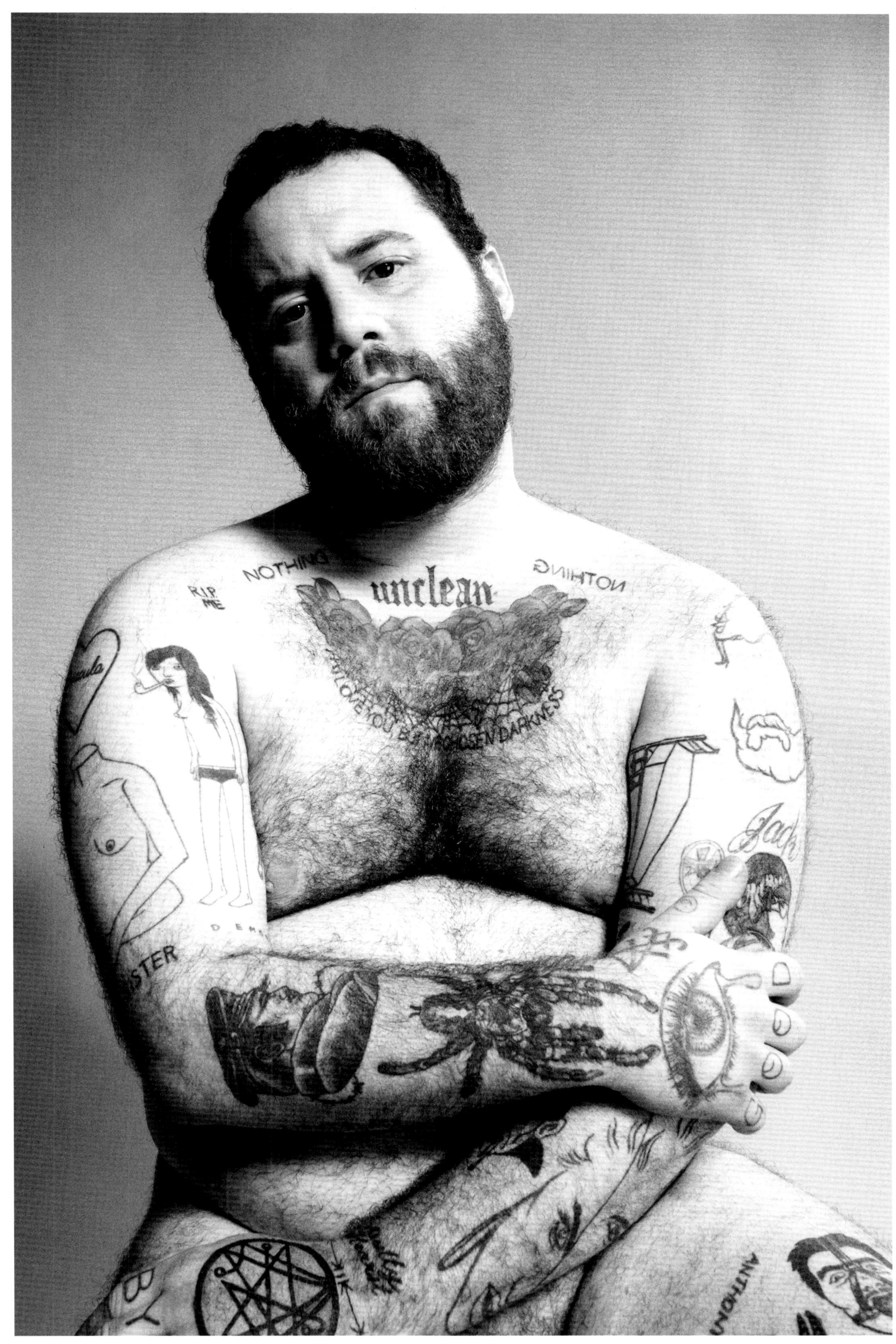

Jake, January 2016

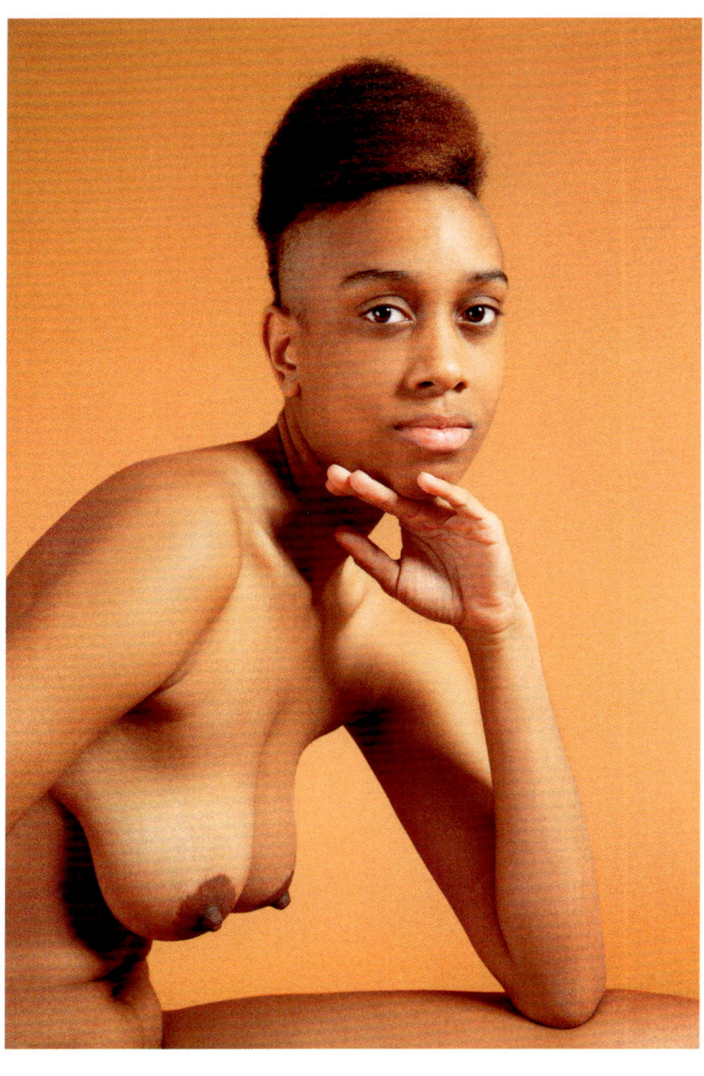

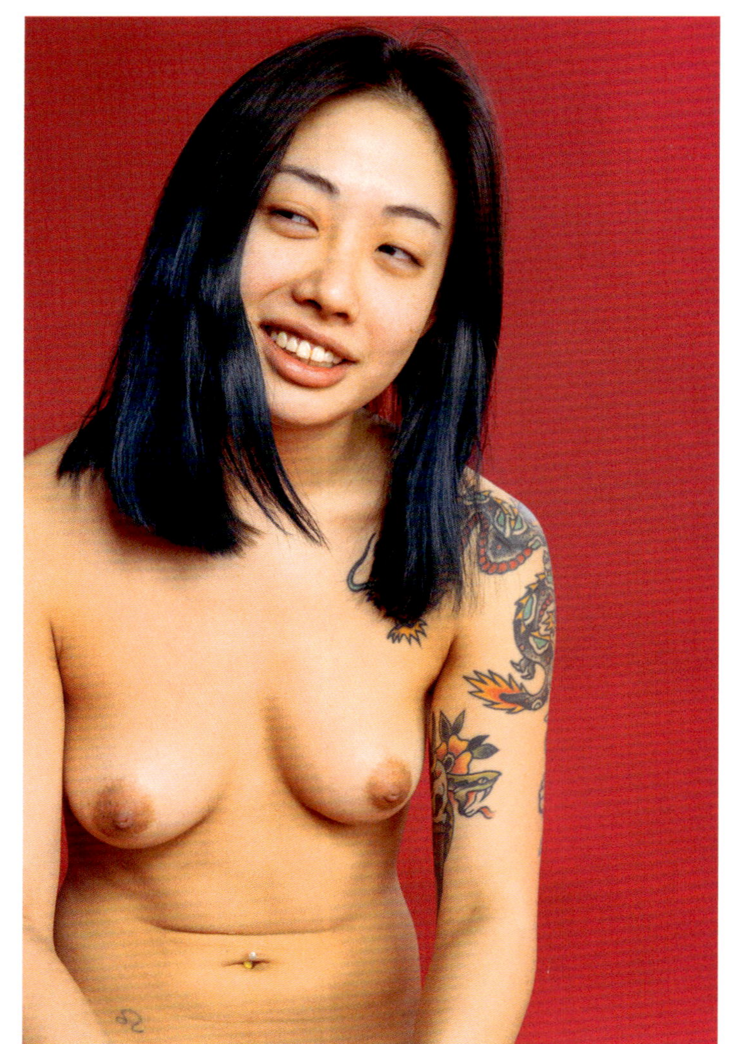

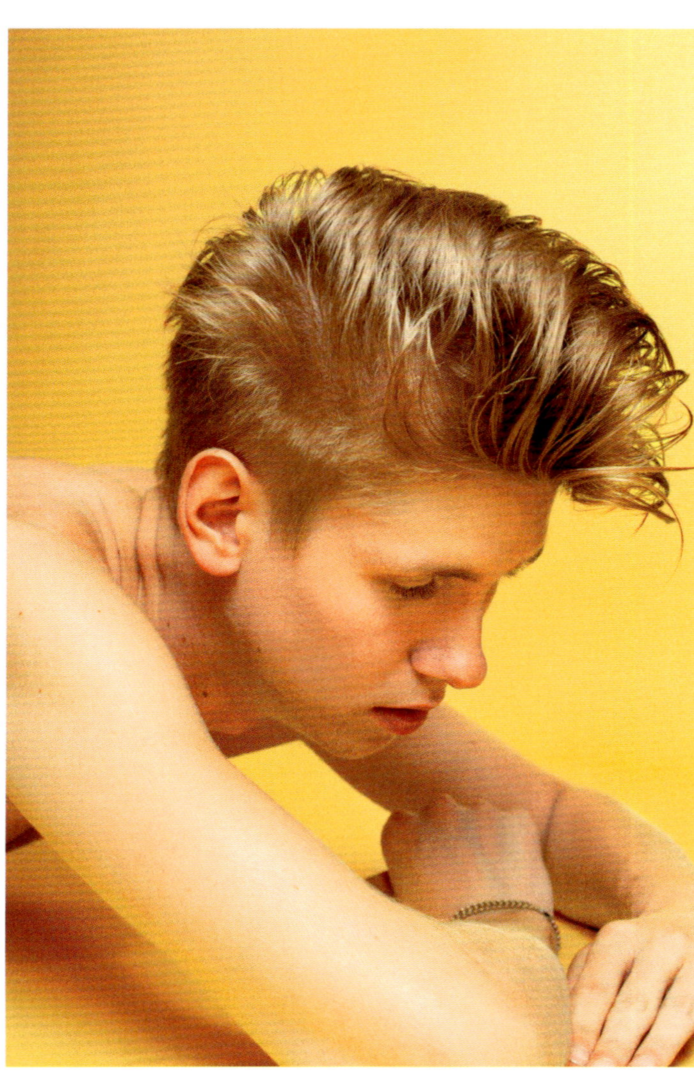

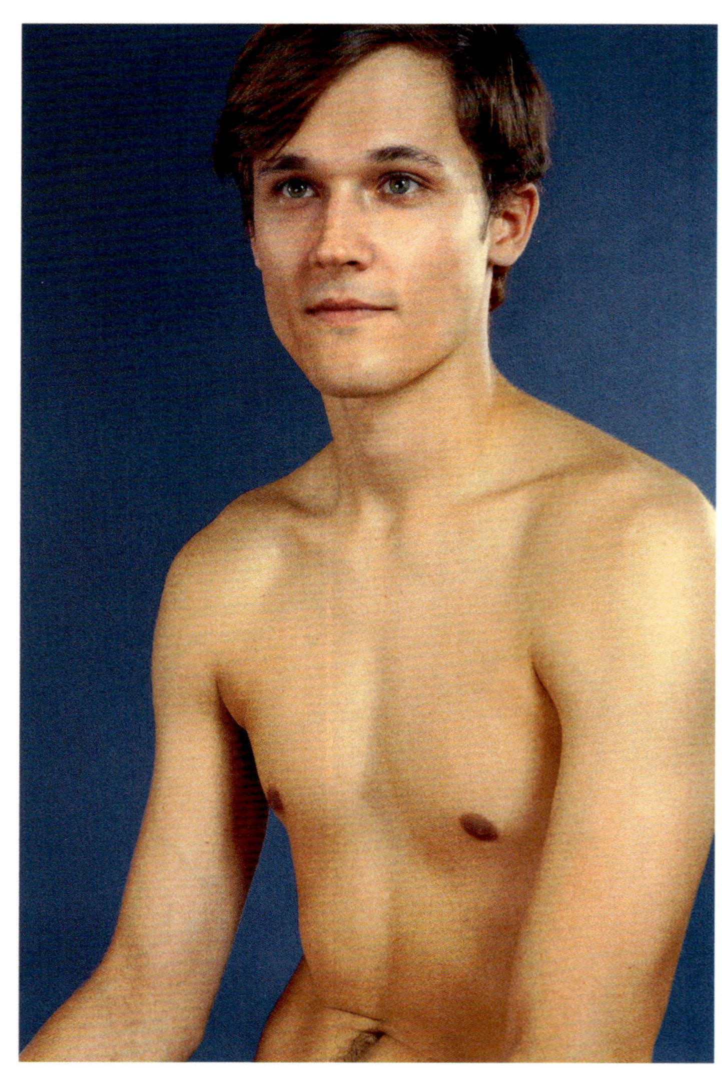

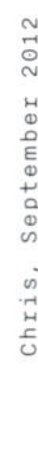

Inny, January 2012   Rei, February 2014   Brennan, September 2009   Chris, September 2012

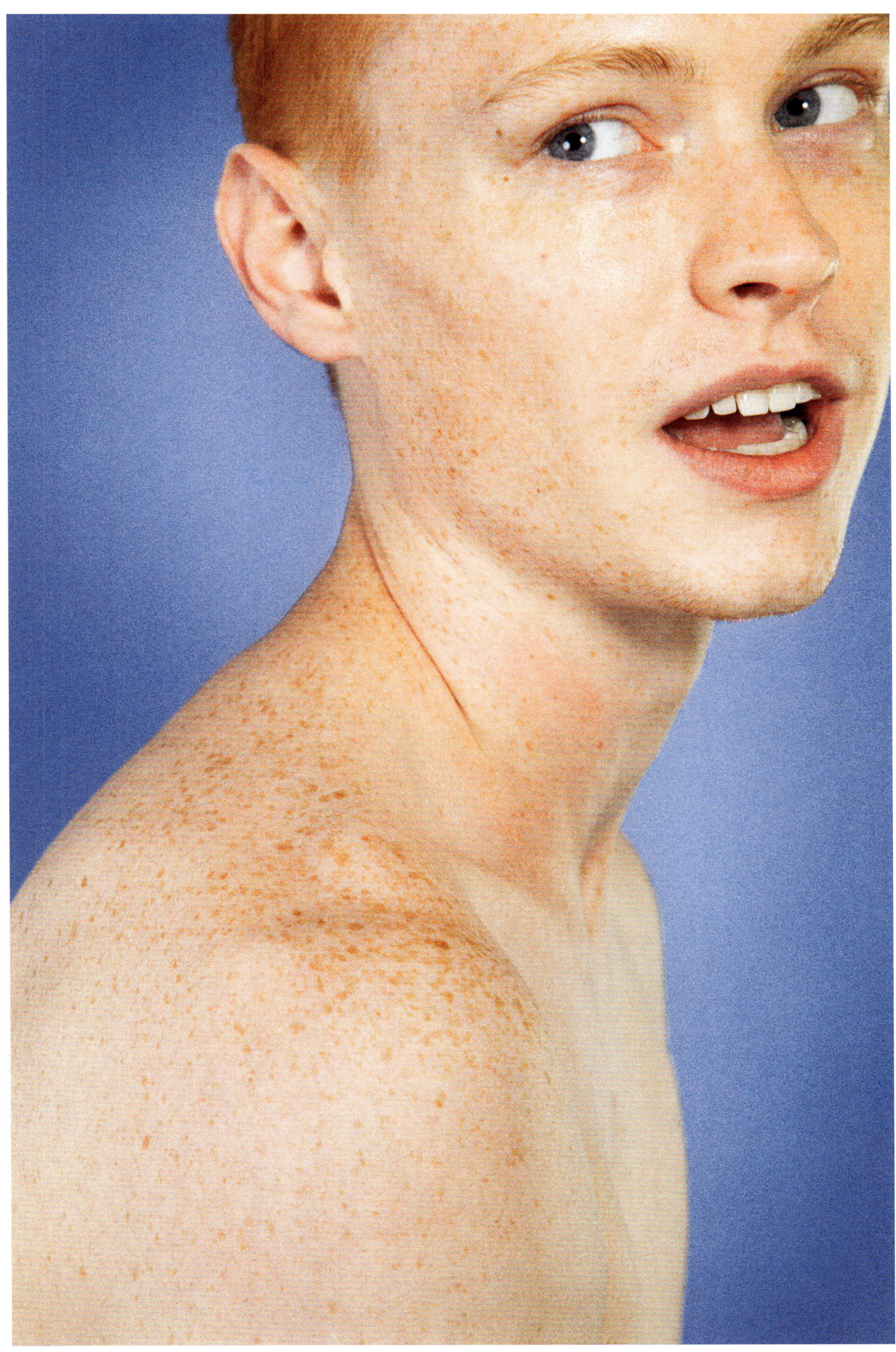

James, November 2013

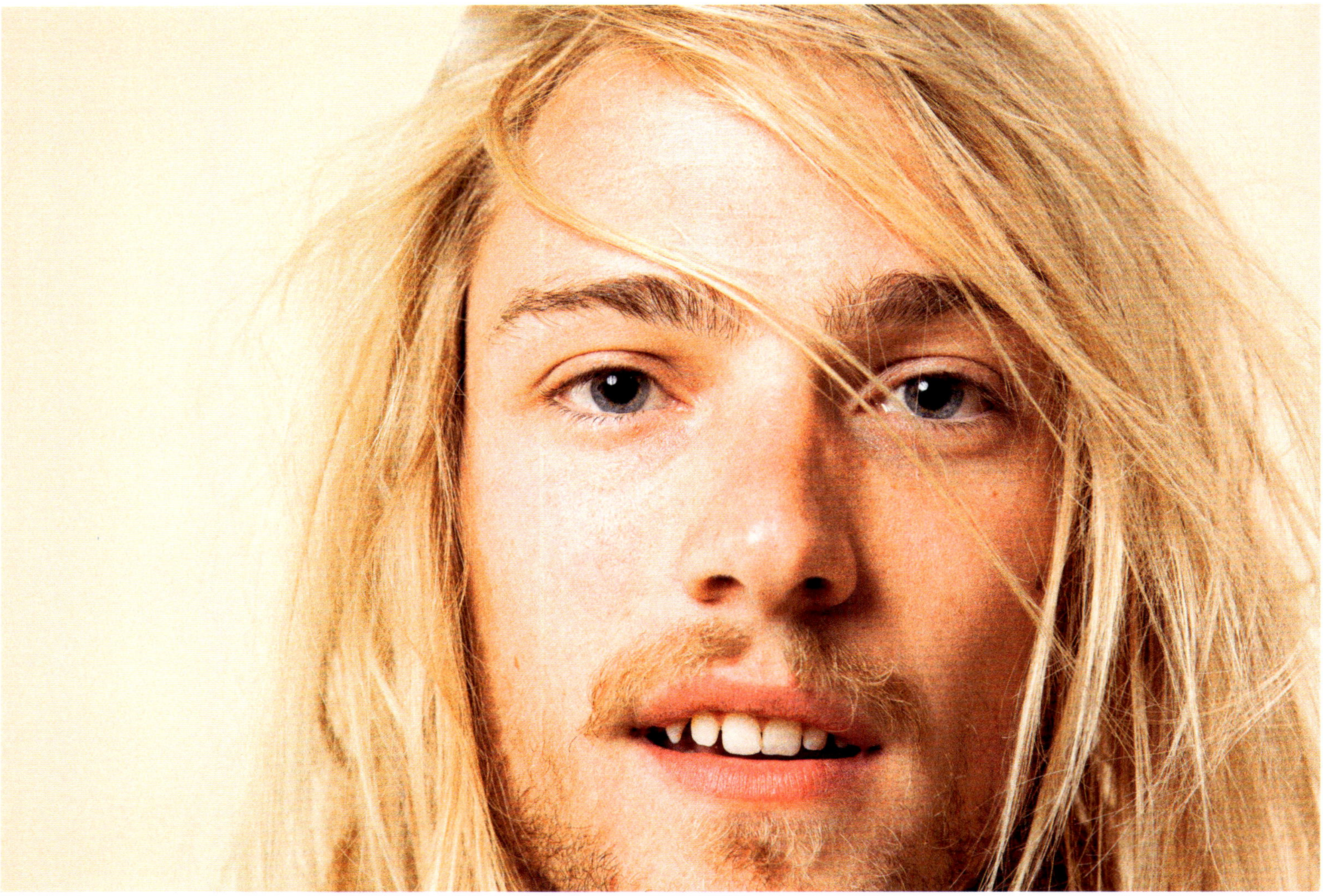

Trevor, August 2010

Elise & Meryl, September 2010

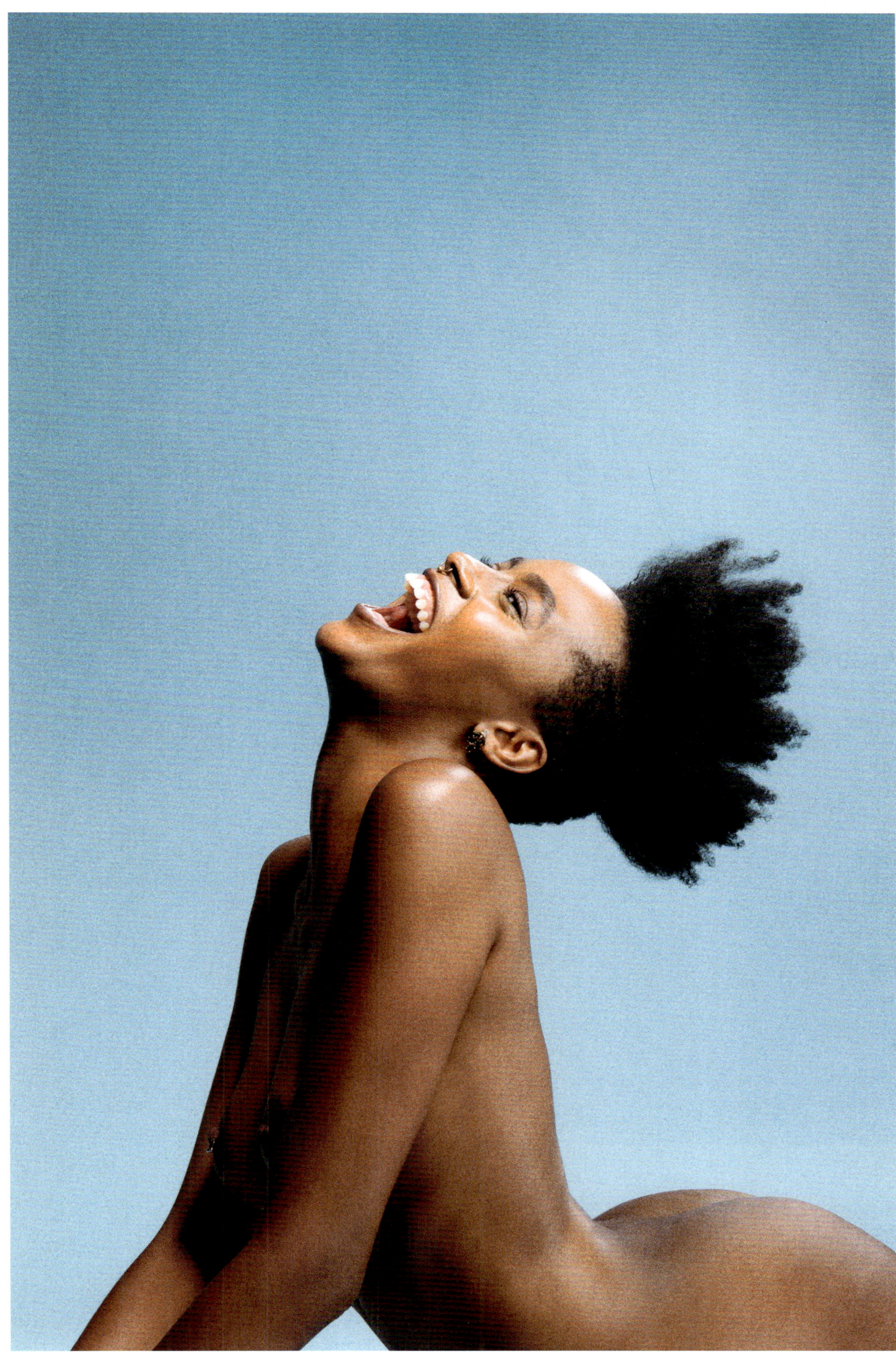

Ronyca, September 2015

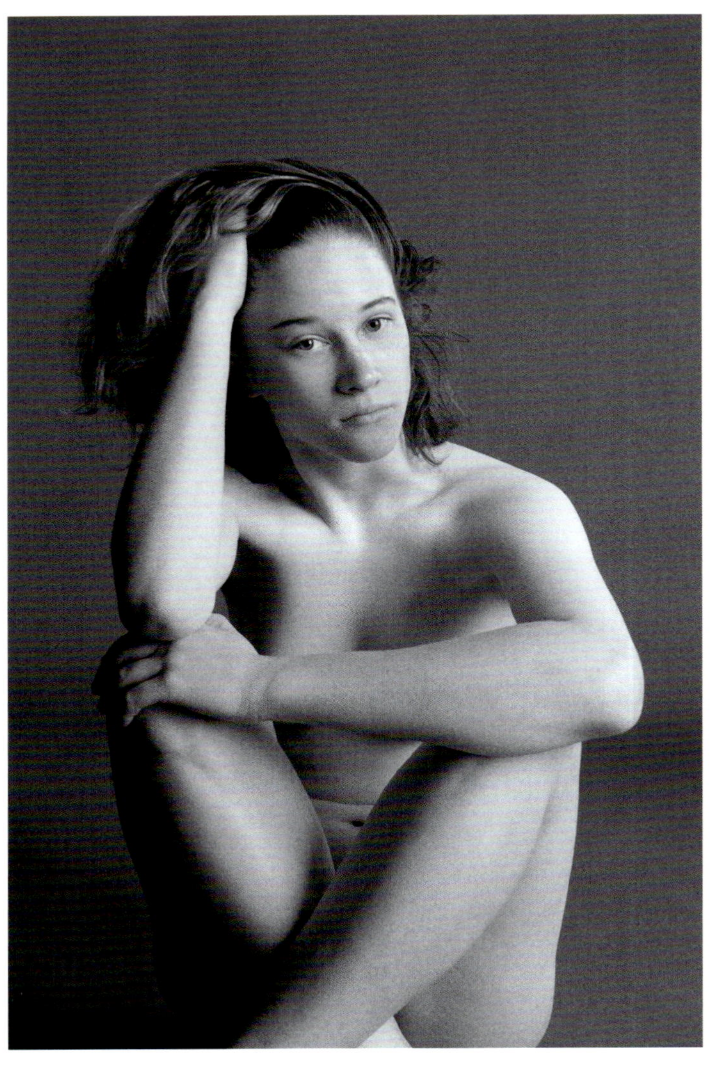

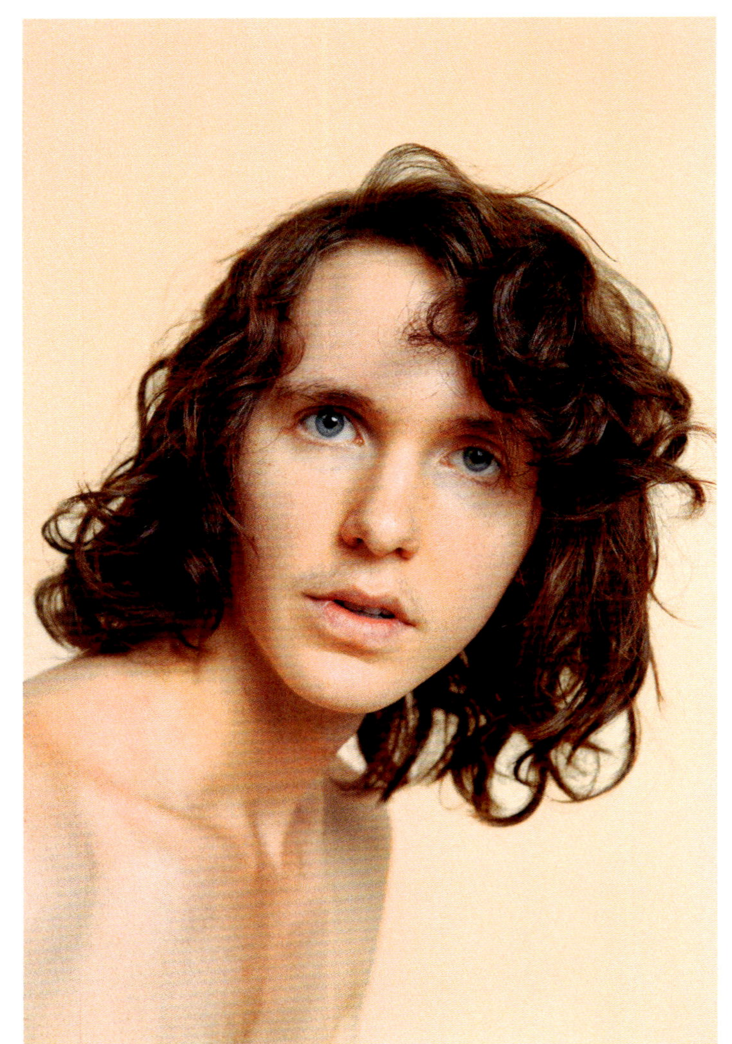

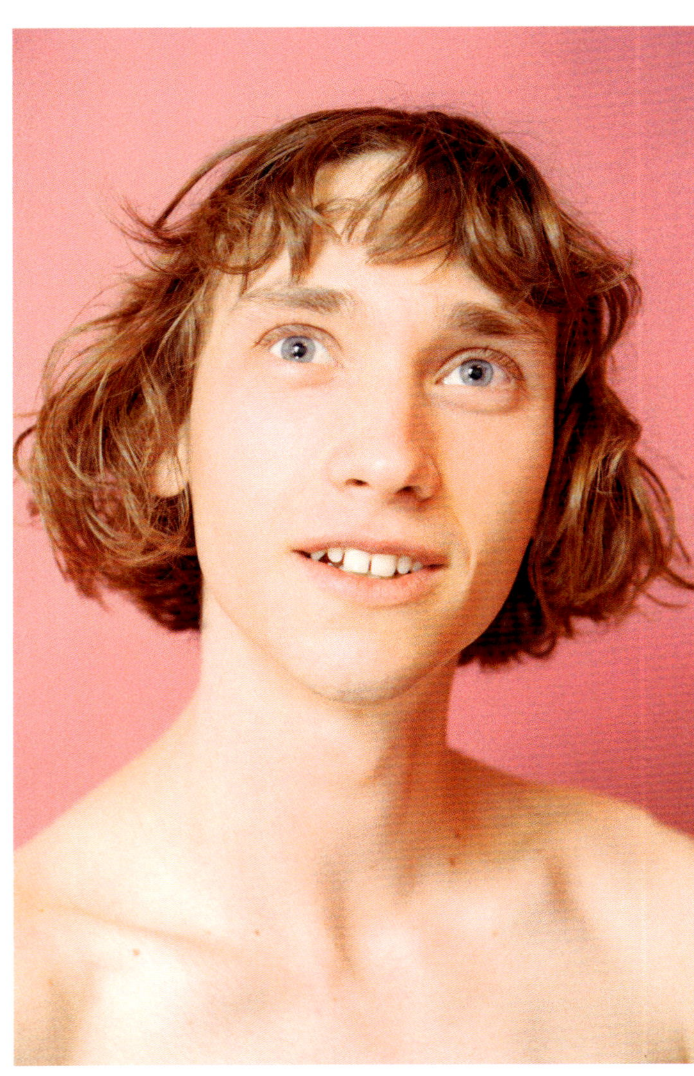

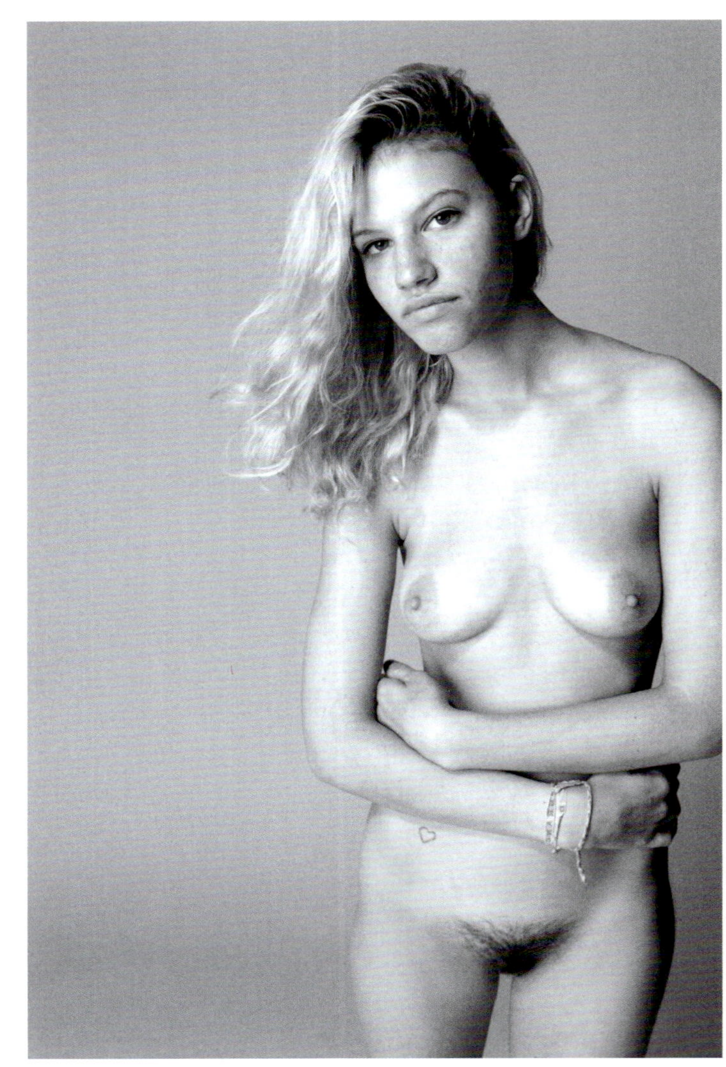

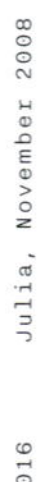

Grace, March 2014   Cody, September 2010   Julian, December 2016   Julia, November 2008

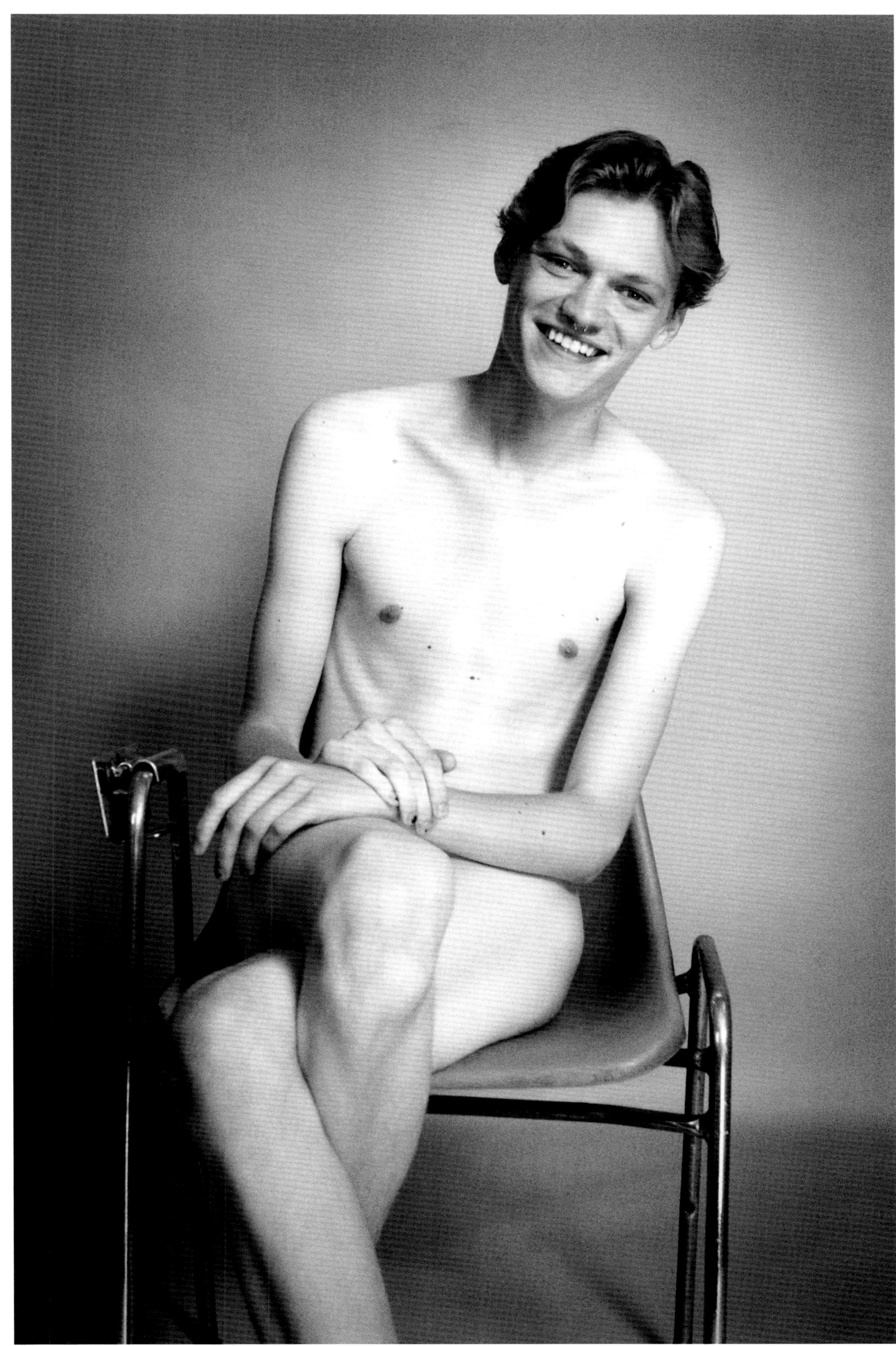

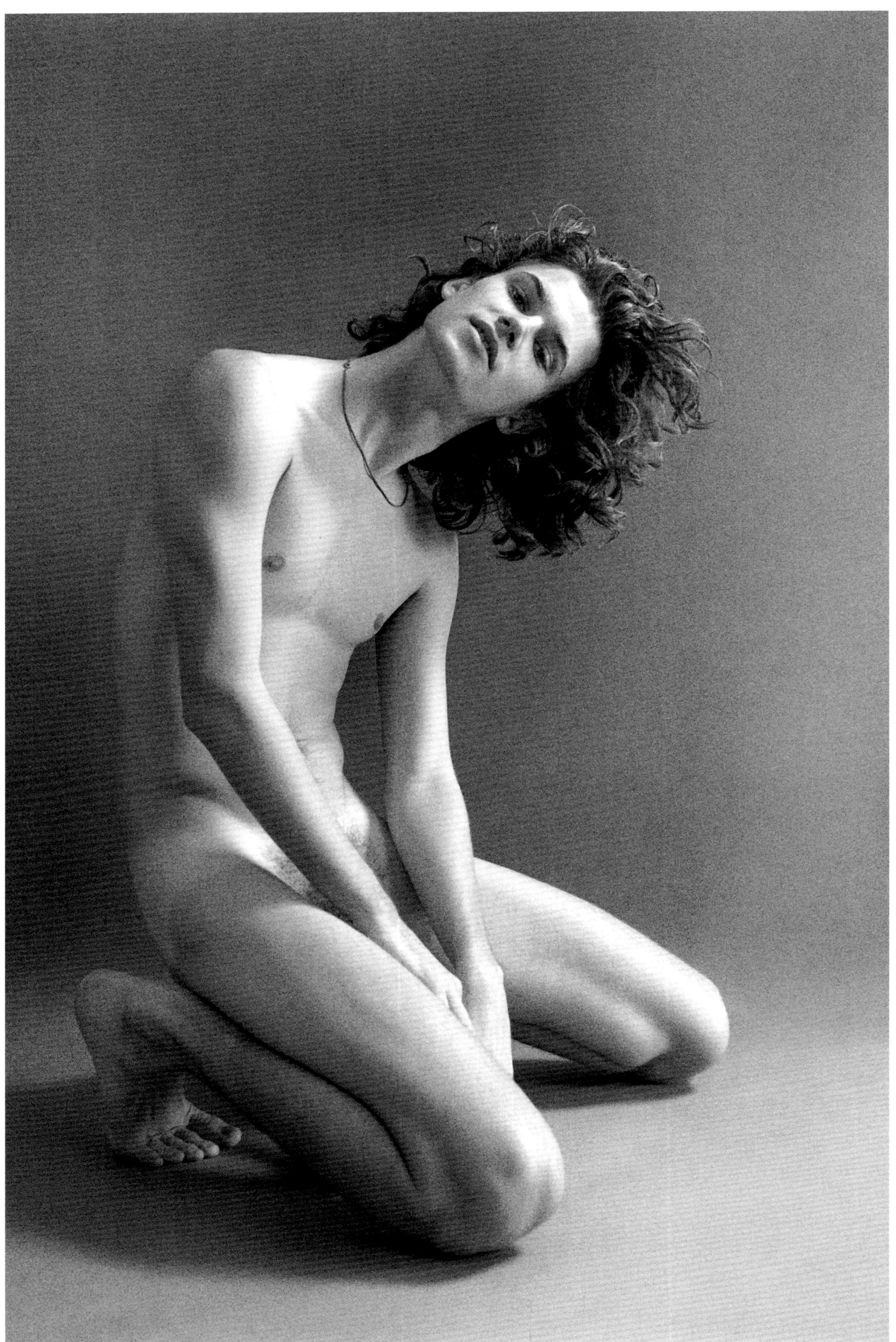

John, September 2016

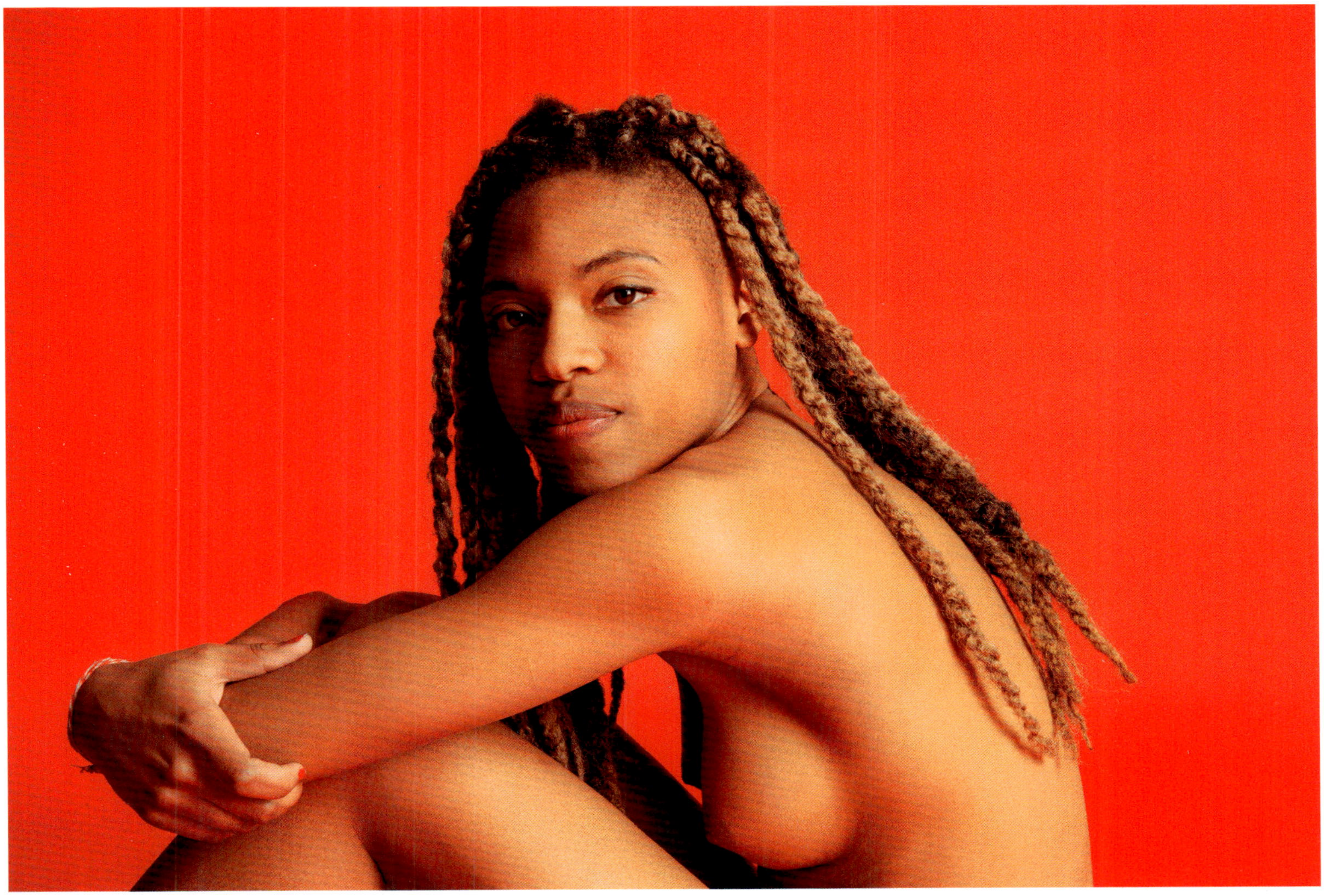

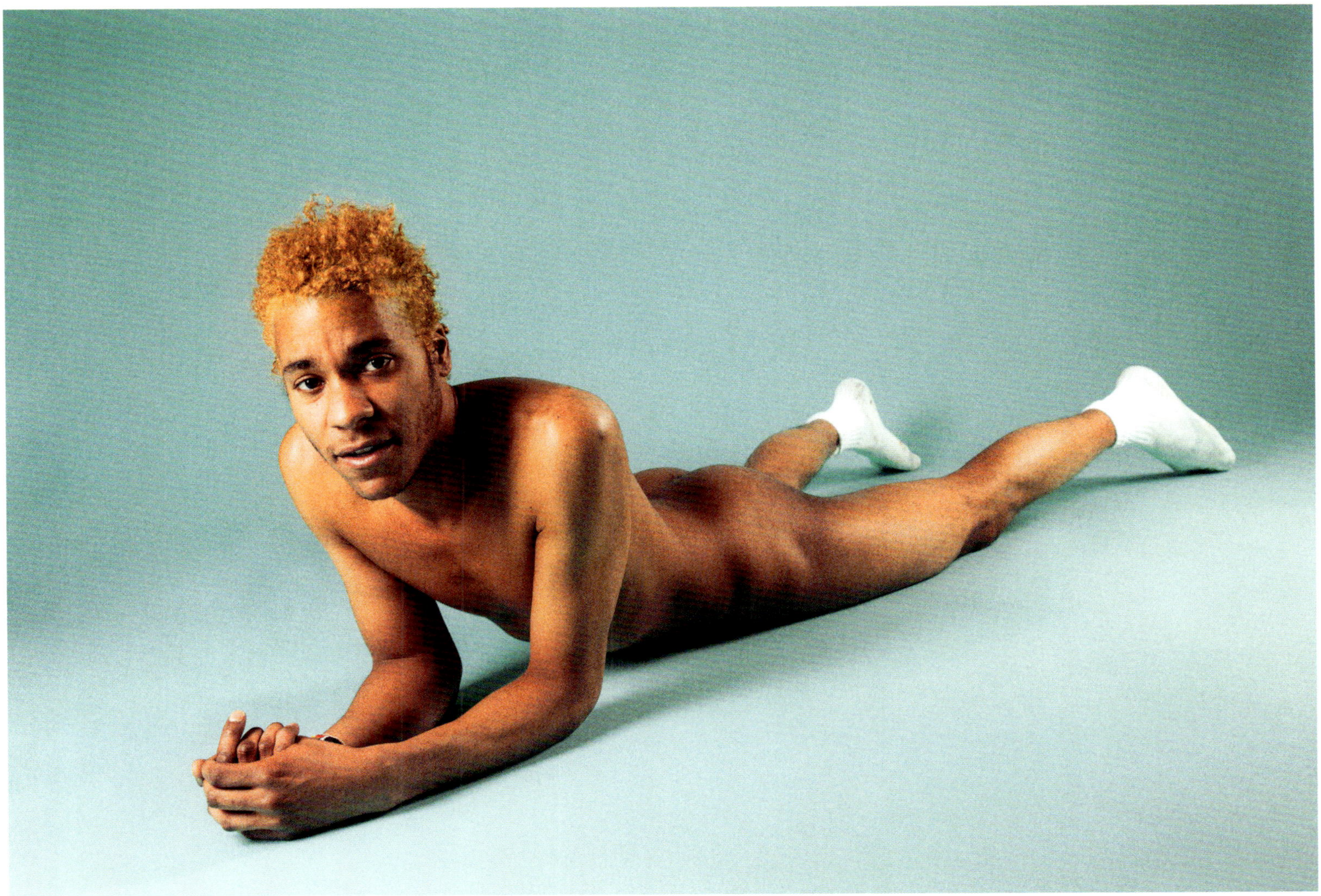

Lynn, May 2014

Devin, November 2011

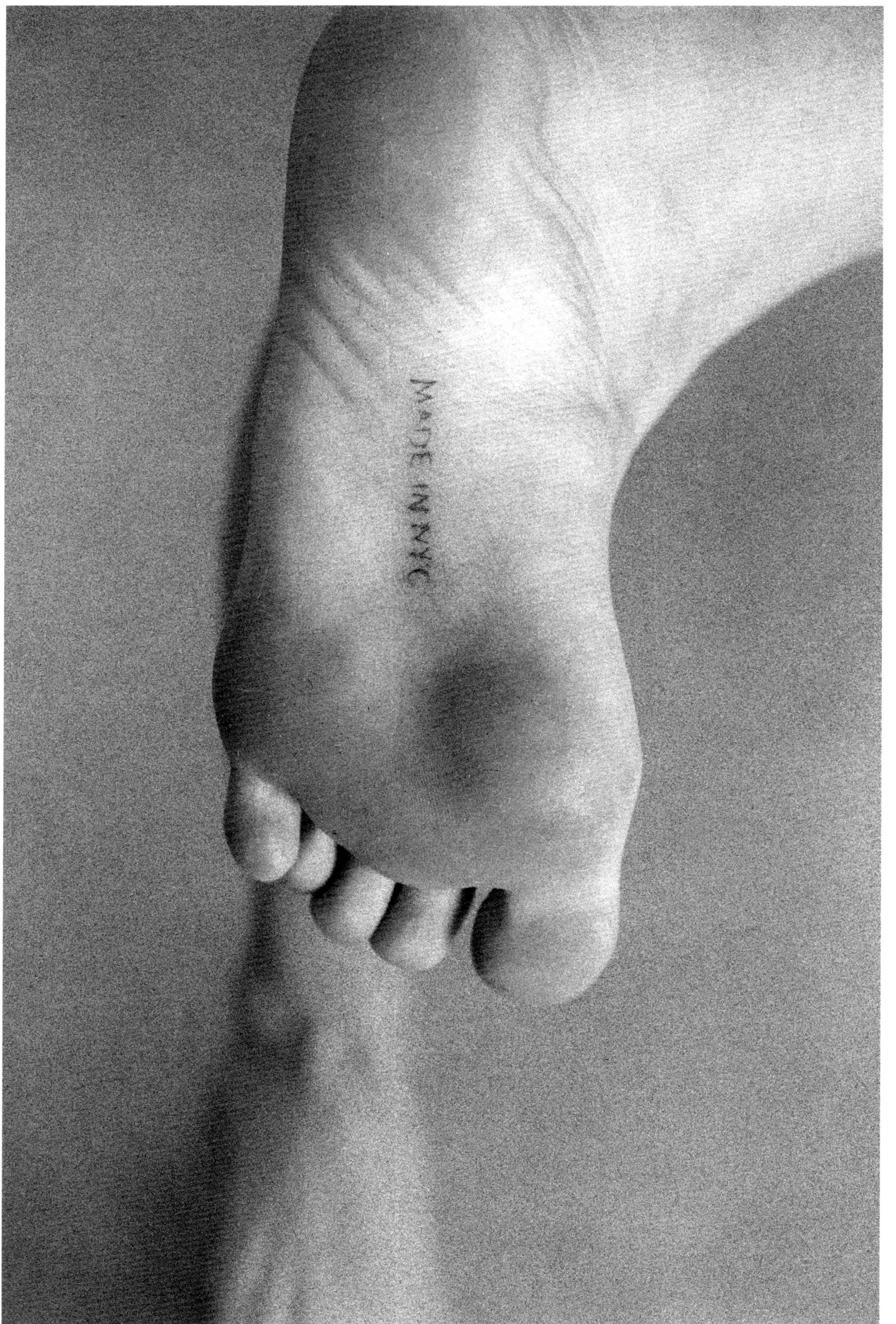

Made in NYC, 2016

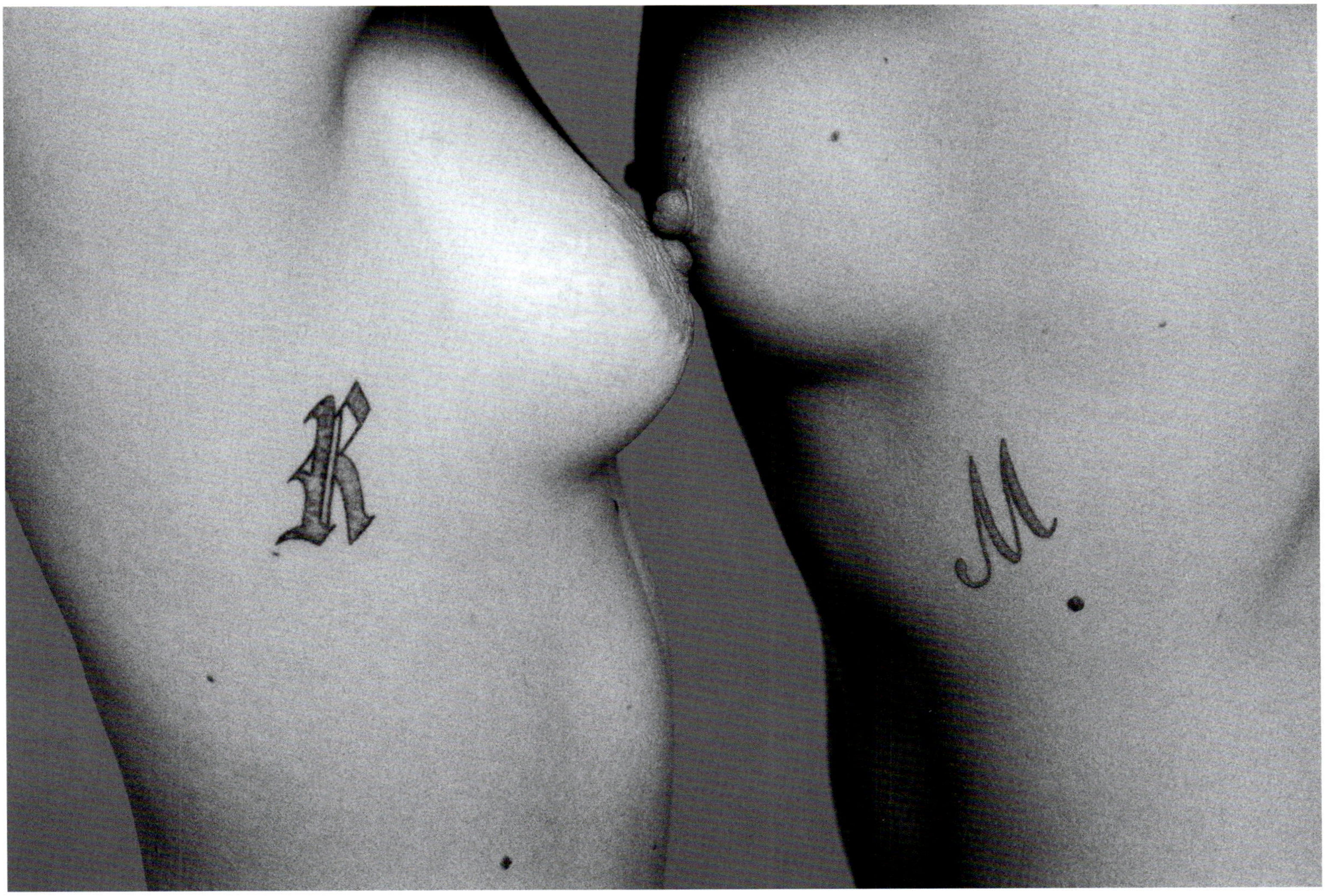

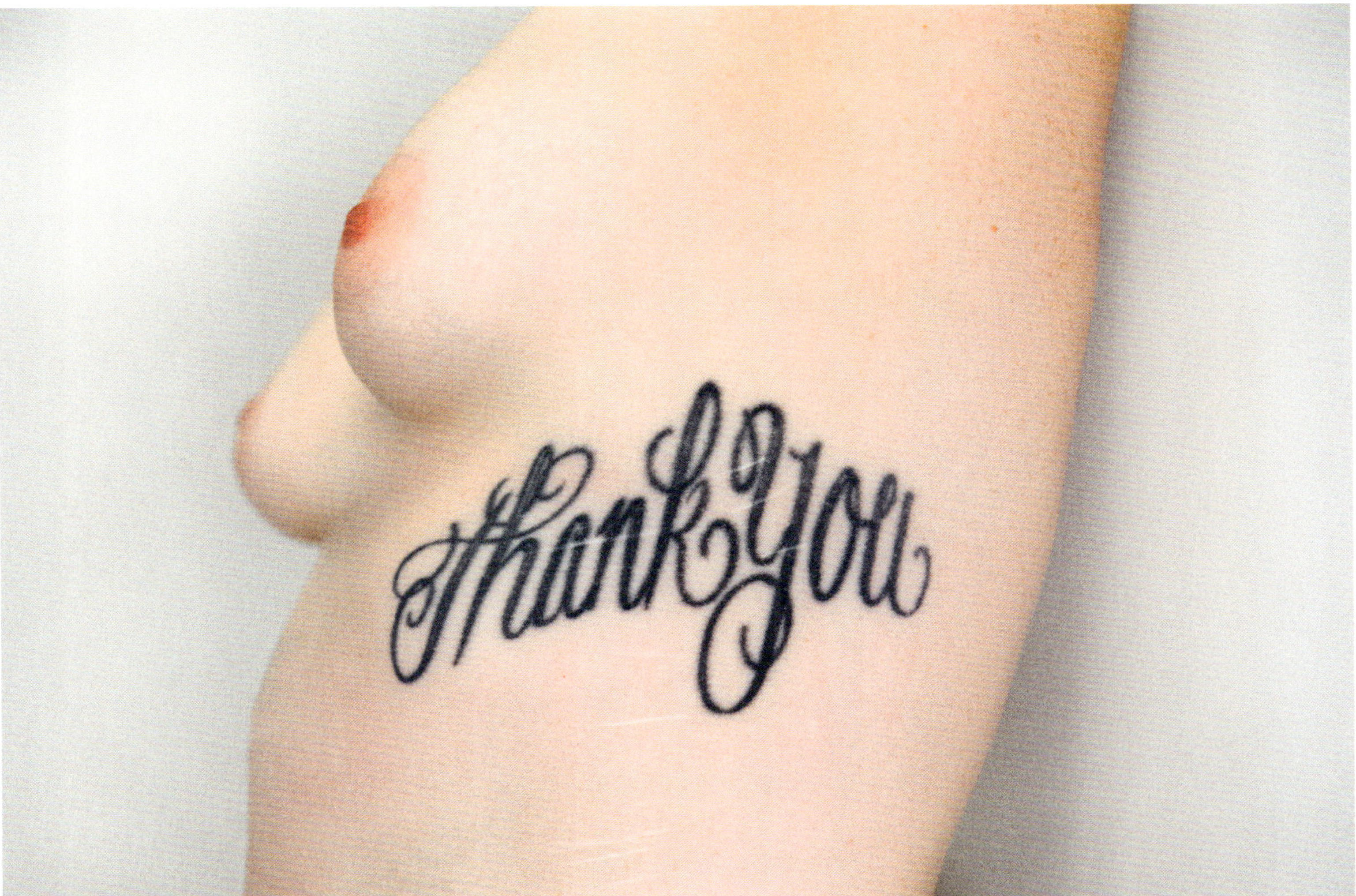

RM, 2010

Thank You, 2019

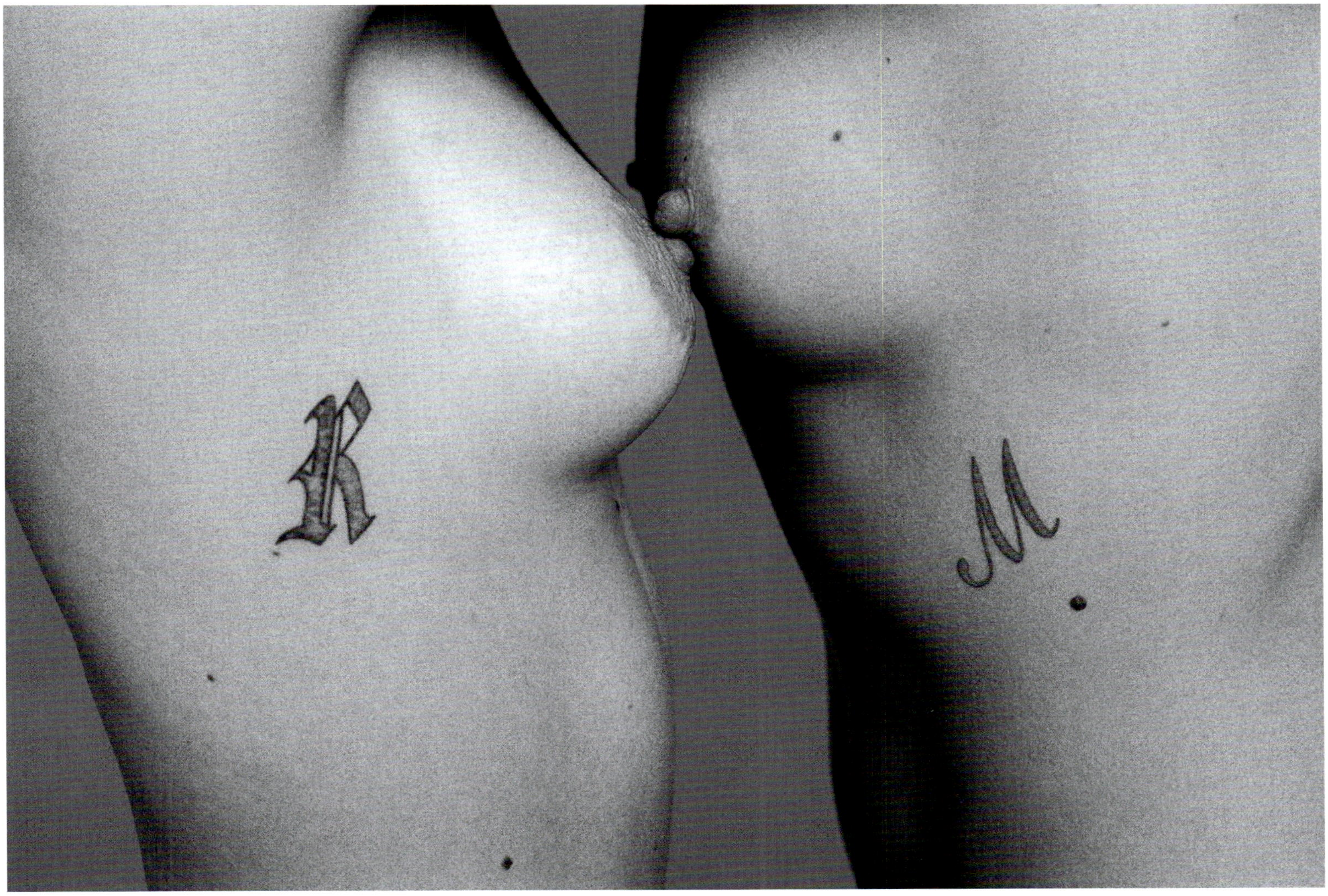

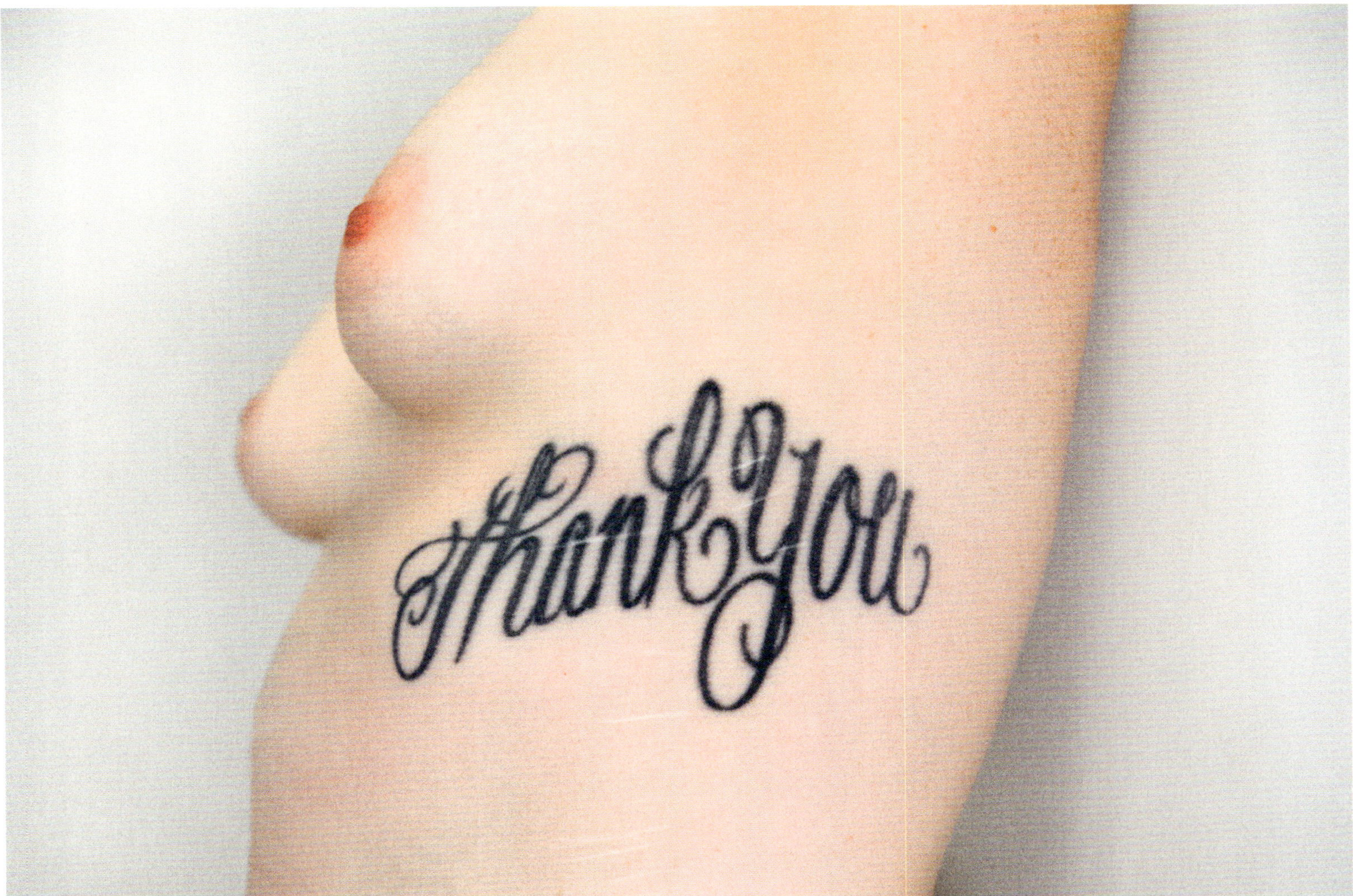

RM, 2010 Thank You, 2019

CHOREOGRAPHERS' NOTES

We know the term "hype girl" from entertainment and music. Hype people break down barriers in order for the audience and the artist to come together. The term also translates to what I did in the studio. As the choreographer or hype girl, my role was to make people's personalities really shine through, and that involved forgetting the elephant in the room, which is that they're nude.

Nudity and sexuality go hand-in-hand within our society. One challenge in this series was, how can we show the human body and not have the first association be sexuality? When a person gets in front of the camera and they don't have any clothes to play with, or to protect them, when you strip everything away, you're left with the raw material of who the person is. The Yearbook photos were really about exhibiting authentic human expression and emotion. Only later would you maybe notice, "Oh, they're nude."

When I first started, I didn't have an intentional technique of how to disarm people. Later, looking back, I'd say my technique was literally just being a human and knowing how to read a room. What time of day is it? Have we had coffee yet? I'm a silly type of gal and comedy is my niche so we're using laughter as medicine. One of my strengths was that I was genuinely interested in everyone and saw what we were doing as a collaboration. I wanted to get to know everyone and make them feel as comfortable as possible. I'd let each person dictate how they wanted to be treated. If someone obviously wanted to dance, I'd be like, "Let's dance." If a person had something they wanted to talk about, I'd lean into that.

We'd start early in the morning and go all day. It was fast-paced, a hectic, fun mess. It was also emotional, even sad, at times. Sometimes people were baring everything and it was like, "Oh, shit. This is deep," and it's 8:00 in the morning. We'd have people scheduled throughout the day, sometimes with only ten minutes in between. I had to learn to navigate that balance of listening and taking on pieces of a person to reflect back to them, so they felt safe in my presence—and then releasing that. I couldn't hold onto all we'd just shared since I had to be fresh for the next person.

After talking about something heavy, who doesn't need a dance party? Even if we were just talking about what someone had for breakfast, there came a time to let loose. We used all sorts of music on set: M.I.A., Frank Ocean, The Strokes, punk-rock. We bumped The Virgins and anything that the model wanted to listen to. Growing up in New York City, we listened to everything. I'd be dancing and mirroring the models from behind the camera. I'd do moves that might ignite their imagination.

When it comes to movement, Michael Jackson is king. He's my number-one, earliest inspiration. As a kid, I was obsessed with his moves, songs, and bravado. Then there's Miss Debbie Allen who's just old school, fun, and awesome. She broke boundaries and taboos as a Black woman dancer owning her own dance company. As far as actors go, I love Viola Davis. Her authenticity on camera is something I sought out in the models. That type of vulnerability is so special and so sacred. In our society, we don't champion vulnerability, so my goal was also to protect it.

One of the most memorable things about the whole experience for me was realizing how exposure to new things can transform your perspective, like how something taboo, like being nude, can become normal. The nudity felt so natural and pure by the end, it became weird to see these people *in clothes*. It was also just so much fun. That's what I think when I see these photos: I wish we could do it again and again and again . . .

—BRANDEE BROWN

When someone walked into the room, the vibe had to be good. It's like the first note of a symphony, it has to be right. We'd set a mood, a spirit. Smile, ask how they're doing. I love people and so does Ryan. Our energy would ping pong; the electricity would make people curious about us. The goal was to feel like there was trust established.

The hour and a half or two hours we'd spend with someone was like a lifetime. So much would be covered between the fun questions and the music and movement. I'm a maniac in the ways that I think and move. I would move as I was speaking and that was a mirror, letting people know that was okay.

We had all these questions prepared. Those lists are burned into my cranium: Do you have brothers and sisters? Who do you feel more connected to, mom or dad? Where are you from? What sports did you play? What's a movie that influenced you lately? What's your favorite karaoke song? What Spice Girl are you? (I'm Ginger.) When's your birthday? (Most people like astrology.) We'd ask questions people couldn't answer with just yes or no. Questions that would provoke a colorful answer, never black and white.

We also had a Rolodex of movements. People love direction when they don't know what to do. Scratch the middle of your back. Try to reach two fingers together, one behind your back, one behind your head. Flailing arms. Donkey kick. Star shape. Little kid throwing oranges. Air Jordan wingspan. Muscleman. Twiggy. Shopping cart dance. Uncle with a handycam. Mime and imagine them. That's the sauce.

Hair flips. Britney Spears is my hair choreographer for life. She taught me you could change the world with your hair when you danced. It's just a fact.

We were trying to give people the freedom to be as spontaneous as possible, to basically play jazz with their bodies. To get the shot, we brought organization (the lists), empathy (meeting people where they're at), and fun. Stand on your head, get crooked and wiry. We were going for truth in movement, which means it's as real as how an animal would move. It's instinctive. Like Marilyn Monroe—her physicality is so fucking good.

I was raised on Jim Carrey. I thought he was my dad until I was ten. Everything he does makes sense to me. Some people get freaked out by Jim Carrey, I think he's a genius. He's like a carnival person and that's in my DNA on my mom's side. My dad's actually a trumpet player. He played for the Philadelphia ballet so we would go see the ballet all the time. I was possessed by dance from the moment I was born but in a non-technical way. I had a ballet phase. I had a modern jazz phase. Then I had a hip-hop dance phase. I'd go to this studio in Philly to try and learn the choreography but I always ended up doing my own thing.

Thinking about it, never once, and I mean never-ever, was there Yearbook day when I felt tired or down. The energy was so consistent. Music was key. We had a really important mix called "Fucking Jump," which was like, level-10 accelerated wile out. Death Grips, Korn, *Helter Skelter*, *Black Skinhead* . . .

Two heads really are better than one. While Ryan got to focus on photography, what's in the frame, which is its own action—it could get super physical—I'd be this extension cord of words and actions. We had our own choreography between us. He might be lying down on the ground, shooting with a crooked neck. And I'd get down and use my arm to cushion his head. It was like we were one body with four legs and two heads.

There were moments when I knew he'd gotten the photo. When the flash was giving me cataracts and people were suspended in the air, acrobatic, *Sports Illustrated*-style. We were no longer in the room, we were transported somewhere else. Those moments felt like half a second and like a really long time.

—LUISA OPALESKY

Special Thanks:
Phoebe Pritchett for casting the majority of this project, Snake Garcia for project managing global installations, Rachel Filler for designing the book layout, and Chris Perez / Ratio 3 Gallery SF for exhibiting the first *Yearbook* installation.

Thank You:
Marc Alain, Marc Armitano, Brandee Brown, Sam Colby, Fiona Alison Duncan, Patrick Dyer, Chris Harth, Thibault Henriet, Jahquira Henry, Jemma Hinkly, Sandy Kim, Nicky Lesser, Tristan Martinez, John McGinley, Michael McGinley, Chad Moore, Luisa Opalesky, George Pitts, Augusto Silva, Sydney Smith, Shea Spencer, Jessica Tang, Christine Ting, Veronica Torres, Helga Traxler, Elena Vazintaris, Isabel Venero, Izzy Wang, Natasha Wong.

Yearbook is installed as a single artwork consisting of between 500-700 photographs. Each presentation of *Yearbook* responds specifically to the unique architecture of the gallery space. The first exhibition in 2013 was installed with wheatpaste. Subsequent exhibitions were installed with high resolution vinyl adhesive prints at 24 x 36 inches.

Yearbook was photographed on a Canon 5D and Nikon D750.

FIRST PUBLISHED IN THE
UNITED STATES OF AMERICA IN 2024 BY
RIZZOLI INTERNATIONAL PUBLICATIONS, INC.
300 PARK AVENUE SOUTH
NEW YORK, NY 10010
WWW.RIZZOLIUSA.COM

PUBLISHER: CHARLES MIERS
EDITOR: ISABEL VENERO
INTERVIEWS: FIONA ALISON DUNCAN
PRODUCTION MANAGER: BARBARA SADICK

DESIGNED BY KAYLEIGH JANKOWSKI

2024 2025 2026 2027 / 10 9 8 7 6 5 4 3 2 1
ISBN: 978-0-8478-6517-8
LIBRARY OF CONGRESS CONTROL NUMBER: 2024931740

PRINTED IN ITALY

VISIT US ONLINE:
FACEBOOK.COM/RIZZOLINEWYORK
X @RIZZOLI_BOOKS
INSTAGRAM.COM/RIZZOLIBOOKS
PINTEREST.COM/RIZZOLIBOOKS
YOUTUBE.COM/USER/RIZZOLINY

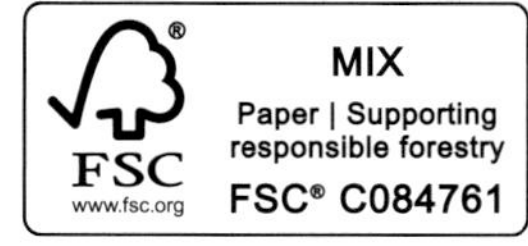

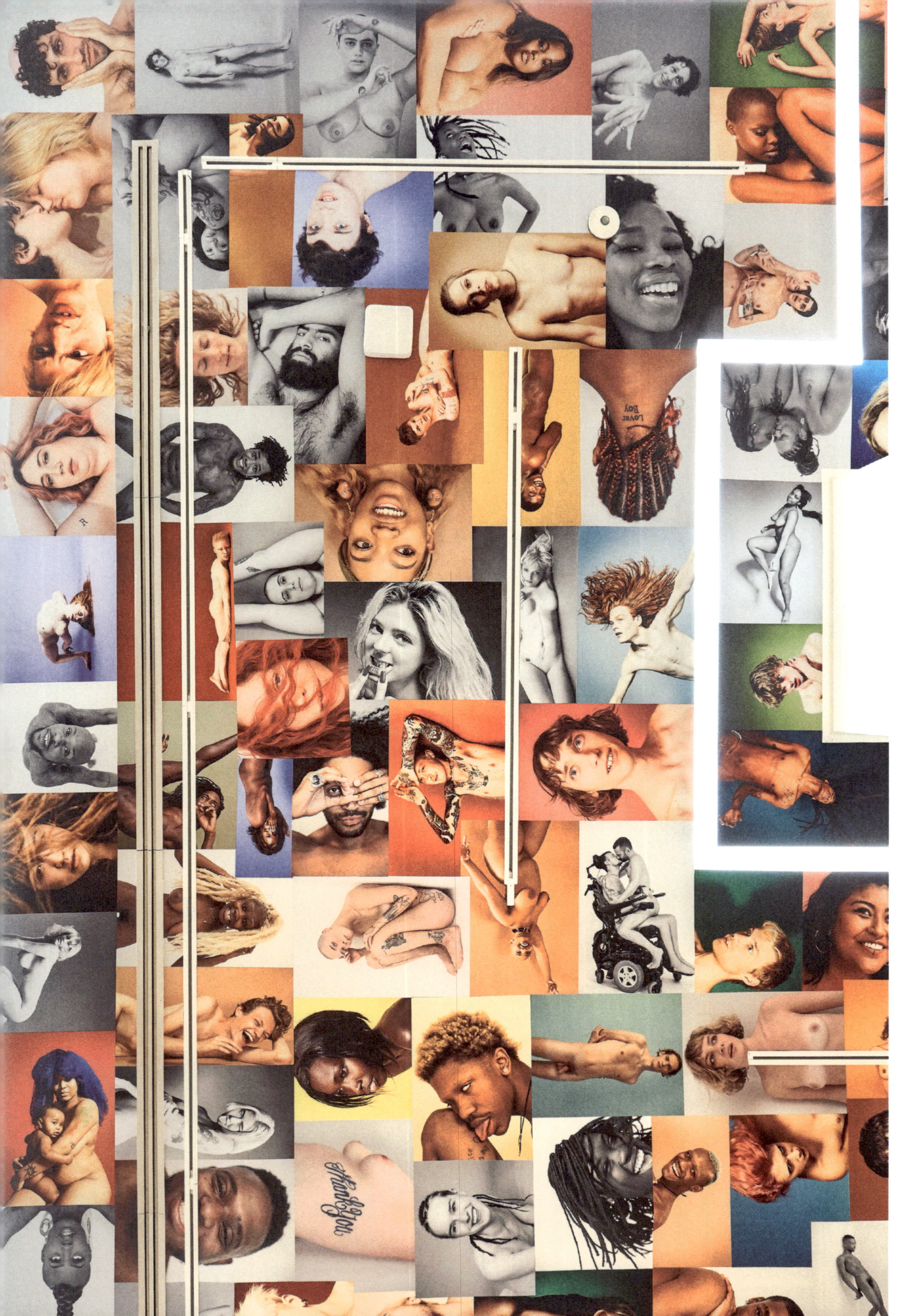